The Palgrave Handbook of Agricultural and Rural Development in Africa

"I would like to congratulate Evans Osabuohien for bringing together so many scholars, especially Africans within the continent and in the Diaspora, to share their insights on relevant issues that matter for the transformation of Africa's agriculture. This transformation is truly a critical facet of Africa's general economic development prospects."
—Jann Lay, *Professor, German Institute of Global and Area Studies (GIGA), Hamburg & University of Goettingen, Goettingen, Germany*

"This is a remarkable book that highlights important and timely agricultural issues affecting Africa's rural poor. In addition to increasing the knowledge base, providing policy-relevant 'food for thought' and pushing forward development efforts, *The Palgrave Handbook of Agricultural and Rural Development in Africa* serves as a solid reference point for future scholars, researchers and policy makers interested in informing and executing disruptive innovations in rural spaces on the African continent."
—Uche Ekhator-Mobayode, *Assistant Professor of Economics, University of Pittsburgh at Bradford, USA*

"An exceptionally rich and comprehensive volume that provides an in-depth view of issues relating to agricultural and rural development in Africa and addresses pertinent policy questions. This is an important book, examining agricultural transformation from different perspectives across different countries on the continent to raise arising concerns, discuss impacts and provide helpful policies and recommendations. Astonishing scholarship, I hope this volume become a standard in the literature on development economics on Africa."
—Samuel Amponsah, *President of the African Finance and Economic Association (AFEA), Institute for International Strategy, Tokyo International University, Japan*

"Unlike the previous publications on the subject, this book brings together the work of people who are concerned and knowledgeable about the dynamics of rural development and the channels through which transformation in agricultural land investments, production, processing, and other value chain activities boost productivity, income and employment for people living and working in rural areas in many African countries. By focusing on agricultural and rural development in Africa, this book has given the plights of poor farmers the special attention and efforts they deserve. Ultimately, the future success of initiatives to alleviate poverty, create employment and increase the livelihood of households in Africa is in the hands of Africans themselves and the competencies of its training institutes and research organizations. It provides a platform for African researchers to showcase their proficiencies in producing high quality research with robust and more widely applicable results."
—Jacinta Nwachukwu, *Professor, Lancashire School of Business and Enterprise, University of Central Lancashire, UK*

"This book, which looks at agricultural and rural development in Africa, is timely and dovetails very well with the current African and international development agenda with respect to African Union Agenda 2063 and the United Nations Sustainable Development Goals (SDGs). Furthermore, the theme of the book is perfectly aligned with the African

Development Bank's High-5 on *Feed Africa* as well as the 2003 Maputo and 2014 Malabo declarations on the Comprehensive Africa Agriculture Development Program (CAADP). The book provides rich background information for policy makers, development partners, students, and researchers. Undeniably, there is something in the book for every person, especially those who have a great interest in agricultural research and rural development."
—Adeleke O. Salami, *Principal Macroeconomist, African Development Bank Group Abidjan, Cote D' Ivoire*

"*The Palgrave Handbook on Agricultural and Rural Development in Africa* addresses relevant and crucial development issues as they pertain to the agriculture sector in African countries. It takes a holistic approach and presents these issues from multidisciplinary and cross-country perspectives. It is with no doubt that this handbook is very timely, insightful and appeals to anyone interested in the development of the agricultural sector and rural economy in Africa and other developing regions."
—Evelyn F. Wamboye, *Associate Professor, Pennsylvania State University, DuBois, USA*

"During the last decades, agricultural and rural development have experienced several 'ups and downs' with respect to the attention of academics, policy and development cooperation. The agricultural sector itself, and its main actors, seems to be too weak to 'hype' itself the attention it deserves. Therefore, it is highly welcome that a large group of overwhelmingly African scholars has tackled the subject in this volume and presents a broad spectrum of views on many of the topics that move the sector. I am optimistic that it will contribute a great deal in maintaining and sustaining the attention!"
—Michael Brüntrup, *Senior Research Fellow, German Development Institute, Bonn, Germany*

"The Agricultural sector is vital to Africa's prosperity and development. This sector employs more than half of the labor force but produces only 15% of GDP, with considerable cross-country variation, indicating that current performance remains below potential. *The Palgrave Handbook of Agricultural and Rural Development in Africa* contains technically rich and policy-relevant chapters that shed light on the performance and challenges of Africa's agriculture sector, particularly, youth employment, agricultural productivity, agricultural value chain, access to financial services, agricultural cooperatives and food security in Africa. Therefore, this book offers an excellent contribution for better understanding of the current state and prospects of Africa's agricultural transformation and generates valuable insights for improved agricultural policymaking on the continent."
—Ramu Govindasamy, *Professor and Chair, Department of Agricultural, Food, and Resource Economics, Rutgers, The State University of New Jersey, USA*

"The 2019 progress report on the attainment of the Sustainable Development Goals (SDGs) in Africa highlights a stark warning: unless serious action is taken by African countries now, most of the SDGs are unlikely to be met in Africa by 2030. It is known that the greatest development challenges in Africa are in the rural areas where about 60% of the population live and where agriculture is by far the main economic activity. It is against this background that the timeliness and importance of this book must be judged. The plea by the authors for agricultural and rural transformation for Africa's development rings loud and clear throughout the book; may it be heeded!"
—Goolam Mohamedbhai, *Former Secretary-General, Association of African Universities; Former President, International Association of Universities; Professor and Former Vice-Chancellor, University of Mauritius, Mauritius*

Evans S. Osabuohien
Editor

The Palgrave Handbook of Agricultural and Rural Development in Africa

Editor
Evans S. Osabuohien
Covenant University
Ota, Nigeria

Witten/Herdecke University
Witten, Germany

ISBN 978-3-030-41515-0   ISBN 978-3-030-41513-6 (eBook)
https://doi.org/10.1007/978-3-030-41513-6

© The Editor(s) (if applicable) and The Author(s), under exclusive license to Springer Nature Switzerland AG 2020, corrected publication 2020
This work is subject to copyright. All rights are solely and exclusively licensed by the Publisher, whether the whole or part of the material is concerned, specifically the rights of translation, reprinting, reuse of illustrations, recitation, broadcasting, reproduction on microfilms or in any other physical way, and transmission or information storage and retrieval, electronic adaptation, computer software, or by similar or dissimilar methodology now known or hereafter developed.
The use of general descriptive names, registered names, trademarks, service marks, etc. in this publication does not imply, even in the absence of a specific statement, that such names are exempt from the relevant protective laws and regulations and therefore free for general use.
The publisher, the authors and the editors are safe to assume that the advice and information in this book are believed to be true and accurate at the date of publication. Neither the publisher nor the authors or the editors give a warranty, expressed or implied, with respect to the material contained herein or for any errors or omissions that may have been made. The publisher remains neutral with regard to jurisdictional claims in published maps and institutional affiliations.

Cover illustration: Michele D'Amico supersky77/Getty Images

This Palgrave Macmillan imprint is published by the registered company Springer Nature Switzerland AG
The registered company address is: Gewerbestrasse 11, 6330 Cham, Switzerland

Foreword by Dr. Badar Alam Iqbal

It gives me the immense pleasure and honour to write a foreword on the book entitled *The Palgrave Handbook of Agricultural and Rural Development in Africa*, edited by Prof. Evans S. Osabuohien.

Agriculture and rural development is the sin-quo-non for every developing economy across the world. Africa is no exception. The editor has chosen a very critical issue of the African continent. Across the developing countries especially in Africa, there is a low level of agricultural transformation along with rural growth and development. This is largely due to inappropriate linkages between agriculture and agro-industries, which are the essential "**spring boards**" for accelerating rural growth and development.

It is an undisputed fact that a country cannot attain economic emancipation unless and until its agricultural sector and rural economies are properly and adequately developed. This could be possible when the country selects and applies proper technology and other modern practices in these sectors. Thus, the major issues, namely poverty, creation of jobs, and low purchasing power, are closely related to agricultural and rural development.

As the editor has rightly opined in the introductory chapter, that transformation suggests the course of change of paradigm, which is a pivotal element of development. In this way, it could be said that transformation goes in tandem with development. Furthermore, rural transformation entails both agricultural and non-agricultural activities, which presupposes that agricultural transformation is subsumed in rural transformation. Therefore, agricultural transformation, agricultural development, rural transformation, and rural development are used to express closely related meaning by various authors in the book.

This book has well-thought and—documented five sections with twenty-six chapters covering the different segments of agriculture and rural development in Africa. Every section is dealing with the major issues within the section that the sectors are facing. The views of the authors are well supported by the citations. The citations are up to date and well inserted at the appropriate places to enhance the academic value of the book.

I do agree with the observations of the editor that "to achieve the desired agricultural transformation and development in Africa, more concerted efforts are required in formulating and implementing policies that will make financial resources available to the agricultural sector; reducing employment bottlenecks; access to agricultural-friendly technologies; adherence to principles guiding land acquisitions, among others. The aforementioned are germane to ensure that the desired agricultural and rural development in Africa are not only sustainable but people-centred".

It is true that the basic purpose and function of agriculture and rural development is to boost the purchasing power of the people and their respective quality of life. These are the essential facets for transformation of traditional economy into modern economy. This could be possible when the required amount of investment is made out in the major segments of the rural economy of the African continent. There is a correct saying that "**rural Africa is the real Africa**" and economic, social, and political emancipation cannot see the light of the day unless and until there is accelerating pace of growth and development in "**rural Africa.**" Thus, the main challenge is the choice of the technology and its application in the agriculture and rural sectors.

The book provides a critical and valuable insight into the structure and function of the agriculture and rural economy in the African region and countries. It is both intensive and extensive. The book is "**light and fruit bearing**" in nature and contents. I must congratulate the editor and all the contributors for providing such a study, which will serve the better cause of agricultural and rural development on the African continent. It will also serve as an eye "**opener**" for planners and policymakers on the continent, who may take into consideration the issues raised and solutions provided, especially in the context of finance, food security, and the land management system. There must be an integrated approach for meeting the rising challenges which the African continent, in general, and the rural economy, in particular, face and which the book unveils to the readers.

Emeritus Prof. Dr. Badar Alam Iqbal
Adjunct Professor, Faculty of Economics and Finance
Monarch University, Zug, Switzerland

Former Extraordinary Professor, North West University
(Vaal Campus), South Africa

Monarch University
Zug, Switzerland

Foreword by Simplice Asongu

It is a consensus both in scholarly and policy circles that after two decades of economic growth resurgence, many lives in Africa have not improved. It is apparent from the attendant literature that many countries in the continent did not achieve the Millennium Development Goals (MDGs) target of halving extreme poverty by 2015. In summary, over the past two decades, while extreme poverty has decreased substantially in other regions of the world, close to half of the countries in Africa were substantially off-track from achieving the MDG extreme poverty target. Post-2015 policy reports and scholarship are also consistent on the view that unless paradigm shifts are taken on board, it is very unlikely that most countries in Africa would achieve most Sustainable Development Goals (SDGs) targets by 2030.

In the light of the above, *The Palgrave Handbook on Agricultural and Rural Development in Africa* is a timely scholarly contribution that provides critical insights into the *Main Issues and Imperatives* that are worth engaging by scholars and policymakers in order to steer Africa towards the achievement of the SDGs. Whereas almost all dimensions of the SDGs are engaged in the book, two specific SDGs merit emphasis. SDG2 (*end hunger, achieve food security and improved nutrition and promote sustainable agriculture*) and SDG 8 (*promote sustained, inclusive and sustainable economic growth, full and productive employment and decent work for all*), which are central elements of the book, clearly articulate the imperative of addressing the challenge of agriculture and food security in the light of growing concerns about job creation, especially among the rural population. The narratives in the book are not exclusively limited to the livelihoods pertaining to primary production. This is essentially because, insights into the non-farm economy and value chains are also provided to articulate the interdependence of agriculture with other sectors of the economy in order to maximize targeted inclusive benefits for society.

The lessons learned from the failed integrated rural development programs in the 1960s are taken into profound account. In essence, policy syndromes and *Main Issues* of the failed rural development dominant paradigms of donors in the immediate post-independence era as well as subsequent structural adjustment and sector-wide paradigms from international financial institutions are addressed in this timely book. Accordingly, policy measures and *Imperatives* proposed in this scholarship acknowledge past lessons surrounding donor-funded investments, which cannot be effective unless there are substantial policy environmental changes. Hence, inter alia, enhanced political will and institutional capacity are some imperatives for the suggested policy initiatives to be sustainably taken on board. The novel approaches to rural transformation and development covered in the book are built on proven and documented contemporary successes on what works for agricultural and rural development. These include: people-centred approaches that are tailored to finding local solutions pertaining to local opportunities and challenges; building a conducive environment for inclusive and responsible investment in the private sector; evidence-tailored solutions that are resilient, inclusive and sustainable; engaging investments and policy concerns with transparency and accountability and strong ownership by stakeholders at the national levels (especially civil society and farming organizations).

In summary, the new paradigms to rural development proposed herein considerably acknowledge the central role of the rural world which, contrary to assumptions pertaining to policy syndromes of failed paradigms, are very different and extremely diverse, complex, and dynamic from one country to another. Hence, the *Issues* raised and *Imperatives* documented in this book for agriculture and rural development carefully engage the fact that the connectedness between the modern economy and the rural population is changing dramatically and hence multifaceted and country-specific approaches are worthwhile.

A relevant common feature that is apparent among the authors of various chapters is that the analyzed findings are succinctly summarized in order to increase readability and accessibility on the part of scholars and policymakers who might need more technical knowhow to grasp the robust empirical analyses and corresponding policy suggestions. Therefore, the book is an easy-to-read and richly policy-relevant scholarship for both non-specialists and specialists.

Prof. Simplice Asongu
The African Governance and Development Institute
Yaounde, Cameroon

Acknowledgments

The editor wishes to most sincerely appreciate the helpful assistance provided by individuals and organizations, which made this research project become a reality right from the ideas formation, conceptualization, proposal stage, review to this beautiful scientific piece. The dedication of the contributing authors of the respective chapters as well as the reviewers is greatly acknowledged.

It is worthy of note that the concept of this research project concretized from my research activities as a Visiting Professor at Faculty of Management and Economics, Witten/Herdecke University (W/HU), Germany with funding from the Alexander von Humboldt Foundation (AvH), Germany. Thus, I deeply appreciate the award from AvH for providing stipend for my stay and that of my family members in Germany, which enhanced my focus and concentration. The helpful assistance from my hosts at W/HU (Dr. Magdalene Silberberger and Prof. Joachim Zweynert) for creating compelling and serene ambience for productive research engagement is appreciated.

The provision of a good working environment by The German Development Institute during my short research stay in June 2019 after my Keynote Speech at the Jan Walliser Memorial Lecture, which facilitated the writing of the preliminary pages of the book, is equally acknowledged. Similarly, I appreciate Covenant University for granting me the permission to embark on research leave that enabled me to stay focused. My sincere appreciation also goes to my former hosts (Dr. Michael Bruentrup, German Development Institute, Bonn and Prof. Jann Lay, German Institute for Global and Area Studies-GIGA, Hamburg) who have remained veritable source of intellectual stimulation over the years.

The call for the book chapters had a wide coverage across the globe, which was facilitated by numerous networks that assisted in disseminating the information. These include: Dr. Kathleen G. Beegle (World Bank), United Nations Conference for Trade and Development Virtual Institute (UNCTAD Vi),

African Finance and Economic Association (AFEA) network, Council for the Development of Social Science in Africa (CODESRIA), Nigerian Economic Society (NES), African Economic Research Consortium (AERC), Young African Researchers in Agriculture (YARA), African Growth and Development Policy Modeling Consortium (AGRODEP), African Political Economy Association, African-German Network of Excellence in Science (AGNES), Swedish Institute, among others.

Furthermore, I remain grateful to faculty and staff of the Department of Economics and Development Studies, Centre for Economic Policy and Development Research (CEPDeR) as well as Regional Centre of Expertise, Ogun (RCE Ogun), Covenant University for valuable insights that helped the *incubation and hatching* of this laudable project. I wish to also acknowledge the inputs and suggestions received from participants and organizers (too numerous to itemize) at various seminars, conferences, and workshops across the world where the ideas, processes, and stages of the research project were discussed.

Finally, I am eternally grateful to the Most High God for the strength and wisdom as well as my family members for their unquantifiable supports that created healthy and fertile ground to nurture and sustain the ideas all through despite other issues contesting for my time and attention.

Ota, Nigeria   Evans S. Osabuohien Ph.D.
2020

Contents

Introduction 1
Evans S. Osabuohien

General and Background Issues

Domesticating the SDGs in Africa for Rural and Agricultural Development: The Case of Devolved Governance 17
Samuel Mwangi Wanjiku, Fred Jonyo, and Milton Alwanga

Youth Employment Challenge and Rural Transformation in Africa 41
Damian Kalu Ude

Impact of Remittances on Agricultural Labor Productivity in Sub-Saharan Africa 67
Kwami Ossadzifo Wonyra and Muriel E. S. Ametoglo

Electricity Access and Agricultural Productivity in Sub-Saharan Africa: Evidence from Panel Data 89
Oluwasola E. Omoju, Opeyemi N. Oladunjoye,
Iyabo A. Olanrele, and Adedoyin I. Lawal

Beyond the Farm Gate: Can Social Capital Help Smallholders to Overcome Constraints in the Agricultural Value Chain in Africa? 109
Oluwaseun Kolade, Oluwasoye Mafimisebi,
and Oluwakayode Aluko

Household Livelihood and Welfare Matters

Large-Scale Land Investments and Household Livelihood in Nigeria: Empirical Insights from Quantitative Analysis — 133
Evans S. Osabuohien, Felicia O. Olokoyo, Uchenna R. Efobi, Alhassan A. Karakara, and Ibukun Beecroft

Agricultural Productivity and Household Welfare in Uganda: Examining the Relevance of Agricultural Improvement Interventions — 153
Nicholas Kilimani, John Bosco Nnyanzi, Ibrahim M. Okumu, and Edward Bbaale

Pattern of Labor Use and Productivity Among Agricultural Households in Nigeria — 175
Popoola A. Olufemi and Adejare A. Kayode

Challenges in Tackling Poverty and Unemployment: Analysis of Youth Employment in Agriculture Program in Alkaleri, Duguri and Gar Rural Communities of Bauchi State, Nigeria — 199
Ruqayya Aminu Gar and Roy Anthony Rodgers

Access to Resources, Transformation and Productivity Interactions

Determinants of the Willingness to Pay for Public Sector Health Care Services: An Empirical Study of Rural and Urban Communities in Nigeria — 219
Lloyd Ahamefule Amaghionyeodiwe

Increasing Agricultural Income and Access to Financial Services through Mobile Technology in Africa: Evidence from Malawi — 247
Angella Faith Montfaucon

Identifying the Gap Between the Demand and Supply of Agricultural Finance Among Irrigation Farmers in Namibia — 263
Elina M. Amadhila and Sylvanus Ikhide

Access to Land and Food Security: Analysis of 'Priority Crops' Production in Ogun State, Nigeria — 291
Ngozi Adeleye, Evans S. Osabuohien, Samuel Adeogun, Siraj Fashola, Oyinkan Tasie, and Gideon Adeyemi

**Rural Transformation Through Savings and Credit
Cooperative Societies in Moshi District, Tanzania**   313
Neema P. Kumburu and Vincent Pande

Employment, Migration and Transformation Nexus

**Rural–Urban Labor Migration and Youth Employment:
Investigating the Relevance of Nigeria's Agricultural Sector
in Employment Generation**   341
Abiodun Elijah Obayelu, Oluwakemi Adeola Obayelu,
and Esther Toluwatope Tolorunju

**Fostering Rural Development and Social Inclusion
in East Africa: Interrogating the Role of Cooperatives**   367
Mangasini Katundu

**Impact of Non-agricultural Activities on Farmers'
Income: Evidence from the Senegalese Groundnut Area**   395
Amadou Tandjigora

**Youth (Un)employment and Large-Scale Agricultural
Land Investments: Examining the Relevance
of Indigenous Institutions and Capacity in Tanzania**   425
Evans S. Osabuohien, Alexander von Humboldt,
Uchenna R. Efobi, Ciliaka M. Gitau, Romanus A. Osabohien,
and Oluwasogo S. Adediran

**Local Politics of Land Acquisitions for Foreign
and Domestic Investments in Tanzania**   457
Godfrey Eliseus Massay

**Agricultural Policy and Food Security in Nigeria:
A Rational Choice Analysis**   475
Opeyemi Idowu Aluko

Processing, Value Chain and Food Security

**Socio-Cultural Factors and Performance of Small-Scale
Enterprise in Agro-Allied Manufacturing Firms in Nigeria**   495
Alidu O. Kareem, Temitope F. Jiboye, Oluwabunmi O. Adejumo,
and Michael O. Akinyosoye

**Labor Processes in Large-Scale Land Investments:
The Case of Sugar Estates in South-Eastern Zimbabwe**   513
Patience Mutopo

**Poverty Reduction, Sustainable Agricultural Development,
and the Cassava Value Chain in Nigeria**   525
Waidi Gbenro Adebayo and Magdalene Silberberger

**Micro-determinants of Women's Participation in Agricultural
Value Chain: Evidence from Rural Households in Nigeria**   553
Kehinde Oluwole Ola

**Job Creation and Social Conditions of Labor
in the Forestry Agro-Industry in Mozambique**   571
Rosimina Ali

**Boosting Non-oil Export Revenue in Nigeria Through
Non-traditional Agricultural Export Commodities: How
Feasible?**   611
Grace O. Evbuomwan, Felicia O. Olokoyo, Tolulope Adesina,
and Lawrence U. Okoye

**Conclusion: Agricultural Investments and Rural
Development in Africa—Salient Issues and Imperatives**   627
Evans S. Osabuohien and Alhassan A. Karakara

**Correction to: Increasing Agricultural Income
and Access to Financial Services through Mobile Technology
in Africa: Evidence from Malawi**   C1
Angella Faith Montfaucon

Index   641

Notes on Contributors

Waidi Gbenro Adebayo is a Doctoral Candidate, Economics at the Faculty of Management and Economics at the Universität Witten/Herdecke in Germany and a visiting Ph.D. Scholar at the Centre for Economic Policy and Development Research (CEPDeR) at Covenant University, Nigeria. He holds a masters degree in philosophy, politics, and economics (PPE) with a major in global economic development, an MBA with specialization in finance and operations management. He is an associate member of the Nigerian Institute of Management (NIM), and a member of the Global Coalition for Abolition of Poverty (GCAP) and, Action for Sustainable Development Coalition (A4SD), and CIVICUS: World Alliance for Citizen Participation. His research interests are in sustainable development, political economy, agricultural economics, human capital development, poverty reduction, inequality, entrepreneurship, and MSME development.

Oluwasogo S. Adediran a member of Faculty at Covenant University in the Department of Economics and Development Studies, where he involves in community service, research, teaching, and mentoring both undergraduate and postgraduate students. He is article editor for SAGE Publications and reviewer for International Business Information Management Association (IBIMA) conferences that are indexed in Web of Science and Scopus. He is involved in a series of research, which has resulted in publications in high impact and world-class Journals locally and internationally and has participated in seminars, conferences, workshops, and short courses. Astute in research in the area of International Economics, Macroeconomics, Applied Econometrics, Financial Economics, Development Economics, and Sustainable Development Goals (SDGs).

Oluwabunmi O. Adejumo is a graduate of Economics of the Obafemi Awolowo University, Ile-Ife with a specialty in the areas of labour and development economics. She is currently a researcher and a lecturer in the same University. She has participated in divers Academic Research & Developmental project aimed at tackling unemployment and scaling up entrepreneurship and vocational skills acquisition for undergraduates in the university where she works and she is also directly involved in Business Development Consultancy Services for companies and corporate organization. Dr. (Mrs.) Adejumo currently has more than 18 published articles at the local and international levels. She has attended several conferences and has been opportune to be a speaker at different academic sessions and fora. She is also a member of professional bodies and networks like The Econometrics Society, and Inter-University Sustainable Development Research Programme. She has served on a number of review board and an associate editor to book projects and journal publications. Her research interest lies in the area of labour issues, sustainable entrepreneurship, sustainable financing, inclusive growth, and sustainable development.

Ngozi Adeleye is a researcher and lecturer in the Department of Economics and Development Studies, Covenant University, Ota, Nigeria. A graduate of Ogun State University, Nigeria and University of Sussex, UK, her research interest revolves around income inequality, financial economics, agricultural economics and issues related to Sustainable Development Goals (SDGs). She is quantitative inclined and has recently published some works relating to her Ph.D. thesis with research findings presented in international conferences/workshops. She is also the tutor and creator of *CrunchEconometrix* www.cruncheconometrix.com.ng a digital platform she designed to teach hands-on econometrics to millions of learners across the world. Her YouTube Channel www.youtube.com/c/CrunchEconometrix has a growing daily subscriber base which serves as a succour to beginners and intermediate users of econometric tools. She is proficient in the use of Stata, EViews, and SPSS analytical softwares. She serves as a reviewer to some international journals.

Samuel Adeogun is the Director of Planning, Monitoring, and Evaluation, Ogun State Ministry of Agriculture. He obtained a Bachelor of Agriculture (Agricultural Economics) and Masters in Agriculture (Agricultural Economics) from the University of Ibadan. Some of his functions involves the development of annual work plan and budget for the agricultural project in Ogun State, monitoring and evaluation of project's major activities, monitoring of project's budget implementation, and preparation of periodic progress reports.

Tolulope Adesina holds a Doctoral Degree and lectures in the Department of Banking and Finance, Covenant University, Ota, Ogun State, Nigeria. She graduated from Obafemi Awolowo University, Ile-Ife with a Bachelor's degree in Economics. She proceeded to the University of Nottingham, the United

Kingdom for a Postgraduate diploma in Economics and Financial Economics. She had her Master's degree in Strategic Financial Management from the University of Derby, the United Kingdom. Prior to her joining Covenant University, she worked with Gods Vineyard Ministries, Nottingham, United Kingdom as an Account Officer for over four years. Her main teaching areas are: Introduction to Banking and Finance, Business Finance, Financial Management and Quantitative Analysis for Financial Decisions. She has research interests in Development Finance, Agricultural Finance, Corporate Finance, and Financial Economics. She has a sizeable number of publications in reputable journals.

Gideon Adeyemi is a Lecturer in the Department of Civil Engineering, College of Engineering, Covenant University, Ota, Nigeria. He obtained his Bachelor of Agriculture from University of Ilorin and M.Sc. in Geographic Information Systems from the University of Ibadan, Certificate in Geo-Information Science and Earth Observation from ITC, Netherlands. He has attended many workshops and conferences both local and international. His research interest includes: Natural resources conservation, Environmental management, Built Environment Design and planning, Land Information Systems, and Sustainable Development.

Michael O. Akinyosoye is a Lecturer at the Institute for Entrepreneurship and Development Studies Obafemi Awolowo University Ile-Ife Nigeria. He holds B.Sc., M.Sc., and M.Phil. in Economics in the Department of Economics Obafemi Awolowo University, Ile-Ife. He is currently on his Ph.D. Programme in the same Department. He has attended many Conferences on Entrepreneurship and has many papers published in reputable Journals locally and internationally. His are of research include Entrepreneurship, Family Business & Retirement Planning, Business Economics, and Entrepreneurship for the Disable.

Rosimina Ali Researcher at the Institute for Social and Economic Studies (IESE) and a Lecturer at the Department of Economics at Eduardo Mondlane University. She holds a Master of Science in Development Economics from the University of London, School of Oriental and African Studies–SOAS (2012). She graduated in Economics from the Department of Economics at Eduardo Mondlane University–UEM (2008). Her areas of research focus on labour markets, employment, inequalities, and productive structures in Mozambique.

Oluwakayode Aluko is a Lecturer in Strategic Management at the De Montfort University. His research and teaching cover areas around Innovation, Strategy and Sustainability. Prior to working in the academia, he had experience in Engineering Consulting and Entrepreneurship. He has been involved in the delivery of a number of development projects both nationally and internationally and contributed towards the delivery of the EU sponsored IAPP project in partnership with Institutions and Industry partners in Turkey in 2016 (Mini-CHIP). He is also now looking to further develop research around Digital/Disruptive Innovation in Developing Economies contexts. He has authored several conference papers and journal publications.

Opeyemi Idowu Aluko is a proficient scholar in the field of Political Science. His research includes Political Economy, Election, Judicial Studies, Security Studies, Comparative Politics, and Research Methodology. Presently, he lectures at Ajayi Crowther University, Oyo, Oyo State, Nigeria. He is a doctoral candidate in the Political Science Department Kwara State University, Malete, Kwara State, Nigeria. He has over 40 publications in reputable outlets national and international. He has presented various research findings in different academic conferences.

Milton Alwanga is a lecturer in the Department of Development Studies in Jomo Kenyatta University of Agriculture and Technology (JKUAT), Kenya where he teaches courses in Development Studies. He is to graduate next year with a Ph.D. in Development Studies from JKUAT. He holds two Master Degrees—M.A. in Development Studies and an M.A. in Philosophy from the University of Nairobi, Kenya. He also holds a BA in economics and Philosophy from the same university. His research interests include: Public–Private sector partnerships, Development Planning and Rural Societies and Change.

Elina M. Amadhila is a Lecturer in the Faculty of Economics and Management Sciences at the University of Namibia Windhoek, Namibia. Dr. Amadhila holds a Ph.D. in Development Finance from Stellenbosch. She also holds a Master of Arts and a Bachelor of Business Administration from the University of Namibia. Her research interests include topics on agricultural finance, education, and barriers to access health care services.

Lloyd Ahamefule Amaghionyeodiwe is a Certified Fraud Examiner (CFE) and a Certified Internal Controls Auditor (CICA) who has several years of experience as a lecturer/professor, researcher, analyst, economist, and consultant. He served as a reviewer for many journals and has a good research record with many publications to his credit. His current research interests include Finance, Small Business Management & IT, and Economics with more focus on Public Sector & Health Economics.

Muriel E. S. Ametoglo is alecturer, researcher, policy analyst, economist, reviewer, and consultant. She was awarded her Ph.D. in Applied Economics with honours, from the Department of Economics and Trade (Hunan University, China). She spent four years as a research fellow in the Department. She also holds both bachelor and master degrees in economics from the Université of Lomé and another Master degree in international monetary economics from Hunan University. Her research interests include the Regional Integration, development economics, Poverty and Inequality,

Econometrics as well as Financing entrepreneurship and Sustainable Development. Dr. Ametoglo has published her research in leading economics journals and has presented her work at numerous conventions.

Edward Bbaale is an Associate Professor of Economics and holds a Ph.D. in Economics. He is also currently the Dean of the School of Economics, Makerere University. Prior to that, Edward also served as a Graduate Programs Coordinator for the School of Economics from 2012 to 2013. He has very rich hands-on experience in economics research with a bias towards development microeconomics. He was in 2010 nominated for the Visiting Research Fellow Position at the Centre for Global Development in Washington D.C. USA, (September 2010–September 2011) and in 2013 he was nominated a Visiting Fellow for the Journal of African Economies, Department of Economics, University of Oxford, UK (April–June 2013). Edward has undertaken several research projects with different grants. He has recently been awarded a 3-month(s) (September–November 2017) post-doctoral scholarship by the Austrian Agency for International Cooperation in Education and Research (OeAD-GmbH).

Ibukun Beecroft is an Economics Researcher and Faculty at Covenant University (CU), Nigeria, from where she holds a bachelor's degree in Economics. She also holds a masters degree from the University of London's School of Oriental and African Studies, United Kingdom, and a Ph.D. from Covenant University, Ota, Nigeria. Her research is centred on Fiscal Studies, Institutions, and Economic Development in Africa. She has collaborated with a number of scholars in her field on various grants and award-winning research projects. Some of these include: Adoption of the Integrated Tax Administration System research (funded by ICTD/NTRN); Large-Scale Agricultural Land Investment project (funded by CODESRIA); Green Industrialization project (funded by UONGOZI); Trade Protectionism research (funded by CEPR/GTA/ACET), among others. She is an international scholar who continuously participates in knowledge sharing through her publications and conference presentations in many parts of the world.

Uchenna R. Efobi obtained his Ph.D. in December 2016 from the College of Business and Social Sciences, Covenant University, Ota, where he holds a Senior Lectureship position. His research focus is on Development, Institutions and International Economics. He has publications in journals and book chapters published by Elsevier, Taylor and Francis, Springer, among others. He is also a qualified Chartered Accountant. He has participated in conferences/workshops in different parts of the world.

Grace O. Evbuomwan is a Fellow of the Farm Management Association of Nigeria (FFAMAN), which, is affiliated to the African Farm Management Association (AFMA) and the International Farm Management Association (IFMA). She is also an Honorary Senior Member of the Chartered Institute of Bankers of Nigeria (HCIB). She trained as an Agricultural Economist and is an experienced Banker. She is widely travelled and has participated in IFMA/AFMA congresses since 1993. She was elected President, African Farm Management Association in 2004, and currently represents West and Central Africa on the Council of the International Farm Management Association. She consulted for the Food and Agricultural Organization of the United Nations (FAO) between 2005 and 2007. She worked for the Central Bank of Nigeria between 1981 and 2008, and retired as an Assistant Director, Development Finance Department, after which she joined the Academia. She has authored over 50 publications.

Siraj Fashola is the Director of Planning Research & Statistics, Ogun State Ministry of Agriculture. He obtained a Bachelor of Agriculture (Agricultural Economics) and Masters in Agriculture (Agricultural Economics and Farm Management) from the University of Agriculture, Abeokuta. His research interests revolve around social/economic research, rural development, and farm advisory services.

Ruqayya Aminu Gar is a lecturer at the Department of Political Science, Bauchi State University, Gadau Nigeria. Obtained B.Sc. Political Science from UNIMAID, Borno State Nigeria, and MSc in Political Science from the International Islamic University Malaysia (IIUM) Malaysia. Currently is a Ph.D. research fellow with the Department of International and Strategic Studies, University of Malaya, Malaysia. She is a Resource Person from 2011 to Date with the Consultancy Services Unit, Political Science Programme, School of General Studies in Abubakar Tatari Ali Polytechnic, Bauchi. She has research interest in International and strategic studies/Government and Development policies.

Ciliaka M. Gitau is an Economist at the World Bank in the Trade, investment, and competitiveness practice. Previously, she was a tutorial fellow in the School of Economics, University of Nairobi. She also holds a Masters of Arts and Bachelor of Arts in Economics from the same University. She is a qualified Certified Public Accountant and Investment and Securities Analyst. Her research focus is on private sector development, international trade and finance, and financial economics. She has published on peer-reviewed journals and participated in several conferences and workshops.

Sylvanus Ikhide is a Professor in Development Finance at the Stellenbosch University Business School. His research interests cut across money, banking and finance, poverty studies, and development finance.

Temitope F. Jiboye is a Lecturer at the Institute for Entrepreneurship and Development Studies Obafemi Awolowo University Ile-Ife Nigeria. She holds B.A. English from Ambrose Alli University, Ekpoma, M.Sc and Ph.D. in International relations with specialty in International Economic Relations in the Department of International Relations Obafemi Awolowo University, Ile-Ife. She has contributed to knowledge by providing information on the features of Entrepreneurial Economic Sustainability to guide business owners in implementing strategic product development policy programs, to guide the government in making economic policies; and also providing theoretical basis for further studies. She has attended many Conferences on Entrepreneurship and has many papers published in reputable Journals locally and internationally with research areas include Entrepreneurship, Family Business & Retirement Planning, Design thinking, and Entrepreneurship for the Disable.

Fred Jonyo is the Chair, Department of Political Science and Public Administration, University of Nairobi. He holds a Doctorate Degree in Political Science and Public Administration from Makerere University, Uganda; Masters in International Politics from the Graduate School of International Relations, Japan and a Bachelors (Hons) Degree in Political Science from University of Nairobi, Kenya. His areas of specialization include; Political Economy, International Relations, National Security, and Strategic Studies.

Alhassan A. Karakara is a postgraduate researcher at the Department of Economics, University of Cape Coast, Ghana. He started researching when he served as a Research Assistant for Educational Network for West and Central Africa (ENWACA), in May–June 2009. He had his first degree in Economics, M.Sc. Economics of Technology and Development as well as Master of Philosophy in Economics all from the University of Cape Coast, Ghana. He has published some articles in peer review journals with other several articles co-authored with Prof. Evans Osabuohien that are under peer review in various Journals. He has served as a discussant and presenter in international conferences across the African Continent. He was a panel in the African Innovation Summit II, in Kigali Rwanda in June 2018. His research interest includes; poverty, economics of innovation and technology, development economics, and international economics with emphasis on developing countries.

Alidu O. Kareem is a Sociologist and Anthropologist trained at Obafemi Awolowo University, Ile-Ife. He obtained bachelor, masters, and doctorate degrees (Sociology & Anthropology) and M.phil. (Bus. Admin.), all from Obafemi Awolowo University, Ile- Ife, Osun state, Nigeria. He has engaged in teaching, research, and community service at Bells University, Ota, Joseph Ayo Babalola University (JABU), Ikeji-Arakeji, Osun State University, Okuku Campus, and presently at Federal University Wukari, Taraba State, in the last 10 years after successfully disengaged from the media industry as Deputy Manager (Distribution and Circulation) with landmark achievement. He had also held several academic and administrative positions in the university, aside from being a member of other university committees. As a scholar in the field of Sociology and Anthropology, he specializes in Industrial Sociology, Human Resource Management, and Gerontology. He had attended both national and international conferences, workshop, and seminars in the field of Sociology and Anthropology. He had also participated in many national research in the area of Political Participation, Political/Religious Violence, Aged Men Relationship with Adolescent Females, Bamako Initiative Programs among others. Dr. Kareem is a member of several professional bodies, such as Chartered Institute of Personnel Management of Nigeria (CIPMN); National Institute for Training and Development (NITAD); West Africa Research and Innovation Management Association (WARIMA), and National Anthropological and Sociological Association (NASA). He has successfully published in both local and international journals with contributions in academic books.

Mangasini Katundu is a senior lecturer at the Moshi Co-operative University (MoCU). He works at the Department of Community and Rural Development specializing in the area of rural development. He holds a Ph.D. and Master of Arts in Rural development from the Sokoine University of Agriculture (SUA), Morogoro Tanzania and a Bachelor of Arts (Hons) in Geography and Environmental Studies from the University of Dar Es Salaam, Tanzania. His research interests include: Agriculture and rural development, rural land reform, rural livelihoods and cooperatives, community-driven development, environment and natural resource management, entrepreneurship development, impact evaluation. Dr. Katundu has been involved in diverse studies either as a team leader or a team member. He has published more than ten papers in internationally recognized peer-reviewed journals. He is an active member of the Organization for Social Science Research in Eastern and Southern Africa (OSSREA) and Union for African Population Studies (UAPS).

Adejare A. Kayode holds Masters and Bachelors Degrees in Agricultural Economics from the University of Ibadan. He has admirable research capability and has participated in a number of research works in Nigeria. He has a number of academic papers in learned journals to his credit.

Nicholas Kilimani is a Lecturer in the Department of Policy and Development Economics, College of Business and Management Sciences, Makerere University in Kampala-Uganda. His is a Postdoctoral Research Fellow at the School of Economics, University of Johannesburg in South Africa and a Nordic African Institute Guest Researcher for 2019. His research interests are in the realm of environmental and development economics with an overall bias on research in a developing country context. He has published a number of outputs in peer-reviewed journals and book chapters. Some of his past research projects include modelling the impact of drought-induced productivity losses, policy relevancy of water resource accounting, and the use of fiscal policy in the management and use of environmental resources. His current projects include the impact of agricultural commercialization on household nutrition, and the impact of electrification on the socioeconomic improvement of households in Uganda.

Dr. Oluwaseun Kolade is a Senior Lecturer in Strategic Management at the Department of Strategic Management and Marketing at De Montfort University (DMU). Prior to joining DMU, he held research and teaching positions at London South Bank University, University of Wolverhampton, and Loughborough University. With a background in engineering and a Ph.D. in International Development, Dr. Kolade's research activities cover the broad areas of transformative entrepreneuring, social capital, entrepreneurship education and SMEs' innovation in turbulent environments, agricultural innovations, and post-disaster preparedness and response. He has published peer-reviewed articles in reputable journals, convened conference panels, and presented his works at various international fora. Dr. Kolade is also a regular blogger and has engaged publicly via several media, including newspapers, TV shows, and social media platforms, on issues relating to poverty, youth unemployment, and inclusive development.

Neema P. Kumburu is a Senior Lecturer at the Moshi Co-operative University (MoCU). She holds a Ph.D. in Business Management from the Sokoine University of Agriculture (SUA), Morogoro Tanzania, a Master of Public Administration (Human Resource Management) and a Bachelor Public Administration (Public Service Management) from the Mzumbe University (MU), Tanzania. She was appointed Acting Dean, Faculty of Business and Information Sciences in 2016 to 2017 and Head of Department, Department of Management from 2010 to 2019. She is currently Director of Bureau of Consultancy Services. She was a Visiting Research Fellow, Fredskorpset [FK] Business Experience Exchange Programme [BEEP], Bunda College of Agriculture, University of Malawi for a period of one year since 2007. She was also a visiting lecturer at the Moshi Catholic University for a period of one year. She has written many scholarly articles and presented in different fora, both nationally and internationally. Her research interests include: rural development, rural livelihoods, co-operatives, farmer's organizations, entrepreneurship, organizational development, governance, strategic management, sustainable development, and public administration and policy.

Adedoyin I. Lawal lectures at the Department of Accounting and Finance, Landmark University, Omu Aran, Nigeria. He holds a Bachelor Degree in Economics from the University of Ilorin, a Masters in Banking and Finance from Bayero University, Kano, and a Ph.D. in Banking and Finance from Covenant University. He has published extensively in reputable journals and book chapters. Dr. Lawal reviews for a number of Journals like *African Development Review* (Wiley); *The Quarterly Review of Economics and Finance* (Elsevier); *International Journal of Emerging Markets* (Emerald Insight); *Cogent Social Sciences* (Taylor and Francis), among others. He is on the Editorial Board of the Binus Business Review (Binus University, Indonesia) and serves as the Editor—in Chief of the Human and Social Science Letters.

Oluwasoye Mafimisebi is a Lecturer in Strategic Management at Leicester Castle Business School, De Montfort University, Leicester, United Kingdom. He received his Ph.D. from the University of Portsmouth. His research interests revolve around risk and crisis management, organizational resilience and business continuity, disaster and terrorism, and business ethics. Dr. Mafimisebi's current research centres on SMEs resilience, Crisis Management, Government as Entrepreneurs, Entrepreneurship Education, African Entrepreneurship, Commercialization of Research and Innovation, Disruptive Innovation and Strategy as Practice. He has published articles in *Journal of Emergency Management*, *International Journal of Mass Emergencies and Disasters*, *Journal of Economics and Sustainable Development*, and *European Journal of Business and Management*, among others.

Godfrey Eliseus Massay is a land rights lawyer who earned his Bachelor of Laws with honours in 2009 from the University of Dar es Salaam. He joined Landesa in May 2017 as Advocacy Manager for Tanzania office a position he held until June 2018 when he was promoted to become Land Tenure Specialist. Before joining Landesa, Mr. Massay worked with Land Rights Research and Resources Institute (HAKIARDHI) for four years and with Tanzania Natural Resources Forum (TNRF) for two and half years. Mr. Massay likes writing and publishing on land rights. In both organizations he implemented and supervised work on land rights literacy, legal aid, research, and policy advocacy. His primary research interests are on land grabbing, land reforms, constitutionalism, foreign investment, natural resources, and agrarian question and gender issues in Tanzania. In September 2018, he published a book chapter on *Land Based Investments in Tanzania: Legal Framework and Realities on the Ground*.

Angella Faith Montfaucon recently completed her doctoral studies at Yokohama National University under Japanese Government MEXT Scholarship. Prior to that she spent four and a half years working at the Reserve Bank of Malawi. During her time at the central bank she received an award for exceptional performance from the central bank governor and has since been active in regional policy through her research. Among others, she contributed to research Seminars organized by the Common Market of Eastern and Southern Africa (COMESA), the African Capacity Building Foundation (ACBF) and the Macroeconomic and Financial Management Institute of Eastern and Southern Africa (MEFMI). Two of her papers published by COMESA's annual Key Issues in Regional Integration volume 4 and volume 5 among other publications in per reviewed journals. During her Ph.D. in Japan, she has continued to present research findings at international conferences and workshops in Europe, Asia, and Africa. Her research is in the areas of financial inclusion, international trade, and international macroeconomics.

Patience Mutopo is a Social Scientist, and she is currently a Senior Lecturer in the Centre for Development Studies, Chinhoyi University of Technology, Zimbabwe. Her work centres on processes of rural development and land reform in Zimbabwe, agrarian transformation, gender analysis, rural livelihoods, and policy analysis. She holds a Ph.D. awarded with a Magna Cum Laude, from the Institute of Social and Cultural Anthropology and the Cologne African Studies Centre, University of Cologne, Germany and the Rural Development Sociology Group, University of Wageningen, The Netherlands. She has also completed a Postdoctoral Fellowship with the University of Cologne Germany, and her research focused on theoretical groundings of the land reform in Zimbabwe. She is a 2017/2018 fellow on the African Science Leadership Initiative, University of Pretoria, South Africa. Dr. Mutopo is a member of the internationally reputable research network, the Land Deal Politics Initiative administered by the Institute of Social Studies, the Hague, the Netherlands, the Institute of Development Studies, University of Sussex, United Kingdom, the Polson Centre for International Development, University of Cornell, USA and the Institute for Poverty, Land and Agrarian Studies, University of the Western Cape, South Africa. She is an active member of the Network on the Legal Empowerment of the Poor that is run concurrently by the Centre for Environment and Development, University of Oslo and the Norwegian Centre for Human Rights. Patience is also a member of the advisory board of Cambridge Publishers, in the United Kingdom. Furthermore, she is an editorial review member of several international reputable journals.

John Bosco Nnyanzi is a Lecturer of Economics at Makerere University after receiving his Doctorate in Economics in 2013 from Johannes Keppler University of Linz. He was also a visiting scholar at the University of Rwanda and a member of professional associations, such as the American Economic Association, where he has attended international conferences on teaching economics and research (Chicago, 2013) and on Economics and Education (Boston, 2012). He was Trade Specialist for the major project, the Northern Corridor Skills Audit, Northern Corridor Integration Projects, (NCIP)–2017. He has research interests ranging from Applied Macroeconomics to Applied Microeconomics, particularly in Development Economics, Capital Markets, Risk Sharing, Agricultural Economics, Economic growth, Regional Integration, Public policy, and, Remittances, inter alia, where he has published over 12 scholarly articles and 10 others still under consideration for publication. He is also a peer reviewer of the *African Journal of Economic and Management Sciences*.

Abiodun Elijah Obayelu started his educational career at the University of Ilorin, Kwara State Nigeria where he obtained Bachelor Degree in Agriculture in 1995. In year 2002, he completed his Master degrees in Business Administration (MBA), and Agricultural Economics (M.Sc.) from University of Ilorin and Ibadan, Nigeria, respectively. Obayelu has his Ph.D. degree in Agricultural Economics from the University of Ibadan. He currently lectures in the Department of Agricultural Economics and

Farm Management, Federal University of Agriculture Abeokuta, Ogun State, Nigeria and an Associate member of Capra International, Canada. He has research interests in Food and Consumer Economics, Resource and Environmental Economics, Production and Development Economics where he has published over 65 scholarly articles. He is a member of the African Growth and Development Policy (AGRODEP) Impact Evaluation Network and editorial board member of the African Journal of Food Nutrition and Development (AJFAND).

Oluwakemi Adeola Obayelu holds a Ph.D. in Agricultural Economics and is a lecturer in the Department of Agricultural Economics, University of Ibadan. She is an applied economist with research foci on gender, food policy, and development economics. She aims to contribute meaningfully to sustainable rural development in Nigeria and globally through research, training, community development, and policy advocacy. She is a member of local and international professional associations including African Growth and Development Modelling Consortium. She has published extensively in reputable peer-reviewed international journals.

Lawrence U. Okoye is a Lecturer in the Department of Banking and Finance, Covenant University Ota, Nigeria. He is actively engaged in teaching and research. He has published over forty scholarly articles in reputable journals and has presented over twenty research papers at major academic conferences across different the globe. Dr. Okoye is a reviewer for many reputable publishers, including Financial Innovation (Springer Nature) and IBIMA (International Business Information Management Association). His major areas of research include Corporate Finance, Financial Economics, and Development Finance. He is member of Nigerian Institute of Management (NIM).

Ibrahim M. Okumu is an Economist with expertise in public finance, informal economy, firm and household level analysis, inequality, economic growth and development, and public sector governance. His research experience has involved understanding the integral role of an effectively functioning public sector on: private sector development; quality of public expenditure; tax evasion; fiscal consolidation; informal economy; inequality; and economic growth and development. He has peer-reviewed publications in; Development Policy Review, African Development Review, and Innovation and Entrepreneurship among others. He is currently a Senior Lecturer at the School of Economics, Makerere University. He is also an Associate Researcher at the Economic Policy Research Center, Makerere University and a Research Affiliate of the Centre for Dynamic Macroeconomic Analysis, University of St Andrews. He holds a Ph.D. in Economics of the University of St Andrews (United Kingdom), M.A. Economics of McMaster University (Canada), and B.A. Economics of Makerere University (Uganda).

Kehinde Oluwole Ola teaches Economics at Samuel Adegboyega University, Ogwa, Edo State, Nigeria. He is a doctoral student at Ambrose Alli University, Ekpoma, Edo State, Nigeria. He has special interest in rural economics and environmental economics. His teaching areas are Statistics, Mathematical Economics, and Operational Research. Kehinde spends most of his free time with his wife (Mercy) and two children (Miracle and Joshua).

Opeyemi N. Oladunjoye is a Nigerian national. He holds a Doctorate degree in Economics from Obafemi Awolowo University, Ile-Ife. Prior to that, he holds Bachelor, Master of Science and Master of Philosophy in Economics from the University of Ilorin and Obafemi Awolowo University respectively. He is a Lecturer in the Department of Economics, Obafemi Awolowo University, Ile-Ife. His research interest is in International Trade and Finance and Energy Economics. He has a number of publications to his credit. He is a member of the Institute of Criminological Studies and Security Management, Nigeria (ICSSM); Nigerian Institute of Training and Development (NITDA) and Ife Development Policy Network, Obafemi Awolowo University, Ile-Ife.

Iyabo A. Olanrele has a Ph.D. in Energy Economics from the Centre for Petroleum Energy Economics and Law (CPEEL), University of Ibadan, Nigeria. Iyabo holds Bachelor and Master's degrees from the University of Ilorin. She works with the Nigerian Institute of Social and Economic Research, and equally a research fellow at CPEEL. She has published in reputable, national and international, journal outlets. The Federal Government of Nigeria has engaged Iyabo in several funded projects and she has attended both local and international conferences. Her main research interests lie in Macroeconomics, Econometrics, Energy Economics, Oil and Gas Economics, and Macroeconometric Modelling.

Felicia O. Olokoyo is an Associate Professor of Corporate Finance and current Director, Centre for Entrepreneurial Development Studies, Covenant University, Nigeria. Her research interest is in Lending Behaviour of Banks, Foreign Direct Investments, Capital Structure, Institutions and Corporate Performance, Corporate Governance, Land-based Investments (LIs), Large-scale Land-based Agricultural Investments (LLAIs), and Development Finance where she has published many scholarly articles and has presented conference/seminar papers in many countries of the world and has won several awards. She is a Fulbright Scholar and Fellow of the Chartered Institute of Bankers of Nigeria (FCIB). She is also a member of the Council for the Development of Social Science Research in Africa (CODESRIA), the International Forum for Democracy and Peace (IFDP), the International Academy of African Business and Development (IAABD) and Global Trade Analysis Project (GTAP), among others.

Popoola A. Olufemi is currently a Junior Research Fellow at the Nigerian Institute of Social and Economic Research (NISER), Ibadan, Nigeria and at the concluding stage of his Ph.D. in the Department of Agricultural Economics, University of Ibadan, Nigeria. He holds a Master's and Bachelor's Degrees in Agricultural Economics from the University of Ibadan and University of Agriculture, Abeokuta, respectively. He has admirable research capability and has participated in a number of research works in Nigeria. His research interests are in the areas of development economics, environmental economics, and agricultural policy. He has a number of academic papers in learned journals to his credit.

Oluwasola E. Omoju holds a Ph.D. in Energy Economics from Xiamen University in China. Prior to that, he holds Bachelor and Masters degrees in Economics from the Universities of Ilorin and Lagos (Nigeria), respectively. He has cognate professional experiences in the financial and think tank sectors. He is currently a Research Fellow at the National Institute for Legislative and Democratic Studies, a think tank that provides research and policy support as well as training to the Nigerian and ECOWAS parliaments. His research interests include energy economics, public financial management, sustainable development, and impact evaluation. His research works have been presented in several fora and published in reputable peer-reviewed journals. He is a recipient of several awards and grants, including the 2014 CODESRIA-CLACSO-IDEAS South-South Collaborative Research Grant, 2017 GDN-EIB Fellowship Grant, and 2018 PEP PAGE II Research Grant.

Romanus A. Osabohien is currently a Lecturer and a Ph.D. candidate in the Department of Economics and Development Studies, Covenant University, Ota, Nigeria. He obtained his Bachelor of Science (B.Sc.) Degree in Economics from Ambrose Alli University, Ekpoma, Nigeria (2011), emerging as the best student in his class; and Master of Science (M.Sc.) Degree in Economics from Covenant University, Ota, Nigeria (2017) and also came top in his class. His core research areas include: Agricultural Economics, Economic Growth and Development with special interest on social protection and employment in the agricultural sector. He has attended and presented research papers in international conferences/workshops and has published peer-reviewed papers in Scopus indexed journals.

Prof. Evans S. Osabuohien is the former Head of Department-HOD (Economics & Development Studies, Covenant University, Nigeria). He was appointed HOD in 2016, emerging as the Youngest HOD in the University. He received Double Promotion to the Rank of a Full Professor of Economics in December 2017, which made him the Youngest Professor in the University. In May 2020, he was recognised as 'One of the 6 Youngest Professors Nigeria Ever Had.' He is an Alexander von Humboldt-AvH Visiting Professor, Faculty of Management & Economics, Witten/Herdecke University, Germany. He is a Visiting Scholar at University of Economics, HCMC, Vietnam. He was a research fellow at German Development Institute, Bonn (2013–2015) with a fellowship from AvH and he held the same fellowship at German Institute for Global and Area Studies, Hamburg (2012/2013). He was a guest Ph.D. Candidate at Lund University, Sweden (2009/2010). He has executed many funded research projects for international organizations. He has research interests in Institutional, International, Land/Agricultural, and Development Economics where he has published two books and over 100 scholarly articles and presented research findings in international conferences/workshops across the globe. He is the pioneer chair, Centre for Economic Policy and Development Research (CEPDeR) and Regional Centre for Expertise (RCE Ogun), Covenant University. He coordinates the collaboration between Covenant University and three international institutions (namely: Witten/Herdecke University, Germany; United Nations Conference for Trade and Development Virtual Institute-UNCTAD Vi, Switzerland; and German Development Institute, Germany). He reviews for many international journals and he is on editorial board of some of them. He is a Guest Editor to *African Journal of Economic and Management Studies (AJEMS)*. He is married with children.

Vincent Pande is a lecturer at the Moshi Co-operative University (MoCU). He is also a University advisor in all matters relating to planning and budgeting. He works under the Department of Community and Rural Development. He has published in the areas of development, population, and co-operative and has experience in teaching and research. His research interests include: rural development, planning, project planning and management, entrepreneurship, population issues, and development. He has also been involved in various consultancy activities.

Roy Anthony Rodgers is a Senior Lecturer with the Department of Strategic and International Studies, University of Malaya, B.A. (Hons) in International Studies and a Master in Strategic and Defence Studies (M.SDS) both from the University of Malaya. He has also taught at the Malaysian Armed Forces Staff College (MAFSC). In 2012 he obtained Ph.D. from the International Islamic University Malaysia (IIUM). He is currently the Head of the Department of Strategic and International Studies, University of Malaya.

Magdalene Silberberger is an Assistant Professor of Development Economics at the Faculty of Management and Economics at Witten/Herdecke University in Germany. She obtained her Ph.D. from the Ruhr-University Bochum, Germany. Her main interest lies in empirical analysis in development and international economics with a focus on trade policy (in particular standards and other non-tariff measures), economic integration (through trade agreements and global value chains), and growth of the Global South, especially Sub-Saharan Africa. Other interests include the role of institutions (local, national, global), political instability, and environmental issues. She has fieldwork experience in several Sub-Saharan African countries such as Ghana, Mozambique, Mauritius, and Cameroon.

Amadou Tandjigora is a Ph.D. student in Economics at the Cheikh Anta Diop University of Dakar where he has done all his university studies. After his Master's degree, he became interested in agricultural and rural issues. He has participated in several scientific meetings in Senegal including the Senegalese Institute of Agricultural Research, the Laboratory of Economic and Monetary Research and abroad especially at the University of Social Sciences and Management of Bamako. He is passionate about research, especially agriculture and related works. He recently published "Industries and Rural Services: The Rural transformation Support in the context of continuing Degradation Agriculture: Evidence from Senegal", in French.

Oyinkan Tasie is an Assistant Professor in the Department of Agricultural, Food, and Resource Economics at Michigan State University. He obtained his postgraduate degrees from the University of Aberdeen and a bachelor's degree from University of Ibadan. Oyinkan's core research interests revolve broadly around issues on Sustainable Development relating to Land access and renewable electricity development in Sub-Saharan Africa; gender and agricultural productivity; and institutional architecture for policy formulation and implementation.

Esther Toluwatope Tolorunju bagged a Ph.D. Degree in Agricultural Economics and Farm Management (with area of specialization in Production, Welfare, and Food Economics) from the Federal University of Agriculture, Abeokuta (FUNAAB). She has M.Agric Degree in Agricultural Economics and Farm Management from FUNAAB, and B.Tech in Agricultural Economics and Extension from the Ladoke Akintola University of Technology, Ogbomoso (LAUTECH). She has eleven (11) publications. Dr. Tolorunju currently works as an Associate Lecturer in the Department of Agricultural Economics and Farm Management at FUNAAB. In 2013, she won the Association of African Universities, "Association Des Universités Africaines", (AAU) research grant in Nigeria. She is a competent user of Microsoft Windows, Word, Excel, Office, Power Point, with working knowledge of SPSS, STATA, and SHAZAM. She manages time according to allocated tasks and ensures their completion, has good organizational and presentation skills.

Damian Kalu Ude is a Ph.D. student of the University of Nigeria, Nsukka and a lecturer in the Department of Economics, Michael Okpara University of Agriculture, Umudike, Nigeria. He is the immediate past coordinator of the Department of Economics, Centre for Continuing Education, Michael Okpara University of Agriculture, Umudike, Nigeria. He was appointed coordinator in 2015. He is the associate editor of the Journal of research in Management and Social Sciences. He has reviewed over 50 articles for national and international journals. He has research interests in Macroeconomic, Public finance, Development Economics, and Energy economics where he has published over 40 scholarly articles and presented research findings in national and international conferences/workshops across Africa.

Samuel Mwangi Wanjiku is pursuing a Ph.D. in Political Science (International Relations) at Tübingen University, Germany. He holds an M.A. in Project Planning and Management—majoring social change—from the University of Nairobi, and a B.A. in Development Studies from Maseno University, Kenya. Samuel worked in Africa for various NGOs in the field of governance, security, and peace building. His research interests include: human security; conflict, fragility, and vulnerability; social inclusion and community development; Sustainable Development Goals (SDGs).

Kwami Ossadzifo Wonyra is an associate professor of Economics at the Department of Economics and Management at Université de Kara in Togo. He holds a Ph.D. in International Economics and also has a postgraduate intermediate-level certificate in "International Trade Policy and Trade Law" from the Trade Policy Training Centre in Africa (TRAPCA) in partnership with Lund University. In addition, he has earned several certificates with the UNCTAD Virtual Institute in the areas of Trade and Poverty (2015); Trade and Gender (2016); Non-Tariff Measures (2017); and Structural Transformation (2018). He serves as consultant on many national and international projects. His research interests focus on trade in services, regional integration, Structural transformation and Industrialization, agricultural economics and development economics. Dr. Wonyra has published extensively in many reputable journals and participated in several international conferences.

LIST OF FIGURES

Domesticating the SDGs in Africa for Rural and Agricultural Development: The Case of Devolved Governance

Fig. 1	SDGs domestication process	24

Youth Employment Challenge and Rural Transformation in Africa

Fig. 1	Trend of youth literacy rate by gender in Africa	56
Fig. 2	Trend of employment in agriculture and employment to population ratio in Africa	56

Impact of Remittances on Agricultural Labor Productivity in Sub-Saharan Africa

Graph 1	Remittances transmission channels in sub-Saharan Africa	71

Electricity Access and Agricultural Productivity in Sub-Saharan Africa: Evidence from Panel Data

Fig. 1	Agriculture, fishing and forestry value added, 1981–2017	90

Beyond the Farm Gate: Can Social Capital Help Smallholders to Overcome Constraints in the Agricultural Value Chain in Africa?

Fig. 1	Conceptual framework: Social capital and mechanisms for overcoming constraints in the agricultural value chain	123

Large-Scale Land Investments and Household Livelihood in Nigeria: Empirical Insights from Quantitative Analysis

Fig. 1	Land tenure system and LLIs nexus	139

Increasing Agricultural Income and Access to Financial Services through Mobile Technology in Africa: Evidence from Malawi

Chart 1	Mobile cellular subscription and crop production in Malawi	252
Chart 2	Percent of respondents across the variables	255
Chart 3	Effect of education of HH head on the probability of having a phone	259

Identifying the Gap Between the Demand and Supply of Agricultural Finance Among Irrigation Farmers in Namibia

Fig. 1	Map of Namibia with regions	272
Fig. 2	The NCT model approach of computer-assisted analysis	276
Fig. 3	Loan amounts in arrears	282

Access to Land and Food Security: Analysis of 'Priority Crops' Production in Ogun State, Nigeria

Fig. 1	Ecological clustering of crops in Ogun State	297
Fig. 2	Output of selected priority crops in Ogun State, Nigeria	308
Fig. 3	Yield per hectare of selected priority crops in Ogun State, Nigeria	308

Rural Transformation Through Savings and Credit Cooperative Societies in Moshi District, Tanzania

| Fig. 1 | Overview of theory of change for rural transformation | 319 |
| Fig. 2 | Role of SACCOS in rural transformation | 322 |

Fostering Rural Development and Social Inclusion in East Africa: Interrogating the Role of Cooperatives

| Fig. 1 | The integrated co-operative Model (ICM) | 383 |

Youth (Un)employment and Large-Scale Agricultural Land Investments: Examining the Relevance of Indigenous Institutions and Capacity in Tanzania

Fig. 1	The top 10 major recipients of land investments in Africa	428
Fig. 2	Analytical framework: Large-scale land deals and employment interaction	433
Fig. 3	Farmers' association and youth employment	450
Fig. 4	Ward tribunal and youth employment	451
Fig. 5	Civilian vigilante group and youth employment	451
Fig. 6	Educational qualification of community leader and youth employment	451

Local Politics of Land Acquisitions for Foreign and Domestic Investments in Tanzania

Fig. 1	Map of Tanzania showing the study area	464

Agricultural Policy and Food Security in Nigeria: A Rational Choice Analysis

Fig. 1	Failed approach	484
Fig. 2	The successful approach	484

Poverty Reduction, Sustainable Agricultural Development, and the Cassava Value Chain in Nigeria

Fig. 1	World cassava production: top 10 producers average 1990–2017	536
Fig. 2	A cassava value chain map	538

Job Creation and Social Conditions of Labor in the Forestry Agro-Industry in Mozambique

Graph 1	Percentage distribution of Occ Pop. with agriculture as their main occupation and by occupational situation, Niassa province, Mozambique, 2008–2009 and 2014–2015	574
Graph 2	Recruitment of the workforce on the forestry plantations, Niassa province, Company A, 2012	588

Boosting Non-oil Export Revenue in Nigeria Through Non-traditional Agricultural Export Commodities: How Feasible?

Fig. 1	Oil export revenue as percent of total export revenue, 2001–2015	616
Fig. 2	Non-oil export revenue as percent of total export revenue, 2001–2015	617

List of Tables

Youth Employment Challenge and Rural Transformation in Africa

Table 1	Descriptive statistics	54
Table 2	Multicollinearity result	55
Table 3	The results of the estimation of rural transformation and youth employment challenge models	57

Impact of Remittances on Agricultural Labor Productivity in Sub-Saharan Africa

Table 1	The expected relationship between the explanatory variables and the Agricultural labor productivity	77
Table 2	Descriptive statistics of the variables	78
Table 3	Correlation matrix	80
Table 4	Results of the impact of remittances on agricultural labor productivity using GMM	81

Electricity Access and Agricultural Productivity in Sub-Saharan Africa: Evidence from Panel Data

Table 1	Panel cointegration tests	97
Table 2	Regression results—impact of electricity access on agricultural productivity	98
Table 3	Panel cointegration tests	99
Table 4	Random effects model of the differential impacts of rural and urban electricity access on agricultural productivity	100
Table 5	Panel unit root test at level	103
Table 6	Panel unit root test at first difference	104
Table 7	Correlated random effects—Hausmann test	105
Table 8	Correlated random effects–Hausmann test	105
Table 9	List of countries in the analysis	106

Large-Scale Land Investments and Household Livelihood in Nigeria: Empirical Insights from Quantitative Analysis

Table 1	Variable names and definitions	143
Table 2	Summary statistics of variables	144
Table 3	Results from double difference (DiD)	146
Table 4	Double difference with fixed effect	147

Agricultural Productivity and Household Welfare in Uganda: Examining the Relevance of Agricultural Improvement Interventions

Table 1	Description of output, input, and farm specific variables	160
Table 2	Mean values of data used in the Stochastic production frontier	162
Table 3	Results of the stochastic frontier model	163
Table 4	Mean values of variables for the of the household consumption model	165
Table 5	Fixed effects model results for productivity on real household consumption per capita	167

Pattern of Labor Use and Productivity Among Agricultural Households in Nigeria

Table 1	Overview of main productivity measures	178
Table 2	A priori expectations for the determinants of labor use	186
Table 3	A priori expectations of the determinants of labor productivity	186
Table 4	Socio-economic characteristics of agricultural households	187
Table 5	Number of labor use during planting and harvesting activities	188
Table 6	Average number of man-days spent on work during planting and harvesting activities	189
Table 7	Average daily wage paid for hired labor for planting and harvesting activities	189
Table 8	Determinants of labor use among agricultural households	190
Table 9	Distribution of labor productivity	193
Table 10	Determinants of labor productivity	194

Determinants of the Willingness to Pay for Public Sector Health Care Services: An Empirical Study of Rural and Urban Communities in Nigeria

Table 1	Sociodemographic characteristics of the respondents	232
Table 2	Location (settlement area), access to health facility, preferred health care services, rating of the cost of health care services and whether cost prevented health facility utilization	233
Table 3	Perceived willingness to pay for improved quality of health services	234
Table 4	Average amount households are willing to pay for improved quality in public sector health care services	236
Table 5	Willingness to pay for improvement of health services (Prices in Naira (₦) for rural respondents)	238

| Table 6 | Willingness to pay for the improvement of health services (Prices in Naira (₦) for Urban respondents) | 239 |

Increasing Agricultural Income and Access to Financial Services through Mobile Technology in Africa: Evidence from Malawi

Table 1	Marginal effects-factors affecting probability of having a loan	256
Table 2	Probability of non-zero agricultural income	257
Table 3	Marginal effects-factors affecting agricultural income and mobile phone ownership	258
Table 4	Probability of a household owning a mobile phone	258

Identifying the Gap Between the Demand and Supply of Agricultural Finance Among Irrigation Farmers in Namibia

Table 1	Population list of green-schemes	273
Table 2	Total loans approved, and the number of applications received between 2012 and 2014	274
Table 3	Loan access distribution	279
Table 4	Range of amounts borrowed by farmers interviewed	279
Table 5	Gap between demand and supply among green-scheme communal farmers in Namibia	280

Access to Land and Food Security: Analysis of 'Priority Crops' Production in Ogun State, Nigeria

Table 1	Average values of the crops	298
Table 2	Hectarage, output and yield pattern of priority crops (2003–2015)	299
Table 3	Ecological clustering of crop production	307

Rural Transformation Through Savings and Credit Cooperative Societies in Moshi District, Tanzania

Table 1	Explanatory variables and the hypotheses included in regression analysis	326
Table 2	Socio-economic characteristics of studied SACCOS	327
Table 3	Members transformation through SACCOS	328
Table 4	Multiple regression on the effects of SACCOS to rural transformation	329

Rural–Urban Labor Migration and Youth Employment: Investigating the Relevance of Nigeria's Agricultural Sector in Employment Generation

| Table 1 | Rural–urban migration and engagement of youths in agriculture | 356 |

Impact of Non-agricultural Activities on Farmers' Income: Evidence from the Senegalese Groundnut Area

Table 1	Incomes shares from the diversification of activities (%)	398
Table 2	Descriptive statistics of farmers' income	409
Table 3	Descriptive statistics of the non-agricultural activity as a secondary activity	410
Table 4	Farmers' non-farm income	410
Table 5	Non-agricultural income in terms of agricultural income	410
Table 6	Descriptive statistics of the number of days devoted to secondary employment	411
Table 7	Farm experience and farmer income	412
Table 8	Farmers' education level	412
Table 9	Farmers' sex	413
Table 10	Age and farmers' income	413
Table 11	Farmers' household size	414
Table 12	Estimations Results	415

Youth (Un)employment and Large-Scale Agricultural Land Investments: Examining the Relevance of Indigenous Institutions and Capacity in Tanzania

Table 1	Large-scale land deals in Tanzania (domestic versus foreign)	429
Table 2	Locations surveyed, # land deals and youth unemployment using ILO's definition of youth	435
Table 3	Summary statistics of selected variables using ILO's definition of youth	437
Table 4	Baseline regression inclusive of presence of NSAs	438
Table 5	Baseline regression inclusive of local institutions	440
Table 6	Baseline regression inclusive of social stability indicators	442
Table 7	Baseline regression, inclusive of quality of community leader	445
Table 8	Sensitivity checks (regression inclusive of only rural sample)	446
Table 9	Sensitivity checks (regression using TOBIT technique)	448

Socio-Cultural Factors and Performance of Small-Scale Enterprise in Agro-Allied Manufacturing Firms in Nigeria

Table 1	Result of reliability test	503
Table 2	Socio-cultural factors influencing performance of SSAMEs in South-western Nigeria	504
Table 3	Mechanism linking socio-cultural factors to SSAMFs performance	505
Table 4	ANOVA results for test of the hypotheses	507

Poverty Reduction, Sustainable Agricultural Development, and the Cassava Value Chain in Nigeria

Table 1	Nigeria—relative poverty headcount (1980–2010)	532

Table 2	Nigeria—urban/rural incidence of poverty by different measures in 2010	532
Table 3	Nigeria—Gini index (inequality index) Nigeria (1985–2010)	532
Table 4	Production share of cassava by region average (1990–2017)	536
Table 5	Nigeria's cassava production, share of world production and gross production value (current million US$)—(1961–2017)	537

Micro-determinants of Women's Participation in Agricultural Value Chain: Evidence from Rural Households in Nigeria

Table 1	Summary of statistics of selected variables	562
Table 2	Probit regression dependent variable: level of involvement	564

Job Creation and Social Conditions of Labor in the Forestry Agro-Industry in Mozambique

Table 1	Percentage of the Occ Pop. in Agriculture, Forestry and Fisheries (AFF) and proportion of the Occ Pop. who gave "peasant" as their main occupation, Sanga and Chimbonila Districts in Niassa Province, 1997 and 2007	574
Table 2	Areas occupied by the forestry companies, Niassa province	580
Table 3	Labor processes in forestry production in Niassa	585
Table 4	Structure of the workforce, Forestry Company A, Niassa, in 2012	589
Table 5	Monthly wage (in Meticais—MT) and percentage of workers paid below the minimum wage, Forestry Company A, Niassa, 2012	593
Table 6	Change in social strata (Part 1) and change in possession of particular goods (Part 2), before and after the entry of the forestry companies, Chimbonila e Sanga districts, Niassa province	603

Boosting Non-oil Export Revenue in Nigeria Through Non-traditional Agricultural Export Commodities: How Feasible?

Table 1	Fixed effect results by commodity	620
Table 2	Random-effects regression result	622

Introduction

Evans S. Osabuohien

In the last two decades, some efforts have been made to examine agricultural transformation (e.g. Goetz et al. 2001) or rural transformation (Rauch et al. 2016) in a given context. However, exploring agricultural transformation in connection to rural transformation and development has not received in-depth investigation. It is also understandable that the agricultural sector (unlike many other sectors) needs to adapt to a given technology as well as consideration for local circumstances and natural conditions for productive and optimal engagement particularly in developing economies. In addition, the issue of land tenure security, which is crucial for agricultural production in African countries, differs in many respects compared to those of other regions (Osabuohien et al. 2015, 2019; Herrmann et al. 2018). The above is akin to the concern of the increasing wave of large-scale agricultural land investments (LALIs) in Africa with over 65% of the total world figure (Osabuohien et al. 2015; Land Matrix Global Observatory [LMGO] 2017), which necessarily need to be knitted into rural spaces where such agricultural activities usually take place.

The aforementioned issues are imperative because in many African countries the agricultural sector is closely related to issues of poverty reduction; employment creation; and the livelihood of many households depend on agriculture especially in rural areas (Osabuohien 2014; Nolte and Ostermeier 2017; Lay et al. 2018). The discourse is also essential for the attainment of

---

E. S. Osabuohien (✉)
Department of Economics and Development Studies & Chair,
Centre for Economic Policy and Development Research (CEPDeR),
Covenant University, Ota, Nigeria
e-mail: evans.osabuohien@covenantuniversity.edu.ng

Alexander von Humboldt Visiting Professor, Witten/Herdecke University, Witten, Germany

some of the targets of the Sustainable Development Goals (SDGs) of the United Nations (such as Goals 1, 2, 8, 10, 11, and 12) and the Agenda 2063 of the African Union. Thus, the role of government (at subnational, national, and regional levels) in terms of stimulating economic activities (both agricultural and nonagricultural sectors) in rural areas cannot be overemphasized. This entails the provision of access to road network, water supply, health, educational, recreational facilities, to mention but a few. The foregoing requires in-depth study both from theoretical and empirical standpoints to unravel the interactions and inform evidence-based policies. This is what this handbook achieves by providing research findings and recommendations from a host of African countries based on a variety of methodological approaches and interdisciplinary orientations.

By simple conceptualisation, rural transformation and development is about improving the overall quality of life in rural areas, which includes agricultural and nonagricultural activities. This involves promoting investments in health, education, and rural infrastructure; effective markets (financial and otherwise); crafting and implementing policies that promote greater inclusivity as well as the empowerment of rural dwellers (such as safety net programs); improving access to market and development of the value chain (Osabuohien and Karakara 2020). On one hand, transformation encapsulates the process of change of pattern usually to a better one, which is a vital hallmark of development. In this wise, it could be said that transformation goes in tandem with development. On the other hand, rural transformation involves both agricultural and nonagricultural activities, which presupposes that agricultural transformation is a subset of rural transformation. Thus, agricultural transformation and agricultural development as well as rural transformation and rural development are used to convey similar nuance by various authors in this book with a view to creating room for multidisciplinary standpoints.

The rest aspects of this introduction contain a synopsis of the respective chapters that are presented in the various parts of the book. This is intended to provide a brief hindsight that is discussed, the approaches utilized, and the key submissions made.

1   THE STRUCTURE OF THE BOOK

The book, which encapsulates 28 chapters, is structured into five different parts. This is with a view to providing the possible interconnections among the various aspects relating to agricultural and rural development in Africa as documented by the array of scholars across Africa and beyond. It is important to note that the highlights of the chapters are presented chronologically based on how they appear in the book and not in the order of relevance.

1.1   Part I: General and Background Issues

The first part provides a broad overview and relevant insights that are related to the issues of agricultural and rural development in Africa. It probes into contemporary discourse on the diverse nature of agricultural and rural development within the lens of a wide range of perspectives in five chapters.

Focusing on the issue of SDGs, Samuel Mwangi, Fred Jonyo, and Milton Alwanga in the chapter "Domesticating the SDGs in Africa for Rural and Agricultural Development: The Case of Devolved Governance" gave useful insights on how SDGs can be domesticated through devolved governance for agricultural and rural development in Africa. Paraphrasing the words of the authors, the development of the agricultural sector in Africa is crucial as it entails the promotion of food security, on the one hand, and the expansion of the productive capacity to meaningfully engage labor, on the other hand, which are germane for rural development. The investigation of ways and manners that the SDGs can be domesticated with a view to crafting a somewhat harmonized synergy requires the understanding of the need for devolved governance that will engender rural development, the authors canvassed. The authors went further to stress that to enhance agricultural development there is the appropriate policy toolkit within the embryo of devolution, which will require frantic efforts to ensure: effective domestication and operationalization of the SDGs; aggregation of the domesticated plans that can measure the achievement of the SDGs.

In the third chapter, Damian Ude brought to light the issue of youth employment in relation to rural transformation in Africa, which is germane given the increasing level of youth unemployment despite enormous resources in the continent. The study achieved its goal by using panel data of 54 countries in Africa for the period between 2010 and 2017. Based on the analysis conducted, the author submitted that youth employment exerts a direct effect on the level of rural transformation (development) in African countries. The level of youth literacy rate was found to be one of the attributive factors for the nature of association that exists between youth employment rate (especially in the agricultural sector) and rural development. Thus, the author posited that the empowerment of the youth through mechanisms such as youth skills development, facilitating rural youth access to land and affordable financial resources, promoting micro, small, and medium enterprises (MSMEs), and provision of social protection and safety net programs, among others, as essential stimuli for rural development in Africa. In related discourse, in the chapter "Impact of Remittances on Agricultural Labor Productivity in Sub-Saharan Africa," Kwami Wonyra and Muriel Ametoglo noted that an increase in the agricultural value-added increases the labor productivity in the agricultural sector in Sub-Saharan Africa (SSA). Thus, there is the need for a greater investment drive in the agricultural sector, through a training and support program for the farmers.

In the chapter that follows, Oluwasola Omoju, Opeyemi Oladunjoye, Iyabo Olanrele, and Adedoyin Lawal examined the impact of electricity access on agricultural productivity by teasing out the impact of urban and rural electricity access on agricultural productivity in 45 SSA countries. Their study established that, between the two variants of electricity access, only the coefficient of urban electricity access turns out positive and significant. This implies that urban electricity access, as expected, impacts on agricultural productivity. Thus, providing electricity access in urban areas may facilitate agricultural productivity. The authors opined that improving the overall electricity access has positive and significant effects on agricultural productivity in SSA countries. Thus, there is the need for policymakers in the region to focus on improving overall electrification to boost agricultural productivity and economic development. They concluded that, rather than prioritizing rural electrification, which solely focuses on the production side of the agricultural value chain, electricity infrastructure intervention in SSA should consider the entire agricultural value chain.

Agricultural land investments affect smallholders processing and value chain gains and this subsequently affects food security. On agricultural value chain development, Oluwaseun Kolade, Oluwasoye Mafimisebi, and Oluwakayode Aluko in the sixth chapter draw the readers' attention to the challenges faced by, and opportunities available to, smallholder farmers beyond the farmgate. The authors noted that for many smallholders, the most consequential, and often the most ignored, constraints exist beyond the farmgate in the value chain. These constraints include the limited access to useful information and low technological capacities for post-production processing and packaging, the challenge of quality requirements and delivery for high-valued markets, limited connections to established market actors, and weak transportation networks. Their study highlighted the critical role of social capital (in its bonding, bridging, and linking forms) in helping farmers to overcome the various constraints in the value chain. In sum, the authors argued that social capital is an important resource that smallholder farmers can deploy to mitigate and overcome their relative resource disadvantage relative to big farms, in accessing and benefitting from the value chain.

1.2 Part II: Household Livelihood and Welfare Matters

This part focuses mainly on households livelihood and welfare effects stemming from agricultural investments, rural transformation, and development. In four different but related chapters, the part delves into issues on the effects that diversity of agricultural activities, agricultural investments, rural transformation, and development have on livelihood and welfare of the households with emphasis on household income, expenditure, employment, poverty reduction, and health issues.

Exploring the implications of large-scale land investments (LLIs) on households welfare in Nigerian communities with LLIs in comparison with communities without LLIs, the seventh chapter by Evans Osabuohien, Felicia Olokoyo, Uchenna Efobi, Alhassan Karakara, and Ibukun Beecroft underscored that, on the average, the total consumption of households in communities with LLIs increased by 4.18% compared to those in communities without LLIs. The authors asserted that households in communities with

LLIs spend less amount of their money on consumption. It was found that an average household spends less money on nonfood expenditure as per capita expenditure on food is higher than nonfood per household. According to the authors, LLIs are mostly located in communities where household average size of plot area is larger and this is what is observed as communities with LLIs have households average plot size (7309) higher than households (5173) in communities without LLIs. Also, on household welfare outcomes, an average household in communities with LLIs has consumption higher than their counterparts in communities without LLIs and change in the period has no effect on the consumption pattern of households. The authors found that despite the fact that there exists a direct negative effect of LLI presence on household total consumption, (notably food and nonfood consumption), there is a likely positive effect from the presence of LLI when considering the combination of other unobserved characteristics such as presence of structures to effectively negotiate and intermediate between landowners and the land investors that may affect the relationship.

In the chapter "Agricultural Productivity and Household Welfare in Uganda: Examining the Relevance of Agricultural Improvement Interventions," Nicholas Kilimani, John Nnyanzi, Ibrahim Okumu, and Edward Bbaale analyzed the growth in agricultural productivity and household welfare in Uganda using three waves of nationally representative data (Living Standards Measurement Study-Integrated Surveys in Agriculture [LSMS-ISA]). The authors demonstrated that the dependency ratio declined from nearly 0.65 in 2009 to less than 0.56 in 2013 implying a changing household composition with households having fewer children than adults and that the observed change could be a positive step toward reducing the negative effects of a higher dependency ratio on household welfare. Furthermore, the authors reiterated that land productivity is important for household welfare improvement. In this regard, they found that a 0.43% increase in land productivity increased real consumption per capita by 0.25% when land productivity is modeled and 0.23% when real value of production per unit of labor is modeled. Also, the wealth of households as measured by livestock ownership in tropical livestock units was found to have increased marginally from 2.32 in 2009 to 2.65 in 2013. The authors also indicated that farmers' technical efficiency and real consumption per capita are related positively. Thus, they conclude that improving technical efficiency of farmers is important to increase production and hence real consumption per capita.

Agricultural labor as a resource could be harnessed for increased productivity if keen interest is focused on the pattern of labor usage in the agricultural sector, as opined by Olufemi Popoola and Kayode Adejare in the chapter "Pattern of Labor Use and Productivity Among Agricultural Households in Nigeria." The authors examined the pattern of labor use and labor productivity among agricultural households in Nigeria and found that the number of workers employed during planting and harvesting activities differ markedly between female-headed and male-headed households.

The chapter observed that female-headed households use more family labor than the male-headed households—the male-headed households use more hired labor during planting and harvesting activities than their female counterpart. Also, labor use is positively influenced by crop output, age of household head, household size, farm size, wage, herbicide use, among others; while labor productivity was low, as the majority was below the mean cut-off point. The authors noted that the allocation of labor usually varies with farming activities; whereas some tasks require skilled hired labor, family labor is sufficient for some as the cost and availability affect the use of hired labor for different agricultural activities.

Carrying out an empirical examination of agricultural youth employment, Ruqayya Gar and Roy Rodgers in the tenth chapter used a qualitative approach to investigate the constraints of a particular agricultural program (the Youth Employment in Agriculture Programme [YEAP]). Their findings indicated that the YEAP uses informational skills and economic resources to train and partially empower youth with very little allowance for managing small-scale agricultural activities. The authors added that a majority of the participants in YEAP disclosed that they received financial aid in the form of the provision of small amount of money (i.e., allowance) to start small-scale poultry farm; such aid is in one way or another seen as a poverty alleviation strategy. The second strategy used by the YEAP to empower youth is informational resources as all the respondents indicated that they were trained by YEAP officials on managing small-scale poultry production, among other activities.

1.3   Part III: Access to Resources, Transformation and Productivity Interactions

The third part, which has five chapters, helps to unravel how access to various forms of resources can interact with agricultural productivity in engendering transformation and development in Africa based on analyses from different countries.

Focusing on health issues, Lloyd Amaghionyeodiwe in the chapter "Determinants of the Willingness to Pay for Public Sector Health Care Services: An Empirical Study of Rural and Urban Communities in Nigeria" examined the determinants of the households' willingness to pay for public healthcare services in Nigeria and evaluates the extent to which these factors affect households' willingness to pay in both the urban and rural areas. Using both primary and secondary data, the author acknowledged that the willingness to pay increased with income in all the cases considered. The author submitted that distance ranks high as one of the most important factors that influences the willingness to pay more in public sector health care services for rural dwellers while quality of care was momentous for urban dwellers.

Still on access to resources and agricultural development nexus, Angella Montfaucon in the chapter "Increasing Agricultural Income and Access to

Financial Services Through Mobile Technology in Africa: Evidence from Malawi" using data from Malawi's Integrated Household Survey (IHS) and the logit model as the empirical analysis noted that a higher number of mobile phones in a household is the key variable that consistently and positively predicts that a household is likely to have access to financial resources (loan in general, a formal loan or an informal loan). Also, the author surmised that households living in the rural area, those with a larger agricultural land size and with access to extension services have a higher probability of nonzero agricultural income than their counterparts who did not have such access. Thus, improved financial inclusion for smallholder households can be achieved through improvements in technology as increased mobile phone usage can lead households into the formal financial sector, which is more regulated and provides customer protection more than the informal avenues.

On a related note, the thirteenth chapter by Elina Amadhila and Sylvanus Ikhide deepens the readers' knowledge on agricultural finance by exploring the agricultural finance gap in Namibia and the causes of such a gap with reference to irrigation farmers. Building on the demand–supply gap theory, the authors engaged a mixed-method analysis and found that more male farmers have access to loans than the female farmers and most of the farmers operate at small-scale than medium-scale level. Also, the authors indicated that small-scale farmers in contract farming projects have access to loans (because of collateral by government) than medium-scale and independent farmers. The authors further observed a marked mismatch between demand and supply of agricultural finance in Namibia, while the gap varies within different loan categories for different types of farmers. Some factors including dishonesty among medium-scale farmers toward agricultural bank (*Agribank*), difficulty in recovering loans from borrowers, among others, according to the authors, are the crucial determinants of financial performance of *Agribank* in Namibia.

Studying access to land and food security in the chapter "Access to Land and Agricultural Production: Analysis of 'Priority Crops' Production in Ogun State, Nigeria," Ngozi Adeleye, Evans Osabuohien, Samuel Adeogun, Siraj Fashola, Onyikan Tasie, and Gideon Adeyemi explored the linkage between access to land and food security in Ogun State, Nigeria especially on the production of crops deemed to be a priority. The authors revealed that cassava is cultivated on a larger farm area of 270,829 hectares with 4.5 million metric tons produced on the average giving a yield of 16.41. Following cassava are maize, yam, cocoyam, potato, rice, melon, and cowpea, in that order. Also, the study revealed that to ensure food security, the State Government encourages the production of several crops (cassava, maize, rice, melon, yam, potato, cocoyam, and cowpea). Further evidence from the chapter reveals that Ogun State has a comparative advantage in the cultivation of cassava in the areas of cultivated land area, productivity, and yield relative to others. Thus, reduction in over-dependence on cassava produce while establishing its comparative advantages on related crops such as yam, potato, cocoyam, and rice will help and State Government has to initiate a long-term agricultural development plan to ensure consistency and continuity of agricultural policies, which are *sine qua non* for food security.

Neema Kumburu and Vincent Pande in the chapter "Rural Transformation Through Savings and Credit Cooperatives Societies in Moshi District, Tanzania" investigate the role of Savings and Credit Cooperative Societies (SACCOS) in facilitating rural transformation and development in Moshi District, Tanzania and accentuated that SACCOS play an important role in facilitating rural transformation by providing financial services in rural areas where most people are not usually served by the formal financial institutions. The authors further confirmed the usefulness of SACCOS in increasing the material welfare of their members in terms of living standards, guaranteed income, enhancement of skills and knowledge, employment as well as leadership and governance. In addition, it was established in their study that SACCOS had effect in transforming rural areas in terms of special loan schemes, rural customer size, direct rural investments, and rural income generation programs. Thus, the authors recommend that cooperative practitioners should make more campaigns and educate rural people on the purpose and benefits of SACCOS.

1.4 Part IV: Employment, Migration and Transformation Nexus

Part IV of the book contains five chapters that connect the issue of employment, migration, agricultural, and rural transformation using empirical evidence from different Africa countries (notably, Kenya, Nigeria, Senegal, Tanzania, and Uganda).

Looking at youth migration and how it affects labor availability for agricultural sector, Abiodun Obayelu, Oluwakemi Obayelu, and Esther Tolorunju in the chapter "Rural–Urban Labor Migration and Youth Employment: Investigating the Relevance of Nigeria's Agricultural Sector in Employment Generation" sought to understand the phenomenon of rural–urban youth migration and employment generation in the agricultural sector as well as migration from the agricultural to nonagricultural sectors. Youth rural–urban migration was found to be largely induced by the expectation of higher wages in the destination, which is attuned with the principle of comparative advantage. The authors indicated that because of low earnings in agriculture and difficulty of obtaining land for agricultural purposes force people to migrate to the cities for jobs from their place of origin, which is mainly rural areas. The authors posited that the proportion of youth or adults in a household who are engaged in agriculture in rural areas is higher than those in urban areas. Furthermore, the authors indicated that rural and urban migration by youths leads to a rise in wage rate due to scarcity of labor for agricultural works in rural areas. In sum, the authors concluded with the following submissions: youth are engaging less in agriculture than the older age group suggesting that they are leaving agriculture for nonagricultural jobs in Nigeria; youth from poorer households and from rural areas with less agricultural potential are more likely to migrate; educated youth who expect better employment in urban areas are more likely to migrate; and most youth migrate with the consent of their parents, who in most cases cover the costs of their migration.

On welfare and rural development interaction, the seventeenth chapter by Mangasini Katundu did an in-depth review on the role of cooperatives in reducing rural poverty and enhancing social inclusion in East African countries, namely: Kenya, Tanzania, and Uganda. The chapter established that cooperatives are an organ for rural development in whichever form and model and can contribute to rural development whether they are weak or strong. The author went ahead to propose the use of Integrated Cooperative Model (ICM) that could be effective in linking the rural poor in terms of production, marketing support, and financial services. The chapter surmised that training is needed on member's roles and responsibilities, knowledge of production, marketing, and management. Also, government intervention is needed especially on areas related to punishing criminals in the cooperative industry. Lastly, the use of ICM, which has proved to be effective in linking the rural poor in terms of production, marketing support, and financial services; education of the members as priority; more investment in cooperatives for training their members especially on how they can work in an ICM within the East African context were recommended by the author.

With respect to the income of farmers and welfare, Amadou Tandjigora in the chapter "Impact of Non-agricultural Activities on Farmers' Income: Evidence from the Senegalese Groundnut Area," used multinomial logit model to assess the hypothesis that nonagricultural revenues have a positive influence on farmers' total revenue in the groundnut producing area of Senegal. The author indicated that the farmers who diversify their activities are more likely to have more income, which verifies the existing literature on the issue. In other words, a farmer exercising a nonagricultural activity that provides him/her a high income cannot have a low total income. Thus, nonagricultural income, even if it is low, has a positive and significant impact on the improvement of total income of the farmers. The author found that other individual variables also have a positive impact on farmers' incomes; that is, the number of days per week spent on nonagricultural activities, age, and level of education. A similar finding was made for the experience in agriculture, justifying that the improvement of agricultural income is rather dependent on the different nonagricultural sources than the seniority in the agricultural practice.

The agriculture sector, which is the main employer of labor in most African countries could be made better with the issue of harnessing LALIs effects on employment. LALIs aim at increasing production, create employment opportunities, and enhance infrastructure development as most of them have such promises particularly employment creation. Thus, Evans Osabuohien, Uchenna Efobi, Ciliaka Gitau, Romanus Osabohien, and

Oluwasogo Adediran in the chapter "Youth Unemployment and Large-Scale Agricultural Land Investments: Examining the Relevance of Indigenous Institutions and Local Capacity in Tanzania," engaged the Living Standard Measurement Study-Integrated Surveys on Agriculture (LSMS-ISA) data for Tanzania and found that communities with LALIs had lower youth employment level of 20.40% compared to the value of 26.90% in communities without LALIs. Also, they observed that in the communities where there is the presence of ward tribunal, the rate of youth employment is clearly higher than communities without ward tribunal. The authors concluded that the variable "land deal" was still consistently displaying an insignificant relationship with youth employment. At least, it can be verified that in communities where there is land deal and ward tribunal, the chances of youth unemployment will be marginally lower. Plausibly, such communities have chances of enhancing the youth employment by 4.9%. They concluded that the presence of Non-State Actors (NSAs), the presence of community tribunals and the frequency of their meetings, the social stability in terms of security, and reduction in social violence and the education of community leaders are important factors that can enhance the presence of land investors in extending their social responsibility of granting employment to the youths in the host community.

In a closely related study involving two investments (one foreign and the other domestic), Godfrey Massay in the chapter "Local Politics of Land Acquisitions for Foreign and Domestic Investments in Tanzania" explored different approaches used in land acquisitions and the perceptions of communities toward such approaches in Chakenge Village of Kisarawe District in the Coastal Region of Tanzania. Focusing on how land deals affect food security based on the cases of two companies (The Sunbiofuels and Gagaja Industries—GI), the author observed that the politicians who were involved have in one way or another gained from their involvement in the land acquisitions either financially or in furtherance of their political interests in their constituencies. It also shows how national policies such as those that promote agriculture and industry sector are driving land acquisition. Community members trust the local investor than the foreign investor.

Using rational choice theory to analyze the political economy dimensions of why agricultural policies deliver below expectation and affect food security in Nigeria; the twenty-first chapter by Opeyemi Aluko found that there are weak agricultural policies that cannot stand the test of time. According to the author, policies have short durations of lifespan especially at the expiration of the political administrators' tenure that initiates the policy. In furtherance, the author indicated that there is subjective rational choice of the political actors and a poor political will to fulfill all the tenets of the policies so made. The author recommended that stakeholders must be incorporated at the policy formulation stage so that the right policy statements and inputs can be included in the schemes and the government should invest in agricultural researches and make adequate use of the outcomes.

1.5 Part V: Processing, Value Chain and Food Security

The last part in six different chapters brings to bear the issues pertaining to agricultural processing, value chain development, and food security in Africa drawing empirical insights from different countries (namely Mozambique, Nigeria, and Zimbabwe). In essence, the part unveils the interconnectedness of processing, marketing, and food security, on one hand, and their relevance for agricultural transformation and rural development, on the other.

Starting off with the chapter "Socio-Cultural Factors and Performance of Small-Scale Enterprise in Agro-Allied Manufacturing Firms in Nigeria," Alidu Kareem, Temitope Jiboye, Oluwabunmi Adejumo, and Michael Akinyosoye examined the influence of sociocultural factors on the performance of selected small-scale agro-allied manufacturing firms in Nigeria. From the analysis carried out by the authors using binary logistic regression, it was found that there was a significant relationship between sociocultural factors and small-scale agro-allied firms in Nigeria. The results also revealed that religious beliefs, burden of extended family, ostentatious lifestyle, and social spending exerted significant influence on the firms investigated. The study concluded that small-scale agro-allied manufacturing firm is multidimensional in nature as it is largely driven by sociocultural factors.

Patience Mutopo in the chapter "Labor Processes in Large-Scale Land Investments: The Case of Sugar Estates in South-Eastern Zimbabwe" studied the labor processes in LALIs with particular reference to sugar estates in Zimbabwe. The study anchored its empirical investigations and philosophical orientation on political economy to show how people are stratified in plantations and the role that different political and economic factors affect the farm workers. The author noted that labor processes are rooted in class dynamics and self-interest sharing modes of production that are a characteristic feature of capitalist agricultural modes of production. It was found that women played a pivotal process in the planting and harvesting of sugarcane. Thus, the author recommended that credible and equal level policy field be created to address the needs of the sugarcane workers so that in the face of LALIs and the changes in the geophysical landscape, policy regimes are created that lead to equity in terms of how sugarcane workers are treated in fast-track and large sugarcane estates in Zimbabwe.

From another different perspective in terms of the type of crop and mode of processing, the chapter "Poverty Reduction, Sustainable Agricultural Development and the Cassava Value Chain in Nigeria" by Waidi Adebayo and Magdalene Silberberger explored the potentials of the cassava crop and its value chain being catalytic for alleviating poverty among cassava farmers and a range of other stakeholders along cassava value chain in Nigeria. The authors noted that investments in activities that enhance the cassava value chain would, among other things, lead to increases in farmers' income. With the use of a high yield, cassava plants and several new industrial uses for processed cassava tuber has transformed it into a sort-after crop by high-end industrial users, the authors added.

Investigating the participation of women in agricultural value chain in farm communities in Edo State of Nigeria, Kehinde Ola in the chapter "Micro-determinants of Women's Participation in Agricultural Value Chain: Evidence from Rural Households in Nigeria" found, from a probit regression, that the level of education, age of women, land inheritance, distance from house to market centers, and community responsibilities as significant micro-determining factors. The author emphasized the need for adult literacy classes among women farmers in the region, and women of ages 35–59 years are crucial to agricultural production and therefore the government should have specialized agricultural extension workers to attend to their farm needs with a view to promoting the participation of women in agricultural value chain.

From the standpoint of political economy and a triangulation between qualitative and quantitative data, and focusing on the organisation and patterns of work, Rosimina Ali in the chapter "Job Creation and Social Conditions of Labor in the Forestry Agro-Industry in Mozambique," explored the somewhat contradiction between employment creation and better social conditions in the current productive structure in Mozambique especially with respect to forestry agro-industry. The author found that the structures of employment and work on the forestry plantations in Niassa Province of Mozambique reflect the more general organisation of productive agro-industrial structures of an extractive nature. The prevalent productive structure is centered on the production of primary products for export, through obtaining vast areas of land and access to water at low cost, and a poorly paid workforce, mostly casual and under precarious conditions. The social reproduction of the labor force is guaranteed by the interdependence and mutual financing of varied forms of labor, paid and/or unpaid, agricultural or not was also stressed by the author.

Grace Evbuomwan, Felica Olokoyo, Tolulope Adesina, and Lawrence Okoye in the chapter "Boosting Non-oil Export Revenue in Nigeria through Non-traditional Agricultural Export Commodities: How Feasible?" indicated that some traditional agricultural export commodities like cocoa and rubber have remained on Nigeria's agricultural export list, while others like groundnut and coffee have drastically reduced from the export list. Carrying out an econometric analysis, the authors recommended a major policy change, which can provide a boost for agricultural exports, which should include effective exchange rate management, among others.

The book ends with a concluding chapter "Conclusion: Agricultural Investments and Rural Development in Africa—Salient Issues and Imperatives", which summaries the key messages emanating from the book both for policy and future research.

References

Goetz, S. J., Jaksch, T., & Siebert, R. (Eds.). (2001). *Agricultural transformation and land use in central and eastern Europe*. Burlington: Ashgate.

Herrmann, R., Jumbe, C., Bruentrup, M., & Osabuohien, E. (2018, July). Competition between biofuel feedstock and food production: Empirical evidence from sugarcane outgrower settings in Malawi. *Biomass and Bioenergy, 114*, 100–111. http://dx.doi.org/10.1016/j.biombioe.2017.09.002.

Land Matrix Global Observatory. (LMGO). (2017). *The online public database on land deals*. Retrieved February 5, 2017, from http://www.landmatrix.org/en/.

Lay, J., Nolte, K., & Sipangule, K (2018). *Large-scale farms and smallholders: Evidence from Zambia* (Kiel Working Paper No. 2098).

Nolte, K., & Ostermeier, M. (2017, October). Labor market effects of large-scale agricultural investment: Conceptual considerations and estimated employment effects. *World Development, 98*, 430–446.

Osabuohien, E. S. (2014). Large-scale agricultural land investments and local institutions in Africa: The Nigerian case. *Land Use Policy, 39*(July), 155–165. https://doi.org/10.1016/j.landusepol.2014.02.019.

Osabuohien, E., Efobi, U. R., Herrmann, R., & Gitau, C. M. (2019). Female labor outcomes and large-scale agricultural land investments: Macro-micro evidence from Tanzania. *Land Use Policy, 82*, 716–728. https://doi.org/10.1016/j.landusepol.2019.01.005.

Osabuohien, E., & Karakara, A. A. (2020). Conclusion: Agricultural investments and rural development in Africa—salient issues and imperatives. In E. Osabuohien (Ed.), *The palgrave handbook of agricultural and rural development in Africa*. Geneva: Palgrave Macmillan. https://doi.org/10.1007/978-3-030-41513-6_28.

Osabuohien, E. S., Gitau, C. M., Efobi, U. R., & Bruentrup, M. (2015). Agents and implications of foreign land deals in East African community: The case of Uganda. In E. Osabuohien (Ed.), *Handbook of research on in-country determinants and implications of foreign land acquisitions* (pp. 263–286). Hershey, PA: Business Science Reference.

Rauch, T., Beckmann, G., Neubert, S., & Rettberg, S. (2016). *Rural transformation in sub-Saharan Africa: Conceptual study* (SLE Discussion Paper 01/2016 – EN). Berlin: Centre for Rural Development (SLE).

General and Background Issues

Domesticating the SDGs in Africa for Rural and Agricultural Development: The Case of Devolved Governance

Samuel Mwangi Wanjiku, Fred Jonyo, and Milton Alwanga

1 Introduction

The formulation of comprehensive global development goals is one task, while domestication of these goals to create a development reality at the local level is another critical task. The fact that the Sustainable Development Goals (SDGs) are common to all states does not mean similar approaches to achieving them. Every country has its own governance structure and development strategies that aim at reaching the global targets. It is not logical to harmonize the vast and diverse development approaches to achieve the SDGs, but instead, we can only think of contextualizing the latter. This understanding of policy downscaling resonates with the definition of localization as "the implementation of supranational policy into projects at the appropriate subnational level to ensure the service delivery to the appropriate level population" (Patole 2018). The chapter focuses on the 17 SDGs and the 169 targets that form the UN 2030 Agenda for Sustainable Development and which picks up from the Millennium Development Goals (MDGs) (United

---

S. M. Wanjiku (✉)
Tübingen University, Tübingen, Germany

F. Jonyo
University of Nairobi, Nairobi, Kenya

M. Alwanga
Jomo Kenyatta University of Agriculture and Technology, Nairobi, Kenya

© The Author(s) 2020
E. S. Osabuohien (ed.), *The Palgrave Handbook of Agricultural and Rural Development in Africa*, https://doi.org/10.1007/978-3-030-41513-6_2

Nations Development Program [UNDP] 2017). The analysis involves the domestication of SDGs in relation to labor and agricultural sectors in enhancing rural development.

The chapter starts by looking at the genesis of international development goals, and the transition from MDGs to SDGs. It continues to examine the performance of Africa in the achievement of SDGs. It then engages the concept of SDGs domestication which is then analyzed in the context of the devolved governance. In particular, the domestication of the SDGs is analyzed in reference to devolved governance using Kenya as the case study.

2   International Development Goals

The genesis of the current SDGs can be traced back to the 1960s international development decade when the first international development agenda within the UN system was established. The 1960s marked the first decade for international development. The 1961 United Nations Development Decade 1710 (XVI), outlined a program for international economic cooperation that emphasized on the promotion of the development process of developing countries. Further, it recognized that the social and economic development among the Third World countries is not only beneficial to those very countries but also to the world peace, security, and prosperity (United Nations 1961). During the 1960s Development Decade, there were proposals for action. For instance, in 1963 there was a joint Declaration of the developing countries on development. From 1970 to 1980 there was a continuation of the 1960s' international development strategy—the second UN development decade. During the 1970s, key events such as declaration on the Establishment of a New International Economic Order (1974) and the World Conference on Agrarian Reform and Rural Development (1979) which gave rise to Food and Agricultural Organization (FAO) (United Nations 2007).

The 1980s marked the third development decade with a special focus on developing countries. It connected discrimination, rights, and development (with more attention to children and women); disarmament and development; and the development of the Least Developed Countries (LDCs). The following international development decade—the 1990s—was featured mainly by the concept of human development that had emerged in the 1980s (United Nations 2018). A shift from the language of "decades of development" to human development indicated improvement in comprehensiveness in development analysis. All through the 1990s, the UN published human development reports. The reports mainly were about, and continue to measure and compare, the Human Development Index (HDI) between countries and regions of the world. HDI puts emphasis on people and their capabilities as an ultimate methodology of assessing a country's development. Analytically, HDI involves development measurement in terms of life expectancy, education, and per capita income. SDGs and MDGs have been the international development agendas for the twenty-first century. Although the international development agenda has existed since the 1960s, in general, the MDGs and SDGs present more quantifiable objectives.

In 2000, the UN General Assembly adopted the Millennium Declaration. The goals and targets that focused on development became the MDGs. The MDGs were mainly an effort to refocus on the long period of deliberation to progress the social and economic development of the LCDs. The goals are grounded on the most demanding development needs of the least developing countries. The goals include (1) To eradicate extreme poverty and hunger; (2) To achieve universal primary education; (3) To promote gender equality and empower women; (4) To reduce child mortality; (5) To improve maternal health; (6) To combat HIV/AIDS, malaria, and other diseases; (7) To ensure environmental sustainability; and (8) To develop a global partnership for development. All eight goals have different but specific targets. The eight MDGs represent the important dimensions of underdevelopment in LDCs. All the UN member states and many international organizations committed to achieving the MDGs by 2015. By region, countries in Sub-Saharan Africa have the least HDI and the most affected these issues of underdevelopment highlighted in the MDGs.

By the end of 2015, ex-post evaluations indicate a varied achievement of MDGs by different African countries. Overall, there was a significant level of MDGs achievement. However, it still remained difficult to achieve some targets due to challenges such as inadequate funding (Abhilaksh 2013; Yibeltal et al. 2017). Despite attracting huge funding, challenges such as management of conflicts and natural disasters took a significant share of resources, that could have otherwise gone into the mainstream development process. A goal such as number 1 (reducing hunger by half) was not achieved (Pingali et al. 2016). Other challenges experienced in the implementation of the MDGs include inadequate understanding, insufficient accounting for trade-offs and low synergies across sectors. Eventually, the inadequate synergy resulted in policy incoherence and had a negative impact on the broader framework. Since 2014, the United Nations member states started a process to evaluate MDGs and think through the post-MDGs. The post-MDGs thinking led to the establishment of the agenda 2015–2030 on SDGs.

2.1 From MDGs to SDGs

The concept of sustainable development did not emerge with the 17 SDGs. Instead, it was a living agenda since the 1992 Earth Summit in Brazil. In the Earth Summit, more than 178 countries adopted Agenda 21 which contains a comprehensive strategic plan to establish an international partnership for sustainable development to both enhance people's livelihoods and protect the environment. Later in the 2002 World Summit on Sustainable Development, the Johannesburg Declaration on sustainable development and the Plan of Implementation was adopted (SDGs Knowledge Platform 2019). This makes it clear that SDGs were still taking shape during the implementation of MDGs.

The establishment of SDGs involved connecting the international development goals to the concept of sustainable development to derive a normative value. As compared with MDGs, SDGs are more elaborative. The goals have been broken down into finer and more specific units—17 goals and 169 targets. They are expected to fill the gaps identified during the implementation of MDGs, including integrating different development sectors in terms of policies and implementation strategies. Thus, the SDGs came as a remedial strategy to establish a comprehensive connection between the thematic areas in the development process. Moreover, the SDGs are a rejuvenation of the concept of sustainable development that has been in existence since the 1992 Earth Summit (Blanc 2015; Patole 2018).

The methodologies of measurement need to adequately accommodate all the targets at all levels right from global, regional, national, and local levels. In order to gather proper evidence-based data, bottom-up monitoring, and evaluation processes and procedures are vital. Other than the bottom-up approach, an analysis of the interconnection between and within SDGs is important. Using network analysis techniques, Blanc (2015) has demonstrated how SDGs are unequally connected. Some goals are strongly connected while others have a weak connection. In terms of numbers, some goals are comparatively more connected to many others. Overall, the attempt to examine the interconnectedness within the SDGs shows an urge to analyze the policy coherence and integration (Pomare 2018). It further signifies the need to reexamine the sectoral anchorage in the implementation of SDGs by different development actors—through the mainstreaming process.

With strong links to a normative concept of sustainability, the SDGs demand more scientific inquiry as compared to MDGs. Every SDG has its own variables; hence, every goal requires its own specific set of practical indices (Yonglong et al. 2016). It is important to note that goals, as well as their targets, have some level of correlation. For instance, the SDG 1, "No, Poverty" can effectively be measured using the guides of HDI. It can also be measured using SDG 7, "affordable and clean energy" and therefore be monitored and evaluated using approaches such as environmental impact assessment, life-cycle costing, natural assert-evaluation, etc. The targets of each specific goals do not specify any methodology of either defining or quantifying them. SDGs thus leave a big room for the application of diverse analytical tools which pose a challenge to effectively combining and aggregating data from the local level, through national level to the international level.

Hitherto, researchers and academicians have an important role in theorizing SDGs as tools for connecting local and international development process and deploying the existing development paradigms into a workable SDG framework. In an attempt to measure the development impact against the SDGs framework, scientific scrutiny of unique relationships between targets of different goals enables the establishment of efficiency metrics. In international development, the analysis requires the use of various dimensions. First is the role of development actors and second is the sectors involved. Different development actors play different roles in different sectors.

The SDGs framework of analysis needs to consider different levels of development in different regions. Specifically, the development-divide between the global north and the global south. The variance in the development levels creates diverse priorities and therefore different strategies of achieving those priorities. For instance, while extreme poverty, hunger, education, and health are the major development issues in most developing countries, an issue such as greenhouse gasses emissions (a non-priority in Third World) is a top priority in the developed world. This does not, however, mean that the development priorities in the global north are completely irrelevant in the global north and vice versa. Rather, this calls for a common, differentiated, and compatible framework that takes into consideration the variance in development models.

SDGs have a place for all the development actors—the state takes the lead role. The state redistributes resources and establishes policy and legal framework necessary for SDGs achievement at the national level. As a key actor, the state creates the policy infrastructure for the other development actors both at national and local levels including the private sector, Civil Society Organizations (CSOs), and the individuals. The private companies contribute to the achievement of SDGs through the market strategies while CSOs contribute chiefly through nonmarket strategies such as humanitarian initiatives. The UN and other international development agencies work with governments (both national and local authorities), NGOs, and private companies in contributing to the attainment of SDGs.

2.2 Achievement of Sustainable Development Goals and Agenda 2063 in Africa

On 31 January, the African Union adopted Agenda 2063. At the continental level, Africa Union has incorporated the "Agenda 2063" (A2063) into the metrics of SDGs. These metrics enable African countries to both understand and compare socioeconomic development among themselves. The achievement of SDGs has generally been perceived as an approach to reaching the long-term African Vision of "Agenda 2063—The Africa We want." There are huge similarities between the two development goals. While SDGs contain 17 goals with 169 targets, Africa's Agenda 2063 has 20 goals with 174 targets. Generally, both development agendas address common elements of development including human capital development, inclusive economic growth, and promotion of environmental conservation and sustainability. However, the SDGs appear to hold more emphasis on the environmental sustainability and management of climate change as compared to Agenda 2063. On the other hand, Agenda 2063 focuses on institutional governance, i.e., democracy, than SDGs. Goals 14 and 15 of A2063, for example, put emphasis on governance, peace, and security. The time frame is also very different. The SDGs have 15 years time frame while Agenda 2063 has a time limit of 50 years—2013–2063. Overall, there is almost 85% overlap between SDGs and Agenda 2063 (SDGs Center for Africa and Sustainable

Development Solutions Network 2018). Due to highly interwoven development issues, the SDGs appear to be short-term goals of Agenda 2063.

According to the Africa SDG Index and Dashboards Report (2018), African states have achieved various SDGs differently. On average, goals 10, 13, 14, and 15 are better met as compared to goals 1, 2,3, 9, and 16. By region, North Africa leads in the SDGs achievement (with an index score of 61.6) followed by Southern Africa (54.8), West Africa (52), East Africa (50.1), while Central Africa (46) lags behind. By countries, Morocco, Tunisia Mauritius, Algeria, and Cape Verde are the 5 major leading African countries while Eritrea, Sudan, Guinea-Bissau, the Democratic Republic of Congo (DRC), Equatorial Guinea, Chad, Somalia, and the Central Africa Republic constitute the least performing countries in achieving the SDGs. In general, the trend shows that war and instability are the key hindrances to SDGs achievement in Africa.

3 Domestication of Sustainable Development Goals

Despite the good conceptualization of the MDGs by governments, it still remains unclear how the goals were contextualized to fit the diversity of the local actors. Many local actors remained unaware of MDGs inasmuch as their output contributed to the achievement of these goals. So far, the situation is the same with SDGs, especially in many third world countries. By the time of the writing of this chapter,there exists no comprehensive mechanism for domesticating SDGs. The Inter-agency and Expert Group on SDG Indicators (IAEG-SDGs), has focused on developing the global statistical framework that is necessary to evaluate the achievement of SDGs. The group appears to establish a bottom-up analytical approach of SDGs that involves disaggregation of indicators metadata by sex, age, race, and ethnicity among other national characteristics. This means combining data from diverse sources to generate a trend (IAEG-SDGs 2016). However, the visibility of an all-inclusive statistical analysis prior to the development of a domestication approach is questionable.

Although the domestication of international development agenda seems to emerge with the establishment of MDGs, the concept connects closely to work on HDI and participatory (people-centered) development that began in the 1980s (see, Chambers 1983; Sen 1985). The domestication process involves enhancing participatory development in achieving international development goals. The success of the integration of "multiple location-based variables" should follow the already effectively shared vision of sustainable development. However, there is a need to create a stronger link between the internationally driven development agendas and the local context prior to analyzing the indicators to avoid the same challenges of MDGs. As Patole (2018) argues in relation to localization of SDGs, data [dis]aggregation for evaluation is crucial to prevent MDGs' implementation limitations. The analysis here starts by examining the state's governance structure as a critical underpinning SDGs domestication variable.

In the domestication process, two major determinants include the general state governance structure and the specific social-economic sectoral policies. Various sectoral policies are certainly designed to suit and function within the political, economic, and administrative structure of the government. In this regard, the analysis focuses on the domestication of SDGs in a devolved governance structure. Domesticating in this context involves linking global development goals, with national and subnational government's development agendas in a manner that establishes paradigmatic transformation and coherence in the design and implementation of development policies. The SDGs domestication process is not only relevant to the developing countries but also among developed countries. Countries such as Germany, Sweden, Japan, Norway, Denmark, Finland, Belgium, and The Netherlands have already initiated a process of aligning SDGs with their national development strategies (Bernstein 2018).

Essentially, domesticating translates to envisioning the SDGs targets to communities, especially those located in the underdeveloped regions. The two major processes involved include (1) SDGs knowledge sharing and (2) Empowerment of local actors to own the implementation of SDGs within their scope. The process also involves bottom-up aggregation of data on SDGs achievement.

3.1 Knowledge Sharing

SDGs knowledge sharing is the starting point of domestication. Local participation depends on how a vision is successfully shared. The roadmap for localizing SDGs outlines awareness-raising to the local actors as one of the necessities for the achievement of the global goals (Global Taskforce 2016). The regional and local governments are better positioned to raise awareness about the meaning and significance of SDGs to their respective local communities. Local governments connect the central government and the communities by closely engaging with CSOs, the private sector, and community-based organizations. Sharing SDG-related knowledge creates a common but differentiated approach to harnessing the power of the local culture.

3.2 Capacity Building

Strengthening local communities is the means and the end of the domestication process. This means building capacities of local development actors to establish a localized measurement framework and use it to analyze the achievement of the SDGs. A report by Global Taskforce of Local and Regional Governments outlines the significance of supporting and enhancing the local actors toward achieving SDGs. Domestication process goes beyond a simple adaption of SDGs at the local level to "finding solutions to the global challenges and objectives at the local level." The extent of SDGs achievement depends on their full ownership by the local communities (Global Taskforce 2018, see also, FAO 2017; Littlewood and Holt 2018). Political-will by the national government is a significant driver for the empowerment of local actors. Empowerment of local actors in this context includes tapping the community's cultural power in achieving the SDGs. Empowerment also means building the capacity of local governments to produce high-quality data and use it in policymaking. To achieve domestication requires the mobilization of human and financial resources both at the national and local level (Fig. 1).

The approach to domesticate SDGs (knowledge sharing and empowerment of the local actors) is dependent on some factors. The two major determinants of the domesticating processes include first, the overall governance structure of a country, i.e., centralized or decentralized and second the specific sector such as health, trade, agriculture, and education. It is thus deducible that the SDGs domestication process in a country with a centralized governance structure would be different from the one with the devolved governance system. Likewise, SDGs link to various development sectors and development actors differently (Blanc 2015; Pomare 2018). SDGs domestication framework thus requires to be comprehensive enough to capture multiple perspectives that reflect the variance in the governance systems and the implementation of development among countries.

An effective domestication process means the local government is taking ownership of SDGs. And this forms another important task of SDGs domestication. The ownership is built in two ways: first, the sharing of SDGs-related knowledge to convince the local actors as the key players. Put differently, developing a shared vision. Second, supporting and empowering local actors

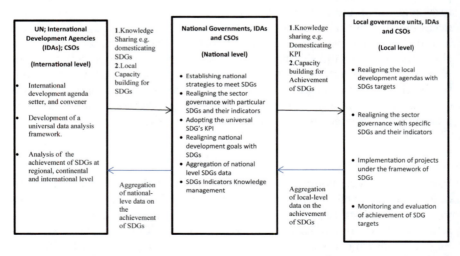

Fig. 1 SDGs domestication process (*Source* Conceptualised by the authors based on information in the literature)

to take responsibility and implement development projects within the SDGs framework. Derived from the above highlighted crucial functions, the study, therefore, defines the domestication of SDGs as creating awareness and enabling the local actors to implement monitor and evaluate the achievement of SDGs.

4 The State's Governance Structure and SDGs Domestication Process

Since the inception of MDGs, it has become a norm that the development process in the developing world is measured against both national and global targets. States have different development strategies and different development objectives. However, the global development goals harmonize the measure of realization of economic development and growth. The two broad forms of state governance structures are centralized governance and decentralized governance. Although a centralized governance system has its own way of SDGs domestication, the focus here is on decentralized governance structure. The idea of decentralization of governance is based on the reasoning that itself is an approach to domestication. Devolution is meant to prioritize subnational planning and resource allocation. Devolution involves decentralization that Mansuri and Vijayendra define as the process of strengthening local governments on both the demand and supply sides (Mansuri and Vijayendra 2013). Worthwhile noting, every sustainable goal and its targets link to multiple governance sectors. As well, good sector governance strongly relates to the generation of high-quality data that is necessary for both accountability and monitoring and evaluation of the SDGs targets (Beegle et al. 2016).

4.1 Devolution and Domestication Process

Since the 1980s, most countries in sub-Saharan Africa have been undergoing reforms with the aim of increasing service delivery and spur economic growth and development to lower levels of poverty. Devolution can be explained as the transfer of power from the central government to devolved systems to perform some duties and is viewed as a key public sector structural reform strategy to enhance service delivery (Muriisa 2008). Devolution or decentralization, in other words, transfers administrative and political powers and financial resources from the central administration to the local governments. This is a long-term practice in the African continent, but which became more pronounced in the 1980s and 1990s when it became the World Bank's reform agenda for developing countries. Thus, decentralization programs in Africa followed the World Bank's recommendations on how to devolve both administrative and political powers as well as resources to local or autonomous levels. This was premised on the fact that social services like education, health, and sanitation for which the central government was responsible, were beginning to deteriorate in many developing countries (World Bank 2015). In addition, these recommendations were based on the argument that decentralization would make the decision-making process much faster and easier and increase the involvement of the local people. These resulted in decisions that are tailored to the needs of the people and reduce corruption, clientelism, which was prevalent in the central government.

The motivation for devolution differs from one country to the other, and from region to region. For instance, from the Soviet Union and Eastern Europe, devolution was part of the political transformation from the central to local government to increase the number of people who were participating in decision-making as opposed to the centralized system where a few participated (Muriisa 2008). In Sri Lanka and South Africa, decentralization came as a response to ethnic and regional conflicts. Treisman (2000) argues that decentralization provides mechanisms through which divided groups are brought into formal, and rule-bound bargaining process. In this case, decentralization of authority and resources acts as a conduit for national unity. In countries like Uganda, Chile, and Cote D'Ivoire, decentralization was meant to improve service delivery.

Devolution is expected to have a positive impact on service delivery within the public service. Potter (2001) argues that devolution is a paradigm shift from previous arrangements that were characterized by persistent failures in the delivery of services. Several studies have been carried out to reaffirm the view that devolution presents the best prospects for the improvement in service delivery regarding access to health services, water and sanitation, education, improved agricultural production, as well as improvement in policing and local justice. Political and economic validation and the effect of devolution of social services has elicited a wide debate in the academic circles (De Vita 1998; Kettle 2000; Muriisa 2008). Both scholars and politicians have justified devolution in the sense that it leads to competitiveness and efficiency which enables the government to have a drastic response to the needs of its citizens. It is argued that transferring responsibilities to local units reduces political and administrative difficulties faced by the central government or its agencies in launching new development programs regarding staff recruitment and locating facilities for new initiatives. Furthermore, devolution enhances the reputation of the government by enabling more institutional heterogeneity, and therefore, address issues of mistrust and enhance legitimacy of government involvement. Moreover, devolution aids in reducing bureaucratic obstacles and facilities people's access to resources and public goods.

Regarding natural resource management, studies have justified devolution on several grounds. Decentralization helps the local residents to identify and prioritize their environmental challenges more precisely, guarantee efficient resource allocation, enhance greater respect for decisions made with the input of the locals such as resource allocation rules, and enable easier monitoring of resource use. Decentralization also gives the marginalized groups more influence on the local policy because it embraces democratic ideals rather than administrative (Larson 2003). Democratic administration calls for representation and downwardly accountable authorities, who hold autonomous and secure spheres of power to make and execute reasonable decisions.

Studies have argued that democratic decentralization of governance system could lead to improved service delivery in the rural setups or marginalized communities (Manor 2004; Besley et al. 2004, 2007). Advocates of devolution of governance structure contend that it gets closer elected government officials at grassroot who are then able to understand the specific preferences and aspirations of the locals for reasonable developmental planning. In addition, devolution has been defended on the grounds that it decentralizes sufficient authority and resources (material, human, and financial), it enhances transparency, accountability, and efficiency in marginalized communities. Manor (2004) observes that direct involvement of the locals in designing, implementation, and monitoring of development initiatives improves productivity both in quality and quantity.

Contrastingly, some authors have established mixed findings regarding devolution and performance of the rural economy (Oommen 2004; Robinson 2007). However, these findings are based on lack of political goodwill in power-sharing, poor mobilization of the locals, lack of accountability of the elected officers, insufficient resources, and technical capacity. In addition, these revelations are not inimical to the devolution of governance itself but largely paid attention to the process. Thus, the achievement of devolution objectives is contingent upon the realization of efficiency in the development process (Robinson 2007).

Historically, successful economic growth and development have been engineered and sustained by rising productivity of labor in the Agricultural sector (Timmer 1988). An increase in agricultural labor productivity in developing agrarian economies plays multiple foundational roles in the wider development process. This is because increased production per employee leads to an increase in food availability per worker. Labor productivity is defined as output per worker (Rebecca 2008). This ration is very vital in the statistical and economic analysis of the country. Labor productivity is an indicator of economic growth, competitiveness and living standards. Therefore, it provides a foundation for social and economic development. Accumulation of capital equipment, improvement of organizational, infrastructure, health, competencies of the workforce, adoption of improved knowledge best explains labor productivity.

The productivity of labor is directly linked to structural change since agricultural labor is the denominator of this variable (Miguel and Pinila 2012). Parameters such as factor endowments and institutional technology determine labor productivity levels. Literature on economic growth as well as on economic history, argues that there exist both proximate and fundamental causes that explain the existence of agricultural labor productivity variations (Crafts 2010). Proximate causes comprise of variables included in the production function of the agricultural sector, except, the labor factor which is already the denominator of labor productivity.

Furthermore, studies have adduced that decentralization of agricultural functions such as the supply of farm inputs, and extension services facilitate easier access to farmers for enhancement of agricultural productivity (Deshpande and Rao 2002; World Bank 2007). For example, devolution of government structures coupled with lane reforms improved agricultural production in states such as West Bengal (Chattopadhyay 2005; Rajasekhar and Manjula 2011).

Both locally, and globally, there is a scarcity of empirical evidence on the role of labor productivity in the context of devolution. In Kenya, empirical evidence indicates that some county governments have facilitated the availability of tools of work such as plowing tractors at a subsidized cost as and other farm inputs such as seeds and fertilizers to small-scale farmers which has enhanced their productivity (Isaboke 2017). Therefore, it is one of the mandates of local governments to assist rural farmers with such tools to boost their production with the aim of poverty alleviation.

In Kenya, there have been reasonable indicators of positive impact in agricultural productivity in many counties. First and foremost, devolution has succeeded in opening up of marginalized areas in Kenya (Mitullah 2013). These areas are mainly from the Arid and semiarid areas. Positive impacts have been realized, especially in infrastructure development (Bosire and Wanjiru 2015), and health delivery (Khaunya et al. 2015). On the other hand, devolution in Kenya has been characterized by several challenges; first, there seems to be a transfer of inefficiencies or wrong policies of the national government being replicated at the county level. Second, there is a replication of elite control or capture of the devolved government (Jonyo 2015; Nyanjom 2011).

At the center of the African development, is the examination of the agriculture and rural transformation agenda. In rural development, agriculture is such a vital sector not only due to its hunger reduction but also the creation of massive employment. In most African countries, it absorbs more than 50% of the labor force. In the effort of achieving the targets, the beginning point is scaling down the Agenda 2030 from a global vision into the local reality. As FAO (2018) informs, the domestication process translates to a transformed commitment between stakeholders in multidisciplinary and cross-sectional engagements.

4.2 Sector Governance: SDGs in Enhancing Rural and Agricultural Development

Land output, and agricultural productivity and rural transformation are intertwined and can best be analyzed as causes and effects of each other in the achievement of SDGs. By region, Sub-Saharan Africa lags behind in these three entangled elements of agricultural transformation and structural change. Structural transformation refers to the declining of the proportion of agriculture in GDP and reducing the gap between agriculture and nonagriculture labor productivity (Timmer 2017). Raising the productivity of agricultural labor is the fundamental cause and effect of structural transformation. Some of the main features of structural transformation include: a declining share of agriculture in the domestic economic output and employment—economic diversification; an increasing share of urban economic activities including both modern services and industries; and, demographic transition and shifting life expectancy (ibid.).

The historical path of structural transformation is associated with reduced food prices. However, the continued financial instability, especially in developing countries coupled with poor means of managing the effects of climatic change, has led to food price anomalies and high uncertainty of the real cost of food. The latter case is an indication of a reversal of structural transformation (Binswanger-Mkhize and McCalla 2010; Timmer 2009). The management of agricultural policy and the efforts toward sustained poverty reduction will obviously be different relative to the success of the dimension taken. Structural transformation is the common path out of poverty for all societies. The transformation process, nonetheless, depends on the productivity increase and the interconnection of both agricultural and nonagricultural sectors (Abraham and Pingali 2017). It is important to highlight that the productivity growth of the agricultural sector is at its highest when that of nonfarm is also at the highest.

The SDG 8 "Promote sustained, inclusive and sustainable economic growth, full and productive employment and decent work for all" has a direct impact on agriculture and labor productivity. Within the domestication process, the local (rural) actors are presumed to be one of the key agents in implementing the labor and agriculture-related SDGs. One of the approaches to measuring agricultural transformation is the use of productivity per hectare against productivity per worker. In other words, the growth of land productivity and labor productivity (rural transformation) is best measured in SDGs-domesticated environment. Nevertheless, the SDG 8 alone cannot capture the complexity of that labor and agricultural productivity as elements of rural transformation. Most of the related dimensions of rural and agriculture development can be captured in other related SDGs and/or their targets. The domestication of SDGs framework serves as a monitoring and evaluation tool that harmonizes the heterogeneity of measuring labor and agricultural productivity.

5 Agricultural Development in the Context of Kenya's Devolution

The 2010 Kenyan constitution (Republic of Kenya 2010) adopted a devolved governance system which introduced key changes with the vibrant shift from a highly centralized to the decentralized arrangement. As envisaged in the constitution, devolution is anchored on the sharing of administrative, political, and fiscal responsibilities between the two levels of governments (national and county). The devolution consists of 47 semi-autonomous units called counties. The 47 counties took responsibility in the management of health, agriculture, urban service, and local infrastructure. Notwithstanding the commitment to openness and involvement of the public in decision-making regarding these services, initially, there was mix-up on the roles and responsibilities of the devolved units. As a result, accountability mechanisms were hindered. In addition, insufficient resources and limited capacity undermined efforts to involve the general public in budget and planning processes as well as getting their feedback (World Bank 2015). Furthermore, a key problem with regard to personnel management. Before devolution had taken effect, there were 4000 agricultural, livestock, and fisheries extension officers at the district level. The devolved units which have now taken charge of extension officers did not absorb them and instead recruited new ones. This led to two parallel extension service system, which remains a burden on the budgets and operations and resulted in total interruption of services in some counties (World Bank 2014).

Agricultural sector plays a critical role in economic growth in Kenya. Sustained agricultural productivity is also essential for hunger and poverty alleviation since the majority (80%) of Kenyans in rural areas are employed by the sector. In addition, the sector contributes 27% of the GDP, 65% of annual earnings from exports, and provides more than 18% of the formal labor force (Republic of Kenya 2017). Like many African countries, women constitute more than 50% of the labor force in the agriculture sector (Asongu et al. 2019; Osabuohien et al. 2019). Despite the importance of agriculture to the Kenyan economy, its contribution to GDP has over the past two decades declined significantly (Karugia et al. 2013). This has been attributed to factors such as the lack of adoption of modern technologies, harsh weather conditions, pests and diseases, poor infrastructure, limited access to credit, post-harvest losses, and market constraints. Furthermore, smallholder farmers in Kenya are characterized by low agricultural production and poverty. According to the Development Initiatives 2016 report, 45.2% of the Kenyan population lives below the poverty line. Moreover, studies show that low off-farm activities in the East Africa region have an adverse effect on agricultural production (Barasa et al. 2019). A more in-depth analysis indicates that rural poverty is higher, with 76.9% of the poor living in rural areas.

In July 2003, in Maputo, Mozambique African Heads of state at the Second Ordinary Assembly of African Union (AU), endorsed a Declaration on agriculture and food security in Africa. It was stipulated that state parties present in the ordinary Assembly of the African Union take steps to increase allocation to agricultural sector development from 2 to 10%. It was noted that without this increase, agricultural productivity in particular food production would stall. Kenya, just like the rest of other East Africa countries, is falling behind in the operationalization of the Maputo Declaration (Alliance for a Green Revolution in Africa [AGRA] 2017). For instance, in Kenya's 2018 budget, the agricultural sector was allocated nearly 4.2% of the national budget, while in the previous fiscal year, 2.3% of the budget was allocated to the same sector. This still remains a low allocation to the agricultural sector.

Kenya's agriculture productivity per worker has largely remained constant, with some decline in other areas. The production of some crops such as maize and other cereals, for instance, has stagnated for the last five years, while that of coffee, sugar cane, fish, and livestock products have recorded a significant drop. This has been partially attributed to a decline in the per capita land owned and cultivated over the years as a result of the piling population pressures and inadequate extension services. In Kenya, more than 30% of the small-scale farmers control less than a one-acre piece of land (USAID 2018).

The fourth schedule of the Kenyan constitution outlines the role of county governments regarding devolution of agricultural function. These include the implementation of national policies relevant to the counties. Specifically, county governments take charge of crop and animal husbandry, livestock sale yards (Markets), abattoirs, animal and plant diseases, and fisheries. To achieve high agricultural growth rates, this schedule stipulates that county governments should provide a conducive environment for the development of the sector. It is the responsibility of both the national and county governments to determine and facilitate the implementation of policies and measures in a way that is premeditated to encourage, support, and promote productivity in the agricultural sector. The need to revitalize agriculture has also been amplified in Kenya's vision 2030 and SDGs.

5.1 *The SDGs Domestication Process in Kenya*

The process of SDGs domestication is distinct from devolution. Nonetheless, the two processes aim to empower the local development actors to identify their own development concerns and take responsibility for their development processes. Both SDGs domestication and devolution use a similar bottom-up strategy where the local communities are the subjects of development. The SDGs domestication process in Kenya is examined through the above highlighted two processes—raising the SDGs awareness to the local development actors and empowering the local development actors to own, implement, and measure the achievement of SDGs.

5.1.1 *Raising Awareness on SDGs*
Both the Kenya government and the CSO appear to make significant progress in raising the awareness of SDGs domestication process. The government has established the County Integrated Development Plan (CIDP) in an effort to link the county governments with SDGs and African Agenda 2063. In its first SDGs implementation evaluation report presented in the 2017 SDGs High-level Political Forum in New York, the Kenyan government demonstrated

significant efforts in creating synergy to raise the awareness of SDGs domestication process. Different agencies involved in the SDGs awareness-raising process include government ministries and departments, county governments, CSOs, development partners, the private sector and special groups such as youths and persons with disabilities. The awareness process highlighted the importance of empowering county government to implement the SDGs effectively.

The official SDGs domestication process in Kenya referred to as "SDGs Road Map" has seven broad thematic areas: identifying stakeholders and establishing partnerships, advocacy and sensitization, domestication, resource mobilization, capacity building, mainstreaming and accelerating implementation, and monitoring and evaluation. The Kenyan government has indeed kicked off the domestication process. The ministry of Devolution and planning provides an institutional framework for implementation as well as monitoring and evaluation of SDGs in Kenya. The national office has established SDGs liaison office with county governors (the secretariat of the Council of Governors) to enhance the alignment of the Mid-term Development agendas with SDGs (Government of Kenya 2017; Council of Governors 2017).

The CSOs have also been on the frontline in advocating for effective domestication of SDGs. The SDGs Kenya Forum is a CSOs platform with over 100 members and works on the adoption of SDGs and the 2030 Development Agenda (SDGs Kenya Forum 2017). CSOs recognize that the ultimate success of the SDGs domestication process is dependent on the cooperation between the national government and the county governments. Other than influencing the policy framework through conducting research and modeling and sharing best practices, some NGOs implement their project with consciousness to the SDGs framework.

5.1.2 Capacity Building for SDGs Achievement

Despite remarkable efforts in raising awareness on the domestication of SDGs, the same has not been translated into implementation. In reality, the coordination between the national government and the county governments is characterized by mixed outcomes. There is a common understanding between the two levels of governance that skilled labor force is a crucial component of economic growth and development. Several counties have initiated capacity building programs in various sectors of their economies. For instance, Kakamega County has an ambitious farmer training program targeting all rural farmers to embrace modern farming methods and therefore, more production (Kakamega County Integrated Development Plan [KCIDP] 2018). A study on the African manufacturing firms revealed that skill acquisition through training has a positive influence on output per worker (Almeida and Carneiro 2008). Skilled labor force has been recognized as a critical source of labor productivity, and therefore training labor force in the agricultural sector will accelerate food production as well as living standards of the rural farmers through increased productivity.

The national government has worked closely with the county government to improve the employment of traditionally marginalized groups including youths and women, especially in rural areas. Policies such as the women enterprise fund, the youth enterprise development fund aim at the promotion of economic activities, most of which are agriculturally based. In addition, to ensure inclusive productivity, 30% of all the public procurement has been reserved for women, youth, and persons with disabilities. Skilled population produces high productivity. The two levels of the government have strengthened technical schools and polytechnics. Skills development has taken a new dimension with the revitalization of national youth empowerment programs such as the National Youth Service (NYS), capacity building initiatives, and the Kenya Youth Empowerment Project (the KYEP). All these are initiatives that have been rolled out in ensuring that the Kenyan youths are empowered through technical skills to enhance productivity.

There have been concerted efforts between the county governments and the national government to initiate infrastructural development across the country. These projects aim at opening up rural areas to improve the connection with urban areas. The increased tarmacking of rural roads has greatly opened the rural areas in some counties has enhanced the market of agricultural products. Most counties in arid and semiarid regions have prioritized the construction of dams, gabions, and water pans in a bid to improve self-reliance in food security and to manage the disastrous effects of the unforeseen disasters such as droughts. Although there has been a significant effort in implementing local development projects, there has been no reference to SDGs, their targets, or SDGs indicators.

County governments have recognized agricultural extension as an avenue for revitalizing rural agriculture as a strategy to reduce poverty (Isaboke 2017). Indeed, most county governments have plans to recruit and deploy many extensional workers to educate farmers on the best farming methods to enhance labor and agricultural productivity. Through extensional services, information is converted into functional knowledge that is instrumental in improving productivity and generation of income. Besides the transfer of technology, extensional workers promote access to nonformal education as well as information services to small-scale rural farmers. This is vital toward enhancing productivity, though also subject to county government institutional development.

Some of the critical development agencies in Kenya have operated in what is seen as an informal SDG-domesticated approach to development. Counties are increasingly becoming the key levels of governance considered when designing international aid. There appears to be an emerging trend of the development partners designing financing models that target the local agencies rather than a country as a whole. Most development agencies have focused on the promotion of labor productivity in the least performing counties. Some counties dragging behind the average development rate include Isiolo, Garissa, Lamu, Marsabit, Wajir, Samburu, Tana River, Moyale, and Turkana. These are the most impoverished counties and mostly located in arid and semiarid regions of the country (see, for instance, World Bank 2018). One of the major challenges Kenya is experiencing a shortage of skills to propel it to become a more internationally competitive and technologically powered business hub. High unemployment and low performance of SMEs among many counties especially those that historically been marginalized experience very low productivity. Like many CSOs, international development authorities have increasingly been concerned with improving agricultural productivity among small-scale farmers and pastoralist communities within the most vulnerable counties. Such an understanding that enables designing of development financing to target specific local governments appears to go the domestication direction.

Although various development agents target local development authorities and communities in their implementation of development projects, there is no precise reference to the specific SDGs and their goals. Definitely, any enhancement of development contributes to the achievement of SDGs, but development is not luck, but rather strategic planning and working within that plan. Without close reference to specific SDGs or their targets, it remains indistinguishable whether development actors are doing their conventional development work, or they are working to achieve the SDGs. Even among the international development financiers, it is difficult to quantify which specific SDGs and targets they aim to achieve, and to what extent while designing their development loans. Generally, there is over-assumption that any act of development will have contributed to the achievement of SDGs come 2030. Such a notion limits both the SDGs knowledge sharing and capacity building for the local actors to achieve SDGs.

5.2 *Challenges of SDGs Domestication in Kenya*

Domestication process within devolution in Kenya is not without difficulties. Although devolution in Kenya is less than 10 years old, there still lacks proper harmony and coordination between the national government and the county governments. Nonetheless, county governments are expected to play the key role in the growth of the agricultural sector—and so to the achievement of the related SDGs. Some of the highlighted issues at the county level include inadequate financing from the national government, staff shortage, insufficient technical support that hampers productivity (Njagi et al. 2015). The most affected departments are the directorates of livestock, veterinary services, and fisheries which have serious labor force shortage at the county, subcounty, and ward levels. In addition, most counties lack necessary infrastructures such as office space and transport and therefore making it difficult for county officials to access and provide services to farmers. There are also challenges with the disbursement of funds to the counties by the national treasury. To boost growth in the sector, there is a dire need to address these constraints especially those associated with low productivity such as low uptake of technology, animal and crop diseases, high input, and credit costs. The major challenge of domesticating the SDGs in Kenya is the financial empowerment of the local actors to take charge of their own development process. Furthermore, there is weak coordination between the devolved authorities and national government, challenges of communication due to high bureaucracy, and lack of synergies among the counties hinder SDGs knowledge sharing.

Even the CSOs that are cognizant of the domestication process, and working within the SDGs framework, use their own measurement tools which makes it difficult to aggregate data to derive any meaningful comparison of SDGs achievement in different counties (see, SDGs Kenya Forum 2017). Most CSOs work parallel to government agencies. Although the language of achieving the SDGs in more prevalent among Non-Governmental Organizations (NGOs), as compared to the government agencies, it still remains a challenge how to use SDGs targets and indicators in measuring the SDGs achievement between the two development actors.

6 Conclusion

As international development goals, SDGs achievement requires a more comprehensive analytical framework—a framework that is inclusive of all development actors. The framework of SDGs domestication. Although domestication of international development goals is a relatively new concept, it is gaining popularity among many development actors. To date, there exists no formal framework of SDGs domestication that captures every development effort made to enable proper measurement of SDGs achievement. Nonetheless, the lack of a formal strategy does not mean different actors do not work to achieve SDGs. Instead, it shows incoherence in measuring SDGs achievements. Sharing the SDGs-related knowledge and empowering the local actors to achieve the SDGs are the two major policy instruments that the domestication process involves. The implementation of the domestication process is, in turn, dependent on two variables; the governance structure and the specific social-economic sector involved.

The devolved governance structure appears to promote the domestication process since it empowers the local actors in the development process. A narrow examination of devolution as a pro-SDGs domestication governance structure would focus on the manner in which the national and the local level government engage to achieve SDGs. This chapter, however, widens the scope of SDGs domestication process to consider the role of non-state agencies in the development which also operates to enhance the achievement of SDGs within a devolved governance structure.

The Kenyan government has made a significant effort in raising awareness and establishing synergies in relation to sharing SDGs-related knowledge. Despite consciousness about SDGs, both the national and local governments there lacks a framework to enhance coordination in implementing and measuring the achievement of SDGs. Mainly because of noncompatibility, of measurements, it is still difficult to estimate how much the government, international development agencies, CSOs, and private sector have contributed to achieving SDGs. Even with the SDGs awareness, there lack comprehensive strategies of empowering local actors to achieve the Goals. The future effectiveness of Africa's SDGs achievement and the agricultural sector, in particular, depends on how well SDGs are domesticated. We thus recommend that any SDGs domestication policy toolbox need to consider:

- A universal framework to measure the achievement of SDGs. The framework should be comprehensive enough to capture SDGs targets and involve all development actors, e.g., inter-governmental, national, the private sector, CSO, at different levels ranging from international to local levels.
- SDGs knowledge management: this involves raising awareness on the meaning and the purpose of working under the consciousness of SDGs. Different actors working to improve labor output in agricultural need to share experience on different approaches within the SDGs framework.
- Capacity building: there is a need to empower the local level governments to adequately take responsibility for the achievement of SDGs. Skills and capacities of international development agencies such as the ability to conduct research and measurement of their own developments are essential to the local development actors. In Kenya, for instance, it is difficult to break down the national-level data on a measure of agricultural productivity output to determine per county data.
- A bottom-up approach to aggregation of data is the best means of measuring the achievement of SDGs.

References

Abhilaksh, L. (2013). *The Millennium Development Goals (MDGs): Challenges for poverty reduction and service delivery in the rural–urban continuum.* World Bank.

Abraham, M., & Pingali, P. (2017). Transforming smallholder agriculture to achieve the SDGs. In L. Riesgo, S. Gomez-Y-Paloma, & K. Louhichi (Eds.), *The role of small farms in food and nutrition security.* New York: Springer.

Alliance for a Green Revolution in Africa (AGRA). (2017). *Africa agriculture status report. The business of smallholder agriculture in sub-Saharan Africa* (issue 5). Nairobi

Almeida, R., & Carneiro, P. (2008). The return to firm investments in human capital. *Labor Economics, 16*(1), 97–106. https://doi.org/10.1016/j.labeco.2008.06.002.

Asongu, S. A., Efobi, U. R., Tanakem, B. V., & Osabuohien, E. (2019). Globalisation and female economic participation in sub-Saharan Africa. *Gender Issues.* https://doi.org/10.1007/s12147-019-09233-3.

Barasa, L. L., Araar, A., Kinyanjui, B. K., Maende, S. O., & Mariera, F. (2019). *Off-farm participation, agricultural production and farmers welfare in Tanzania and Uganda* (Working Paper of the Partnership for Economic Policy (PEP) No. 2019-01).

Beegle, K., Luc-Christiaensen, Dabalen, A., & Gaddis I. (2016). *Poverty in a rising Africa: Overview*. Washington, DC: World Bank.
Bernstein, J. (2018). Drawing on good Sustainable Development Goals practices – Options for Sweden. Komm 2018/00568.
Besley, T., Pande, R., Rahman, L., & Rao, V. (2004). The politics of public good provision: Evidence from Indian local governments. *Journal of the European Economic Association, 2*(2-3), 416–426.
Besley, T., Pande, R., & Rao, V. (2007). Political economy of panchayats in south India. *Economic and Political Weekly, 42*(8), 661–666.
Binswanger-Mkhize, H., & McCalla, A. F. (2010). The changing context and prospects for agricultural and rural development in Africa. In P. L. Pingali, & R. E. Evenson (Eds.), *Handbook of agricultural economics* (4: pp. 3571–3712). Oxford: Elsevier B.V.
Blanc, L. D. (2015). Towards integration at last? The Sustainable Development Goals as a network of targets. *Sustainable Development, 23*, 176–187.
Bosire, M., & Wanjiru, G. (2015). *Animating devolution in Kenya, the role of the judiciary*. IDLO Nairobi: International Development Law Organization.
Chambers, R. (1983). *Rural development: Putting the last first*. Harlow, UK: Pearson Education.
Chattopadhyay, A. K. (2005). Distributive impact of agricultural growth in rural West Bengal. *Economic and Political Weekly, 40*(53), 5601–5610.
Council of Governors. (2017). *Annual devolution report*. Accessed on www.cog.co.org.
Crafts, N. (2010). The contribution of new technology to economic growth: Lessons from economic history. *Revista de Historia Economical, Journal of Iberian and Latin American Economic History, 28*(3), 409–440.
Deshpande, R. S., & Rao, V. M. (2002). Food security in drought-prone areas. *Economic and Political Weekly, 37*(35), 3677–3681.
De Vita, C. (1998). *Nonprofits and devolution; what do we know?* Washington, DC: Urban Institute Press.
Food and Agricultural Organization (FAO). (2017). FAO and SDGs indicators: Measuring up to the 2030 Agenda for Sustainable Development. I6919EN/1/02.17.
Food and Agricultural Organization (FAO). (2018). *Transforming food and agriculture to achieve SDGs. 20 interconnected actions to guide decision-makers*. Rome.
Global Taskforce. (2016). Roadmap for localizing the SDGs: Implementation and monitoring at subnational levels. gtf2016.org.
Global Taskforce. (2018). Towards the domestication of the SDGs: Local and regional governments' report to the 2018 High Level Political Forum.
Government of Kenya. (2017). *Ministry of Devolution and Planning Report: Implementation of the Agenda Vision 2030 for Sustainable Development in Kenya*. Nairobi, Kenya: Government Printer.
IAEG-SDGs. (2016). Resolution adopted by the General Assembly on Work of the Statistical Commission pertaining to the 2030 Agenda for Sustainable Development (A/RES/71/313).
Isaboke, J. M. (2017). Drivers of labor productivity in flower farms in Naivasha, Kenya. *Sustainable Agriculture Research, 6*(4), 117–123.

Jonyo, F. (2015). *The constitution, parliament and governance systems*. Nairobi: The Centre for Parliamentary Studies and Training.

Kakamega County. (2018). Kakamega County Integrated Development Plan. Accessed February 18, 2019, from https://kakamega.go.ke/download/county-integrated-development-plan-2018-2022/.

Karugia, J. Massawe, S., Guthiga, P., & Macharia, E. (2013). Agricultural productivity in EAC region (1965–2010): Trends and determinants. In *International Symposium and Exhibition on the Agricultural Development in the EAC Partner States* (Vol. 50).

Kettle, D. (2000). The transformation of governance: Globalization, devolution, & the role of government. *Public Administration Review, 60*(6), 488–497.

Khaunya, M., Wawire, B., & Chepngeno, V. (2015). Devolved governance in Kenya, Is it a false start in democratic decentralization for development? *International Journal of Economics, Finance and Management, 4*(1), 27–37.

Larson, A. M. (2003). Decentralization and forest management in Latin America: Towards a working model. *Public Administration and Development, 23,* 211–222.

Littlewood, D., & Holt, D. (2018). How social enterprises can contribute to the Sustainable Development Goals (SDGs) – A conceptual framework. In N. Apostolopoulos, H. Al-Dajani, D. Holt, P. Jones, & R. Newbery (Eds.), *Entrepreneurship and the Sustainable Development Goals. Contemporary Issues in Entrepreneurship Research, 8* (pp. 33–46). Bingley: Emerald.

Manor, J. (2004). Democratization with inclusion: Political reforms and people's empowerment at the grassroots. *Journal of Human Development, 5*(1), 5–29.

Mansuri, G., & Vijayendra, R. (2013). *Localizing development: Does participation work?* Washington, DC: World Bank. https://doi.org/10.1596/978-0-8213-8256-1.

Miguel, M. R., & Pinila, V. (2012). *Why did agricultural labor productivity not converge in Europe from 1950 to 2005?* (Working Paper 25).

Mitullah, W. V. (2013). *Development ideals and reality, bridging the gap through devolution*. Nairobi: Clarion.

Muriisa, R. K. (2008). Decentralization in Uganda: Prospects for improved service delivery. *Africa Development, 33*(4), 83–95.

Njagi, T., Kirimi, L., Onyango, K., & Nthenya, K. (2015). *The status of the agricultural sector after devolution to county governments*. Retrieved September 18, 2018, from http://www.tegemeo.org/images/downloads/publications/policy_briefs/Policy%20brief%20No%2013.pdf.

Nyanjom, O. (2011). *Devolution in Kenya's new constitution* (pp. 1–30) (Constitution Working Paper No. 4).

Oommen, M. A. (2004). *Deepening decentralised governance in rural India: Lessons from the People's Plan Initiative of Kerala* (Working Paper No. 11). Kerala: Centre for Socio-Economic and Environmental Studies.

Osabuohien, E., Efobi, U. R., Herrmann, R., & Gitau, C. M. (2019). Female labor outcomes and large-scale agricultural land investments: Macro-micro evidence from Tanzania. *Land Use Policy, 82,* 716–728. https://doi.org/10.1016/j.landusepol.2019.01.005.

Patole, M. (2018). Domestication of SDGs through disaggregation of KPIs. *Economies, 6,* 15. https://doi.org/10.3390/economies6010015.

Pingali, P., Witwer, M., & Abraham, M. (2016). Getting to zero hunger: Learning from the MDGs for the SDGs. In P. D. Y. Lalaguna, C. M. D. Barrado, & C. R.

F. Liesa (Eds.), *International Society and Sustainable Development Goals* (pp. 175–202). Pamplona, Spain: Thomson Reuters Aranzadi.

Pomare, C. (2018). A multiple framework approach to Sustainable Development Goals (SDGs) and entrepreneurship. In N. Apostolopoulos, H. Al-Dajani, D. Holt, P. Jones, & R. Newbery (Eds.), *Entrepreneurship and the Sustainable Development Goals. Contemporary Issues in Entrepreneurship Research, Volume 8* (pp. 11–31). Bingley: Emerald.

Potter, J. G. (2001). *Devolution and globalization: Implications for local decision makers.* Paris: Organization for Economic Cooperation and Development (OECD).

Rajasekhar, D., & Manjula, R. (2011). *Decentralised governance and service delivery affordability of drinking water supply by gram panchayats in Karnataka.* ISEC Monograph 23. Bangalore: Institute for Social and Economic Change (ISEC).

Rebecca, F. (2008). *Labor productivity indicators comparison of two OECD databases productivity differentials & the Balassa-Samuelson effect.* Retrieved September 9, 2018, from http://www.oecd.org/sdd/labor-stats/41354425.pdf.

Republic of Kenya. (2010). *Kenyan Constitution (2010).* Government Printer: Nairobi.

Republic of Kenya. (2017). *Economic review of agriculture.* Government Printer: Nairobi.

Robinson, M. (2007). Does decentralization improve equity and efficiency in public service delivery. *IDS Bulletin, 38*(1), 7–17.

SDGs Center for Africa and Sustainable Development Solutions Network. (2018). Africa SDG Index and Dashboards Report Summary.

SDGs Kenya Forum. (2017). Voluntary National Review (VNR) of Progress on Sustainable Development Goals (SDGs) in Kenya.

SDGs Knowledge Platform. (2019). Sustainable Development Goals. Accessed January 2, 2019, from https://sustainabledevelopment.un.org/sdgs.

Sen, A. (1985). *Commodities and capabilities.* Amsterdam: Elsevier.

Timmer, C. P. (1988). The agricultural transformation. *Handbook of Development Economics, 1,* 275–331.

Timmer, P. C. (2009). *A world without agriculture: The structural transformation in historical perspective.* Washington, DC: American Enterprise Institute.

Timmer, P. C. (2017). Food security, structural transformation, markets and government policy. *Asia & the Pacific Policy Studies, 4*(1), 4–19.

Treisman, D. (2000). *Decentralization and the quality of government.* Retrieved February 21, 2019, from https://www.imf.org/external/pubs/ft/seminar/2000/fiscal/treisman.pdf.

United Nations. (1961). Resolutions adopted on the Second Committee.

United Nations. (2007). A prehistory of the Millennium Development Goals: Four decades of struggle for development in the United Nations. Vol. XLIV No. 4 2007.

United Nations. (2018). UN documentation: Development. Accessed June 30, 2019, from http://research.un.org/en/docs/dev/intro.

United Nations Development Program. (2017). *Policy brief, Sustainable Development Goals, post-2015, localizing SDGs in Kenya, building on the lessons learned from the MDGs, What role can the UN system play in the process?* Nairobi: UNDP Nairobi Printer.

USAID. (2018). *Agriculture and food security.* Retrieved from https://www.usaid.gov/kenya/agriculture-and-food-security.

World Bank. (2007). *World Development Report 2008: Agriculture for development*. Washington, DC: World Bank.

World Bank. (2014). *The evolution of Kenya's devolution: What's working well, what could work better*. Information Note for World Bank Staff. Washington, DC: World Bank.

World Bank. (2015). *Practical approaches for county governments to facilitate public participation in the planning and budget process* (Kenya Devolution Working Paper 6). Nairobi, Kenya: World Bank.

World Bank. (2018). Kenya: World Bank Approves $50 million to boost Kenya's small and medium enterprises. Retrieved February 21, 2019, from https://www.worldbank.org/en/news/press-release/2018/06/15/kenya-world-bank-approves-50-million-to-boost-kenyas-small-and-medium-enterprises.

Yibeltal, A.,Wim, V. D., Owain, D. W., & Hill, P. S. (2017). Successes and challenges of the Millennium Development Goals in Ethiopia: Lessons for the Sustainable Development Goals. *BMJ Global Health, 2*(2), e000318.

Yonglong, L., Nebojsa, N., Martin, V., & Anne-Sophie, S. (2016). Five priorities for the UN Sustainable Development Goals. Brief for GSDR – 2016 Update.

Youth Employment Challenge and Rural Transformation in Africa

Damian Kalu Ude

1 Introduction

Africa is said to be the world's most youthful continent. Africa has the youngest and fastest growing population. The median age of the population in Africa is 18.3 years old. Each year, over 11 million young Africans are entering the labor market. Presently, the continent is facing an employment crisis of lack of jobs for the teeming youth. Most Africans of working age have no access to social protection schemes such as unemployment compensations and hence cannot afford not to work even if the returns to labor are very low. It is also argued that around 80% of African youth are in vulnerable employment (International Development Research Centre 2018).

One of the most defining challenges of the twenty-first century will be to provide productive and decent jobs to more than 40 million additional people who enter the global labor market every year (Brussels Rural Development Briefings 2011). For Africa, this is a race against time. By 2035, the number of Africans joining the working-age population will exceed that of the rest of the world combined. According to the International Monetary Fund (IMF) (2015) "Regional Economic Outlook: Sub-Saharan Africa," the region will need to create about 18 million jobs per year until 2035 to absorb this growing labor force. The stakes are high. Africa's growth rates have outperformed the global rate over the last decade, but job creation has not kept pace. Moreover, the gap between Africa's youth and decent work has

---

D. K. Ude (✉)
Department of Economics, Michael Okpara University of Agriculture, Umudike, Nigeria
e-mail: dk.ude@mouau.edu.ng

© The Author(s) 2020
E. S. Osabuohien (ed.), *The Palgrave Handbook of Agricultural and Rural Development in Africa*, https://doi.org/10.1007/978-3-030-41513-6_3

not reduced. Nevertheless, youth employment has the potential to become Africa's most powerful development engine. According to the International Labor Organization (ILO)'s "World Employment and Social Outlook: Trends 2015," Sub-Saharan Africa has the highest labor force participation of all regions, estimated at 70.9%—compared with a global average of 63.5% in 2014. Unemployment stood at 7.7% in 2014, while the youth unemployment rate in the continent was 11.8% in 2014; only East Asia and South Asia had lower rates at 10.5 and 10.0%, respectively.

Tactlessly, Africa's population and labor force has continued to grow rapidly, but opportunities for decent employment are expanding at a slower pace (Adesugba and Mavrotas 2016; Osabuohien et al. 2019). Sub-Saharan Africa has the youngest and fastest growing population. The median age of the population in Africa is 18.3 years old and in Asia it is 30 years old (37.0 in China, 26.6 in India). Youth are two or three times more likely than adults to be unemployed. This is because the majority of youth are jobless or do not participate in labor markets (United Nations [UN] 2015). As a consequence, high youth unemployment rates seem to act as a disincentive for youth to participate in the labor force. The youth unemployment rate is double the adult unemployment rates in Sub-Saharan Africa and over five times higher in South-East Asia and the Pacific. The majority of working youth are poor and employed in vulnerable, low-quality jobs, often in the informal sector (ILO 2013). According to the African Development Bank (AfDB) (2015), the gap between the number of labor market participants and available wage job opportunities widens by approximately eight million annually. Young Africans are disproportionately affected by the slow growth in jobs, and projections suggest that even under the most favorable growth conditions, less than a quarter of the roughly 350 million young Africans entering the labor force by 2035 will find wage employment in the formal sector. Many young people will need to create their own jobs through entrepreneurial activities to avoid escalating challenges associated with unemployment (AfDB 2015).

At the same time, growing populations, urbanization, and rising incomes of the urban working population are fueling increased demand for food and agricultural products in the region, featuring more diverse, high value, and processed foods including meat, dairy, and horticulture. However, because of prevailing low productivity levels, Africa's agricultural production systems have not evolved proportionally to keep up with this growing demand. Consequently, an increasing share of the continent's food demand is being met through food imports, which is estimated at US$68 billion annually according to the African Transformation Report (2017). Improving the capacity and productivity of local producers to recapture this growing food market could accelerate economic growth and create jobs for young people on the farm and in off-farm activities including improved seed, fertilizer and machinery service provision, as well as in post-harvest handling, marketing, and food manufacturing.

In Sub-Saharan Africa, the youth unemployment rate, at almost 12%, is twice that of adults (ILO 2014). Due to the large and growing child and youth populations—those aged below 25 made up over 63% of the population in 2010, expected to remain above 50% by 2050 (United Nations Population Division [UNPD] 2012)—the absolute number of unemployed youths continues to grow. Additionally, vulnerable employment and working poverty are particularly pressing issues in Sub-Saharan Africa, with by far the highest rates of both compared with any other region. Estimated at 77% in 2013 (ILO 2014), "vulnerable employment" encompasses own-account workers (i.e. those self-employed) and unpaid contributing family workers (i.e. those working on a family farm or for a family business without a wage). These workers are employed under relatively precarious circumstances, with no formal employment arrangements or access to social protection benefits or programs, putting them at relatively high risk of poverty and vulnerable to the effects of economic cycles. It is also argued that in many Sub-Saharan countries vulnerable employment also includes precarious wage labor mainly in agricultural sector and processing of agriculture products in formal and informal sectors, which even the wage workers in formal labor market tend to receive below the minimum wage established by law due to the organization of work and production. "Working poverty," estimated at 40% in 2012, 43% in 2013, 41% in 2015, and 36% in 2017 at the US$1.25/day level (ILO 2013, 2018), describes those who continue to live in poverty despite their wages or income. The nature of the challenge can be seen in terms of both risks and opportunities.

The high number of African youths who are unemployed or unable to make ends meet through jobs and businesses are often seen as a threat to social stability. However, overcoming youth unemployment and working poverty is a chance for significant, positive change. Inclusive growth that fosters economic opportunities for youth, and their meaningful engagement in social and political life should be seen as an opportunity for innovation, growth, development, and sustainability, at the individual, household, and national levels. Adolescence and young adulthood are key moments to interrupt the intergenerational transmission of poverty (Shepherd et al. 2011). Evidence suggests, for example, that long spells of unemployment or underemployment in informal work can have permanent repercussions on future productivity and employment (Guarcello et al. 2007). A lack of early economic opportunities can undermine asset building and life satisfaction (World Bank 2013).

Conversely, smoother and quicker transitions from school to adequate, sustainable jobs or small businesses can have positive, long-lasting effects. Yet sub-Saharan African youth face a range of barriers to accessing good economic opportunities, constraining their ability to build sustainable livelihoods and escape poverty. Among these are limited numbers of formal jobs, low levels of literacy, education, and work-relevant skills (Sparreboom and Staneva 2014);

and a lack of access to assets (Markel and Panetta 2014), including land, and to financial services (Demirgüç-Kunt and Klapper 2012). These barriers are cross-cut by social, economic, and political biases against youth (Banks and Sulaiman 2012; Markel and Panetta 2014; MasterCard Foundation 2014). It is important to note the heterogeneity of "youth" as a group. First, it reflects the same diversity as the population in general.

Marginalized youth—including young women, but also youth with disabilities, youth from minority populations, youth living in remote rural areas and urban slums, and others—face particular challenges in accessing work and risk being trapped in vulnerable employment and working poverty. Second, as "transition" is the defining feature of youthhood, there is additional diversity within the group, whether defined according to the United Nations' 15–24 age range or the wider ranges often adopted by national governments. An 18-year-old may be in school and/or training, and/or working for herself and/or for others. She may be living with parents, alone, or with a partner and/or her own children dependent on her. And transitions are not always unidirectional: a period of self-employment can precede finishing school, for example. This diversity in young people's status and experience adds a layer of complexity to both data-gathering and programming, but understanding "youth segments" is crucial to successful interventions (Resnick and Thurlow 2015).

The African economic landscape has faced a dramatic change since the 1960s with a very quick process of urbanization. However, even if the urban population increased tenfold in Africa, the continent remains predominantly rural (around 60–65% of the population). As clearly stressed by the High-level Panel on the Post-2015 Development Agenda, unemployment and youth employment remain probably today's major global issue with sustainable development related to climate change (United Nations [UN] 2013). In relative terms, the youth employment challenge affects every region—developed as well as developing countries—a feature stressed by the World Development Report 2013 on "Jobs" (World Bank 2012). Due to the characteristics of its demographic trends, Africa is the region of the world where this challenge is—and will increasingly be—a deep concern: 60% of the world's labor force growth between 2010 and 2050 will be in Africa; 60% of the African population today are under 25; African youth weights 35% of the economically active population; and only in the next 15 years, nearly 400 million youth will enter the labor market of the continent.

From the foregoing, the study is poised to investigate youth employment challenge and rural transformation in Africa as well as analyzes dimensions of issues in agricultural and rural development in Africa using involution hypothesis in panel analysis and focusing on youth unemployment. Specifically, Sect. 1 discusses the background information and the key objective of the study while Sect. 2 establishes some empirical background issues on youth employment and Africa's rural transformation. Section 3 expatiates the method of analysis and Sect. 4 deals with the estimated results and discussion of findings. Finally, Sect. 5 is the conclusion of the study. The study concludes by exploring some of the prospects and policies for enhancing youth employment in Africa.

2 Some Background Issues on Youth Employment and Africa's Rural Transformation

The 15–24-year-old age group represents 20% of Africa's population today and, unlike in other regions, this youth share will remain high and stable (19% in 2050). In absolute terms, Africa's youth will grow from nearly 200 million in 2015 to nearly 400 million in 2050, and its share in the labor force will remain the highest in the world, even if following a declining trend. The entire youth population in Africa represent 37% today—in comparison with 30% in India, 25% in China, and 20% in Europe—it should still account for 30% in 2050 (ILO 2016) (Raghav and Vani 2017).

Issues related to youth employment in developing countries, particularly those connected to agricultural transformation policies in Africa south of the Sahara, have attracted much attention in recent years (see Headey et al. 2010; Henley 2012; Brooks, Zorya, Gautam, and Goyal 2013; Brooks, Zorya, and Gautam 2013; Resnick and Thurlow 2015; Collier and Dercon 2014, among others; Adesugba and Mavrotas [2016] also provide a discussion of these issues). At the same time, recent years have witnessed a demographic transition across many developing countries from high to low levels of fertility and mortality and migration to urban areas. An important development associated with this transition is the decrease in dependency ratios in rural areas—a demographic dividend that can enhance growth. Conversely, migration to urban areas results in labor shortages in the agricultural sector, which in turn may lead to greater mechanization and higher wages (Keats and Wiggins 2016). The debate on youth unemployment globally, and in Africa in particular, hinges also on the differential pattern of structural change of economies, which works against the creation of "good" jobs (McMillan et al. 2014; McMillan and Rodrik 2011). Despite economic growth, structural change in Africa is still minimal and, for the most part, fails to create high-productivity jobs (McMillan et al. 2014). It has been suggested that one of the reasons for low labor productivity in Africa is its comparative advantage based on the exploitation of natural resources. As McMillan and Rodrik (2011) rightly argue, countries with such an advantage face the risk of an underdeveloped process of structural transformation that results from an overdependence on natural resources for development.

The rural transformation agenda is about improving the overall quality of life in rural areas. This entails promoting investments in health, education, and rural infrastructure; having in place efficient rural financial markets; designing policies that promote greater gender equity and the empowerment of rural people, especially the most vulnerable through designing and implementing effective safety net programs; improving market access of small-scale farmers in innovative markets and strengthen their involvement in the whole value chain (Brussels Rural Development Briefings 2011). However, for all this to happen, it is necessary to ensure effective institutions for rural development and public and private investments in agricultural research and extension to provide a continuous stream of yield-enhancing technologies that can be profitably adopted by farmers.

The core of the rural transformation agenda is defined by the following major imperatives:

a. Reducing poverty and inequalities, not only those inherited from past policy decisions and social structures, but also the new poverties, gaps, and inequalities being created each day by the process of rapid change itself.
b. Ensuring food security, accelerating agricultural development, and securing a relevant role of and opportunities for small-scale producers and family farmers in national and global value chains.
c. Creating more and better jobs and economic self-sufficiency in rural areas, including in small towns and intermediate cities. Rural economic diversification is a major driver of job creation. At the same time, rural labor markets are notoriously imperfect and they represent a huge challenge that needs to be urgently addressed.
d. Meeting the climate change and environmental challenge, enhancing environmental services, making much more efficient use of scarce natural resources such as land and water, promoting renewable sources of energy that can only be created in rural areas, and leveraging a green agenda for new jobs and sources of income for the poor.
e. Stimulating the growth of rural towns and intermediate cities and strengthening the links between them and their rural hinterlands.
f. Managing the complex and sensitive issue of rural–urban migration.
g. Securing universal access by rural populations to basic public services including education, health, housing, fresh water, electricity, transport, and communications, with improving quality standards.
h. Developing land reform and land tenure systems that balance objectives of social equity, economic growth, and environmental sustainability, and that can evolve rapidly as many young and better-educated people join new nonfarm rural jobs or emigrate out of rural areas.
i. Securing widespread access to efficient and sustainable financial services and capital, without which the benefits of the rural transformation cannot be realized in full. This requires a significant expansion of financial resources and budgets, as well as major improvements in the efficiency and institutional sustainability of rural financial systems.
j. Promoting innovation, research, and development focused on the needs of rural people and rural producers and firms and making much better use of the opportunities offered by ICTs.

k. Putting in place social support schemes including cash transfers, pensions, employment guarantees, and subsidies for the most vulnerable that secure the basic human dignity of every rural dweller. It is important to reaffirm that poverty eradication and social inclusion will lead to better long-term outcomes and will be more sustainable if they rest on localized, inclusive economic growth, complemented, and not replaced by social support schemes.

Young people are increasingly linked to targeted agriculture and food security interventions. Specifically, it is also argued that in many parts of Mozambique, Uganda, Ethiopia, Zimbabwe, and South Africa, many people get evolved in diversified activities or forms of work even in casual forms. In general, in Africa, the argument is that the combination of agricultural value chains, technology and entrepreneurship will unlock a sweet spot for youth employment (Santiago et al. 2017). However, the existing policy narratives and program approaches linking youth, agricultural development, and food security are problematic. First, they frame issues such as limited access to land and credit as youth-specific, ignoring the structural nature of these constraints; that is, in most situations, these issues affect other social groups as well as youth. They also conflate situations where young people may be systematically discriminated against in their access to productive resources, with circumstances in which young people, by virtue of being young, are more likely to have fewer assets, less status, and less access to resources than older people. Second, they assume that the opportunity to engage with value chains is open to all young people independent of the rural environment in which they live and their individual circumstances. Third, they accept a broad conception of entrepreneurship, to the point where any income generating activity is seen as reflecting entrepreneurial behavior. Fourth, they rely on essentialist thinking, suggesting that all young people share particular characteristics, such as being "innovative" of having a particular mindset. Finally, they tend to conceive of young people as isolated economic agents, ignoring the fact that their economic activity is deeply embedded in and dependent on networks of family and social relations (Flynn and Sumberg 2017).

Unfortunately, agriculture is widely perceived by many young Africans as unattractive—an obvious result of the historical low profitability and drudgery associated with traditional agricultural practices. Even those young people with a predilection for agriculture typically lack the skills and/or access to productive resources to effectively take advantage of opportunities in the rapidly evolving agricultural and food system (UN 2015). Also, many of the youth-in-agriculture initiatives across the continent have neither been scaled up nor have they yielded the desired results. This is partly due to the fact that most initiatives are occurring within a limited evidence base and much of the existing narratives are largely devoid of the inputs of the young people they are intended to serve (Losch et al. 2012).

The notion of rural transformation is a useful way to conceptualize the core processes of economic growth and rural development. Structural transformation can be understood as several interrelated components. It is often conceptualized as beginning with agricultural productivity growth, led by productive farmers with enough land to generate marketable surpluses. This growth results in income gains which stimulate demand for goods and services from nonfarm sectors. Rural–urban migration is stimulated by increasing demand for nonfarm labor, driving urbanization. The gradual movement of labor from farm to nonfarm activities is reflected in a declining share of agriculture in total gross domestic products (GDP) and employment. Less efficient farmers are likely to exit farming first, driving net efficiency gains. The movement of labor from agricultural to other sectors may enable land consolidation, as more efficient producers obtain land from less efficient producers (reflecting its higher marginal value for the more efficient farmers) (Sitko and Chamberlin 2016).

Across the economic system, structural transformation results in productivity increases through two main channels: first, aggregate labor productivity rises as labor migrates from less productive to more productive economic activities; second, productivity growth may occur within sectors, as a result of technological development. Within agriculture, such growth is driven by the exodus of less efficient labor, abetted by technical innovation, scale economies, shifts to higher value commodities (driven, in turn, by the changing demands of urbanizing populations) and improving market infrastructure and supporting services.

Empirical evidence (McMillan et al. 2014) on how this process has played out in recent decades in the developing world highlights several important stylized facts. First, while agriculture's share of GDP and employment has been decreasing across the developing world, the rate of decrease has been relatively small, and agriculture is still the dominant sector. Second, there are very distinct regional variations in the transformation process: only in Asia (and particularly in a few countries, e.g. Vietnam, China) has surplus labor moved from agriculture into more productive sectors (e.g. manufacturing, high-value services). In Latin America and, especially, Africa, the more limited movement of labor out of agriculture has been into lower value services and the informal economy, offsetting the productivity growth that has taken place within agriculture and dampening overall levels of economic growth (McMillan et al. 2014). In the case of Africa in particular, the phenomenon of urbanization without industrialization has been well documented (Jedwab 2011, 2013). Third, these stylized patterns are reflected to a certain extent in patterns of growth within the agricultural sector; while Asia has seen agricultural productivity growth, rates of growth have been much lower for Latin America and Africa. The agricultural growth that has taken place in these regions has largely come through area expansion, rather than productivity increases (Gollin et al. 2016).

Despite the reduction in agriculture's share of GDP (not forgetting the forward and backward linkages of agricultural-industrialization processes), there are sizeable populations that will remain in rural areas and will be dependent to some degree on agriculture. This is particularly true for Africa, where the population of young people is projected to increase by 95 million between 2015 and 2030 (UN 2015), the majority of whom will live in rural areas. In contrast, the youth populations of Latin America, North Africa, and the Middle East are reducing or growing at a much lower rate (ibid.); but even in Asian countries where agriculture's share of employment has seen the largest reductions, the absolute number of people in rural areas will remain very high for the next decades. By 2050, 2.8 billion people will still live in rural areas, and South Asia and Africa will account for two-thirds (Losch et al. 2012). Given the annual volume of new labor market entrants in rural areas, along with the limited absorption capacity of urban economic sectors (particularly in Africa), current thinking is that millions of young people in the developing world will need to find viable employment in the (farm and non-farm) rural economy.

However, given the exploitation of natural resources through FDI in many countries with land use conflicts and changes in people's livelihoods, agricultural land is already a scarce resource in many rural areas of the developing world. In Africa, it was traditionally assumed that cropland was an abundant resource, available to meet the food and other needs of growing populations. However, recent work has shown that surplus land is highly concentrated, with as much as 90% of Africa's unutilized arable land located in just six to eight countries (Chamberlin et al. 2014). In the list of land-scarce countries, are some of the continent's most populous ones, including Nigeria, Ethiopia, and Uganda (ibid.).

Population increase plays an important part in growing land scarcity. Over the past decades, farms in Africa have become smaller. For example, in east and southern Africa, the arable land area has increased "only marginally over the 1980–2010 period, but the percentage of households engaged in agriculture has grown threefold" (Jayne et al. 2014, p. 3). In addition to rural population growth, the allocation of land to transnational corporations and domestic businesses for large-scale ventures can shape farming households' access to land (Chinsinga and Chasukwa 2012; Sitko and Chamberlin 2016). There are other factors that make land relatively scarce including the quality of the natural resources and settlement patterns which concentrate near market infrastructure: in Africa, "82% of the population is found to reside in only 20% of total rural land area, and 62% reside within just 10% of this area" (Jayne et al. 2014).

Asia is even more densely populated and has also witnessed a significant decline in farm size: South Asian farms have decreased on average from 2.01 ha to 1.19 ha per holding, while in China and South-East Asia land area per farm has decreased from 2.08 ha to 1.58 ha (Headey and Jayne 2014).

Asian agriculture responded to increasing land pressure with technological change (mainly fertilizer varieties and irrigation) and as a result, increased total agricultural output and land and labor productivity, despite shrinking farm size (ibid.). This dynamic has not been observed in Africa.

Compared to Asia and Africa, Latin America has significantly more land availability per capita, and in the case of South America, the average hectares per holding have actually increased since the 1970s (probably due to forest clearance). However, Latin America also has the greatest inequality in land ownership, with very large farm owners coexisting with small-scale farmers. Further, as mentioned above, Latin America has been relatively unsuccessful in increasing agricultural output and productivity since the 1970s (Ferreira et al. 2013).

Economic opportunities for rural youth in changing agri-food systems: Thinking beyond the plot, the foregoing changes imply that (a) the number of young people in rural areas will increase dramatically throughout the developing world over the next few decades, particularly in Africa; (b) only a small proportion of this youth bulge will be absorbed by the nonfarm sector in urban areas (again, particularly in Africa); and (c) rising levels of relative land scarcity mean that not all of the rural young people entering the labor force will be able to operate their own farms. It will therefore be increasingly important to understand the scope for stimulating viable economic opportunities in both the farm and nonfarm rural economies. A narrow focus on "youth as the farmers and agri-entrepreneurs of tomorrow" will be insufficient at best and disastrous at worst.

Beyond growing land scarcity and the transformation of national economies, globalization has also meant a restructuring of agri-food systems and changes in the opportunity set available within rural areas (Asongu, et al. 2019). At the production end, a focus on local and national markets (nurtured by import substitution policies in the 1960s and 1970s) has given way to increased interest in export-oriented ventures, including traditional export crops (e.g. coffee, cocoa, tea, sugar, cotton, and palm oil); high-value agricultural products such as fresh fruit, horticultural products, and cut flowers and "flexi-crops" such as soy, sugar, and grains for the production of food, ethanol, and livestock feed (Bernstein 2010). Systematic evaluation of where and what the resulting opportunities are, and to whom they might be open, should form a critical component of a youth-relevant research agenda. For instance, growth in export-oriented agriculture may displace cereal production, thus reshaping opportunities for young people. In addition, investments in some crops and value chains may create more employment opportunities than others: for example, Deininger and Byerlee (2011) suggest that "Oil palm and (manual) sugarcane generate between 10 and 30 times more jobs per hectare than does large-scale mechanized grain farming." This is somewhat related to the submission of Herrmann et al. (2018) for the case of Malawi.

The discussion of rural transformations has shown how demographic developments change agricultural production contexts in paradoxical ways.

For instance, as a result of African urban population growth—and increasing demand for food—the potential for commercial agricultural production increases. Yet, increasing rural population densities at the same time put farm sizes under pressure (Jayne et al. 2014). Such trends have important ramifications, particularly for the economic geography of cereal-based agri-food systems, whose profitability generally depends on economies of scale, and therefore relatively large land areas but also on ready access to markets.

Figure 2 distinguishes four types of economic geographies for cereal production, based on the resource quality and access to markets. The basic idea is that market access (represented vertically in the figure) is a fundamental conditioner of production possibilities and choices, following a logic similar to that proposed by Von Thünen in 1826 (Von Thünen 1966). In areas close to markets, where land prices are high, horticulture and other high-value products are likely to have a comparative advantage over land-demanding cereal production. Hence, the commercial importance of cereal production is likely to be greatest in areas with moderate market access.

A second dimension, reflecting agricultural production potential, distinguishes good and poor biophysical endowments. Natural resource quality is less critical in highly accessible, peri-urban areas, where the returns to investment in irrigation and the inputs to address resource quality deficiencies are high. In very remote areas, even good quality soils and climate may not be enough to make production more commercially oriented, as the fundamental limitation is market access. Within areas of moderate market access, however, such differences may be important, with better biophysical endowments associated with greater likelihood of commercially viable production.

Population growth and development of transportation infrastructure are important drivers that alter the context of agricultural production, enlarging markets and their geographical reach. Directly and indirectly, these forces stimulate investments in increased productivity, influencing the dynamics of rural areas in terms of production orientations, economically viable production options, crop choices, land access regulations, and so on.

3   Method of Analysis

Due to the characteristics of its demographic trends, Africa is the region of the world where youth employment challenge and rural transformation are—and will increasingly be—a deep concern: 60% of the world's labor force growth between 2010 and 2050 will be in Africa; and only in the next 15 years, nearly 400 million youth will enter the labor market of the continent. The study will analyze most of these dimensions of youth employment issues in Africa's agricultural and rural transformation using panel analysis.

Panel (data) analysis is a statistical method, widely used in social science, epidemiology, and econometrics to analyze two-dimensional (typically cross sectional and longitudinal) panel data. The data are usually collected over time and over the same units and then a regression is run over these two dimensions.

The total number of independent states in Africa is 54. Alphabetical list of the entire 54 African countries used in this chapter are Algeria, Angola, Burundi, Benin, Burkina Faso, Botswana, Central African Republic, Cote d'Ivoire, Cameroon, Republic of Congo, Democratic Republic of Congo, Comoros, Cabe Verde, Djibouti, Egypt, Eritrea, Eswatini, Ethiopia, Gabon, Ghana, Guinea, The Gambia, Guinea-Bissau, Equatorial Guinea, Kenya, Liberia, Libya, Lesotho, Morocco, Madagascar, Mali, Mozambique, Mauritania, Mauritius, Malawi, Namibia, Niger, Nigeria, Rwanda, Sudan, Senegal, Sierra Leone, Somalia, South Sudan, Sao Tome and Principe, Seychelles, Chad, Togo, Tunisia, Tanzania, Uganda, South Africa, Zambia, and Zimbabwe.

3.1 The Model

There has been considerable recent discussion of the changes that are taking place in rural development both in terms of the nature of the changes underway within rural economies and in terms of the approaches adopted toward rural policy. The predominant characterization is of a single change, commonly from an approach focused fundamentally on the agricultural sector toward one focused on rural territories and more diversified economic activity (Van der Ploeg et al. 2000; Leon 2005; OECD 2006). However, we argue that there has been a steadier process of economic and social change in rural areas over a longer period of time.

The four predominant models of rural development. The immediate postwar model centered on the agricultural sector. Increasing food production was the first priority and other objectives, such as enhancing rural employment and services, were seen as following directly from the production support given to the agricultural sector. But through time the approach has changed, shifting to multisectoral, territorial, and local approaches. The multisectoral policy recognizes the limits to agricultural production support and sees agriculture as one of several economic sectors through which the development objectives can be attained. The focus may still be on farming, but there is encouragement for agricultural diversification. The territorial approach recognizes the wider interactions within the rural economy and the importance of social and environmental as well as economic issues. Finally, the differentiation between rural areas and the variation in individual circumstances within areas promotes a search for actions that recognize the specificity of solutions at most local levels. These changes have reflected both forces fundamentally associated with national economic change and other factors more governed by local circumstances. And they have major implications for the methodologies that are relevant for the analysis of rural problems and the evaluation of policies (Hodge and Midmore 2008).

The study follows the variables on the work by Rauch et al. (2016) and Losch (2016) on structural transformation to boost youth labor demand in Sub-Saharan Africa: The role of agriculture, rural areas and territorial development. Thus, the study employs static linear model with unobserved heterogeneity to examine youth employment challenge and rural transformation in Africa.

3.1.1 The Model for Rural Transformation

$$\text{ssa\_affv}_{it} = \lambda_1 + \lambda_2 \text{ssa\_ylr}_{it} + \lambda_3 \text{ssa\_eag}_{it} + \lambda_4 \text{ssa\_epr}_{it} + \lambda_5 \text{ssa\_rupt}_{it} + \eta_1 + \varepsilon_{it} \quad (1)$$

Transforming the model by taking the first difference

$$\Delta \text{ssa\_affv}_{it} = \lambda_1 + \lambda_2 \Delta \text{ssa\_ylr}_{it} + \lambda_3 \Delta \text{ssa\_eag}_{it} + \lambda_4 \Delta \text{ssa\_epr}_{it} + \lambda_5 \Delta \text{ssa\_rupt}_{it} + \varepsilon_{it} \quad (2)$$

$\varepsilon_{it} = \upsilon_i + \omega_{it}$

3.1.2 The Model for Youth Employment Challenge

$$\text{ssa\_yemp}_{it} = \beta_1 + \beta_2 \text{ssa\_ylr}_{it} + \beta_3 \text{ssa\_eag}_{it} + \beta_4 \text{ssa\_rupt}_{it} + \eta_2 + \mu_{it} \quad (3)$$

Transforming (3) by taking the first difference

$$\Delta \text{ssa\_yemp}_{it} = \beta_1 + \beta_2 \Delta \text{ssa\_ylr}_{it} + \beta_3 \Delta \text{ssa\_eag}_{it} + \beta_4 \Delta \text{ssa\_rupt}_{it} + \mu_{it} \quad (4)$$

$\mu_{it} = \upsilon_i + \omega_{it}$

The key trick is that by taking differences we have eliminated the unobserved heterogeneity term η_i from the model. And the new differenced Eqs. (2) and (4) satisfy all the necessary assumptions to guarantee consistency of the OLS estimator. In particular, given the assumptions that $E(\Delta \nu) = 0$ and $\text{Cov}(\Delta \nu, \Delta X) = 0$. Thus, we can simply apply OLS to the differenced equation and obtain consistent estimates of λ and β.

where,

ssa_affv is Agriculture, forestry, and fishing, value-added to GNI per capita (constant 2010 US$) (proxy for rural transformation). This shows how agricultural productivity impacts rural development through the per capita income of the rural population.

ssa_ylr is Literacy rate, youth (ages 15–24), gender parity index (GPI)

ssa_eag is Employment in agriculture (% of total employment) (modeled ILO estimate)

ssa_epr is Employment to population ratio, 15+, total (%) (modeled ILO estimate)

ssa_rup is Rural population (% of total population)

ssa_yemp is Employment to population ratio, ages 15–24, total (%) (modeled ILO estimate)

see Rauch et al. (2016) and Losch (2016)

υ_i are the individual-specific, time-invariant effects which are fixed over time., whereas ω_{it} are time-varying random component.

If υ_i are unobserved, and correlated with at least one of the independent variables, then it will cause omitted variable bias in a standard OLS regression. However, panel data methods, such as the fixed effects estimator or alternatively, the first-difference estimator can be used to control for it.

The data were sourced from World Bank database (by indicator) from 2010 to 2017.

The intuition behind including youth literacy rate as the explanatory variable in both models is because it is well documented in development literature that human capital is a critical variable for transformation and development (see Romer 1990), while other variables are control variables in both models.

The chapter expects $\lambda_1>0$, $\lambda_2>0$, $\lambda_3>0$, $\lambda_4>0$, $\lambda_5>0$ while $\beta_1>0$ $\beta_2>0$, $\beta_3>0$, $\beta_4>0$.

4 Results and Discussion

The results of the estimation are presented below.

The descriptive statistics output shows that valid observation across the variables is 26. The skewness values for all the variables suggest that the degree and direction of asymmetry is normal distribution sine all the values for skewness are either approximately zero or negative (Table 1). The Kurtosis is a measure of the heaviness of the tails of a distribution. The result shows that ssa_ylr and ssa_yemp have normal distributions while ssa_affv, ssa_eag, ssa_epr, and ssa_rup have light tailed distribution. The Jarque-Bera results suggest that the errors across the variables are normally distributed since all the values are less than 5.99.

The multicollinearity result of Table 2 suggests that no multicollinearity exists between the variables.

Table 1 Descriptive statistics

	SSA_AFFV	SSA_YLR	SSA_EAG	SSA_EPR	SSA_RUP	SSA_YEMP
Mean	1.75E+11	0.849021	63.22519	62.96755	66.87814	44.65380
Median	1.69E+11	0.842225	64.38565	63.06090	67.13304	44.62319
Maximum	2.81E+11	0.907580	67.50158	63.72051	72.13104	46.49994
Minimum	9.88E+10	0.805290	57.40157	62.12377	60.98208	42.85592
Std. Dev.	5.96E+10	0.025801	3.737128	0.481489	3.366756	0.868571
Skewness	0.309453	0.244193	−0.378949	−0.212273	−0.171378	0.332035
Kurtosis	1.751495	2.786570	1.553921	1.864190	1.838877	2.992449
Jarque-Bera	2.103626	1.847615	2.887682	1.592828	1.587828	0.477800
Probability	0.349304	0.397005	0.236019	0.450943	0.452072	0.787494
Sum	4.55E+12	22.07454	1643.855	1637.156	1738.832	1160.999
Sum Sq. Dev.	8.87E+22	0.016642	349.1531	5.795787	283.3762	18.86038
Observations	26	26	26	26	26	26

Table 2 Multicollinearity result

Variables	Correlation coefficient	Decision
ssa_affv & ssa_ylr	0.799324	No multicollinearity
ssa_affv & ssa_eag	−0.583002	No multicollinearity
ssa_affv & ssa_epr	0.696674	No multicollinearity
ssa_affv & ssa_rup	−0.494881	No multicollinearity
ssa_ylr & ssa_eag	−0.776984	No multicollinearity
ssa_ylr & ssa_epr	0.426994	No multicollinearity
ssa_aylr & ssa_rup	−0.318276	No multicollinearity
ssa_eag & ssa_epr	−0.743793	No multicollinearity
ssa_eag & ssa_rup	−0.641299	No multicollinearity
ssa_yemp & ssa_ylr	−0.780197	No multicollinearity
ssa_yemp & ssa_eag	0.651816	No multicollinearity
ssa_yemp & ssa_rup	0.220631	No multicollinearity

4.1 Trend Outcome

The result also suggests an upward trend in youth literacy rate in Africa. However, there existed minor stable fluctuation between the years 2000 and 2007 and the upward trend continues thereafter. More so, the result also shows that there has been a sustainable advancement in rural transformation in Africa within the period under investigation (Fig. 1).

Where, ssa_ylrm is Literacy rate, youth male (% of males ages 15–24)

ssa_ylrf is Literacy rate, youth female (% of males ages 15–24)

After disaggregation of youth by sex, the figure suggests that youth male literacy rate has consistently been higher than the youth female literacy rate in Africa. However, 2016 data suggests that the gap is fast narrowing. Youth male literacy rate in 1985 and 2016 were 71.59 and 78.93 while youth female literacy rate was 54.68 and 71.63 for the period (Fig. 2).

The figure shows that employment in agricultural sector has shown some downward trend since 1991 till date. This may not be unconnected with rural–urban drift witnessed in the past three decades in Africa. However, employment to population ratio has been relatively stable over the period under investigation (from 63.10 in 1991 to 63.30 in 2017) (Table 3).

4.2 Effect of Employment to Population Ratio, 15+, on Rural Transformation in Africa

The result suggests that employment to population ratio, 15+, has a great positive influence on rural transformation in African countries. Since the composition of youth is 15+, it implies that if more youth are meaningfully engaged, it would also guarantee faster rural transformation. This could be because most youth dwell in rural areas in Africa. However, increase in the rural population has an inverse effect on rural transformation. High illiteracy rate and rural–urban drift in Africa could explain this outcome. This means that increase in

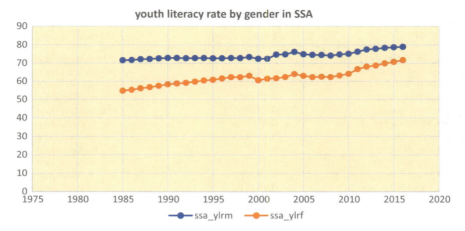

Fig. 1 Trend of youth literacy rate by gender in Africa

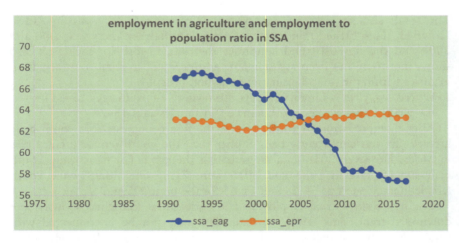

Fig. 2 Trend of employment in agriculture and employment to population ratio in Africa

rural population would engender a decline in rural transformation. This is in line with the findings by (Santiago et al. 2017) for Africa and contradicts the finding by (Gollin et al. 2016) for Latin America and Africa.

4.3 *Effect of Youth Literacy Rate and Employment in Agriculture on Youth Unemployment in Africa*

The result shows that youth literacy rate has an inverse relationship with youth unemployment rate. The result implies that an increase in the level of education of the youth would be a great factor in reducing youth unemployment

Table 3 The results of the estimation of rural transformation and youth employment challenge models

Effect of employment to population ratio, 15+, on rural transformation in Africa			Effect of youth literacy rate and employment in agriculture on youth unemployment in Africa		
Dependent variable: D(ssa_affv)			Dependent variable: D(ssa_yemp)		
Variables	Coef	t-Start	Variables	Coef	t-Stat
D(ssa_ylr)	−3.66	−0.62	D(ssa_ylr)	−11.15	−3.27
D(ssa_eag)	−3.76	−0.26	D(ssa_rup)	0.37	4.97
D(ssa_epr)	1.14	3.5	D(ssa_eag)	−0.19	−3.07
D(ssa_rup)	−1.64	−11.11	_cons	41.17	9.01
_cons	6.06	2.53			

rate in Africa. This is because an increase in the level of education among the youth enhances their technical know-how and employability. By extension, this could also enhance rural transformation. More so, the result also suggests that an increase in employment in the agricultural sector would lead to a decline in youth unemployment rate in Africa. However, the result also shows that an increase in rural population would aggravate youth unemployment rate in Africa. This is true because an increase in rural population would put pressure on rarely existing employment opportunities in Africa. This finding is in tandem with the findings by Losch et al. (2012), McMillan et al. (2014).

The economic and employment opportunities that will arise in urban and nonfarm sectors are likely to remain limited, and particularly so in Africa. This, combined with fears about future food security, underpins the interest of policymakers, planners, and development professionals in what is being portrayed as youth-inclusive rural transformation.

It is reasonable to expect that both within and between social groups and rural situations, rural transformation will create opportunities for some and challenges for others. Dorward's "hanging in," "stepping up," and "stepping out" framework provides a useful perspective on the different potential pathways for rural people faced with rural transformation (Dorward 2009). Those who either "hang in" or "step up" might remain or become producers in their own right; work as wage labor on farms, or in other associated agricultural (formal or informal) businesses; and/or operate businesses that are in some way associated with agriculture. Those who "hang in" often only maintain their farming activities, whereas those who "step up" increase their land and/or labor productivity.

4.4 Discussion of Keys to Youth Employment Challenge and Rural Transformation in Africa

Recognizing agriculture as a viable employment option is even more challenging when economic and social restrictions related to access to productive resources (for instance, land, credit, and improved seeds) are considered.

All these limitations are exacerbated for young women who, in general, have no prospect of land access due to rules of inheritance, and who know that they will mainly have to work for their husbands (ILO 2016). Although the government considers rural educated youth as instrumental in bringing about a transformation in agricultural skills, knowledge, and productivity, it has not effectively addressed either the attitude of many young people toward agriculture or the obstacles preventing their entry into the sector (Oyebola et al. 2019).

To create opportunities commensurate with the number of young people who will need employment, constraints on the acquisition of capital, land, and skills must be removed or relaxed.

A few selected initiatives are delineated below.

Allowing alternative forms of collateral, such as chattel mortgages, warehouse receipts, and the future harvest, can ease the credit constraints especially for young farmers. The OHADA7 Uniform Act on Secured Transactions, in effect in 17 Sub-Saharan African countries, was amended at the end of 2010 to allow borrowers to use a wide range of assets as collateral, including warehouse receipts and movable property such as machinery, equipment, and receivables that remain in the hands of the debtor. Leasing also offers young farmers some relief, as it requires either no or less collateral than typically required by loans. A case in point is DFCU Leasing in Uganda, which gave more than US$4 million in farm equipment leases in 2002 for items such as rice hullers, dairy processing equipment, and maize milling equipment. Some out-grower arrangements prefinance inputs and assure marketing channels. In Mozambique, Rwanda, Tanzania, and Zambia, Rabo Development (a subsidiary of Rabobank) offers management services and technical assistance to financial institutions, which, in turn, finance supply chains with a range of agricultural clients.

The two aspects of land administration that matter most to young entrants to the labor force are the need to improve the security of tenure and the need to relax controls on rental. Land redistribution will also enhance young people's access to land. In general, policies and measures that help the poor to gain access to land will also help young people.

The growing food demand in Africa is a major avenue for agro-processing, which can easily be developed using small and medium-sized entities (SMEs). This option requires less capital, is more labor-intensive and facilitates the proliferation of units in rural boroughs and small towns, offering employment and entrepreneurial opportunities, local value-added and new incomes. Agro-processing SMEs can also facilitate the resolution of post-harvest problems, which are a significant issue in AFRICA resulting in a loss of revenue for farmers.

In the Niger Delta of Nigeria, for instance, the International Fund for Agricultural Development (IFAD)-supported Community Based Natural Resource Management Program is promoting a new category of entrepreneur-cum-mentor called the "N-Agripreneur." These N-Agripreneurs own and run medium-scale enterprises at different stages of food value chains. They deliver business development services to producers, especially young people, who are interested in agro-based activities, such as farming as a business, small-scale processing, input supply, and marketing.

In order to enable young people to respond to the environmental, economic, and nutrition challenges of the future, they must develop suitable capacities. A case in point is ICTs which can develop young people's capacities while improving communication and easing access to information and decision-making processes. Investing in extending these technologies to rural areas, in particular targeting young people—who are generally more adaptable to their use—has allowed them to keep themselves up-to-date with market information and new opportunities.

In sum, there is an abundance of remunerative employment opportunities for the youth in rural areas that could dispel the mirage through imaginative government policies.

Another harsh reality is that the informal economy is the only professional horizon for eight in 10 young workers in Africa. Young African women are even more likely to work informally than young men. African young people work hard, but with low productivity, pay, protection, and perspectives. On average, 72% of the youth population in Africa live on less than $2 per day. Self-employment and entrepreneurship are often the only employment options available to youths, including graduates. The highest proportion of potential youth entrepreneurs in the world is to be found in sub-Saharan Africa (60%). Unfortunately, 32% of these young individuals are necessity-driven entrepreneurs. Entrepreneurship is perceived as a survival strategy and not a business opportunity.

New avenues will have to be opened in African youth labor markets. For instance, Africa's food markets alone are projected to increase from $313 billion in 2010 to $1 trillion in 2030. But in order to attract and retain young people, Africa's agriculture will need to upgrade and become more appealing. Agro-industries would have high multiplier effects in terms of youth employment creation.

4.5 *An Inclusive Approach with Sectoral Linkages*

Africa does not lack diagnoses and strategies, but there is also a need for integrated methodologies to implement them. The following (7Cs) suggest an inclusive approach for policy and program actions on youth employment.

i. Concept

It is fundamental to take a holistic view and include decent work and youth employment creation as a central objective in national development strategies. It is the role of the governments to ensure a supportive macroeconomic environment, provide sustainable and resilient infrastructure, help build human capital, and improve the business environment to unleash private initiative at all levels as the private sector provides some 90% of the jobs in the world.

Any policy priority setting should also take into account the fact that the youth are not a homogenous group. Special attention should be paid to adolescent girls and young women, rural youth and youths with disabilities, as they face additional constraints that impact their possibilities to secure decent work opportunities.

ii. Coordination
Unlocking the transformative potential of young people and accelerating youth employment creation require strong policy coordination among ministries responsible for economic policies such as planning, finance, trade, industry, agriculture, and those responsible for education and training, labor market policy, and social protection.

Employers' and workers' organizations are important partners for policy and program development, and can help by strengthening links between business, education, and promoting the rights of young people at work.

iii. Credit
Across the board, youth and young women in particular face the most difficulties in gaining access to financial services. Every day, so many young African entrepreneurs are not deemed creditworthy because they do not have enough savings or a track record with formal savings institutions. Furthermore, funds are not available to provide the five million or so youths who are expected to start a business every year in Africa over the next 10 years with a grant of $100, which is about the average amount given in pilot programs. Access to credit should be improved for sustainable youth enterprises, in particular micro, small, and medium-sized enterprises, cooperatives, and social enterprises. This may include grants, subsidizing credit, guaranteeing loans, and supporting microcredit initiatives, together with encouraging the use of innovative tools for financial inclusion, such as mobile banking, payment platforms, and digitalized payments (Akinyemi et al. 2019; Ejemeyovwi et al. 2019; Karakara and Osabuohien 2019).

iv. Competences
Education and vocational training, including apprenticeship, are essential for improving Africa's youth productive capacities. To make education and training relevant, institutional and financial arrangements should build solid bridges between the world of learning and the world of work. Bringing together government, business, labor, training providers, and youth representatives at the local level is the most direct route to secure the relevance of training to the needs of enterprises and labor markets.

v. Cooperation
It has been calculated that a 1% increase in intra-African trade will result in a 1.47% reduction in overall youth unemployment. Also, a 1% increase in intra-African trade will lead to 1.67 and 1.46% reduction in female and male

youth unemployment rates, respectively. Deepening inter-African exchange is key to promoting regional production for regional markets as well as for regional operations that supply global markets. Regional cooperation is the name of the game.

vi. Communication

Regular institutional communication and highly participatory approaches are essential to support policies and programs aimed at improving the employment prospects of young people. Representatives of the young people who are affected by policies toward youth employment should have a say in their design and implementation. Direct involvement of the youth in the elaboration and implementation of policies and programs supporting their employment will be the real game changer for the way forward.

vii. Control

The performance of the youth employment objectives should be systematically measured to enable verification of overall success or failure of national policies and action plans to promote youth employment. Given the limited resources, this provides vital feedback for improving policy, program, and project design as well as strategic fund reallocations.

In sum, every decent job for a young African man or woman is a step toward the development of Africa. This is not only an agenda for governments, but also for business, trade unions, regional institutions, and international development cooperation. Nobody can do it alone. Such a feat also requires innovative mechanisms for the direct participation of young women and men as well as engagement with them. Nothing can be done without the youth. Empowering the youth is developing Africa. This may come quickly if youth employment becomes the litmus test of Africa's development policies.

5 Conclusion

The new interest in young people as economic agents within Africa's agri-food systems is to be welcomed. However, discourses, policy, and programs that construct and focus on youth-specific constraints and opportunities, and privilege entrepreneurship and imaginaries of millions of rural youth "pulling themselves up by the bootstraps" are likely to fail. They ignore structural constraints and processes and the importance of social structures as enablers and constrainers. International agricultural research should rather root its engagement with young people in an analysis of rural transformation and its dynamic interplay with rural social structures within Sub-Saharan Africa and national contexts.

The understanding of emergent patterns of rural transformation in Africa, the youth-related propositions and the analytical framework presented above have important implications for the study of young people's economic opportunities in agri-food systems. There is a need to step back from the premise that research needs to explain whether, or how, rural young people can be enticed into small-scale agriculture. Projected rural population increases and the need for economically viable farm sizes capable of producing surpluses for rapidly growing urban centers suggest neither a countryside devoid of youth nor the need for a massive effort to retain rural youth in agriculture. Rather, to enable the identification of youth-specific constraints to sustainable rural livelihoods (and the subsequent formulation of intervention strategies), there is a need to shift attention toward the diverse ways in which contemporary young people engage with the rural economy. An important challenge for research is therefore to understand (emerging) patterns of young people's engagements with agricultural production and related economic activities, and whether or how this varies across young people of different continents, countries, and by extension social categories.

REFERENCES

Adesugba, M. A., & Mavrotas, G. (2016). *Delving deeper into the agricultural transformation and youth employment nexus: The Nigerian case* (Nigeria Strategy Support Program Working Paper 31). Washington, DC: International Food Policy Research Institute.

African Development Bank (AfDB). (2015). *African economic outlook. Regional development and spatial inclusion*. Tunis: African Development Bank.

African Transformation Report. (2017). *"Transformation in a generation" African centre for economic transformation*. https://acetforafrica.org/publication_type/african-transformation-report-2017/.

Akinyemi, O., Efobi, U., Asongu, S., & Osabuohien, E. (2019). Renewable energy, trade performance and the conditional role of finance and institutional capacity in sub-Sahara African Countries. *Energy Policy, 132*, 490–498.

Asongu, S. A., Efobi, U. R., Tanakem, B. V., & Osabuohien, E. (2019). Globalisation and female economic participation in sub-Saharan Africa. *Gender Issues*. https://doi.org/10.1007/s12147-019-09233-3.

Banks, N., & Sulaiman, M. (2012). *Problem or promise? Harnessing youth potential in Uganda* [pdf]. BRAC Youth Watch Series. Accessed September 20, 2018, from www.brac.net/sites/default/files/YW%202012.pdf.

Bernstein, H. (2010). *Class dynamics of agrarian change*. Boulder: Kumarian Press. Google Scholar.

Brooks, K., Zorya, S., & Gautam, A. (2013). *Employment in agriculture: Jobs for Africa's youth* (2012 Global Food Policy Report 49–57). Washington, DC: International Food Policy Research Institute, Budina.

Brooks, K., Zorya, S., Gautam, A., & Goyal, A. (2013). *Agriculture as a sector of opportunity for young people in Africa* (World Bank Policy Research Working Paper 6473). Washington, DC: World Bank.

Brussels Rural Development Briefings. (2011). *Major drivers for rural transformation in Africa. Brussels Rural Development Briefings a series of meetings on ACP-EU Development issues* (Briefing No. 24).

Chamberlin, J., Jayne, T. S, & Headey, D. (2014). Scarcity amidst abundance? Reassessing the potential for cropland expansion in Africa. *Food Policy, 48*, 51–65. Google Scholar, Crossref, ISI

Chinsinga, B., & Chasukwa, M. (2012). Youth, agriculture and land grabs in Malawi. *IDS Bulletin, 43*, 67–77. Google Scholar, Crossref, ISI.

Collier, P., & Dercon, S. (2014). African agriculture in 50 years: Smallholders in a rapidly changing world? *World Development, 63*, 92–101.

Deininger, K., & Byerlee, D. (2011). *The rise of large farms in land abundant countries: Do they have a future?* (Policy Research Working Paper No. 5588). Washington, DC: The World Bank. Google Scholar, Crossref.

Demirgüç-Kunt, A., & Klapper, L. (2012). *Measuring financial inclusion: The Global Findex Database* [pdf]. (Policy Research Working Paper 6025). Washington, DC: World Bank. Accessed September 20, 2018, from http://elibrary.worldbank.org/doi/pdf/10.1596/1813-9450-6025.

Dorward, A. (2009). Integrating contested aspirations, processes and policy: Development as hanging in, stepping up and stepping out. *Development Policy Review, 27*, 131–146. Google Scholar, Crossref, ISI.

Ejemeyovwi, J. O., Osabuohien, E. S., Johnson, O. D., & Bowale, E. I. K. (2019). Internet usage, innovation and human development nexus in Africa: The case of ECOWAS. *Journal of Economic Structures, 8*(5). https://doi.org/10.1186/s40008-019-0146-2.

Ferreira, P., De Abreu Pessoa, S., & Veloso, F. A (2013). On the evolution of total factor productivity in Latin America. *Economic Inquiry, 51*, 16–30. Google Scholar, Crossref, ISI.

Flynn, J., & Sumberg, J. (2017). Youth savings groups in Africa: They're a family affair. *Enterprise Development and Microfinance*. https://doi.org/10.1177/0030727017724669. Google Scholar, Crossref.

Gollin, D., Jedwab, R., & Vollrath, D. (2016). Urbanization with and without industrialization. *Journal of Economic Growth, 21*, 35–70. Google Scholar, Crossref, ISI.

Guarcello, L., Manacorda, M., Rosati, F., Fares, J., Lyon, S., & Valdivia, C. (2007). Schoolto-work transitions in sub-Saharan Africa: An overview. In M. Garcia & J. Fares (Eds.), *Youth in Africa's labor market, directions in development*. World Bank: Washington, DC.

Headey, D., Bezemer, D., & Hazell, P. B. (2010). Agricultural employment trends in Asia and Africa: Too fast or too slow? *The World Bank Research Observer, 25*(1), 57–89.

Headey, D. D., & Jayne, T. S (2014). Adaptation to land constraints: Is Africa different? *Food Policy, 48*, 18–33. Google Scholar, Crossref, ISI.

Henley, D. (2012). The agrarian roots of industrial growth: Rural development in South-East Asia and Sub-Saharan Africa. *Development Policy Review, 30*(1), 25–47.

Herrmann, R., Jumbe, C., Bruentrup, M., & Osabuohien, E. (2018). Competition between biofuel feedstock and food production: Empirical evidence from sugarcane outgrower settings in Malawi. *Biomass and Bioenergy, 114*(July), 100–111.

Hodge, I., & Midmore, P. (2008). Models of rural development and approaches to analysis evaluation and decision-making. Économie rurale [En ligne], 307 | septembre–octobre 2008, mis en ligne le 01 septembre 2010, consulté le 30 avril 2019. http://journals.openedition.org/economierurale/406; DOI: https://doi.org/10.4000/economierurale.406.

International Development Research Centre. (2018). *Putting youth employment at the heart of growth*. Canada: Supporting Inclusive Growth.

International Labour Organization (ILO). (2013). *Global employment trends for youth 2013: A generation at risk* [online]. Geneva: ILO. Accessed October 3, 2018, from www.ilo.org/global/research/global-reports/globalemployment-trends/youth/2013/lang–en/index.htm.

ILO. (2014). *Global employment trends 2014: The risk of a jobless recovery* [online]. Geneva: ILO. Accessed October 3, 2018, from www.ilo.org/global/research/global-reports/global-employment-trends/2014/WCMS_233953/lang–en/index.htm.

ILO. (2018). *Structural transformation to boost youth labour demand in sub-Saharan Africa: The role of agriculture, rural areas and territorial development.* Geneva: ILO.

International Monetary Fund (IMF). (2015). *"Regional economic outlook: Sub-Sahara Africa" dealing with the gathering clouds.* World Economic and Financial Surveys.

Jayne, T. S., Chamberlin, J., & Headey, D. D. (2014). Land pressures, the evolution of farming systems, and development strategies in Africa: A synthesis. *Food Policy, 48*, 1–17. Google Scholar, Crossref, ISI.

Jedwab, R. (2011). *African cities and the structural transformation: Evidence from Ghana and Ivory Coast.* Paper presented at Centre for the Studies of African Economies Annual Conference, 2011. Google Scholar.

Jedwab, R. (2013). *Urbanization without structural transformation: Evidence from consumption cities in Africa.* Unpublished working paper. Department of Economics, George Washington University. Google Scholar.

Karakara, A. A., & Osabuohien, E. (2019). Households' ICT access and bank patronage in West Africa: Empirical insights from Burkina Faso and Ghana. *Technology in Society, 56*, 116–125.

Keats, S., & Wiggins, S. (2016). *Population change in the rural developing world: Making the transition. Research reports and studies.* London: Overseas Development Institute.

Leon, Y. (2005). Rural development in Europe: A research frontier for agricultural economists. *European Review of Agricultural Economics, 32*(3), 301–317.

Losch, B. (2016). *Structural transformation to boost youth labour demand in sub-Saharan Africa: The role of agriculture, rural areas and territorial development* (Working Paper No. 204). International Labour Organization.

Losch, B., Fréguin-Gresh, S., & White, E. T. (2012). *Structural transformation and rural change revisited: Challenges for late developing countries in a globalizing world.* Washington, DC: World Bank. Google Scholar, Crossref.

Markel, E., & Panetta, D. (2014). *Youth savings groups, entrepreneurship and employment* [online]. London: Plan UK. Accessed September 20, 2015, from www.plan-uk.org/resources/documents/494816/.

MasterCard Foundation. (2014). *2013–2014 youth think tank report: Engaging young people* [pdf]. Toronto: The MasterCard Foundation. Accessed September 20, 2018, from www.mastercardfdn.org/ytt2014.

McMillan, M., Rodrik, D., & Verduzco-Gallo, I. (2014). Globalization, structural change, and productivity growth, with an update on Africa. *World Development, 63*, 11–32. Google Scholar, Crossref, ISI.

McMillan, M. S., & Rodrik, D. (2011). *Globalization, structural change and productivity growth* (Working Paper 17143). New York: National Bureau of Economic Research.

OECD. (2006). *The new rural paradigm: Policies and governance*. Paris: Organisation for Economic Co-operation and Development.
Osabuohien, E., Efobi, U. R., Herrmann, R., & Gitau, C. M. (2019). Female labor outcomes and large-scale agricultural land investments: Macro-micro evidence from Tanzania. *Land Use Policy, 82*, 716–728.
Oyebola, P. O., Osabuohien, E., & Obasaju, B. (2019). Employment and income effects of Nigeria's agricultural transformation agenda. *African Journal of Economic and Management Studies*. https://doi.org/10.1108/AJEMS-12-2018-0402.
Raghav G., & Vani S. K. (2017). *Are prospects of rural youth employment in Africa a mirage? Food and agricultural organisation in Rwanda*. Accessed online October 1, 2018. http://www.ipsnews.net/2017/11/prospects-rural-youth-employment-africa-mirage/.
Rauch, T., Beckmann, G., Neubert, S., & Rettberg S. (2016). *Rural transformation in sub-saharan Africa – Conceptual study*. SLE Discussion Paper 01/2016 – EN. Centre for Rural Development (SLE), Berlin.
Resnick, D., & Thurlow, J. (2015). *African youth and the persistence of marginalization: Employment, politics and prospects of change*. New York: Routledge.
Romer, P. (1990). Endogenous technological change. *Journal of Political Economy, 98*(5), s71–s102.
Santiago, R., Jens, A., & Lone, B. (2017). *Rural transformation, cereals and youth in Africa: What role for international agricultural research?* Accessed online October 2, 2018. https://doi.org/10.1177/0030727017724669.
Shepherd, A., Scott, L., & CPRC. (2011). *Tackling chronic poverty: The policy implications of research on chronic poverty and poverty dynamics* [online]. London: Chronic Poverty Research Centre. Accessed October 4, 2018, from www.chronicpoverty.org/publications/details/tackling-chronic-poverty1.
Sitko, N.J., & Chamberlin, J. (2016). The geography of Zambia's customary land: Assessing the prospects for smallholder development. *Land Use Policy, 55*, 49–60. Google Scholar, Crossref, ISI.
Sparreboom, T., & Staneva, A. (2014). *Is education the solution to decent work for youth in developing economies? Identifying qualifications mismatch from 28 school-to-work transition surveys* [pdf]. Work4Youth Publication Series No. 23. Geneva: ILO. Accessed September 20, 2018, from www.ilo.org/wcmsp5/groups/public/—dgreports/—dcomm/documents/publication/wcms_326260.pdf.
UN. (2015). *Youth population trends and sustainable development*. Population Facts 2015/1. New York: UN Department of Economic and Social Affairs, Population Division. Google Scholar.
UNPD (Population Division of the Department of Economic and Social Affairs of the United Nations Secretariat). (2012). *World population prospects: The 2012 revision* [webpage]. Accessed October, 4, 2018. https://www.un.org/en/development/desa/population/publications/pdf/ageing/2012PopAgeingandDev_WallChart.pdf.
United Nations. (2013). *World population ageing 2013 ST/ESA/SER.A/348*. United Nations Department of Economic and Social Affairs, Population Division 2013. https://www.un.org/en/development/desa/population/publications/pdf/ageing/WorldPopulationAgeing2013.pdf.
Van der Ploeg, J., Renting, H., Brunori, G., Knickel, K., Mannion, J., Marsden, T., et al. (2000). Rural development: From practices and policies towards theories. *Sociologia Ruralis, 40*(4), 391–408.

Von Thünen, J. H. (1966). *Von Thünen's 'Isolated state'* (English edition). Oxford: Pergamon Press. Google Scholar.

World Bank. (2012). *World Development Report 2012: Gender Equality and Development*. World Bank. © World Bank. https://openknowledge.worldbank.org/handle/10986/4391. License: CC BY 3.0 IGO. https://openknowledge.worldbank.org/handle/10986/4391.

World Bank. (2013). *World Development Report 2013: Jobs* [online]. Washington, DC: World Bank. Accessed October 4, 2018, from http://econ.worldbank.org/external/default/main?contentMDK=23044836&theSitePK=8258025&piPK=8258412&pagePK=8258258.

Impact of Remittances on Agricultural Labor Productivity in Sub-Saharan Africa

Kwami Ossadzifo Wonyra and Muriel E. S. Ametoglo

1 INTRODUCTION

The world economic expansion in the 1980s and the 1990s created economic opportunities in developed countries. This encouraged many people in the least developed countries to migrate to these destinations (Castles et al. 2002). For semi-skilled or unskilled workers in sub-Saharan African countries, this situation provided opportunities to earn a living abroad and escape poverty. As a result, a significant increase in the remittances sent to home countries has been observed.

International migrant remittances are the portion of revenue sent by people working abroad to their countries of origin. Remittances receive considerable attention in recent years because they became a rising source of external finance, especially in developing countries. Remittances are defined as the monetary transfers sent from overseas migrants to their relatives back home.

Evidence shows that the remittances flow to developing countries was above US$441 billion, an amount that is three times the volume of official aid flows to developing countries. In Sub-Saharan Africa (SSA), Nigeria is first on the list of remittance receivers' countries in 2015, with US$20.8 billion followed by Ghana and Senegal (Ratha et al. 2016). Remittances sent by international African migrants were 37.2 billion US$ in 2016 compared

---

K. O. Wonyra
FASEG, Université de Kara, Kara, Togo

M. E. S. Ametoglo (✉)
School of Economics and Trade, Hunan University, Changsha, China

© The Author(s) 2020
E. S. Osabuohien (ed.), *The Palgrave Handbook of Agricultural and Rural Development in Africa*, https://doi.org/10.1007/978-3-030-41513-6_4

with only 4.8 billion US$ in 2000. (World Bank 2018). This represents a substantial portion of the GDP for most sub-Saharan countries (in Liberia, they represent more than 20%) while providing a significant share of disposable income for many households (Agarwal and Horowitz 2002).

First, remittances provide income for the family to cater for food, education, and health needs as well as for land acquisition. Therefore, remittances improve the human capital (Rapoport and Docquier 2006; Baldé 2011) and productivity of labor in the home countries. Second, changes in labor productivity are a robust indicator of economic growth, living standards, competitiveness and poverty reduction (Asongu et al. 2019). Third, as the majority of people in SSA are working in the primary sector, the funds sent to households, especially in rural areas, will stimulate the productivity of labor in the agricultural sector (McCullough 2017). Even if the portion of the agricultural sector in the GDP has declined between 1981 and 2017 in the region (from 22.21 to 16.22, respectively), agriculture is still the major economic sector in several SSA countries (41.3% in Togo, 49.2 in Guinea-Bissau, 60.3 in Sierra Leone) (World Bank 2018).

In SSA, several studies investigate the effects of international remittances on the home countries. The literature finds a positive relationship with respect to economic growth (Lartey 2013) with other socio-economic variables such as: human development (Adenutsi 2010); human capital formation (Gyimah-Brempong and Aside 2015 for Ghana; Gubert et al. 2015 for Mali; Kifle 2007 for Eritrea); financial development (Aggarwal et al. 2010; Gupta et al. 2009; Ngozi et al. 2017; Fromentin 2017); in the long term, poverty, and income inequality reduction (Agwu et al. 2018 for Senegal; Bang et al. 2016 for Kenya; Anyanwu and Erhijakpor 2010; Adams et al. 2008; for Nigeria). Regarding health, remittances contribute to the improvement of health outcomes in the region, such as the construction of clinics (Martin et al. 2002; Adenutsi 2010). Moreover, Williams (2017) finds evidence of a positive association between remittances and democratic institutions in 45 SSA countries. The estimates reveal that a one standard deviation increase in remittance flows improves democratic institutions by around 0.32 standard deviations.

A number of studies have hypothesized the remittance and development linkage, including Adenutsi (2010); Osabuohien and Efobi (2013) and Efobi et al. (2015). Even though these empirics have highlighted the importance of remittances in SSA, only few have investigated the remittances and agricultural labor productivity nexus. The remittance–agricultural labor productivity nexus is important in SSA as the relationship informs us on the effects on the recipient household members who participate in the agricultural sector, and the effects on poverty (De Janvry and Sadoulet 2010; Christiaensen et al. 2011; Osabuohien and Efobi 2013, 2014). Furthermore, little attention has been made to relate the discourse to the agricultural sector. The contribution of this paper is two-fold. First, we provide evidence for the agricultural labor supply effect of remittances in Sub-Saharan Africa. Second, we use a system-GMM to underscore new evidence on remittances–agricultural labor productivity in SSA as we show that remittances have a strong negative impact on agricultural labor productivity.

The results reveal that remittances have a strong negative impact on agricultural labor productivity. The analysis also finds that higher GDP per capita and human capital generate a lower agricultural labor productivity. Furthermore, it provides evidence of a positive link between trade openness and labor productivity in the primary sector.

The remainder of the paper is organized as follows. Section 3 describes the previous relevant literature; Sect. 4 presents the data, the model and the methodology; Sect. 5 discusses our results; Sect. 6 concludes and provides the policy implications.

2 A Thematic Review

2.1 *Thematic Framework*

We provide here a review of the frameworks describing the relationship between remittance and labor.

2.1.1 The Neoclassic Theory of Labor–Leisure Framework

For the neoclassic theory, remittances affect the arbitration between labor and leisure. Let's assume that an individual's daily utility depends on her consumption during that period and on hours of leisure enjoyed. The *labor–leisure framework* states than an individual's choice between labor and leisure due to an increase in non-labor income (such as remittance) will decrease the supply of labor in the labor market. This is because as its non-labor income increased, the individual will raise her demand for leisure, and reduce labor because there are only 24 hours in a day (Nicholson and Snyder 2016).

Moreover, the neoclassical model argues that the *reservation wage* is a fundamental concept of participation in the labor force. An individual's participation in the labor market is motivated by the *reservation wage*, the lowest wage rate at which a worker would be disposed to accept a specific job offer. The worker will reject any job offer, which presents a lower wage (even though the job offers the same kind of work and the same working conditions). An increase in the individual's non-labor income (such as remittances) raises his or her reservation wage and reduces his willingness to participate in the labor force (Cox-Edwards and Rodríguez-Oreggia 2009). Atkinson and Stern (1981) suggest that, as remittances raise the recipient's reservation wages, they also augment the number of job offers rejected by this individual, while they could increase the number of vacancies for other job seekers.

2.1.2 Remittance-Led Growth Hypothesis
Many studies have investigated the relationship between remittances and output productivity, known as the "Remittance-led growth hypothesis" (Osabuohien and Efobi 2013; Efobi et al. 2019). The evidence suggests that remittance can affect productivity and the growth through several channels. First, remittances can improve the welfare of the receiving households by influencing their decisions on consumption (of domestic or foreign goods). Second, remittance is a source of investment, especially in education and health and thus contributes to the development of human capital (Osabuohien and Efobi 2014).

2.1.3 Remittances and the Goods and Labor Markets
Remittances can influence the labor productivity through the *goods market*. These funds generate an increase in the level of aggregate demand in the home country, as recipients can increase their consumption. By doing so, the output will rise, causing the appreciation of the country's exchange rate. This will channel resources to the non-tradable goods sector, which requires abundant labor, but with a labor productivity lower than that of the tradable goods sector. As a result, the average labor productivity will decline (Lartey et al. 2008).

On the labor market, the migration of labor to developed countries diminishes the workforce in SSA, especially in rural areas. However, the inflows of remittances sent by the migrants' increase the investment and the capital stock in the recipient country. The combination of these two effects can enhance the labor–capital ratio and improve the overall productivity of the economy, involving the labor productivity (Al Mamun et al. 2015, 2016).

2.2 *Transmission Channels*

In Graph 1, we describe three channels through which remittances could impact agricultural labor productivity in SSA.

First, the remittances received increase the income of the individuals and households in the home country. They can increase their health and education expenditures. In the rural areas, the improvement of human capital and the access to better information will increase the productivity of the farmers and the workers in the agricultural sector.

Second, recipients can use their remittances to buy land and livestock, to augment their production. Such a situation will require additional workers or an increase in productivity of the existing labor force. Thus, agricultural labor productivity rises.

Lastly, for most recipients, remittances offer insurance for present and future adverse shocks. These funds expand the reservation wage of the recipients who participate in the agricultural labor market. With a high reservation wage set, these individuals experience a low incentive to work and an appetite for leisure. This will decrease the overall production in the agricultural market as well as the individual labor productivity.

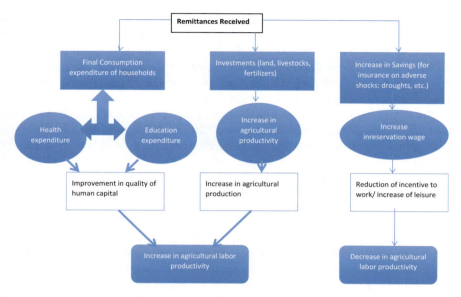

Graph 1 Remittances transmission channels in sub-Saharan Africa (*Source* Authors)

3 Empirical Literature Review

There does not appear to be a consensus in the economic literature on the impacts of remittances sent on productivity, labor productivity and agricultural labor productivity in the home countries.

3.1 Impact of Remittance on Productivity

Despite the vast literature on the subject, the remittance-led growth effects are ambiguous.

Some studies suggest a positive impact of remittance on economic output and growth. Over the long term, migrant funds can have a positive effect on growth in Sub-Saharan countries and provide additional tax revenues and improve social transfers (Gonzalez-Garcia et al. 2016). Furthermore, remittances boost consumption and expenditure on health, education, and nutrition, which support a rise in long-term productivity (Mohapatra and Ratha 2011).

Gbenou (2015), examining the macroeconomic impact of remittance in WAEMU countries, discover two aspects. On one hand, migrant remittances have a stabilizing role, as they have a counter-cyclical effect in relation to the volatility of the output gap. On the other hand, remittances have a positive impact on actual production per capita.

Lartey (2013), using a dynamic panel estimate for 36 countries in Sub-Saharan Africa, discovers that there is a positive relationship between remittances and growth through two channels: the consumption smoothing effect and the investment channel.

To measure the economic impact of remittances, Nsiah and Fayissa (2011) perform several methods (developed panel unit-root tests, cointegration tests, and Panel Fully Modified OLS (PFMOLS)) on the annual data from 1985 to 2007 for 64 countries consisting of 29 from Africa, 14 from Asia, and 21 from Latin America and the Caribbean region. They prove a positive, long-run impact of remittances on growth in the regions.

Another strand of studies shows the negative effects of remittance on growth. Singh, Markus, and Kyung-woo (2009), in the case of sub-Saharan Africa, find that the adverse effects of remittances on growth are significant, and occur through a decline in labor supply.

Studies such as Donou-Adonsou and Lim (2015) do not find any existence of relationship between the two variables. Indeed, Donou-Adonsou and Lim (2015), using the Westerlund Error Correction Model for panel time series over 1975–2011, indicate that remittance flows into WAEMU have no long-run impact on income per capita. The authors argue that remittance funds received in the home countries are utilized for consumption purposes. Even though remittance-recipients can make the choice to work less, they would be unlikely to have a significant impact on output in African countries with high levels of underemployment (Mohapatra and Ratha 2011).

3.2 Impact of Remittance on Agricultural Productivity

Even if funds remitted foster the overall productivity in home countries, do they really affect productivity in the agricultural sector? For the positive effects of remittance on agricultural productivity, Fayssia and Nsiah (2005) examine the aggregate impact of remittance on agriculture, using panel data from 18 Latin American countries for the period of 1980–2005; they discover that, in countries where financial system was less developed, remittance had a significant impact on agriculture. Remittances could supply the necessary funds to purchase fertilizers and improve agricultural output. Studies report that remittances were used to enhance the quality of agricultural land, to acquire agricultural inputs, and invest in agricultural equipment (Ellis 2003). Studying the effects of remittances in Pakistan, Ali et al. (2018) find that remittance received from European countries has a positive effect on agricultural GDP in the long run, while remittances from US, Canada, and Australia showed a negative effect.

Conversely, recipient-Households utilize income from remittances in consumption or education, rather than productive agricultural investment (Lipton 1980). The findings of Lipton on the negative effects of remittances on agricultural productivity were supported by various country-specific case studies. Likewise, Miluka et al. (2010) find that migration boosts consumption, but reduces agricultural labor inputs among Albanian farm households. Quisumbing and Mcniven (2010), employing 20-year panel data from the Philippines, discover that, for receiving households, remittances have no impact on investment in land nor on agricultural assets.

3.3 Impact of Remittance on Labor Supply and Productivity

Remittances have an influence on the individual labor supply and aggregate labor force participation.

3.3.1 Positive Effects

Remittance inflow encourages the household members to invest in self-employment opportunities, rather than searching for a waged employment (Shapiro and Mandelman 2016). Evidence shows that in Egypt, international migration raises the number of self- employed workers but does not affect the overall employment of the remaining members of migrant-sending households (Arouri and Nguyen 2018). Yang (2008) observes that remittance-receiving households increase their working hours in self-employment, and are more likely to start a relatively capital-intensive activity. Migrants' earnings sent to the home country encourage the development of private entrepreneurship by providing capital for business (Ratha 2003; Moneygram 2010; Zvezda 2011; Yang 2011).

The impact of remittance on labor productivity might differ in the short run and in the long run. Indeed, Akter (2018), using data over the 1976–2014 period for Bangladesh, observed a significant positive effect of remittance on the labor productivity, through capital accumulation. Bangladeshi households save a share of their remittances, which turns into investment in productive sectors.

3.3.2 Negative Effects

Some studies (e.g., Chami et al. 2005) have highlighted that remittances could have a possible negative effect on the recipient's effort because of the issue of asymmetric information. Chami et al. (2005) reveal that as remittance increases, recipients are less eager to get a small income from work. If the remittance transfers augment the reservation wage of non-migrating family members and lower the opportunity cost of leisure, it may reduce the incentives to work (Amuedo-Dorantes and Pozo 2006). Narazani's (2009) study show the evidence that, in response to substantial remittance receipts, salaried non-migrant employees switch income for leisure when they get in Albania;. Similar findings for Mexican women in the informal sector and non-paid work in rural areas (Amuedo-Dorantes and Pozo 2006). The above will reduce labor force participation.

Studying the economic effects of international remittances on household spending decisions in El Salvador, Acosta (2006) shows that remittances have a negative effect on adult female labor supply, while the effect is positive for middle-aged males.

Azizi (2018) used a vast data for 122 developing countries from 1990 to 2015, to investigate the impacts of workers' remittances on human capital and labor supply. The results revealed that remittances decrease the female labor force participation rate but do not affect the male labor force participation rate. Moreover, evidence reveals that women from high-migration states become less likely to work relative to women from low-migration states in rural households in Mexico (Hanson 2007).

Guha (2013), applying a Dynamic Stochastic General Equilibrium (DSGE) Model in Bangladesh, asserts that with an increase in international remittances, the households and remittance-recipients will work less and have more leisure, as the remittance income compensates the loss in the wage income. This will result in a decline in labor supply and a decline in output. Justino and Shemyakina (2012) discover that, for Tajikistan, individuals in remittance-receiving households are less likely to participate in the labor market. Even when they work, they reduce their working hours. Moreover, if mostly well-educated people emigrate, remittances could be connected to a downturn in the labor market.

3.4 Impact of Remittance on Agricultural Labor Productivity

Although a number of empirics over the last two decades shed light on the impact of remittances, there is a gap in the literature on the relationship between remittances and labor productivity with respect to the agricultural sector. Remittances sent by migrants can be used to increase the land, livestock, as well as the human capital of rural household members. The relationship between remittances and agricultural labor productivity is complex. Rozelle et al. (1999) were among the first researchers to study the connection between migration, remittances and agricultural labor productivity. Their results depict that a combination of remittances and urbanization increase the need to foster agricultural productivity.

On one hand, agricultural productivity can be negatively affected by remittances, as rural household members reduce their labor force participation. On the other hand, remittances might help rural households to surmount production constraints and increase labor productivity (Damon 2010; Miluka et al. 2010). Azam and Gubert (2002) pointed out that remittances have two functions in the agricultural sector. First, they provide new technological machines for farm households. Second, they function as an insurance mechanism for farm households. The authors argue that the more reliable this mechanism, the greater the incentive to reduce the agricultural workforce and labor productivity in the community.

4   ECONOMETRIC FRAMEWORK

4.1 Econometric Model and Data

We use the following function:

$$\text{ALP} = f(K, H, X) \tag{1}$$

where ALP represents agricultural labor productivity, K, the international remittances received, H, the human capital, and X, the other explanatory factors.

The specific equation is:

$$\text{ALP}_{i,t} = \alpha_0 + \alpha_1 \text{ALP}_{i,t-1} + \alpha_2 \text{REMIT}_{i,t} + \sum_{j}^{i} \mathbf{X}'_{ijt} \delta_j + \vartheta_i + \mu_{i,t} \quad (2)$$

where ALP is the agricultural labor productivity, REMIT denotes the log of personal remittances received as a percentage of GDP. The term $\mathbf{X}'$ is a vector for control variables, ϑ_i is an unobserved individual effect, and μ_{it} is an unobserved white noise disturbance. The control variables are Life expectancy at birth, the degree of openness, the manufacturing value added, Human capital, GDP per capita, the agricultural added value, Gross fixed capital formation. Our dataset comprises 39 SSA countries from 2000 to 2016.

Next, Following Dzeha et al. (2017), we argue that, as people reach their retirement, they become less productive and need more remittance for their consumption. We interact remittance and the life expectancy at birth to assert its effect on agricultural productivity. We create a dummy variable for countries with a life expectancy ratio greater than 55 years as "1," and those with less than 55 years as "0."

$$\text{LP}_{i,t} = \alpha_0 + \alpha_1 * \text{LP}_{i,t\_1} + \alpha_2 * \text{REMIT}_{i,t} + \alpha_3 * (\text{REMIT}_{i,t} * \text{LIFEEXP}_{i,t})$$
$$+ \sum_{j}^{i} \mathbf{X}'_{ijt} \delta_j + \vartheta_i + \mu_{i,t} \quad (3)$$

The variables in the regression are:

Agricultural labor productivity measured by the share of agricultural employment in the real agricultural value added. We use sectoral employment data from Global Employment Trend from ILO (GET-Sector ILO) and the National Accounts Aggregates Database from UNSTAT.

Personal remittances received comprise personal transfers and compensation of employees in current US dollars. Personal transfers consist of all current transfers in cash or in kind made or received by resident households to or from nonresident households. Compensation of employees refers to the income of border, seasonal, and other short-term workers who are employed in an economy where they are not residents and of residents employed by nonresident entities.

GDP per capita (current US$) is the gross domestic product divided by population. GDP is the sum of gross value added by all resident producers in the economy plus any product taxes and minus any subsidies not included in the value of the products. It is calculated without making deductions for depreciation of fabricated assets or for depletion and degradation of natural resources. An increase in the GDP per capita will increase the demand for goods, which in turn will spur the domestic agricultural production and the agricultural labor productivity.

Trade openness measured by trade is the sum of exports and imports of goods and services measured as a share of gross domestic product. We expect that a greater openness to trade will increase the agricultural labor productivity in SSA. This was confirmed by the findings of Hassine Belhaj, Robichaud, and Decaluwe (2010). They observe that opening up to foreign trade promotes productivity growth and that poverty can drop under the agricultural trade liberalization scheme.

Life expectancy at birth indicates the number of years a newborn infant would live if prevailing patterns of mortality at the time of its birth were to stay the same throughout its life. It reflects the overall mortality level of a population, and summarizes the mortality pattern that prevails across all age groups in a given year. Life expectancy is a measure of good health. In Sub-Saharan Africa, diseases such as malaria, HIV-AIDS, and malnutrition can be fatal for the population and reduce the total level of labor supply. Moreover, these very common illnesses can simply have non-fatal effects on workers in the labor market. Rather than diminishing the labor force, these diseases severely weakened the individuals' productivity. Cole and Neumayer (2006). Thus, a country with a longer life expectancy indicates better health for its citizens, thus an increase in the agricultural labor productivity.

The manufacturing value added; Manufacturing refers to industries belonging to ISIC divisions 15–37. Value added is the net output of a sector after adding up all outputs and subtracting intermediate inputs. It is calculated without making deductions for depreciation of fabricated assets or depletion and degradation of natural resources. An increase in the manufacturing value added suggests a relative decrease in other sectors such as the agricultural one, thus a reduction in the agricultural labor productivity.

The Human capital, Enrollment in primary education, both sexes (number). It is the Total number of students enrolled in public and private primary education institutions regardless of age. Usually, farmers obtain necessary knowledge through an educational system. There is evidence that, in areas where educated people are higher, agricultural labor productivity grows faster (Gutierrez 2000). Education allows workers and farmers to adopt innovative techniques, which will increase their productivity (Jamison and Moock 1984).

The agricultural added value: Agriculture corresponds to ISIC divisions 1–5 and includes forestry, hunting, and fishing, as well as cultivation of crops and livestock production. Value added is the net output of a sector after adding up all outputs and subtracting intermediate inputs. It is calculated without making deductions for depreciation of fabricated assets or depletion and degradation of natural resources. As the share of agriculture value increases, the agricultural labor productivity rises, following a spur of the production of agricultural goods.

Gross fixed capital formation (% of GDP). It includes land improvements (fences, ditches, drains, and so on); plant, machinery, and equipment purchases; and the construction of roads, railways, and the like, including schools, offices, hospitals, private residential dwellings, and commercial and

Table 1 The expected relationship between the explanatory variables and the Agricultural labor productivity

Explanatory variables	Expected sign
Agricultural labor productivity (past value)	Positive (+)
Personal remittances received	Ambiguous
GDP per capita (current US$)	Positive (+)
Openness degree	Positive (+)
Life expectancy at birth	Positive (+)
the manufacturing value added	Negative (−)
The Human capital	Positive (+)
The agricultural added value	Positive (+)
Gross fixed capital formation	Positive (+)

Source Computed by the Authors

industrial buildings. This variable captures all investment spending on sustainable machinery and materials purchases. For Romer (2006), an increase in the fixed capital formation could lead to an optimal combination of labor and capital which, in turn, increases labor productivity, as supported by the classic Cobb–Douglas type production function. Thus, we expect this variable to have a positive effect on agricultural labor productivity.

The data on remittance as well as the control variables are taken from the World Bank World Development Indicators. All variables were used in their natural logarithm form. Table 1 summarizes the expected relationship of each explanatory variable with our dependent variables.

4.2 Empirical Strategy

We will use a dynamic panel data model design. A dynamic panel has two advantages. First, static panel regression process may omit variables which are connected to income distribution, such as cultural, historical, and economic development. Yet, these factors usually do not change over time. Taking difference can remove these invariants with time variables and individual unobserved effects, solving the problem of missing variables. Secondly, taking the differences can eliminate reverse causality. As indicated by Reuveny and Li (2003), the inclusion of the lagged values of inequality helps to control for some excluded but potentially important variables in the model.

The inclusion of the lagged dependent variable as one of the regressors suggests a problem of endogeneity. This renders the OLS estimator biased and inconsistent. This bias is of great concern because of the short temporal dimension of the data set used. For the fixed effects (FE) estimator, the within transformation wipes out the μ_i but $\hat{y}_{i,t}$ will still be correlated with $\vartheta_{i,t}$ even if the $\vartheta_{i,t}$ are not serially correlated. The same problem occurs with the random effects GLS estimator (Anderson and Hsiao 1982; Sevestre and Trognon 1985).

One solution to address such issue will be the use of the General Method of Moments (GMM) (Arellano and Bond 1991; Arellano and Bover 1995;

Blundell and Bond 1998). The GMM estimator addresses issues of lagged dependent variables, unobserved fixed effects, endogenous independent regressors, as well as presence of autocorrelation across and within individuals or countries (Roodman 2009). Another important advantage is that, with a GMM, it is easy to obtain parameter estimates that are robust to heteroskedasticity of unknown form (Blundell and Bond 1998).

The following moments' conditions below associated with System-GMM allow for the estimation of the coefficients of the model

$$E(\vartheta_i) = 0, E(\mu_{i,t}) = 0, E(\mu_{i,t}\vartheta_i) = 0, \quad \text{for } i = 1,\ldots,N \text{ and } t = 2,\ldots,T$$

$$E(\mu_{i,t}\mu_{i,s}) = 0, \quad \text{for } i = 1,\ldots,N \text{ and } \forall t \neq s$$

$$E[(\text{ALP}_{i,t})(\mu_{i,t})] = 0, \quad \text{for } i = 1,\ldots,N \text{ and } t = 2,\ldots,T$$

$$E[(\text{ALP}_{i,t-1})(\mu_{i,t})] = 0, \quad \text{for } i = 1,\ldots,N \text{ and } t = 2,\ldots,T$$

$$E[(\text{REMIT}_{i,t})(\mu_{i,t})] = 0, \quad \text{for } i = 1,\ldots,N \text{ and } t = 2,\ldots,T$$

$$E[(X_{i,t})(\mu_{i,t})] = 0, \quad \text{for } i = 1,\ldots,N \text{ and } t = 2,\ldots,T$$

5 Empirical Results and Discussion

Table 2 displays the descriptive statistics of the variables. It shows that the average level of the natural log of agricultural labor productivity is 13.52. On average, the natural log of remittance is 18. The average GDP per

Table 2 Descriptive statistics of the variables

Variable	Observations	Mean	Standard deviation	Minimum	Maximum
Agricultural productivity (log)	663	13.53	1.10	11.56	17.71
Remittances (log)	663	18.00	2.27	9.35	23.77
Life expectancy	663	55.86	5.95	38.69	74.35
Openness degree	663	80.05	42.67	6.04	351.11
Gross fixed capital formation	663	21.78	11.95	1.10	145.75
GDP per capita	663	1756.78	2900.52	111.36	22,742.38
Manufacturing added value to GDP	663	11.16	7.13	0.24	36.57
Agricultural added value (log)	663	20.79	1.22	18.50	25.07
Enrolment in primary education	663	2,619,286	3,674,481	67,825	22,861,884

Source Computed by the Authors

capita per year is approximately 1756 US dollars while the highest value of GDP per capita recorded is 22,742 US dollars, suggesting a great disparity in the standard of living across Sub-Saharan countries. The number of years a newborn infant would live on average, in the selected countries is 55.85 years. The maximum manufacturing added value is 36.57% per GDP with a variability of 7.13%.

Table 3 depicts the bivariate correlations among the variables. With a coefficient correlation of 0.09, remittances are weakly positively correlated with agricultural labor productivity.

Life expectancy, openness degree, and agricultural added values also present a weak relationship with agricultural labor productivity, while gross capital formation and GDP per capita have a moderate association with agricultural labor productivity.

Agricultural labor productivity negatively correlates with manufacturing added value and human capital. As the share of manufacturing in the total production or the level or education of individuals goes up, the agricultural labor productivity goes down.

In Table 4, Column 1 shows the results of the basic model with the lagged dependent variable, revealing a positive relationship. Previous agricultural labor productivity has a 93.4% positive impact on current agricultural labor productivity. The past value of the agricultural labor productivity accounts for the path-dependent nature of current values.

The estimates signal that, on average, an increase in remittance inflows in Sub-Saharan will result in a decrease in agricultural labor productivity. Thus, it suggests that the impact of remittance on agricultural labor productivity is negative. This is because remittances received are often used for consumption rather than for capital accumulation. The recipients have the tendency to substitute remittances to their own income, by decreasing their labor participation rate in the agricultural sector. This is consistent with Mamun and Nath (2010) who found that, in case of an increase in remittances, households substitute labor with leisure. Chami et al. (2003) reported that only a smaller part of remittance funds is saved or invested, and mostly in "not necessarily productive" such as housing, land, and jewelry.

Moreover, Bussolo and Medvedev (2008) support that, with a rise in non-labor income through remittances, people can consume more goods and leisure and thus their labor supply is diminished. This is also in line with the findings of the West African Economic and Monetary Union, where most received funds are devoted to the consumption of (imported) goods and services and leisure (BCEAO 2013). Remittances encourage dependence vis-à-vis transfers to beneficiaries in developing countries (Lipton 1980; Binford 2003; Chami et al. 2003), encourage the emigration of people of working age, leading to a massive exodus of the workforce, leading to a reduction in labor supply.

Table 3 Correlation matrix

	1	2	3	4	5	6	7	8	9
1 Agricultural productivity	1								
2 Remittances	0.09	1							
3 Life expectancy	0.02	−0.01	1						
4 Openness degree	0.06	−0.14	0.22	1					
5 Gross fixed capital formation	0.30	−0.09	0.34	0.22	1				
6 GDP per capita	0.33	−0.09	0.29	0.39	0.26	1			
7 Manufacturing added value	−0.13	0.08	0.04	−0.02	−0.18	0.12	1		
8 Agricultural added value	0.16	0.43	−0.03	−0.27	−0.09	−0.04	0.08	1	
9 Enrolment in primary education	−0.06	0.31	−0.18	−0.26	−0.06	−0.33	0.03	0.58	1

Source Computed by the Authors

Table 4 Results of the impact of remittances on agricultural labor productivity using GMM

	1	2
Lag of agricultural labor productivity	0.934*** (22.86)	0.995*** (16.47)
Remittances	−0.011* (1.70)	−0.019** (2.38)
Life expectancy	0.039 (0.50)	−0.103 (0.89)
Trade openness	0.059*** (2.16)	0.073*** (2.60)
Gross fixed capital formation	0.023 (0.68)	−0.020 (0.45)
GDP per capita	−0.034* (1.75)	−0.056** (2.23)
Manufacturing added value to GDP	−0.003 (0.13)	0.013 (0.59)
Agricultural added value	0.055*** (3.44)	0.055*** (3.39)
Enrolment in primary education	−0.021* (1.86)	−0.019 (1.63)
Remittances × life expectancy		0.005** (2.17)
Observations	624	624
AR (1)	0.029**	0.023**
AR (2)	0.801	0.799
Sargan test	0.136	0.115

Standard errors in parentheses ***$p<0.01$, **$p<0.05$, *$p<0.1$
Source Computed by the Authors

Furthermore, in most Sub-Saharan countries, remittances are channeled through informal means. The formal financial sector does not actively capture these funds and cannot allow an optimal mobilization of remittances into productive investments in the agricultural sector. Therefore, these remittances fail to release their full potential in the improvement of the labor productivity, especially in the agricultural sector.

As in Sub-saharan countries, the remittances boost the consumption of foreign goods, our findings diverge from that of McCullough (2017), who shows that the funds sent to households, especially in rural areas, stimulate the agricultural labor productivity. Our findings also differ from the findings of Rozelle et al. (1999), that for the Chinese context, remittances raise the demand for food and foster agricultural labor productivity.

An increase in the agricultural added value increases the labor productivity in the sector. This is due to the fact that the more the added value of agriculture increases, the more the contribution to growth arises. Also, as producers accumulate more wealth, the higher is the likelihood to use more cultivation techniques and inputs, which improve the productivity. Moreover, a country's openness degree has a positive effect on the labor productivity in the agricultural sector by boosting the agricultural added value to the economy.

GDP per capita and human capital have a negative impact on agricultural labor productivity. A low skill level of the workforce and a weak capacity of expertise in production techniques can explain these results. These findings present a case for an intensification of training for the agricultural labor. In this sense, remittances could contribute to improving human capital. Our results are in line with Schultz (1964), who considers that human capital can enhance productivity only in modern, rather than traditional agriculture. In Sub-Saharan Africa, the agricultural sector requires a technological transformation (Osabuohien et al. 2019; Oyebola et al. 2019).

Life expectancy is not significant in our regressions. However, remittances received in countries with high life expectancy (beyond 55 years), can augment the agricultural labor productivity. In countries with high life expectancy, old farmers and workers in the agricultural sector share their skills with their family members or with the young generation of workers. This transfer of knowledge amplifies the labor productivity in the sector.

6   Conclusion and Policy Implications

This chapter set out to offer an analysis of the remittance–labor productivity relationship in the agricultural sector in Sub-Saharan Africa with a comprehensive dataset, comprising data for 39 countries from 2000 to 2016. It uses a panel analysis and generalized method of moments (GMM) techniques to address issues such as that of lagged dependent variables, unobserved fixed effects, endogenous independent regressors, as well as the presence of heteroskedasticity and autocorrelation across and within individuals or countries.

We find robust estimates proving a significant and negative impact of remittance on agricultural labor productivity, which implicates that with an increase in non-labor income through remittances, individuals can consume more goods and leisure (i.e., the income effect dominates) and thus their labor supply is reduced. The results also suggest that GDP per capita and human capital reduce labor productivity, while trade openness improves it, in the agricultural sector.

In the second part, we examine how the interaction of remittance and life expectancy at birth affects the remittance–agricultural labor productivity nexus. The evidence shows that the interaction effect is tempered in countries with high life expectancy.

Our results present several policy implications.

Diaspora management: Countries need to create schemes to manage labor migration, to support the remittance fund and incite the migrants to invest directly in productive sectors. *Invest in technology and agribusiness*: An improvement in technological equipment in agriculture, a rise in agribusiness activities, and the training of unskilled or rural workers will increase the output in the agriculture sector as well as its labor productivity.

Vocational training in agriculture: alongside the formal education system, farmers and households in rural areas in Sub-Saharan Africa can receive additional practical knowledge and trainings in higher vocational schools and specialized agricultural institutions.

Policy design: In designing agricultural policies, countries in SSA should take into account the role of remittance transfers in addressing the labor productivity. In order to increase agricultural labor productivity through remittances received from abroad, their uses should be reoriented. Indeed, the negative impact obtained as a result could be interpreted as if the transfers are often directed toward consumption expenditure (e.g., health and education) and not toward investments in the agricultural sector. Although transfers help to ensure health and education costs, it is equally important that they help reorient the workforce toward skills training in the agricultural sector. It will therefore be necessary to channel these remittances into a new dimension: that of investment can increase productivity in the agricultural sector and whose multiplier effects will boost the growth of African economies whose agricultural sector contributes up to 40% of GDP. Given the growing importance of the transfer of migrant funds in economic development, especially in developing countries, the results of this study would help redefining the phenomenon of migration flows on the agricultural labor force.

Appendix: List of the 39 Countries

Angola, Benin, Burkina Faso, Botswana, Burundi, Cameroon, Chad, Congo Brazzaville, Equatorial Guinea, Ethiopia, Gabon, Gambia, Ghana, Guinea-Bissau, Guinea, Ivory Coast, Kenya, Liberia, Lesotho, Mauritania, Madagascar, Mauritius, Malawi, Mali, Mozambique, Nigeria, Niger, Rwanda, South Africa, Senegal, Sierra Leone, Swaziland, Tanzania, Togo, Uganda, Congo Kinshasa, Zambia, Zimbabwe.

References

Acosta, P. (2006). *Labor supply, school attendance and remittances from international migration: The case of El Salvador* (World Bank Policy Research Working Paper 3903).

Adams, R., Jr., Cuecuecha, A., & Page, J. (2008). *The impact of remittances on poverty and inequality in Ghana* (World Bank Policy Research Working Paper No. 4732. 1-39).

Adenutsi, D. E. (2010). Do international remittances promote human development in poor countries? Empirical evidence from sub-Saharan Africa. *The International Journal of Applied Economics and Finance, 4*(1), 31–45. Accessed June 14, 2018 from https://mpra.ub.uni-muenchen.de/29347/.

Agarwal, R., & Horowitz, A. W. (2002). Are international remittances altruism or insurance? Evidence from Guyana using multiple-migrant households. *World Development, 30*(11), 2033–2044.

Aggarwal, R., Demirgüç-Kuntm, A., & Pería Maria, S. M. (2010). Do remittances promote financial development? *Journal of Development Economics, 96*(2), 255–264. https://doi.org/10.1016/j.jdeveco.2010.10.005.

Agwu, G. A., Yuni, D. N., & Anochiwa, L. (2018). Do remittances improve income inequality? An instrumental variable quantile analysis of the Senegalese case. *International Migration, 56*(1), 146–166.

Akter, S. (2018). Impact of remittance on domestic labor productivity in Bangladesh. *Progressive Agriculture, 29*(1), 33–44. https://doi.org/10.3329/pa.v29i1.37478.

Ali, A., Saeed, M. Z., Imran, M. A., Mushtaq, K., & Ghafoor, A. (2018). Investigation of the impact of foreign remittance on agricultural development in Pakistan: A time series analysis. *Pakistan Journal of Applied Economics, 28*(1), 131–146.

Al Mamun, M., Sohag, K., Samargandi, N., & Yasmeen, F. (2016). Does remittance fuel labor productivity in Bangladesh? The application of an asymmetric non-linear ARDL approach. *Applied Economics, 48*(50), 4861–4877. https://doi.org/10.1080/00036846.2016.1167825.

Al Mamun, M., Sohag, K., Uddin, G., & Shahbaz, M. (2015). Remittance and domestic labor productivity: Evidence from remittance recipient countries. *Economic Modelling, 47*, 207–218. https://doi.org/10.1016/j.econmod.2015.02.024.

Amuedo-Dorantes, C., & Pozo, S. (2006). Migration, remittances, and male and female employment patterns. *American Economic Review, 96*(2), 222–226.

Anderson, T., & Hsiao, C. (1982). Formulation and estimation of dynamic models using panel data. *Journal of Econometrics, 18*, 47–82.

Anyanwu, J. C., & Erhijakpor, A. E. O. (2010). Do international remittances affect poverty in Africa? *African Development Review, 22*, 51–91. https://doi.org/10.1111/j.1467-8268.2009.00228.x.

Arellano, M., & Bond, S. (1991). Some tests of specification for panel data: Monte Carlo evidence and an application to employment equations. *Review of Economic Studies, 58*, 277–297.

Arellano, M., & Bover, O. (1995). Another look at the instrumental variable estimation of error-components models. *Journal of Econometrics, 68*(1), 29–51.

Arouri, M., & Nguyen, C. V. (2018). Does international migration affect labor supply, non-farm diversification and welfare of households? Evidence from Egypt. *International Migration, 56*(1), 39.

Asongu, S. A., Efobi, U. R., Tanakem, B. V., & Osabuohien, E. (2019). Globalisation and female economic participation in sub-Saharan Africa. *Gender Issues.* https://doi.org/10.1007/s12147-019-09233-3.

Atkinson, A. B., & Stern, N. H. (1981). On labor supply and commodity demands. In A. Deaton (Ed.), *Essays in the theory and measurement of consumer behavior* (pp. 265–296). New York: Cambridge University Press.

Azam, J. P., & Gubert, F. (2002). Those in Kayes: The impact of remittances on their recipients in Africa. *Revue Economique, 56*, 1331–1358.

Azizi, S. (2018). The impacts of workers' remittances on human capital and labor supply in developing countries. *Economic Modelling, 75*, 377–396. https://doi.org/10.1016/j.econmod.2018.07.011.

Baldé, Y. (2011). The impact of remittances and foreign aid on savings/investment in sub-Saharan Africa. *African Development Review, 23*(2), 247–262.

Bang, J. T., Mitra, A., & Wunnava, P. V. (2016). Do remittances improve income inequality? An instrumental variable quantile analysis of the Kenyan case. *Economic Modelling, 58*, 394–402.

BCEAO. (2013). Synthèse des résultats des enquêtes sur les envois de fonds des travailleurs migrants dans les pays de l'UEMOA.

Binford, L. (2003). Migrant remittances and (under) development in Mexico. *Critique of Anthropology, 23*(3), 305–336.

Blundell, R., & Bond, S. (1998). Initial conditions and moment restrictions in dynamic panel data models. *Journal of Econometrics, 87*(1), 115–143.

Bussolo, M., & Medvedev, D. (2008). Do remittances have a flip side? A general equilibrium analysis of remittances, labor supply responses and policy options for Jamaica. *Journal of Economic Integration, 23*(3), 734–764.

Castles, S., Staeheli, L., & Davidson, A. (2002). Citizenship and migration: Globalization and the politics of belonging. *Economic Geography, 78*(3), 392. https://doi.org/10.2307/4140816.

Chami, R., Fullenkamp, C., & Jahjah, S. (2003). *Are immigrant remittance flows a source of capital for development?* (IMF Working Paper (WP/03/189)).

Chami, R., Fullenkamp, C., & Jahjah, S. (2005). Are immigrant remittance flows a source of capital for development? *IMF Staff Papers, 52,* 55–81.

Christiaensen, L., Demery, L., & Kuhl, J. (2011). The (evolving) role of agriculture in poverty reduction – An empirical perspective. *Journal of Development Economics, 96*(2), 239–254.

Cole, M., & Neumayer, E. (2006). The impact of poor health on total factor productivity. *The Journal of Development Studies, 42*(6), 918–938. https://doi.org/10.1080/00220380600774681.

Cox-Edwards, A., & Rodríguez-Oreggia, E. (2009). Remittances and labor force participation in Mexico: An analysis using propensity score matching. *World Development, 37*(5), 1004–1014. https://doi.org/10.1016/j.worlddev.2008.09.010.

Damon, A. (2010). Agricultural land use and asset accumulation in migrant households: The case of El Salvador. *Journal of Development Studies, 46*(1), 162–189. https://doi.org/10.1080/00220380903197994.

De Janvry, A., & Sadoulet, E. (2010). Agricultural growth and poverty reduction: Additional evidence. *The World Bank Research Observer, 25*(1), 1–20.

Donou-Adonsou, F., & Lim, S. (2015). An empirical analysis of remittance flows into West African Economic and Monetary Union: A panel time-series approach. *Applied Economics, 48*(11), 1018–1029. https://doi.org/10.1080/00036846.2015.1093080.

Dzeha, G. C. O., Abor, J. Y., Turkson, F. E., & Agbloyor, E. K. (2017). Do remittances matter in accelerating labor productivity and capital accumulation? In N. Biekpe, D. Cassimon, & A. W. Mullineux (Eds.), *Development finance— Innovations for sustainable growth* (pp. 251–283). Switzerland: Palgrave Macmillan.

Efobi, U., Asongu, A., Okafor, C., Tchamyou, V. & Tanakem, B (2019, March). Remittances, finance and industrialization in Africa. *Journal of Multinational Financial Management, 49,* 54–66.

Efobi, U. R., Osabuohien, E. S., & Oluwatobi, S. (2015). One dollar, one bank account: Remittance and bank breadth in Nigeria. *Journal of International Migration and Integration, 16*(3), 761–781.

Ellis, F. (2003). *A livelihoods approach to migration and poverty reduction.* Paper Commissioned by the Department for International Development (DFID).

Fayssia, B., & Nsiah, C. (2005). *Can remittances spur economic growth and agricultural development? Evidence from Latin American countries.* Working Paper Series. Department of Economic and Finance.

Fromentin, V. (2017). The long-run and short-run impacts of remittances on financial development in developing countries. *The Quarterly Review of Economics and Finance, 66,* 192–201. https://doi.org/10.1016/j.qref.2017.02.006.

Gbenou, K. D. A. (2015). Impacts macroéconomiques des transferts de fonds des migrants dans les pays de l'UEMOA. *Journal of Development Studies, 48*(8), 1009–1025.

Gonzalez-Garcia, J., Hitaj, E., Viseth, A., & Yenice, M. (2016). *Sub-Saharan Africa migration: Patterns and spillovers*. Washington, DC: International Monetary Fund Spill Over Notes.

Gubert, F., Chauvet, L., Mercier, M., & Mesplé-Somps, S. (2015). Migrants' HTAs and local development in Mali. *Scandinavian Journal of Economics, 117*(2), 686–722.

Guha, P. (2013). Macroeconomic effects of international remittances: The case of developing economies. *Economic Modelling, 33*, 292–305. https://doi.org/10.1016/j.econmod.2013.04.016.

Gutierrez, L. (2000). *Why is agricultural labour productivity higher in some countries than others? 2000 annual meeting, July 30–August 2, Tampa, FL 21741, (Agricultural and Applied Economics Association)*.

Gupta, S., Pattillo, C. A., & Wagh, S. (2009). Effect of remittances on poverty and financial development in sub-Saharan Africa. *World Development, 37*(1), 104–115.

Gyimah-Brempong, K., & Aside, E. (2015). Remittances and investment in education: Evidence from Ghana. *The Journal of International Trade & Economic Development, 24*, 2.

Hajra, R., & Ghosh, T. (2018). Agricultural productivity, household poverty and migration in the Indian Sundarban Delta. *Elementa Science of the Anthropocene, 6*(1), 3. https://doi.org/10.1525/elementa.196.

Hanson. G. H. (2007). Emigration, remittances and labor force participation in Mexico. ITD Documento de Trabajo ITD, 28.

Hassine Belhaj, N., Robichaud, V., & Decaluwe, B. (2010). *Agricultural trade liberalization, productivity gain, and poverty alleviation: A general equilibrium analysis* (Working Paper 519). Economic Research Forum.

Jamison, D., & Moock, P. (1984). Farmer education and farm efficiency in Nepal: The role of schooling, extension services, and cognitive skills (English). *World Development, 12*(1), 67–86.

Justino, P., & Shemyakina, O. (2012). Remittances and labor supply in post-conflict Tajikistan. *IZA Journal of Labor & Development, 1*(1). https://doi.org/10.1186/2193-9020-1-8.

Kifle, T. (2007). Do remittances encourage investment in education? Evidence from Eritrea. *GEFAME Journal of African Studies, 4*, 1.

Lartey, E. K. K. (2013). Remittances, investment and growth in sub-Saharan Africa. *The Journal of International Trade & Economic Development, 22*(7), 1038–1058.

Lartey, E. K. K., Mandelman, F., & Acosta, P. A. (2008, March). *Remittances, exchange rate regimes, and the Dutch disease: A panel data analysis* (FRB of Atlanta Working Paper No. 2008–12).

Lipton, M. (1980). Migration from rural areas of poor countries: The impact on rural productivity and income distribution. *World Development, 8*(1), 1–24. https://doi.org/10.1016/0305-750x(80)90047-9.

Mamun, A. K., & Nath K. H. (2010). *Workers' migration and remittances in Bangladesh*. Accessed July 15, 2018 from http://www.shsu.edu/~tcq001/paper_files/wp10-02_paper.pdf

Martin, P., Susan, M., & Patrick, W. (2002). Best practice options: Mali. *International Migration, 40*, 87–99.

McCulloughm, E. B. (2017). Labor productivity and employment gaps in sub-Saharan Africa. *Food Policy, 67*, 133–152.

Miluka, J., Carletto, G., Davis, B., & Zezza, A. (2010). The vanishing farms? The impact of international migration on Albanian family farming. *The Journal of Development Studies*, *46*(1), 140–161. https://doi.org/10.1080/00220380903197978.

Mohapatra, S., & Ratha, D. (2011). *Remittance markets in Africa* (English). Directions in development; Finance. Washington, DC: World Bank.

Moneygram. (2010). *Remittance trends and the role of money transfer organizations*. Presentational Materials Dated July 20, Moneygram International, Minneapolis, MN.

Narazani. E. (2009). *Labor supply, remittances and the new flat tax in Albania*. Global Development Network Southeast Europe.

Ngozi, A., Evans, O., & Ebenezer, B. (2017). *Journal of Contextual Economics, 137*, 173–192.

Nicholson, W., & Snyder, C. (2016). *Microeconomic theory*. Boston, MA: Cengage Learning.

Nsiah, C., & Fayissa, B. (2011). Remittances and economic growth in Africa, Asia, and Latin American-Caribbean countries: A panel unit root and panel cointegration analysis. *Journal of Economics and Finance, 37*(3), 424–441. https://doi.org/10.1007/s12197-011-9195-6.

Osabuohien, E. S., & Efobi, U. R. (2013). Africa's money in Africa. *South African Journal of Economics, 81*(2), 292–306.

Osabuohien, E. S., & Efobi, U. R. (2014). Africa's money in Africa: Human and physical capital dimensions. In S. Sahoo & B. K. Pattanaik (Eds.), *Global diaspora and development: Socioeconomic, cultural and policy perspectives* (pp. 87–104). New Delhi: Springer.

Osabuohien, E., Efobi, U. R., Herrmann, R., & Gitau, C. M. (2019). Female labor outcomes and large-scale agricultural land investments: Macro-micro evidence from Tanzania. *Land Use Policy, 82*, 716–728.

Oyebola, P. O., Osabuohien, E., & Obasaju, B. (2019). Employment and income effects of Nigeria's agricultural transformation agenda. *African Journal of Economic and Management Studies*. https://doi.org/10.1108/AJEMS-12-2018-0402.

Quisumbing, A., & McNiven, S. (2010). Moving forward, looking back: The impact of migration and remittances on assets, consumption, and credit constraints in the rural Philippines. *Journal of Development Studies, 46*(1), 91–113. https://doi.org/10.1080/00220380903197960.

Rapoport, H., & Docquier, F. (2006). The economics of migrants' remittances. In K. Arrow & M. Intriligator (Eds.), *Handbook of the economics of giving, altruism and reciprocity* (Vol. 2, pp. 1135–1198). Elsevier-North Holland.

Ratha, D. (2003). Workers' remittances: An important and stable source of external development finance. In *Global development finance 2003, striving for development finance*. Washington, DC: The World Bank.

Ratha, D. K., Plaza, S., & Dervisevic, E. (2016). *Migration and remittances fact book 2016 (English)*. Washington, DC.: World Bank Group.

Rempel, H., & Lobdell, R. A. (1978). The role of urban-to-rural remittances in rural development. *The Journal of Development Studies, 14*(3), 324–341. https://doi.org/10.1080/00220387808421678.

Reuveny, R., & Li, Q. (2003). Economic openness, democracy, and income inequality: An empirical analysis. *Comparative Political Studies, 36*(5), 575–601.

Romer, D. (2006). *Advanced macroeconomics*. Mcgraw Hill Series Economics (4th ed.). New York: McGraw-Hill Education.

Roodman, D. (2009). A note on the theme of too many instruments. *Oxford Bulletin of Economics and Statistics, 71*(1), 135–158.

Rozelle, S., Taylor, J. E., & DeBrauw, A. (1999). Migration, remittances, and agricultural productivity in China. *American Economic Review, 89*(2), 287–291. https://doi.org/10.1257/aer.89.2.287.

Schultz, T. (1964). Transforming traditional agriculture. *The Economic Journal, 74*(296), 996. https://doi.org/10.2307/2228861.

Sevestre, P., & Trognon, A. (1985). A note on autoregressive error components models. *Journal of Econometrics, 28*(2), 231–245. https://doi.org/10.1016/0304-4076(85)90122-8.

Shapiro, A. F., & Mandelman, F. S. (2016). Remittances, entrepreneurship, and employment dynamics over the business cycle. *Journal of International Economics, 103*, 184–199.

Singh, R. J., Markus, H., & Kyung-woo, L. (2009). *Determinants and macroeconomic impact of remittances in sub-Saharan Africa* (IMF working paper WP/09/216).

Williams, K. (2017). Do remittances improve political institutions? Evidence from sub-Saharan Africa. *Economic Modelling, 61*, 65–75.

World Bank. (2018). *World development indicators*. Washington, DC: World Bank.

Yang, D. (2008). International migration, remittances, and household investment: Evidence from Philippine migrants' exchange rate shocks. *Economic Journal, 118*, 591–630.

Yang, D. (2011). Migrant remittances. *Journal of Economic Perspectives, 25*(3), 129–52. https://doi.org/10.1257/jep.25.3.129.

Zvezda, D. (2011). Emigration from the South Caucasus: Who goes abroad and what are the economic implications? *Post-Communist Economies, 23*(3), 377–398. https://doi.org/10.1080/14631377.2011.595135.

Electricity Access and Agricultural Productivity in Sub-Saharan Africa: Evidence from Panel Data

Oluwasola E. Omoju, Opeyemi N. Oladunjoye, Iyabo A. Olanrele, and Adedoyin I. Lawal

1 Introduction

The important role of the agriculture sector in sub-Sahara African (SSA) economies cannot be overemphasized because the region is largely recognized as agrarian with agriculture and natural resources usually the mainstay of the economies. The agricultural sector in SSA is important due to its role in economic activities, employment generation, food security, poverty reduction and rural economic transformation (Oyebola et al. 2019; Osabuohien et al. 2019). According to Organization for Economic Cooperation and Development/Food and Agricultural Organization ([OECD/FAO] 2016),

---

O. E. Omoju
National Institute for Legislative and Democratic Studies (National Assembly), Abuja, Nigeria

O. N. Oladunjoye
Department of Economics, Obafemi Awolowo University, Ile-Ife, Nigeria

I. A. Olanrele
Nigeria Institute of Social and Economic Research (NISER), Ibadan, Nigeria

A. I. Lawal (✉)
Department of Accounting and Finance, Landmark University, Omu-Aran, Nigeria

the agriculture sector in SSA accounts for an average of 15% of gross domestic products (GDP) in 2014, ranging from less than 3% in Botswana to over 50% in Chad. This underscores the limited diversification of the economic structure in some parts of the region, and high dependence on the sector. Similarly, the sector contributes about 56.7 and 57.1% of male and female employment, respectively, according to the World Bank's (2019) World Development Indicators (WDI). In addition, the sector is seen as a priority for poverty eradication, standard of living improvements, and structural transformation (Diao et al. 2010), as well as the attainment of the Sustainable Development Goals (SDGs) in the region.

Despite the criticality of the sector to attaining the development potentials of the region, agriculture productivity (measured as agriculture, forestry, and fishing value added as a percentage of GDP) has been declining over the years (see Fig. 1 in the Appendix). The absolute value of agriculture value added rose by 380.79% from $62.7 billion in 1981 to $301.2 billion in 2017, but its proportion as a percentage of GDP fell from 18.8 to 15.8% over the same period. Vast differences in agricultural productivity also exist among countries in the region, suggesting differences in governance structure, macroeconomic and agricultural policies, infrastructure development and institutional capabilities (OECD/FAO 2016). The experience of successful countries in terms of drivers of agricultural productivity can be useful for other countries in the region.

Several studies have been conducted on the underlying causes of declining agricultural productivity (Dar and Gowda 2013; Fugile and Rada 2013). Moreover, recent studies have focused on the impacts of specific infrastructure interventions on agricultural productivity (Knox et al. 2013).

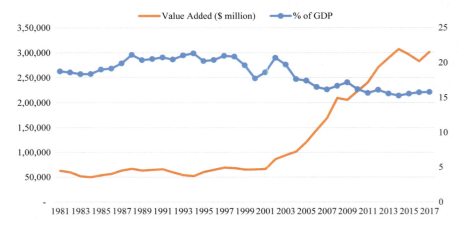

Fig. 1 Agriculture, fishing and forestry value added, 1981–2017 (*Source* The authors' using data from World Development Indicators [World Bank 2019])

Many of the studies on how improving electricity access influence agricultural productivity and rural development are focused on Asia (Fan et al. 2000, 2002, 2004; Khandker and Koolwal 2010). Among the few studies on sub-Sahara Africa such as the Energy Sector Management Assistance Program (ESMAP) (2007), Adu et al. (2018), and Mensah (2018), emphasis has always been on micro-level impact evaluations and household data (Bernard 2012), with limited studies on the macro-level impacts of electricity access on agricultural productivity in the region. Micro-level analyses of the impacts of electrification on agriculture are limited to specific agriculture or household welfare indicators, and do not provide an aggregate assessment of the impacts of electrification on the agriculture sector. Empirical studies on the macro-level analysis of the impact of electricity access on agricultural productivity, including those looking at the relative impact of urban and rural electrification in sub-Sahara Africa, are scanty. These are the gaps in the current literature that this study fills.

This study contributes to the literature in two ways. First, we examine the impact of electricity access on agricultural productivity in sub-Sahara Africa from a cross-country and macro perspective, as against the micro-level analysis and impact evaluation studies that are common in the literature. Micro-level analyses are focused on a small subset or indicator of the agriculture sector and fail to provide a comprehensive understanding of the impacts of electrification. Second, unlike the previous studies in the literature that examine the impact of aggregate electricity access on agricultural output and productivity, this study separately estimates the impacts of rural and urban electrification on agricultural productivity. The research questions for this study are as follows:

(i) What is the impact of electrification on agricultural productivity in sub-Sahara Africa?
(ii) Do rural and urban electrification have similar effects on agricultural productivity in the region?

The remainder of the chapter is structured as follows. Section 2 is the literature review while Sect. 3 focused on the theoretical framework, methodology and data sources. Section 4 presents and discusses the results while Sect. 5 concludes the paper and provides some policy implications.

2 Literature Review

The theoretical literature that governs this research is rooted in the growth hypothesis framework that stresses the positive effects of improved electricity supply/consumption on growth (You et al. 2019; Pavel et al. 2018). The theory stresses that rural electrification will affect growth through improved productivity in three aspects. First, when household electrification shortens time spent on collecting and preparing fuel, it increases the productive capacity of households via improved technology and market-based work (Trotter 2016; Onyeji et al. 2012). Second, access to electricity enhances the job creation potentials of the economy especially for the self-employed, and in particular among women (Dinkelman 2011; Grogan and Sadanand 2011; Asongu et al. 2019). Lastly, electrification can induce a shift from agro-allied jobs to non-agro-allied that relate to increase in productivity (Barron and Torero 2017; Singh and Vermaak 2018).

A plethora of studies have empirically investigated the impact of electricity on agricultural productivity in Africa and beyond. For instance, Scott et al. (2019) examined the impact of bioenergy development and electricity access on sustainable agricultural output in Denmark. They used a Global Bioenergy Partnership framework, which calibrates sixteen sustainability indicators subdivided into three key pillars of sustainability—environmental, social and economic over the period 2010–2015. Their results show that the provision of energy from both bioenergy and electricity offers some desirable benefits such as reduction in GHG emissions, income generation and jobs for the rural population, decrease in fossil fuels consumption and increased diversity of the national energy supply. The above can be related to the findings of Herrmann et al. (2018) for Malawi with respect to the existence of competition between bioenergy (biofuel feedstock from sugarcane) and food production.

Ozturk (2017) examined the relationship among food, energy and water resources for the economies of Botswana, Ethiopia, Kenya, South Africa, Sudan and Senegal based on data from 1980 to 2013. The study employed three separate panel analysis within a non-linear regression framework to investigate the food-energy-water nexus. The study observed that energy poverty in the sub-region significantly undermines agricultural sustainability endeavor.

Singh and Vermaak (2018) examined the impact of rural electrification on gender and labor market for two emerging economies of India and South Africa by employing two identification strategies: Propensity Score Matching and Panel Fixed Effects estimation techniques. The study noted that though electrification has the potential of inducing growth, evidence abounds to show that electrification can shift labor force from engaging in agro-allied activities to non-agro-allied activities. This is so as it offers rural households' opportunities to diversify away from agriculture by engaging in other non-agro-allied ventures (Oyebola et al. 2019). This implies that rural electrification can impact negatively on agricultural productivity.

Assunção et al. (2017) examined the impact of electrification on agricultural productivity and deforestation in Brazil. The study used county-level census data over five-year periods from 1970 to 2006 and employed instrumental variables technique. Agricultural productivity was mainly measured by crop production per hectare while electricity data is measured based on the location and date of construction of hydro-power plants and transmission substations. The study showed that electrification increased crop productivity enabled farmers to expand farming, and shift from land-intensive activities to capital- and labor-intensive activities.

Leon Esteban et al. (2018) assessed the impact of electricity access on health, education and agricultural productivity in rural areas of Colombia. Using data from a national agriculture census and three-stage least square method, the study found that electrification has a positive effect on agricultural productivity. Khandker and Koolwal (2010) found positive effect of electrification on agricultural prices in Bangladesh. But the study found a weak impact of electrification on agricultural productivity.

Series of studies on the impact of electrification on agricultural productivity with focus on Asia showed mixed results (Fan et al. 2000, 2002, 2004). While Fan et al. (2000) found limited impact of rural electrification on agricultural productivity in India, Fan et al. (2004) found investment in rural electrification to have the second-largest impacts on productivity in Thailand after agricultural research. On the extreme, Fan et al. (2002) did not find evidence of electrification effects on agricultural productivity in China.

The divergent findings on the impact of rural electrification partly depend on the dataset and econometric models and techniques used by the studies (Torero 2015). Some studies use data from household survey while others use secondary data. Several methods, ranging from fixed effects to instrumental variables and randomized control trials, have also been used in the literature.

The present study differs from the existing line in the literature in two major ways. We examine the impact of electricity access on agricultural productivity in sub-Sahara Africa from a cross-country and macro perspective, diverging from the existing literature which concentrates mainly on household data and micro-level analysis. And unlike the current literature, we estimate the differential impacts of rural and urban electricity access on agricultural productivity.

3   Theoretical Framework and Methodology

This study adopted the endogenous growth theory to investigate the impact of electricity access on agricultural productivity in SSA. This is explored through the production function where the aggregate output is a linear function of aggregate capital stock. The underlying assumption here is that electricity access has the capacity to have a greater influence on the efficiency of both capital and labor in the long run. As such, output is assumed to be an increasing function of aggregate capital given the level of technology and that it is a composite variable incorporating both physical and human capital.

Drawing from the theoretical framework, this study considered a simple *AK* model production function where aggregate output is a linear function of aggregate capital stock:

$$Y = AK \tag{1}$$

Where: Y is aggregate output, A is the efficiency of production (electricity access), K is volume of capital stock. Output per capital in Eq. (1) is given as:

$$\frac{Y}{L} ELA \cdot \frac{K}{L} \tag{2}$$

Where other parameters remained the same, except for ELECT, which is electricity access. Equation (3) represent the intensive form of Eq. (2) as follows:

$$y_t = (ELECT)k_t \tag{3}$$

The average and marginal product of capital in Eq. (3) are constant at the level $ELECT > 0$. Capital (k_t) in a broad sense can be decomposed into human capital (k_H^β) and the physical capital $\left(k_p^\psi\right)$ as stated by Lucas (1988).

$$\text{Thus}, k_t = \left(k_H^\beta, k_p^\psi\right) \tag{4}$$

Furthermore, physical capital is decomposed into domestic investment and foreign reserve accumulation, such that

$$k_p^\psi = f(DI, FDI)^\psi \tag{5}$$

If ψ is the element of the power of k (physical capital) and φ and θ are the elasticities of *DI (domestic investment)* and *FDI (foreign direct investment)*, therefore,

$$\varphi, \theta \epsilon \psi; \text{ then } k_p^\psi = (DI^\varphi, FDI^\theta) \tag{6}$$

Similarly, incorporating Eqs. (4) and (5) into Eq. (3) and substituting for k_p^ψ as presented in Eq. (6), we obtain

$$y_t = ELECTk_H^\beta DI_p^\varphi FDI_p^\theta \tag{7}$$

where $\beta, \varphi,$ and θ are elasticities of human capital, domestic capital stock and foreign direct investment.

Taking logarithms of Eq. (7), the study generated the following dynamic production function:

$$\ln y_t = \ln ELECT + \beta \ln k_H + \varphi \ln DI_P + \theta \ln FDI_P \tag{8}$$

The estimated derived equation is as follows:

$$\ln AGP_t = \beta_0 + \beta_1 \ln ELECT + \beta_2 \ln k_H + \beta_3 \ln DI_P + \beta_4 \ln FDI_P + X_i + \mu_t \tag{9}$$

Where (y_t) is the output indicator represented by agricultural productivity (*AGP*). The measure of agricultural productivity here adopted is the agricultural value added as share of GDP (*AGRVAGR*). *TELECT* is a measure of national electricity access, rural electrification is depicted by *ELECTR*, and urban electrification is denoted by *ELECTU*.[1] Capital (k_H) is human capital (labor force participation rate), (DI_P) is domestic investment and (FDI_P) is foreign direct investment as a share of GDP and X_i are other exogenous policy variables (lending rate and domestic credit to private sector as a share of GDP).[2] Therefore, Eq. (9) is the base line model.

Thus Eq. (9) becomes;

$$\ln AGP_{ijt} = \beta_0 + \beta_1 ELECT_{ijt} + \beta_2 \ln LFP_{ijt} + \beta_3 \ln DI_{ijt} + \beta_4 \ln FDI_{ijt} \\ + \beta_5 \ln LENDR_{ijt} + \beta_6 \ln DCPS + \mu_{it} \quad (10)$$

Where: Subscript i and j represent the countries in the SSA, t represents the time, β_0 represents the intercept while $\beta_1 \ldots \beta_6$ represent the coefficients of the explanatory variables.

The model a priori expectation are $\beta_1, \beta_2, \beta_3, \beta_4, \beta_6 > 0$, $\beta_5 < 0$. This implies that access to electricity, labor force participation rate, domestic investment, foreign direct investment and domestic credit to private sector are expected to have positive impact on agricultural productivity, except for lending rate that is expected to exert a negative effect.

The scope of the study covers SSA countries. Small-scale agricultural activities are predominant, contributing an average of about 15% of GDP. The 45 countries in this cross-country analysis are chosen based on data availability and are listed in the appendix (Appendix, Table 9). All dataset was collected from the World Development (WDI) of the World Bank (2019), and span from 1980 to 2017.

To estimate the model specified in Eq. (10), the various time series properties of the model were checked. This include the panel unit root tests (Levin, Lin and Chu [LLC], Im, Pesaran and Shin [IPS], Fisher's Panel ADF and PP, and Hadri LM), and the long-run cointegration of the series in the model. The Pedroni, Kao and Johansen-Fisher panel cointegration tests are used to ascertain the long run relationship among the variables. A panel regression analysis was employed to estimate objectives 1 and 2.

4 Presentation and Discussion of Results

This section discusses the various empirical findings of the study, with particular emphasis on the time series properties of the variables and the analysis of the estimated effects of electricity access on agricultural productivity in sub-Sahara Africa.

4.1 Panel Stationarity Tests

Since the characteristics of the 45 SSA countries involved in this study are likely to be homogenous in nature, there is the need to subject all the macroeconomic variables to unit root tests. The Levin, Lin and Chu (LLC) panel unit root test; Im, Pesaran and Shin (IPS) panel unit root test, Fisher's

Panel ADF and PP tests as well as Hadri LM test were used to investigate for the presence of unit root in the panel data. The lag length for each of the variable is automatically selected by Schwartz Information Criterion (SIC). The Newey-West method was equally applied to choose the optimal lag length. The macroeconomic variables subjected to panel unit root tests include national electricity access (TELECT), rural electrification (ELECTR), urban electrification (ELECTU), agricultural value added as a percentage of GDP (AGRVAGR), foreign direct investment (FDI), domestic credit to private sector (DCPS), lending rate (LENDR), private gross fixed capital formation (PGFCF) and labor force participation rate (LFP).

The results showed that the variables were strictly stationary at levels and after first differencing.[3] However, lending rate (LENDR) was observed to be stationary at second difference with the LLC test. The essence of the panel unit root test is to ascertain the order of integration of the macroeconomic variables used for this study which plays a pivotal role in model specification and the policy inferences.

4.2 Impact of Electricity Access on Agricultural Productivity

This section presents the various estimation results of the impact of national electricity access (*TELECT*) on agricultural value added as share of GDP growth rate, as well as other macroeconomic variables outlined in Sect. 3. This is done to achieve the stated objective 1 of the study.

4.2.1 Panel Cointegration Test

Having established the level of integration of the macroeconomic variables, the long-run cointegration relationship among the variables was determined. The Pedroni, Johansen-Fisher as well as Kao panel cointegration tests were employed for this purpose (Table 1). The cointegration tests showed that there is a long-run relationship among the variables. Specifically, the Pedroni cointegration test results showed that in all the 11 Pedroni's statistics, six significantly reject the null hypothesis of no cointegration (Part A). Hence, the presence of cointegration among the macroeconomic was established. On the other hand, the Johansen-Fisher cointegration test revealed the existence of at least five cointegration equations among the variables used in the study (Part B). Similarly, in Part C, the outcome of the Kao panel cointegration test reinforces the validity of the Pedroni cointegration test which established the existence of long-run co-movement among the variables used. This is because the Kao cointegration test which is a residual-based test revealed that the panel residual of the variables used is negative and statistically significant.

In selecting between two alternative models in estimating the effects of electricity access on agricultural productivity, the Hausmann test based on the fixed and the random effects models was adopted[4] (see Green 2012). The probability of the Hausmann test (0.8830) is higher than the conventional 5% level of significance (Appendix, Table 7), leading to the non-rejection of

Table 1 Panel cointegration tests

Part A: Pedroni residual cointegration test

Series: AGRVAGR DCPS TELECT FDI LENDR LFP PGFCF

	Statistic	Prob.	Weighted statistic	Prob.
Panel v-statistic	−1.040	0.851	−3.850	0.999
Panel rho-statistic	−0.556	0.289	1.332	0.908
Panel PP-statistic	−30.288	0.000	−26.40	0.000
Panel ADF-statistic	−8.795	0.000	−6.305	0.000
Alternative hypothesis: individual AR coefs. (between-dimension)				
Group rho-statistic	3.871	0.999		
Group PP-statistic	−40.582	0.000		
Group ADF-statistic	−4.916	0.000		

Part B: Johansen-Fisher cointegration test

Series: AGRVAGR DCPS TELECT FDI LENDR LFP PGFCF

Hypothesized No. of CE(s)	Fisher Stat.* (from trace test)	Prob.	Fisher Stat.* (from Max-Eigen test)	Prob.
None	341.1	0.0000	292.1	0.0000
At most 1	225.5	0.0000	117.0	0.0000
At most 2	131.3	0.0000	98.85	0.0000
At most 3	65.33	0.0000	53.45	0.0000
At most 4	58.10	0.0000	49.98	0.0000
At most 5	34.15	0.0052	27.90	0.0325
At most 6	25.60	0.0599	25.60	0.0599

*Probabilities are computed using asymptotic Chi-square distribution

Part C: Kao residual cointegration tests

Series: AGRVAGR DCPS TELECT FDI LENDR LFP PGFCF

	t-Statistic probability	t-Statistic probability
ADF	−2.116476	0.0172
Residual variance	119.4665	
HAC variance	28.64821	

Source Authors' computations

the null hypothesis. Consequently, the conclusion that the SSA economies are not homogenous was rejected, while the random effects model was employed for estimating the effect of electricity access on agricultural productivity in Sub-Sahara Africa.

Table 2 Regression results—impact of electricity access on agricultural productivity

Dependent variable: AGRVAGR

Variable	Coefficient	Std. Error	t-Statistic	Prob.
C	−13.73084	8.199556	−1.674583	0.0947
LOG(TELECT)	0.845395	0.336076	2.515490	0.0122
LOG(DCPS)	−1.051972	0.547372	−1.921861	0.0552
LOG(FDI)	−0.009626	0.026421	−0.364317	0.7158
LOG(LENDR)	−0.606445	0.709274	−0.855022	0.3930
LOG(LFP)	4.266982	1.855081	2.300160	0.0219
LOG(PGFCF)	0.253531	0.775031	0.327123	0.7437
Effects specification				
			SD	Rho
Cross-section random			0.895910	0.0154
Idiosyncratic random			7.166808	0.9846

Source Authors' computations

4.2.2 Random Effects Regression

This section presents the empirical estimates of the impact of electricity access on agricultural productivity as presented in Table 2.

National electricity access (*TELECT*) is positive and significantly related to agricultural productivity. Specifically, a 1% increase in level of electricity access will lead to about 0.84% increase in the level of agricultural productivity in sub-Sahara Africa. The results of the study with respect to the positive impact of electrification on agricultural productivity is in line with a priori expectation and support earlier findings by studies such as Assunção et al. (2017), Khandker et al. (2009, 2012). Providing electricity access enables farm mechanization, creates value-added product from agricultural commodity, preserves agricultural commodities for selling in higher-value markets, etc.

Furthermore, labor force participation (*lnLFP*) has a positive significant effect on agricultural productivity. This suggests that human capital development is supportive of improvement in agricultural productivity in SSA. All the other variables do not have a significant effect on agricultural productivity.

4.3 Differential Impacts of Urban and Rural Electrification on Agricultural Productivity

The second objective of the study is to estimate the differential impacts of urban and rural electrification on agricultural productivity. This and other relevant analyses are herein discussed.

4.3.1 Panel Cointegration Tests

The long-run relationship of the model is presented in Table 3. The Johansen-Fisher cointegration test (Part A) revealed the existence of at least five cointegration equations among the variables. On the other hand, the

Table 3 Panel cointegration tests

Part A: Johansen-Fisher panel cointegration test

Series: AGRVAGR DCPS FDI LENDR LFP PGFCF ELECR ELECU

Hypothesized No. of CE(s)	Fisher Stat.* (from trace test)	Prob.	Fisher Stat.* (from Max-Eigen test)	Prob.
None	178.7	0.0000	73.89	0.0000
At most 1	107.1	0.0000	100.8	0.0000
At most 2	127.5	0.0000	119.1	0.0000
At most 3	93.69	0.0000	87.77	0.0000
At most 4	48.26	0.0000	43.58	0.0000
At most 5	47.84	0.0000	40.51	0.0001
At most 6	27.85	0.0058	19.57	0.0756
At most 7	26.54	0.0090	26.54	0.0090

*Probabilities are computed using asymptotic Chi-square distribution

Part B: Kao residual cointegration test

Series: AGRVAGR DCPS FDI LENDR LFP PGFCF ELECR ELECTU

	t-Statistic probability	t-Statistic probability
ADF	−2.727882	0.0032
Residual variance	124.2203	
HAC variance	29.58735	

Source Authors' computations

Kao cointegration test (Part B) which is a residual-based test revealed that the panel residual of the variables used in the study is negative and statistically significant ($t=-2.72$; $p<0.05$). The outcome of the Kao panel cointegration test reinforces the validity of the Johansen-Fisher cointegration test. This established the existence of a long-run relationship of at least five equations among the variables.

The Hausmann test was used to determine the viability of either the fixed or random effect model in estimating the differential impacts of rural or urban electricity access on agricultural productivity (see Appendix, Table 8). The probability of the chi-square statistics (0.9524) is higher than the conventional 5% significance level, leading to the conclusion that the random effects model is the appropriate model in this regard.[5]

4.3.2 Differential Impacts of Rural and Urban Electricity Access on Agricultural Productivity

This section presents the empirical estimates of the impacts of rural and urban electricity access on agricultural productivity as presented in Table 4. The study found that, between the two variants of electricity access, only the coefficient of urban electricity access *(lnELECTU)* turns out positive

Table 4 Random effects model of the differential impacts of rural and urban electricity access on agricultural productivity

Dependent variable: AGRVAGR

Variable	Coefficient	Std. Error	t-Statistic	Prob.
C	−14.36497	8.504860	−1.689031	0.0920
LOG(ELECTR)	0.185863	0.287062	0.647466	0.5177
LOG(ELECTU)	0.620906	0.302125	2.055131	0.0405
LOG(DCPS)	−1.167042	0.613893	−1.901051	0.0580
LOG(FDI)	−0.015828	0.027780	−0.569758	0.5692
LOG(LENDR)	−0.028638	0.054758	−0.522989	0.6013
LOG(LFP)	3.613270	1.977815	1.826900	0.0685
LOG(PGFCF)	1.263011	0.957008	1.319750	0.1877
Effects specification				
			SD	Rho
Cross-section random			0.273213	0.0014
Idiosyncratic random			7.360761	0.9986

Source Authors' computations

and significant. A 1% increase in the level of urban electricity access causes agricultural productivity to rise by about 0.62% in sub-Sahara Africa, suggesting that providing electricity access in urban areas may facilitate agricultural productivity.

The effect of rural electricity access, though correctly signed at about 0.19%, turns out insignificant. The insignificant impact of rural electricity access on agricultural productivity in sub-Sahara Africa goes further to reveal the level of weak infrastructural development, like rural electrification, and the limited impact on agricultural productivity. Although this result is contrary to expectation as rural electrification is expected to impact productivity in rural areas where they are implemented, it is in line with Barnes and Binswanger (1986) which found that the impact of rural electrification on agricultural productivity were not as huge as anticipated by planners.

However, this could suggest that rural electrification leads to movement of skilled workers and other resources from agriculture sector towards blue and white-collar jobs, corroborating earlier findings by Akpandjar and Kitchens (2017). Furthermore, the importance of electrification to the agriculture sector in rural regions may not be overly pronounced due to affordability issues and limited productive use of electricity in rural areas. This has been initially suggested by Chakravorty et al. (2014) and Grimm et al. (2016). According to the studies, providing electrification is not only the main issue, rather it is the reliability of supply and the ability of households to afford it (Chakravorty et al. 2014; Grimm et al. 2016). Thus, efforts should be made to ensure that farmers and rural dwellers have access to electricity and are able to use it for productive purposes.

5 Implications of Findings and Conclusion

Despite the important role of the agriculture sector in African economies, the sector's value added as share of GDP has been declining over the years, raising concerns about the challenges to rural development, poverty reduction and attainment of the SDGs in the region. Various studies have attempted to understand the reasons for the decline as well as policy interventions that could enhance the performance of the sector.

This study examines the impact of electricity access on agricultural productivity in sub-Sahara Africa. Specifically, it analyses how national, rural and urban electricity access influence agricultural productivity using panel data regression methods. The data for the study was obtained from the World Development Indicator while panel cointegration techniques and random effects were used to analyze the data.

The study finds that improving national electricity access has positive and significant effects on agricultural productivity in sub-Sahara Africa. The results also show that urban electricity access has a positive and significant impact on agricultural productivity, while rural electrification does not. This implies that policymakers in the region should focus on improving overall electrification to boost agricultural productivity and economic development. The policy narrative of prioritizing rural electrification to promote agricultural and rural development may be inadequate.

In terms of policy, rather than prioritizing rural electrification which solely focuses on the production side of the agricultural value chain, electricity infrastructure intervention in sub-Sahara Africa should consider the entire agricultural value chain. Recent electrification projects in sub-Sahara Africa have emphasized the importance of rural electrification for agriculture and rural development as well as poverty reduction. While this is a noble idea, agricultural productivity would be largely enhanced if the higher ends of the value chain such as processing and marketing are supported with adequate electricity infrastructure.

One of the main limitations of this study is data availability. The study was confronted with the problem of data unavailability for some variables in most of the countries in sub-Sahara Africa which resulted in the estimation of an unbalance panel data. Data on other agriculture-related variables such as government expenditure on the agriculture sector and institutional policies are not available and therefore excluded from the model. Going forward, we believe the analysis will be enriched by using more sophisticated techniques such as Generalized Method of Moments (GMM), which can address issues of potential endogeneity inherent in the model.

Future studies on the subject can take on these limitations. Besides, future studies should also investigate the transmission mechanism or channels through which electrification impact agricultural productivity. There are other important questions that require further research going forward. What kind of electricity access interventions/projects brings the most benefits for agricultural productivity? How can farmers be encouraged to use electricity more productively? How long does it take for the impact of electricity access on agricultural productivity to take effect? What complementary policies would enhance the impact of electricity access on agricultural productivity? Future research should endeavor to look at these questions to advance the frontiers of research on the subject.

Notes

1. National electricity access (TELECT) is the electricity indicator adopted in analysing objective 1. At a disaggregated level, objective 2 employed urban electricity access (ELECTU) and rural electricity access (ELECTR) to analyse the differential effects of electricity on agricultural productivity.
2. Domestic private investment is measured by private gross fixed capital formation as share of GDP (PGFCF).
3. See Appendix, Tables 5 and 6.
4. The null hypothesis is that the preferred model is the former, and the alternative hypothesis is the latter. This takes the form of comparing the parameter estimates of fixed effects with the random effects model (Green 2012) (see Appendix, Table 7). The conclusion that SSA economies are not homogenous was rejected. Thus, the random effects model was employed for estimating the effect of electricity access on agricultural productivity in Sub-Sahara Africa.
5. The null hypothesis of no individual effects was tested against the alternative hypothesis that individual effects are not equal to zero. The probability of the Hausmann test ($p>0.05$) was observed leading to the acceptance the null hypothesis at approximately 1% level of significance (see Table 8 in the Appendix). Therefore, the conclusion that SSA economies are not homogenous was rejected.

Appendix

See Fig. 1, Tables 5, 6, 7, 8 and 9.

Table 5 Panel unit root test at level

Variable	Levin, Lin and Chu test			Im, Pesaran and Shin test		Fisher ADF test			Fisher PP test			Hadri LM test	
	Individual intercept	Individual intercept with trend	None	Individual intercept	Individual intercept with trend	Individual intercept	Individual intercept with trend	None	Individual intercept	Individual intercept with trend	None	Individual Intercept	Individual Intercept with Trend
Ln(TELECT)	−16.58	−7.92	2.84	−10.44	−11.66	−8.88	−10.07	12.83	−14.63	−26.12	13.89	22.37	17.89
(p-Value)	(0.000)	(0.000)	(0.990)	(0.000)	(0.000)	(0.000)	(0.000)	(1.000)	(0.000)	(0.000)	(1.000)	(0.000)	(0.000)
Ln(ELECTR)	−6.46	−5.04	−0.54	−3.14	−8.96	−2.05	−8.00	8.57	−8.11	−26.16	6.56	20.77	14.53
(p-Value)	(0.000)	(0.000)	(0.293)	(0.000)	(0.000)	(0.020)	(0.000)	(1.000)	(0.000)	(0.000)	(1.000)	(1.000)	(1.000)
Ln(ELECTU)	−6.72	3.77	−0.82	−4.37	−6.62	−3.75	−7.09	11.33	−7.91	−20.23	14.50	22.10	14.38
(p-Value)	(0.000)	(0.999)	(0.204)	(0.000)	(0.000)	(0.001)	(0.000)	(1.000)	(0.000)	(0.000)	(1.000)	(0.000)	(0.000)
AGRVAGR	−16.95	−12.27	−19.58	−22.43	−15.71	−20.65	−17.91	−19.37	−27.72	−39.18	−31.32	2.08	12.21
(p-Value)	(0.000)	(0.000)	(0.000)	(0.000)	(0.000)	(0.000)	(0.000)	(0.000)	(0.000)	(0.000)	(0.000)	(0.019)	(0.000)
Ln(DCPS)	−2.02	−2.14	2.08	−0.02	−0.51	0.26	0.09	3.61	−0.18	0.45	4.62	14.39	14.56
(p-Value)	(0.021)	(0.016)	(0.981)	(0.493)	(0.304)	(0.604)	(0.538)	(0.999)	(0.429)	(0.676)	(1.000)	(0.0000)	(0.1656)
LENDR	5.42	17.17	0.14	−2.61	−2.86	−2.77	−2.72	0.85	−6.38	−5.12	−1.37	7.65	5.25
(p-Value)	(1.000)	(1.000)	(0.559)	(0.004)	(0.002)	(0.002)	(0.002)	(0.805)	(0.000)	(0.000)	(0.080)	(0.000)	(0.000)
Ln(LFP)	−7.00	−5.82	−1.84	−3.26	−4.26	−2.83	−3.68	0.75	5.72	4.16	−3.58	15.95	9.79
(p-Value)	(0.000)	(0.000)	(0.033)	(0.000)	(0.000)	(0.002)	(0.000)	(0.776)	(1.000)	(1.000)	(0.000)	(0.000)	(0.000)
FDI	−5.27	−5.81	−7.16	−6.39	−6.78	−6.44	−6.58	−7.20	−9.76	−10.60	−9.64	7.65	5.25
(p-Value)	(0.000)	(0.000)	(0.000)	(0.000)	(0.000)	(0.000)	(0.000)	(0.000)	(0.000)	(0.000)	(0.000)	(0.000)	(0.000)
PGFCF	−2.97	−3.01	−1.73	−2.56	−3.20	−2.58	−3.83	−0.05	−4.26	−5.53	0.89	9.67	13.00
(p-Value)	(0.001)	(0.001)	(0.045)	(0.005)	(0.000)	(0.004)	(0.000)	(0.479)	(0.000)	(0.000)	(0.814)	(0.000)	(0.000)

Source Authors' computation (2019)

Table 6 Panel unit root test at first difference

Variable	Levin, Lin and Chu test			Im, Pesaran and Shin test		Fisher ADF test			Fisher PP test			Hadri LM test	
	Individual intercept	Individual intercept with trend	None	Individual intercept	Individual intercept with trend	Individual intercept	Individual intercept with trend	None	Individual intercept	Individual intercept with trend	None	Individual Intercept	Individual Intercept with Trend
Ln(TELECT)	–	–	–	–	–	–	–	–	–	–	−18.86	–	–
(p-Value)	–	–	–	–	–	–	–	–	–	–	(0.000)	–	–
Ln(ELECTR)	–	−17.10	–	–	–	–	–	−21.82	–	–	−32.78	–	–
(p-Value)	–	–	–	–	–	–	–	(0.000)	–	–	(0.000)	–	–
Ln(ELECTU)	–	−24.01	−20.01	–	–	–	–	−20.61	–	–	–	–	–
(p-Value)	–	(0.000)	(0.000)	–	–	–	–	(0.000)	–	–	–	–	–
AGRVAGR	–	–	–	–	–	–	–	–	–	–	–	–	–
(p-Value)	–	–	–	–	–	–	–	–	–	–	–	–	–
Ln(DCPS)	–	–	−25.20	−17.79	−13.66	−16.99	−14.11	−22.46	−25.47	−29.48	−32.95	1.82	5.73
(p-Value)	–	–	(0.000)	(0.000)	(0.000)	(0.000)	(0.000)	(0.000)	(0.000)	(0.000)	(0.000)	(0.030)	(0.000)
LENDR	−11.96**	−12.09**	−39.21**	–	–	–	–	−21.45	–	–	–	–	–
(p-Value)	(0.000)	(0.000)	(0.000)	–	–	–	–	(0.000)	–	–	–	–	–
Ln(LFP)	–	–	–	–	–	–	–	−9.59	−5.34	−2.65	–	–	–
(p-Value)	–	–	–	–	–	–	–	(0.000)	(0.000)	(0.000)	–	–	–
FDI	–	–	–	–	–	–	–	–	–	–	–	–	–
(p-Value)	–	–	–	–	–	–	–	–	–	–	–	–	–
PGFCF	–	–	–	–	–	–	–	−21.09	–	–	−33.65	–	–
(p-Value)	–	–	–	–	–	–	–	(0.000)	–	–	(0.000)	–	–

Source Authors' computation (2019)

Table 7 Correlated random effects—Hausmann test

Correlated random effects—Hausmann test
Test cross-section random effects

Test summary	Chi-Sq. statistic	Chi-Sq. d.f.	Prob.
Cross-section random	2.367244	6	0.8830

Cross-section random effects test comparisons

Variable	Fixed	Random	Var (Diff.)	Prob.
LOG(TELECT)	1.061537	0.845395	0.117772	0.5288
LOG(DCPS)	−0.709840	−1.051972	0.675997	0.6773
FDI	−0.021544	−0.009626	0.000466	0.5810
LOG(LENDR)	0.124702	−0.606445	2.090123	0.6130
LOG(LFP)	−1.366746	4.266982	159.248301	0.6553
LOG(PGFCF)	−0.976535	0.253531	1.188755	0.2592

Source Authors' computation (2019)

Table 8 Correlated random effects–Hausmann test

Correlated random effects—Hausmann test

Test summary	Chi-Sq. statistic	Chi-Sq. df	Prob.
Cross-section random	2.128974	7	0.9524

Cross-section random effects test comparisons

Variable	Fixed	Random	Var (Diff.)	Prob.
LOG(ELECTR)	0.120760	0.185863	0.332356	0.9101
LOG(ELECTU)	0.740017	0.620906	0.312291	0.8312
LOG(DCPS)	−0.380373	−1.167042	1.328323	0.4949
FDI	−0.021210	−0.015828	0.000644	0.8320
LENDR	−0.009439	−0.028638	0.005306	0.7921
LOG(LFP)	−4.914742	3.613270	202.202269	0.5487
LOG(PGFCF)	−0.140974	1.263011	1.687699	0.2798

Source Authors' computation (2019)

Table 9 List of countries in the analysis

S/N	Country	S/N	Country
1	Benin	24	Rwanda
2	Burkina Faso	25	Seychelles
3	Cape Verde	26	Somalia
4	Cote d'Ivoire	27	Sudan
5	The Gambia	28	Swaziland
6	Ghana	29	Tanzania
7	Guinea	30	Uganda
8	Guinea-Bissau	31	Zambia
9	Liberia	32	Zimbabwe
10	Mali	33	Djibouti
11	Niger	34	Ethiopia
12	Nigeria	35	Lesotho
13	Senegal	36	Mozambique
14	Sierra Leone	37	Mauritius
15	Togo	38	Mauritania
16	Angola	39	Malawi
17	Botswana	40	Madagascar
18	Cameroon	41	Kenya
19	Burundi	42	Sao Tome and Principe
20	Central African Republic	43	South Africa
21	Chad	44	Eritrea
22	Comoros	45	Gabon
23	Namibia		

References

Adu, G., Dramani, J. B., & Oteng-Abayie, E. F. (2018). *Powering the powerless: Economic impact of rural electrification in Ghana*. Final Report No. E-33415-GHA-2. International Growth Center, UK.

Akpandjar, G., & Kitchens, C. (2017). From darkness to light: The effect of electrification in Ghana, 2000–2010. *Economic Development and Cultural Change, 66*(1), 31–54.

Asongu, S.A., Efobi, U.R., Tanakem, B.V. & Osabuohien, E. (2019). Globalisation and female economic participation in sub-Saharan Africa. *Gender Issues*. https://doi.org/10.1007/s12147-019-09233-3.

Assunção, J., Lipscomb, M., Mobarak, A. M., & Szerman, D. (2017). *Agricultural productivity and deforestation in Brazil*. Working Paper. USA: Virginia University.

Barnes, D. F., & Binswanger, H. P. (1986). Impact of rural electrification and infrastructure on agricultural changes, 1966–1980. *Economic and Political Weekly, 21*(1), 26–34.

Barron, M., & Torero, M. (2017). Household electrification and indoor air pollution. *Journal of Environmental Economics and Management, 86*(C), 81–92. https://doi.org/10.1016/j.jeem.2017.07.007.

Bernard, T. (2012). Impact analysis of rural electrification projects in sub-Sahara Africa. *The World Bank Research Observer, 27*(1), 33–51.

Chakravorty, U., Pelli, M., & Marchand, B. U. (2014). Does the quality of electricity matter? Evidence from rural India. *Journal of Economic Behavior and Organisation, 107*, 228–247.

Dar, W. D., & Gowda, C. L. L. (2013). Declining agricultural productivity and global food security. *Journal of Crop Improvement, 27*(2), 242–254.

Diao, X., Hzell, P., & Thurlow, J. (2010). The role of agriculture in African development. *World Development, 38*(10), 1375–1383.

Dinkelman, T. (2011). The effects of rural electrification on employment: New evidence from South Africa. *American Economic Review, 101*, 3078–3108.

ESMAP. (2007). *Maximisation des retombe´es de l'electricite´ en zones rurales: Application au cas du Senegal* (ESMAP Technical Paper 109/07). Washington, DC: World Bank.

Fan, S., Hazell, P., & Thorat, S. (2000). Government spending, growth, and poverty in rural India. *American Journal of Agricultural Economics, 82*(4), 1038–1051.

Fan, S., Jitsuchon, S., & Methakunnavut, N. (2004). *The importance of public investment for reducing rural poverty in middle-income countries: The case of Thailand* (DSGD Discussion Paper 7). Washington, DC: International Food Policy Research Institute.

Fan, S., Zhang, L., & Zhang, X. (2002). *Growth, inequality, and poverty in rural China: The role of public investment* (Research Report 125). Washington, DC: International Food Policy Research Institute.

Fugile, K. O., & Rada, N. E. (2013). *Resources, policies and agricultural productivity in sub-Sahara Africa* (Economic Research Report No. 145). Economic Research Service, United States Department of Agriculture.

Green, H. (2012). *Econometric analysis* (7th ed.). Upper Saddle River, NJ: Prentice Hall.

Grimm, M., Munyehirwe, A., Peters, J., & Sievert, M. (2016). A first step up the energy ladder? Low cost solar kits and household's welfare in rural Rwanda. *World Bank Economic Review, 31*(3), 1–25.

Grogan, L., & Sadanand, A. (2011). Rural electrification and employment in poor countries: Evidence from Nicaragua. *World Development, 43*, 252–265.

Herrmann, R., Jumbe, C., Bruentrup, M., & Osabuohien, E. (2018, July). Competition between biofuel feedstock and food production: Empirical evidence from sugarcane outgrower settings in Malawi. *Biomass and Bioenergy, 114*, 100–111.

Khandker, S. R., Barnes, D. F., & Samad, H. A. (2012). The welfare impacts of rural electrification in Bangladesh. *The Energy Journal, 33*(1), 187–206.

Khandker, S. R., Barnes, D. F., Samad, H. A., & Minh H. N. (2009). *Welfare impacts of rural electrification: Evidence from Vietnam* (Policy Research Working Paper 5057). The World Bank.

Khandker, S. R., & Koolwal, G. B. (2010). How infrastructure and financial institutions affect rural income and poverty: Evidence from Bangladesh. *Journal of Development Studies, 46*(6), 1109–1137.

Knox, J., Daccache, A., & Hess, T. (2013). *What is the impact of infrastructural investments in roads, electricity and irrigation on agricultural productivity?* Systematic Review CEE 11-007, Collaboration for Environmental Evidence and DFID.

Leon Esteban, A. F., Kafarov, V., Guerrero, I., Cortes, A., Rosso Ceron, A. M., & Duarte, M. M. (2018). Assessment of access to electricity and the health, education and agricultural productivity effects in rural areas of Colombia. *Chemical Engineering Transactions, 70*, 1219–1224. https://doi.org/10.3303/CET1870204.

Lucas, R. (1988). On the mechanics of economic development. *Journal of Monetary Economics, 22*, 3–42.

Mensah, J. T. (2018). *Jobs! Electricity shortages and unemployment in Africa. Background paper to the "Regional Study on Electricity Access in Sub-Sahara Africa"*. The World Bank.

OECD/FAO. (2016). Agriculture in sub-Sahara Africa: Prospects and challenges for the next decade. In *OECD-FAO agriculture outlook 2016–2025*. Paris: OECD Publishing.

Onyeji, I., Bazilian, M., & Nussbaumer, P. (2012). Contextualizing electricity access in sub-Sahara Africa. *Energy for Sustainable Development, 16*(4), 520–527. https://doi.org/10.1016/j.esd.2012.08.007.

Osabuohien, E., Efobi, U. R., Herrmann, R., & Gitau, C. M. (2019). Female labor outcomes and large-scale agricultural land investments: Macro-micro evidence from Tanzania. *Land Use Policy, 82*, 716-728. https://doi.org/10.1016/j.landusepol.2019.01.005.

Oyebola, P. O., Osabuohien, E., & Obasaju, B. (2019). Employment and income effects of Nigeria's agricultural transformation agenda. *African Journal of Economic and Management Studies*. https://doi.org/10.1108/AJEMS-12-2018-0402.

Ozturk, I. (2017). The dynamic relationship between agricultural sustainability and food- energy-water poverty in a panel of selected sub-Sahara African countries. *Energy Policy, 107*, 289–299. https://doi.org/10.1016/j.enpol.2017.04.048.

Pavel, A., Moldovan, B., Neamtu, B., & Hintea, C. (2018). Are investments in basic infrastructure the magic wand to boost the local economy of rural communities from Romania? *Sustainability, 10*(3384), 1–32.

Scott, N., Ravn, J., Stupak, I., & Jørgensen, U. (2019). Dynamic sustainability assessment of heat and electricity production based on agricultural crop residues in Denmark. *Journal of Cleaner Production, 213*, 491–507. https://doi.org/10.1016/j.jclepro.2018.12.19.

Singh, S., & Vermaak, C. (2018). Rural electrification, gender and the labor market: A cross-country study of India and South Africa. *World Development, 109*, 346–359. https://doi.org/10.1016/j.worlddev.2018.05.016.

Torero, M. (2015). The impact of rural electrification: Challenges and ways forward. *Revue D'économie Du Développement, 23*, 49–75.

Trotter, P. A. (2016). Rural electrification, electrification inequality and democratic institutions in sub-Sahara Africa. *Energy for Sustainable Development, 34*, 111–129. https://doi.org/10.1016/j.esd.2016.07.008.

You, J., Kontoleon, A., & Wang, S. (2019). Identifying a sustained pathway to multi-dimensional poverty reduction: Evidence from two Chinese provinces. *The Journal of Development Studies, 55*(1), 137–158.

World Bank. (2019). *World Development Indicators* (online database). Washington, DC: The World Bank.

Beyond the Farm Gate: Can Social Capital Help Smallholders to Overcome Constraints in the Agricultural Value Chain in Africa?

Oluwaseun Kolade, Oluwasoye Mafimisebi, and Oluwakayode Aluko

1 Introduction

Majority of scholarly studies on smallholder agriculture typically focus on factors influencing productivity at the farm gate. As such, studies have focused mainly on the impact of technological innovations on conditions and factors of agricultural production (see for example, Muzari et al. 2012; Geta et al. 2013; Folberth et al. 2014; Abate et al. 2015; Oyebola et al. 2019). Scholars have addressed concerns about soil productivity and wider environmental implications, as well as the creation of high yield varieties of crops and animal breeds for improved productions (Feder and Umali 1993; Kebede et al. 1990; Knowler and Bradshaw 2007). However, it is increasingly recognised that technologies aimed at increasing yield and productivity are limited with regard to their overall impact on livelihoods of smallholders. It is possible for farmers to significantly improve farm outputs as a result of technology adoption, without achieving proportionate increase in profit and income. Farmers in

---

O. Kolade (✉) · O. Mafimisebi · O. Aluko
Leicester Castle Business School, De Montfort University, Leicester, UK
e-mail: seun.kolade@dmu.ac.uk

O. Mafimisebi
e-mail: oluwasoye.mafimisebi@dmu.ac.uk

O. Aluko
e-mail: oluwakayode.aluko@dmu.ac.uk

developing countries have spoken about severe losses incurred at harvest time, as a result of failure to transport their produce to the market, and lack of capacity to store and process raw produce (Kolade and Harpham 2014; Kolade et al. 2014).

As a result of the above concerns, there is increasing interest among scholars and practitioners to explore constraints faced by smallholders beyond the farm gate, and what technological, institutional and practical supports can be used for smallholders to benefit more from the agricultural value chain. Researchers have observed that poverty reduction interventions targeted at smallholder farmers must include not only the goal of enhanced productivity, but also the need to improve their access to markets (Cavatassi et al. 2011; Fischer and Qaim 2012; Markelova et al. 2009). However, there is a need for better understanding of the challenges of farmers' participation in organised value chains (Briones 2015). These challenges include high transaction costs associated with the production, quality standard requirements and delivery for high-value markets (Cavatassi et al. 2011); lack of information on prices and technologies; lack of connections to established market actors (Markelova et al. 2009), and highly expensive third-party certifications (Barrett et al. 2002). Several scholars have argued that these challenges can be mitigated by farmers' collective action in cooperatives and producer groups (Fischer and Qaim 2012; Markelova et al. 2009). This chapter brings together a broad spectrum of scholarly interests with a view to synthesising a new framework to analyse the challenges and opportunities for smallholders in the value chain. The rest of the chapter is organised as follows. First, we highlight the impact of technological innovations on farm productivity review constraints to smallholder participation in the agricultural value chain. We then go on to examine the role of social capital in overcoming these barriers to smallholders in the value chain. We conclude with a framework that captures the interactions between various forms of social capital and constraints to farmers in the value chain.

2 Technological Innovations, Productivity and Value Addition in Smallholder Agriculture

2.1 Impact of Technological Innovations on Farm Productivity

Agricultural innovations can be classified by form, by impact on economic agents, or by embeddedness in goods and products. This section discusses the impact of technological innovation on farm productivity, that is, those that fall mainly within the groups of yield increasing and cost-reducing innovations. These include ICT, mechanical, biotechnological and chemical innovations that help farmer to optimise input and maximise output at the farm gate. Sunding and Zilberman (2000) proposed a classification based on three categories: form, impacts on economic agents, and embodiments in goods and products. The form category include mechanical innovations such as tractor combines, biological and biotechnological innovations, chemical innovations, agronomic innovations, and informational innovations. Based on the impacts on economic agents, agricultural innovations are divided into yield increasing, cost-reducing, quality-enhancing, risk-reducing and environmental-protection increasing innovations. Finally, on the basis of embodiment in goods and products, there are two types: embodied and disembodied innovations.

Ogutu et al. (2014) examined the impact of ICT-based Market information System (MIS) on farm productivity in Kenya. Their research highlighted limited access to finance as a limiting factor to farmers' willingness to engage with innovation and technology that could improve their farm productivity. Using a robust set of data from participating and non-participating farmers in a World Bank sponsored ICT-MIS farm project, they examined the impact of the adoption of technological innovation on farm productivity. Their research identified a significant number of advantages for farmers who engaged with this technology. These advantages include increased farm input such as increased purchase of seed and fertiliser indicating improved resources utilisation and efficiency which were in agreement with (Kiiza et al. 2011). Furthermore, participating farmers also experienced increased output in the form of increased value of output per man-day coupled with reduced total labour per acre when compared with non-participants. Other benefits harnessed by the participating farmers include reduced transaction cost and time leading to increased commercialisation hence enabling these farmers to better participate in the market economy. The research also highlighted need for further dissemination of this technology citing its capacity to not only enhance the overall productivity of small-hold farmers but also its ability to better include them in the economy while generating better value for them.

Aker (2008) examined the impact of the introduction of new search technology on price dispersion of grains in Niger. Using two robust datasets of primary and secondary data covering prices, transaction costs, agricultural production and rainfall as well as time-series data on gas prices, cell phone coverage, road quality the research included 395 traders across 35 markets. Their findings suggested a negative relationship between cell phone introduction and reduced-price dispersion with a significant 21% reduction in price dispersion in markets with cell phone coverage compared to those without. Furthermore, there were even stronger effects for markets that were further apart, and vice versa meaning the further apart that markets were, the greater influence of the cell phone introduction on price dispersion reduction; similar results were identified for markets with bad road networks. The research identified that on the initial introduction of cell phones there wasn't any significant influence however, this changed with increased coverage and began to diminish when market coverage reached about 75%. The research provides "empirical evidence of the importance of information for market performance and welfare, suggesting that access to information particularly via information technology - can have important policy implications" (Aker 2008, p. 40). The research highlighted that little attention is paid to information technology on comparison to other basic human needs highlighting the tremendous contribution of access to information as critical to helping to address other plaguing human issues especially food availability.

Okello et al. (2010) examined the contribution of new technology models especially mobile phones to smallholder's farmers' productivity and welfare. This has been a particularly increasing trend in developing economies. A number of studies (Aker 2008; Chigona et al. 2009) have highlighted the link between access to market information and farmers' productivity. Okello et al. (2010) surveyed 256 small-hold farmers making use of transaction cost theory; their findings highlighted that the introduction of new technology models was helpful in reducing opportunistic behaviour while improving efficiency of markets input and output. Their research further implied that "new generation ICT-based can bring about progress in smallholder farm sector by resolving market-information related constraints" (Okello et al. 2010).

Furuholt and Matotay (2011) investigated the developmental role of mobile phone technology among farmers in Tanzania; their work drew from the research of Sein and Harindranath (2004) which highlighted the immense contribution of technology to development particularly in developing countries. Other scholars have examined the influence of technology on the development of rural settlement, highlighting the impact on improved communication and information flow, and the positive impact on crop income and poverty alleviation strategies (Chapman and Slaymaker 2002; Furuholt and Matotay 2011; Kassie et al. 2011; Sife et al. 2010).

There are other types of new technologies that can enhance agricultural productivity in developing countries particularly in Africa. Some of these are already seeing application for example in Nigeria where drones are have been used to map potential land expansion for rice cultivation and in South Sudan where satellite technology/imaging has been to design farming irrigation schemes as well as provide information on crop growth and other environmental changes (Juma 2016). There is evidence that suggest growing use of biotechnology to enhance agricultural productivity in Africa. For instance, as of 2014, Burkina Faso, Sudan and South Africa collectively planted more than 3.3 million hectares of cotton making use of transgenic crops. This meant a 57.5% increase in cotton production for Burkina Faso from the previous year. The impact was even more significant in South Sudan where the percentage increase in production was about 300% from 2012 to 2013 and in South Africa where over 3.3 million hectares of land was cultivated in 2014 (James 2014). Transgenic cotton crops have enhanced resistance hence they are able to resist other predatory species. Biotechnology has been quite beneficial to agriculture as has been mobile technology as other research as shown. When combined with other innovations in high yielding crops, improved innovation, etc., it results in significant increase in agricultural production

(Juma 2016). While the main benefit of transgenic crops is to reduce problems of crop diseases and pest, however, their use invariably has significant impact on productivity (Bloom et al. 2002).

2.2 Innovation and Agricultural Value Addition

While innovation and value chain can be complimentary, they are distinct concepts. Innovation is often described as a new way of doing things while value chains are the interlinked activities/process that help transform inputs into outputs while making the finished products available to the consumers.

Norton (2014) defined a value chain as "a set of linked activities that work to add value to a product; it consists of actors and actions that improve a product while linking commodity producers to processors and markets". This definition easily compliments that of (Porter 1985) which highlighted that value chain is the processes involved in transforming inputs into output such that the outputs have greater value than the original cost of the input. In an agricultural context value chain can be understood to be "the sequence of interlinked agents and markets that transforms inputs and services into products with attributes that consumers are prepared to purchase" (Devaux et al. 2018). In developing countries, Agricultural value chain would usually feature two models; an informal or traditional model where smallholders transfer products to local middle men who in turn sell them to local stores. The other model is a more formal process where large farms or organised smallholder groups deliver same or similar products possibly of a more uniform quality or better packaging to commercial wholesalers who may then sell to superstores or export overseas. It is important to note that while agricultural value chains may have common features, there are distinctive features in each sub-sector, owing to a combination of specific quality requirements and unique links (Norton 2014).

Devaux et al. (2018) noted that agricultural research had often been confused with innovation. They further highlighted the difference stating that "research is concerned with the production of new knowledge, which may or may not be used in practice while innovation is concerned with the processes of change in the production and marketing of goods and services; changes that may or may not be driven by research" (Devaux et al. 2018, p. 100). World Bank (2011) defined innovation in agricultural context as "the process by which individuals or organisations master and implement the design and production of goods and services that are new to them, irrespective of whether they are new to their competitors, their country, or the world" (World Bank 2011, p. 2). Agricultural research was considered to be the fundamental source of farm innovation in the 1970s during which the aim was to boost farm productivity and improve the welfare of farmers and consumers. The idea was to have research knowledge flow through "innovation pipelines" research institutes around the globe to farmers (Biggs 1990). The lapse in the innovation pipeline idea has however been improved over time leading to an efficient interplay between research institutes and farmers (Devaux et al. 2018).

Devaux et al. (2018) described value chain as a significant update in the development of relationships among all agricultural stakeholders (producers, traders, processors and consumers). This is because improving the performance of agricultural value chains stands to benefit large numbers of people. Some of the benefits accrued from value chain development include poverty reduction, income and employment generation, economic growth, environmental performance, gender equity and other development goals.

The foregoing literature provides insights into how innovation can be complimentary to the development of agricultural value chain. In some instances, the development of value chain can be an act of innovation where such activities were not already present. Furthermore, individual activities/processes within a value chain can be further improved which will also be acts of innovation. This however does not emphatically equate both concepts.

3 Constraints to Smallholder Participation in the Agricultural Value Chain

3.1 Information and Technological Constraints

Several authors have discussed the technological challenges faced by the agricultural sector; these challenges can be summarised into lack of capital for research and developments; absence of technological readiness; the need for co-innovation to enhance technology adoption; the need for interdisciplinary research to enhance knowledge development (Hall et al. 2014; Maine and Garnsey 2006; Maine and Seegopaul 2016).

In addition to these, Adeoti and Sinh (2009) examined the constraints that farmers face with respect to technology. Their research highlighted that previous research has discussed the significant benefits of technology particularly in reducing farmers' poverty. Despite this significant impact, they identified some constraint faced by farmers as the access to technologies that can improve the productivity of farm produce, poor infrastructure development and in some instances, the problem in unequal access leading to opportunistic behaviour and marginalisation.

Dahabieh et al. (2018) suggested that technological innovation could be considered in two categories; one if which technology uncertainty is high and the other in which technology uncertainty is low. The former would require novel research while the later would be only require existing technology to be applied to unresolved problems (Broring et al. 2006; Garcia and Calantone 2002; O'Connor 1998).

3.2 Financial Constraints

Smallholders have limited ability to undertake farm investment required to access high-valued markets (Hartarska and Nadolnyak 2012). In effect, financially constrained farmers are unable to overcome some of the critical challenges associated with moving their produce beyond the farm gate. These includes severe agency costs in financial markets (Korajczyk and Levy 2003) and poor cash flow. Financial constraints hinder smallholders' access to knowledge, expertise and innovation capabilities that can be deployed to improve farm operations. These constraints aggravate poverty because of inability of farmers to engage in productive farming by which they income in the value chain (Barry et al. 2000; Dethier and Effenberger 2012; Singh-Peterson and Iranacolaivalu 2018).

In context of African countries, smallholder farmers face increased financial constraints in acquiring the infrastructure, farm equipment and technology required to make their business competitive (Mather et al. 2013). The risky nature of agricultural production that makes farms performance projection difficult is partly responsible. Climate change, political instability, communal clashes and environmental crises aggravate smallholders' inability to engage in other productive activities necessary to complement farm incomes.

Furthermore, farmers face a great variety of weather, pest, disease, input supply, and market-related risks resulting in the instability of their income (Farzaneh et al. 2017; Meuwissen et al. 2001). In a vicious cycle, this in turn inhibits most smallholders' capacity to generate sufficient cash flows and incomes for themselves. Previous studies report that cash holdings and cash flows are valuable for financially constrained smallholders than for large farms which are often financially unconstrained (Barry et al. 2000; Hartarska and Nadolnyak 2012; Korajczyk and Levy 2003). In addition, smallholders, unlike large farms, find it difficult to raise capital because of high cost of funding, availability of few venture capital firms, and the fact that commercial banks require stiff collaterals (Hart and Lence 2004; Markelova et al. 2009). Much of the literature centres on the financial constraints facing farmers without adequate consideration for potential implications for poverty, unemployment and inequality. Increased collateral requirements typically worsen access for credit for smallholders especially among the vulnerable groups and exacerbate poverty and unemployment (Briggeman et al. 2009). However, even when lenders or funders demand different requirements such as viable business plans, statement of cash flow and overall business financial statements, most smallholders lack the capacity to meet these requirements.

A clear significant insight from existing research is that smallholders often lack the resources, dynamic capabilities and strategic innovation vital to ensure profitable farm operations and enhanced competitiveness. There is limited appreciation of the scale of the problem and broader impacts on smallholders' ability to engage in productive farming. The existence and magnitude of financial constraints for smallholders are non-negligible.

(Briggeman et al. 2009) estimate that the value of production is 3% lower in financially constrained farm compared with those that are not financially constrained. Financial constraints also limit the capacity of smallholders to grow because of inadequate investment in equipment and technology that are vital for scaling farm operations (Barry et al. 2000; Corsi et al. 2017). In most cases, financially constrained smallholders often used off farm spousal income to increase investment on farm operations (Hartarska and Mai 2008). This has considerable implications for poverty reduction and inequality. Smallholders facing financial constraints do not invest and grow in the same manner as unconstrained farmers. The broader implication is that issue patterns for unconstrained large farm and constrained smallholders are substantially different. For example, at land preparation stage, while most smallholders are doing land preparations with those practising conservation farming having dug their holes and applied manure, large farms with substantial farm inputs and equipment such as tractors and large personnel are in the process of tiling their land. This shows how large farms gain an advantage over smallholders.

Previous studies show that smallholders also face significant difficulty in accessing post-harvest finance, leading to severe household liquidity constraints which usually compel them to sell the bulk of their produce at harvest when prices are extremely low (Gashayie 2015). This clearly widens the inequality gap between smallholders and large farms. Because financial constraints do not affect all farmers uniformly, there is a need to pay attention to the extent of effective financing constraints that different smallholders face. Clearly, most smallholders hold their wealth in non-liquid assets (for example, livestock and household goods), risking loss via theft, fire and other man-made or natural disasters. This can aggravate poverty and inequality for most smallholder farmers. By contrast, large farms can afford insurance and price hedging to overcome constraints associated with loss in the agricultural value chains and destruction of assets because of man-made or natural disasters.

3.3 Quality Constraints

According to the Food and Agriculture Organisation (FAO), the world population is projected to reach 9.3 billion by 2050. Thus, to feed this greatly increased population, food production must increase by 70%—down to 60% in an update of the report (Alexandratos and Bruinsma 2012). Research maintains that improved food production techniques are a necessity, albeit this remains an underestimated issue especially how it impacts most farmers and their livelihoods (Corsi et al. 2017). High-value agriculture has increased substantially in the past two recent decades but characterised by highly vertically coordinated supply chains. In perspective, during the past two decades, the global trade in food and agricultural products is increasing and has almost doubled from USD$243 billion in 1980 to USD$720 billion in 2005 (Crossley et al. 2009). The rise of high-value agricultural markets has been accompanied by large and rapid structural changes. (Maertens and Swinnen 2009) maintain that international food chains is largely dominated by a few large commercial farms and food multinationals. This is partly attributed to the quality of produce and quality control systems in large commercial farms compared with smallholders' production.

While stringent quality requirements are essential to improve food standards and access to international markets, smallholders do not have the necessary resources to process their produce in meeting quality standards and requirements. Unlike large commercial farms, smallholders have limited capabilities and resources to ensure strict compliance to food standards and regulations. Consequently, this limits their capacity to engage, participate and integrate in these high-value supply chains and agricultural markets. One significant point is that high-value chains are characterised by the use of stringent food quality and food safety standards, products of high value, the importance of private standards, public regulations and requirements (Maertens and Swinnen 2009). Quite clearly, smallholders are disadvantaged in several ways, compared with large commercial farms, in meeting these expectations and requirements.

For example, fresh food exports to the European Union (EU) have to meet a range of stringent public requirements including labelling requirements, regulations concerning contamination in food, general hygiene rules, traceability requirements, and marketing standards (Bureau and Swinnen 2017). In addition, private standards often established by large food companies, which are not legally mandatory, play an essential role in agro-food trade. These private standards also extend to food quality and safety specifications and include ethical as well as environmental standards. The broader implication is that these requirements affect farmers in different ways. In practice, despite growing market opportunities, there is a possibility that smallholders will be squeezed out because of compliance with food safety regulations and standards. Likewise, we acknowledge that large commercial farms have the capacity to meet private standards such as food safety governance, quality control systems, food safety regulations and standards because of their large scale, expertise, and resources. In conclusion, smallholders face high quality control costs due to their small scale and quite often their inability to develop quality control systems. Hence, it is evident that the emerging high-value chains that frequently involve strict standards and new procurement systems of agribusiness may further exacerbate market access for smallholders (Omamo and Lynam 2003; Reardon et al. 2009; Oyebola et al. 2019).

3.4 Transportation Constraints

Transportation is indispensable to linking farmers to the markets as well as economic development in developing countries. Previous studies found that transport operations are a basic component of agricultural supply and value chains, and that transportation networks can be the decisive factor for the success or failure of farmers particularly in rural areas (Baker et al. 2015; Barrett 2008; Crossley et al. 2009; Gashayie 2015). In many of the world poorest countries, transportation networks are largely inadequate. This holds true for most African countries. The construction of roads is an essential tool towards improving farm productivity and profitability.

Moreover, the availability of good transportation networks provide farmers with better physical access to markets and other social amenities such as education and health care services. The prevailing literature on the linkages between agriculture and transportation claim that with transportation access farmers can improve their market access and produce more for themselves and the market (Fischer and Qaim 2012; Mather et al. 2013). Poor transportation networks disproportionately affect smallholder farmers particularly in terms of access to market and linkages with other actors in the agricultural value chain. However, transportation by itself cannot have a decisive impact on poverty, inadequate transportation networks has the ability to intensify inequalities and deepen poverty if its negative externalities are not appropriately managed (Briggeman et al. 2009; Wiggins et al. 2010). Transportation is largely recognised as a major driver of the agricultural value chains. Thus, transportation constraints such as poor road networks inhibit farmers' ability to move their produce beyond the farm gate in most African countries. This clearly disconnects smallholders from the agricultural value chains and constitutes a barrier to the development of efficient and profitable agribusiness. We posit that improving road networks and providing direct transportation intervention that allows smallholders in rural areas to move their produce to reach collection centres and markets more promptly can stimulate economic development. Furthermore, transportation improvements reduce damage to perishable crops and operating costs for vehicle users, and provide greater opportunities for smallholders to participate actively in the agricultural value chains.

3.5 Market Constraints

There is widespread consensus that many of the world's poor still directly or indirectly depend on agriculture as their main occupation and source of incomes, most of them are small-scale farmers (Fischer and Qaim 2012; Swamy and Dharani 2016). More than two billion people live on less than US$2 a day (World Bank 2015) and market-based solutions such as agricultural value chain interventions have become increasingly popular to reach this population and facilitate their entrance into larger markets, providing a means to improve their economic welfare (Rutherford et al. 2016; Staritz 2012). Smallholders could improve their livelihoods if they had better access to viable markets for their agricultural outputs. Research has also linked improved access to agricultural markets serves as a powerful tool for economic growth in African countries. For example, in regions such as sub-Saharan Africa, where 70% of all population rely on agriculture for their livelihood, and 80% of all the farms are less than two hectares in size, smallholder farmers can turn their surpluses into income only if they have the ability to gain access to markets (International Food Policy and Research Institute [IFPRI] 2002). Increased incomes, in turn, support food security and help to alleviate poverty (Corsi et al. 2017). This clearly suggests why addressing market constraints facing farmers especially smallholders is essential and should be seen as policy intervention issue.

In addition to building up farmers' production capabilities, improving their access to markets has become a vital element in strategies to promote rural development and poverty reduction (Fischer and Qaim 2012). Smallholders face multiple market failures that impede them from taking advantage of market opportunities. In particular, smallholders live in remote areas with poor infrastructure and face high transaction costs that significantly reduce their incentives for market participation (Barrett 2008; Fischer and Qaim 2012). In addition, previous studies have also shown that smallholders typically with few assets have limited access to services, including effective extension and rural credit, which are important preconditions for upgrading production systems (Reardon et al. 2009; Wiggins et al. 2010). The lack of basic infrastructure in rural areas where most smallholders live often contribute to high transaction costs that limit smallholders' access to markets.

Much of the literature on market access highlights the pervasive imperfections of markets in developing countries. Lack of information on prices and technologies, lack of connections to established market actors, distortions or absence of input and output markets, and financial constraints often make it difficult for small farmers to take advantage of market opportunities (Markelova et al. 2009; Wuepper and Sauer 2016). There are other several issues such as distance to road/town, household ownership of transportation assets, and access to market price information that determine farmers' market access. For example, smallholders often do not have access to market price information necessary to improve farmers' bargaining power with intermediaries and thus improve both participation probability and sales quantities.

By contrast, large farms have access to market price information and therefore have higher market participation. Likewise, research has linked household ownership of transportation assets to improvement in the market participation of farmers (Mather et al. 2013). In addition, distance to road/town is another conventional explanation for observing a low market participation in sub-Saharan Africa (Barrett 2008). There is a valid reason to question whether heterogeneity in smallholder resource endowments might constrain a significant number of poor smallholders from taking advantage of lower market access costs. Furthermore, the question that arises for agricultural policy is whether market access and financial constraints are complementary or substitutes. This raises the question about whether an increase in public good-type investments to improve market access is a sufficient condition to enable a significant number of smallholders to escape poverty and gain competitive advantage. The existence of linkages between market access and poverty or resource endowments demands that farmers must produce what markets want. We argue that smallholder farmers must create an entrepreneurial culture in rural communities where "farmers produce for markets rather than trying to market what they produce" (Lundy et al. 2002, p. 3) in order to break market constraints. Creating an entrepreneurial culture, building resource capabilities and fostering strategic innovation through adequate support from policymakers remain vital to overcoming market constraints.

4 Overcoming Constraints in the Agricultural Value Chain: The Role of Social Capital

According to Bourdieu and Wacquant (1992), social capital is defined as "the sum of the resources, actual or virtual, that accrue to an individual or a group by virtue of possessing a durable network of more or less institutionalized relationships of mutual acquaintance and recognition" (Bourdieu and Wacquant 1992, p. 119). Social Capital is recognised as a key livelihood asset in the sustainable livelihood framework. It is a key means by which individuals and communities can overcome vulnerabilities by transforming structures and processes to achieve livelihood outcomes (Krantz 2001). Social capital is classified into *bonding* social capital between people with similar socio-economic characteristic and family and religious identities; *bridging* social capital among people belonging to different ethnic, social and religious groupings; and *linking* social capital between citizens and those in authorities (Claridge 2013). It is measured by norms of trust and reciprocity (Stone 2001). In the following, we examine the impact of social capital and collective action on various constraints to smallholder agriculture.

4.1 Overcoming Market Constraints

As highlighted in the foregoing, one of the major constraints to smallholder access to new markets is the economy of scale and lack of capacity to meet the requirements for standardisation of products. Collective action can help farmers improve their market position through delivery of in-house training and inputs, the use of group marketing to strengthen their bargaining power, and the pooling together of labour resources to achieve economies of scale and meet quality standards (Gyau et al. 2014). However, collective action requires certain thresholds, including leadership and membership strength of groups, in order to be effective in achieving marketing goals. Majority of farmer groups in developing countries tend to be in their earlier stages of development, typically with less than 50 members. While smaller groups often have higher internal cohesion, larger groups can achieve economies of scale (Markelova et al. 2009). One way to combine both advantages of smaller and larger groups is for small groups to federate with smaller and similar farmer groups within a region or country. This is an example of bridging social capital. In Nigeria, for example, local smallholder farmer groups came together under the aegis of Cassava Growers Association of Nigeria (Kolade and Harpham 2014). They consistently fared better than farmers who are not members of cooperatives. Nevertheless, the impact of the umbrella organisation is mixed. The mixed success reflects the reality that the impact of collective action for market access can be limited by other factors, including the availability and use of post-harvest technology for value addition (Gyau et al. 2014), as well as other institutional factors.

4.2 Collective Action for Post-harvest Processing, Storage and Packaging

To add value to raw produce, farmers require access to, and competence in, post-harvest technologies to store, process and transform farm produce (Abass et al. 2014; Affognon et al. 2015). Access to better post-harvest technologies are sometimes linked with uptake of improved high-breed varieties (Omotilewa et al. 2018). Failure to access post-harvest technologies typically result in severe post-harvest losses, due to insect and fungal infestation (Mendoza et al. 2017) or pressure to sell produce at significant losses to middlemen. Farmers' cooperatives offer an effective pathway for smallholder farmers to access and utilise technologies for value addition, which in turn give them better opportunities to break the barriers to high-value markets both domestically and internationally.

In Rwanda, the government encouraged coffee growers, most of them owning less than 1 ha of land, to form cooperatives. They were supported with subsidised Coffee Washing Stations (CWS) installed throughout the country. These enable smallholder to de-pulp, wash, and dry cherries in order to produce high quality coffee for international high-end markets (Issa and Chrysostome 2015). In spite of this, less than 25% of Rwandan smallholders belonged to farmers' cooperatives, suggesting a lack of awareness of the opportunities, or general scepticism. In the Ugandan case of the Nyabyumba Farmer Group located in Kabale district in south-western Uganda, potato farmers were able to utilise their bonding and bridging social capital to overcome quality constraints to supplying Nandos, a multi-national fast food restaurant in Kampala. Between September 2003 and December 2004, the farmer group was able to drastically reduce rejection rate for their produce from 80% to less than 10% (Kaganzi et al. 2009).

In general, farmers' cooperatives enable smallholders to create dynamic communities of practice by which they can support innovation, adaptation and resilience in the value chains (Lowitt et al. 2015).

4.3 Harnessing Linking Social Capital for Institutional Reforms and Policy Interventions

Smallholder farmers constitute a significant proportion of the population in developing countries. In Nigeria, the agriculture sector employs about two-thirds of the entire labour force. Yet, the sector has suffered perennial neglect from successive governments, in terms of budgetary allocations and relevant policy instruments to support and incentivise smallholder farmers. By coming together in federated associations, smallholder farmers can deploy their collective synergy to effect necessary policy changes and institutional reforms. A South African study revealed that smallholder farmer groups were able to use their linking social capital to access opportunities to receive implements, production inputs and training (Taruvinga et al. 2017). In the Rwandan example previously highlighted, farmers cooperatives were able to enjoy better access to funding, technical and institutional support provided by the Rwandan government, compared to individual farmers who were not members of cooperatives (Issa and Chrysostome 2015). In general, farmer groups are better positioned, through their organisation and sheer number to influence government policies and access opportunities both in the domestic and international markets.

The foregoing discussion highlights the activities and mechanisms by which smallholder use their bonding, bridging and linking social capital to overcome barriers and access opportunities in the agricultural value chain. The interactions between the various forms of social capital, associated activities and constraints in the value chain are captured in Fig. 1.

The framework above highlights the contributions of various forms of social capital towards overcoming constraints to smallholders in the agricultural value chain. First, farmer groups are able to harness their bonding social capital to share relevant and critical information about the market and new techniques and technology that can help them add value to their produce. The group also provides an auspicious platform to develop and improve competence in the use of new technologies. Similarly, bridging social capital- such as those seen in federated organisations- enable farmers to generate better economies of scale, and use group marketing to strengthen their bargaining position in high-value markets. They can also use bridging social capital to reduce the cost and risk of ownership of machineries, while benefitting optimally from them. Finally, smallholders can use their linking social capital to gain better access to governments and thereby engineer institutional reforms, and access or influence new opportunities for funding and technical support.

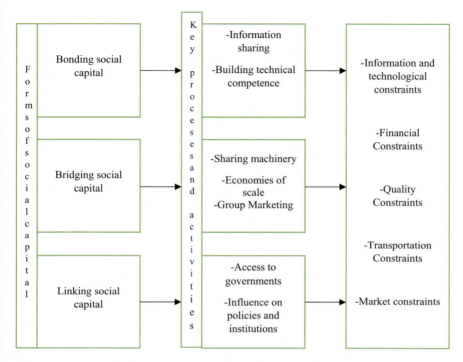

Fig. 1 Conceptual framework: Social capital and mechanisms for overcoming constraints in the agricultural value chain (*Source* The Authors)

5 Conclusion and Future Research Agenda

In this chapter, we have drawn attention to the challenges faced by, and opportunities available to, smallholder farmers beyond the farm gate. This is in the light of the recognition that most of the extant research on smallholders tend to focus more on innovations and opportunities for farmers to improve their productivity. While the research on farmers' productivity has continuing relevance and resonance, there is need for more attention from scholars and practitioners to give more attention to empirical investigations and practical interventions aimed at activities and opportunities for farmers in the agricultural value chain. Here, we highlighted the critical role of social capital—in its bonding, bridging and linking forms—in helping farmers to overcome the various constraints in the value chain. In summary, we argue that social capital is an important resource smallholder farmers can deploy to mitigate and overcome their relative resource disadvantage relative to big farms, in accessing and benefitting from the value chain. Among others, farmer groups can pool funds together to procure necessary inputs and equipment necessary for improved productivity. We proposed a conceptual framework, which we aim to test, and hope other researchers can test and expand, in future empirical investigations.

References

Abass, A. B., Ndunguru, G., Mamiro, P., Alenkhe, B., Mlingi, N., & Bekunda, M. (2014). Post-harvest food losses in a maize-based farming system of semi-arid savannah area of Tanzania. *Journal of Stored Products Research, 57,* 49–57. https://doi.org/10.1016/j.jspr.2013.12.004.

Abate, T., Shiferaw, B., Menkir, A., Wegary, D., Kebede, Y., Tesfaye, K., et al. (2015). Factors that transformed maize productivity in Ethiopia. *Food Security, 7*(5), 965–981. https://doi.org/10.1007/s12571-015-0488-z.

Adeoti, J. O., & Sinh, B. T. (2009). Technological constraint and farmers' vulnerability in selected developing countries (Nigeria and Vietnam). In *7th International Conference 2009* (p. 29).

Affognon, H., Mutungi, C., Sanginga, P., & Borgemeister, C. (2015). Unpacking postharvest losses in sub-Saharan Africa: A meta-analysis. *World Development, 66,* 49–68. https://doi.org/10.1016/j.worlddev.2014.08.002.

Aker, J. C. (2008). Does digital divide or provide? The impact of cell phones on grain markets in Niger. *SSRN.* https://doi.org/10.2139/ssrn.1093374

Alexandratos, N., & Bruinsma, J. (2012). World agriculture towards 2030/2050: The 2012 revision. *Food and Agriculture Organization of the United Nations, 12,* 146. https://doi.org/10.1016/S0264-8377(03)00047-4.

Baker, D., Cadilhon, J., & Ochola, W. (2015). Identification and analysis of smallholder producers' constraints: Applications to Tanzania and Uganda. *Development in Practice, 25*(2), 204–220. https://doi.org/10.1080/09614524.2015.1007924.

Barrett, C. B. (2008). Smallholder market participation: Concepts and evidence from eastern and southern Africa. *Food Policy, 33*(4), 299–317. https://doi.org/10.1016/j.foodpol.2007.10.005.

Barrett, H. R., Browne, A. W., Harris, P. J. C., & Cadoret, K. (2002). Organic certification and the UK market: Organic imports from developing countries. *Food Policy, 27,* 301–318. https://doi.org/10.1016/S0306-9192(02)00036-2.

Barry, P. J., Bierlen, R. W., & Sotomayor, N. L. (2000). Financial structure of farm business under imperfect capital markets. *American Journal of Agricultural Economics, 82*(4), 920–933.

Biggs, S. D. (1990). A multiple source of innovation model of agricultural research and technology promotion. *World Development, 18*(11), 1481–1499.

Bloom, N., Griffith, R., & Van Reenen, J. (2002). Do R&D tax credits work? Evidence from a panel of countries 1979–1997. *Journal of Public Economics, 85*(1), 1–31.

Bourdieu, P., & Wacquant, L. (1992). Interest, habitus, rationality. In *An Invitation to Reflective Sociology* (pp. 115–140). University of Chicago Press.

Briggeman, B. C., Towe, C. A., & Morehart, M. J. (2009). Credit constraints: Their existence, determinants, and implications for U.S. farm and nonfarm sole proprietorships. *American Journal of Agricultural Economics, 91*(1), 275–289. https://doi.org/10.1111/j.1467-8276.2008.01173.x.

Briones, R. M. (2015). Small farmers in high-value chains: Binding or relaxing constraints to inclusive growth? *World Development, 72,* 43–52. https://doi.org/10.1016/j.worlddev.2015.01.005.

Broring, S., Leker, J., & Ruhmer, S. (2006). Radical or not? Assessing innovativeness and its organisational implications for established firms. *International Journal of Product Development.* https://doi.org/10.1504/IJPD.2006.009363.

Bureau, J.-C., & Swinnen, J. F. M. (2017, December). EU policies and global food security. *SSRN, 16,* 106–115. https://doi.org/10.2139/ssrn.2961695.
Cavatassi, R., González-flores, M., Winters, P., Andrade-Piedra, J., Espinosa, P., & Thiele, G. (2011, May). Linking smallholders to the new agricultural economy: The case of the Plataformas de Concertacion in Ecuador. *Journal of Development Studies, 47,* 1545–1573. https://doi.org/10.1080/00220388.2010.536221.
Chapman, R., & Slaymaker, T. (2002). *ICTs and rural development: Review of the literature, current interventions and opportunities for action. In ICTs and rural development* (Working Paper). https://www.odi.org/sites/odi.org.uk/files/odi-assets/publications-opinion-files/2670.pdf.
Chigona, W., Chigona, A., Ngqokelela, B., & Mpofu, S. (2009). MXIT: Uses, perceptions and self-justifications. *Journal of Information, Information Technology and Organizations, 4,* 001–016. https://doi.org/10.28945/123.
Claridge, T. (2013). *Classifications of social capital.* Social Capital Research & Training. http://www.socialcapitalresearch.com/explanation-types-social-capital.
Corsi, S., Marchisio, L. V., & Orsi, L. (2017, June). Connecting smallholder farmers to local markets: Drivers of collective action, land tenure and food security in East Chad. *Land Use Policy, 68,* 39–47. https://doi.org/10.1016/j.landusepol.2017.07.025.
Crossley, P., Chamen, T., & Kienzle, J. (2009). *Diversification booklet number 10.* Rome. Retrieved from http://www.fao.org/3/a-i0525e.pdf.
Dahabieh, M. S., Bröring, S., & Maine, E. (2018). Overcoming barriers to innovation in food and agricultural biotechnology. *Trends in Food Science & Technology, 79,* 204–213. https://doi.org/10.1016/J.TIFS.2018.07.004.
Dethier, J.-J., & Effenberger, A. (2012). Agriculture and development: A brief review of the literature. *Economic Systems, 36*(2), 175–205. https://doi.org/10.1016/j.ecosys.2011.09.003.
Devaux, A., Torero, M., Donovan, J., & Horton, D. (2018). Agricultural innovation and inclusive value-chain development: A review. *Journal of Agribusiness in Developing and Emerging Economies.* https://doi.org/10.1108/JADEE-06-2017-0065.
Farzaneh, M., Allahyari, M. S., Damalas, C. A., & Seidavi, A. (2017). Crop insurance as a risk management tool in agriculture: The case of silk farmers in northern Iran. *Land Use Policy, 64,* 225–232. https://doi.org/10.1016/j.landusepol.2017.02.018.
Feder, G., & Umali, D. L. (1993). The adoption of agricultural innovations: A review. *Technological Forecasting and Social Change.* https://doi.org/10.1016/0040-1625(93)90053-A.
Fischer, E., & Qaim, M. (2012). Linking smallholders to markets: Determinants and impacts of farmer collective action in Kenya. *World Development, 40*(6), 1255–1268. https://doi.org/10.1016/j.worlddev.2011.11.018.
Folberth, C., Yang, H., Gaiser, T., Liu, J., Wang, X., Williams, J., et al. (2014). Effects of ecological and conventional agricultural intensification practices on maize yields in sub-Saharan Africa under potential climate change. *Environmental Research Letters, 9*(4), 044004. https://doi.org/10.1088/1748-9326/9/4/044004.
Furuholt, B., & Matotay, E. (2011). The developmental contribution from mobile phones across the agricultural value chain in rural Africa. *The Electronic Journal of Information Systems in Developing Countries, 48*(1), 1–16. https://doi.org/10.1002/j.1681-4835.2011.tb00343.x.

Garcia, R., & Calantone, R. (2002). A critical look at technological innovation typology and innovativeness terminology: A literature review. *Journal of Product Innovation Management.* https://doi.org/10.1016/S0737-6782(01)00132-1.

Gashayie, A. (2015). Agricultural finance constraints and innovative models experience for Ethiopia: Empirical evidence from developing countries. *Research Journal of Finance and Accounting, 6*(7), 39–50.

Geta, E., Bogale, A., Kassa, B., & Elias, E. (2013). Productivity and efficiency analysis of smallholder maize producers in southern Ethiopia. *Journal of Human Ecology.* https://doi.org/10.1080/09709274.2013.11906554.

Gyau, A., Franzel, S., Chiatoh, M., Nimino, G., & Owusu, K. (2014). Collective action to improve market access for smallholder producers of agroforestry products: Key lessons learned with insights from Cameroon's experience. *Current Opinion in Environmental Sustainability, 6*, 68–72. https://doi.org/10.1016/j.cosust.2013.10.017.

Hall, J., Bachor, V., & Matos, S. (2014). Developing and diffusing new technologies: Strategies for legitimization. *California Management Review.* https://doi.org/10.1525/cmr.2014.56.3.98.

Hart, C. E., & Lence, S. H. (2004). Financial constraints and farm investment: A Bayesian examination. *Journal of Business and Economic Statistics, 22*(1), 51–63. https://doi.org/10.1198/073500103288619403.

Hartarska, V., & Mai, C. (2008). Financing constraints and the family farm: How do families react? Valentina Hartarska and Chi Mai. In *Southern Agricultural Economics Association Annual Meeting* (p. 20). Dallas, TX.

Hartarska, V., & Nadolnyak, D. (2012). Financing constraints and access to credit in a postcrisis environment: Evidence from new farmers in Alabama. *Journal of Agricultural and Applied Economic, 44*(4), 607–621.

IFPRI. (2002). *Essays: Time to stop dumping on the world's poor.*

Issa, N., & Chrysostome, N. J. (2015). Determinants of farmer participation in the vertical integration of the Rwandan Coffee Value Chain: Results from Huye District. *Journal of Agricultural Science, 7*(9), 197–211. https://doi.org/10.5539/jas.v7n9p197.

James, C. (2014). *Global status of commercialized biotech/GM crops: 2014.* Executive summary, brief 49.

Juma, C. (2016). *Innovation and its enemies: Why people resist new technologies.* Oxford University Press.

Kaganzi, E., Ferris, S., Barham, J., Abenakyo, A., Sanginga, P., & Njuki, J. (2009). Sustaining linkages to high value markets through collective action in Uganda. *Food Policy, 34*(1), 23–30. https://doi.org/10.1016/j.foodpol.2008.10.004.

Kassie, M., Shiferaw, B., & Muricho, G. (2011). Agricultural technology, crop income, and poverty alleviation in Uganda. *World Development.* https://doi.org/10.1016/j.worlddev.2011.04.023.

Kebede, Y., Gunjal, K., & Coffin, G. (1990). Adoption of new technologies agriculture: The case of Tegulet-Bulga Shoa Province in Ethiopian District. *Agricultural Economics, 4*, 27–43.

Kiiza, B., Pederson, G., & Lwasa, S. (2011). The role of market information in adoption of agricultural seed technology in rural Uganda. *International Journal of ICT Research and Development in Africa (IJICTRDA), 2*(1), 29–46. Retrieved from https://econpapers.repec.org/article/iggjictrd/v_3a2_3ay_3a2011_3ai_3a1_3ap_3a29-46.htm.

Knowler, D., & Bradshaw, B. (2007). Farmers' adoption of conservation agriculture: A review and synthesis of recent research. *Food Policy, 32*(1), 25–48. https://doi.org/10.1016/j.foodpol.2006.01.003.

Kolade, O., & Harpham, T. (2014). Impact of cooperative membership on farmers' uptake of technological innovations in Southwest Nigeria. *Development Studies Research, 1*(1), 340–353. https://doi.org/10.1080/21665095.2014.978981.

Kolade, O., Harpham, T., & Kibreab, G. (2014). Institutional barriers to successful innovations: Perceptions of rural farmers and key stakeholders in southwest Nigeria. *African Journal of Science, Technology, Innovation and Development, 6*(4), 339–353. https://doi.org/10.1080/20421338.2014.966039.

Korajczyk, R. A., & Levy, A. (2003). Capital structure choice: Macroeconomic conditions and financial constraints. *Journal of Financial Economics, 68*(1), 75–109. https://doi.org/10.1016/S0304-405X(02)00249-0.

Krantz, B. L. (2001, February). *The sustainable livelihood approach to poverty reduction: An introduction.* https://www.sida.se/contentassets/bd474c-210163447c9a7963d77c64148a/the-sustainable-livelihood-approach-to-poverty-reduction_2656.pdf.

Lowitt, K., Hickey, G. M., Ganpat, W., & Phillip, L. (2015). Linking communities of practice with value chain development in smallholder farming systems. *World Development, 74,* 363–373. https://doi.org/10.1016/j.worlddev.2015.05.014.

Lundy, M., Ostertag, C. F., & Best, R. (2002). *Value adding, agroenterprise and poverty reduction: A territorial approach for rural business development.* Rural Agroenterprise Development Project Paper. Cali, Colombia.

Maertens, M., & Swinnen, J. F. M. (2009). Trade, standards, and poverty: Evidence from Senegal. *World Development, 37*(1), 161–178. https://doi.org/10.1016/j.worlddev.2008.04.006.

Maine, E., & Garnsey, E. (2006). Commercializing generic technology: The case of advanced materials ventures. *Research Policy.* https://doi.org/10.1016/j.respol.2005.12.006.

Maine, E., & Seegopaul, P. (2016). Accelerating advanced-materials commercialization. *Nature Materials.* https://doi.org/10.1038/nmat4625.

Markelova, H., Meinzen-Dick, R., Hellin, J., & Dohrn, S. (2009). Collective action for smallholder market access. *Food Policy, 34*(1), 1–7. https://doi.org/10.1016/j.foodpol.2008.10.001.

Mather, D., Boughton, D., & Jayne, T. S. (2013). Explaining smallholder maize marketing in southern and eastern Africa: The roles of market access, technology and household resource endowments. *Food Policy, 43,* 248–266. https://doi.org/10.1016/j.foodpol.2013.09.008.

Mendoza, J. R., Sabillón, L., Martinez, W., Campabadal, C., Hallen-Adams, H. E., & Bianchini, A. (2017). Traditional maize post-harvest management practices amongst smallholder farmers in Guatemala. *Journal of Stored Products Research, 71,* 14–21. https://doi.org/10.1016/j.jspr.2016.12.007.

Meuwissen, M. P. M., Huirne, R. B. M., & Hardaker, J. B. (2001). Risk and risk management: An empirical analysis of Dutch livestock farmers. *Livestock Production Science, 69*(1), 43–53. https://doi.org/10.1016/S0301-6226(00)00247-5.

Muzari, W., Gatsi, W., & Muvhunzi, S. (2012). The impacts of technology adoption on smallholder agricultural productivity in sub-Saharan Africa: A review. *Journal of Sustainable Development.* https://doi.org/10.5539/jsd.v5n8p69.

Norton, R. (2014). Agricultural value chains: A game changer for small holders | Devex. Retrieved October 15, 2018, from https://www.devex.com/news/agricultural-value-chains-a-game-changer-for-small-holders-83981.

O'Connor, G. C. (1998). Market learning and radical innovation: A cross case comparison of eight radical innovation projects. *Journal of Product Innovation Management*. https://doi.org/10.1111/1540-5885.1520151.

Ogutu, S. O., Okello, J. J., & Otieno, D. J. (2014). Impact of information and communication technology-based market information services on smallholder farm input use and productivity: The case of Kenya. *World Development*, 64(104482), 311–321. https://doi.org/10.1016/j.worlddev.2014.06.011.

Okello, J. J., Ofwona-Adera, E., Mbatia, O. L. E., & Okello, R. M. (2010). Using ICT to integrate smallholder farmers into agricultural value chain: The case of DrumNet project in Kenya. *International Journal of ICT Research and Development in Africa (IJICTRDA)*. https://doi.org/10.4018/jictrda.2010010102.

Omamo, S. W., & Lynam, J. K. (2003). Agricultural science and technology policy in Africa. *Research Policy*, 32(9), 1681–1694. https://doi.org/10.1016/S0048-7333(03)00059-3.

Omotilewa, O. J., Ricker-Gilbert, J., Ainembabazi, J. H., & Shively, G. E. (2018, June). Does improved storage technology promote modern input use and food security? Evidence from a randomized trial in Uganda. *Journal of Development Economics*, 135(2017), 176–198. https://doi.org/10.1016/j.jdeveco.2018.07.006.

Oyebola, P. O., Osabuohien, E., & Obasaju, B. (2019). Employment and income effects of Nigeria's agricultural transformation agenda. *African Journal of Economic and Management Studies*. https://doi.org/10.1108/AJEMS-12-2018-0402.

Porter, M. E. (1985). Competitive advantage. In *Competitive advantage: Creating and sustaining superior performance*. https://doi.org/10.1182/blood-2005-11-4354.

Reardon, T., Barrett, C. B., Berdegué, J. A., & Swinnen, J. F. M. (2009). Agrifood industry transformation and small farmers in developing countries. *World Development*, 37(11), 1717–1727. https://doi.org/10.1016/j.worlddev.2008.08.023.

Rutherford, D., Burke, H., Cheung, K., & Field, S. (2016). Impact of an agricultural value chain project on smallholder farmers, households, and children in Liberia. *World Development*, 83, 70–83. https://doi.org/10.1016/j.worlddev.2016.03.004.

Sein, M. K., & Harindranath, G. (2004). Conceptualizing the ICT artifact: Toward understanding the role of ICT in national development. *Information Society*. https://doi.org/10.1080/01972240490269942.

Sife, A. S., Kiondo, E., & Lyimo-Macha, J. G. (2010). Contribution of mobile phones to rural livelihoods and poverty reduction in Morogoro region, Tanzania. *The Electronic Journal of Information Systems in Developing Countries*. https://doi.org/10.1002/j.1681-4835.2010.tb00299.x.

Singh-Peterson, L., & Iranacolaivalu, M. (2018, March). Barriers to market for subsistence farmers in Fiji – A gendered perspective. *Journal of Rural Studies*, 60, 11–20. https://doi.org/10.1016/j.jrurstud.2018.03.001.

Staritz, C. (2012). *Value chains for development? Potentials and limitations of global value chain approaches in donor interventions*. Vienna.

Stone, W. (2001). *Measuring social capital: Towards a theoretically informed measurement framework for researching social capital in family and community life. Australian Institute of Family Studies* (Vol. 52). https://doi.org/ISSN: 1440-4761.

Sunding, D., & Zilberman, D. (2000). The agricultural innovation process: Research and technology adoption in a changing agricultural sector. *Handbook of Agricultural Economics.* https://doi.org/10.1016/S1574-0072(01)10007-1.

Swamy, V., & Dharani, D. (2016). Analyzing the agricultural value chain financing: Approaches and tools in India. *Agricultural Finance Review, 76*(2), 211–232. https://doi.org/10.1108/AFR-11-2015-0051.

Taruvinga, B., Ndou, P., Hlerema, I. N., Maraganedzha, T. L., Du Plooy, C. P., & Venter, S. (2017). Fostering linking social capital for successful agricultural development projects in South Africa. *Agrekon, 56*(1), 28–39. https://doi.org/10.1080/03031853.2017.1283243.

Wiggins, S., Kirsten, J., & Llambí, L. (2010). The future of small farms. *World Development, 38*(10), 1341–1348. https://doi.org/10.1016/j.worlddev.2009.06.013.

World Bank. (2011). *Agricultural innovation systems: An investment sourcebook. World Bank Series.* Washington, DC. https://doi.org/10.1596/978-0-8213-8684-2.

World Bank. (2015). *World development indicators.* Washington, DC.

Wuepper, D., & Sauer, J. (2016, July). Explaining the performance of contract farming in Ghana: The role of self-efficacy and social capital explaining the performance of contract farming in Ghana: *Food Policy, 62*, 11–27. https://doi.org/10.13140/RG.2.1.3567.0169.

Household Livelihood and Welfare Matters

Large-Scale Land Investments and Household Livelihood in Nigeria: Empirical Insights from Quantitative Analysis

Evans S. Osabuohien, Felicia O. Olokoyo, Uchenna R. Efobi, Alhassan A. Karakara, and Ibukun Beecroft

1 Introduction

There is an increase in the volume of Large-scale Agricultural Land Investments (or Large-scale Land Investments—[LLIs]) across the world, with most of them in developing countries, especially in Africa. More than half of the reported LLIs under the framework of land lease/concession across the world are concentrated in Africa. For example, 376 of the total 681 LLIs reported cases are located in the African continent (Nolte et al. 2016).[1] Large-scale agricultural land investment in African land transactions raises concerns about the impacts on the local households and smallholders welfare in locations where they are situated. The implications of these LLIs occurrence are numerous, ranging from dispossession of ancestral lands, reduction in households livelihood, displacement of

---

E. S. Osabuohien (✉)
Department of Economics and Development Studies & Chair,
Centre for Economic Policy and Development Research (CEPDeR),
Covenant University, Ota, Nigeria
e-mail: evans.osabuohien@covenantuniversity.edu.ng

Alexander von Humboldt Visiting Professor,
Witten/Herdecke University, Witten, Germany

F. O. Olokoyo
Department of Banking and Finance, Covenant University, Ota, Nigeria

Centre for Entrepreneurial Development Studies, Covenant University, Ota, Nigeria

© The Author(s) 2020
E. S. Osabuohien (ed.), *The Palgrave Handbook of Agricultural and Rural Development in Africa*, https://doi.org/10.1007/978-3-030-41513-6_7

household agricultural activities, (un)employment concerns due to loss of agricultural jobs, poverty and food security, poor compensations, and environmental pollution, among others (Deininger et al. 2011; Osabuohien 2014; Mutopo et al. 2015; Osabuohien et al. 2015, 2019).

There is emerging and relevant empirical evidence, especially in the African context, that evaluates the implication of the presence of LLIs on households that reside in communities where they are located. Some of the concerns in such evaluation are partly the issue of data lapses, data inaccuracies, and data hoarding at various national levels across Africa, which makes it difficult to provide empirical evidences on the subject matter. This study is among the few that provides new empirical insights on the implications of LLIs on households with a focus on a specific African country—Nigeria. The choice of Nigeria is motivated mainly because it is among the top twenty (20) LLIs recipient countries globally, and among the top ten (10) in Africa (Land Matrix Global Observatory [LMGO] 2017). Whereas other countries in Africa (e.g., Ethiopia, Ghana, Mozambique, South Sudan, Tanzania, and Zambia) that are LLI destinations have received considerable research efforts, not much is known for Nigeria, in terms of the implications. Furthermore, Nigeria is among the very few countries in Africa with nationally representative data like the Living Standards Measurement Study-Integrated Surveys on Agriculture (LSMS_ISA),[2] which contain relevant information on communities, households and agricultural activities, and which will be relevant for statistical analysis of the relationship as considered in this study.

Using the Difference-in-Difference (*DiD*) technique, which is a tool in the quasi-experimental research design, this study tests the causal-effect relationships of the presence of LLIs in households communities on their livelihood. Specifically, the main objective of this study is to examine the effects of LLIs on households livelihood (using consumption and expenditure proxies approach) in communities with LLIs in comparison with those in communities without LLIs in Nigeria. Stemming from the objective, this paper answers the broad research question: In what way does consumption expenditure of households in communities with LLIs differ from their counterparts in other communities? The above

---

U. R. Efobi
College of Business and Social Sciences (CBSS) & Centre for Economic Policy and Development Research (CEPDeR), Covenant University, Ota, Nigeria

A. A. Karakara
School of Economics, University of Cape Coast, Cape Coast, Ghana

I. Beecroft
Department of Economics & Development Studies & Centre for Economic Policy and Development Research (CEPDeR), Covenant University, Ota, Nigeria

research question is crucial in understanding the welfare[3] implications of LLIs on households in LLIs communities compared to those in communities without LLIs. Basically, consumption gives better understanding of households welfare outcome compared to income (Herrmann et al. 2018; Osabuohien et al. 2019). Thus, this study proceeds with the hypothesis that households in communities with LLIs have increased welfare than their counterparts in communities without LLIs.

Three measures of livelihoods are adopted in this study, which include total household expenditure, food expenditure, and non-food expenditure. The estimation suggests that on the average, households in communities with LLIs have higher total consumption, food, and non-food consumption outcome compared to households in communities without LLIs. Thus, this research makes an important contribution to literature by focusing on the micro impacts of the presence of LLIs on the livelihood of households and host communities, as extant studies (like Cotula 2012) have examined the *drivers* (i.e., determinants) of LLIs at the global level. Studies that have considered the welfare implications of LLIs on host communities are mainly reports (Deininger and Songwe 2009; Daniel and Mittal 2009; Cotula et al. 2009; Dessy et al. 2012). Also, unlike some previous studies (like Herrmann and Grote 2015; Mutopo et al. 2015; Herrmann et al. 2018) that looked at the implications of LLIs within a country based on one or two cases, this study considers a plurality of cases to provide a general outlook of the implication of LLIs and compares households in communities with and without LLIs.

The remainder of the study is distributed as follows: the second section considers the review of related literature and theoretical underpinning, which is immediately followed by the analytical technique and data sources in the third section. The fourth section includes the results and discussions, and the paper is concluded in the fifth section.

2   Land Investments and Employment Nexus

This section briefly reviews literature that explores the relationship between land investments and households livelihood using a synchronic approach. It also underscores the framework upon which the analysis in the study is built.

2.1   *Review of the Interactions Between Large-Scale Land Investments and Employment*

Large-scale Land Investments (LLIs) is often conflated with the term "land grabbing." Though both terms are similar, there is a line of demarcation between them. Land grabbing entails taking possession of and/or controlling a scale of land for commercial/industrial agricultural production that is disproportionate in size in comparison to the average land holding in the region (Hall 2011). "Land grabbing" in simple form is a situation where locally used land is leased or sold to foreign investors. However, LLIs involves the acquisition of land of 200 hectares and above (usually through lease, and in few cases purchase) of land for mainly agricultural purpose (Land Matrix Global Observatory [LMGO] 2017).[4] Thus, not all LLIs lead to land grabbing.

Among the possible drivers of LLIs in Africa are the relatively cheap prices of arable land. For instance, land in Zambia (that happens to be the most expensive in Africa) is only one-eighth the price of similar land in Argentina or Brazil, and less than one-twentieth of that in Germany (Osabuohien et al. 2013). Some other drivers include the increasing use of biofuels, global economic crises, supports from national government especially those from advanced countries, and rising food prices (Cotula et al. 2009; Deininger et al. 2011; Nolte et al. 2016; Osabuohien et al. 2019). Väth and Kirk (2014) acknowledged that the demand for LLIs in Africa is largely driven by the desire for food and fodder, industrial raw materials, biomass, or purely by financial speculation. Also, most foreign governments are striving to secure reliable water and food supply as a way of insulation against tighter and more volatile markets, while the private sector expects to cash-in on promising positive returns from agriculture (Badiane 2011; Cotula 2011). LLIs in Africa's land transactions raise concerns about the impacts on the locals and smallholder farmers in areas where they are located.

Some existing studies on LLIs have largely focused on exploring the risks associated with its presence, in terms of the infringement on the rights and livelihood of the poor. Okuro (2015) noted that large-scale land acquisition might further jeopardize the welfare of the poor by depriving them of the safety net function that this type of land and water use fulfills. Aigbokhan and Ola (2015) further concluded that a particular LLI deal in Nigeria (i.e., Presco Industries in Edo state) was not able to improve the livelihood of the people of the community where they are located through employment, while other authors (e.g., Cotula et al. 2009) find the opposite in relation to different outcome variables (food security and rural development). However, the welfare impacts of LLIs in Africa have raised serious concerns among researchers with some looking at the implications of LLIs on water rights and livelihoods (Smaller and Mann 2009; Williams et al. 2012). Cotula et al. (2009) have acknowledged the potentials of land investments, but warned that these may not be handy if host governments fail to build capacities to negotiate better terms for their people. In terms of the effects on employment, Food and Agricultural Organization (FAO) (2012) found that foreign investments in the agricultural sector in Ghana contributed to more than 180,000 jobs between 2001 and 2008. In contrast, Schoneveld et al. (2011), who studied acquisition of land for a plantation for biofuel production in Ghana, found increasing rural poverty—especially affecting women and migrants—as LLIs land acquisition was focused on customary land and therefore deprived households of their livelihood resources. The above is akin to earlier observation made by Ato (2010) regarding the issue of property rights institutions in African countries.

Other studies like Khadjavi et al. (2017) and Nolte and Ostermeier (2017) found that LLIs have effect on the employment nature of communities with high LLIs rate than communities with low LLIs rate. They (Nolte and

Ostermeier 2017) use two different sets of data (LMGO & LSMS_ISA) in their analysis by comparing high LLIs communities with low LLIs communities. Khadjavi et al. (2017), closely looked at social capital and LLIs, where they compare communities near LLIs and communities farthest to LLIs, and reached a similar conclusion.

Proponents of LLIs have encouraged the inflow of land investors as a veritable tool for development based on agreed terms between the investors and the owners of the land (Haberl et al. 2009). However, the underlining tone of land deals in Africa can be seen as "selfish ambitions," which involves the cultivation of agricultural products and exporting same to country of origin of the land investors, thereby resulting in local food security threats. Some of the cases emphasising the consequences of LLIs include Ghana, which has witnessed an increase in LLIs with promises to be involved in plantation development plans and engage smallholder farmers through an out-grower agreement; however, such schemes are yet to be observed (Schoneveld et al. 2011). In addtion, the investor's competition with local indigenes for the inadequate infrastructure has been experienced in host communities. More so, it has been noted that LLIs can be driven by corruption in governance. ElHadary and Obeng-Odoom (2013) concluded that the aim of the state in *land grab* transactions is more for the purpose of amassing wealth and power than for public interest. Holden and Pagel (2013) observed that a sizeable number of deals remain "questionable" in terms of the size and questioned whether they have actually been finalized and implemented.

Osabuohien et al. (2015) and Osabuohien et al. (2019) respectively studied Uganda and Tanzania with the LSMS_ISA data, as proposed in this current study. However, in the former, focus was placed mainly on the implications of LLIs on the communities, while the latter considered the impact of LLIs on female labour market outcomes. For empirical studies in Nigeria, Ariyo and Mortimore (2012) made some efforts using the case of Shonga in Kwara State and focusing on the effects of LLIs on youth employment. Very few other studies in Nigeria that have considered LLI include: Mustapha (2011), Odoemene (2012), Osabuohien (2014), and Olokoyo et al. (2015). Both Mustapha (2011) and Odoemene (2012) were also focused on Shonga, Kwara State in which the activities of the white Zimbabwean farmers, food and human security issues were examined, respectively. Aigbokhan and Ola (2015), which was on Edo state equally looked at LLIs and its impact on household livelihood by considering Obaretin and Ologbo estates. That of Osabuohien (2014) was quite a nationally representative analysis; the author essentially emphasized the role of local institutions in influencing the location of LLIs in Nigerian communities. In Olokoyo et al. (2015), the impact of land deals on income sustainability of smallholder farmers and owners of land was studied in a rural community in Ogun state. Thus, this present study takes the literature on LLIs forward by providing empirical analysis on the implications of LLIs on households in communities in Nigeria where LLIs are located. Overall, this study brings a different perspective to the LLIs debate by considering the effects of LLIs on households livelihood in Nigeria.

2.2 Theoretical Underpinning on the Effects of Land Investments

Different theories predict different impacts (positive or negative) of large-scale land acquisitions on smallholder farmers. Some theories conclude that the effect of land acquisition is strongly influenced by the type of land tenure system in place. In weak land tenure system for instance, large-scale land acquisitions could lead to a public open-access property regime to private property system. The so-called Enclosed Model predicts that the shift from communal to private property will lead to the displacement of smallholders, lower labor opportunities and overall lower standards of living for smallholders. It (enclosure theory) predicts that large-scale acquisition of land frequently entails the expropriation of customary land right-holders. Some writers critically looked at the effects of foreign land acquisitions in Sub-Saharan Africa (De Schutter 2011; Anseeuw et al. 2012) per the enclosure theory and concluded that, peasant displacement, decline in standard of living, rise in rent and surplus, agriculture becoming less labor-intensive than in communal management, national income rises, net flow of labor out of agriculture are some of the results of LLIs.

The Evolutionary Theory of property rights, as summarized by Platteau (1996), shows how in a land market, there is movement from communal to private property as soon as the national and international commercial pressure on rural land creates new market opportunities. The theory predicts that once land assumes a scarcity value, the demand for land should increase which strengthens land security for smallholders. The evolution is considered as spontaneous and that the state still plays an important role as the actor formalizing and consolidating the new system. This theory is based on the observation of the shortcomings of communal rights as opposed to private property. Demsetz (1967) argued that new property rights takes place in response to the desires of interacting persons for adjustment to new benefit–cost possibilities.

A theoretical framework by Deininger et al. (2011) considers the Welfare Enhancing Approach, which is in line with the evolutionary theory of property rights, but differs by assuming that the property rights are already well established and enforced (Ato 2010). Hence, land investment can lead to mutually beneficial outcomes for both investors and smallholders or community. This can happen in twofold; smallholders can benefit from land rental and contract farming in one hand while in the other hand wage payment would allow landless members of the community such as women to benefit from the labor hours they supply. Large-scale land investments can improve infrastructure, market access, boost production, lead to rural development, create labor opportunities, and increases welfare. All these theories share the similar view that is espoused in this paper—that the effect of large-scale land acquisitions is strongly influenced by the type of land tenure system in place—which is displayed in Fig. 1.

This framework follows that of the welfare enhancing theory, in that the LLIs in this study area have promises that will benefit the households in the communities where such LLIs are located. Thus, these LLIs can be welfare enhancing for the households in host communities. Figure 1 shows the theoretical framework the study adopts. It goes with the assumption that property rights are already well defined, the market for lands functions competitively, and information is accessible to all involved parties (land investors and community members). There is evidence that in terms of investment involving large-scale land acquisitions in countries where land rights are unclear and insecure; the disadvantages often outweigh the few benefits to the local community, especially in the short run (Liu 2014; Oyebola et al. 2019). This assumption in the study area (Nigeria) is germane given the fact that Nigeria is an African country where the government has institutionalized controls over land acquisition and usage. The land administration policy spelled out rules on acquisition and use of large-scale land. There are instances where government gets involved in LLIs dealings with community members. With the assumption that property rights are already defined, the relationship between smallholders (land owners) and investors can be welfare enhancing for all parties without need for a regulatory intervention. Where some of the conditions are not met, the state or government will need to intervene to strengthen the property rights system, the market functioning or the transparency among parties.

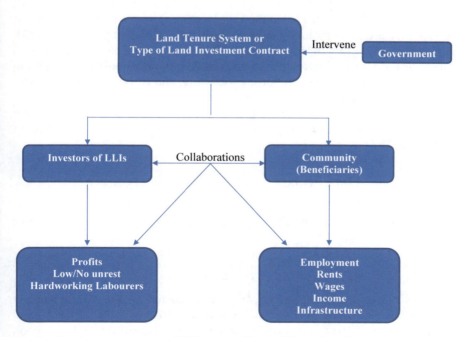

Fig. 1 Land tenure system and LLIs nexus (*Source* The authors')

As shown in Fig. 1, as land investors and community members collaborates for the success of LLIs, both parties enjoy some benefits. If the land contract system is good and there is good collaboration between investors and community members, the LLI investors stand the chance of making good profits; enjoy hardworking labor with virtually no labor unrest as community members who are employed tend to see the project as one of their own. On the other hand, such LLIs tend to create employment for such members of the community where it is located, land owners can enjoy rents, wages are paid to labor who has no land to enjoy rent, incomes are earned, smallholders may enjoy agricultural technology spillover from the LLIs and LLIs calls for good roads and other infrastructures. Proceeds from the sale of lands could be a means to community economic well-being when the monies are used well in productive investments. Furthermore, community members may create business enterprises to service the LLI Company and its workers. Community members may depend on the company's products that can be traded and petty selling of items to workers as means of livelihood. LLIs companies may also engage in corporate social responsibility projects, which benefit the households. Where such benefits are not forthcoming or where such land contracts raise tendencies the state or government intervene to correct the anomalies.

The analytical framework of this study is germane to the study area for some reasons. First, most of the LLIs in Nigeria are found to have created employment for the communities where they are located (Ariyo and Mortimore 2012; Osabuohien 2014; Aigbokhan and Ola 2015; Osabuohien et al. 2015). Second, LLIs acquisitions have affected community welfare in terms of improvement in houses they live in, community infrastructures etc. (Aigbokhan and Ola 2015). Aigbokhan and Ola (2015) specifically found that the Presco Industries in Obaretin and Ologbo Estates in Edo State has led to more households acquiring motor cycles, TV set, air conditions, good water, and so on, which they previously do not have before the company came to the community. Third, many community members are found to operate businesses in the area of petty trading with the LLIs in Nigeria, thus, enhancing rural entrepreneurship (Aigbokhan and Ola 2015).

3 Data Sources and Analytical Technique

This section highlights the sources of the data utilized in the study and the technique employed in analyzing the data with a view to achieving the objective of the study.

3.1 Data

This study uses data from the LSMS_ISA conducted by the World Bank in collaboration with Nigeria's National Bureau of Statistics (NBS). The dataset, structured questionnaires, manuals (interviewer and supervisor) and codebook are available on World Bank (LSMS_ISA)'s website. The LSMS_ISA data for

Nigeria covers the 36 States of Nigeria plus the Federal Capital Territory-FCT, Abuja. The data is grouped into: community, households, and agriculture for the two segments (i.e., post-planting and post-harvest) of the survey. For the purpose of this study, the community and the household levels data is used, which will involve merging the two sets of data for the latest two waves, notably: Wave 2 (2012–2013) and Wave 3 (2015/2016). There are 500 Enumeration Areas (EAs) sampled from the total of 774 Local Government Areas (LGAs) in Nigeria (including urban and rural areas) in the 36 States and FCT. An EA is a constituent of an LGA; Nigeria runs three tiers of government: the Federal, State, and Local.

The analysis is at the household level, while information on the EAs (e.g., EA codes) is used in categorizing communities with LLIs and those without it. Thus, for the purpose of this study, a community is used synonymously with an EA. One of the advantages of the LSMS_ISA data is that information about the location (i.e., codes for EA and LGA) and the codes for households is unique in data files in both waves. This makes the combination of the data to show time dimension possible using the relevant identification codes for the households and EAs.[5]

3.2 Difference-in-Difference (DiD) Approach

The quasi-experimental design based on Difference-in-Difference (*DiD*) technique, is used as the main analytical tool.[6] Experimental studies are those that are intended to test causal–effect relationships (hypotheses) in a tightly controlled setting by separating the cause from the effect in time, administering the cause to one group of subjects (the "treatment group") but not to another group ("comparison group"), and observing how the mean effects vary between subjects in these two groups (Bhattacherjee 2012). In a typical experimental design, subjects should be randomly assigned to each group. If random assignment is not followed, then the design becomes quasi-experimental (Kothari 2004). This study is unique and novel as it looked at the welfare effects of LLIs by comparing communities with and without LLIs, which other studies did not. Thus, the sample of the study includes communities where the LLIs are located (experimental communities) versus communities without LLIs (control group). In this study, we are not interested in the random assignment of communities according to LLI presence. This is because the sites of LLI are predetermined by a multiplicity of reasons, including the investors' decision and some other observable characteristics that improve the conduciveness of the community for investment.

The *DiD* estimation is an important impact evaluation technique that estimates the counterfactual for the change in outcome for the population (i.e., households) in communities with LLIs by calculating the change in outcome for the households in communities without LLIs, and estimating the difference. This estimation technique is helpful because it takes into consideration any differences between the two groups that are constant over time.

The *DiD* technique's applicability is conditional on group fixed effect and time fixed effect. In this case, the *intervention* of interest is the presence of LLIs in communities that are represented in the LSMS_ISA dataset. For the *DiD* estimation to be successful, both groups of interest should have similar time trends and there is no anticipation of policy intervention, or regional shocks that will make the groups to be non-comparable. The study has overcome this challenge since the communities of interest are exposed to similar macroeconomic atmosphere and general economic policy. With regards to the time period being similar across groups, the last two waves: namely, the second (2012/2013) and the third (2015/2016) waves of the LSMA_ISA are used.[7]

To apply the *DiD* technique, there are two *states of affairs*, $S=0$; 1 (in the case of this study, communities with LLIs$=1$ and those without it$=0$) and two periods, $t=0$ (first wave of the LSMS_ISA); 1 (second wave of the LSMS_ISA). This can be written heuristically as:

$$W = \begin{cases} 1 & \text{if } S = 1, t = 1 \\ 0 & \text{if otherwise} \end{cases} \quad (1)$$

From Eq. (1), the causal relationship of interest can be expressed as:

$$Y_{st} = \alpha + \rho W_{st} + \gamma_s X_s + \tau T_t + \epsilon_{st} \quad (2)$$

The time-invariant community fixed effect and the common time trend can be differenced out as:

$$\tilde{Y}_s = Y_{s1} - Y_{s0} = \rho(W_{s1} - W_{s0}) + \epsilon_{s1} - \epsilon_{s0} \quad (3)$$

Then the difference-in-difference is taken as:

$$Y^{DiD} = \tilde{Y}_1 - \tilde{Y}_0 = Y_{11} - Y_{10} - (Y_{01} - Y_{00}) - \rho(W_{11} - W_{10} - (W_{01} - W_{00})) \\ + \epsilon_{11} - \epsilon_{10} - (\epsilon_{01} - \epsilon_{00}) \quad (4)$$

This can be simplified as:

$$Y^{DiD} = \rho + \epsilon_{11} - \epsilon_{10} - (\epsilon_{01} - \epsilon_{00}) \quad (5)$$

Ideally, the final result from *DiD* is:

$$Y^{DiD} = \rho \quad (6)$$

3.2.1 Definition of the Variables
The variables of interest for this study are presented in Table 1.

Apart from the classification of the communities of the household across their locations in communities with LLIs and without LLIs, the other variables of interest (including the outcome and explanatory variables) are all sourced from the World Bank's LSMS_ISA data. The outcome variable is justified as a measure of household welfare considering that it captures the expenditure dimension of income, compared to income that are mostly under reported in survey data (Osabuohien et al. 2019). The other explanatory variables were included

Table 1 Variable names and definitions

Variable	Code	Description
Share of children	share_child	This is the share of children that are living in the household to the total number of individuals in the household
Share of female	share_female	This is the share of female that are living in the household to the total number of individuals in the household
Household assets	hh_assetnos	This is the total number of household assets that are owned in the household. It is a count variable
Age of household	age	This is the average age of the total individuals that are living in the household
Plot area cultivated	plot_area	This is the size (area) of the household land that are cultivated. It is GPS measure in square meters
Land harvest	land_harv	This measures the quantity of the agricultural produce harvested by the household in previous year
Hh expenditure	hhexp_pcap	This is the average total household expenditure per capita. It includes both food and non-food expenditure in a week. The value is measured in the local currency unit (Naira)
Food expenditure	fdexp_pcap	This is the average total food expenditure of the household in a typical week. The value is measured in the local currency unit (Naira)
Non-food expenditure	ndfd_exppcap	This is the value of the non-food expenditure of the household in a typical week. The value is measured in the local currency unit (Naira)
Large scale investment	LLI	This is a dummy variable, where households in communities with LLI occurrence are classified as 1 and those in communities without LLIs are classified as 0

Source Authors' compilation using information from LSMS_ISA

considering the literature (e.g., Glewwe 1991; Mansour 2012) that considers the determinants of households welfare.

4 Results and Discussions

In this section, the results from the empirical analysis are presented and discussed. It starts with the results from descriptive statistics of the main variables of interest.

4.1 *The Summary Statistics*

The summary statistics of the main variables of interest are presented in Table 2. The mean and standard deviation for each of the variables used in the empirical analysis are also included in the table.

From Table 2, the main outcome variables of interest (i.e., total expenditure, food expenditure, and non-food expenditure) show that, on the average, the

Table 2 Summary statistics of variables

Variable	All		Households in communities with LLIs		Households in communities without LLIs	
	Mean	Std. Dev.	Mean	Std. Dev.	Mean	Std. Dev.
share_child	0.637	0.455	0.677	0.444	0.636	0.455
share_female	0.527	0.474	0.555	0.472	0.526	0.474
hh_assetnos	0.206	0.544	0.18	0.221	0.207	0.549
Age	17.911	20.13	15.159	16.85	17.964	20.185
plot_area	5213.03	15,810.56	7308.856	10,534.15	5172.88	15,896.42
land_harv	523.006	2339.484	440.123	784.189	524.325	2355.955
hhexp_pcap	3.616	8.165	2.992	7.383	3.628	8.179
fdexp_pcap	3.286	8.147	2.686	7.362	3.297	8.161
ndfd_exp-pcap	0.331	0.324	0.306	0.223	0.331	0.325

Source Authors' computation using LSMS_ISA dataset

entire households per capita expenditure across these categories of expenditure are about 4 and less than 1 for non-food expenditure, which is about 3500 for total household expenditure and less than 100 naira for non-food expenditure. It is important to note that apart from the low values of food and non-food expenditure, as well as the total expenditure, the per capita value of the variables show the total amount that are spent by the household as a share of the total number of individuals in the household. Entirely, the households spend less money on non-food expenditure in an average week.

The mean values of the other explanatory variables are also displayed in Table 2 and are discussed as follows: the mean share of children in the household is about 64%, and for households in communities with (and without) LLIs it is about 68 and 64%, respectively. The share of female is about 53% for the entire households, and 56% for those households in communities with LLIs and 53% for those in communities without LLIs. The number of assets owned by the household, which is also another measure of endowment, is low for the entire households and those in communities with (and without) LLIs. This shows that generally, the households are less endowed. The average age of the household is 18 years: 15 years for those in communities with LLIs, and 18 years for those in communities without LLIs. The average size of the households' plot area is 5213 square meters, which is larger for households in communities with LLIs (7309) compared to those in communities without LLIs (5173). For the farm yield, there is an average of 523-plot yield, which is more for households in communities without LLIs compared to those in communities with LLIs.

4.2 Empirical Results

4.2.1 The Average Treatment Effect—DiD

The average treatment effect (ATE) measures the outcome variable, in this case, the households' total expenditure, food and non-food expenditure in LLI communities compared to those in communities without LLIs. This comparison will help to understand the average difference in the outcome variables between households that reside in communities with (and without) LLIs.

In a regression setup, the equation for examining the impact policy change is equal to:

$$Hh.\,Consumption_i = \beta_0 + \beta_1 t + \beta_2 D + \beta_3 (D \times t) + \beta_4\, controls + \cdots \quad (7)$$

Where "t" denotes a dummy variable for the period and D equals to one for those in the communities with LLI and zero otherwise. The parameter of interest is β_3, which is a dummy variable that equals to "1" for those observations in the treatment group across the period.

The results of the difference-in-difference are presented in Table 3 and suggest that on the average, the total consumption of households in communities with LLIs increased by 4.18% compared to those in communities without LLIs. Focusing on the direct effect of the dummy variable that measures the period and LLI presence, the coefficient of the former suggest that it is not statistically significant at the traditional significant levels of 1 and 5%. This result suggests that the change in the periods had no effect on the different measures of household welfare. The coefficient on LLIs shows that, even in the absence of any change in the period, households in communities with LLIs spend less amount of their money on consumption, as measured using the three outcome variables. Possibly, the increase in the policy variable can be traced to the fact that there are some time-invariant community characteristics that most likely relates with the presence of LLIs to impact positively on households total consumption. The LLI variable, at its initial value, has a negative impact on household consumption (both total, food, and non-food consumption). The total effect is that, household welfare, measured by total consumption and consumption of food and non-food items, in LLIs communities are higher than non-LLIs communities. Thus, a household from an LLI community is expected to have increased consumption than their counterpart in non-LLI community. Perhaps, the presence of LLI in a community could help in increasing the food hub of the community as food may be abundant in such community. The occurrence of LLI could also offer jobs to the local people, hence incomes will be earned and more food can be consumed.

4.2.2 Controlling for the Household Fixed Effect

The next step is to consider the consistency of the result when controlling for those unobserved household effects that potentially affect the relationship of

Table 3 Results from double difference (DiD)

	Total Hh exp.	Total Hh food exp.	Total Hh non-food exp.
Year	0.181	−0.237	0.156
	(0.291)	(0.547)	(0.366)
Lli	−1.216**	−2.514*	−1.213***
	(0.044)	(0.095)	(0.005)
lli*year	4.184**	7.629***	4.202***
	(0.034)	(0.000)	(0.000)
share_child	−0.402	−0.458	−0.411
	(0.111)	(0.439)	(0.106)
share_female	0.102	0.190	0.121
	(0.502)	(0.599)	(0.422)
hh_assetnos	0.322*	0.662**	0.329*
	(0.073)	(0.027)	(0.061)
Age	−0.011**	−0.002	−0.012**
	(0.042)	(0.905)	(0.029)
Lnplot	−0.057	−0.157	−0.054
	(0.266)	(0.214)	(0.285)
Lnharv	0.047*	0.057	0.047*
	(0.100)	(0.407)	(0.098)
Constant	0.573	−0.785	5.315***
	(0.258)	(0.512)	(0.000)
R-squared	0.036	0.017	0.036

Note: ***, **, and * indicate significant at 1, 5 & 10 percent. *Source* Authors' computation using LSMS_ISA dataset

interest. From the result reported in Table 4, it is still evident that there is a significant improvement in the volume of household welfare when considering the location of the household in communities with LLIs and other time-invariant factors. The LLI variable remained negative at its initial value, which is the same with the earlier explanation. Precisely, the magnitude of the coefficient of the presence of LLI on total household expenditure, total food expenditure, and total non-food expenditure were at similar range as those presented in Table 3.

The result from this study is consistent with the result for Herrmann (2017), who observed that there is a positive household effect of the presence of land investments in Tanzania. Herrmann (2017) identified two main channels through which this effect is possible. They include: the employment channel and the consumption channel. The author noted that the presence of investors improves the employment status of households in locations where they are situated through their contract farming and out-grower schemes. For the consumption channel, the author observed that the presence of LLIs increases the stock of local goods for sale within the community, which increases the consumption of households. However, it differs from that of Osabuohien et al. (2019) who focused mainly on female labor outcomes in Tanzania. One good explanation for the difference in the result is that the authors focused on only female-headed

Table 4 Double difference with fixed effect

	Total Hh exp.	Total Hh food exp.	Total Hh non-food exp.
Year	0.187	−0.120	−0.228
	(0.273)	(0.794)	(0.563)
Lli	−1.113*	−1.800*	−2.252*
	(0.064)	(0.100)	(0.100)
lli*year	3.746*	6.341***	6.783***
	(0.058)	(0.004)	(0.000)
share_child	−0.386	−0.038	−0.418
	(0.124)	(0.954)	(0.478)
share_female	0.094	0.088	0.168
	(0.533)	(0.781)	(0.642)
hh_assetnos	0.373**	0.748***	0.748**
	(0.039)	(0.000)	(0.019)
Age	−0.011**	0.004	−0.001
	(0.047)	(0.783)	(0.939)
Lnplot	−0.097*	−0.230*	−0.230*
	(0.072)	(0.081)	(0.081)
Lnharv	0.045	0.021	0.058
	(0.110)	(0.776)	(0.405)
Constant	0.598	−1.476	−0.745
	(0.237)	(0.272)	(0.534)
R-squared	0.044	0.022	0.022

Note: ***, **, and * indicate significant at 1, 5 & 10 percent. *Source* Authors' computation using LSMS_ISA dataset

households in their analysis given a somewhat gender discrimination in terms of employment, salary structure, and business profit structure in Tanzania.

5 Conclusion

This study sets out with the motivation to provide further empirical evidence on the nexus between large-scale land investments (LLIs) and household livelihood using the case of Nigeria. The study is deemed essential because unlike other LLIs destination countries in Africa (e.g., Ethiopia, Kenya, Mozambique, Tanzania, and Zambia) that have received sizeable analyses on the implications of LLIs on households; evidences indicate that considerable focus has not been on Nigeria. This objective is crucial as it underscores with a view to providing empirical analysis on the implications of LLIs on households welfare outcomes.

Based on the analysis carried out in the study using difference-in-difference technique, it was found that in an average week, households spend less money on non-food expenditure as per capita expenditure on food is higher than non-food as per household. Also, LLIs are mostly located in communities where household average size of plot area is larger and this is what is observed as communities with LLIs have households average plot size (7309) higher than households (5173) in communities without LLIs.

In addition, on household welfare outcomes, an average household in communities with LLIs has consumption higher than their counterparts in communities without LLIs and change in period has no effect on the consumption pattern of households. There is significant improvement in the volume of household welfare in communities with LLIs. Thus, the results from this study offer policy recommendations that will be useful in addressing the issue of LLIs. Government and policy makers should look at land rights and household access to land and offer regulations that will be better fit to help benefit the households. This will help reduce rural poverty and enhance consumption by the households.

The main issue from this research is that despite that there exists a direct negative effect of LLI presence on household total consumption, food and non-food consumption, there is a likely positive effect from the presence of LLI when considering the combination of those unobserved characteristics that may affect the relationship. This finding implies that the issue of LLI should not be considered from only the perspective of the LLI presence and what it offers the community, but there should be a combination of other important community and household variables, such as the presence of structures to effectively negotiate and intermediate between land owners and the foreign investors, to ensure an inclusive policy to enhance the outcomes of displaced land owners. Other important structures like this are necessary to ensure that LLIs are beneficial to their host communities.

As suggestions for further studies, other approaches such as fixed effect regression technique, which can capture the within-group variation over time with a view to further exploring the relationship between LLIs (i.e., the predictor) and the welfare of households (i.e., the outcome variables) can be adopted. This will complement the analysis carried out in this study that used the difference-in-difference (DiD) technique. Thus, such analysis can consider cross-community differences in livelihood and LLIs, by clustering the analysis by the community, which will help in identifying the individual household effect from the presence of LLIs across communities. It could also cover other areas like employment that are crucial for household livelihood and with other technique like propensity sore matching especially for cross-section component.

Acknowledgments The research on which this work is based was made possible by the Research Grant [Ref: MRI/CTR 6/2017] from the Council for the Development of Social Science Research in Africa (CODESRIA). The first author acknowledges the Research Fellowship Award [Ref: 3.4-1147508-NGA-GF-P] and Equipment Subsidy Grant to the Centre for Economic Policy and Development Research-CEPDeR [Ref: 3.4-8151/19 047] from the Alexander von Humboldt Foundation. The authors appreciate the reviewers as well as CODESRIA resource persons and evaluator for their helpful comments on the earlier drafts. The views expressed are the authors'.

Notes

1. Evidences show that over 80% of LLI goes to the agricultural sector. Besides the activities of foreign investors with respect to LLIs, it has been observed that domestic investments are equally important (Nolte 2014; Osabuohien et al. 2015).
2. Other Sub-Saharan African (SSA) countries with LSMS_ISA data include: Burkina Faso, Ethiopia, Malawi, Mali, Niger, Tanzania, and Uganda. See http://go.worldbank.org/BCLXW38HY0 for details.
3. In this study, household welfare is taken almost synonymously with households livelihood. This is given the fact that consumption expenditure is a reflection of the utility of the households, which has direct relationship with their welfare status (Herrmann et al. 2018; Osabuohien et al. 2019).
4. Some others like Cotula et al. (2009), conceptualized LLIs as deals/acquisitions involving outright purchases and lease of land areas over 1000 hectares. This study follows the definition by LMGO (2017) of LLIs as above 200 hectares because 200 hectares is quite sizable enough given the recommended land per household of 2 hectares in Africa.
5. More details are in the basic information document (BID) and respective questionnaires for the data on LSMS_ISA website (http://go.worldbank.org/P6XWWYUIB0).
6. The analysis can also be done using fixed effect regression technique that can exploit the within-group variation over time. In this case, the fixed effect model can explore the relationship between the predictor and the outcome variables (in terms of household welfare) within the community of the households. This kind of analysis could also support the difference-in-difference (*DiD*) as it can help in controlling for own community characteristics that may or may not influence the predictor variables. Thus, the analysis can also consider cross-community differences in welfare and LLIs, by clustering the analysis by the community, which will help in identifying the individual household effect from the presence of LLIs across communities. With a view to staying focus and space constraint, this study only utilized the *DiD* technique. Hence, future studies can complement the present study using the fixed effect regression as well as other technique such as propensity sore matching (PSM).
7. For robustness, we use Wave 1 as the baseline so that possible contaminations from other interventions happening in the communities is minimized. More so, we use three levels of differences (namely: 1st & 2nd; 2nd & 3rd; 1st & 3rd Waves).

References

Aigbokhan, B., & Ola, K. (2015). Foreign land acquisitions, households' livelihood with some evidences on Nigeria. In E. Osabuohien (Ed.), *Handbook of research on in-country determinants and implications of foreign land acquisitions* (pp. 287–305). Hershey, PA: Business Science Reference.

Anseeuw, W., Wily, L. A., Cotula, L., & Taylor, M. (2012). Land rights and the rush for land: Findings of the global commercial pressures on land research project. In T. Bending & D. Wilson (Eds.). Rome: ILC, IIED, CIRA.

Ariyo, J. A., & Mortimore, M. (2012). Youth farming and Nigeria's development dilemma: The Shonga experiment. *IDS Bulletin, 43*(6), 58–66.

Ato, K. O. (2010). *The politics of property rights institutions in Africa*. New York: Cambridge University Press.

Badiane, O. (2011, December). Foreign direct investment in land and agriculture-based poverty reduction strategies in Africa. In F. Wouterse, K. Deininger, H. Selod, O. Badiane, J., Swinnen, J. von Braun, & D. Zilberman (Eds.), *Foreign direct investment in land in West Africa: The status quo, lessons from other regions, implications for research*. IFPRI—West and Central; Africa Office Thematic Research Note 01.

Bhattacherjee, A. (2012). *Social science research: Principles, methods, and practices*. USF Tampa Bay Open Access Textbooks Collection. Book 3.

Cotula, L. (2011). *Land deals in Africa: What is in the contracts?* London: IIED.

Cotula, L. (2012). The international political economy of the global land rush: A critical appraisal of trends, scale, geography and drivers. *Journal of Peasant Studies, 39*(3–4), 649–680.

Cotula, L., Vermeulen, S., Leonard, R., & Keeley, J. (2009). *Land grab or development opportunity? Agricultural investment and international land deals in Africa*. London and Rome: IIED/FAO/IFAD.

Daniel, S., & Mittal, A. (2009). *The great land grab: Rush for world's farmland threatens food security for the poor*. The Oakland Institute. Available from http://www.rrojasdatabank.info/landgrab3.pdf.

Deininger, K., Byerlee, D., Lindsay, J., Norton, A., Selod, H., & Stickler, M. (2011). *Rising global interest in farmland*. Washington, DC: The World Bank.

Deininger, K., & Songwe, V. (2009). Foreign investment in agricultural production: Opportunities and challenges. *Agricultural and Rural Development Notes, Issue 45*.

Demsetz, H. (1967). Toward a theory of property rights. *The American Economic Review, 57*(2), 347–359.

De Schutter, O. (2011). How not to think of land-grabbing: Three critiques of large-scale investments in farmland. *Journal of Peasant Studies, 38*(2), 249–279.

Dessy, S., Gohou, G., & Vencatachellum, D. (2012). *Foreign direct investments in Africa's farmlands: Threat or opportunity for local populations?* (CIRPEE Working Paper No. 12-03). https://doi.org/10.2139/ssrn.1991290.

ElHadary, Y. A., & Obeng-Odoom, F. (2013). Conventions, changes, and contradictions in land governance in Africa: The story of land grabbing in North Sudan and Ghana. Project Muse.

Food and Agricultural Organization (FAO). (2012). *Trends and impacts of foreign investment in developing country agriculture: Evidence from case studies*. Rome: Food and Agriculture Organization of the United Nations.

Glewwe, P. (1991). Investigating the determinants of household welfare in Cote d'Ivoire. *Journal of Development Economics, 35*(2), 307–337.

Haberl, H., Erb, K.-H., Krausmann, F., Berecz, S., Ludwiczek, N., Martínez-Alier, J., et al. (2009). Using embodied HANPP to analyse teleconnections in the global land system: Conceptual considerations. *Journal of Geography, 109*(2), 119–130.

Hall, R. (2011). Land grabbing in Southern Africa: The many faces of the investor rush. *Review of African Political Economy, 38*, 193–214.

Herrmann, R. (2017). Large-scale agricultural investments and smallholder welfare: A comparison of wage labour and outgrower channels in Tanzania. *World Development, 90*, 294–310.

Herrmann, R., & Grote, U. (2015). Large-scale agro-industrial investments and rural poverty: Evidence from sugarcane in Malawi. *Journal of African Economies, 24*(5), 645–676.

Herrmann, R., Jumbe, C., Bruentrup, M., & Osabuohien, E. (2018). Competition between biofuel feedstock and food production: Empirical evidence from sugarcane outgrower settings in Malawi. *Biomass and Bioenergy, 114,* 100–111.

Holden, J., & Pagel, M. (2013). *Transnational land acquisitions—What are the drivers, levels, and destinations, of recent transnational land acquisitions?* London: Nathan Associates LTD.

Khadjavi, M., Sipangule, K., & Thiele, R. (2017). *Social capital and large-scale agriculture investment: An experimental investigation in Zambia* (Kiel Working Paper No. 2056).

Kothari, C. R. (2004). *Research methodology: Methods and techniques.* 2nd Rev. ed. New Delhi: New Age International (P) Ltd.

Land Matrix Global Observatory (LMGO). (2017). *The online public database on land deals.* Retrieved February 5, 2017 from http://www.landmatrix.org/en/.

Liu, P. (2014). *Impacts of foreign agricultural investment on developing countries: Evidence from case studies* (FAO Commodity and Trade Policy Research Working Paper No. 47).

Mansour, W., (2012). *The patterns and determinants of household welfare growth in Jordan: 2002–2010* (World Bank Policy Research Working Paper No. 6249).

Mustapha, A. R. (2011). White Zimbabwean farmers in Nigeria: Exceptional farmers or spectacular support? *African Affairs, 110*(441), 536–561.

Mutopo, P., Chiweshe, M. K., & Mubaya, C. P. (2015). Large-scale land acquisitions, livelihoods, and gender configurations in Zimbabwe. In E. Osabuohien (Ed.), *Handbook of research on in-country determinants and implications of foreign land acquisitions* (pp. 130–144). Hershey, PA: Business Science Reference.

Nolte, K. (2014). Large-scale agricultural investments under poor land governance in Zambia. *Land Use Policy, 38,* 698–706.

Nolte, K. Chamberlain, W., & Markus, G. (2016). *International land deals for agriculture. Fresh insights from the land matrix: Analytical report II.* Bern, Montpellier, Hamburg, Pretoria: Centre for Development and Environment, University of Bern; Centre de coopération internationale en recherche agronomique pour le développement; German Institute of Global and Area Studies; University of Pretoria; Bern Open Publishing.

Nolte, K., & Ostermeier, M. (2017, October). Labour market effects of large-scale agricultural investment: Conceptual considerations and estimated employment effects. *World Development, 98,* 430–446.

Odoemene, A. (2012). White Zimbabwe farmers in Nigeria: Issues in "New Nigerian" land deals and the implication for food and human security. *African Identities, 10*(1), 63–76.

Okuro, S. O. (2015). Land grab in Kenya: Risk and opportunities. In *Environment, agriculture and cross-border migrations* (pp. 105–120). Dakar: CODESRIA Publication.

Olokoyo, F. O., George, T. O., Efobi, U., & Beecroft, I. (2015). Land deals and sustainable income: The case of a rural community in Ogun State, Nigeria. In E. Osabuohien (Ed.), *Handbook of research on in-country determinants and implications of foreign land acquisitions* (pp. 322–336). Hershey, PA: Business Science Reference.

Osabuohien, E. S. (2014, July). Large-scale agricultural land investments and local institutions in Africa: The Nigerian case. *Land Use Policy, 39,* 155–165.

Osabuohien, E. S., Efobi, U. R., Herrmann, R. T., & Gitau, C. M. (2019). Female labor outcomes and large-scale agricultural land investments: Macro-micro evidence from Tanzania. *Land Use Policy, 82,* 716–728. https://doi.org/10.1016/j.landusepol.2019.01.005.

Osabuohien, E. S., Gitau, C. M., Efobi, U. R., & Bruentrup, M. (2015). Agents and implications of foreign land deals in East African community: The case of Uganda. In E. Osabuohien (Ed.), *Handbook of research on in-country determinants and implications of foreign land acquisitions* (pp. 263–286). Hershey, PA: Business Science Reference.

Osabuohien, E. S., Ogundipe, A., & Efobi, U. R. (2013). The land rush in Africa: Implications and institutional panacea. In E. E. Oku & K. O. Asubonteng (Eds.), *Harnessing land and water resources for improved food security and ecosystem services in Africa* (pp. 92–106). Accra: United Nations University—Institute for Natural Resources in Africa.

Oyebola, P. O., Osabuohien, E., & Obasaju, B. (2019). Employment and income effects of Nigeria's agricultural transformation agenda. *African Journal of Economic and Management Studies*. https://doi.org/10.1108/AJEMS-12-2018-0402.

Platteau, J.-P. (1996). The evolutionary theory of land rights as applied to sub-Saharan Africa: A critical assessment. *Development and Change, 27*(1), 29–86.

Schoneveld, G. C., German, L. A., & Nutakor, E. (2011). Land-based investments for rural development? A grounded analysis of the local impacts of biofuel feedstock plantations in Ghana. *Ecology and Society, 16*(4). http://dx.doi.org/10.5751/ES-04424-160410.

Smaller, C., & Mann, H. (2009). *A thirst for distant lands: Foreign investment in agricultural land and water*. International Institute for Sustainable Development. Foreign Investment for Sustainable Development Program, Canada. Available from http://www.iisd.org/pdf/2009/thirst_for_distant_lands.pdf.

Väth, S. J., & Kirk, S. (2014). *Do contract farming and property rights matter for rural development? Evidence from a large-scale investment in Ghana*. MAGKS Joint Discussion Paper Series in Economics No.16.

Williams, T. O., Gyampoh, B., Kizito, F., & Namara, R. (2012). Water implications of large-scale land acquisitions in Ghana. *Water Alternatives, 5*(2), 243–265.

Agricultural Productivity and Household Welfare in Uganda: Examining the Relevance of Agricultural Improvement Interventions

Nicholas Kilimani, John Bosco Nnyanzi, Ibrahim M. Okumu, and Edward Bbaale

1   Introduction and Rationale

Agriculture in sub-Saharan Africa remains a strong candidate for driving growth, alleviating poverty, and enhancing food security (Asfaw et al. 2012). Improving the productivity, profitability, and sustainability of smallholder farming is therefore one critical pathway for improved welfare for the majority of the region's population (World Bank 2008). What is vital to note is that achieving agricultural productivity growth will not be possible without developing and disseminating yield-enhancing technologies since it is no longer feasible to meet the needs of the increasing population through the expansion of cultivable area (Asfaw et al. 2012). Agricultural research and technological improvements are considered as the vehicles through which agricultural productivity can be increased. A combination of those would result in income growth, asset accumulation, rural employment creation, and overall welfare improvement. In the absence of such innovations, poverty as well as meeting the demand for food will inevitably result in environmental and natural resource degradation as farmers encroach on forests and wetlands in search for fertile "virgin" land.

Tittonell and Giller (2013) note that food production in sub-Saharan Africa is failing to keep up pace with population growth as the region has the lowest land and labor productivity rates in the world, with annual growth in cereal yields averaging only 10 kg of grain per hectare per year. While cereal yields in most of the developed and developing economies have steadily risen during the last 50 years, yields in the sub-Saharan African region have stagnated around 1 ton per hectare or less. Similarly, the average yield of tuber crops is reported to be around 8 tons per hectare, making it the lowest in the world, and only increasing at a rate of 50 kg per hectare per year over the past half century (Tittonell and Giller 2013). Analysis of growth in harvested area shows that food production in the region increases at an annual rate of 2%, while average population growth rate is 3%. If sub-Saharan Africa is to rely on agriculture for socioeconomic transformation, agricultural production as of necessity has to increase at an annual rate of 4–7% (Breman and Debrah 2003). This could be achievable considering that technological progress in tropical agriculture in combination with more favorable socioeconomic contexts has allowed food production to increase substantially in Latin America and Asia during the last two to three decades (Tittonell and Giller 2013). Evidence shows that much of the increase could be attributable to increased input use and genetic advances through plant breeding (Hall and Richards 2013). As the yield ability of major crop varieties available for tropical environments keeps rising, the stagnating average yield observed in most African countries means that yield gaps are widening across the continent.

Technological improvements in agriculture are therefore believed to be the most important pathway for reducing rural poverty in many agrarian economies such as those in Sub-Saharan Africa (SSA) (Mendola 2007; Kijima et al. 2006; Kassie et al. 2011). For many of these countries, agriculture provides the leading source of employment and is a major contributor to the GDP of many developing countries national income. In Uganda's case, the sector contributes at least 40% of the GDP, approximately 85% of export earnings, and employs over 70% of the labor force (Government of Uganda 2018). This is in addition to the fact that nearly 90% of the population lives in rural areas, and directly derives its livelihood from subsistence agriculture.

The literature on the direct benefits of improved agricultural technologies points to the importance of such interventions in improving the welfare outcomes of the majority population that lives off agriculture in many of the developing countries. Studies by de Janvry and Sadoulet (2001) and Irz et al. (2001) detail the associated welfare gains from improved technology uptake such as raising incomes of especially the farm households and the indirect benefits of raising employment, wage rates of the functionally landless laborers and by the reduced prices of food. Whereas the use of productivity enhancing technologies in agriculture presents positive socioeconomic outcomes, very few studies interrogate the impact of interventions that support a general uptake of improved production technologies in agriculture (Mendola 2007).

In recognition of the importance of agriculture, public investment is being undertaken in agricultural research and development with the view to increasing agricultural productivity and stimulate growth in many developing countries (Diiro et al. 2015; Doss 2006). In fact, under the Government of Uganda's Plan for Modernization of Agriculture (PMA), the National Agriculture Research System in collaboration with international research centers has generated a wide range of improved technologies and management practices that have been disseminated to farmers through the National Agricultural Advisory Services and several other private service providers. Thus, it is expected that adoption of modern technologies such as improved crop varieties coupled with modern agronomic practices is expected to increase farm-level productivity and improve livelihoods of farm households in developing countries.

It is important to note that many of the impact studies related to modern agricultural technologies have largely been conducted for single staple crops such as maize, groundnuts, wheat, and rice. In addition, such studies are limited to small case studies in particular regions of the respective study areas (see e.g., Asfaw et al. 2012; Becerril and Abdulai 2010; Minten and Barrett 2008; Cairns et al. 2013; Kassie et al. 2011; Otsuka 2000; Rahman 1999). Therefore, it has not been proven about the extent of welfare outcomes if interventions are implemented on a larger scale with several mini-components within the intervention, as is the case with Uganda's programs on improving agricultural productivity. This chapter therefore contributes to the literature by presenting evidence on the impact of a sustained effort by the Government of Uganda to implement series of agricultural enhancing production technologies on agricultural productivity and welfare outcomes of agricultural households in Uganda.

Empirical evidence already shows that adoption of improved agricultural technologies enhances household well-being in developing countries (see e.g., Abro et al. 2014; Mendola 2007; Kijima et al. 2006; Ali and Abdulai 2010; Kassie et al. 2011). For instance, Kijima et al. (2006) and Kassie et al. (2011) found that adoption of upland rice and modern groundnut varieties were crucial for increasing agricultural income and therefore poverty reduction among rural households in Uganda. In this chapter, we investigate whether or not the various interventions meant to improve agricultural productivity have had any impact on the efficiency of agricultural production as well as improvement in the overall household welfare.

1.1 Description of a Recent Agricultural Productivity Enhancing Program

Uganda's sustained economic growth rate has translated into a significant reduction in household poverty levels, from 56.4 in 1992/93 to less than 19.7% in 2015/16 (Uganda Bureau of Statistics 2016). However, household incomes for majority of the population have remained low despite the reduction in absolute poverty. Despite the growth in per-capita income from US$320 over the past quarter century, rising to US$550, this is still among the lowest in the world. Against such a background, the Government of Uganda has overtime, undertaken several agricultural productivity enhancing programs with the most recent being the Operation Wealth Creation (OWC).

The OWC program proponents contend that one of the reasons for the stagnation in household incomes is the failure by households in Uganda, as is indeed the case with other parts of Africa to engage in commercial agricultural activities beyond subsistence farming. The Government of Uganda launched OWC in 2013 with a focus on raising household incomes for poverty eradication and sustainable wealth creation. The OWC activities include the sensitizing and mobilization of farmers to engage in commercial agricultural activities. The program activities entail distribution of planting and breeding inputs, post-harvest and bulking equipment, provision of processing equipment to farmers, and provision of credit services. The intervention operates countrywide with structures from the district to the Constituency level in 18 Zones. Zonal Coordinators oversee the activities of the Constituency Coordinators who, through a participatory approach, work with the Local Government leaders and the population to identify relevant enterprises at the household level and coordinate with line agencies and departments to ensure the systematic execution of the interventions.

The remainder of this chapter is organized as follows: Sect. 2 presents a brief description of the data and the research methods, while Sect. 3 discusses the findings of the study. Section 4 presents a highlight of recent evidence on the constraints to technology adoption in the agricultural sector in Uganda. The conclusion is presented in Sect. 5.

2 Methodology

Increasing agricultural productivity in Africa remains central to the continent's socioeconomic transformation. The existing literature is a little limited in providing evidence as to the linkages between productivity and welfare outcomes that result from multiple and large-scale interventions. We thus examine whether the various government interventions to boost agricultural productivity are making any impact and if that in turn is affecting household welfare. First, we assess issues of technical inefficiency before further analysis is undertaken.

2.1 Data

We employ the 2009/2010, 2011/2012, and 2013/2014 waves of the nationally representative household panel surveys conducted by the World Bank and the Uganda Bureau of Statistics (UBOS) under the Living Standards Measurement Study-Integrated Surveys in Agriculture (LSMS-ISA) initiative. The LSMS-ISA data is both quantitative and qualitative and it contains detailed household level information on a set of socioeconomic as well as community level characteristics (Uganda Bureau of Statistics).[1] It contains approximately 3200 representative households from urban, rural, and main regions of the country (North, East, West, and Central regions). Given our focus, the sample includes only farming households, defined as households who reported involvement in agricultural activities through ownership and/or cultivation of land for the period spanning the survey. The descriptive analysis presented in this chapter in Sects. 3–5 is based on the full samples of the baseline surveys, which were carried out in 2009/2010. Our final sample at baseline thus consists of 2930 households in Uganda. After excluding the non-panel and non-farming households, the final sample size of the panel used for the estimations is 1587 farming households. Overall, sample, attrition between the three waves was rather low. Data was cleaned, following which, variables were constructed.

Family labor was used as proxy for labor use in agricultural production. The choice of measurement is based on the fact that the largely smallholder nature of agriculture predisposes majority households to rely on family labor rather than hired labor in the conduct of their agricultural activities. The value of farm capital is the sum of the value of farm implements used for cultivation (see, Abro et al. 2014). A land quality index was developed using the farmers' self-reported slope and fertility of their plots (see e.g., Bachewe 2009). To calculate the average land quality index, we assigned a value of 1 for a plot with flat slope, 2 for gentle slope and 3 a hilly slope and 4 for steep slopes for every household. Similarly, if the land is very fertile a value of 1 for good soil, 2 for fair soil, and 3 for poor soil was assigned. Then multiplying the slope and fertility indicator of the plots, a plot with a value of 1 has the best land quality, while 12 would indicate the lowest quality. Other combinations of quality indicators are in between 1 and 12.

Given the importance of water in agricultural production, this was measured by the amount of rain recorded during the respective survey year. The role of dissemination of agricultural technologies through information provision under the National Agricultural Advisory Services (NAADS) was investigated using a dummy variable that checked whether any household member participated in government extension program during the respective survey periods. Under these programs, farmers are provided with information on agricultural production, agricultural prices, agro-processing, crop marketing, livestock marketing, fish production, livestock production, meat, and milk production, as well as prevention and treatment of crop and animal diseases. Households that recorded having received advice on the different program activities were taken as participants in the extension program. Human capital was measured by the years of schooling for the head of the household. Finally, we used real consumption per capita in the analysis of household welfare (see e.g., Dercon et al. 2012). Livestock ownership in tropical livestock units (TLUs) calculated by the Food and Agricultural Organization (FAO) (2011) was also directly used in the fixed effects regression.

2.2 Analysis of the Productivity Impacts on Agricultural Output

Following Aigner et al. (1977), Abro et al. (2014), we use the following deterministic production frontier, which is formally expressed as:

$$y = f(x, t; \beta) * \exp\{v - u\} \tag{1}$$

where y scalar of output produced is, $f(x, t; \beta)$ is the deterministic part of the stochastic production frontier with technology parameter vector β to be estimated for the underlying technology. $x = (x_1, x_2, \ldots, x_n) \geq 0$ is an input vector, t is a time trend serving as a proxy for technical change, and $u \geq 0$ represents output-oriented technical inefficiency. v are assumed to be independently and identically distributed random errors ($N(0, \sigma_v^2)$), and are independent of u. u are nonnegative random variables, associated with technical inefficiency in production, which are assumed to be independently and identically distributed exponential half-normal variables $\{u \sim [N(0, \sigma_u^2)]\}$ From Eq. (1), the rate of technical change can be computed as:

$$\Delta TC = \frac{\partial \ln f(x, t; \beta)}{\partial t} \tag{2}$$

ΔTC is greater than one, less than one, or equal to zero as technical change shifts the production frontier up, down or, leaves it unchanged, respectively. ΔTC can therefore be interpreted as an outward shift in the production frontier over time. Similarly, the rate of change of technical efficiency (ΔTE) can be measured by:

$$\Delta TE = -\frac{\partial u}{\partial t} \tag{3}$$

ΔTE has a value greater than one, less than one, or equal to zero as technical inefficiency declines, remains unchanged, or increases through time, respectively. ΔTE can therefore be interpreted as the rate at which a producer moves toward or away from the production frontier, which itself may be shifting through time (Kumbhakar and Lovell 2000). Following Coelli et al. (2005), Kumbhakar and Lovell (2000), Abro et al. (2014), we use a semi-logarithmic Cobb–Douglas function to empirically estimate Eq. (1) as follows:

$$\ln y_{it} = \alpha_0 + \alpha_1 \text{rain}_{it} + \alpha_2 \text{labour}_{it} + \alpha_3 \text{landsize}_{it} + \alpha_4 \text{lquality}_{it} + \alpha_5 \text{cfert}_{it} + \alpha_6 \text{farmcap}_{it} +$$
$$\alpha_7 \text{educ}_{it} + \alpha_8 \text{oxen}_{it} + \alpha_9 \text{extension}_{it} + \gamma_1 t + \frac{1}{2}\gamma_2 t^2 + \epsilon_{it} \quad (4)$$

ϵ_{it} is the composite error term of u_{it} and v_{it}. In the literature, several time-varying specifications for the technical inefficiency error components have been used. However, we follow Battese and Coelli (1992) and later Abro et al. (2014) for a non-linear specification to separate the time effects.

$$u_{it} = \eta u_i = \{\exp[-\eta(t-T)]\}u_{it}, \quad (5)$$

η is an unknown scalar parameter, and T is the last period for which observations for the i-th household are obtained. This model assumes that u_{it} decreases, remains constant or increases, as $\eta > 0$, $\eta = 0$ or $\eta < 0$, respectively. Setting $\eta = 0$ provides the time-invariant model. On the other hand, $\eta > 0$ implies that households tend to improve their level of efficiency over time and vice versa. v_{it} is assumed to be independently and identically distributed $N(0, \sigma_v^2)$ random errors. Moreover, v_{it} and u_{it} are assumed to be independently distributed. Based on these assumptions, the probability density function of the composite error term ϵ_{it} and its log likelihood function can be derived for the model using maximum likelihood. The predicted value of technical efficiency for producer i in period t is the conditional expectation of the inefficiency component in the error term.

$$TE_{it} = E\left[\exp\left(-u_{it}/\epsilon_{it}\right)\right] = \left\{\frac{1 - \Phi[\eta \sigma_i^* - (\mu_i^*/\sigma_i^*)]}{1 - \Phi(\mu_i^*/\sigma_i^*)}\right\} \exp\left[-\eta \mu_i^* + \frac{1}{2}\eta^2 \sigma_i^{*2}\right] \quad (6)$$

$$\mu_i^* = \frac{\mu \sigma_v^2 - \eta' \sigma^2}{\sigma_v^2 + \eta' \eta \sigma^2},$$

$$\sigma_i^{*2} = \frac{\sigma_v^2 \sigma^2}{\sigma_v^2 + \eta' \eta \sigma^2}$$

and $\Phi(\bullet)$ is the distribution function of a standard normal random variable (see Coelli et al. 2005; Kumbhakar and Lovell 2000: Battese and Coelli 1992).

The dependent variable in Eq. (4) is the real value of production for all crops produced (y_{it}) by a farmer household for a given period. Several independent variables are identified as input in the production process. Variables that are supposed to be directly used in the production of crops (conventional inputs) are chosen. These variables have to also be under the control of the farmer's decision (Lovell 1993). t indicates the survey year which is a proxy for Hicks-neutral technical progress. The description of independent variables is shown in Table 1. The amount of seed and other costs of productions (such as hired labor, payment for improved seed, land rental cost among

Table 1 Description of output, input, and farm specific variables

Variables	Description
Output ln y_{it}	Natural logarithm of real value of production
ln rain$_{it}$	The natural logarithm of the amount of rainfall 12 months during the survey
labor$_{it}$	The number of family members involved faming activity
ln farmsize$_{it}$	The natural logarithm of area cultivated (acres)
ln lquality$_{it}$	The natural logarithm of land quality index for farmer
ofert$_{it}$	Amount of fertilizers used, kilograms
oxen$_{it}$	Number of ploughing oxen owned
edu$_{it}$	Years of schooling for the head of the household
farmcap$_{it}$	The value of farm capital owned by the household in Shillings
ext$_{it}$	Value of 1 if farmer uses extension services, 0 otherwise
T	The survey year which is a proxy for Hicks-neutral technical progress
$\propto$	Parameters to be estimated
γ	Parameters to be estimated
ϵ_{it}	The composite error term as defined in Eq. (4)

Source Authors' extraction from LSMS_ISA Panel data

others) are also integral to the production process. However, these were not considered because less than 5% of sample recorded to have used them.

2.3 Analysis of Productivity Impacts of Agricultural Productivity on Household Welfare

This part of the chapter undertakes an analysis of the link between growth in productivity and real per capita household consumption. Consumption per capita per household was used as an indicator of household welfare and living standards. Following Abro et al. (2014), Simler et al. (2004), we, estimate the determinants of household real consumption per capita. The identification strategy is the unobserved effects model of Wooldridge (2009) and Greene (2003) and used by Abro et al. (2014). Formally:

$$lnc_{it} = \alpha_i + \varphi prod_{it} + \beta x_{it} + \epsilon_{it} \qquad (7)$$

where lnc_{it} is the natural logarithm of real household consumption per capita of household i, at time t, α_i is random individual-specific (unobserved) effects, β is a vector of parameters to be estimated, x_{it} represent exogenous regressors which serve as controls. $prod_{it}$ represents the indicators of productivity gains of farming households. The idiosyncratic error terms (ϵ_{it}) are assumed to be uncorrelated with the exogenous variables (x_{it}). Equation (5) is estimated using panel estimators since we believe that time-invariant unobserved household characteristics of a household are likely to correlate with the idiosyncratic error terms (ϵ_{it}).

The indicators of productivity such as land productivity and labor productivity were directly estimated from the raw data while the estimates of technical efficiency for the farming households were derived from a stochastic frontier model (see Abro et al. 2014). The productivity indicators are endogenous since they are correlated with other factors. This violates the crucial assumption of exogeneity of regressors. To obtain unbiased and consistent estimators, the Two-Stage Least Squares (2SLS) approach is employed. The instrumental variables Z_{it} were obtained based on the key identification criterion, i.e., that they should be correlated with $prod_{it}$ and second, that they should be uncorrelated with ε_{it}. Formally, we express $prod_{it}$ as a function of a vector of exogenous variables (Z_{it}) to be used as instruments and the other vector of exogenous variables (x_{it}) used in Eq. (7);

$$prod_{it} = \psi_1 Z_{it} + \psi_2 x_{it} + v_{it} \qquad (8)$$

v_{it} is assumed to be uncorrelated with Z_{it} and x_{it}. The key identification criteria for Z_{it} to serve as good instruments is that at least one of the coefficients of the variables in with Z_{it} must not have $\psi_1 = 0$. Thus, the test for the null hypothesis $H_0 : \psi_1 = 0$ against the alternative hypothesis $H_1 : \psi_1 \neq 0$ was carried out. We used six variables (planted area in acres, dummy variables for: if a household experienced a drought shock, if a farmer reported theft of agricultural assets/output, a dummy if a household reported an unusually high level of crop pests and diseases, a dummy variable if a household member participated in the NAADS extension program, a dummy if a household experienced serious illness of household member) to instrument technical efficiency. Land productivity was instrumented by a dummy variable if crops were affected by drought and a household reported an unusually high level of crop pests and diseases. Labor productivity on the other hand was instrumented using a dummy variable if crops were affected because a farmer or someone in the family was ill, a dummy variable if farmers participated in the extension program. The identification criteria for all instruments are also fulfilled

3   Findings

3.1   Descriptive Statistics for the Stochastic Frontier Model

Table 2 presents a summary of the data on the different variables used in the stochastic frontier. Farmers' real value of output was used as a dependent variable in the stochastic frontier model. It consistently rose across all survey years from nearly UGX 153,196 in 2009, peaking at nearly UGX 240,000 in survey year 2011, but later declining by 17.4% in 2013. Ownership of farm capital in real terms, years of schooling, increased over time. However, fertilizer use declined sharply, perhaps owing to the increase in prices. Land quality increased, and so did the ownership of oxen, labor remained constant. Participation in the extension program remained very low. Cultivated land area decreased from 6.9 acres in 2009 to 4.6 in 2013. It is worth noting that the decline in planted area was also accompanied by an increase in average land quality from 4.64 in 2009 to 3.48 in 2013.[2] Results of the descriptive

Table 2 Mean values of data used in the Stochastic production frontier

	2009	2011	2013
Value of output (UGX '000)	153,196	238,676	203,278
Value of farm capital (UGX '000)	72,834	74,772	81,309
Total planted area (acres)	6.60	5.39	4.60
Total rainfall during survey	1066.46	1131.57	1213
Land quality index	4.64	3.33	3.48
Land productivity	46,976	51,123	53,220
Labor productivity	73,728	78,857	96,548
Land labor ratio	3.15	1.86	2.06
Family labor	2.44	5.85	2.6
Hired labor (Yes=1)	0.24	0.22	0.24
Number of bulls & Oxen	2.32	2.99	2.65
Fertilizer use (kg)	89.9	94.33	91.13
Years of schooling HH head	6.87	5.73	7.28
Participation in extension program (Yes=1)	0.07	0.04	0.03

Source Calculated by the authors from the LSMS-ISA panel data

analysis show that the amount of annual rainfall increased from 1066 m^3 in 2009 to 1213 m^3 in 2013.

What is important to note from the summary statistics is the fact that growth in the value of output is determined in a large part by the increase in quantity and quality of factors. This is nowhere best demonstrated than by the nature of fluctuation in the value of output between 2011 and 2013. Note the values of labor, land quality, farm capital, and amount of rainfall. In Table 2, we can note that labor productivity which is the ratio of the real value of production to the number of family labor increased by 24%. This productivity increase was raised by other factors of production, underscoring the role of technology in enhancing productivity. Similarly, labor productivity for the median farmers also showed a significant increase over the survey years. Average land productivity (real value of production in UGX per acre) increased albeit moderately from approximately UGX 47,000 in 2009 to UGX 53,000 in 2013, translating into 11.3% increase. This happened mainly due to the presence of extreme observations in the data. The median land productivity improved over time by nearly 95%.

The median land–labor ratio declined from 1.50 in 2009 to 1.30 in 2013. For a given amount of area cultivated, land–labor ratio declined mainly on account of changes in the amount of family labor during the survey period. This points to the fact that land is largely a fixed factor. Thus, with any increase in labor force, the land–labor ratio will necessarily decline. This implies that maintaining any level of output would require improving factor productivity. The foregoing analysis makes it clear that for the median farmer's labor productivity and land productivity showed tremendous improvement over the period spanning the data. This lends to credence to the view that despite the challenges surrounding the implementation of

Table 3 Results of the stochastic frontier model

Explanatory variables	Coefficient	Std error	T Statistic	P>z
Constant	4.626	0.637	7.262	0.000
Family labor	0.020	0.006	3.333	0.000
Number of bulls and oxen	0.065	0.167	0.389	0.980
Amount of fertilizer (kg)	0.311	0.017	18.294	0.000
Log of planted area (acres)	0.159	0.025	6.36	0.000
Log of land quality index	−0.070	0.021	−3.33	0.000
Education of household head (years)	0.069	0.022	3.136	0.000
Log of annual rainfall	0.109	0.023	4.739	0.000
Value of farm capital (UG '000)	0.029	0.059	0.491	0.613
Participation in extension program	0.036	0.386	0.093	0.351
Time	0.023	0.015	1.533	0.079
Time squared	−0.002	0.00091	−2.196	0.000
$\hat{\mu}$	0.24	0.84	0.285	0.840
$\hat{\eta}$	0.056	0.01	5.60	0.000
$\hat{\sigma}^2$	0.557	0.16	3.481	0.000
$\hat{\gamma}$	0.300	0.12	2.50	0.012
$\hat{\sigma}_u^2$	0.338	0.15	2.253	0.000
$\hat{\sigma}_v^2$	0.152	0.04	3.800	0.000

Note Log likelihood = −116.573; Wald chi² (12) = 1655.50; Prob > chi² = 0.0000
Source Estimated from the model by the authors

public interventions to enhance agricultural productivity in Uganda, the results show marked improvement over time. These findings are also consistent with Tafesse et a. (2011), Abro et al. (2014) on the growth in crop yield in Ethiopia, and policies on productivity growth, and Kassie et al. (2011) on the impact of agricultural technologies uptake in Uganda.

3.2 Results of the Stochastic Frontier Model

Table 3, presents the findings of the estimated stochastic frontier model. The Wald test shows that the explanatory variables are jointly significant enough in explaining the dependent variable. This suggests that the estimated model is a good fit for the observed data. The maximum likelihood estimator of the stochastic frontier model uses the observed information matrix (OIM) method of handling heteroscedasticity problems during the estimation of the variance–covariance matrix. Besides, all the explanatory variables have the expected sign. The value of $\hat{\eta}$ is highly significant indicating that technical efficiency improves over time at the rate of 0.056. In other words, the degree of inefficiency decreases over time by the same factor. The variation in the inefficiency term $\hat{\gamma}$ also explains 30% of the total variance in the composite error term.

As expected, the real value of output increases with the amount of cultivated land and is statistically significant at 1%. However, given the inelastic supply of land, it is important that productivity enhancing technologies be put in place to limit the over reliance on planted area as a way of increasing output. In this regard, an effort to improve the quality of land through improved land management practices is one possible intervention. The coefficient rainfall amount to real value of output is also high. This underscores the role of rainfall in enhancing the performance of agricultural output. This finding provides a key message given the rain-fed nature of the agricultural sector. It implies that had the rainfall been dismal during the survey period, output could have been affected. This finding highlights what usually happens during drought episodes (see e.g., FEWSNET 2012). The recurrence of drought and erratic rainfall significantly effects agricultural output and productivity of farmers. Indeed, the country has had pervious episodes of drought, which have affected crop production. The implication is that interventions geared toward sustainable agricultural activity should promote the development of alternative water sources for production. There should be development of water harvesting, development of ground water sources, and investment in irrigation infrastructure that currently stands at less than 5%. Hagos et al. (2010), Abro et al. (2014) emphasize the role of investment in irrigation and or improved water management technologies in increasing the income of farmers.

Participating in government extension programs is insignificant in contributing to increasing the real value of output. However, education was found to be highly significant with the expected sign. The insignificance of extension program participation in influencing output can be understood from the lack of response from households in utilizing the different programs. This could partly be the reason for the government of Uganda decision to restructure the program in 2013. Among the reasons for the decision was to ensure effective delivery was to include provision of agricultural inputs beyond the production and pricing information, which the National Agricultural Advisory Services used to provide. As expected, the proxy for labor (family labor) is highly significant in influencing the growth output. The implication is that in peak seasons, shortage of labor may reduce output significantly. This finding highlights a key issue that has implications for the performance of especially the school going family members of households. Given that farming households depend largely on family labor, a number of families compel members of a school going age to tend to gardens during planting and harvesting period of the season. With regard to farm capital, the average real value of farm capital rose significantly over the surveyed years, its impact on output is insignificant.

Although the sign of the coefficient is positive as expected, it is insignificant in driving the value of output. Given the limited use of ox ploughs among Ugandan farming households, this result seems to be expected. Besides, the average holding of bulls and oxen is approximately 3 for the entire survey period. In addition, given that many households are smallholder farmers, owning more ploughing ox is not an option, with many in the ox-ploughing areas preferring to share, while those outside the ox-ploughing areas prefer to hire tractors. The use of fertilizer is highly significant as expected. The non-monotonous Hicks-neutral technical progress is indicated by the time trend, with a coefficient of 0.023. This implies that technical progress increase by 2.3% on average per year. The negative coefficient of time squared indicates that the rate of technical progress decreases over time. The findings are consistent with results of recent studies done in similar developing country settings by Abro et al. (2014), Bachewe (2009) using household survey data. In the next section, we investigate the role of agricultural productivity improvement in improving household welfare household poverty is relevant for public policy making.

3.3 Results of the Fixed Effects Model on the Impact of Productivity Improvement on Household Welfare

Table 4 presents the summary statistics of variables in our household consumption model. The average age of household head is approximately 45 years. Male headship slightly declined over the survey years from 70% in 2009 to 68%. The data also showed that dependency ratio declined from nearly 0.65 in 2009 to less than 0.56 for other survey years. This implies that household composition is changing with households having fewer children than adults. This could be a positive step toward reducing the negative effects of a higher dependency ratio on household welfare. However, we can note that total household size has not changed much standing at an average 6 members. The number of households that reported participating in different kinds of off-farm activities stood at 80% for 2009 and 2011 before declining to 50%. Distance to the nearest station where they could access public transport in kilometers declined over time indicating a significant improvement in transport services and infrastructure. On average, the wealth of households as measured by livestock ownership in TLUs rose marginally from 2.32 in 2009 to 2.65 in 2013.

Table 4 Mean values of variables for the of the household consumption model

Variable	2009	2011	2013
Real consumption per capita	51,406	50,689	31,462
Sex of head household (1 = Male, 0 otherwise)	0.7	0.68	0.681
Age of the head of the household	43.9	46.18	45.38
Head's years of schooling	6.83	5.74	7.28
Household size	4.79	6.85	7.13
Dependency ratio	0.65	0.57	0.56
Number of livestock	2.32	2.99	2.65
Non agriculture income (1 = Yes, 0 otherwise)	0.88	0.88	0.5
Technical efficiency	0.59	0.64	0.69
Distance to bus station (km)	3.03	2.85	1.13

Source Computed from the model

As Table 4 shows, mean real consumption per capita declined from nearly UGX 51,000 to UGX 31,000 in 2013. This could be attributed to among others, micro and macroeconomic shocks that resulted in price increases as well as the increase in the household size. As an indicator of productivity, technical efficiency of farmers grew from 53 to 69% during 1994–2009. The link between real consumption per capita and technical efficiency reveals that technical efficiency and real consumption per capita are positively correlated. This suggests that improving technical efficiency of farmers is important to increase production and hence real consumption per capita. In this regard, a panel fixed effects model was estimated to rule out the possibility of unobserved household characteristics such as preference and taste being correlated with the exogenous regressors. The choice of fixed effects over random effects was also supported by Hausman test for random effects (the last row of Table 5).

We have estimated four models with model 1 using technical efficiency of farmers as an indicator of productivity while Model 2 used labor productivity. The land productivity indicator was used for the third model, while model 4 decomposes real value of production per unit of labor into real value of production per land cultivated and land cultivated per unit labor. Land cultivated per unit of labor indicates the relative shortage of land. The lower is the ratio; the higher is the shortage of land for a unit of labor. The rationale for this decomposition is that it is not always clear whether to use labor or land productivity as the explanatory variables in the regression (see Abro et al. 2014; Irz et al. 2001). This has particularly been cited to be the case in many parts of Africa where agricultural activity is dependent on family labor especially the female household members (Asongu et al. 2019; Osabuohien et al. 2019). The Wald test indicates that the coefficients are jointly and statistically significant from zero. The coefficients of the productivity variables in the four models are also statistically significantly at 5 or 1% level of significance. Besides, many of the coefficients of other variables used as controls have the expected sign and individually significant at 10% or less level of significance.

The findings from the alternative models show that productivity has a positive and significant impact on real household consumption per capita. Model 1 shows that, on average, a 10% increase in technical efficiency increases household consumption per capita by nearly 15%. Model 2 indicates that, on average, when labor productivity went up by 0.43 US cents, while real consumption per capita increased by nearly 0.21%. Model 3 and 4 also show that land productivity is important for household welfare improvement. We find that a 0.43 US cents increase in land productivity increases real consumption per capita by 0.25 and 0.23% for model 3 and 4, respectively. These findings are supported by previous studies by cross-country studies on Africa (see Thirtle et al. 2001; Kassie et al. 2014). Increasing the productivity of farmers is thus key in improving household welfare. These results point to

Table 5 Fixed effects model results for productivity on real household consumption per capita

	Model 1	Model 2	Model 3	Model 4
Technical efficiency	a,b2.21** (0.913)			
Logarithm of labor productivity (UGX/labor)		0.21** (0.087)		
Logarithm of land productivity (UGX/acre)			0.25** (0.103)	0.23* (0.131)
Land to family labor ratio				0.10* (0.054)
Sex of the head of the household	0.18* (0.099)	0.15* (0.088)	0.08** (0.032)	0.09** (0.038)
Household head's years of schooling	0.12*** (0.044)	0.11** (0.042)	0.10** (0.044)	0.15*** (0.035)
Age of the head of the household	0.029* (0.017)	0.01 (0.029)	0.00 (0.000)	0.00 (0.000)
Household size	−0.08** (0.038)	−0.13* (0.078)	−0.12* (0.064)	−0.11 (0.157)
Dependency ratio	−0.09** (0.044)	−0.18* (0.062)	−0.15 (0.201)	−0.13* (0.07)
Non-agriculture income (1 = Yes, 0 = No)	0.1* (0.059)	0.11 (0.171)	0.17* (0.097)	0.21* 0.117
Livestock ownership	0.05 (0.046)	0.025 (0.021)	0.00 (0.000)	0.000 (0.000)
Distance to bus station (km)	−0.013* (0.007)	−0.02* (0.011)	−0.01* (0.005)	−0.05** (0.02)
Constant	5.36* (2.777)	5.11* (3.059)	4.11* (2.258)	4.25* (2.272)
Overall Wald test statistic	184,361	182,434	180,134	181,481
R-squared	0.2	0.28	0.22	0.25
corr(a_i, Xb)	−0.43	0.08	−0.04	−0.02
F test that all $a_i=0$	1.84	1.74	1.85	1.86
Wald test statistic for random effects	1567.7*	883.7*	951.41*	632.16*

Note (a)* significant at 1%, ** significant at 5%, *** significant at 10%. The dependent variable for all models is the logarithm of real consumption per capita; (b)The elasticity of technical efficiency with respect to real consumption per capita is 1.43

the need to put into place a comprehensive package of interventions in order to bolster the agricultural productivity enhancing programs.

Specific interventions could include the provision of quality farm inputs, deliberate steps to intensify agricultural extension services, alongside knowledge dissemination on critical agronomic practices. Evidence shows that access to extension service enhances the adoption of improved agricultural technologies by reducing supply-side constraints that arise from frictions in the information market (Wossen et al. 2017, 2015). Essentially, access to extension services exposes farmers to new technologies and provides a vehicle for educating them about the best agronomic practices (see Anderson and Feder 2007). Such measures result in a reduction in the gap between potential and actual yields (Anderson and Feder 2007).

In addition to the current practice of providing farmers with inputs, farmers should be afforded credit facilities that are linked to the purchase of agricultural inputs. This would mitigate the possibility of credit misappropriation, a practice that has variously jeopardized the effectiveness of public interventions in agriculture. The key mechanism for such an arrangement should be the development and strengthening of farmer cooperatives, whose subscription still remains low. Cooperatives are widely regarded as a vital institutional innovation that can mitigate the constraints that impede smallholders' access to market (Abebaw and Haile 2013; Verhofstadt and Maertens 2014; Ma and Abdulai 2016). Fundamentally, cooperatives can relax the liquidity constraints that farmers face by providing credit support for their members. Secondly, they also affect agricultural technology adoption and household welfare by providing market information as well as offer a better market price for their produce (Wossen et al. 2017). Abebaw and Haile (2013) found a strong positive impact of cooperative membership on fertilizer adoption. Similarly, cooperative membership in rural China was found to have a positive and significant impact on apple yields, net returns, and household income (Ma and Abdulai 2016).

While evidence points to the positive impact of improved technologies in boosting farm productivity, resulting in improved household welfare, the challenge here, as has already been established elsewhere in Sub-Saharan Africa is that the adoption rates are low on a wide range of interventions. For instance, the use of irrigation, fertilizer, coupled with improved seed varieties can be critical ingredients for boosting agricultural productivity. However, these remain low. Previous evidence shows that only 28% of the land area allocated to maize growing is actually planted with improved varieties (Langyintuo et al. 2010). Furthermore, an average farmer applies only about 8 kg per hectare of fertilizers compared to 101 kg per hectare for South Asia and over 145 kg per hectare in the developed world (Morris et al. 2007; World Bank 2010).

4 Constraints to Uptake of Productivity Enhancing Technologies in Uganda[3]

This section provides a discussion of recent evidence on the constraints to the uptake of agricultural productivity enhancing technologies in Uganda. Among the issues that require attention is the need for farm households to be aware of the availability of improved seed varieties, if they are to test and determine their performance relative to other cultivars. In the absence of such information, the farmer has no opportunity to choose the technology. Several household specific, institutional, and regional variables determine access to agro-inputs. These include institutional variables such as agricultural research, extension, markets, farmer-to-farmer seed exchange, and membership to farmer organizations. Farmers with access to extension services, input markets and farmer organizations, or to nongovernmental organizations (NGOs) and research centers have been found to face lower constraints in accessing quality inputs. Indeed, Shiferaw et al. (2015) show that prior experience with obtaining seed from research/extension centers and buying seed from traders have a strong bearing on relaxing the seed access constraint. This implies that farmers who have previously obtained their seed stock from extension and local agro-dealers are less likely to face seed supply constraints. This may range from saving and recycling of seed to better relationships that allow farmers to subsequently access seed from a particular source. Membership to crop production groups also significantly reduces the probability of facing constraints relating to seed supply. Shiferaw et al. (2015) underscore the importance of both formal and informal seed systems in technology diffusion in rural areas and networking among farmers in overcoming the problem of access to improved seed (also see Arega and Manyong 2007; Shiferaw et al. 2008).

Farmers' ability to access improved technology is also affected by their endowment of certain marketing assets and regional effects. In particular, ownership of a means of transport says, a bicycle significantly increases the probability of a farmer having access to improved seeds. A bicycle being a key low-cost transport can facilitate local mobility and linkages with input and output markets. Such is its importance given the fact that distance to markets and agricultural extension centers is cited as an impediment to farmer access to some of the improved agricultural technologies.

Shiferaw et al. (2015) also find that while the probability of facing a capital constraint in buying improved inputs is expected to depend on several factors such as asset ownership, education, market linkages, past income, social capital, among others, one of the key variables that was identified as having a reducing effect on the likelihood of facing a capital constraint was group membership. Collective action in terms of membership to a crop production group (farmer cooperative) is a form of social capital that improves access to liquidity in the case of capital-constrained households that need to finance the purchase of inputs. Such groups are critical for farm households to overcome idiosyncratic constraints that result from imperfections in rural markets.

Overall, Shiferaw et al. (2015) note that adoption of productivity enhancing technologies in Uganda is constrained by imperfect markets for information and access to improved inputs and capital. This finding is a departure from several studies on agricultural technologies adoption, which assume that non-adopting farmers make decisions on technology choice under full information. That assumption implies that the decision by a farmer not to adopt a given innovation is made from an informed comparative assessment of its potential performance on the farm. Shiferaw et al. (2015) thus recommend that information asymmetry can be overcome by the development of strong links between farmers and local input dealers, extension services, and membership to farmer groups. They further note that development and consolidation of farmer group membership has the desired effect of overcoming both information and capital constraints.

Shiferaw et al. (2015) highlight the importance of market access, household assets, human capital, and farm size in overcoming certain constraints to agricultural technology adoption. This then implies that in the absence of public intervention, resource-poor farm households may potentially lag behind in the adoption of new farming technologies. This may have the consequence of condemning such households to permanent subsistence production and hence poverty. Given the hidden nature of demand for new technologies, improvements in farmer education and supply of improved inputs and rural finance can make substantial improvements in the scale of adoption of modern technologies. That in turn has the desirable consequence of improving productivity, nutrition, and food security for overcoming rural poverty.

5 Conclusion

This chapter analyzed the growth in agricultural productivity and household welfare using three waves of nationally representative panel data for Uganda. Overall, the study confirms evidence from previous studies on the impact of adoption of improved agricultural technologies as a key mechanism for enhancing agricultural income and general welfare of rural households. However, the scale of technology adoption is constrained by low accessibility and use of improved seeds, market infrastructure, and limited access to production information which is provided through agricultural extension services as well as the low subscription rates to cooperatives. This is a major constraint to any efforts to improve the rate of adoption of agricultural technologies. Evidence shows that cooperatives facilitate the pooling of different resources such as credit, information, and labor among members, all of which create economies of scale and hence improve welfare. In fact, studies show that agricultural cooperatives can play a vital role in technology adoption in the presence of high transaction costs and low bargaining power as is the case in developing countries (Abebaw and Haile 2013; Ma and Abdulai 2016). In addition, the findings show that agricultural productivity enhancing technologies such as the use of irrigation, is currently being used by a limited number of households. Most households were also found to possess fewer and a less productive farm implements. Given that the majority of the population is engaged in agriculture, one sure way of improving household income and hence welfare is through interventions that can boost agricultural productivity. It is thus important that the design of interventions covers other sectors that support agriculture such as the provision of infrastructure to support water for production is key. Further research is needed to analyze the full potential of adopting agricultural productivity enhancing technologies, by undertaking a quantification of its indirect effects, say on employment food prices as well as the nutritional benefits.

Notes

1. http://microdata.worldbank.org/index.php/catalog/2663. Osabuohien et al. (2015) have also used the data.
2. The index ranges from 1 to 12. The closer it is to one, the higher is the quality of land, while the closer the index to 12, the lower is the quality of the index.
3. This section draws extensively from Shiferaw et al. (2015).

References

Abebaw, D., & Haile, M. G. (2013). The impact of cooperatives on agricultural technology adoption: Empirical evidence from Ethiopia. *Food Policy, 38,* 82–91.

Abro, A. Z., Alemu, B. A., & Hajra, A. M. (2014). Policies for agricultural productivity growth and poverty reduction in rural Ethiopia. *World Development, 59,* 461–474.

Aigner, D., Lovell, C. A. K., & Schmidt, P. (1977). Formulation and estimation of stochastic frontier production function models. *Journal of Econometrics, 6*(1), 21–37.

Ali, A., & Abdulai, A. (2010). The adoption of genetically modified cotton and poverty reduction in Pakistan. *Journal of Agricultural Economics, 61,* 175–192.

Anderson, J., & Feder, G. (2007). Agricultural extension. In R. Evenson & P. Pingali, (Eds.), *Handbook of agricultural economics* (Vol. 3, pp. 2343e2378: Chapter 44).

Arega, A. D., & Manyong, V. M. (2007). The effect of education on agricultural productivity under traditional and improved technology in Northern Nigeria: An endogenous switching regression analysis. *Empirical Economics, 32*(1), 141–159.

Asfaw, S., Shiferaw, B., Simtowe, F., & Lipper, L. (2012). Impact of modern agricultural technologies on smallholder welfare: Evidence from Tanzania and Ethiopia. *Food Policy, 37,* 283–295.

Asongu, S. A., Efobi, U. R., Tanakem, B. V., & Osabuohien, E. (2019). Globalisation and female economic participation in sub-Saharan Africa. *Gender Issues.* https://doi.org/10.1007/s12147-019-09233-3.

Bachewe, F. N. (2009). *The state of subsistence agriculture in Ethiopia: Sources of output growth and agricultural inefficiency.* Ph.D. dissertation, University of Minnesota, USA.

Battese, G. E., & Coelli, T. J. (1992). Frontier production functions, technical efficiency and panel data: With application to paddy farmers in India. *The Journal of Productivity Analysis, 3,* 153–169.

Becerril, J., & Abdulai, A. (2010). The impact of improved maize varieties on poverty in Mexico: A propensity score-matching approach. *World Development, 38*(7), 1024–1035.

Breman, H., & Debrah, S. K. (2003). Improving African food security. *SAIS Review, XXIII,* 153–170.

Cairns, J. E., Hellin, J., Sonder, K., Araus, J. L., MacRobert, J. F., Thierfelder, C., et al. (2013). Adapting maize production to climate change in sub-Saharan Africa. *Food Security, 5,* 345–360.

Coelli, T. J., Rao, D. P., O'Donnell, C. J., & Battese, G. E. (2005). *Introduction to efficiency and productivity analysis.* New York, USA: Springer Science Business Media.

de Janvry, A., & Sadoulet, E. (2001). World poverty and the role of agricultural technology: Direct and indirect effects. *Journal of Development Studies, 38*(4), 1–26.

Dercon, S., Hoddinott, J., & Woldehanna, T. (2012). Growth and chronic poverty: Evidence from rural communities in Ethiopia. *Journal of Development Studies, 48*(2), 238–253.

Diiro, G. M., Ker, A. P., & Sam, A. G. (2015). Agricultural technology adoption and Nonfarm earnings in Uganda: A semiparametric analysis. *The Journal of Developing Areas, 49*(2), 145–162.

Doss, C. R. (2006). Analyzing technology adoption using microstudies: Limitations, challenges, and opportunities for improvement. *Agricultural Economics, 34*(3), 207–219.

FAO. (2011). *Guidelines for the preparation of livestock sector reviews: Animal production and health guidelines.* Food and Agricultural Organization, No. 5. Rome.

FEWSNET. (2012). *A climate trend analysis of Uganda: Famine early warning systems network.* Accessed April 25, 2018 from http://pubs.usgs.gov/fs/2012/3062/FS2012-3062.pdf.

Government of Uganda. (2018). *Background to the budget for the 2017/2018 financial year.* Kampala, Uganda: Government of Uganda, Ministry of Finance, Planning and Economic Development.

Greene, W. H. (2003). *Econometric analysis* (5th ed.). Upper Saddle River, NJ, USA: Prentice Hall.

Hagos, F., Awulachew, S. B., Loulseged, M., & Yilma, A. D. (2010). *Poverty impacts of agricultural water management technologies in Ethiopia.* Addis Ababa, Ethiopia: International Water Management Institute (IWMI), East Africa and Nile Basin Office.

Hall, A. J., & Richards, R. A. (2013). Prognosis for genetic improvement of yield potential and water-limited yield of major grain crops. *Field Crops Research, 143,* 18–33.

Irz, X., Thirtle, C., Lin, L., & Wiggins, S. (2001). Agricultural productivity growth and poverty alleviation. *Development Policy Review, 19*(4), 449–466.

Kassie, M., Shiferaw, B., & Muricho, G. (2011). Agricultural technology, crop income, and poverty alleviation in Uganda. *World Development, 39*(10), 1784–1795.

Kassie, M., Jaleta, M., & Mattei, A. (2014). Evaluating the impact of improved maize varieties on food security in Rural Tanzania: Evidence from a continuous treatment approach. *Food Security, 6,* 217–230. https://doi.org/10.1007/s12571-014-0332-x.

Kijima, Y., Matsumoto, T., & Yamano, T. (2006). Nonfarm employment, agricultural shocks, and poverty dynamics: Evidence from rural Uganda. *Agricultural Economics, 35*(3), 459–467.

Kumbhakar, S. C., & Lovell, C. A. K. (2000). *Stochastic frontier analysis.* Cambridge: University Press.

Langyintuo, A. S., Mwangi, W., ADiallo, O., MacRobert, J., Dixon, J., & Bänziger, M. (2010). Challenges of the maize seed industry in Eastern and Southern Africa: A compelling case for private–public intervention to promote growth. *Food Policy, 35,* 323–333.

Lovell, C. A. K. (1993). Production frontiers and productive efficiency. In H. O. Fried, C. A. K. Lovell, & S. S. Schmidt (Eds.), *The measurement of productive efficiency: Techniques and applications* (pp. 3–67). New York: Oxford University Press.

Ma, W., & Abdulai, A. (2016). Does cooperative membership improve household welfare? Evidence from apple farmers in China. *Food Policy, 58*, 94–102.

Mendola, M. (2007). Agricultural technology adoption and poverty reduction: A propensity-score matching analysis for rural Bangladesh. *Food Policy, 32*, 372–393.

Minten, B., & Barrett, C. B. (2008). Agricultural technology, productivity, and poverty in Madagascar. *World Development, 36*(5), 797–822.

Morris, M., Kelly, V. A., Kopicki, R., & Byerlee, D. (2007). *Promoting increased fertilizer use in Africa: Lessons learned and good practice guidelines*. Washington, DC: World Bank.

Osabuohien, E., Efobi, U. R., Herrmann, R., & Gitau, C. M. (2019). Female labor outcomes and large-scale agricultural land investments: Macro-micro evidence from Tanzania. *Land Use Policy, 82*, 716–728.

Osabuohien, E. S., Gitau, C. M., Efobi, U. R., & Bruentrup, M. (2015). Agents and implications of foreign land deals in East African community: The case of Uganda. In E. Osabuohien (Ed.), *Handbook of research on in-country determinants and implications of foreign land acquisitions* (pp. 263–286). Hershey, PA: Business Science Reference. https://doi.org/10.4018/978-1-4666-7405-9.ch013.

Otsuka, K. (2000). Role of agricultural research in poverty reduction: Lessons from the Asian experience. *Food Policy, 254*, 447–462.

Rahman, S. (1999). Impact of technological change on income distribution and poverty in Bangladesh agriculture: An empirical analysis. *Journal of International Development, 11*(7), 935–955.

Simler, K. R., Mukherjee, S., Dava, G. L., & Datt, G. (2004). *Rebuilding after war: Micro-level determinants of poverty reduction in Mozambique* (Research Report 32). Washington, DC: International Food Policy Research Institute.

Shiferaw, B., Kebede, T., Kassie, M., & Fisher, M. (2015). Market imperfections, access to information and technology adoption in Uganda: Challenges of overcoming multiple constraints. *Agricultural Economics, 46*(4), 475–488.

Shiferaw, B., Kebede, T. A., & You, Z. (2008). Technology adoption under seed access constraints and the economic impacts of improved pigeon pea varieties in Tanzania. *Agricultural Economics, 39*(3), 1–15.

Tafesse, A. S., Dorosh, P., & Asrat, S. (2011). *Crop production in Ethiopia: Regional patterns and trends* (Ethiopia ESSP II Working Paper No. 0016). Addis Ababa, Ethiopia: Development Strategy and Governance Division, International Food Policy Research Institute, Ethiopia Strategy Support Program II.

Thirtle, C., Irz, X., Lin, L., McKenzie-Hill, V., & Wiggins, S. (2001). *Relationship between changes in agricultural productivity and the incidence of poverty in developing countries* (Report No. 7946 27/02/2001). UK: Department for International Development (DFID).

Tittonell, P., & Giller, K. E. (2013). When yield gaps are poverty traps: The paradigm of ecological intensification in African smallholder agriculture. *Field Crops Research, 143*, 76–90.

UBOS. (2016). National accounts [Online]. Accessed March 2, 2018, from http://www.ubos.org/statistics/macro-economic/national-accounts.

Verhofstadt, E., & Maertens, M. (2014). Can agricultural cooperatives reduce Poverty? Heterogeneous impact of cooperative membership on farmers' welfare in Rwanda. *Applied Economic Perspectives and Policy, 2014*, 1–21.

Wooldridge, J. M. (2009). *Introduction to econometrics: A modern approach* (4th ed.). Mason, OH: South Western Educational Publishing.

World Bank. (2008). *World development report 2008: Agriculture for development*. Washington, DC: World Bank.

World Bank, World Development Indicators. (2010). http://data.worldbank.org/Datacatalog/World-Development-Indicators.

Wossen, T., Berger, T., & Di Falco, S. (2015). Social capital, risk preference and adoption of improved farm land management practices in Ethiopia. *Agricultural Economics, 46,* 81–97.

Wossen, T., Abdoulaye, T., Alene, A., Haile, M. G., Feleke, S., Olanrewaju, A., et al. (2017). Impacts of extension access and cooperative membership on technology adoption and household welfare. *Journal of Rural Studies, 54,* 223–233.

Pattern of Labor Use and Productivity Among Agricultural Households in Nigeria

Popoola A. Olufemi and Adejare A. Kayode

1 Introduction

Labor is an essential input entering the production process. The pattern and intensity of its use has generated a lot of attention from the viewpoint of increasing productivity and employment. It has been observed that the necessary condition for sustainable economic growth and development of every arm of national economy as well as agriculture is an efficient use of basic production resources that is labor, land, and capital (Bervidova 2002). Nigeria's agriculture is dominated by smallholders, whose farm size varies between 0.10 and 5.99 hectares (Adepoju and Salman 2013). They make use of traditional technologies and the main source of labor is human labor that can be in the form of family labor, hired labor, and cooperative labor.

The availability of labor has been found to have influence on agricultural activities such as planting precision, better weed control, timely harvesting, and crop processing (Oluyole et al. 2007). However, seasonality of agricultural activities causes fluctuation in the quantity of labor use for these activities, and this implies that labor uses in agriculture are different across different farm operations. Farming operations vary in the gender distribution of labor and responsibility around the world (Sachs 1996). Furthermore, farm labor is a major source of employment opportunity for the rural labor force in Nigeria. Evidence abound that there has been a steady decline in the

P. A. Olufemi (✉)
Innovation and Technology Policy Department, Nigerian Intitute of Social and Economic Research (NISER), Ibadan, Nigeria

A. A. Kayode
Department of Agricultural Economics, University of Ibadan, Ibadan, Nigeria

percentage in farm labor supply in Nigeria. Declining farm labor supply is compounded by the fact that the agricultural sector, with a few exceptions, has the worst poverty conditions (Ruben and van der Berg 2001). More so, socio-economic conditions in most rural communities in Nigeria are generally poorer than what obtains in the cities: hence rural–urban migration has been a strategy adopted by many in a bid to escape poverty (Okali et al. 2001). This indicates that shortage in farm labor can consequently lead to low farm productivity, which eventually culminates in food insecurity and poverty among rural farming communities. Globally, it has been observed that there is an increase in women participation in the labor market including agricultural sector (FAO 2011). However, women's growing labor force participation does not necessarily mean an improvement in their employment status relative to men or in their well-being. In agriculture, women's employment status depends on gendered power relations in access to and control of productive assets (especially land), labor, services, and/or jobs. Even women with land rights under customary, religious, and/or civil law are often unable to exercise their rights and farm independently (Food and Agricultural Organization-FAO 2011; Osabuohien et al. 2019).

The issues of how many laborers are working in non-agricultural production and how many in farming is of interest to many policy makers (Kwan 2009). This became important because the socio-economic condition of rural people may be uplifted by attaining the goals of increased productivity, employment opportunities, and income redistribution, which agricultural labor is capable of providing (Faridi and Basit 2011). Also, allocation of resources can as well determine the level of productivity. Resources are scarce, agricultural households must decide how to use those resources (labor in this case) for their optimum benefit. Resources are used in order to produce one good or service, those resources become unavailable for any other purpose. Mohammed-lawal and Omotesho (2004) submitted that an effective management of available resources through an efficient resource allocation pattern will enable a farming household to get as much income as possible from its production and consequently improve its economic access to food required by its members. Therefore, to understand how agricultural households allocate and utilize labor resource become important.

In Nigeria, several studies have looked into the issue of labor productivity. For example, Okoye et al. (2008) and Anyaegbunam et al. (2010) examined the effects of inputs on the productivity of labor while Ogunniyi et al. (2012) and Umar et al. (2010) considered the differences in the productivity between males and females in their assessments. Furthermore, Rufai et al. (2018) examined the gender analysis of input utilization and agricultural labor productivity in Nigeria. However, this present study examines the pattern of labor use and labor productivity using nationally representative data, LSMS-ISA data. This study also employed the two-stage least squares regression estimation technique to address endogeneity issues arising from labor use and labor productivity.

According to the National Bureau of Statistics, a short analysis of labor productivity in Nigeria between 2010 and 2014 affirmed that measuring the productivity of labor is an important way to understand the dynamics occurring in the labor market, and useful in providing insights to policy makers regarding trends in unemployment, job creation, and wages (NBS 2014). Ultimately, these have implications for higher economic output and poverty reduction. This chapter extends the frontiers in extant literature by providing empirical evidence on pattern of labor use by gender of household head and productivity of labor among agricultural households in Nigeria, taking into consideration planting and harvesting activities.

Thus, the main objective of this study is to examine the pattern of labor use and productivity among agricultural households in Nigeria. Specifically, the study profiles the pattern of labor use among agricultural households, examine factors influencing the labor use among the agricultural households, estimate labor productivity, and identify the determinants of labor productivity.

This chapter is structured as follows: a brief on key issues in related literature, the methodology showing the study area, type and source of data, sampling procedure and sample size, and the analytical techniques used. This is followed by results and discussion section, conclusion and recommendations.

2 Key Issues in the Related Literature

2.1 Measures of Productivity

There are many different productivity measures. The choice between them depends on the purpose of productivity measurement and, in many instances, on the availability of data. Broadly, productivity measures can be classified as single factor productivity measures (relating a measure of output to a single measure of input) or multifactor productivity (MFP) measures (relating a measure of output to a bundle of inputs). Another distinction, of particular relevance at the industry or firm level is between productivity measures that relate some measure of gross output to one or several inputs and those which use a value-added concept to capture movements of output (OECD 2001). Table 1 was restricted to the most frequently used productivity measures. These are measures of labor and capital productivity, and multifactor productivity measures either in the form of capital-labor MFP, based on a value-added concept of output, or in the form of capital–labor–energy–materials MFP (KLEMS), based on a concept of gross output. Among those measures, value-added based labor productivity is the single most frequently computed productivity statistic, followed by capital-labor MFP and KLEMS MFP.

Productivity measures are subdivided into partial or total measures.

Partial Factor Productivity: Partial measures are the amount of output per unit of a particular input. Commonly used partial measures are yield (output per

Table 1 Overview of main productivity measures

Type of output measure	Type of input measure			
	Labor	Capital	Capital and labor	Capital, labor and intermediate inputs (energy, materials, services)
Gross output	Labor productivity (based on gross output)	Capital productivity (based on gross output)	Capital-labor MFP (based on gross output)	KLEMS multifactor productivity
Value added	Labor productivity (based on value added)	Capital productivity (based on value added)	Capital-labor MFP (based on value added)	–
	Single factor productivity measures		Multifactor productivity (MFP) measures	

Source Organization for Economic Cooperation and Development (OECD) Productivity Manual (2001)

unit of land), labor productivity (output per economically active person [EAP] or per agricultural person-hour). Yield is commonly used to assess the success of new production practices or technology. Labor productivity is often used as a means of comparing the productivity of sectors within or across economies. It is also used as an indicator of rural welfare or living standards since it reflects the ability to acquire income through sale of agricultural goods or agricultural production (Block 1995; Oyebola et al. 2019).

Total Factor Productivity (TFP) is the ratio of an index of agricultural output to an index of agricultural inputs. The index of agricultural output is a value-weighted sum of all agricultural production components. The index of agricultural inputs is the value-weighted sum of conventional agricultural inputs. These generally include land, labor, physical capital, livestock and chemical fertilizers and pesticides.

2.2 Labor Productivity

The productivity of labor is earlier captured as a partial productivity measure. It can be measured in physical and financial term as a ratio of output to input. Thus, physical term was estimated by dividing output level with labor use in man-days while financial labor productivity is computed as the ratio of total value of output in Naira to the cost of labor used.

$$\text{Labor productivity} = \frac{\text{output}}{\text{labor input}}$$

2.3 Measuring Labor Utilization

Method of measuring labor utilization as developed by Bervidova (2002) is adapted in this study. On the basis that if labor represents a purposeful human activity, then the most exact indicator of the utilized labor amount would be the spent energy of muscles (in physical work) and brain (in psychical work). To measure the amount of energy spent in common work activity is, however, practically non-productive. That is why substitution ways of the utilized human labor qualification are used, which show a higher or lower level of inaccuracy. Most often human labor consumption is expressed in time units. The advantage is simplicity and comparability. At the level of agriculture as a branch of national economy, it is, however, more suitable to express the amount of consumed work by the number of workers. Nevertheless, it is necessary to consider the fact that there exist various obstacles in work (e.g., sickness leave), holidays, and differing efficiency of particular workers and so on. The results of the utilized labor as well as the amount of labor can be expressed in monetary units by means of the total labor costs. The total labor costs represent the price of labor as a production factor, considering also its complexity, demands responsibility or scarcity. It is then suitable to use this way of measurement of the utilized labor for evaluation of its productivity from the viewpoint of the application of created production in the market.

It can be concluded that in expressing the amount of the utilized labor for the purposes of labor productivity evaluation from the technological point of view, it is possible to use physical units, and in judging of the utilized labor efficiency from the viewpoint of its results application in the market, monetary units are more suitable (Bervidova 2002).

3 Review of Empirical Studies on Pattern of Labor Use

The role of agricultural labor markets within the wider macro labor market is interesting (Donnellan et al. 2012). A study by Timmer (1988) suggests that the agricultural labor is commonly seen as a buffer in economic development. When other sectors of the macroeconomic prosper, the agricultural sector tends to release the work force without reducing output. However, in times of recession, the sector tends to absorb more labor, thus avoiding more dramatic unemployment problems. The literature on the institutional frameworks of agricultural labor markets is thin. Most studies examining the institutional setting of agricultural labor markets tend to refer to developing countries. Such studies typically examine the failing of the institutions and the consequent effect for the productivity and efficiency of the agricultural sector.

Studies in Nigeria context that examined the pattern of labor use include Awotodunbo (2008), Simonyan and Obiakor (2012), Oluyole et al. (2013), Osugiri et al. (2012). Awotodunbo (2008) studied labor use pattern among farmers in Ife Central Local Government Area of Osun State and the results revealed that majority of the farmers employed between 11 and 30 laborers per season while none of the respondents employed hired laborers for the whole farm work. The study also showed that labor is rarely available and rarely used by the respondents. A correlation analysis revealed that farmers' age, labor cost, and labor input productivity were positively correlated with labor use pattern and the relationship was statistically significant in each case at 5% level. In a similar study, Oluyole et al. (2013) examined labor structure and its determinants among cocoa farmers in Nigeria. They found out that ninety-four percent of the farmers utilized hired labor for farm clearing while 61.0 and 51% of the farmers utilized family labor for harvesting and on-farm cocoa processing, respectively. All the farmers used male labor for farm clearing while 60.0% utilized female labor for harvesting and the result of the multi-variate regression analysis shows that there is a significant relationship between labor structure and farm size, wage rate, and labor cost.

Osugiri et al. (2012) studied population dynamics, labor, and smallholder farmers' productivity in Southeast Nigeria. They found that though farming is a profitable venture but is still at subsistence level. The study showed further that about 46% of the farmers could not afford or access the use of fertilizers and modern inputs required for agricultural intensification prevalent in the area. The tenure arrangement was by inheritance which caused much land fragmentations and pressure on limited arable land. Labor had the highest average factor cost due to high cost of hired labor. The regression result showed that farm size and fertilizer application are significantly and positively correlated with crop production. Conversely, population density and cropping density and labor were significant but negatively correlated with crop output.

Moreover, Simonyan and Obiakor (2012) analyzed household labor use in yam production in Anambra West Local Government Area of Nigeria. They found that age, education, household size, farm size, wage rate, hired labor, credit, cooperative membership, and occupational status were all statistically and significantly determined the household labor use in the study area. Moreover, labor, seed yam and fertilizer were found significantly to determined yam output among the household. The technical efficiency of households in the study area was found to be determined by age, education, household size, extension contact, and gender of the household head. Akanni and Dada (2012) investigated effects of labor use patterns on productivity of cocoa farms in south western Nigeria using descriptive statistics and stochastic efficiency frontier function. The results of the study revealed that majority of the farms sampled (80%) were less than 5 hectares in size and sharecropping was the most dominant of the labor types on the farms. The study further reported that adult male labor constituted about 69% of the total labor—use on the plantations and the majority of the labor was involved in the application of agrochemicals and harvesting of cocoa pods. Also, the quantity of harvested cocoa beans, size of cleared understoreys, and quantity of applied agrochemicals significantly affected (at 5% level) the labor-use efficiency in cocoa plantations. Moreover, the results also show that poor remunerations often discourage prospective farm labor from participating in cocoa production.

Furthermore, Anyiro et al. (undated) examined labor-use efficiency among the smallholder yam farmers in Abia State, Nigeria using descriptive statistic and stochastic frontier function. The result of the empirical study revealed that farm households provided an average of 336 man-days used in yam production activities and 36.66% of the sampled farmers used hired labor while family labor, share croppers, and exchange labor provided the balance labor (63.34%) required. The Cobb–Douglas functional form of labor-use frontier estimates shows that the quantity of harvested yam, size of cleared farm land and quantity of fertilizer applied significantly affected the amount of labor used in yam production at 10.0, 5.0, and 1.0% level of significance, respectively. Furthermore, the socio-economic determinants of labor-use efficiency were age, education, farm size, gender, labor wage, and household size which were statistically significant at 1.0% risk level except the coefficient of age which was significant at 5.0% risk level. The result showed that the estimated farm labor-use efficiency ranged from 0.20 to 0.97 with a mean labor-use efficiency value of 0.76.

The issue in the literature revealed that there is a relationship between pattern of labor use and household socio-economic characteristics and this study will further contribute to this growing literature by examining the pattern of labor use through a gender perspective.

4 Review of Empirical Studies on Factors Affecting Pattern of Labor Use

Adejare and Arimi (2013) examined the determinants of labor use for selected tree crops in Oyo and Ondo States, Nigeria. They identified the sources of labor used by tree crop farmers to be self, family, hired and informal/exchange labor. Average annual labor used by tree crop farmers was 62.7±21.6 man-days and there was a significant difference in labor use among farmers in the two states. Labor used by farmers in Oyo state was significantly influenced by contact with extension agents and use of labor-saving device. On the other hand, seven variables were significant predictors of labor used for tree crop production by farmers in Ondo state and these include family size, farm location and contact with extension agents, number of dependents, years of experience, membership of farmers association, and use of labor-saving devices. Use of labor-saving devices influenced labor use among tree crop farmers in the two states.

Agwu et al. (undated) examined factors influencing youth participation in agricultural labor in Abia state, Nigeria. The study employed descriptive statistics and probit model in the analysis of the data. The study reveals that in bush clearing and mound making males were participated majorly while female's percentage in the participation of all other farm operations outnumbered those of men. The study estimated the determinants of agricultural labor participation among youths in the study area and the coefficients of education, income from non-agricultural sources, occupation of the parents, education of the father, farm size and the rate of mechanization influenced agricultural labor participation among the youths in the study area and only the coefficient of farm size had a positive sign, the other variables had negative relationship. The study recommended that the cost of mechanization should be made affordable among other things to attract youths in agricultural participation.

It is observed from the literature that among the factors influencing pattern of labor use are the contact with extension agents, family size, farm location, number of dependents, years of experience, membership of farmers association, and use of labor-saving devices. This study will make use of some of these variable and go further to include sector and zone to observe regional disparity in labor use.

5 Review of Empirical Studies on Factors Affecting Labor Productivity

Okoye et al. (2008) examined the determinant of labor productivity on smallholder cocoyam farmers in Anambra State. They found out that fertilizer, cocoyam setts, capital, and farmer experience to be positively and significantly related to labor productivity at 5% level. Farm size and household size had a negative relationship with labor productivity and significant at 5% level. The coefficients for manure and education were negative but not significant. The results call for policies aimed at increasing planting materials, fertilizer, capital inputs, encouraging experienced farmers to remain in production, birth control measures and access to productive resources to small scale cocoyam enterprises.

Changkid (2008) examined labor use efficiency of rice farming in Thailand with emphasis on the central plain. Results showed that labor use was inefficient in Thai rice farming since the value of the marginal product of labor was less than wage rate. The result also indicated that there were decreasing returns to scale in rice production.

Shittu et al. (2014) examined labor use efficiency in food crop production by farmers in Ogun State, Nigeria. The study examined the pattern (sources and contract form) of labor use and the effects on production efficiency of food crop farms in Ogun State, Nigeria. The most widely used form of labor was family labor and hired labor. Hired labor was mostly employed on annual and/or job specific contracts. The mean labor use by farmers in the sample was 72.6 man-day/ha and 34.6% of which were supplied by household members, 33.5% by labor hired on annual contract, 14.5% by labor hired on job specific contract and the rest (10.8%) by daily paid contract. They concluded that labor use irrespective of engagement type with the exception of family labor increases technical efficiency.

It has been observed from the literature that fertilizer, planting material, capital, farmer experience, Farm size, and household size significantly related to labor productivity. Therefore, this study will employ fertilizer, planting material, farm size and household size to examine factor influencing labor productivity.

6 Methodology

6.1 Study Area

The study area is Nigeria. The country is made up of 36 States and the Federal Capital Territory (FCT), Abuja with 774 Local Government Areas (LGAs). She has a population of 178.5 Million (World Bank 2019) and is located in West Africa on the Gulf of Guinea between Benin and Cameroon; lying between latitudes 4° 1′ and 13° 9′ N and longitudes 2° 2′ and 14° 30′ E. Nigeria's climate is arid in the north, tropical in the center, and equatorial in the South. Mean maximum temperatures are 30–32 °C in the south and 33–35 °C in the North. High humidity is characteristic from February to November in the South and from June to September in the North. Low humidity coincides with the dry season. Annual rainfall decreases northward; rainfall ranges from about 2000 millimeters in the coastal zone (averaging more than 3550 millimeters in the Niger Delta) to 500–750 millimeters in the north (Federal Research Division: Country Profile, July 2008).

6.2 Type and Source of Data

The study made use of secondary data. The General Household Survey (GHS) of the National Bureau of Statistics (NBS) was used. The survey was implemented in collaboration with the World Bank Living Standards Measurement Study (LSMS) team as part of the Integrated Surveys on Agriculture (ISA) programme and was recently revised to include a panel component (GHS-Panel). The 2012/2013 round of the survey was used as it was the most recent available at the time of carrying out this research. The 2015/2016 and 2018/2019 rounds were not available at the time of this study. Data extracted from the 2012/2013 cross-section include: socioeconomic characteristics, household characteristics, labor use, planting and harvesting activities, assets, etc.

6.3 Sampling Procedure and Sample Size

The GHS-Panel sample is a two-stage probability sample: First Stage: The EAs were selected based on probability proportional to size (PPS) of the total EAs in each state and FCT, Abuja, and the total households listed in those EAs. A total of 500 EAs were selected using this method. Second Stage: The second stage was the selection of households. Households were selected randomly using the systematic selection of ten (10) households per EA. This involved obtaining the total number of households listed in a particular EA, and then calculating a Sampling Interval (S.I) by dividing the total households listed by ten (10). The next step was to generate a random start 'r' from the table of random numbers, which stands as the 1st selection. Consecutive selection of households was obtained by adding the sampling interval to the random start. Determination of the household-level sample size was based on experience gained from previous GHS rounds, in which 10 households per EA are usually selected and give robust estimates. In all, 500 clusters/EAs were canvassed and 5000 households were interviewed. These samples were proportionally selected in the states such that different states had different samples sizes (NBS 2014).

7 ANALYTICAL TECHNIQUES

7.1 Descriptive Statistics

Descriptive statistics was used to explain the socio-economic characteristics of the agricultural households in Nigeria. This includes the use of frequency tables, means, and percentages.

7.2 Partial Productivity Measure

Labor productivity: This was measured by finding the ratio of the crop output obtained to the man-day of labor employed, which is expressed in Eq. (1) as follows:

$$\text{Labor productivity} = \frac{\text{Output}}{\text{Number of labor use (man day)}} \quad (1)$$

Based on the mean labor productivity, any household that has a productivity value that below the mean value will be consider less productive and those having equal and above the mean are considered to be productive.

7.3 Two Stage Least Squares Regression

The two-stage least squares regression technique was used to identify the determinants of labor use and labor productivity among agricultural households in Nigeria. Two stage least squares regression (2SLS) is a method of extending regression to cover models which violate ordinary least squares (OLS) regression's assumption of recursivity, especially models where the researcher must assume that the disturbance term of the dependent variable is correlated with the cause of the independent variable.

A structural model of the determinants of labor use and productivity is defined in the equation below.

$$C_1 = \alpha_0 + \alpha_1 c_2 + \alpha_2 z_1 + \cdots + \alpha_k z_{k-1} + \mu_i \quad (2)$$

C_1 labor use/productivity
c_2 Explanatory variables for determinants of labor use/labor productivity
z_1 Vector of exogenous variables
z_k Variable not in (2) but exogenous
μ_i Error term.

A reduced form model for labor use/productivity (c_2) is specified as:

$$c_2 = \pi_0 + \pi_1 z_1 + \cdots + \pi_{k-1} z_{k-1} + \pi_{zk} + v_2 \tag{3}$$

The variables C1 and c2 are endogenous variables to be determined within the model while the explanatory variables are both the exogenous and endogenous variables included in the model.

For the purpose of addressing possible endogeneity, previous empirical studies (Tassew 2000; Abdulai and Regmi 2000; Jacoby 1993) were consulted to identify instrumental variables to be included in the model. The set of instruments used are the number of young children aged between 10 and 15, number of children aged between five and nine years, numbers of children aged below five years, adults above 60 years old and adult daily field wage for hired labor.

7.3.1 Determinants of Labor Use

Y = Quantity of labor (in man-days) used by ith agricultural household for production (Adult Equivalent Unit [AEU]: Male 15 years or older = 1; Female 15 years or older = 0.8; Male or female 14 years or under = 0.5 [Takane 2008]); β = Vector of unknown parameters; e = Random error term; X = explanatory variables.

The variables are:

Y = labor use (man-days); X_1 = Output (kg); X_2 = Gender (1 = male, 0 = female); X_3 = Age of household head (years); X_4 = Household size; X_5 = Marital status (1 = married, 0 if otherwise); X_6 = Farm size (square meter); X_7 = Wage rate (₦); X_8 = Extension contact (1 = has access, 0 if otherwise); X_9 = Pesticide use (1 = used, 0 if otherwise); X_{10} = Herbicide use (1 = used, 0 if otherwise); X_{11} = mechanization (1 = equipment used, 0 if otherwise); X_{12} = Cropping system (1 = mixed cropping, 0 if otherwise); X_{13} = Credit access (1 = has access, 0 if otherwise); X_{14} = sector (1 = rural, 0 if otherwise); X_{15} = North East (1 = North East, 0 if otherwise); X_{16} = North West (1 = North West, 0 if otherwise); X_{17} = South East (1 = South East, 0 if otherwise); X_{18} = South-South (1 = South-South, 0 if otherwise); X_{19} = South West (1 = South West, 0 if otherwise).

The a priori expectations for the determinants of labor use are presented in Table 2.

Table 2 A priori expectations for the determinants of labor use

Variable	Source	Expected sign
Output	Osugiri et al. (2012)	−
Age of household head	Simonyan and Obiakor (2012)	+
Household size	Canwat (2012)	+
Farm size	Oluyole et al. (2013), Osugiri et al. (2012)	+
Wage rate	Oluyole et al. (2013)	+
Extension contact	Adejare and Arimi (2013)	−
Pesticide use	Adejare and Arimi (2013)	−
Herbicide use	Adejare and Arimi (2013)	−
Mechanization	Adejare and Arimi (2013)	−
Credit access	Simonyan and Obiakor (2012)	+

Source Authors' compilation

Table 3 A priori expectations of the determinants of labor productivity

	Source	Expectation sign
Age	Okoye et al. (2008)	−
Household size	Okoye et al. (2008)	−
Fertilizer use	Okoye et al. (2008), Mbam and Edeh (2011)	+
		+
Seed	Okoye et al. (2008), Mbam and Edeh (2011)	+
		+
Farm size	Okoye et al. (2008), Mbam and Edeh (2011)	−
		−

Source Author's compilation

7.3.2 Determinants of Labor Productivity

The explanatory variables included in the model are:

X_1 = Age of household head (Years); X_2 = Marital status ($D=1$ if married; 0 otherwise); X_3 = Household size (Number); X_4 = quantity of fertilizer used (Kg); X_5 = quantity of seed (kg); X_6 = Pesticide use (kg); X_7 = Herbicide use (litre); X_8 = Hired labor wage (₦); X_9 = Farm size (m²); X_{10} = Cropping system ($D=1$ if mixed cropping; 0 otherwise); X_{11} = Credit access ($D=1$ if has access; 0 otherwise).

The a priori expectations for the determinants of labor productivity are presented in Table 3.

8 Results and Discussion

8.1 Socio-Economic Characteristics of the Households

Table 4 presents the socio-economic characteristics of agricultural households in Nigeria. The average age of male household head was 50.74 ± 14.83 years. This was significantly different for female household head which was 59.65 ± 12.69 years. This implies that male-headed households are still

Table 4 Socio-economic characteristics of agricultural households

Characteristics	Male-headed household (N= 3934)	Female-headed household (N= 684)
Age		
≤34	498 (12.7)	36 (5.26)
35–54	1973 (50.2)	206 (30.12)
55–74	1172 (29.8)	333 (48.68)
≥75	291 (7.4)	109 (15.94)
Mean	50.74±14.83	59.65±12.69
Marital status		
Married	3651 (92.81)	58 (8.49)
Divorced/separated	74 (1.88)	70 (10.23)
Widowed	98 (2.49)	529 (77.34)
Single	111 (2.82)	27 (3.95)
Household size		
1–3	557 (14.16)	319 (46.64)
4–6	1430 (36.35)	265 (38.74)
7–9	1249 (311.75)	74 (10.82)
10–12	590 (15)	23 (3.36)
>12	108 (2.75)	3 (0.44)
Mean	7.18	4.31
Sector		
Urban	1175 (29.87)	260 (38.01)
Rural	2759 (70.13)	424 (61.99)

Note Figures in parenthesis are percentages
Source Authors' computation LSMS-ISA data

economically active than their female counterpart. Most of the women in female-headed households are widowed. This is a likely reason for the age difference because households in Nigeria are patriarchal. Furthermore, the age structure in households affects their decision to engage in strenuous agricultural activities with implication on labor availability and use. They are mostly married with an average household size of 7 and 4 members for male-headed and female-headed households, respectively. It is assumed that married households would have some stability in terms of ready access and availability of family labor. The preponderance of large households is typical in Nigeria's rural areas and could affect decisions of these households in hiring labor to augment family labor in agricultural production. As explained by Omotesho et al. (2014), increases in total household size will result in a decrease in hired labor use. The distribution of agricultural households by sector shows that agricultural households are predominantly in rural areas.

8.2 Labor Use in Agricultural Production

Table 5 presents a comparative perspective of labor use, number of days spent on work and average daily wage for hired labor in various agricultural activities across male-headed and female-headed households. The agricultural activities considered were planting and harvesting activities.

Table 5 Number of labor use during planting and harvesting activities

Type of labor	Planting		Harvesting	
	Male-headed households	Female-headed households	Male-headed households	Female-headed households
Family labor	5928 (36.3)	607 (37.5)	5749 (51.2)	686 (76.4)
Hired men	7482 (45.8)	606 (37.5)	3538 (31.5)	143 (15.9)
Hired women	2250 (13.8)	379 (23.4)	1602 (14.3)	63 (7.0)
Hired children	671 (4.1)	26 (1.6)	338 (3.0)	6 (0.7)
Total number	16,331 (100)	1618 (100)	11,227	100.0

Note Figures in parenthesis are percentages
Source Authors' computation LSMS-ISA data

8.2.1 Number of Labor Use for Planting and Harvesting Activities

Allocation of labor usually varies with farming activities. While some tasks require skilled hired labor, family labor is sufficient for some and sometimes both. The cost and availability may affect the use of hired labor for different agricultural activities. Table 5 presents the number of labor use for planting and harvesting activities. Results showed that male-headed households mostly use hired men for planting activities (45.8%) followed by family labor (36.3%). On the other hand, female-headed households used equal proportion of hired men and family labor for planting activities. It can be concluded that agricultural households for planting activities predominantly use hired men. This might be due to the labor-intensive nature of planting activities. For harvesting activities, female-headed households used more family labor (76.4%) than male-headed (51.2%). It could be concluded that family labor is mostly used for harvesting activities irrespective of the sex of household head, as this might not be as strenuous and laborious as planting activities.

8.2.2 Average Number of Days Spent on Work by Agricultural Labor

Table 6 presents the average number of days spent on work by agricultural labor on planting and harvesting activities. Hired men for planting activities spent an average of 11 man-days across the sex of household head. Hired men spent an average of 6.3 man-days in male-headed households and about 4 man-days in female-headed households. This implies that family labor spend longer man-days than hired men for planting activities. For harvesting activities, the type of labor that is predominantly used is family labor. An average of 11.8 and 11.5 man-days for male-headed and female-headed households, respectively, were spent on harvesting activities. Hired men irrespective of the sex of the household head spent shorter number of man-days. This further supports the fact that harvesting activities are mostly done using family labor. The reasons for this might be due to the high cost of engaging hired labor in Nigeria and the type of activity to be carried out, which appear slightly different from that of other Sub-Saharan African countries like Tanzania (Osabuohien et al. 2019).

Table 6 Average number of man-days spent on work during planting and harvesting activities

Type of labor	Planting		Harvesting	
	Male-headed household	Female-headed household	Male-headed household	Female-headed household
Family labor	11.09	11.17	11.77	11.46
Hired men	6.33	3.93	4.13	3.20
Hired women	3.55	3.20	3.90	2.68
Hired children	3.21	2.83	3.59	2.00

Source Authors' computation LSMS-ISA data

Table 7 Average daily wage paid for hired labor for planting and harvesting activities

Type of labor	Planting		Harvesting	
	Male headed household (₦)	Female headed household (₦)	Male headed household (₦)	Female headed household (₦)
Hired men	4392.32	3836.04	1589.15	1202.27
Hired women	1105.53	1255.39	1197.79	971.43
Hired children	624.86	600.00	731.04	300.00

Source Authors' computation LSMS-ISA data

8.2.3 Average Daily Wage for Hired Labor

The average daily wage for hired labor for planting and harvesting activities is presented in Table 7. Results showed that male labor receive higher wages on the average than female labor for planting activities. It was as high as ₦4392.32 for hired men in male-headed households and ₦3836.04 in female-headed households for planting activities. This is because women are not able to engage in more strenuous agricultural activities and this might be the reason for the wage differential. The average daily wage rate was lowest for hired children across the households. Similarly, for harvesting activities, hired men had higher wages than hired women, though the difference was not significant across male-headed and female-headed households. This implies that average daily wage is usually higher for planting activities than harvesting and hired male labor usually earn more than hired female labor irrespective of the sex of the household head.

9 Determinants of Labor Use Among Agricultural Households

The determinants of labor use among agricultural households are presented in Table 8. The result showed that crop output, age of household head, mixed cropping system, credit access, North East, South East and South West geo-political zones have a positive influence on labor use while

Table 8 Determinants of labor use among agricultural households

	Male headed household	Female headed household
	Coefficient	Coefficient
Mechanization	−5.397***	−4.152**
	(1.674)	(1.453)
Output	0.027***	0.043***
	(0.005)	(0.008)
Age of household head	0.490***	0.96***
	(0.0643)	(0.177)
Household size	0.060	0.069*
	(0.019)	(0.036)
Marital status	0.213	−0.879
	(0.6401)	(0.9107)
Farm size	−0.292***	−0.138**
	(0.053)	(0.07)
Ln (Wages)	−0.2580***	−0.621***
	(0.00684)	(0.0324)
Extension contact	0.176	0.847
	(0.591)	(0.844)
Herbicide use	0.271	−4.708***
	(0.166)	(0.509)
Mixed cropping	0.639***	0.544***
	(0.056)	(0.078)
Credit access	1.580**	1.164*
	(0.763)	(0.654)
Rural	−0.218	1.804***
	(0.225)	(0.32)
North East	2.059***	0.672
	(0.474)	(0.702)
North West	−0.608*	2.003**
	(0.325)	(0.664)
South East	1.300**	2.003*
	(0.608)	(0.741)
South-South	−0.523*	1.957***
	(0.296)	(0.47)
South West	1.685*	−1.185**
	(0.934)	(0.587)
Constant	6.173***	14.607***
	(1.828)	(3.015)
	Wald chi2(17) = 2091.80	Wald chi2(17) = 945.54
	Prob > chi2 = 0.0000	Prob > chi2 = 0.0000
	R-squared = 0.0645	R-squared = 0.3290

Note ***, **, * represent significant levels at 1%, 5% and 10% respectively. Standard error in parenthesis
Source Authors' computation LSMS-ISA data

mechanization, farm size, wage rate and being an agricultural household living in North West and South-South had a negative effect on labor use among the male headed households.

Similarly for female-headed households, crop output, age of household head, household size, credit access, residing in a rural area and being resident in North-West, South-East and South-South positively influence labor use while mechanization, farm size, wage rate, pesticide use, mixed cropping and being an agricultural household living in South-West have negative effects on labor use.

Output has positive and significant influence on labor use in male-headed and female-headed agricultural households. This implies that a one percent increase in output is associated with 0.027 percent and 0.043 percent increase in labor use in male-headed and female-headed households respectively. This can be explained that as agricultural households' output increases, the more the income received from sale of the output and this will enable the households to employ more labor for the planting and harvesting activities. This finding is expected and is in agreement with Oluyole et al. (2013) that found a positive relationship between farm income and labor use. The Age of household head is significant and positively related to labor use in male-headed agricultural households. An increase of one year in the age of household head will result in an increase in labor use by 0.490 and 0.96 man-days for male and female headed households respectively. The positive linkage between labor use and the age of the household head can be probably attributed to the fact that as household head increase in age, he/she is more experienced about the labor requirements and might not have required strength to cope with the rigors of farming and as such, increase labor use. This result is in line with the findings of Simonyan and Obiakor (2012) that found a positive and significant relationship between age and household labor use.

The household size is significant and positively related to labor use in female-headed households. An increase in household size by one person will lead to an increase in labor use by 0.069 man-days. This result is in agreement with Canwat (2012) who found a positive significant relationship between household size and labor use. Farm size is significant and negatively related to labor use in both male-headed and female-headed households. The plausible reason for this is that as the area under cultivation increases, household heads might engage in mechanized farming and use less of human labor. This result contradicts the findings of Oluyole et al. (2013) who pointed out that large sized farms would require more labor than small sized farms, and *vice versa*.

Wage is significant and negatively related to labor use in both households. The coefficient of wage indicates that for every additional naira in wages paid to the hired labor, labor use decreases in male-headed and female-headed households. This result corroborates Oluyole et al. (2013) that found that wage rate negatively affected labor use. This is quite obvious because wage rate determines the extent to which labor could be used particularly hired labor. When wage rate is low, more labor could be employed and vice versa. The coefficient of use of herbicide has a negative and significant relationship with labor use in female-headed households but not significant among the male headed households. A unit increase in quantity of herbicide use will lead to decreases in labor use by an average of 4.7 man-days. This is because herbicide is category as one of labor-saving devices therefore the use of herbicide will reduce the number of human labor use and man day spent in agricultural operation. Similarly, the use of machinery also has a negative and significant relationship with labor use in male and female-headed households. This result is in agreement with Adejare and Arimi (2013) that found that labor saving devices reduce labor use.

The coefficient of mixed cropping system was positive and significant for male-headed and female-headed households. A possible reason for this is that mixed cropping involves planting a number of crops at the same time and as such would require more labor for cropping activities. The coefficient of access to credit is significant and positively related to labor use in both households. An increase in access to credit by agricultural household is expected to increase labor use by 1.58 percent man-days and 1.16 percent man-days in male headed and female-headed households respectively than those that have no access to credit. This result is expected because access to credit provides an opportunity for households to hire labor in addition to that of family labor thus resulting in more labor use. This finding corroborates Simonyan and Obiakor (2012) that found that household labor use increases with credit access. The coefficient of rural sector was found to be positively and significantly influence labor use among female-headed agricultural households. This implies that being an agricultural household living in a rural area is associated with 1.8 man-days increase in labor use in female-headed households than those in urban areas. The coefficient of North West and South-South were significant and negatively related to labor use in male headed household while the coefficient of North East, South East and South West were significant and positively related to labor use. In female headed households, the coefficient of North West, South East, and South South were significant and positive while only the coefficient of South West was significant and negative. This might be as a result of labor availability differentials that exist in these regions.

10 Labor Productivity

Table 9 presents the estimates of labor productivity among agricultural households. The results showed that 60.7% of male-headed households and 53.8% of female-headed households have a labor productivity of less than 0.2. This implies that majority of the agricultural households are less productive. The mean labor productivity index was used as the cut-off point (0.44). Any household below this cut-off point of 0.44 was considered less productive and household with and above the point is considered as productive. Based on this, 75.5% of male-headed households are less productive compared to

Table 9 Distribution of labor productivity

Productivity ratio	Male-headed household		Female-headed household	
	Frequency	Percent	Frequency	Percent
<0.2	860	60.69	106	53.81
0.20–0.39	211	14.89	15	7.61
0.40–0.59	126	8.89	20	10.15
>0.59	220	15.53	56	28.43
Total	1417	100	197	100
Mean	0.45		0.41	
Less productive	1070	75.51	142	72.08
Productive	347	24.49	55	27.92
Mean	0.45		0.41	
Combined mean (cut-off)	0.44			

Source Authors' computation LSMS-ISA data

72.1% in female-headed households. Overall, labor productivity among agricultural households in Nigeria is low.

11 Determinants of Labor Productivity Among Agricultural Households

The determinants of labor productivity are presented in Table 10. The factors that determine labor productivity among male-headed households were fertilizer use, improved seed usage and farm size. Only mixed cropping system significantly influenced labor productivity among female-headed households. Fertilizer use had a positive and significant ($p < 0.01$) relationship with labor productivity in male-headed households. This implies that an increase in quantity of fertilizer used increases the productivity of labor in male-headed households. Upton (1973) posited that fertilizer use increases productivity of both labour and land simultaneously resulting in what is regarded as neutral process innovation. This result is consistent with findings of Okoye et al. (2008), where they found that an increase in fertilizer use led to an increase in labor productivity. Farm size had a negative and significant ($p < 0.1$) relationship with labor productivity. This implies that as the size of farm increases, labor productivity reduces. The quantity of seed has a positive and significant effect ($p < 0.01$) on labor productivity in male headed households. This shows that an increase in quantity of seed used increases labor productivity in male-headed households. Access to credit by male-headed households was positive and significant ($p < 0.1$) with labor productivity.

The coefficient of mixed cropping system has a positive and significant ($p < 0.05$) influence on labor productivity in female headed households. This indicating that being a female headed household practicing mixed cropping is more likely to increase labor productivity. This is consistent with the findings

Table 10 Determinants of labor productivity

	Male headed household	Female headed household
	Coefficient	Coefficient
Mechanization	2.197	11.4229
	(5.205)	(8.536)
Age	0.301	0.3369
	(0.378)	(0.499)
Marital status	−1.762	−6.7229
	(1.216)	(6.260)
Household size	2.402	−1.6176
	(1.853)	(1.148)
Fertilizer use	1.543***	2.8273
	(0.222)	(6.038)
Quantity of seed (Kg)	3.073***	1.6303
	(0.925)	(1.290)
Pesticide use	−1.886	2.7619
	(3.779)	(1.718)
Farm size	-8.011***	−2.73859
	(2.34)	(2.184)
Mixed cropping	-1.269	4.9009**
	(1.134)	(3.584)
Credit access	1.796*	3.20354
	(1.079)	(2.838)
Constant	8.558.62	-1.13902
	(7.247)	(7.766)
	Wald chi2(10) = 12846.26	Wald chi2(10) = 56.07
	Prob > chi2 = 0.0000	Prob > chi2 = 0.0000
	R-squared = 0.4896	R-squared = 0.567

Note ***significant at 1% level, **significant at 5% level, and *significant at 10% level
Source Authors' computation LSMS-ISA data

of Rufai et al. (2018) where labor productivity increased among female farmers who practiced multiple cropping.

12 Conclusion and Recommendation

The study examines the pattern of labor use among agricultural households in Nigeria. Labor productivity was also examined and the factors influencing it. Allocation of labor usually varies with farming activities. The cost and availability may affect the use of hired labor for different agricultural activities. Hired men are predominantly used by agricultural households for planting activities while family labor is mostly used for harvesting activities irrespective of the sex of household head. Average number of man-days spent on work and wages during planting and harvesting activities also vary depending on the type of activity to be carried out. Wages are usually higher for hired men than hired women. The study established that labor use is positively influenced by crop output, age of household head, household size, farm size, credit access, cropping system, among others. Labor productivity is also low and below the maximum that can be obtained from existing level of labor use. Factors that affect labor productivity were quantity of fertilizer used, seeds and type of cropping system employed. Since labor productivity can be enhanced by the use of fertilizers and improved seeds, government should therefore make these inputs available to agricultural households. Agricultural households' productivity is a critical issue in the pursuit of sustainable agricultural production in Nigeria, therefore, the introduction of labor-saving technologies such as the use of herbicide, fertilizers and seeds into agricultural production activities should be encouraged so as to achieve optimum labor use and increase labor productivity.

References

Abdulai, A., & Regmi, P. (2000). Estimating labour supply of farm households under non-separability: Empirical evidence from Nepal. *Agricultural Economics, 22*(2000), 309–320.

Adejare, G. T., & Arimi, K. (2013). Determinants of labor use for selected tree crops in Oyo and Ondo States, Nigeria. *New York Science Journal, 6*(8), 76.

Adepoju, A. A., & Salman, K. K. (2013). Increasing agricultural productivity through rural infrastructure: Evidence from Oyo and Osun States, Nigeria. *International Journal of Applied Agricultural and Apicultural Research, 9*(1&2), 1–10.

Agwu, N. M., Nwankwo, E. E., & Anyanwu, C. I. (undated). Determinants of agricultural labor participation among youths in Abia State, Nigeria. *International Journal of Food and Agricultural Economics, 2*(1), 157–164.

Akanni, K. A., & Dada, A. O. (2012). Analysis of labor use patterns among small-holder cocoa farmers in South Western Nigeria. *Journal of Agricultural Science and Technology, B2,* 107–113.

Anyaegbunam, H. N., Okoye, G. N., Asumugha, M. C., Ogbonna, T. U., Madu, N. N., & Ejechi, M. E. (2010). Labour productivity among small- holder cassava farmers in South East agro ecological zone, Nigeria. *African Journal of Agricultural Research, 5*(21), 2882–2885.

Anyiro, C. O., Emerole, C. O., Osondu, C. K., Udah, S. C., & Ugorji, S. E. (undated). Labor-use efficiency by smallholder yam farmers in Abia State Nigeria: A labor-use requirement frontier approach. *International Journal of Food and Agricultural Economics, 1*(1), 151–163.

Awotodunbo, A. A. (2008). Labor use pattern among farmers in Ife central local government area of Osun State. *International Journal of Agricultural Economics & Rural Development, 1*(2), 84–92. https://www.lautechaee-edu.com/journal/ijaerd2/ijaerd2.11.pdf.

Bervidova, L. (2002). Labor productivity as a factor of sustained economic development of the CR agriculture. Czech University of Agriculture, Prague, Czech Republic. *Agricultural Economics, 48*(2), 55–59.

Block, S. A. (1995). The recovery of agricultural productivity in sub-Saharan Africa. *Food Policy, 20*(5), 385–405.

Canwat, V. (2012). Modelling seasonal farm labor demand: What can we learn from rural Kakamega district, western Kenya? *International Journal of Development and Sustainability, 1*(2), 195–211.

Changkid, N. (2008). Labor use efficiency of rice farming in Thailand with emphasis on the central plain. *Suratthani Rajabhat Journal, 1*(2), 73–82.

Donnellan, T., Hanrahan, K., & Henness, T. (2012). *Defining an institutional framework for the labor market* (Factor Markets Working Paper No. 24).

FAO. (2011). *The role of women in agriculture* (ESA Working Paper No. 11–02). Agricultural Development Economics Division, The Food and Agriculture Organization of the United Nations. www.fao.org/economic/esa.

Faridi, M. Z., & Basit, A. B. (2011). Factors determining rural labor supply: A micro analysis. *Pakistan Economic and Social Review, 49*(1), 91–108.

Jacoby, H. (1993). Shadow wages and peasant family labour supply: An econometrics application to the peruvian sierra. *Review of Economic Studies, 60*(4), 903–921.

Kwan, F. (2009). Agricultural labor and the incidence of surplus labor: Experience from China during reform. *Journal of Chinese Economic and Business Studies, 7*(3), 341–361.

Mbam, B. N., & Edeh, H. O. (2011). Determinants of farm productivity among smallholder rice farmers in Anambra State, Nigeria. *Journal of Animal and Plant Sciences, 9*(3), 1187–1191.

Mohammed-lawal, A., & Omotesho, O. A. (2004). Resource allocation in food crop production and farming household food security in Kwara State. *Agro Search, 6*, 15–21.

National Bureau of Statistics—NBS. (2014). Labour productivity in Nigeria (2010–2014): A short analysis. https://www.nigerianstat.gov.ng/pdfuploads/nbs%20Labour%20productivity%20summary%20rport%202010-2014.pdf.

OECD. (2001). *Measuring productivity: Measurement of aggregate and industry-level productivity growth*. http://oecd.org/sdd/productivity-stats/2352458.pdf.

Ogunniyi, L. T., Ajao, O. A., & Adeleke, O. A. (2012). Gender comparison in production and productivity of cocoa farmers in Ile Oluji local government area of Ondo state, Nigeria. *Global Journal of Science Frontier Research Agriculture Biology, 12*(5), 59–63.

Okali, D., Okpara, E., & Olawoye, J. (2001, October). *Rural–urban interactions and livelihood strategies: The case of Aba and its region, southeastern Nigeria*. Working Paper Series on Rural–Urban Interactions and Livelihood Strategies, Human Settlements Programme, IIED.

Okoye, B. C., Onyenweaku, C. E., Ukoha, O. O., Asumugha, G. N., & Aniedu, O. C. (2008). Determinants of labor productivity on small-holder cocoyam farms in Anambra State. *Scientific Research and Essay, 3*(11), 559–561.

Oluyole, K. A., Adebiyi, S., & Adejumo, M. O. (2007). An assessment of the adoption of cocoa rehabilitation techniques among cocoa farmers in Ijebu east local government area of Ogun state. *Journal of Agricultural Research and Policies, 2*(1), 56–60.

Oluyole, O. A., Dada, K. A., Oni, O. A., Adebiyi, S., & Oduwole, O. O. (2013). Farm labor structure and its determinants among cocoa farmers in Nigeria. *American Journal of Rural Development, 1*(1), 1–5.

Omotesho, K. F., Muhammad-Lawal, A., & Ismaila, D. E. (2014). Assessment of hired labor use and food security among rural farming households in Kwara State, Nigeria. *Journal of Agricultural Sciences, 59*(3), 353–361.

Osabuohien, E., Efobi, U. R., Herrmann, R., & Gitau, C. M. (2019). Female labor outcomes and large-scale agricultural land investments: Macro-micro evidence from Tanzania. *Land Use Policy, 82*, 716–728.

Osugiri, I. I., Ugochukwu, A. I., Onyemauwa, C. S., & Ben Chendo, G. N. (2012). Population dynamics, labor and small holder farmers' productivity in south east Nigeria. *Journal of Economics and Sustainable Development, 3*(12), 95–101.

Oyebola, P. O., Osabuohien, E., & Obasaju, B. (2019). Employment and income effects of Nigeria's agricultural transformation agenda. *African Journal of Economic and Management Studies.* https://doi.org/10.1108/AJEMS-12-2018-0402.

Ruben, R., & van den Berg, M. (2001). Non-Farm employment and rural poverty alleviation in rural honduras. *World Development, 29*(2), 549–560.http://www.elsevier/com/locate/worlddev.PII:S0305-750X(00)00107-8.

Rufai, A. M., Salman, K. K., & Salawu, M. B. (2018). Input utilization and agricultural labor productivity: A gender analysis. In A. Shimeles, A. Verdier-Chouchane, & A. Boly (Eds.), *Building a resilient and sustainable agriculture in sub-Saharan Africa.* Cham: Palgrave Macmillan.

Sachs, C. (1996). *Gendered fields: Rural women, agriculture and environment.* Boulder, CO: Westview Press.

Shittu, A. M., Adewuyi, S. A., Sowemimo, H. K., & Fapojuwo, O. E. (2014). Labour use efficiency in food crop production by farmers in Ogun State, Nigeria. *World Journal of Agricultural Sciences, 2*(3), 034–039. http://wsrjournals.org/journal/wjas.

Simonyan, J. B., & Obiakor, C. T. (2012). Analysis of household labor use in yam production in Anambra West local government area of Anambra State, Nigeria. *PAT 2, 8*(1), 1–16. http://www.patnsukjournal.net/currentissue.

Takane, T. (2008). Labor use in smallholder agriculture in Malawi: Six village case studies. *African Study Monographs, 29*(4), 183–200.

Tassew, W. (2000). *Economic analysis and policy implications of farm and off-farm employment: A case study in the tigray region of Northern Ethiopia* (Doctoral dissertation). Wageningen University, Wageningen.

Timmer, C. P. (1988). The agricultural transformation. In H. Chenery & T. N. Srinivasan (Eds.), *Handbook of development economics* (Vol. 1, pp. 275–331). Amsterdam: Elsevier Science.

Umar, H. S., Luka, E. G., & Rahman, S. A. (2010). Gender based analysis of labour productivity in sesame production in Doma local government area of Nasarawa State, Nigeria. *Patnsuki Journal, 6*(2), 61–68.

Upton, M. (1973). *Farm management in Africa. Principles of production and planning.* London: Oxford University Press.

World Bank. (2019). "Nigeria population, total". https://data.worldbank.org/country/nigeria.

Challenges in Tackling Poverty and Unemployment: Analysis of Youth Employment in Agriculture Program in Alkaleri, Duguri and Gar Rural Communities of Bauchi State, Nigeria

Ruqayya Aminu Gar and Roy Anthony Rodgers

1 Introduction

In development discuss, the concept of poverty and unemployment has transformed and extended beyond its traditional form. From a basic concept that was only grounded on income levels and poverty lines. The notion of poverty in particular has changed to embrace a multi-dimensional approach with consideration given to non-income dimensions such as health, education, housing, and so on (Callander et al. 2012). Therefore, effective poverty and unemployment reduction plans are generally seen as attributes of good governance. This is significant for all countries, particularly Nigeria that is recognised with a large portion of population that is highly poor and unemployed. Indeed, plan targeted at poverty and unemployment reduction ought to be a condition that improve countries development (Grindle 2004). The principle goal and process that established the Youth Employment in

---

R. A. Gar (✉) · R. A. Rodgers
Department of International and Strategic, Studies University Malaya UM Malaysia, Kuala Lumpur, Malaysia

R. A. Gar
Department of Political Science, Bauchi State University Gadau (BASUG) Nigeria, Gadau, Nigeria

Agriculture Programme (YEAP) in Nigeria was to have a direct impact on the extent and depth of poverty and unemployment. However, this aim remains only a mirage, as majority of the populaces predominantly in the rural areas of Alkaleri, Duguri, and Gar of Bauchi State in Nigeria remain extremely poor and unemployed. Unemployment especially among youth has continued to multiply annually in hundreds reflecting the higher number of youths that are incapable to sponsor their education. The persistent escalations in food and fuel prices has put more hardship to the masses. This demand for the need to assess the YEAP in terms of its contributions on its set objectives and goals of poverty and unemployment reduction in Alkaleri, Duguri, and Gar rural areas. By investigating what is constraining, in achieving the targeted goals of the YEAP. This is an activity that requires research and critical analysis which this study aimed at. In an overview, this study is divided into five sections, section one provides introduction of the study. Section 2 broadens the view on poverty by considering critical conceptualizations and analysis on poverty and unemployment in Sub-Saharan Africa, Nigeria and Bauchi State, Sect. 3 presents important literature review of the poverty and unemployment reduction programs in Nigeria. The data collection techniques and methodology for this study is discussed in Sect. 4. While Sect. 5 presents the results and concludes the study.

2   Conceptual Explanations

Brief clarification on the key concepts used in the study is provided in this section.

Poverty: People live in poverty when their earnings are not adequate for their well-being and when these conditions prevent them from taking part in activities which are an accepted part of daily life in that society (Adibe 2014). Thus, an individual is poor if his or her income level falls below some minimum level required to meet daily basic necessities (Ferreira et al. 2015). These explanations of poverty stress low-income levels despite the significance of other elements that are not quantifiable in monetary terms such as access to health care and societal stigmatization (Adibe 2014). There are fundamentally three current definitions of poverty in common usage: absolute poverty, relative poverty, and social exclusion. Absolute poverty is defined as the insufficiency of resources with which to keep body and soul together. Relative poverty expresses income or resources in relation to the average. Relative poverty is grounded on household expenditures. Per capita expenditures that are less than two-thirds of the poverty line are measured to be poor, while those above are non-poor. Relative measure has been the Nigerian NBS official poverty measure, but to better understand Nigerian measure of poverty, absolute poverty is considered by the NBS to relate Nigeria's poverty rates with other countries (NBS 2010). Additionally, the notion "poverty" has been defined from several approaches by scholars of different ideological perspectives. For instance, the United Nations Development Program (UNDP) describes poverty as that income level below which a minimum nutritionally sufficient diet together with essential non-food requirements are not affordable. Poverty is grouped by UNDP in three comprehensive classes as contained in the universally established definition to mean absolute poverty, relative and material poverty. Absolute poverty means the inability to provide such physiological subsistence (i.e., foods, shelter, clothing, potable water, safety, healthcare service, basic education, transportation, and gainful employment) to the extent of being incapable to protect human dignity. People under this category receive scarce income and their ability to make savings is zero.

Relative poverty means inadequate income to enhance active participation in societal activities to the extent that it limits the actualization of one's potentials. In this category of poverty, the minimum requirement of an individual is determined by caloric intake of square meters of shelter per person. Poverty here means inability of one to satisfy his basic social needs. Material poverty is the deprivation of physical assets such as cash-crop trees, land, animal husbandry, etc. (Laderchi et al. 2003). Poverty remain one of the major socio-economic problem affecting many countries of the world, mostly the developing regions of the globe. Remarkably, with the prompt and unprecedented increase in globalization, poverty has reduced significantly in the world both in number and in proportion regrettably, not all regions have made remarkable progress in reducing poverty. Sub-Saharan Africa (SSA) has lagged behind other regions with regard to poverty reduction (Castañeda et al. 2016). In addition, nearly 60% of the world's one billion extremely poor people reside in Sub-Saharan Africa (SSA), India, Bangladesh, and China (Heger et al. 2018). In the same vein (Thorbecke 2013). Points that since the 1980s, there was no significant progress recorded in poverty reduction where almost half of the population remained below the poverty line from 1981 to 2005 when compared to South Asia (SAS).

It is obvious that SSA's performance on poverty reduction since 1981 has not been even. Though the poverty incidence rate at the $1.25 level puffed-up by about 6.6% between 1981 and 1996, it essentially dropped to 6.0% during 1996–2005, and further by 3.6% between 2005 and 2010. Conversely, at 9.2 and 8.4%, the rates of poverty declined during 1996–2005 and 2005–2010 remained, respectively, faster for South Asia (SAS) a region that has also experienced generally high rate of poverty. Currently, SSA has indeed reversed its course since 1993, with the $1.25 poverty rate falling by some 10% by 2010, this progress appears quite stable, until in 2008 when an insignificant reduction rate was seen in which was related to the global crisis (World Bank 2014). Relatively, however, poverty reduction in SAS was about twice that level, at 21%. This is similar with the $2.50 standard as well, with SSA's poverty incidence decreasing by 6% between 1993 and 2010; over the same period, however, SAS's poverty rate dropped by 12%. Therefore, with a generally higher poverty frequency than in SSA at the $2.50 standard, and notwithstanding the important growth in SSA since the mid-1990s, SAS has certainly been rising up, demonstrating merely a little higher level of poverty prevalence than in SSA (Fosu 2013).

Nigeria like other African countries remains one of the most fertile lands with abundant natural and material resources. This was, however, expected to foster development and substantial improvements in Socio-economic well-being but unfortunately, these expectations never materialized and regrettably, these resources remain mismanaged. This could be seen in a huge amount of money set aside every year in form of budgetary allocation to various sectors of the economy but without translating into a tangible project with capacity to accommodate the economic needs of the public. Statistics of the Nigeria's earning from its oil sale reveal that throughout the previous three decades, the country received over US $300 billion from oil sources which should have been transformed into a substantial socio–economic development of the country. Not surprisingly, Nigeria's basic social indicators has currently been ranked the 25th poorest country in the world (Siddig et al. 2014).

In addition to the recent significance improvement with rising trends in its Gross Domestic Product (GDP), in the past decade, with the latest GDP of $500 billion in 2013, yet this has not been transformed positively to enhance employment and decrease poverty among the populace (Oginni et al. 2013; Oyebola et al. 2019; Yusof 2014). This is demonstrated by the high level of poverty and unemployment manifested across a significant proportion of the people in the various segment of Nigeria's rural areas. Some scholars relate this problem to the failure of both state and federal governments to utilize their allocated share from the oil and other revenue accruable to both states and federal government. This has been acknowledged in the poor households earning across Nigeria where majority of the household earned less than US$2 per day. For instance, in States like Edo, Delta, Gombe, Sokoto, Zamfara, Kano, Bayelsa, and Rivers have 62.6, 60.1, 60.9, 65.2, 69.7, 61.5, and 5.1%, respectively, of the number of households among the total number of their population that could not earned up to two Dollars per day. Other states have over 80% of their households that could not earned two dollar per day. This category of states includes, Ondo (81.89%), Ekiti (81.%), Enugu and Abia (both having 80.7%), Ebonyi (88.9%), Katsina (92.8%), and Yobe (94.3%). While the Federal Capital Territory FCT Abuja and Lagos State have the lowest poverty rate with 43.3 and 46.8%, respectively (Akanbi and Du Toit 2011).

Nigeria is the largest oil producer in Africa, sixth in the world and has the second-largest gas reserves in the world in addition to many valuable solid mineral deposits, such as kaolin, tin, limestone, zinc, iron ore, coal, and barite, lead and gypsum, most of which are in the northern part of the country. However, the population remain poor particularly in the northern part which is also blessed with fertile land that yield both food and cash crops such as cassava, yam, cereals, cotton, groundnut, beans, vegetables, variety of fruits, and cattle, fish and dairy products. Despite abundance of mineral and human resources, poverty continues to rise in Nigeria with 60.9% (99,284,512) of Nigerians living in absolute poverty, incapable of affording a minimal standard of food, clothing, and shelter. While those living below $1 per day are 61.2%; the Gini-coefficient measure of income inequality rose from 0.429 in 2004 to 0.447 in 2010, whereas Nigerians living in extreme poverty rose from 6.2% in 1980 to 38.7% in 2010 (Khan and Cheri 2016) Consistently, the percentage of people living in poverty rose from 27.2% in 1980 to 46.3% in 1985, dropped to 42.7% in 1992 and then increased to 65% in 1996. By 2010, the poverty level was at 69%, indicating that about 112.47 million Nigerians are living below the poverty line and climbing further to 93.9% in 2010 (Babatunde et al. 2011; NBS 2010). In addition, food poverty incidence in Nigeria was 50.23% while the vulnerability to food poverty incidence was 61.68% and the vulnerability to food poverty/food poverty ratio was 1.228. This shows the need for policies and programs that will optimally reduce food poverty and vulnerability in Nigeria to target more on the food poor to break the burden of underdevelopment in Nigeria (Ozughalu 2016).

In Northern Nigeria where Bauchi State is located, regardless of the existence of many economic resources such as tin, kaolin, a variety of agricultural products, and a huge fertile land, the people remain in abject poverty paving the way to crisis in forms of insurgency, electoral violence, and law breaking, joblessness, crime, illiteracy, maternal mortality, early marriage and, recently, terrorism (Abiodun et al. 2019). Three out of the six geopolitical zones in Nigeria are in the northern part of the country and they have the worst ratio of poverty compared to the other zones. The Northwest with 77.7%, North-central having 67.5% and Northeast with 76.3%. The economy remains very poor and the living standard of the populace have continued to worsen due to high rate of poverty, this creates more hardship that adds to the suffering conditions of the people particularly the masses (Khan and Cheri 2016).

Unemployment: the concept 'unemployment' refers to the condition of people who are without jobs. Also, the unemployed are described by the International Labor Organization (ILO) as numbers of the economically active population who are without work but available for and seeking work, comprising people who have lost their jobs and those who have willingly left work. This exists when members of the labor force wish to work but cannot get employments (Okafor 2011).

Similarly, youth unemployment, therefore, could be defined as the collection of youths with different background, seeking and able to work but cannot find any. Once the supply of labor outshines the demand for labor, it results to unemployment. Following the lack of sufficient employment prospective in the formal sector, youth may be constrained to engage in casual work and other unorthodox livelihood sources, thus leading to underemployment. Moreover, in Nigeria's unemployment situation, the young school leavers of all categories are the most vulnerable. This jobless youths fit to the major workforce of the economy but are being wasted as they strive for job ceaselessly without success. In addition, unemployment is a global trend, however it transpires generally in developing countries of the world, associated to social, economic, political, and psychological magnitudes. Therefore, huge youth unemployment in any country is a sign of multifaceted problems (Gibb and George 1989; Onah 2001; Echebiri 2005).

3 Poverty and Unemployment Reduction Programs in Nigeria

In the early stages after Nigeria achieved independence, effort to reduce poverty and unemployment by both previous and current Nigerian government have initiated series of Programs. The National Accelerated Food Production Program and Nigerian Agricultural and Co-operative Bank during Gowon's administration in (1972) was established to fund agriculture from the profits of oil boom but failed, the country remains burdened with import dependency and food insecurity. Operation Feed the Nation by General Obasanjo from (1976 to 1979) followed a related pattern by using newly university graduates to teach farmers in the rural areas about modern ways of farming, but this terminated without transforming into positive impact due to inadequate manpower and resources (Eneh 2011). The Shagari's Green Revolution program (1979–1983) had two major goals: reducing food importation into the country, in so doing to improve the capacity of Nigerian farmers to feed the nation, and diversifying Nigerian farming into the production of cash crops and fibre aimed at modernization of farming activities in the country. Despite the huge amount of money invested to fund the program estimated at over 2 billion naira nevertheless, it ended up a failure due to corruption. The General Buhari's Go Back to Farm Project (1983–1985) recorded some initial success especially in Rivers State under Governor Fidelis Onyakhilome's School to Farm project but the success was short-lived as it could not be continued when the regime was ended. "The Directorate of Food, Roads and Rural Infrastructure Employment," the "Directorate for Foods, Roads and Rural Infrastructure," the "Better Life Program," "Peoples Bank," "Community Bank," and the "National Economic Reconstruction Fund" of Babangida's regime (1985–1993) was planned to offer feeder roads, potable drinking water, and modern facilities in rural areas which claimed about 1.9 billion naira ended up in vain. The Poverty Alleviation Program (National Poverty Eradication Program) (NAPEP), the sectorial reform agenda and the "Vision 2020" initiated by Obasanjo's second tenure (1999–2007), Yar'Adua's Seven Point Agenda and the transformation Agenda of President Goodluck Jonathan also failed to improve the well-being of Nigerians despite incorporating poverty reduction as their major goal. These schemes consumed trillions of Naira (Nigeria's currency) that failed to rescue Nigerians from devastating poverty that continues to upsurge (Cheri 2014).

Moreover, other programs include the Subsidy Reinvestment and Empowerment Program (SURE-P): Community Services Women and Youth Employment (CSWYE), were all initiated p 2012 by the Goodluck Jonathan administration to reduce unemployment among the people. As well as to complement different employment strategies and mainstream employment in all sectors targeting poor. Nigerian men aged 18–35 and women aged 18–50, with no other source of income and with only a secondary school education. The SURE-P has slightly reduced some of the problems associated with unemployment and helped in trying to boost some economic activities across the country. However, most of the jobs offered to the trainees were not relevant to their course of study. The SURE-P programs have been politicized and hijacked by selfish politicians providing jobs to only their associates. The exclusion of the physically challenged youths in SURE-P Program was a key obstacle that threatens its success in all parts of the country. Most of the projects executed by SURE-P, were the same projects awarded to different ministries before the advent of the program, thus, approval of funds for the programs became problematic thereby making it almost impossible to achieve its aim of empowering Nigerian youths. With insufficient welfare package and corruption, the SURE-P had done merely below expectation to improve the economy of the country (Nwosu et al. 2018).

Similarly, the Home-Grown School Feeding (HGSF) program being part of a N500 billion (US$2 billion) Social Investment Program to reduce poverty and improve the health and education of children and other weak groups. The HGSF program was first directed in 2004 and provides free school meals obtained from local farmers. The food was generally delivered in the form of a hot, balanced meal at lunch, containing at least one-third of the recommended dietary allowance of nutrients. The program was extended in 2016–2020 to the national level, targeting 155,000 beneficiaries to support Nigerian states government in feeding more than 24 million school children, making it the largest school feeding program of its kind in Africa. Although the program seems to be a good one; however, challenges of mismanagement and corruption jeopardize the ultimate goals and achievement of the program. Cooks employed by for the HGSF program are normally unqualified on food and nutrition, kitchen hygiene, and environmental sanitation. The majority of the cooks do not have health certificates. They also do not receive any on-the-job training to enhance their services. Many of the school prepare food under trees, this has an adverse consequence on the hygienic environment desirable for food preparation to protect the overall health status of the beneficiaries as well as teaching and learning. Additionally, because benefitting schools lack dining halls where meals are served, pupils use their classrooms as dining rooms. This is quite alarming as pupils soils their books and also make the classrooms untidy for academic work. This obstructs good teaching and learning and also postures severe health threats for the children. In addition to these programs, international, aid-based schemes such as Structural Adjustment Program (SAP), African Growth and Opportunity Act (AGOA), and a four years medium term plan initiated by the formal president of Nigeria Aremu Olusegun Obasanjo, for the period of 2003–2007, i.e., the National Economic Empowerment and Development Strategy (NEEDS), Millennium Development Goals (MDGs) and several others funded by international organizations were initiated, funded, but poorly implemented (Marfo et al. 2017; Osabuohien et al. 2018).

Generally, youths have great potentials and in order to harness these potentials, there is the need to make the right investments in their skills to provide them with appropriate tools, to create their own jobs and provide decent employment to others. Youths have great roles to play in agricultural development, in Nigeria youth are seen to be the most active working group. Despite efforts from various government regimes in Nigeria to implement several agricultural development programs to reduce poverty and unemployment across Nigeria for the benefit of all citizens, especially youths. And though Nigeria's economy has sustained to witness considerable economic growth during the past few years, this has not turned into poverty reduction and job creation, especially for youth. Because very few out of the four to five million youth who search for jobs in the labour market annually finds formal employment. Therefore, being part of the federal government Agricultural Transformation Agenda to create employment and development for youth. The Federal Ministry of Agriculture and Rural Development (FMARD) initiated a national (Osabuohien et al. 2018; Oyebola et al. 2019). Also, the Food and Agriculture Organization of the United Nations (FAO) partners with the FMARD to reinforce capabilities at federal and state level to implement YEAP, and has delivered technical support in developing an investment plan, which has since been allocated approximately US$235 million by the Government. FAO provides support to the Government in the design and implementation of YEAP, focusing on the creation of an enabling policy environment. This involves embracing agricultural policies and programs for youth and women; enabling institutional environment through the promotion of inter-institutional collaboration and partnership; promotion of youth-friendly information and communication technologies for knowledge management and dissemination; and facilitation of training initiatives that teach agricultural business and life skills for young agricultural entrepreneurs for the selected priority value chains (Akinlade et al. 2011).

Also, that more than 37% of youths in Nigeria were engaged in Agriculture, with over 50% of those between 15 and 24 years of age, participating in various income generating activities within the agricultural sector. Similarly, YEAP, has empowered 30,000 youths in area-based priority value chains and had received about 34,000 applications from market-oriented producers from twelve participating States comprising Akwa Ibom, Bauchi, Gombe, Imo, Kaduna, Kastina, Lagos, Niger, Ogun as well as the Federal Capital Territory (FCT). Agro further states that about 250 youths were selected per state at the first stage of the program. The participants were trained in various value chains, including rice, aquaculture, poultry, maize, tomato, wheat, sorghum, apiculture, soya bean, cassava, groundnut, oil palm, snailery (rearing of snails), grass cutter, and multiple value chains, such as welding and fabrication, repairs and maintenance (Agro 2015).

Obviously, these programs are worthy effort by the federal government of Nigeria in the struggle to minimize poverty and unemployment particularly among youth and other vulnerable groups within diverse Nigerian communities. However, the success of these initiatives and their main goal remains at limbo, since poverty and unemployment appear increasing. It is a fact that the National Bureau of Statistics reports that as of 2017, the unemployment rate for the working age population in Nigeria rise from 16.20% to 23.13 in 2019 (Lucky and Sam 2018). This is problematic to the well-being of the people. Similarly, poverty, unemployment, and inequality remain significant problems in Nigeria (Adeleye et al. 2018). The country is described with a per capita gross domestic product of US$1437, in 2010, a fairly higher than that of sub-Saharan Africa of US$1311. Nevertheless, 68% of the Nigerian population lives on less than US$1.25 per day as compared with 48% in sub-Saharan Africa (Siddig et al. 2015). Equally, in 2016, nearly 13 million Nigerians still suffer from hunger. The high occurrence of hunger in rural areas is connected with low agricultural growth, poor road infrastructure, limited access to safe water and sanitation, and inadequate health and education services (Rietveld and Bruinsma 2012). The rate of poverty has been increasing in Nigeria over the years, from 54.7% in 2004—60.9% in 2010 National Bureau of Statistics (NBS 2010). Having understood the various strategies of poverty alleviation, the next section will outline the methodology for this study. About 23.22% of children in Nigeria are living in extreme child poverty while 70.31% of children in the country are in complete child poverty. The report further points that there is a pronounced child deprivation in education, health, nutrition, child protection, water, and sanitation. Both poverty and unemployment are more noticeable in the rural areas than in the urban areas and in Northern Nigeria than in Southern Nigerias (Ogwumike and Ozughalu 2018; Adetola and Olufemi 2012).

4 Methodology

Mostly, research plan involves a choice of a proper outline for specific study, this in many reseachers view such as Merriam, the plan should be "comfortable or match with the worldview, personality and skills" (Merriam 2009). It is this processes that involve the selection of proper framework and methodology of any research that Denzin and Lincoln called "strategies of inquiry." Therefore, it is within this notion that this study adopted a qualitative method, this method allows a researcher to understand some aspects of social life, experiences, and attitudes of individuals, using words or discussions with varying methodological practices (Denzin and Lincoln 2011; McCusker and Gunaydin 2015).

This study utilized data from direct interviews with the youth beneficiaries from Alkaleri, Gar and Duguri rural areas and field observations in the study area. The interviews were conducted with seven youth been the only beneficiaries of the skills acquisitions program in Alkaleri, Gar and Duguri rural communities and three officials from the Federal Ministry of Agriculture and Rural Development (FMARD) with Bauchi State Agricultural Development Program BSADP that facilitated the YEAP initiatives. The interviews were audio-taped, transcribed, and analyzed using a qualitative research methodology guided by Consensual Qualitative Research (CQR) (Hill et al. 2005; Hill 2012; Daniels et al. 2015).

The participants were distributed in the following manner; ($n=10$) men and women. Three ($n=\#3$) of the ten participants were beneficiaries from Alkaleri, three ($n=\#3$) from Gar, ($n=\#1$) one from Duguri, and ($n=\#3$) three were officials from the (BSADP), While some of these participants allowed their names to appear in the study report, some declined due to the nature and position of their work. As a result, the researcher gave all the participants pseudonyms to protect their identities. The essence of selecting these youth beneficiaries and officials is because their knowledge and experience will provide appropriate information that helped to identify, examine, as well as articulate the problems of the efforts made by Nigeria's Federal government initiative as it concerns the Youth Employment Program in Agriculture (YEAP), on the struggle against poverty and unemployment reduction in rural communities across Nigeria. Additionally, secondary data were obtained and used as supporting details to the primary data of this study. Materials from published sources such as journal articles from the internet online portals and database such as that of the Nigeria National Bureau of statistics. The central ideas, and main results were presented, discussed.

5 Findings

5.1 Strategies used by the Youth Employment in Agricultural Program (YEAP)

5.1.1 Economic Resources

When questioned about the strategies employed by YEAP to empower youth in reducing poverty and unemployment, about ten interviewees (F1, #F2, #F3, #B1G, #B2G, #B3G, #B4A, #B5A, #B6A, and #B7D) from all the three selected rural areas (Alkaleri, Gar, and Duguri) expressed related views and disclosed that they received financial aid from the Youth Employment in Agricultural Program (YEAP) in form of the provision of small amount of money/allowance to start up small scale poultry farm, such aid is in one way or another seen as a poverty alleviation strategy for them. For instance, one Gar respondent mentioned that he received assistance from the YEAP when he related the following: "I received little allowance as financial assistance from the YEAP after they train us on how to start up a small scale poultry farm" (Gar respondent #B2G).

Similarly, all of the Alkaleri, and Duguri interviewees emphasized that financial support and skills on the individual are significant strategies for poverty and unemployment reduction. According to them, funding such as capital to start up the poultry farming and the skills was of paramount importance. To lessen poverty and unemployment, the interviewees also stressed that a person must be diligent. In addition to the above skills and the availability of financial support, all interviewees from Alkaleri, Duguri, and Gar were conscious of the importance of education as a crucial element for poverty and unemployment alleviation. Although some of the interviewees had low academic accomplishment, all of them were aware of the importance of education as a key element to alleviate poverty and unemployment. As such, the interviewees struggled hard to ensure that they further their education to a significant level to avoid stagnating into the cycle of poverty and unemployment. Government's assistance in the form of essential goods that will facilitate the community's daily life and assist them toward generating more income play a critical role. It can help them to improve their ability to remain competitive in a challenging environment. Support in the form of financial capital and product technology seem to be more effective if the government tries to act as a facilitator in forming or creating a joint venture with companies or individuals who are knowledgeable and experienced in the business. Direct support to youth is essential to build their confidence and strengthen their capacity in pursuing potentials. This condition can ultimately avoid any mismanagement of the assistance received (Leng et al. 2018).

5.1.2 Informational Resources

The second strategy used by the YEAP to empower youth is informational resources, all the respondents (F1, #F2 #F3, #B1G, #B2G, #B3G, #B4A, #B5A, #B6A, and #B7D) from the three selected rural areas of Alkaleri, Gar, and Duguri expressed connected opinions and unveiled that they were trained by YEAP officials on managing small scale poultry production such as farming, rearing, fishing, and rice cultivation. Some respondents from Alkaleri, and Duguri, state the following: "I was trained by the facilitators of the YEAP on how to start doing fishing and rearing" (Alkaleri, respondent #B5A). Also, a Duguri respondent also shared the same statement, about how the officials of the YEAP trained and informed the beneficiaries. One of the most important strategy used by YEAP was training and skill acquisition to help us and improve the youths to be empowered and become more viable. Also, they noted the need to study more, gain more credentials to establish their own business and other firms will be of more benefits (Duguri respondent #B7D).

Another Gar respondent #B1G states that with the training and skill acquisition from YEAP, being hardworking and exploring more job opportunities would be a workable strategy to alleviate poverty and unemployment, this respondent recommended that one should create connections with successful people in order to learn from them and be viable to get self-employed as well as get others employed without relying on the scarce government jobs. Technical education and vocational training need to be frequent and efficiently with a focus toward improving the quality of qualifications. This is vital toward providing a viable alternative to enable individuals to realize their full potential, according to their own preference and talent. This principle necessitates a renewed focus on championing the interests of each and every community, to make sure no one is left behind or marginalized in the course of the nation's development. Poverty and unemployment strategies must be motivated on the enhancement of human skills, innovativeness, and knowledge of the poor (Hatta and Ali 2013).

5.2 Factors that Pose Threat to YEAP on Tackling Poverty and Unemployment Among Youth in Alkaleri, Duguri and Gar Rural Communities

From the findings, the respondents, #F1, #F2, #F3, #B4A, #B5A, #B7D, #B2G, and #B3G frequently stressed that YEAP assistance to them was a good effort, however they were not fully empowered to start up the small scale farming efficiently due to inadequate stipend offered to them by YEAP at the end of the trainings. Similarly, most of the respondents expressed the need for YEAP to expand its scope to target more youths considering the growing number of poverty and unemployment among the people, which has stood as an obstacle to the youth empowerment as well as the core goal of the YEAP to reduce poverty and unemployment within the rural areas. Equally, respondent's #F1, #F2, #F3, #B4A, #B3G, and #B7D, from all the three selected rural areas agreed that, inadequate coverage of the target beneficiaries considering the large population of more than 461,200 people with larger number of unemployed youth in these rural communities and insufficient funding, are major problems, even the seven selected beneficiary youth were not fully empowered to start up effectively; therefore, the capability and strength to expand the program need to be considered in designing poverty and unemployment alleviation so that YEAP can achieve its objectives. Five of the respondents highlighted that assistance in the form of financial aid, and training are able to touch and make some changes to their lives. However, the kinds of assistance provided need to follow main concern. First, adequate financial capital, and expansion of targeted beneficiaries, because youth's self-readiness is very impressive among the huge poor and unemployed youths as well as the selected beneficiaries. However, due to poor motivation, monitoring and coordination, the seriousness and confidences of the beneficiaries and youths has become weaken and depressed. Thus, regular motivation and development of monitoring and evaluation strategies are of utmost importance.

Thus, the time has come for scholars and policy-makers to revisit and redefine the concepts and strategies employed in policy making as regards reducing poverty and unemployment. Poverty and unemployment strategies require a comprehensive and efficient grounding that incorporates sufficient resources and capacity to meet its goals in reaching out to majority of the targeted beneficiaries (Leng et al. 2018). Generally, this is crucial because until a more appropriate conceptualization and efficient strategies with full capacity to meet majority of target beneficiaries in reducing poverty and unemployment is projected, it would continue to be a great challenge to formulate and implement the correct types of poverty and unemployment reduction strategies to reach out to the target beneficiaries. Generally, to make the situation less challenging considering the heterogeneous nature of the Nigerian populace comprising people from diverse ethnicities with Hausa–Fulani, Yorubas, and Igbos being the three most dominant ethnic groups in the country. Such ethnic diversity in the Nigerian social structure will in turn reveal the way different socio-cultural and economic conditions tend to shape and define poverty and unemployment. In this regard, due considerations should also be given to ethnicity when deliberating on strategies that can help to poverty and unemployment reduction.

6   Conclusion

Since political independence in 1960 until currently, the Nigerian government has embarked on numerous poverty and unemployment alleviation policies to reduce poverty and unemployment particularly in rural areas. In the last decade, however, poverty and unemployment incidence have continued to worsen, thus resulting in another effort by the YEAP being the focus of this study.

Considering the densely contextual population, unemployment, and poverty ratio that characterized all the three rural areas of Alkaleri, Gar, and Duguri of Bauchi state Nigeria; the forms of poverty and unemployment reduction programs of YEAP ranging from economic and informational resource provision perspective, including skills and training with small financial assistance for the targeted beneficiaries investigated and understood by this study is a commendable effort. However, there is the need for more unique ways toward reconceptualizing and understanding efficient strategies to lessen and mitigate the limitations that depressed the goals of poverty and unemployment reduction by YEAP in the rural areas of Gar, Duguri, and Alaleri. Poverty and unemployment reduction strategies of YEAP has been hindered by insufficient financial capital for its beneficiaries, inadequate monitoring, inefficient coordination and evaluation, as well as poor coverage and outreach of the majority of the poor and unemployed population. These are vital requisite to poverty and unemployment reduction strategies for such densely populated areas with multi-ethnic society like Alkaleri Gar and Duguri and Bauchi State in general.

Moreover, considering the increasing number of the population being extremely poor especially the youth. This study recommends that the poverty and unemployment reduction strategies of YEAP should be revisited, extended, and tailored toward providing sufficient financial capital for its beneficiaries, efficient training and skills, frequent monitoring, efficient coordination and evaluation, as well as proper coverage and outreach for the majority of the poor and unemployed population. In addition to the particular needs of people in relation to the dimension of housing, education, healthcare that is considered most relevant to them.

References

Abiodun, T. F., Onafowora, O., & Ayo-Adeyekun, I. (2019). *Alarming rate of child poverty in northern Nigeria: Implications for national security.*

Adeleye, N., Osabuohien, E., Bowale, E., Matthew, O., & Oduntan, E. (2018). Financial reforms and credit growth in Nigeria: Empirical insights from ARDL and ECM techniques. *International Review of Applied Economics, 32*(6), 807–820.

Adetola, A., & Olufemi, P. (2012). Determinants of child poverty in rural Nigeria: A multidimensional approach. *Global Journal of Human-Social Science Research, 12*(12-A): 38–52.

Adibe, J. (2014). MINT, re-based GDP and poverty: A commentary on the identity crisis in Africa's "Largest" economy. *African Journal of Business and Economic Research, 9*(1), 119–134.

Agro Nigeria Report. (2015). *FG to empower 30,000 Nigerian youths via the first phase of YEAP.*

Akanbi, O. A., & Du Toit, C. B. (2011). Macro-econometric modelling for the Nigerian economy: A growth–poverty gap analysis. *Economic Modelling, 28*(1–2), 335–350.

Akinlade, R. J., Yusuf, S. A., Omonona, B. T., & Oyekale, A. S. (2011). Poverty alleviation programme and pro-poor growth in rural Nigeria: Case of Fadama II project. *World Rural Observations, 3*(1), 27–33.

Amirah, N. A., Asma, W. I., Muda, M. S., & Amin, W. A. A. W. M. (2013). Safety culture in combating occupational safety and health problems in the Malaysian manufacturing sectors. *Asian Social Science, 9*(3), 182.

Babatunde, R. O., Olagunju, F. I., Fakayode, S. B., & Sola-Ojo, F. E. (2011). Prevalence and determinants of malnutrition among under-five children of farming households in Kwara State, Nigeria. *Journal of Agricultural Science, 3*(3), 173–181.

Callander, E. J., Schofield, D. J., & Shrestha, R. N. (2012). Towards a holistic understanding of poverty: A new multidimensional measure of poverty for Australia. *Health Sociology Review, 21*(2), 141–155.

Castañeda, A., Doan, D., Newhouse, D., Nguyen, M. C., Uematsu, H., & Azevedo, J. P. (2016). *Who are the poor in the developing world?* The World Bank.

Cheri, L. (2014). Job creation, poverty reduction, and conflict resolution in north eastern Nigeria. *IOSR Journal of Humanities and Social Science, 19*(3), 31–35.

Daniels, J. A., Angleman, A. J., & Grinnan, E. (2015). Standardizing research methods on violent offenders: Perpetrator-motive research design and consensual qualitative research. *Aggression and Violent Behavior, 21*, 125–132.

Denzin, N. K., & Lincoln, Y. S. (Eds.). (2011). *The Sage handbook of qualitative research*. Sage.

Development. *International Small Business Development Journal, 8*(3), 10–12.

Echebiri, R. N. (2005, July 21–22). *Characteristics and determinants of urban youth unemployment in Umuahia, Nigeria: Implications for rural development and alternative labor market variables*. A Paper presented at the ISSER/Cornell/World Bank conference on "Shared Growth in Africa" held in Accra, Ghana.

Eneh, O. C. (2011). Failed development vision, political leadership, and Nigeria's underdevelopment: A critique. *Asian Journal of Rural Development, 1*(1), 63–69.

Ferreira, F. H., Chen, S., Dabalen, A., Dikhanov, Y., Hamadeh, N., Jolliffe, D., & Serajuddin, U. (2015). *A global count of the extreme poor in 2012: Data issues, methodology and initial results*. The World Bank.

Fosu, A. K. (2013). Institutions and African economies: An overview. *Journal of African Economies, 22*(4), 491–498.

Gibb, A. A., & George, M. (1989). The design of extension and related support services for small-scale enterprise. *International Small Business Journal, 8*(3).

Grindle, M. S. (2004). Good enough governance: Poverty reduction and reform in developing countries. *Governance, 17*(4), 525–548.

Hatta, Z. A., & Ali, I. (2013). Poverty reduction policies in Malaysia: Trends, strategies and challenges. *Asian Culture and History, 5*(2), 48.

Heger, M., Zens, G., & Bangalor, M. (2018). *Does the environment matter for poverty reduction? The role of soil fertility and vegetation vigor in poverty reduction*. Washington, DC: The World Bank.

Hill, C. E. (2012). *Consensual qualitative research: A practical resource for investigating social science phenomena*. Washington, DC: American Psychological Association.

Hill, C. E., Knox, S., Thompson, B. J., Williams, E. N., Hess, S. A., & Ladany, N. (2005). Consensual qualitative research: An update. *Journal of Counseling Psychology, 52*(2), 196. http://www.schoolsandhealth.org/News/Pages/Nigerian-Vice-President-launches-National-School-Feeding-Programme.aspx; http://allafrica.com/stories/201702130517.html.

International Labor Organization. (2007). *Global employment trends*. Geneva: International Labor Office.

Khan, A., & Cheri, L. (2016). An examination of poverty as the foundation of crisis in Northern Nigeria. *Insight on Africa, 8*(1), 59–71.

National Bureau of Statistic (NBS). (2010). www.nigerianstat.gov.ng.

Laderchi, C. R., Saith, R., & Stewart, F. (2003). Does it matter that we do not agree on the definition of poverty? A comparison of four approaches. *Oxford Development Studies, 31*(3), 243–274.

Leng, K. S., Samsurijan, M. S., Gopal, P. S., Malek, N. M., & Hamat, Z. (2018). Urban poverty alleviation strategies from multi-dimensional and multi-ethnic perspective: Evidences from Malaysia. *Kajian Malaysia, 36*(2), 43–68. https://doi.org/10.21315/km2018.36.2.3.

Lucky, L. A., & Sam, A. D. (2018). Poverty and income inequality in Nigeria: An illustration of Lorenz curve from NBS survey. *American Economic & Social Review, 2*(1), 80–92.

Marfo, E. O., Amoako, K. O., Antwi, H. A., Ghansah, B., & Mohammed Baba, G. (2017). Corporate social responsibility: Institutional behavior differences in extractive industry. In *International journal of engineering research in Africa* (Vol. 33, pp. 194–215). Trans Tech Publications Ltd.

Martin, G., Danzig, A. B., Wright, W. F., Flanary, R. A., & Orr, M. T. (2016). *School leader internship: Developing, monitoring, and evaluating your leadership experience.* New York: Routledge.

McCusker, K., & Gunaydin, S. (2015). Research using qualitative, quantitative or mixed methods and choice based on the research. *Perfusion, 30*(7), 537–542.

Merriam, S. B. (2009). *Qualitative research: A guide to design and implementation; revised and expanded from qualitative research and case study application in education.* USA.

Nwosu, E. O., Ojonta, O., & Orji, A. (2018). Household consumption expenditure and inequality: Evidence from Nigerian data. *International Journal of Development Issues.*

Oginni, A., Ahonsi, B., & Ukwuije, F. (2013). Are female-headed households typically poorer than male-headed households in Nigeria? *The Journal of Socio-Economics, 45,* 132–137.

Ogwumike, F. O., & Ozughalu, U. M. (2018). Empirical evidence of child poverty and deprivation in Nigeria. *Child Abuse and Neglect, 77,* 13–22.

Okafor, E. E. (2011). Youth unemployment and implications for stability of democracy in Nigeria. *Journal of sustainable Development in Africa, 13*(1), 358–373.

Onah, F. O. (2001). Urban unemployment situation in Nigeria. In E. O. Ezeani & N. N. Elekwa (Eds.), *Issues in urbanization and urban administration in Nigeria* (pp. 154–167). Enugu: Jamo Enterprises Presented at the Youth Employment Summit, Alexandria, Egypt, and 13 pages.

Osabuohien, E., Adeleye, N., & Osabohien, R. (2018, October). *Developing an African Growth and Opportunity Act (AGOA) country strategy for Nigeria.* Technical report submitted to African Capacity Building Foundation (ACBF)/National Institute for Legislative and Democratic Studies (NILDS).

Osabuohien, E., Okorie, U., & Osabohien, R. (2018). Rice production and processing in Ogun State, Nigeria: Qualitative insights from Farmers' association. In E. Obayelu (Ed.), *Food Systems sustainability and environmental policies in modern economics* (pp. 188–216). Hershey, PA: IGI Global. https://doi.org/10.4018/978-1-5225-3631-4.ch009.

Oyebola, P. O., Osabuohien, E., & Obasaju, B. (2019). Employment and income effects of Nigeria's agricultural transformation agenda. *African Journal of Economic and Management Studies.* https://doi.org/10.1108/AJEMS-12-2018-0402.

Ozughalu, U. M. (2016). Relationship between household food poverty and vulnerability to food poverty: Evidence from Nigeria. *Social Indicators Research, 125*(2), 567–587.

Rietveld, P., & Bruinsma, F. (2012). *Is transport infrastructure effective? Transport infrastructure and accessibility: Impacts on the space economy.* Springer Science & Business Media.

Siddig, K., Aguiar, A., Grethe, H., Minor, P., & Walmsley, T. (2014). Impacts of removing fuel import subsidies in Nigeria on poverty. *Energy Policy, 69,* 165–178.

Siddig, K., Minor, P., Grethe, H., Aguiar, A., & Walmsley, T. (2015). *Impacts on poverty of removing fuel import subsidies in Nigeria.* The World Bank.

Thorbecke, E. (2013). The interrelationship linking growth, inequality and poverty in sub-Saharan Africa. *Journal of African Economies, 22*(Suppl. 1), i15–i48.

World Bank. (2012). *POVCALNET 2012.* Available at http://iresearch.worldbank.org/PovcalNet/index.htm.

World Bank. (2014). *POVCALNET 2014.* Available at http://iresearch.worldbank.org/PovcalNet/index.htm.

Yusof, R. (2014). Democracy, and rural development in Nigeria: Challenges and prospects. In *The UUm international conference on governance* (p. 215).

Yusof, Y., Ibrahim, Y., Muda, M. S., & Amin, W. A. A. W. M. (2012). Community based tourism and quality of life. *Review of Integrative Business and Economics Research, 1*(1), 336.

Yusof, Y., Muda, M. S., Amin, W. A., & Ibrahim, Y. (2013). Rural tourism in Malaysia: A homestay program. *China–USA Business Review, 12*(3), 300–306.

Access to Resources, Transformation and Productivity Interactions

Determinants of the Willingness to Pay for Public Sector Health Care Services: An Empirical Study of Rural and Urban Communities in Nigeria

Lloyd Ahamefule Amaghionyeodiwe

1 Introduction

The plummeting of the Nigerian economy in the 1980s and 1990s ushered in a set of reforms and policies to help revive many of the dwindling sectors, one of which is the health sector. One of such reforms was the introduction of user charges in public sector health care facilities, which involves out-of-pocket payments by Public health care consumers (Mbanefoh et al. 1996). This adoption of user charges has been questioned on many grounds, one of which, is the willingness and ability to pay for these services, especially given the high rate of poverty being experienced in the Nigerian economy (Amaghionyeodiwe 2008). Despite government's efforts to reduce poverty, this user charges in public health facilities in Nigeria have led to huge out-of-pocket expenses on public health care seekers (Mbanefoh et al. 1996). They assert that these out-of-pocket expenses constitute a significant portion of households' health expenditure in Nigeria. This increase in household spending tends to conflict with the poverty reduction policy of the government. With an increasing trend in the proportion of Nigerians living in poverty (both in the rural and urban areas) as indicated by the

---

L. A. Amaghionyeodiwe (✉)
Department of Business and Economics, York College,
City University of New York, Jamaica, NY, USA
e-mail: lamaghionyeodiwe@york.cuny.edu

incidence of poverty data, questions about the ability and Willingness to Pay (WTP) for these health care services by the households become pertinent (Amaghionyeodiwe 2008). Available data from the National Bureau of Statistics (2016, 2017) reports that about 62.6% of Nigerians are living in absolute poverty. Of this, 69.0% accounts for poverty in the rural area while that of the urban area is 51.2%. Also, the GINI index stood at 43 points in 2015 indicating a wide range of income inequality with the Nigerian economy.

Out-of-pocket payments affect the ability of many low- and middle-income households and individuals to satisfy their basic needs, thus sinking them more into poverty (Amaghionyeodiwe 2008). Accordingly, the ever-increasing trend in the poverty rate does influence the households' ability and WTP these charges in Nigeria hence making out-of-pocket payments for health care services a very enormous challenge in Nigeria especially as it affects the rural area dwellers.

To worsen this issue of the WTP is the fact that the first level of health care provision and prevention of diseases, the Primary Health Care (PHC) services, being provided by the local governments have been reduced to non-existent as many of the dispensaries, health clinics, and health centers are non-functional. According to the Viewpoint of the Vanguard Newspaper (December 20, 2016, p. 10), Opaluwah, stated that "a recent newspaper reports indicate that only 2500 of 30,000 Primary Healthcare centers in Nigeria are functional." This implies that the services provided by PHC centers of the local governments are virtually non-existent. And where they exist, the quality of care being provided has been an issue of concern. This portrays a huge danger to access to modern health care by those in the grassroots especially the rural area dwellers vis a vis the urban dwellers. Most rural dwellers have had to travel to the nearest health facility (which may probably be in an urban area) to seek for help thereby incurring more out-of-pocket expenses as travel cost. This, most times, tends to discourage access to modern health care by the rural dwellers and conversely encourage the demand for self-care (including traditional herbalists or healers).

The above raises questions on the quality of care being provided, access to modern health care, income to make the out-of-pocket payments, the rural–urban dichotomy in health care demand, among others. These factors tend to have some effects on the ability and willingness of both the rural and urban households to make the necessary out-of-pocket payments in their demand for modern health care. Accordingly, and as its own contribution to literature, this study examines the factors that determine the households' WTP for public health care services in Nigeria as well as evaluate the extent to which these factors affect households' WTP in both the urban and rural areas. This was done using primary data as well as econometric analysis. The rest of the chapter is organized as follows: Section two contains the stylized facts on health care in Nigeria. Section three is the literature review, section four comprises the methodology while section five presents the result and analysis, and section six concludes the chapter.

2 Stylized Facts on Health Care in Nigeria

According to the Federal Ministry of Planning (1956), Federal Ministry of Health (1988, 1996) and as entrenched in Nigerian constitution, Nigeria's National Health Care System is structured as follows: PHC; Secondary Health Care (SHC); Tertiary Health Care (THC); and Referral System. There are also private nongovernmental (profit and nonprofit organizations) health care providers. The federal government focusses on the tertiary and apex referral institutions like the National Hospital, the Specialist/Teaching Hospitals, and the interventionist Federal Medical Centers. The state government provides for secondary health care system. Each state government's secondary health facility serves as the administrative headquarters supervising health care activities of the PHC units. Secondary health care provides specialized services to patients referred from the PHC level. It operates in- and out-patient health care services. These services include general medical, surgical, pediatric patients as well as community health services. It also provides adequate supportive services such as laboratory, diagnostic, blood bank, rehabilitation, and physiotherapy. The PHC is largely the responsibility of the local governments with the support of state ministries of health. It provides general health services at preventive, curative, and promotive levels to the populace. It also acts as the entry point of the health care system. Private medical practitioners provide health care services at this level. Also, noting that traditional medicine is widely used, and that there is no uniform system of traditional medicine in the country but what exits are wide variations with each variant strongly bound to the local culture and beliefs. The local health authorities, where applicable, seek the collaboration of the traditional practitioners in promoting their health programs such as nutrition, environmental sanitation, personal hygiene, family planning, and immunization. The federal, state, and local governments coordinate their efforts in such a way as to provide the citizens with effective health services at all levels.

Over the past years, the Nigerian government has spent less than 3% of its annual budget on health services. For instance, data from https://knoema.com/atlas/Nigeria, showed that Nigeria's health expenditure as a share of GDP fluctuated substantially (between 3.3 and 4.0%) in recent years, it increased through 2001–2015 period ending at 3.6% in 2015. In terms of health expenditure per capita for Nigeria, it increased from 16 US dollars in 2001 to 97 US dollars in 2015 growing at an average annual rate of 17.09%. Nigeria government health expenditure as a share of general government expenditure fluctuated substantially (between 2.7 and 5.8%) in recent years, it increased through 2001–2015 period ending at 5.3% in 2015. Private expenditure on health as a share of total health expenditure for Nigeria was 73.7% in 2015. Though, it fluctuated substantially (between 73.1 and 79.9%) in recent years, it decreased through 2001–2015. Out of pocket expenditure as a share of current health expenditure fluctuated substantially between 71.4 and 75% from 2001 to 2014 and by 2015, it was 72.2% (https://knoema.com/atlas/Nigeria—accessed January 12, 2019).

Consequently, there has been a declining trend in the Nigeria's health indicators. For instance, available data from UNICEF (n.d.) showed that the life expectancy of Nigerians though increased from 39.8 years in 1967 to 53.4 years in 2016, growing at an average annual rate of 0.60%, is below the African average. Under-5 mortality rate of Nigeria fell gradually from 307.4 deaths per thousand live births in 1967 to 104.3 deaths per thousand live births in 2016. While, infant mortality rate of Nigeria fell gradually from 182.8 deaths per thousand live births in 1967 to 66.9 deaths per thousand live births in 2016. Neonatal Mortality Rate (NMR) of Nigeria fell gradually from 71.4 deaths per thousand live births in 1967 to 34.1 deaths per thousand live births in 2016. With respect to hospital beds per 1000 people, Nigeria hospital beds were at level of 0.5 units per thousand people in 2004, down from 1.2 units per thousand people in 2000, this is a change of 58.33%. Births attended by skilled health staff as a share of total number of births fluctuated substantially (between 30.8 and 47.3%) and in recent years, it decreased through 1999–2013 period ending at 35.2% in 2013 (UNICEF, n.d.-a).

According to data from United Nations International Children's Emergency Fund (UNICEF), in 2015, Nigeria's NMR was 34 deaths per 1000 live births. NMR in rural areas was 44 deaths per 1000 live births and 34 deaths per 1000 live births in urban areas with an urban-to-rural ratio of 0.82. Furthermore, in rural areas, 38% of women made at least 4 antenatal care (ANC) visits compared to 75% in urban areas. Coverage of skilled attendance at birth was 23% in rural areas, compared to 67% in urban areas. About 8% of newborns in rural areas received postnatal care (PNC) within 2 days after birth, compared to 25% in urban areas. Most mothers among richest households (86%) made at least four ANC visits, compared to 18% of mothers from the poorest households. Only 6% of mothers in the poorest households had a skilled attendant at birth, compared to 85% of mothers in the richest households. Furthermore, 34% of newborns in the richest households receive PNC within 2 days after birth, compared to 3% among the poorest households (UNICEF, n.d.-b).

In 2005, Nigeria launched a federally funded National Health Insurance Scheme (NHIS), designed to facilitate fair financing of health care costs through risk pooling and cost-sharing arrangements for individuals. The scheme claimed to have issued 5 million identity cards, covering about 3% of the population. In 2010, under the National Health Insurance Act 2008, the national health insurance started a rural community-based social health insurance program (RCSHIP). Most of the enrollees, however, are individuals working in the formal sector and the community scheme still leaves large gaps among the poor and informally employed (Osabohien et al. 2019).

From the data above, the GDP has been growing while there have been some increases in both the government expenditure on health and household's out-of-pocket expenditure on health while the various socio demographic variables experienced fluctuating trend and these fluctuations showed some biasness with respect to rural and urban areas. This has implications on the household's behavior toward paying for public sector health care demand, thus the need for this study to empirically examine the households' WTP for public health care services in general and more specifically, which factors affect this WTP in both the urban and rural areas.

3 Literature Review

3.1 Consumer Willingness to Pay

Lavy and Germain (1994) defined WTP (among others), as how much an individual is willing to pay to have his travel cost reduced by some kilometers as well as improvement in the quality of the available health services in existing public facilities. The issue of WTP has received renewed attention as a method of measuring the benefit of health care interventions (Johannesson et al. 1991, 1993). The WTP assumes that the maximum amount of money an individual is willing to pay for a commodity is an indicator of the utility or satisfaction to her of that commodity. Dupuit (1844) stated that the maximum sacrifice, which each consumer would be willing to make to acquire an object can be taken as the measure of utility of that object. Thus, the only real utility is what people are willing to pay. Yoder (1989) distinguished between the WTP and the ability to pay. Although, they may not directly covary, they are both influenced by some factors of which income and the quality of health care are very important. Ching (1995), using a mixed/conditional logit parameterization of the health care demand model to study user charges, demand for children's health care and access across income groups in the Philippines confirmed that the poor are more sensitive to price changes than the rich. This has implications for the WTP.

According to Alpizar et al. (2003), Johnston et al. (2015) and Champ et al. (2017) markets do not exist for nonmarket goods and services such as clean air and water, health and environmental amenities and, hence, their economic value, which is deciphered from how much people would be willing to pay for them, is not revealed in market prices hence several studies that have been carried out in developing countries to examined the factors that influence and or determine the WTP. For instance, Akter (2008) examined the determinants of WTP for Safe Drinking Water in rural Bangladesh. In Akter's study, households living in different highly arsenic concentrated areas in Bangladesh were asked for their WTP for the collection of arsenic safe drinking water using an open-ended WTP question. The study estimates an average WTP of US$9 per year for safe drinking water which is less than one percent of the average annual household income. Furthermore, the result showed that the WTP amounts varied significantly with respondents' levels of mass media exposure, standards of living (measured through the types of latrine used by households), respondents' age, number of children in each household, the levels of education of the adult family members, and distance of arsenic-free drinking water source.

Ayifah (2010) using the Contingent Valuation Method (CVM) investigated the WTP for the Prevention of Mother to Child Transmission (PMTCT) of the acquired immunodeficiency syndrome (AIDS)/human immunodeficiency virus (HIV) (usually referred to as HIV/AIDS), as well as the determinants of pregnant women's WTP for PMTCT of HIV/AIDS in three antenatal care centers in Ghana (Atua Government Hospital, St. Martins Deporres Hospital-Agormanya and the Central Regional Hospital-Cape Coast). His estimation method was logit and Ordinary Least Squares (OLS) regression. The author's findings indicate that income is the most significant factor that affects the WTP for PMTCT of HIV/AIDS. Other factors such as HIV/AIDS status, distance to antenatal clinic, age, and marital status were also shown to have effect on the WTP for HIV/AIDS, though the results were not robust. Wondimu and Bekele (2011)'s study investigated the determinants of households' WTP for quality water supply, using the CVM in the factory villages of Wonji Shoa Sugar Estate, Ethiopia. Using a close-ended format questionnaire with additional close-ended format, and open-ended follow-up questions which is closer to the market scenario respondents are familiar with as well as the Tobit model, they found that income of the household, education level of the respondent, reliability on existing water supply, respondent perception about quality of the existing water supply, household family size, and age of the respondent are significant variables that explain WTP.

Donfouet et al. (2011) did a study of rural Cameroon where many people have no access to quality health care services. Their study was on the determinants of the WTP for community-based prepayment scheme in rural Cameroon using a CVM. Their findings showed that age, religion, profession, knowledge of community-based health insurance, awareness of usual practice in rural areas, involvement in association and disposable income are the key determinants of WTP for a prepayment health scheme. Also, their findings had two important implications: first, there is substantial demand for a community health care prepayment scheme by rural poor households in Cameroon; second, rural households are averse to health shocks and hence they are willing to sacrifice monthly premium payments to protect themselves (and their households) from unforeseen health-related risks. Halkos et al. (2012)'s study was on the coastal line of an area in Central Greece (Volos) where some beaches failures to meet the standards of the Blue Flag program. Their objective was to determine the factors affecting WTP for an improvement quality (environment, water as well as recreation activities) program using a contingent valuation survey. Among their findings was that the major variables affecting respondents' WTP were related to previous environmental behavior. Also, income, age, gender, coastal recreational activities, and environmental quality of the site were significant in determining the people's WTP for quality improvement of coastal zone. Applying data from a web-based survey conducted in mainland China, Shen (2012) examined the determinants of consumers' WTP for seven different product categories awarded with China Environmental Label and compare the mean WTP estimates among these categories. The Interval Regression method is used for estimation. Among the findings was that sociodemographic characteristics such as gender, age, education, and household income are found to be important factors to affect Chinese consumers' WTP amounts. Also, Chinese consumers who regard environmental conservation as being more important than life convenience, who believe purchasing the eco-labeled products is good for the environment, and who have the experience in purchasing eco-labeled products are willing to pay more for those products with environmental label or eco-label.

Biadgilign et al. (2015)'s study was on the determinants of WTP for the retreatment of insecticide-treated mosquito nets in rural area of eastern Ethiopia. They conducted a community-based cross-sectional study in Gursum district in Eastern Ethiopia. They used multivariable regression analyses using the Tobit model were used to test the theoretical validity of elicited WTP. Their findings indicate that average monthly income and those households who live within a distance in 30 min to the health facility were determinant for WTP. Javan-Noughabi et al. (2017) did a study on Iran where they identified the determinant factors on WTP for health services using the WTP for health status with different severity level and identify determinant factors on WTP. They applied the multivariate regression analyses using OLS to examine the effect of socio-demographic factors on WTP. Their results showed that the mean of WTP increases at severe health status while monthly income was a key determinant of WTP for internal preferences and caring externalities. Lasebew et al. (2017)'s study was to determine WTP for Social Health Insurance (SHI) among health workers and to determine factors associated with WTP in Addis Ababa, Ethiopia. They conducted an institution-based, cross-sectional study from April to December 2016, on 420 health workers who work at St. Paul's Hospital Millennium Medical College. Data was collected using a semi-structured self-administered questionnaire. A multivariate analysis was done, and the findings indicate that significant associations were found between WTP and perceived quality of health care services under SHI while socio-demographic variables, such as monthly salary, did not show a significant association with WTP. An important finding from their study was that those who spend large amount of money previously were more willing to pay. This, they opined might be because of their belief that the SHI membership reduces direct out of pocket expenditure.

Succinctly, conclusions from the various studies discussed pointed to the fact that factors such as age, gender, education, household income, severity of illness, proximity to the nearest medical Centre distance, among others; do have an influence on the WTP for health care utilization.

4 Methodology

4.1 The Model

The framework for this study is a model in which utility depends on the consumption of health care and of goods other than health care. If an illness is experienced, individuals decide whether to seek medical care or not. The benefit from consuming health care is an expected improvement in health status, while the cost of medical care implies a reduction in the consumption of other goods and services.

This is based on the theory of consumer behavior, which utilizes the utility theory. This theory provides a methodological framework for the evaluation of alternative choices made by individuals, firms, and organizations, Doumpos and Zopounidis (n.d.). Utility refers to the satisfaction that each choice provides to the decision maker (in this case the consumer). Thus, utility theory assumes that any decision is made on the basis of the utility maximization principle, according to which the best choice is the one that provides the highest utility (satisfaction) to the decision maker. In this case, the individual or consumer must decide how much of each of the many different choices (goods and services) to make (consume) in order to get the highest possible level of satisfaction (total utility) subject to his/her available income and the prices of the goods/services. In all cases the utility that the decision maker gets from selecting a specific choice is measure by a utility function U, which is a mathematical representation of the decision maker's system of preferences such that: $U(x) > U(y)$, where choice x is preferred over choice y or $U(x) = U(y)$, where choice x is indifferent from choice y—both choices are equally preferred. One important assumption of utility theory is that decision makers are willing to trade one choice for another, Doumpos and Zopounidis (n.d.). This is what was applied to this study.

Individuals have to decide not only whether to seek care but also what type of care they wish to demand. They are able to choose from the finite set of alternative providers, one of which is self-treatment. Each provider offers an expected improvement in health (efficacy) for a price. The quality of an alternative provider is defined as the expected improvement in health as a result of that provider's medical care. The price of an alternative includes both monetary outlays and private access costs such as the opportunity cost of travel time. Based on this and their incomes, individuals choose the alternative that yields the highest expected utility.

Let the expected utility conditional on receiving care from provider j be given by Eq. (1) as follows:

$$U_i = U(H_i, C_i). \qquad (1)$$

where U_j is the expected utility conditional on receiving care from provider j

H_j is the expected health status after receiving treatment from provider j and

C_j is a consumption net of the cost of obtaining care from provider j.

Gertler et al. (1987) defined quality of health care by establishing a relationship between a person's health status before obtaining professional medical care (with self-treatment) (H_0) and after obtaining health care from provider j (H_j). For instance, quality of provider j's care, Q_j can be defined as the difference between health status after and before receiving treatment from provider j. This is represented as $Q_j = H_j - H_0$. Solving for H_j then gives us a relationship between after-treatment health status, pre-treatment health status, H_0 and quality of care. This is specified in Eq. (2) as:

$$H_i = Q_i + H_0 \qquad (2)$$

As specified in (2), quality of health care is assumed to be a function of both providers' and individuals' characteristics. This is because it is not an objective measure but an individual's assessment of the expected improvement in health status. As such it varies with such individual characteristics as severity of illness, education, perceived quality of treatment, age, and sex.

Under the self-care alternative $H_j = H_0$, implying that $Q_0 = 0$. This implicitly normalizes the health care production function so that the quality of a provider's care is measured relative to the efficacy of self-care. Consumption expenditures (net of expenditures on medical care) are derived from the budget constraint. The total price of medical care includes both the direct payments to the provider and the indirect cost of access (like the opportunity cost of travel time). Let P_j be the total price of provider j's care and Y is income, so that the individual or consumer's budget constraint is expressed as:

$$C_j + P_j = Y \qquad (3)$$

With $C_j > 0$ required for the jth alternative to be feasible. Substitution of Eq. (3) into (1) for C_j yields the conditional indirect utility function indicated in Eq. (4) as follows:

$$U_j = U(H_j, Y - P_j). \qquad (4)$$

From this income affects utility through the consumption term and that the price of medical care (P_j) is forgone consumption. Based on the above and also, given that the individual has $j+1$ feasible alternatives (with the $j=0$ alternative being self-care). The unconditional utility maximization problem can then be specified in Eq. (5) as,

$$U^* = \max(U_0, U_1, \ldots, U_j) \qquad (5)$$

where U^* is maximum utility. This is subject to the budget constraint in Eq. (3).

The solution to Eq. (5) gives the alternative that is chosen and when there are random terms in the model, the probability that each alternative is chosen. The probability that an alternative is chosen equals the probability that this choice yields the highest utility among all the alternatives. Thus, the probability that an alternative is chosen can then be interpreted as the demand function in a discrete choice model (Li 1996). These demand functions can then be used to solve for the unconditional indirect utility functions and the expenditures or cost functions. From the expenditure or cost function, the equivalent variation of a change in the price of public sector health care services can then be computed. This is defined as the additional income or amount needed to keep a household as well off (after the improvement) as before, when there is a price change (Gertler et al. 1987; Gertler and Van der Daag 1988, 1990; Alderman and Gertler 1989).

Equivalent variation of a price change is one of the measures used to evaluate the effect of policy changes on consumer's behavior (Varian 1992). A consumer may be made worse off or better off by the policy change (in this study, a change in the price of public sector health care services). For instance, if the policy change affects the price level, all things being equal, the WTP for that change in policy by the consumer may be affected. Equivalent variation uses the current prices as the base and asks the question: what income changes at the current prices would be equivalent to the proposed change in terms of its impact on the consumer's utility. That is, what income level will make the consumer remain on his original or initial utility level? Note that the effect of a price change involves both an income effect and a substitution effect (Varian 1992). The weight of these effects affects both the utility level and the value of the expenditure function. The equivalent variation of a change in price is derived from the value of the expenditure function, which is defined from the demand function in Eqs. (6) and (7) as:

$$Y^0 = y(P^1, U^*) \qquad (6)$$

and

$$Y^1 = y(P^0, U^*) \qquad (7)$$

where

U^* is maximum utility
P^0 is the initial price
P^1 is the new price
Y^0 is the minimum expenditure necessary to achieve the new post-price change utility level
Y^1 is that expenditure necessary to achieve the new level of utility with the initial price.

Hence, in the case of a price rise from P^0 to P^1, the equivalent variation of the price increase can be defined in Eq. (8) as:

$$\text{EV} = y(P^1, U^*) - y(P^0, U^*) \qquad (8)$$

This EV is defined as the area under or below the Hicksian demand curve and can be represented in Eq. (9) as:

$$\text{EV} = \int_{P^0}^{P^1} D(P^0, U^*) dP^0 \qquad (9)$$

For this study, two commodities are considered. They are health care and other goods. The increase in the price of health care is likely to reduce the demand for other goods and services by the consumer. This is based on the premise that the consumer is faced with a relatively constant income level. To measure this impact on the consumer welfare the equivalent variation framework is used. If the expenditure function is of the form $y(P^0, U^0)$, then the amount the consumer will be willing to pay for improvements, that is, the WTP in the health care services in order to remain at the same level of utility is given by:

$$\text{WTP} = y(P^1, U^*) - y(P^0, U^*) \qquad (10)$$

Which is the area under the demand curve and is measuring the equivalent variation (EV). This implies that:

$$\text{WTP} = \text{EV} = \int_{P^0}^{P^1} D(P^0, U^*) dP^0 \qquad (11)$$

The equivalent variation of a price rise can be described as the amount the individual would require to voluntarily forgo a proposed price increase to prevent such an individual from welfare deterioration. That is, it is the willingness to accept compensation (Freeman 1993).

For this study, the choice of the equivalent variation framework is justified for two main reasons: firstly, it measures the income change at current prices and is much easier for decision makers to judge the value of a currency (in this case the Naira), for instance, at current prices than at some hypothetical prices. Secondly, if we are comparing more than one proposed policy change it keeps the base price fixed at the status quo for each new policy. This makes it a more appropriate measure for comparison among a variety of projects.

4.2 Data Requirements and Sources

The study utilized both primary and secondary data. The secondary data were sourced from the publications of the Central Bank of Nigeria (CBN), National Bureau of Statistics (formerly Federal Office of Statistics), Federal Ministry of Health, publications from UNICEF, World Bank, and World Data Atlas from knoema.com. The primary data used were individual, household, and community based. A multistage sampling design was adopted for the sampling process. This involved both stratified random and cluster-sampling techniques. The choice of these sampling techniques was based on the fact that the Nigerian population is heterogeneous but internally homogeneous. The first stage was the selection of the strata to be sampled. The second stage was the selection of clusters. The third stage was the selection of the households to be interviewed. The six geopolitical zones in Nigeria, namely: Southwest, Southeast, South-south, Northeast, Northwest, and North-central, were used as the strata. From each stratum, a state was chosen based on which clusters were drawn. The states were chosen irrespective of the variations in their population for balance purposes. Each of the Local Government Areas (LGAs) in the states was assumed to constitute a natural cluster. A local government area from each state capital, which is more cosmopolitan, with a fairly high population, and a fairly developed social infrastructure, made up the urban cluster while the LGAs on the outskirts were rural. One of the merits of this survey method was that since households that were interviewed lived in clusters, it was easy to collect community level information. For instance, it was easy to link a community to a specific health facility where most of the households living within the cluster went to obtain treatment and this makes it easier to estimate the distance to the health facilities. Moreover, it was easy to collect market prices of consumption goods from the communities.

Of the six geopolitical zones, a state each was randomly chosen. These were made independently in the different strata. In all, 18 LGAs were sampled. Enumerators in these LGAs helped in the gathering of these data. From each state, 1650 (750 for rural; 600 for urban; and 300 for the third LGA) households were randomly selected and in all a total of 9900 households were interviewed (involving 29,700 individuals) using questionnaires. The difference in the sample size was to help capture more of the rural dwellers' response. This was premised on the fact that rural area dwellers tend to be faced with shortage of modern health care facilities and professionals and as such experience lower life expectancy and poorer health status than the urban dwellers. Out of this, 7920 valid questionnaires (that is, those properly answered) were returned. This represents a response rate of 80%. Accordingly, this total of 7920 questionnaires was used for the analysis. Households were randomly selected from both rural and urban areas. The questionnaires were administered in such a way that information obtained from the nearest cluster, was linked to a specific household in the cluster. The data were for both outpatients and inpatients in both rural and urban areas. Households and/or patients were randomly selected from each public sector health facility. The above household survey was supplemented by a health facility survey.

The survey collected socioeconomic information such as household consumption, demographic characteristics, time use, income and consumption, education, and health status. The health statistics provided a detailed description of health care and the incidence of morbidity thirty days prior to the survey date including information on the length of illness, choice of treatment (self, doctor, traditional healer), type of health facility visited (public or private, clinic or hospital), expenditure on consultation and drugs, travel time and cost. The facility survey collected information about infrastructure (beds, vehicles, laboratory, and operating rooms), personnel (number of doctors, nurses, and medical assistants), availability of health services and drugs (number of hours per person per week, type of services provided, and stock of available drugs), and fees charged. Other information about the average consultation time, net expenditure per visit, percentage of people reported ill or injured, government health spending, and the cost recovered were also sorted.

Apart from household questionnaires, facility questionnaires were also administered to some health facilities. Facilities were selected for interviewing based on proximity to a household cluster (this is a geographic area such as a village or neighborhoods of a city). The questions were generally structured questions in which multiple options were provided to the respondents. The questions were made as simple as possible. The questionnaires were administered in such a way that information obtained from the nearest cluster, was linked to a specific household in the cluster. The data were for both outpatients and inpatients in both rural and urban areas. Households and/or patients were randomly selected from each public sector health facility.

The household sample included both individuals who do not report as well as those who reported an illness within four weeks of the survey. The reason for the focus on the preceding one month is that several studies have shown that the longer the recall period, household expenditures and consumption tend to diminish (Scott and Amenuvegbe 1990; Deaton 1997).

5 Result and Analysis

5.1 *Background Characteristics of Respondents*

Table 1 contains the sociodemographic characteristics of the respondents. The three major tribes dominated in the survey. These are Ibo (21.7%), Yoruba (20.6%), and Hausa (23.5%) while the other minor tribes constituted 34.2%. In terms of the household head, 82.8% of the households were headed by the father (male) while 12.2% was headed by the mother (female), and others constitute 3.5% with 1.5% not giving any response.

Table 1 Sociodemographic characteristics of the respondents

Tribe of respondents (%)	
Ibo	21.7
Yoruba	20.6
Hausa	23.5
Others[a]	34.2
Head of household (%)	
Male	82.8
Female	12.2
Others[b]	3.5
Location (settlement area) of respondents (%)	
Urban	58
Rural	42
Age group of sick respondents (%)[c]	
Children	59.0
Adults	37.6
Mean household monthly income by income quartile (in Nigerian Naira)[d]	
Quartile 1 (Lowest)	6885.95
Quartile 2	24,762.48
Quartile 3	59,116.02
Quartile 4 (Highest)	88,106.20
Mean household monthly health care spending by income quartile (in Nigerian Naira)	
Quartile 1 (Lowest)	807.21
Quartile 2	1907.01
Quartile 3	3070.11
Quartile 4 (Highest)	5198.77
Number of respondents	7920

Note
[a]This includes other tribes like Tiv, Idoma, Itsekiri, Efik, Ibibio, Edo, etc
[b]No Response constituted 1.5% of the respondents
[c]No Response constituted 3.4% of the respondents
[d]No Response constituted 3.0% of the respondents
The average exchange rate was US$1 to N135
Source Author's computation

The urban resident respondents were 58.0% while the rural resident was 42.0%. Children (59.0%) constituted a larger percentage of those who were sick implying that many of those who reported sick were those in the active service and this might be an indicator of the healthiness of the country. Majority of the respondents (52.6%) belonged to the lowest income group earning an average monthly income of ₦6885.98 (US$51). This amount is less than the minimum wage of public civil servants which is ₦8500 (US$62.96) at the time of the survey. Only about 3.7% of the respondents belonged to the highest income group earning on average, a monthly income of ₦88,106.20 (US$652.64). This indicates the likelihood that a high percentage of the low-income earners are often sick compared to the high-income earners. This may be adduced to the fact that high-income

Table 2 Location (settlement area), access to health facility, preferred health care services, rating of the cost of health care services and whether cost prevented health facility utilization

Location (Settlement)	Urban	Rural
Access to health facility (%)		
Far	40.0	43.9
Near	55.8	45.8
No response	4.2	10.3
Total	100.0	100.0
χ^2	352.62	
Preferred health care services (%)		
Self-treatment	15.7	10.8
Traditional healer	1.4	28.2
Private facility	30.6	9.8
Government facility	27.5	25.9
Pharmacy/drug Shop	14.5	14.6
Others	10.3	10.7
Total	100	100
Rating of the cost of health care services (%)		
Too low	17.1	10.0
Low	15.5	12.6
Moderate	25.6	20.8
High	21.7	29.5
Too high	19.0	20.1
No response	1.1	7.0
Total	100	100
χ^2	118.95	
Whether cost prevented health facility utilization (%)		
Yes	37.8	62.2
No	64.2	35.8
Total	100	100
χ^2	166.16	

Source Computed from the survey data

earners are exposed to better nutrition, shelter, environment, etc., and they (the high-income earners) have a higher ability to pay for better health care services than the low-income earners.

On access and location, Table 2 shows that there was a significant difference in the responses of the rural and urban dwellers as is indicated by the value of the chi-square. Most of the households who reside in the urban areas tend to have more access to the health facility utilized than their counterparts in the rural areas. This can be adduced to the fact that there are more health facilities in the urban areas than in the rural areas, especially with respect to private health facilities. Most of those in the rural area's respondents, preferred government health facilities as well as the self-care option, traditional medicine and pharmacy and/or drug shops, respectively (Table 2).

Table 2 further indicated that most of the respondents in the urban areas perceived the cost of care as being moderate compared to those from the rural dwellers. The disparity in the rating of the cost of care between the urban and rural areas showed a significant difference given the value of the chi-square and was also manifest when most (64.2%) of the urban respondents indicated that they were not constrained by cost in their utilization of health care services while 62.2% of those in the rural area were constrained from utilizing health care services due to the cost (Table 2). The result of the chi-square showed that there was a significant difference in these perceptions.

5.2 *Perceived Willingness to Pay*

WTP has been defined by Lavy and Germain (1994) to include, among others, how much an individual is willing to pay to have an improvement in the quality of the available health services in existing public sector health facilities. Thus, from the sample data as contained in Table 3, 81.3% of the respondents

Table 3 Perceived willingness to pay for improved quality of health services

	Yes	*No*	*Undecided*	*Total*
Are you willingness to pay for improved quality of health services? (%)	81.3	13.6	5.1	100.0
Location and perceived willingness to pay (%)				
Urban	55.5	17.6	26.9	100.0
Rural	24.5	60.2	15.3	100.0
χ^2	148.55			
Education and perceived willingness to pay (%)				
No education	16.0	63.8	20.2	100.0
Primary	19.6	49.6	30.8	100.0
Secondary	11.5	50.2	38.3	100.0
Modern II	62.6	21.1	16.3	100.0
N.C.E	58.3	15.2	26.5	100.0
OND/HND	54.1	20.3	25.6	100.0
University	87.1	10.9	2.0	100.0
Others	35.9	32.3	31.8	100.0
Income and perceived willingness to pay (%)				
Quartile 1 (Lowest)	9.4	55.9	40.5	
Quartile 2	16.8	28.2	24.4	
Quartile 3	31.7	11.1	20.1	
Quartile 4 (Highest)	42.1	4.8	15.0	
Total	100.0	100.0	100.1	
Perceived willingness to pay and payer of health care services received				
Father	51.8	18.1	30.1	100.0
Mother	30.0	48.6	21.4	100.0
Self	7.9	23.3	68.8	100.0
Government	0.0	0.0	100.0	100.0
Others	10.3	10.0	79.7	100.0

Source Computed from the survey data

were willing to pay for improved quality of health care services in government health facilities while 13.6% were not willing and 5.0% were undecided.

Furthermore, there was a significant difference between respondents' perception on their WTP, especially with respect to urban and rural areas. For instance, majority (64.2%) of the respondents from the rural areas were not willing to pay, while most of those in the urban areas showed the WTP (Table 3). A possible reason for the high-perceived WTP by majority of those in the urban areas vis-à-vis those of the rural areas may be the educational level of the respondents. Most of the urban dwellers tend to be better educated and as such are likely to appreciate the importance of improved quality in public sector health care facilities than the less-educated rural populace. An illustration of this can be found in Table 3, which shows that those with higher education were willing to pay more for improved quality in health care services received relative to those with lower level of education. Another factor influencing WTP, especially with respect to rural and urban populace is income. And from Table 3, of all the sampled households who were willing to pay more, most of them were from the high-income quartile while few were from the low-income quartile. This shows that the high-income earners will tend to spend more for improved quality in the public health care service they received, since the proportion to their income spent on health may be less compared to that of the low-income rural dwellers.

This agrees to the fact that the lesser the proportion of a household's income spent on the consumption of health care the more they will be willing to pay more for the services received. Conversely, the higher the proportion of a household's income spent on the consumption of health care the less willing such a household will be to pay an additional money price for the health care services received. In terms of the perceived WTP and the payer of the health care services received, most of the cases where households were willing to pay more were cases in which the father, as the head of the family, was the payer of the health care services received by any member of the household (Table 3). The better educated an individual is, the more the tendency for him to cherish the merits of quality health care, as a result, he will be willing to pay more. This tends to explain why majority of those who were willing to pay more were those with higher level of education, while those with lower education were willing to pay a lesser amount (Table 4). For instance, those with lower education were willing to pay about 1.51% of their income monthly for improved quality in public sector health care services.

This trend was similar with respect to income and WTP where most of the households who were willing to a higher increase were those from the high-income quartile (Table 4). For instance, respondents in the lowest income quartile were willing to pay an average of 1.68% of the income monthly while those in the highest income quartile were willing to pay 9.96% of their income. For those in the low-income quartile, they were willing to pay a lesser amount than those in the high-income quartile. This consents to

Yoder (1989) assertion that the WTP can only be enhanced where there is the ability to pay. This invariably shows that the higher the level of income, the higher the educational qualification tends to be, the more the household becomes appreciative of the quality of health care received and subsequently the more the WTP for any increase in the cost (money price) of care. In terms of location, there was a significant difference between the amount which the respondents in rural and urban areas were willing to pay as can be seen from the value of the chi-square in Table 4. In fact, more of the urban households sampled indicated their WTP a higher amount relative to the rural households. The rural households were willing to pay an average of ₦407.13 monthly relative to ₦1105.06 which the urban households were willing to pay. This represents about 3 and 5.5% of their monthly income, respectively.

A possible explanation for this can be that those in the urban areas tend to be exposed to better government infrastructure and services than those in the rural areas; this thus serves as an incentive for them to appreciate government activities and consequently will be willing to pay more. Hence, the government should intensify her efforts in increasing the spread of her

Table 4 Average amount households are willing to pay for improved quality in public sector health care services

Education and average amount households are willing to pay for improved quality in public sector health care services

Level of education	Percentage of income households are willing to pay
No education	1.51
Primary	1.85
Secondary	2.28
Modern II	3.76
N.C.E	5.70
OND/HND	8.55
University	10.84

Income and average amount households are willing to pay for improved quality in public sector health care services

Income quartile	Percentage of income households are willing to pay
Quartile 1 (Lowest)	1.68
Quartile 2	4.87
Quartile 3	5.80
Quartile 4 (Highest)	9.96

Location and average amount households are willingness to pay for improved quality in public sector health care services

Location	Average amount households are willing to pay (in Naira)
Urban	1105.06
Rural	407.13
$\chi^2 = 148.55$	

Source Computed from the survey data

infrastructures, especially, to the rural areas. More functional health centers, dispensaries, and health posts should be established in the rural areas. More boreholes should also be sunk in the rural areas. This will enhance their access to potable water and good sanitation, thereby reducing the incidence of diseases, and consequently reduce the pressure on government health facilities. This will not only enhance the quality of service, it will also serve as an incentive for the rural dwellers, whose WTP more for government health care service will increase.

5.3 Willingness to Pay

In evaluating the WTP, the welfare neutral prices were calculated. The welfare neutral prices were derived from the equivalent variation experiments. On the distance effect (which was measured in hours) the simulation was conducted assuming that the nearest public health facility is half an hour away. The scenarios considered for distance include how much an individual is willing to pay to have his travel costs reduced by three-quarter hours; reduced by one-quarter hours; reduced by half, and finally reduced to zero. The second set of scenario considers the price of consultation, that is what will be the welfare neutral price when the price of consultation is reduced by half and when the price is reduced to zero.

The WTP for improved quality in existing public sector facilities was similarly analyzed. The quality variables used were drug (D); personnel (P); service (S); and infrastructure (I). The starting point for this was a situation in which the public sector facility has the lowest quality variables. And for initial values, the lowest quality rating was first used, and then successively the WTP for improving these variables to the highest quality rating was computed. The simulation analysis was done assuming that the nearest public sector health facility is one hour away from the community. The results are presented in Table 5 (for rural respondents) and Table 6 (for urban respondents). The table shows the additional amount which individuals are willing to pay. Each simulation is computed using the mean individual characteristics for three different values of income namely, the Sample Mean Income (SMI), SMI minus the Sample Standard Derivation (SMI1), and SMI plus the Sample Standard Derivation (SMI2). And for counterfactual purposes, the WTP in the model without quality variables, using the mean individual characteristics was also computed. These results are represented in the last column of Tables 5 and 6 and it is denoted by SMI WQ.

Table 5 shows the WTP amount for the rural respondents and it shows a positive trend with income in all the scenarios considered. The representative household (using the Sample Monthly Mean Income) is willing to pay 2.25% of their income to have their travel time (distance) to the nearest public health facility reduced to zero. For the lower income levels, they were willing to pay as much as 2.78% of their income to have their travel time (distance)

Table 5 Willingness to pay for improvement of health services (Prices in Naira (₦) for rural respondents)

SCENARIO		SMI1	SMI	SMI 2	SMI WQ
		10,497.06	18,964.19	38,432.32	18,964.19
Distance	Reducing the travel time (distance) by one-quarter (¹/₄) hour	120.50 (1.15)	129.50 (0.68)	135.50 (0.35)	135.50 (0.71)
	Reducing the travel time (distance) by half (¹/₂) hour	135.50 (1.29)	153.50 (0.81)	164.00 (0.43)	165.50 (0.87)
	Reducing the travel time (distance) by three-quarter (³/₄) hour	291.30 (2.78)	326.50 (1.72)	537.00 (1.40)	404.50 (2.13)
	Reducing the travel time (distance) to zero hours	291.30 (2.78)	426.50 (2.25)	578.00 (1.50)	404.50 (2.13)
Price	Reducing price by 50% or halving price	113.00 (1.08)	216.75 (1.14)	250.00 (0.65)	116.00 (0.61)
	Reducing price by 100% or zero-price	116.75 (1.11)	423.50 (2.23)	427.30 (1.11)	222.00 (1.17)
Quality	Improving drug availability from the lowest quality rating (D=0) to the highest quality rating (D=1)	119.75 (1.14)	149.75 (0.79)	197.75 (0.51)	N/A
	Improving service from the lowest quality rating (S=0) to the highest quality rating (S=1)	117.50 (1.12)	141.50 (0.75)	161.00 (0.42)	N/A
	Improving infrastructure from the lowest quality rating (I=0) to the highest quality rating (I=1)	112.25 (1.07)	225.00 (1.19)	134.75 (0.35)	N/A
	Improving personnel from the lowest quality rating (P=0) to the highest quality rating (P=1)	112.15 (1.07)	252.05 (1.33)	122.75 (0.32)	N/A
	Improving drug availability and service from the lowest quality rating (D=S=0) to the highest quality rating (D=S=1)	145.25 (1.38)	149.50 (0.79)	238.75 (0.62)	N/A
	Improving drug availability and infrastructure from the lowest quality rating (D=I=0) to the highest quality rating (D=I=1)	132.50 (1.26)	100.00 (0.53)	157.75 (0.41)	N/A
	Improving service and infrastructure from the lowest quality rating (S=I=0) to the highest quality rating (S=I=1)	127.25 (1.21)	183.50 (0.97)	130.75 (0.34)	N/A
	Improving drug availability, service and infrastructure from the lowest quality rating (D=S=I=0) to the highest quality rating (D=S=I=1)	211.25 (2.01)	345.75 (1.82)	594.50 (1.55)	N/A

Note N/A: Not Applicable
SMI Sample Mean Income
SMI1 Sample Mean Income minus the Sample Standard Deviation
SMI2 Sample Mean Income plus the Sample Standard Deviation
SMIWQ Sample Mean Income without the quality variables. This is for counterfactual purposes
Percentage of income are in parenthesis
The average exchange rate was US$1 to ₦135

Table 6 Willingness to pay for the improvement of health services (Prices in Naira (₦) for Urban respondents)

SCENARIO		SMI 1	SMI	SMI 2	SMI WQ
		10,497.06	18,964.19	38,432.32	18,964.19
Distance	Reducing the travel time (distance) by one-quarter (¹/₄) hour	102.60 (0.98)	139.55 (0.74)	185.50 (0.48)	185.50 (0.98)
	Reducing the travel time (distance) by half (¹/₂) hour	145.60 (1.39)	173.54 (0.92)	244.01 (0.63)	145.25 (0.77)
	Reducing the travel time (distance) by three-quarter (³/₄) hour	341.80 (3.36)	476.43 (2.51)	597.00 (1.55)	454.50 (2.40)
	Reducing the travel time (distance) to zero hours	341.02 (3.25)	476.50 (2.51)	597.24 (1.55)	454.50 (2.40)
Price	Reducing price by 50% or halving price	150.00 (1.43)	175.50 (0.93)	181.50 (0.47)	177.00 (0.93)
	Reducing price by 100% or zero-price	167.05 (1.59)	195.55 (1.03)	397.3 (1.03)	298.04 (1.57)
Quality	Improving drug availability from the lowest quality rating (D=0) to the highest quality rating (D=1)	259.25 (2.47)	250.75 (1.32)	387.76 (1.01)	N/A
	Improving service from the lowest quality rating (S=0) to the highest quality rating (S=1)	255.25 (2.43)	293.75 (1.55)	421.00 (1.10)	N/A
	Improving infrastructure from the lowest quality rating (I=0) to the highest quality rating (I=1)	251.35 (2.39)	298.10 (2.10)	413.75 (1.08)	N/A
	Improving personnel from the lowest quality rating (P=0) to the highest quality rating (P=1)	251.75 (2.40)	358.01 (1.59)	489.75 (1.27)	N/A
	Improving drug availability and service from the lowest quality rating (D=S=0) to the highest quality rating (D=S=1)	196.25 (1.87)	301.50 (1.89)	388.10 (1.01)	N/A
	Improving drug availability and infrastructure from the lowest quality rating (D=I=0) to the highest quality rating (D=I=1)	240.00 (2.29)	156.25 (0.82)	414.35 (1.08)	N/A
	Improving service and infrastructure from the lowest quality rating (S=I=0) to the highest quality rating (S=I=1)	196.40 (1.87)	244.25 (1.29)	385.00 (1.00)	N/A
	Improving drug availability, service and infrastructure from the lowest quality rating (D=S=I=0) to the highest quality rating (D=S=I=1)	294.32 (2.80)	428.10 (2.26)	698.20 (1.82)	N/A

Note N/A: Not Applicable
SMI Sample Mean Income
SMI Sample Mean Income minus the Sample Standard Deviation
SMI Sample Mean Income plus the Sample Standard Deviation
SMIWQ Sample Mean Income without the quality variables. This is for counterfactual purposes
Percentage of income are in parenthesis
The average exchange rate was US$1 to ₦135

to the nearest public health facility reduced to zero while the higher income earners were willing to pay 1.5% of their income. For the urban respondents, the low-income earners, representative household and the higher income earners were willing to pay 2.2, 2.5, and 1.6% of their income, respectively to have improvements in distance to the nearest health facility. For a reduction in the price of consultation by 100% (that is, reducing it to zero) or by reducing it by half, the representative households in the rural areas were willing to pay 1.08 and 2.23% of their income, respectively while those of the urban areas were willing to pay 0.9 and 1.03% percent of their income.

The quality variables tend to be more significant for the urban respondents as the representative households were willing to pay 2.26% of their income to have quality of care improved by having an improved infrastructure, drug availability and efficient and diverse services. Their rural counterparts were willing to pay 1.82%. Furthermore, the representative households in the rural areas were willing to pay 0.79% of their income to have the health facility stocked with the basic drugs (that is, drug availability). This was slightly lower than those of the urban respondents, which was 1.32% of their income. While for the provision of efficient and diverse services, they (the rural respondents) were willing to pay additional 0.75% of their income and those from the urban area were willing to pay 1.55% for the same level of services being provided. And for improved infrastructure, they were willing to pay 1.19% of their income as against the 2.10%, which the urban respondents were willing to pay. With respect to personnel, the representative households (in the rural areas) were willing to pay 1.33% of their income to have more qualified personnel treat them in the public health facilities while their urban counterparts were willing to pay 1.89% of their income for the same purpose.

An implication of this is that households are somewhat more concerned with the quality of health care services provided by the public sector health facility. Similarly, for households in the higher income level of our sample, they were willing to pay more for the improved quality variables. For instance, to have the quality of care improved by having an improved infrastructure, drug availability, and efficient and diverse services, the rural high-income respondents were willing to pay 1.55% of their income while those of the urban were willing to pay 1.82% of their income.

Though the estimation result shows the importance of the quality of health care services provided by the health facility, the income effect, which is more significant for distance or price than for the quality variables indicates that for the representative households, distance plays a more important role in determining the WTP for the rural respondents while the urban respondents were more concerned about the quality of care in public health facilities. Also, as a percentage of income, the WTP for the price of consultation and distance decreases as income increases while for the quality variables, this percentage increases as income increases for both the urban and rural respondents. This tends to support the notion that the rich households are more concerned with the quality of health care services than with distance or price.

On the counterfactual simulation, which was done without the inclusion of the quality variables (SM1WQ), the urban representative households were willing to pay more, precisely 2.40% of their income to have their travel time (distance) reduced to zero or even have the travel time reduced by three-quarter hour while those of the rural areas were willing to pay 2.13% of their income. An inherent implication of this is that without the quality variables, households prefer to pay more to have their travel time reduced than to have the price of consultation reduced. This implies that distance plays a significant role in influencing the choice of health care provider to utilize by both the rural and urban respondents.

From the analysis, the WTP increased with income in all the cases considered. Also, it is apparent that the poor (low-income earners) in both rural and urban suffers more from the out-of-pocket payments as it tends to reduce their utilization level of public sector health care services. Distance ranks high as one of the most important price factors that influences the WTP more in public sector health care services for rural dwellers while quality of care was momentous for urban respondents. A reduction in distance or travel time tends to be directly related to the magnitude of out-of-pocket and time cost for traveling to a health facility to obtain care. This implies that a reduction in distance to public sector (and possibly private) health facilities will enhance the utilization rate of both facilities. While on the contrary, it will discourage the use of self-care when an illness occurs thus, more functional health facilities should be established.

6 CONCLUSION

The study investigated the factors that determine the households' WTP for public health care services in Nigeria and evaluate the extent to which these factors affect households' WTP in both the urban and rural areas. The study used primary data collected from the six randomly selected states from the six geopolitical zones of the federation. The analysis was based on a subsample of those household members who reported being ill and or sick during the four weeks preceding the survey. Both descriptive statistics and simulation analysis were used in the study. Simulations were carried out using various policy assumptions. The descriptive statistics made use of percentages, frequency distributions, graphs, tables, among others. Among the findings from the descriptive statistics was that majority (75.8%) of the respondents signified their WTP more for health care services while 24.2% did not signify such WTP. Also, most of the rural respondents rated the cost of care in public sector health facilities, on the average, to be moderately high while most of the urban dwellers rated it to be moderately low. The disparity in these ratings was mainly due to the education and income levels, which was skewed positively toward urban respondents. Majority (81.3%) of the respondents were willing to pay more for improved quality in the health care services provided and they are also willing to pay as much as an average of 15% increase in price. The educated and high-income earners were willing to pay more than those with low education and income. Also, rural dwellers were willing to pay less compared to the urban populace. A major reason for this is the disparity in their education and income levels, which favor the urban populace. In most of the cases, education, income level, location (settlement area), religious as well as traditional beliefs influenced most of the health care decisions of the respondents. The simulations exercise showed that households are willing to pay about two percent of their monthly income for improvements in drug and service availability. They are also willing to pay more for improving their access to the public sector facility. Furthermore, the poor in both rural and urban suffers more from the out-of-pocket payments as it tends to reduce their utilization level of public sector health care services. Distance a major determinant of the factor that influences the WTP public sector health care services for rural dwellers while quality of care was a significant factor for urban respondents. A reduction in distance or travel time tends to be directly related to the magnitude of out-of-pocket and time cost for traveling to a health facility to obtain care. An implication of this is that it will discourage the use of self-care when an illness occurs thus, more functional health facilities should be established.

Based on the findings of the study, it is suggested that the government should endeavor to bring public sector health facilities closer to the people especially in the rural areas. The establishment of new public sector health care facilities can do this. Though, recently, the federal government built more public sector health centers across the country, more public health centers can still be established and should be effectively managed as many of the existing ones have deteriorated considerably. Government should introduce price discrimination in public health facilities where fees in clinics in poorer villages and communities (especially rural areas) can be set at different levels than fees in rich communities (urban areas). And as long as the user fee is below the welfare neutral prices the policy will be welfare improving for everyone. This type of price discrimination the clinics in richer villages or areas (urban areas) will be self-financing, while the facilities in poorer villages (rural areas) require a subsidy. Given that the representative households are willing to pay more for improved quality (drug availability, efficient and require services, infrastructure, and qualified personnel) as well as increased access to health care facilities. Thus, there is the need for the government to improve on the quality of care in the public sector health facilities. Also, since households are willing to pay for improved quality of care in public sector hospitals and the government can thus increase the fees marginally and ensure that the revenue from such an increase is used to improve the quality of care by ensuring there are adequate drug availability, skilled personnel, and better infrastructures in these health facilities. The above suggestion is thus, of great importance since the consequence of lack of care is lifelong as it affects the individual's lifetime stock of human capital.

References

Akter, S. (2008). Determinants of willingness to pay for safe drinking water: A case study in Bangladesh. *Asian Journal of Water, Environment and Pollution, 5*(3), 85–91.

Alderman, H., & Gertler, P. (1989). *The substitutability of public and private health care for the treatment of children in Pakistan* (LSMS Working Paper No. 57). Washington, DC: World Bank.

Alpizar, F., Carlsson, F., & Martinsson, P. (2003). Using choice experiments for non-market valuation. *Economic Issues-Stoke on Trent, 8*(1), 83–110.

Amaghionyeodiwe, L. A. (2008). Determinants of the choice of health care provider in nigeria. *Health Care Management Science, 11*, 215–227.

Ayifah, E. (2010). Determinants of the willingness-to-pay for HIV/AIDS prevention: The case of mother-to-child transmission in selected hospitals in Ghana. *Retrovirology, 7*(Suppl. 1), P137.

Biadgilign, S., Reda, A. A., & Kedir, H. (2015). Determinants of willingness to pay for the retreatment of insecticide treated mosquito nets in rural area of eastern Ethiopia. *International Journal for Equity in Health, 14*, 99. https://doi.org/10.1186/s12939-015-0249-9.

Central Bank of Nigeria. (Various Years-a). Annual Report and Statement of Account. Abuja.

Central Bank of Nigeria. (Various Years-b). Statistical Bulletin. Abuja.

Champ, P. A., Boyle, K. J., & Brown, T. C. (Eds.) (2017). *A primer on nonmarket valuation*, 2nd Edn. The Economics of Non-Market Goods and Resources. The Netherlands: Springer, Dordrecht.

Ching, P. (1995). User fees, demand for children's health care and access across income groups: The Philippine case. *Social Science and Medicine, 14*(1), 37–46.

Deaton, A. (1997). *The analysis of household survey: A microeconometric approach to development policy.* Baltimore: The John Hopkins University Press.

Donfouet, H. P. P., Makaudze, E., Mahieu, P. A., & Malin, E. (2011, September). The determinants of the willingness-to-pay for community-based prepayment scheme in rural Cameroon. *International Journal of Health care Finance and Economics, 11*, 209.

Doumpos, M., & Zopounidis, C. (n.d.). *Utility theory.* Retrieved from https://www.referenceforbusiness.com/management/Tr-Z/Utility-Theory.html.

Dupuit, J. (1844) De la mesure de l utilite des travaux publics. Annales des pouts et chaussees 8, pp. 79–84 [Translated by Barback, R. H (1952)]. On the Measurement of Utility of Public Works. International Economic Papers 2, pp. 83–110.

Federal Ministry of Planning, Nigeria. (1956). *The First Nigerian National Development Plans.* Lagos: Federal Ministry of Planning.

Federal Ministry of Health. (1996). *The national health plan 1996–2000.* Abuja: FMOH.

Federal Ministry of Health, Nigeria. (1988, October). *The national health policy and strategy to achieve health for all Nigerians.* Lagos: Federal Ministry of Health.

Freeman III, A. M. (1993). *The measurement of environmental and resource values: Theory and methods.* Baltimore, Maryland: Resources for the Future.

Gertler, P., Locay, L., & Sanderson, W. (1987). Are user fees regressive? The welfare implications of health care financing proposals in Peru. *Journal of Econometrics, 36*, 67–88.

Gertler, P., & Van der Gaag, J. (1988). *Measuring the willingness to pay for social services in developing countries* (Living Standard Measurement Study (LSMS) Working Paper No. 45). Washington, DC: The World Bank.

Gertler, P., & Van der Gaag, J. (1990). *The willingness to pay for social services in developing countries* (Living Standard Measurement Study (LSMS) Working Paper No. 29). Washington, DC: The World Bank.

Halkos, G., & Matsiori, S. (2012, August). Determinants of willingness to pay for coastal zone quality improvement. *The Journal of Socio-Economics, 41*(4), 391–399.

Javan-Noughabi, J., Kavosi, Z., Faramarzi, A., & Khammarnia, M. (2017). Identification determinant factors on willingness to pay for health services in Iran. *Health Economics Review, 7*, 40. https://doi.org/10.1186/s13561-017-0179-x.

Johannesson, M., Johansson, P., Kristrom, B., & Gerdtham, U. (1993). Willingness to pay for antihypertensive therapy—Further results. *Journal of Health Economics, 12*, 95–108.

Johannesson, M., Jonsson, B., & Borgquist, L. (1991). Willingness to pay for antihypertensive therapy—Results of a Swedish pilot study. *Journal of Health Economics, 10*, 461–474.

Johnston, R., Rolfe, J., Rosenberger, R., & Brouwer, R. (2015). *Benefit transfer of environmental and resource values: A guide for researchers and practitioners*. New York, NY: Springer.

knoema.com. (N.L.). *World atlas fact dataset, 2019: Nigeria*. Retrieved from https://knoema.com/atlas/Nigeria/topics/Health.

Lasebew, Y., Mamuye, Y., & Abdelmenan, S. (2017). Willingness to pay for the newly proposed social health insurance among health workers at St. Paul's Hospital Millennium Medical College, Addis Ababa, Ethiopia. *International Journal of Health Economics and Policy, 2*(4), 159–166. http://www.sciencepublishinggroup.com/j/hep; https://doi.org/10.11648/j.hep.20170204.13.

Lavy, V., & Germain, J. (1994). *Quality and cost in health care choice in developing countries* (LSMS Working Paper No. 105). Washington, DC: The World Bank.

Li, M .(1996). *The demand for medical care, evidence from urban areas in Boliva* (The Living Standard Measurement Study (LSMS) Working Paper No. 123). Washington, DC: The World Bank.

Mbanefoh, G. F., Soyibo, A., & Anyanwu, J. C. (1996, August 27–29). *Health care financing reforms*. Paper presented at the Training Workshop on Health Care Financing in Nigeria Issues and Options, Department of Economics, University of Ibadan.

National Bureau of Statistics. (2016). *Nigeria poverty profile report 2010*. Accessed August 14, 2018, from http://www.nigeriastat.gov.ng.

National Bureau of Statistics. (2017). *Nigerian gross domestic product report 2017*. Accessed August 14, 2018, from http://www.nigeriastat.gov.ng.

Opaluwah, A. S. (2016, December). *Health care delivery: Imperatives for change*. Vanguard Nigeria Viewpoint. Retrieved from https://www.vanguardngr.com/2016/12/health-care-delivery-imperatives-change/.

Osabohien, R., Osuagwu, E., Osabuohien, E., Ekhator-Mobayode, U., Matthew, O., & Gershon, O. (2019). Household access to agricultural credit and agricultural production in Nigeria: A PSM model. *South African Journal of Economic and Management Sciences, 22*(1), a2688. https://doi.org/10.4102/sajems.v22i1.2688.

Ryan, M., Rateliffe, J., & Tucker, J. (1997). Using willingness to pay for value alternative model of antenatal care. *Social Science and Medicine, 44*(3), 371–380.

Scott, C., & Amenuvegbe, B. (1990). *Effect of recall duration on reporting of household expenditure: An experimental study in Ghana; social dimension of adjustment in sub-Saharan Africa* (World Bank Working Paper No. 6). Washington, DC: World Bank.

Shen, J. (2012, March). Understanding the determinants of consumers' willingness to pay for eco-labeled products: An empirical analysis of the China environmental label. *Journal of Service Science and Management, 5,* 87–94. http://dx.doi.org/10.4236/jssm.2012.51011.

United Nations International Children's Emergency Fund (UNICEF). (n.d.-a). *Nigeria: Key demographic indicators.* Retrieved from https://data.unicef.org/country/nga/.

United Nations International Children's Emergency Fund (UNICEF). (n.d.-b). *Maternal and newborn health disparities: Nigeria.* Retrieved from https://data.unicef.org/wp-content/uploads/country_profiles/Nigeria/country%20profile_NGA.pdf.

Varian, H. R. (1992). *Macroeconomic analysis* (3rd ed.). New York, USA: W. W. Norton.

Wondimu, S., & Bekele, W. (2011). Determinants of individual willingness to pay for quality water supply: The case of Wonji Shoa Sugar Estate, Ethiopia. *WIT Transactions on Ecology and the Environment, 153,* 59–70.

Yoder, R. A. (1989). Are people willing and able to pay for health services? *Social Science and Medicine, 29,* 35–42.

Increasing Agricultural Income and Access to Financial Services through Mobile Technology in Africa: Evidence from Malawi

Angella Faith Montfaucon

1 Introduction

Smallholder farmers are the world's largest group of working-age poor. Nearly a billion people who work in agriculture and more than 500 million family farms produce more than 80% of the world's food (United Nations Development Programme [UNDP] 2015). Given the high number of people who depend on agriculture for their livelihoods and the vulnerable conditions many of these workers face, efforts to improve productivity and working conditions in agriculture could have considerable positive impacts on human development. Better access to finance may result in higher yields, more diverse production and fewer losses. However, institutional finance is normally available only to those with enough

---

The original version of this chapter was revised: A disclaimer note has been added. The correction to this chapter is available at https://doi.org/10.1007/978-3-030-41513-6_29

The findings, interpretations, and conclusions expressed in this chapter are those of the author(s) and do not necessarily reflect the views of the World Bank or any of my current nor former affiliations.

A. F. Montfaucon (✉)
World Bank, Washington, DC, USA

Southern African Institute for Economic Research (SAIER), Zomba, Malawi

© The Author(s) 2020, corrected publication 2020
E. S. Osabuohien (ed.), *The Palgrave Handbook of Agricultural and Rural Development in Africa*, https://doi.org/10.1007/978-3-030-41513-6_12

land or assets to use as collateral, resulting in financial exclusion of most of the rural population in most developing countries (Maitray et al. 2014). Banking sectors in developing countries lend a smaller share of their loan portfolios to agriculture compared to agriculture's share of gross domestic products (GDP). This limits investment in agriculture by both farmers and agro-enterprises.

According to the International Finance Corporation (2014), only 1% of bank lending in Africa goes to the agricultural sector vis-à-vis the sector's employment of approximately 55% of the population. Africa's agriculture sector is characterized by a high percentage of smallholder farmers cultivating low-yield staple food crops on small plots with a minimal use of inputs. Despite impressive economic growth in the last two decades, poverty reduction in Africa has remained limited and non-inclusive. As noted by Page and Shimeles (2015), the missing link between this growth and poverty reduction in Africa's is growth in agriculture. The agriculture sector is a key to achieving inclusive growth (Kanu et al. 2014). This is because it consists mostly of smallholder farmers, the majority of whom are women. The major characteristics of smallholder production systems are the following: use simple and outdated technologies, low returns, high seasonal labor fluctuations, and women playing a vital role in production. These characteristics of poor productivity of the agriculture sector in Africa have been a concern for decades as noted in the African Development Bank (AfDB) publication by Kanu et al. (2014). Improvements thereof are essential to achieve pro-poor economic opportunities. Further, small-scale agriculture is better placed to initiate growth due to demonstrated positive linkages with the non-farm sectors of an economy (Rapsomanikis 2015).

Malawi is still an agro-based economy and the sector majorly determines the pace and direction of overall economic growth. Malawi's economically active population in agriculture as of 2014 was 78.2% (African Development Bank Group; African Union Commission; United Nations 2015). In the 2010 Malawi country survey by the World Bank, respondents indicated that education (41%) and agriculture development (37%) would contribute most to poverty reduction in Malawi. In the 2013 country survey, agriculture development was top with 42% and education at 39% (The World Bank Group 2013). Increasing levels and quality of education, including enhancing skills in biotechnology to increase agricultural productivity, will be important to raising productivity in the agriculture sector.

The agricultural sector in Malawi can be categorized into estate agriculture sector and smallholder sector, with the latter accounting for 60% of agriculture GDP. Smallholder agriculture remains a vital source of livelihoods for most of the rural population (Herrmann et al. 2018). Of the smallholder farmers, 97% grow maize, and more than half of households grow no other crop (The World Bank Group 2010). Farming remains one of the most important sources of income in Malawi, with 90% of households involved in farming and 66% of them farm mainly for consumption. The sector is generally characterized by low and stagnant yields, overdependence on rain-fed agriculture thus high vulnerability to weather-related shocks, low level of irrigation development, and low uptake of improved farm inputs (Government of Malawi 2009).

Statistics from World Bank Development Indicators between 1960 and 2017 show that the trend in agriculture forestry, and fishing value added as percentage of GDP in Malawi is above both world and Sub-Saharan Africa (SSA) averages. Between 1995 and 2016, the Malawi average was 32% against 18% and 4.5% in the same period for SSA and the World, respectively. Although this ratio has been decreasing in recent years, Malawi's dependency remains relatively high. For instance, in 2002, this percentage was 39, 21, and 5% for Malawi, SSA, and the World, respectively. In 2017 however, these numbers were at 26, 16, and 4%, respectively. Although lower, agriculture still plays a more dominant role in the Malawian economy than most of the world. Given the predominance of the agricultural sector, financial services in the rural areas are therefore critical to support the productive activities. Increased access to credit can help farmers overcome short-run liquidity challenges and potentially increase adoption of more efficient and/or more effective agricultural technologies. George et al. (2011) suggest that farmers often need credit for working capital at the beginning of the growing season to purchase inputs and prepare land and capital and to invest in equipment such as tractors or drip irrigation.

Despite this being the case, access to financial services for farmers remains a challenge for several African countries. This is demonstrated in studies for Namibia (Amadhila and Ikhide 2016), Nigeria (Adekoya 2014), and Malawi (FinMark Trust 2012) to mention a few. This is mainly due to challenges in serving the rural population from the supply side, and lack of adequate financial literacy and awareness, on the demand side. Financial service suppliers in general have vast challenges serving the lower income households. These risks are however heightened when it comes specifically to smallholder farmers as they face greater exposure to droughts and floods, higher transactions costs, weak physical infrastructure, seasonality in production, land constraints, and greater price volatility. Information Communication Technology (ICT), on the other hand, has the potential to increase the availability of rural finance (European Investment Bank 2016). A report by the U.S. Agency for International Development (USAID) released in 2015 found that in Malawi the mobile phone was the most common form of ICT used by Agricultural SME owners and about half of them had a smartphone (U.S. Agency for International Development [USAID] 2015). This provides a potential access point for financial services through such services as mobile banking. Rapsomanikis (2015) for instance, observed that in Kenya, better access to credit enabled the adoption of better agricultural technologies.

Given the above backdrop, this chapter discusses and empirically analyzes the factors that determine access to loans for households in Malawi. Specifically, it addresses the question if access to a mobile phone increases the likelihood of access to credit. This is important so that ICT developments can leverage financial inclusion efforts for those in rural areas. It further investigates whether households with a mobile phone have higher agricultural income and some factors that affect mobile phone ownership as a proxy for digital financial inclusion. Similar studies have been conducted in other parts of Africa such as Ghana and Burkina Faso, where Karakara and Osabuohien

(2019) found that ownership of an ICT gadget has the probability of increasing the degree of bank patronage in both countries. Such empirical studies, however, have not yet been tackled for Malawi, and this chapter aims at filling this gap with possible policy recommendations. A more detailed review of the literature is presented later in the chapter.

The rest of the chapter is organized as follows. Section 2 describes the financial inclusion stance in Malawi and the agricultural sector and takes a brief review of the literature. Section 3 outlines the data and methodology while Sect. 4 discusses the empirical results. Section 5 concludes the study and draws some policy implications.

2 Financial Inclusion for Smallholder Farmers

2.1 State of Financial Inclusion

In Africa, formal financial services are dominated by banks most of which are foreign, with the industry being highly concentrated (European Investment Bank 2016). With this low depth in the financial sector, the lack of bank infrastructure (bank branches and ATMs) is significant, more particularly in the rural areas. Credit can be obtained for agricultural purposes from formal and informal sources. The informal type of agricultural credit refers to credit from moneylenders, friends, relatives, and the like. Whenever small farmers need emergency loans or small investment funds, they often resort to moneylenders in the absence of formal financial services (Varghese 2005).

Historically, smallholder farmers hardly had any formal access to financial credit in Malawi. A case in point is the Smallholder Agricultural Credit Administration (SACA) which operated from 1973 to 1992, under the Ministry of Agriculture. SACA channeled credit to smallholders through groups (Farmers Clubs) and achieved high recovery rates, averaging over 90%. In Malawi, formal financial institutions concentrate services in urban areas and employ traditional lending technologies based on collateral requirements which the poor often cannot afford. The FinScope survey of 2014 revealed that 46% of the population was excluded from both formal and informal financial products in Malawi. About 33% were formally banked and 7% served by other formal non-bank institutions, while a total of 14% used informal services only. Small informal financial service providers using group methodology are the most important forms of finance in rural areas (FinScope 2014).

Most of the financially excluded live at subsistence level and the biggest barrier to the uptake of financial products and services are affordability, i.e., insufficient/low/irregular income and fear of having debt or the inability to pay back borrowed money (FinScope 2014). Ngalawa (2014) records that in 2011; only 11.8% of total loans in Malawi were obtained from a bank. As of 2014 however, this amount increased to 20% (FinScope 2014). Most adult Malawians however still keep their money at home (81%), at an informal savings and credit group (14%) and at informal saving group (*chipereganyu*,

10%) (Chirwa and Mvula 2014). Financial exclusion is most prevalent and somewhat stagnant among low-income population in Malawi.

USAID (2014) found that in surveyed Agricultural SME's in Malawi, borrowing from "friends, family friends, family or colleagues" was the most common main source of loans for nearly half of those that were borrowing (42.5%). This was followed by banks (15.0%), MicroFinance Institutions (10.0%), and informal lenders, such as *Katapila* (10.0%). One of the reasons is transaction costs remain high in the country, due to low economic activity and low-traded volumes of agricultural inputs and output. Commercial banks and microfinance institutions consider lending to the agricultural sector to be a risky investment, preferring to lend to nonfarm sectors. Innovation in products and delivery channels creating value for both suppliers and farmers demanding the services is needed.

The cost of providing financial services in rural areas has been somewhat addressed by the use of electronic communications. Given the challenges faced by traditional financial services providers, ICT services present a viable solution as they offer an effective, less costly means to promote financial inclusion and literacy, since the channels lessen the need for financial services providers to erect expensive physical presence. The potential of ICT development in improving financial inclusion for smallholder farmers is discussed in the next subsection.

2.2   ICT Development: Leverage for Financial Inclusion

Digital Financial Services (DFS) offers an effective, less costly means to promote financial inclusion. ICT's can streamline production knowledge and market information flows between stakeholders in the agriculture sector, help to develop crop insurance against adverse weather shocks and crop failures; be used to get information to farmers, particularly smallholder farmers who could otherwise be out of reach and improve access to financial services through digital finance. Financial services can be accessed using a variety of electronic instruments, including mobile phones. With these, payments and transfers, as well as credit, savings, insurance, and even securities, can be offered digitally to the excluded and underserved customers (Lauer and Lyman 2014). This is because many people in developing countries, including those in rural areas, have access to mobile phones and therefore potentially to DFS. The 2016 World Development Report by the World Bank reports that nearly 70% among the poorest 20% of households, have a mobile phone (The World Bank 2016).

In Malawi, 69% of adults (6.5 million adults) have access to a mobile phone. According to the World Bank's World Development Indicators (WDI), about 34 out of 100 people in Malawi had an active mobile cellular subscription as of 2014, and the trend has been increasing since 2001. Crop production has been similarly increasing, though more volatile. A correlation

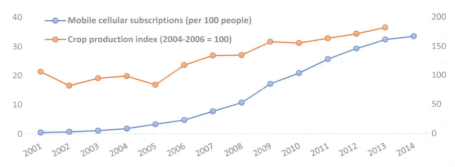

Chart 1 Mobile cellular subscription and crop production in Malawi (*Note* Left-hand axis is cellular subscriptions and right-hand axis crop production index. *Source* World Bank Development Indicators)

is seemingly evident in Chart 1. This suggests that mobile phone access has a potential to improve agricultural output and therefore agricultural income. This aspect will further be empirically investigated in Sect. 3 of the chapter.

According to the 2014 FinScope Survey, only 4% of adults in Malawi used mobile money services actively, while the 96% who did not use mobile money, reported lack of awareness of mobile money services as the main barrier. This compares unfavorably with other countries such as Kenya, Rwanda, Tanzania, and Uganda where 66% of the combined adult population use mobile money on an active basis (GSMA 2018). While in Tanzania 50% of mobile phone owners actively use mobile money systems. The most commonly used DFS payment services in Malawi are domestic money transfers, air time top-ups, and bill payments. However, the usage of mobile money payments which would facilitate financial inclusion such as person to person (P2P) and person to business (P2B) are quite low in terms of volumes, with a proportion of 6% each of total volume compared to airtime which accounts for 83% of total volume (Nkuna et al. 2018). The low adoption of P2P and P2B payments therefore limit the effectiveness of the mobile money channel to enhancing financial inclusion.

2.3 Brief Review of the Literature

There have been considerable studies on credit access in the agricultural sector for Africa. Adekoya (2014) found that farm size membership of a social organization and off farm income had positive significant influence on the amount of credit the household can secure. Awotide et al. (2015) used a tobit regression to analyze the relationship between access to credit and technical efficiency among cocoa farmers in Southwest Nigeria. The results showed that amount of credit obtained, membership of a farmers' association, amount of fertilizer used, educational status, and the amount of chemical used has significant influence on cocoa productivity.

Masawe (1994) in a study on Tanzania pointed out that agricultural credit is considered an important factor in stimulating agricultural production, particularly among smallholder farmers. Feder et al. (1990) find that difficulties in accessing credit in rural areas of developing economies unfavorably affect farm output. By removing credit constraints, the income of farmers would improve considerably. Ibrahim and Bauer (2013) mentioned that the most significant interventions provided by microfinance institutions in the support of agriculture are the supply of improved seedlings, fertilizer, and cash loans. Anang et al. (2016) explore access to agricultural microcredit in Ghana using household survey data. They found that gender, household income, farm capital, improved technology adoption, contact with extension, the location of the farm, and awareness of lending institutions in the area the influence access to agricultural microcredit in Northern Ghana. Similar findings are found by Dzadze et al. (2012).

In Malawi, several studies have substantiated the need for increased access to agricultural finance. For instance, in a study on the efficiency of smallholder agriculture in Malawi, farmers who were members of extension/market/credit-related organizations exhibited higher levels of efficiency (Tchale 2009). Another study found that credit access increased economic efficiency among potato farmers in Dedza district of Malawi (Maganga et al. 2013). A study with small farmer groundnut production identified five major production constraints including lack of finance but found that access to both savings and credit increased due to Village Savings and Loans clubs (Dalzell 2015). Access to finance is also a significant factor for households to diversify income streams from the agricultural sectors and have enterprises in other sectors. A study by Nagler and Naudé (2014) found access to credit to have an empirically significant relationship in Malawi and Ethiopia, for households to start nonfarm enterprises.

Some examples of digital financial inclusion in agriculture include a mobile technology-based insurance on purchased inputs (certified seed, fertilizer, and crop protection products) that protects farmers against bad weather shocks in Kenya. Mobile phones are used to scan the barcode of products purchased by farmers and M-PESA is used for payout at the end of the growing season in case of bad weather. Another example is *mFarmer*, an initiative to support the development of mobile agricultural value-added services (Agri VAS) in four countries: India, Kenya, Mali, and Tanzania. The Agri VAS, developed by mobile network operators, is designed to offer information on crop cultivation and market prices to farmers. These and more are well documented in the 2018 handbook on Digital Financial Services for Agriculture (SIA et al. 2018).

The literature indeed reveals the importance of credit for increased productivity in various levels of agriculture. However, the aspect of ICT has so far not been adequately addressed in the literature, especially on the impact of access to credit and agricultural income. This chapter fills that gap and brings policy focus to the same.

3 DATA AND METHODOLOGY

Data from the Malawi National Statistical Office (NSO) Integrated Household Survey (IHS) of 2010–2011 is used in the study. The data had a sample of over 12,000 households. Of those in the sample, 82% were residing in the rural areas, and 13% responded as having a loan. The dependent variable of interest takes only two values (a dichotomous variable), denoting an event or non-event and coded as 1 and 0, respectively. The model assesses the probability of either a 1 or a 0. In this case, have loan or no loan. Below are models that describe the response probabilities thus:

$$y_i \in \{0, 1\} \tag{1}$$

and have a model that gives Eq. (2):

$$\Pr(y_i = 1) \tag{2}$$

of the dependent variable y_i. In this study, $y_i = 1$ if a household has a loan, and 0 if not. The stochastic behavior of Y is described by the probability of a given response,

$$\Pr(Y = 1|X) = G(\beta_0 + \beta_1 x_1 + \ldots + \beta_k x_k) \tag{3}$$

which is here taken to depend on a vector-valued variable X, where x is full set of explanatory variables, and G is a cumulative distribution function (cdf) taking values strictly between 0 and 1.

Specifically, the logit model is where G is:

$$G(z) = \exp(z)/[1 + \exp(z)]^2 \tag{4}$$

The logit assigns higher probability values to individuals with 1 and lower probability to individuals with 0. G is a proxy for that probability. The question the model is answering is what values of regressors are associated with higher values of G and what values of regressors are associated with lower values of G.

The dependent variable question is: *Did any member of your household access a loan from any provider (formal or informal)?* The explanatory variables are as follows:

Total number of mobile phone handsets in a household: This is our variable of interest. It is the number of mobile phones in a household. We expect a positive relationship with loan acquisition.

Access to extension services: Extension officers play a critical role in ensuring that farmers stay informed. Studies such as Dzadze et al. (2012) found this to be the case and it is worth investigating for Malawi. This is expected to be positively related to credit acquisition.

Age of household head: The young are more likely to save and/or borrow more for investment while the old may not. Additionally, from the supply side, creditors may not be as willing to borrow to the very old. Thus, age can be expected to have a positive influence on credit up to a certain level.

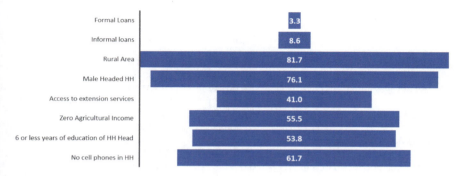

Chart 2 Percent of respondents across the variables (*Source* Author calculation from IHS)

Area of residence: This is whether respondents reside in a rural area or an urban area. It can be expected that residents of rural areas are less likely to have access to financial services.

Highest education of household head: This measures the number of years of schooling for the head of the respondent household. Some studies conducted in areas where there was higher formal education found that there was a negative relationship with credit usage due to more educated individuals having enough money and not in need of loans (Sebopetji and Belete 2009). On the other hand, more educated farmers may have more information and thus higher access to credit. Thus, the result may be ambiguous.

Other variables include household agricultural land size, household income, sex of household head, total agricultural income, and well-being self-assessment. In alternative models, we investigate formal and non-formal loans, whether having a loan affects agricultural income and some factors that determine whether a household has a mobile phone or not.

Chart 2 shows some statistics of the respondents in the survey data to be used. A total of 11.9% of respondents in the data reported to have had a loan (formal + informal [3.3 + 8.8% in Chart 2]) while nearly 62% reported to having no mobile phone in the household (Chart 2).

4 Discussion of Results

4.1 Loan Acquisition

The results reveal that a higher number of mobile phones in a household is the only variable that consistently and positively predicts that a household is likely to have a loan in general, a formal loan or an informal loan. The latter include loans from relative, neighbor, grocery store, religious grouping, or a loan shark (*katapila*). The dependent variable was taking the value zero if the respondent had zero amount of formal (informal) loan and 1 otherwise. Table 1 details all the results. The effect of the number of mobile phones is more pronounced for formal loans compared to informal loans as discussed further below.

Table 1 Marginal effects-factors affecting probability of having a loan

	Loan	Formal	Informal
Reside (1 = urban)	−0.0109	0.00617	−0.0158**
	(0.00875)	(0.00461)	(0.00711)
Household agricultural land size	−0.00149	0.00138	−0.00189
	(0.00378)	(0.00189)	(0.00308)
Highest education of HH head	0.00327***	0.00213***	−0.00000326
	(0.000834)	(0.000399)	(0.000706)
Other income (HH Total)	−2.82e-08	−1.90e-08	3.99e-09
	(2.84e-08)	(1.29e-08)	(2.53e-08)
Total # of cell phone handsets in HH	0.0278***	0.00819***	0.00862***
	(0.00333)	(0.00126)	(0.00306)
Sex of household head (1 = female)	−0.00432	0.00777*	−0.0151**
	(0.00774)	(0.00447)	(0.00593)
Well-being self-assessment	−0.00934**	0.00898***	−0.0212***
	(0.00391)	(0.00190)	(0.00338)
Age of household head	−0.00163***	0.000130	−0.00163***
	(0.000227)	(0.000115)	(0.000190)
Total agricultural income	6.86e-09	−1.10e-09	4.60e-09
	(1.79e-08)	(6.51e-09)	(1.83e-08)
Access to extension services	0.0227***	0.0131***	0.00631
	(0.00661)	(0.00362)	(0.00530)
Observations	12,364	12,364	12,364

Note Standard errors in parentheses. (***), (**), and (*) indicate 1, 5, and 10% significance level, respectively
Source Author's estimation

The higher the education of a household head, the more likely they are to have a formal loan. This can be expected since a more educated household is more likely to have information and understand the formal financial sector. A higher well-being self-assessment and access to extension services also increase the probability of having a loan. These results are consistent with those of Adekoya (2014) among others.

The households without a mobile phone have 2.5 and 8.1% probability of getting a formal and informal loan, respectively. This reveals that informal loans are more accessible. Approximately 34.1% of households had 1 or 2 phones and their probability of having a formal loan was found to be 36.6% higher for formal loans and 18.8% higher for informal loans compared to households with no phones. This evidence suggests that phone ownership can draw people from the informal financial sector. The effect of number of phones in a household remained consistent when estimated among rural and urban household separately, revealing that among somewhat similar conditions, having one or more phones in a household still improves the probability of having a loan. Notably in urban areas, the average effect of increasing phone ownership by one is 31.1 and 28.4% for rural areas.

Other factors that increase the probability of having a loan, in general, are the education of the household head, and access to extension services. On the other hand, well-being self-assessment and age of the household head predict the contrary. Interestingly, a female-headed household had a 0.6% higher probability of having a formal loan while the same had a 1.5% lower probability of getting an informal loan. The model was tested and revealed that it predicts over 50% of the data. Other factors such as income were also controlled for.

4.2 Agricultural Income

We then turned the question around, to predict from the data some of the factors that affect agricultural income, with phone ownership again being our variable of interest. The dependent variable was zero or non-zero agricultural income, and 55% of respondents had zero agricultural income at the time of the survey. The empirical results show that a household with a phone is 4% more likely to have some agricultural income than a household without. The effect of having a loan is much larger, with a household that has a loan (formal or informal) having 10.1 percentage points higher probability of a non-zero amount of agricultural income than a household without, as displayed in Table 2.

In addition, Table 3 shows that households living in the rural area, those with a larger agricultural land size and with access to extension services had a higher probability of non-zero agricultural income than their counterparts. The result on those in the rural area is mainly due to the large number of residents in the rural areas in the raw data, and consequently, those in the rural areas are involved in agricultural activities than those in the urban, and therefore more likely to have some amount of agricultural income. Thus, this result may not necessarily be a result of rural and urban areas themselves but rather the result of the sampling. Further, we observe that female-headed households are less likely to have any amount of agricultural income or a mobile phone.

4.3 Mobile Phone Ownership

Finally, we assess the factors that affect phone ownership among households in the sample. The dependent variable is mobile phone or no mobile phone, which took the value of 1 and 0, respectively, such that the number of mobile phones in the household is not considered in this case. We find

Table 2 Probability of non-zero agricultural income

	Phone?	Loan?	Urban area?	Extension services?
Yes	0.454***	0.418***	0.125***	0.535***
	(0.0088)	(0.0054)	(0.0077)	(0.0077)
No	0.419***	0.519***	0.525***	0.363***
	(0.00665)	(0.014)	(0.00526)	(0.00611)
Observations	12,364	12,364	12,364	12,364

Note Standard errors in parentheses. (***), (**), and (*) indicate 1, 5, and 10% significance level, respectively
Source Author's estimation

Table 3 Marginal effects-factors affecting agricultural income and mobile phone ownership

	Agricultural income	Mobile phone ownership
Reside (1 = urban)	−0.392***	0.299***
	(0.00985)	(0.0123)
Household agricultural land size	0.0202***	−0.00373
	(0.00493)	(0.00438)
Highest education of HH head	−0.000352	0.0377***
	(0.00115)	(0.000852)
Sex of household head (1 = female)	−0.0855***	−0.0334***
	(0.0101)	(0.00954)
Age of household head	0.000156	0.00102***
	(0.000271)	(0.000255)
Access to extension services	0.155***	
	(0.00876)	
Phone (1 = Having a phone)	0.0300***	
	(0.00990)	
Total agricultural income		0.000000793***
		(8.96e-08)
Observations	12,364	12,364

Note Standard errors in parentheses. (***), (**), and (*) indicate 1, 5, and 10% significance level, respectively
Source Author's estimation

Table 4 Probability of a household owning a mobile phone

	Urban area?	Male head of HH?
Yes	0.668***	0.378***
	(0.0126)	(0.00589)
No	0.305***	0.333***
	(0.00510)	(0.0111)
Observations	12,364	12,364

Note Standard errors in parentheses. (***), (**), and (*) indicate 1, 5, and 10% significance level, respectively
Source Author's estimation

that respondents who live in the urban area, households with a higher agricultural income and households headed by someone with higher education or a higher age, have a higher probability of owning a phone. Table 4 shows the respective probabilities for each group of respondents in each of these covariates. Living in the rural area decreases the probability by 36.3%, presumably due to infrastructure limitations in the areas that limit coverage. On the other hand, in agreement with Table 3, we calculate the numerical difference between male and female-headed households and find that female-headed households were found to have a 4.5% less probability of owning a mobile phone.

The effect of education was significantly increasing with the number of years of schooling as shown in the predictive margins in Chart 3. Those with

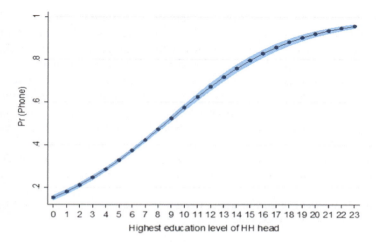

Chart 3 Effect of education of HH head on the probability of having a phone (*Source* Author's estimations)

a university education almost certainly owning a phone with a probability of 96% while those without any education had a 15% likelihood.

5   Conclusion and Policy Recommendations

The chapter provides new evidence on the factors that predict the likelihood of a household having a loan in Malawi with specific focus on developments in ICT technology proxied by mobile phone access. We further assess the effect of phone ownership on agricultural income and some barriers to mobile phone technology access.

The results of the study reveal that households with more mobile phone handsets are more likely to have a loan than household without, with a higher number of mobile phone handsets impacting the likelihood of having a formal loan more than an informal loan. Those without a mobile phone are nearly three times more likely to have an informal loan than a formal one. These observations are further confirmed as households with a mobile phone and those with a loan (formal or informal) have a higher chance of having a non-zero amount of agricultural income and finally, those who live in urban areas and households headed by someone who is more educated, are more likely to own a mobile phone.

The policy implication of these results is that improved financial inclusion for smallholder households can be achieved through the improvements in technology. The results reveal that increased mobile phone usage can lead households into the formal financial sector which is more regulated and provides customer protection more than the informal means. However, rural households have almost half the probability of having a phone than urban ones, and female-headed households as well as less educated household have a lower probability of phone ownership This gives insights to the type of households that can be targeted and the characteristics that may lead to slower update to digital financial inclusion. Thus, inclusion of these households by the telecommunication sector is paramount to improving their financial inclusiveness as well as agricultural incomes. Further, outreach policies targeted to the these households will also improve the inclusiveness of such members.

Further studies using an updated survey or panel survey can be done to track these households over time and assess whether the results still hold.

Acknowledgments The author acknowledges the assistance of Dumisani Moyo on some of the initial data processing.

References

Adekoya, O. (2014). The patterns and determinants of agricultural credit use among farm households in Oyo State, Nigeria. *Asian Economic and Financial Review, 4,* 1290–1297.

African Development Bank Group, African Union Commission, & United Nations. (2015). *African statistical yearbook 2015.* Denmark: African Development Bank Group (AfDB); African Union Commission (AUC); United Nations (UN).

Amadhila, E., & Ikhide, S. (2016). Constraints to financing agriculture in Namibia. *African Review of Economics and Finance, 8*(2), 82–112.

Anang, B., Bäckman, S., & Sipiläinen, T. (2016). Agricultural microcredit and technical efficiency: The case of smallholder rice farmers in Northern Ghana. *Journal of Agriculture and Rural Development in the Tropics and Subtropics, 117,* 189–202.

Awotide, D. O., Kehinde, A. L., & Akorede, T. O. (2015). Metafrontier analysis of access to credit and technical efficiency among smallholder cocoa farmers in Southwest Nigeria. *International Business Research, 8,* 132–144.

Dalzell, H. (2015). *The production of ready to use therapeutic food in Malawi: Contextual constraints faced by farmers and possible policy remedies.* Valid Nutrition.

Dzadze, P., Osei, M. J., Aidoo, R., & Nurah, G. K. (2012). Factors determining access to formal credit in Ghana: A case study of smallholder farmers in the Abura-Asebu Kwamankese district of central region of Ghana. *Journal of Development and Agricultural Economics, 4,* 416–423.

European Investment Bank. (2016). *Banking in sub-Saharan Africa: Recent trends and digital financial inclusion.* Kirchberg: European Investment Bank.

Feder, G., Lau, I., Lin, J., & Luo, X. (1990). The relationship between credit and productivity in Chinese agriculture: A microeconomic model of disequilibrium. *American Journal Agricultural Economics, 72,* 1151–1157.

FinMark Trust. (2012). *Status of agricultural and rural finance in Malawi.* Johannesburg: FinMark Trust.

FinScope. (2014). *FinScope consumer survey Malawi 2014.* Fin Mark Trust. Retrieved from https://finmark.org.za/finscope-consumer-survey-malawi-2014/.

George, T., Bagazonzya, H., Ballantyne, P., Belden, C., Birner, R., Castello, R., et al. (2011). *ICT in agriculture: Connecting smallholders to knowledge, networks, and institutions*. The World Bank Group. Retrieved from http://documents.worldbank.org/.

Government of Malawi. (2009). *The Agriculture Sector Wide Approach (ASWAp): Malawi's prioritized and harmonized agricultural development agenda*. Lilongwe: Ministry of Agriculture and Food Security, Republic of Malawi.

GSMA. (2018). *2017 state of the industry report on mobile money*. London: Groupe Speciale Mobile (GSM). Retrieved from www.gsma.com/mobilemoney.

Herrmann, R., Jumbe, C., Bruentrup, M., & Osabuohien, E. (2018). Competition between biofuel feedstock and food production: Empirical evidence from sugarcane outgrower settings in Malawi. *Biomass and Bioenergy, 114*(July), 100–111.

International Finance Corporation. (2014). *Access to finance for smallholder farmers*. Washington, DC: International Finance Corporation World Bank Group.

Ibrahim, A. H., & Bauer, S. (2013). Access to micro credit and its Impact on farm profit among rural farmers in dryland of Sudan. *Global Advanced Research Journal of Agricultural Science, 2*(3), 88–102.

Kanu, B. S., Salami, A. O., & Numasawa, K. (2014). *Inclusive growth: An imperative for African agriculture*. Tunis-Belvedere: African Development Bank (AfDB) Group.

Karakara, A. A., & Osabuohien, E. S. (2019). Households' ICT access and bank patronage in West Africa: Empirical insights from Burkina Faso and Ghana. *Technology in Society, 56*, 116–125.

Lauer, K., & Lyman, T. (2014). Digital financial inclusion: Implications for customers, regulators, supervisors, and standard-setting bodies. *CGAP/World Bank brief*. Retrieved from http://documents.worldbank.org/curated/en/770291468338664476/pdf/952100BRI0Box30l0Inclusion0Feb02015.pdf.

Maganga, A., Edriss, A., & Matchata, G. (2013). Economic efficiency, Allen / Uzama and Morishima elasticities of smallholder agriculture in Dedza District, Malawi. *Journal of Central European Agriculture, 14*, 604–617.

Maitray, P., Mitraz, S., Mookherjeex, D., Motta, A., & Visariak, S. (2014). *Financing smallholder agriculture: An experiment with agent-intermediated microloans in India* (HKUST IEMS Working Paper No. 2015–23).

Masawe, J. (1994). Agricultural credit as an instrument of rural development in Tanzania: A case study on the credit programme for tractorization of small-scale agriculture in Morogoro region. *African Study Monographs, 15*, 211–226.

Nagler, P., & Naudé, W. (2014). *Non-farm enterprises in rural Africa: New empirical evidence* (Policy Research Working Paper 7066). World Bank Group.

Ngalawa, H. (2014). A portrait of informal sector credit and interest rates in Malawi: Interpolated monthly time series. *African Finance Journal, 16*, 64–81.

Nkuna, O., Lapukeni, A., Kaude, P., & Kabango, G. (2018). The role of commercial banks on financial inclusion in Malawi. *Open Journal of Business and Management, 6*, 813–832.

Page, J., & Shimeles, A. (2015). Aid, employment and poverty reduction in Africa. *African Development Review, 27*, 17–30.

Rapsomanikis, G. (2015). *The economic lives of smallholder farmers: An analysis based on household data from nine countries*. Rome: Food and Agriculture Organization of the United Nations.

Sebopetji, T. O., & Belete, A. (2009). An application of probit analysis to factors affecting small-scale farmers' decision to take credit: A case study of the Greater Letaba Local Municipality in South Africa. *African Journal of Agricultural Research, 4,* 718–723.

SIA, Mastercard Foundation, & IFC. (2018). *Handbook on digital financial services for agriculture.* Strategic Impact Advisors (SIA), Mastercard Foundation and International Finance Corporation (IFC). Retrieved from www.ifc.org/financialinclusionafrica.

Tchale, H. (2009, September). The efficiency of smallholder agriculture in Malawi. *The African Journal of Agricultural and Resource Economics, African Association of Agricultural Economists, 3*(2), 1–21.

The World Bank. (2016). *World development report 2016: Digital dividends.* Washington: The World Bank Group.

The World Bank Group. (2010). *Malawi—Country economic memorandum: Seizing opportunities for growth through regional integration and trade—Summary of main finding and recommendations.* Washington, DC: The World Bank Group. Retrieved from https://openknowledge.worldbank.org/handle/10986/2954.

The World Bank Group. (2013). *Malawi country opinion survey report.* Washington, DC: The World Bank Group. Retrieved from http://hdl.handle.net/10986/19107.

U.S. Agency for International Development (USAID). (2015). *Agribusiness SMEs in Malawi: Assessment of small and medium enterprises in the agricultural sector and improved access to finance in Malawi.* Washington, DC: U.S. Agency for International Development (USAID).

United Nations Development Programme (UNDP). (2015). *Human development report 2015.* New York: United Nations Development Programme (UNDP).

Varghese, A. (2005). Bank-moneylender linkage as an alternative to bank competition in rural credit markets. *Oxford Economic Papers, 57*(2), 315–335.

Identifying the Gap Between the Demand and Supply of Agricultural Finance Among Irrigation Farmers in Namibia

Elina M. Amadhila and Sylvanus Ikhide

1 Introduction

Agricultural finance refers to finance which is used for crop and livestock production (Vitoria et al. 2012). Formal financial institutions such as commercial banks and even venture capital funds and private equities refrain from providing finance to small businesses more especially to those in the agricultural sector due to the risk involved (Coates and Hofmeister 2012), information asymmetry and lack of expertise (Amadhila and Ikhide 2016). Furthermore, lending policies are not written to fit specific target groups; for example, terms of payment, duration, and security. This has caused difficulty in the provision of finance more especially for those engaged in small-scale agriculture (Ofei 2001, cited by Samuel et al. 2012). In view of the fact that the Agricultural Bank of Namibia is the only formal institution set up with a mandate to provide finance to farmers in Namibia, the motivation for this chapter follows from this realism, in order to determine the magnitude of the agricultural SME finance gap and causes of such a gap.

E. M. Amadhila (✉)
Faculty of Economics and Management Sciences,
University of Namibia, Windhoek, Namibia

S. Ikhide
Stellenbosch University Business School, Cape Town,
South Africa
e-mail: Sylanus.Ikhide@usb.ac.za

© The Author(s) 2020
E. S. Osabuohien (ed.), *The Palgrave Handbook of Agricultural and Rural Development in Africa*, https://doi.org/10.1007/978-3-030-41513-6_13

Although past works already provide valuable information with regards the Small and Medium-Scale Enterprise (SME) finance gap in countries such as Ghana (Abor and Biekpe 2006) and South Africa (Underhill Corporate Solutions 2011), this information is very generalized (Lopez de Silanes et al. 2015) as it does not concentrate on precise sectors or concentrate only on views from the supply-side (Ramlee and Berma 2013) but not the demand side. Few studies that have concentrated on the agricultural sector are either conducted in countries outside the border of Africa such as Australia (Watson et al. 2009) or provide information on different countries in one report and numerous times this information does not include Namibia (Doran et al. 2009). This chapter goes beyond the norm in previous research in the literature, to describe and explain in more nuanced detail by making use of hard data from Agribank to estimate the finance gap quantitatively. This is combined with a qualitative approach which involves narratives from interviews (from both the demand and supply-side) that highlight and illustrate key issues to gain a profound understanding of the matter as opposed to the pure use of secondary information by similar studies in the literature (see Cressy 2002); or the use of survey questionnaires (Watson et al. 2009). It is believed that this methodology will deliver new insights for planners, policymakers, researchers, and others involved in the agricultural sector, in order to provide empirical evidence to the challenges faced in the agricultural sector.

Following this introduction, the objectives of this chapter are to estimate the magnitude of the agricultural SME finance gap; and identify reasons behind such a gap in the Namibian context.

2 Conceptualization of the Agricultural SME Finance Gap

SMEs fall between two financing arrangements namely microfinance institutions and large corporations. Microfinance institutions have emerged to serve the smallest enterprises commonly referred to as microenterprises and banking institutions emerged to serve large corporations (De la Torre et al. 2010; the International Finance Corporation [IFC] 2010). SMEs fall between these two markets and this explains the finance gap. Tschach (2002) explored the problem of credit market segmentation based on graphical analysis and noted that although there is no literature that explains why no such institutions exist which offer medium-sized loans to medium-sized enterprises at "medium" interest rates. There is an argument that SMEs are too small thus unattractive for formal sector banks, for this reason they have no access to either formal or informal-sector financing.

The Agricultural SME finance gap for farmers is referred to as the lowest three segments. The three lowest segments are semi-commercial smallholders, commercial smallholders and medium-sized farmers. All three segments have difficulty accessing formal finance especially when producing staple crops and seeking for medium and long-term financing. This paper refers to agricultural SMEs as communal, semi-commercial, commercial smallholders, and medium-sized farmers engaged in primary crop and horticultural production in communal areas in Namibia and these are the focus in this paper.

Doran et al. (2009) described the agricultural finance gap as a "missing middle" which means that loans are rarely provided in the range between where small amount of finance requested end (USD 5000) and where large amounts of finance commence (USD 500,000). This means that agricultural SMEs usually borrow funds that are lower or fall between USD 5000 and USD 500,000 and thus are referred to as the missing middle.

Data that shows specific figures of the finance gap in Africa is very little and this explains why the financial development gap is regarded as stark (Allen et al. 2012; Adeleye et al. 2018; Akinyemi et al. 2019). Access to formal credit in many African countries is restricted to larger urban centers, where collateral requirements are high (Karakara and Osabuohien 2019). Microfinance institutions have taken financial services to millions of previously un-bankable clients and failed to reach poorer rural areas and/or smallholder agricultural producers (Salami et al. 2010; Osabuohien and Karakara 2018). The efforts of the government to fund inputs for SMEs at reduced costs have led to unreliable supplies and rationing, by and large favoring large farmers (Minot 1986), and when microfinance institutions decide to finance SMEs, this comes at extortionate interest rates (Tschach 2002; Milder 2008).

3 Demand and Supply Gap Analysis: A Review

According to the Consultative Group to Assist the Poor [CGAP] (2013), there is no exact data on the demand for agricultural finance except that based on estimations. This makes the percentage of smallholders with access to finance difficult to quantify especially in African countries. For example, in Zimbabwe, the scale of demand is uncertain as there is no comprehensive data available for agricultural credit although there is evidence of a strong, but unmet, demand for credit among small-scale and medium-scale farmers. The unmet demand for credit is instigated by the limited supply of credit and its prohibitive cost. Farmers expressed no interest in applying for agricultural loans due to fear of not being able to pay back (Vitoria et al. 2012).

In Pakistan, it was found that total agricultural credit disbursements have increased from nearly Rs45 billion in the fiscal year 2000–2001 to more than Rs166 billion in 2009–2010. Despite such increase, growth in the supply of agricultural credit has fallen behind the growth in its demand (Arshad 2011). The continued shortage of institutional credit has led to increased farmer reliance on the informal credit market (Arshad 2011).

Although there are studies (as cited above) that have demonstrated that demand is more than the supply, most studies that have estimated the finance gap in microfinance literature tend to overestimate (Anand and Rosenberg 2008). The problem with overestimation is that one runs the risk of making the unrealistic assumption that every person in the identified population would have an outstanding microloan all the time. The present approaches used to determine the potential demand for microfinance take into account the population and income levels (Anand and Rosenberg 2008). This means that population-based estimates divide population by average household size, on the supposition that there will be one microloan per household, more or less (The World Bank 2006; Bruck 2006). Others decrease the overall poor population by suggesting a percentage of those who are "economically active" or "economically able" or "the working poor," and these are assumed to be potential borrowers (Ehrbeck 2006).

Anand and Rosenberg (2008) argue that the estimator of potential borrowers is too broad and needs further reductions. To think that each poor person in the identified population would require a microloan would be overambitious. Many poor people do not actually want microloans, even if they meet the requirements for them. They may not be willing to commit to the terms and conditions of the loan including the repayment plan and prefer to be financed through savings, loans from family, informal savings or they simply may have no good use for borrowed funds.

Furthermore, country-specific estimates do not begin with the poor population, but with the number of micro entrepreneurs, retrieved from survey or census data (Navajas and Tejerina 2006; Tejerina and Westley 2007). Reinke (2004) points out that the methods used to estimate finance demand have significant faults because many people who want to start SMEs do not want to be in debt. They would rather wait until they have accrued enough of their own assets before they start a business. The perceived gap in the market is therefore limited, and much smaller than the estimates (Anand and Rosenberg 2008; Hes and Polednáková 2013). People who desire and meet the requirements for loans are not necessarily borrowing all the time. For example, between 2003 and 2004, MFIs and the government of Bangladesh reported 23.8 million members, but only two-thirds were active borrowers. This raises the suspicion that demand estimates are overstated (Anand and Rosenberg 2008).

The World Bank estimates for the mid-1980s postulate that the need-versus-availability gap is worsened by the fact that only around a third of the institutional disbursements go to small and marginal farmers (De 2010). Lack of access to finance is a major bottleneck for agricultural development (Hartig et al. 2014) and financial penetration is low when it comes to agricultural finance particularly in Namibia (Amadhila and Ikhide 2016). Traditional commercial banks and other financial institutions are reluctant to finance farmers, in particular small farmers.

Given the debate surrounding the demand estimates for SME credit, it is clear that establishing the demand potential of microfinance or SME finance in the developing countries is not as forthright. There is evidence that a gap between the demand for finance and supply exist. This chapter focuses specifically on farmers who have applied for loans than the entire population of farmers to estimate the finance gap. The theory guiding this paper is therefore that of demand and supply gap analysis of finance.

4   Reasons for the Existence of the Finance Gap

The "unique nature" of agricultural businesses is often viewed as a justification by financial institutions for not willing to finance agriculture and as a result of a finance gap. This was found by the IFC's study in 2010 using literature review, as well as numerous primary interviews with SME banking experts and practitioners worldwide. It was found that agricultural SMEs face special challenges and opportunities because finance for agricultural purposes in general involves higher transaction costs due to the greater distances, lower population densities, and lower quality infrastructure encountered in serving rural areas, which discourages smaller transactions (IFC 2013).

Similarly, addressing the historical background of agricultural finance in West Africa, Doligez et al. (2010) posits that the reach of financial services for agricultural farms remains quite far limited because of the territorial dispersion of borrowers, distance from places of residence to places of business, isolation of some regions, and low population densities in many rural situations, which increase financial services transaction costs. Further problems such as the small size of the unit amount to be managed for the various transactions (deposits and loans), which are often not profitable given the unit costs of the individual records that must be borne by the financial intermediaries were also identified. More unique features such as the weakness of human capital available locally which increases the management constraints on institutions and the financial discipline often referred to as the "culture of credit," where a loan is sometimes treated as if it were a grant—or an entitlement—all explain the limited reach of financial services. In Bangladesh, The World Bank (2008) report adds weather risks as an additional challenge in serving farmers because of the uncertainty involved.

The policy review and recommendation document that intended to elaborate on the G-20 SME Finance Sub-Group using various case studies attributed that the SME finance gap exists because many SMEs in different sectors may not have the security required for conventional collateral-based bank lending, nor high enough returns to attract risk investors, while their financial requirements are too large for the type of finance that they require (International Finance Corporation 2011; Amiss 2012).

The IFC (2012) report using case study models based on background stocktaking report by Rabobank International Advisory services for IFC, that an assessment of agricultural SMEs creditworthiness is expensive for financial institutions that in most cases it surpasses the profits they can make. As the farmer grows from a smallholder to a specialized farmer, the bank must analyze all the details of the business. To cover such costs, loans must be significantly larger, reaching a size that significantly exceeds the absorption capacity for capital of the SME—hence the financing gap.

The Organization for Economic Co-operation Development (OECD) (2006) carried out a qualitative study and circulated a questionnaire to officials in all member countries as well as to many nonmembers (over 100 economies in all) to gain some perceptions into factors influencing the provision of financing to the SME sector. The aim of the paper was to analyze the SME finance gap. The report posits that many non-OECD countries report a widespread shortage in SME finance and one of the main reason is that if commercial banks have possibilities of earning higher returns by lending to other borrowers other than SMEs, they will be unwilling to develop the skills required to lend to SMEs and thus will not be very motivated to lend to SMEs. This is demonstrated in India by De (2010) drawing from past studies and previous research which posited that commercial banks failed to reach a target of 18% lending to farmers by 3.7% because other sectors such as information technology and real estate have entered the realm of priority sector lending and as a result increased the competition for institutional credit.

Abor and Biekpe (2006, p. 71) argue that "the presence of the 'finance gap' is mainly a result of the existence of information asymmetries between lenders and borrowers which should be improved. Information asymmetries refer to the disparity between the information available to businesses seeking capital and suppliers of capital who are typically assumed to be at an informational disadvantage with respect to insiders of the business." When lenders do not have enough information about the borrower and are uncertain about his ability to pay back, the lender may deny credit to such a borrower even if he is creditworthy. Within the context of information asymmetry, two issues are identified by Stiglitz and Weiss (1981). These are adverse selection and moral hazard. Under adverse selection, there is incomplete information between the buyer and the seller. As a result, lenders cannot differentiate between a high-quality business and a low-quality business and adverse selection can result. Moral hazard refers to a borrower taking advantage of a situation by taking risks that s/he will not pay for. Owners can benefit economically by, for example, redirecting borrowed funds to invest in higher risk businesses than those approved by the lenders. This means that both SMEs (borrowers) and financial institutions create the finance gap through SMEs unwillingness to share full information but also the fact that financial institutions prioritize where the high returns will come from.

5 How the Finance Gap Can Be Addressed

Addressing issues of how to reduce the finance gap, Milder (2008) examined innovative value chain finance applications that emphasizes models tailored to SMEs that fall within the rural finance gap from U.S.-based social investment fund Root Capital, which lends directly to rural grassroots in Uganda. Milder (ibid.) opined that in order to close the finance gap, commercial financial institutions have the potential to respond to the demand of various financial services through agricultural value chain financing. These financing mechanisms could be (1) shifting local lending practices where agricultural banks provide loan guarantees (Loan guarantees are when an Agricultural bank forms a relationship with a good number of local banks, and the local banks enter into a risk-sharing agreement whereby agricultural bank guarantees a portion of any losses from loans lent to farmers that pertain to the agreement) and (2) risk-sharing with local banks with the objective of attracting local banks to farmers and getting banks to accept other forms of collateral besides fixed asset collateral (see Milder 2008).

Drawing examples from many countries worldwide, Doran et al. (2009) argue that in order to shrink the financing gap, the common theme presented is to work with the private sector to remove frictions of various kinds, thus improving the balance between risk, cost, and return. A number of initiatives suggested are:

i. Non–Governmental Organizations (NGOs) with a financial focus, and a business development culture should create linkages and network in at least the early stages of the business among financial suppliers, women and men producers, buyers, and other service providers;
ii. Multilateral donors can be key sponsors of financial sector reform programs working with national governments and central banks. Reforms can focus on specific institutions such as agricultural development banks or on stimulating competition in rural finance;
iii. Innovative financing mechanisms such as warehouse receipts and leasing by donors and international financial institutions (IFIs);
iv. Struck of alliances between commercial banks and nonfinancial distribution networks: for example, of irrigation equipment or mobile phone services;
v. Socially responsible investors of various kinds either working directly or in conjunction with banks; and
vi. Foundations and socially oriented banks offering limited and temporary guarantees on a commercial basis.

Implementation of these initiatives and other efforts is required with careful examination of what's working and what's not in order to successfully reduce the finance gap.

Estimating the link between credit to SMEs and growth on income per capita and assessing the potential impact that closing the credit gap for women-owned SMEs can have on economic development, Stupnytska et al. (2014) reason that improved access to financing when complemented with business training and mentoring will bring about productive use of capital. Our view is that proper training to farmers will not only allow productive use of capital but also the sustainability of their farms in the long-run.

6 Methodology

This research is guided by the significance of the phenomena of interest. A mixed-method approach was adopted. The research was mixed in the sense that both hard data on financial outlay (SUPPLY) from the loaning organization (AGRIBANK), the volume of loans applications and desired amounts over the approved amounts for offered loans (DEMAND) were used to estimate the finance gap. In-depth semi-structured interview(s) were used to gain insights on the reasons for the finance gap. Following literature on access to finance for agriculture, on the supply-side, the study investigates the number of farmers applying and receiving loans, influences of key factors to approve a loan, and the amounts of loans granted. Similarly, on the demand-side, the study collected data from farmers to find out the number of farmers applying and receiving loans, amounts borrowed and problems experienced with receiving finance.

7 Sample and Site Selection

To identify the reasons behind the finance gap (second objective), purposive-judgment sampling was employed in choosing the participants (i.e., farmers in green-schemes and outside green-schemes and Agribank key personnel). Purposive sampling is a non-probability sampling in which respondents are chosen according to the researcher's judgments as to their suitability for the project also referred to as judgment sampling. (Sarantakos 2005). According to the Agricultural Bank of Namibia, small-scale farmers (SSF) are those who are farming in 3–6 ha and medium-scale farmers (MSF) are those who are farming with 12Ha. The farmers were selected based on these criteria as the focus of the study was on small and medium-scale farmers in crop production.

The green-scheme is an initiative conducted by the Ministry of Agriculture, Water and Forestry not only to encourage the development of irrigation based agronomic production in Namibia with the aim of increasing the contribution of agriculture to the country's Gross Domestic Product and to simultaneously achieve the social development and upliftment of communities located within suitable irrigation areas, but to also promote the human resources and skills development within the irrigation sub-sector to possibly enhance cross-border investment and facilitate the exchange of relevant and limited resources with neighboring countries. The Ministry obtains commercial farm land, develops it alone or jointly with a private investor. The land is utilized by farmers with contract agreements with the Ministry. and the commercial enterprise qualifies for incentives. Farmers in the schemes grow maize, cabbage, tomatoes, onions, butternuts, groundnuts sweet potatoes, and watermelons (Ministry of Agriculture, Water and Forestry 2008).

The following is the population list of the green-schemes (with small and medium-scale farmers) that the researcher was presented with by the Agricultural Business Development office[1] (Agribusdev) in Windhoek, Namibia.

To ensure unbiased representation of the green-schemes in terms of the location of regions in the country, one green-scheme was selected per region, i.e., Etunda, Hardap, and Ndonga-linena green-scheme projects. In addition to green-scheme farmers, independent farmers who are farming outside the green-scheme projects were also interviewed to reduce bias.[2]

On the supply-side, the study focused mainly on Agribank and the Ministry of Agriculture hard data as these are the institutions mainly responsible for financing agricultural activities in Namibia. Key personnel were also interviewed at these institutions to provide further insights.

8 Research Measures and Sample Size

Following approval by the University of Stellenbosch ethics committee and by the Agricultural Bank of Namibia, a total of 28 interviews were conducted on the demand-side to answer the qualitative question of the study which was the question of what causes of the finance gap. Depending on the availability of farmers and convenient time for the researcher and participants in various regions, 6 interviews were from Ndonga linena irrigation scheme, 6 from Hardap irrigation green-scheme and 6 from Etunda irrigation scheme. In addition, a total of 13 independent farmers from the same regions were interviewed with Oshana region added. The 13 farmers were namely: Second chance garden, Eugene farming, Path garden, S&T Veg all in Omusati region, Pozere and Gamade gardens in Kavango region, and 4 individual farmers from Oshana region. It is important to note that, of the 6 Hardap green-scheme interviews, three (medium-scale farmers) are operating inside the green-schemes but not receiving financial assistance from Agribank because either they do not want finance from Agribank or were not successful in securing finance adding to the number of independent farmers to be 13.

On the supply-side, two key informant interviews were conducted at Agribank offices. These interviews were held with the manager of lending at the Head office in Khomas region and regional manager at Oshakati branch in Oshana region. The third interview was conducted at the Ministry of Agriculture, Water and Forestry at head offices in Windhoek (capital city of

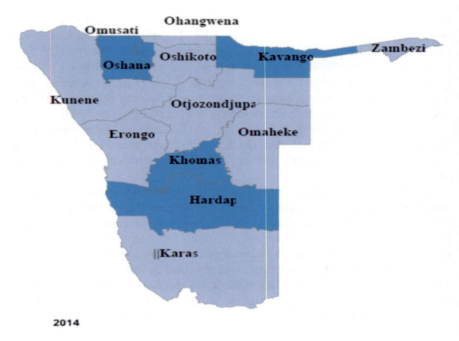

Fig. 1 Map of Namibia with regions (*Source* Authors' Construction using Stat Planet Software)

Namibia). Because Agribank is subsidized by the government, it was deemed necessary to also include the Ministry of Agriculture, Water and Forestry (MAWF). The Agricultural Business Development, an entity in charge of managing the operations of the green-schemes in the country that are financed by Agribank was also interviewed. See Map (Fig. 1) for the location of the specified regions highlighted.

9 Justification of Sample Size

The aim was to capture depth and richness rather than representativeness (see Padgett 1998, p. 50). The main reason to conduct 28 interviews was to gain an in depth-understanding followed by repetitions in the interviews. After talking to 20 people, there were repetitions in the answers provided by participants, thus reaching data saturation. Furthermore, because the population of farmers operating with valid contracts in the various green-schemes on the demand-side is small (see Table 1), a small sample size also resulted. Nevertheless, given the small population in Namibia, findings in this paper give enough evidence in the Namibian context.

Table 1 Population list of green-schemes

Green-scheme	Number of farmers (with valid contracts) in a green-scheme	Region
Etunda green-scheme irrigation project	9	Omusati region
Uvhunguhungu green-scheme irrigation project	10	Kavango region
Hardap green-scheme irrigation project	13	Hardap region
Ndonga-linena green-scheme irrigation project	28	Kavango region
Shadikongoro irrigation project	13	Kavango region

Source Agricultural Business Development Agency (AGRIBUSDEV), Northern Industry, Windhoek

10 Research Procedures

Participants were given informed consent forms to read, ask any questions linked to the study and sign the consent forms before the researcher could commence with the interview. Participants were interviewed in English. The collected data is reported in such way that the identity of individuals is not disclosed. Interviews lasted between 30 and 45 minutes each. The data was collected at the interviewee's places of work and were taped, with the agreement of the interviewees, transcribed for analysis and privacy of the participants was ensured.

11 Data Analysis Process

For the quantitative part, Agribank's hard data was used to estimate (i.e., a value of a variable outside a known range from values within a known range by assuming that the estimated value follows logically from the known values (s.n. 2016)), the number of applications received (see Table 2) using a 70%[3] approval rate. This means, the known facts in Table 2 (loans approved) data were used to determine the unknown facts (number of applications received) in order to determine the gap between demand and supply. In Table 2, the demand and supply gap is defined as the difference between the total number of applications received and the total number of applications approved between the years 2012 and 2014. For example (based on estimations) the total number of applications received for the affirmative loan action scheme were 9, 9, and 4 in 2012, 2013, and 2014 respectively while the total number of applications approved were 6, 6, and 4 in 2012, 2013, and 2014, respectively. This means that the total number of applications received were 22 (for the three-year period) while those approved were 15 which gives a difference of 7 applications not approved.

Table 2 Total loans approved, and the number of applications received between 2012 and 2014

Loan type	2012				2013				2014					
	No. of loans approved	Amounts granted (N$)	% of amount granted	Number of applications loan applications received	No. of loans approved	Amounts granted (N$)	% of amount granted	Number of applications loan applications received	No. of loans approved	Amounts granted (N$)	% of amount granted	Number of applications loan applications received	Demand and supply gap
Affirmative action loan Scheme	6	12,243,675.00	5	9	6	22,752,200	9	9	3	14,715,132	5	4	7
Commercial	112	188,671,858.60	70	160	86	92,633,501.78	36	122	176	196,563,140	65	251	159
Corporate	1	760,200		1	11	97,007,000.00	38	16	3	25,445,000	8	4	6
Close corporation									2	497,712	0	3	1
Co-operatives	3	4,014,400	1	4									1
Green-scheme (communal)	436	62,333,436.02	23	623	221	28,764,407.84	11	316	370	56,828,666.66	19	529	441
Post-settlement fund	47	3,372,950	1	67	115	14,563,792.00	6	164	79	9,504,944.90	2	113	103
Total	605	271,396,519.62	100	864	439	255,720,901.62	100	627	633	303,544,09.67	98	904	718

Source Agricultural Bank of Namibia (2012, 2013, 2014)

To obtain the finance gap in monetary terms, the average size of loans (received) multiplied by price, i.e., amount granted for each particular year determined demand (Demand refers to the total amounts/funds applied for). Using the total amounts granted by Agribank[4] (supply), we determined the difference between demand and supply to get finance gap (see Table 5 in the results section).

The total number of applications approved was divided with the percentage approval rate of 70% (see example of Formula 1) and this determined the total number of applications received annually. For example:

Formula 1: Using an approval rate of 70% to determine the total number of applications received for the year 2012 led to 864 applications received. The following formula was used:

$$\frac{605\,(\textit{total number of applications approved for the year } 2012)}{X\,(\textit{total number of applications received})} = 70\% \quad (1)$$

$$\frac{605}{0.7} = X; \therefore X \approx 864 \quad (2)$$

To estimate the total number of loan applications received for each loan type (or each type of farmer, as estimated in Formula 3), the total number of loans approved for a particular loan type was divided with the total number of all loan types approved for the year multiplied by the total number of applications received for a particular year. For example:

$$\frac{\textit{total number of applications approved for a particular loan type } (6)}{\textit{total number of all loan types approved for the year } (605)} * 864 = 9 \quad (3)$$

9 is the total number of applications received for an affirmative action loan type.

Furthermore, descriptive statistical methods using cross tabulations were also used to analyze the amounts in arrears by farmers. Guangwen (2008) also used descriptive statistics using cross tabs on a study he did on microfinance demand in China and this motivated us to do the same.

To analyze the qualitative data of the study, it is contended that if qualitative research is to bring about meaningful and useful results, it is imperative that the material to be analyzed is analyzed in a systematic manner (Attride-Stirling 2001; Pope et al. 2014). In this paper, content and thematic analyses were the main techniques for data analysis of the interviews. To support the analysis, the software ATLAS.ti was used. For a computer-assisted analysis, Friese (2014) suggests the use of the NCT approach - Noticing things, Collecting things and Thinking about things (see Fig. 2).

Noticing things refers to the process of discovering information related to the question asked when reading through transcripts, field notes, etc. After data collection, interviews were transcribed, read through, cleaned, and uploaded into the ATLAS.ti software.

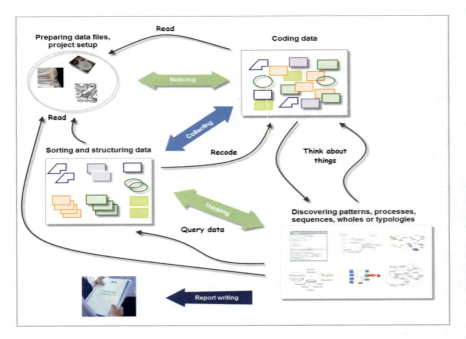

Fig. 2 The NCT model approach of computer-assisted analysis (*Source* Friese 2014, p. 15)

Collecting things refers to the process of specifying information you have discovered and grouping those that belong together or have the same name. This is referred to as coding. Codes relevant to the research question such as *high demand, low supply, loan default, poor repayment* were created. Coding refers to categorizing and combing the data for themes, ideas, and categories and then marking similar passages of text with a code label (Cooper and Schindler 2011). Code families were established (i.e., causes of the finance gap) and data were systematically scrutinized to see ways in which families were portrayed. This study employed an open coding with an inductive framework approach.

Thinking about things refers to the ability to reflect about things that you have noticed and collected in order to find patterns and associations in the data. The categories were developed through repetitive review of the data. During this process subcategories or new categories of themes were identified and analysis continued until no new categories emerged. The research question memo related to the research question was created and linked to the various types of codes identified in the data in order to add transparency to the analysis.

The benefits of using the NCT method analysis enable an analyst to work in a methodical manner (Friese 2014, pp. 13–14). The main aim is to put all the findings together and gain a coherent understanding of the phenomenon.

12   Limitations of the Study

It is important to note some of the limitations of this study. First, given the highly dispersed country that Namibia is, this study was conducted with limited resources among a small purpose judgment sampling method, which limits the ability to generalize to all participants in the broader population on the demand-side. Second, the data on applications received was not available at the time therefore the method of extrapolation was used to come up with these figures. Thirdly, because the percentage approval rate is not disaggregated for different types of loans, the paper used the 70% average approval rate over the three-year period across all loan types to estimate the number of applications received. These limitations may have created weak features of this paper.

13   Criteria for Judging the Quality of the Research

According to Yin (2009, p. 40), there are criteria to consider in judging the quality of the research. These are: construct validity, internal validity, external validity, and reliability. For this study, quality was ensured by doing the following:

For construct validity, multiple sources of evidence, i.e., interviews and document analysis were used. The secondary data documents provided the necessary information to make cross-references for the inferences.

For external validity, results in this study may only be generalized to relevant theory that was used in carrying out the study and not to the population.

The reliability of data for this study is solely attributed to the answers given by the interviewees. A mechanical recording device was used with permission. Procedure on how this study was carried out has been documented to allow collection and analysis by another researcher.

Internal validity is about establishing causal relationships. Because this study did not measure any relationships internal validity is therefore not suitable for this type of study.

14   Results

14.1   Brief Background and Characteristics of Agribank

Agricultural Bank of Namibia (Agribank) started operations in 1907. It is a state-owned institution which provides loans for agricultural and fisheries-related economic activities ranging from small, medium to large scale farmers.

When Agribank processes a credit application from a customer, the following minimum information is needed (Agribank annual report, 2014):

- Comprehensive identity of the borrower;
- Evidence of the borrower's legal ability to borrow;

- Ability to repay including the timing and source of repayment and evidence of verification thereof;
- Description of the terms of credit obligation;
- Assessment of major risks and key litigants;
- Credit checks;
- Overview of the facility and collateral; and
- Documentary evidence of review and approval process.

The government provides collateral and subsidized loans (through Agribank) for small-scale farmers employed in the green-schemes. These farmers (many of who practice subsistence farming), first go through agricultural training (including but not limited to seed production and crop production) for one year. Once employed in the green-scheme, the financial management of the farms is managed by a service provider appointed by the government who handles the financials on behalf of farmers after they are employed in the green-schemes meaning that farmers don't deal directly with the loans although these Agribank loans are their obligations. This is consistent with results found by Koranteng (2010) on financing smallholder farmers in South Africa: the case of the IDC-KAT river citrus development scheme. Koranteng (2010) found that farmers employed at the Industrial Development Corporation (IDC) development scheme receive finance from IDC but it is controlled by Riverside Company who acts as a service provider. Medium-scale farmers on the other hand are expected to provide their own collateral if they intend to borrow money from the bank.

15 Characteristics of Borrowers Interviewed and Loan Access Distribution

Farmers in the green-schemes have signed renewable lease agreements for five years with the ministry and many (from interviews conducted) are between the ages of 24–55. All farmers interviewed have employed only up to a maximum of 5 people but only on a temporary basis because of the nature of the work that it is seasonal and the sizes of the plots are not big enough to allow one to be assisted by a lot of people. In addition, more males have access to loans than females and most farmers are small-scale farmers than medium-scale farmers. Table 3 shows the loan access distribution among farmers interviewed.

From Table 3, there is a clear indication that small-scale farmers in contract farming projects have access to loans (because of collateral by the government) than medium-scale and independent farmers. One independent farmer narrated as follows: *as independent farmers we are producing in high quantity compared to green-scheme farmers but then green-scheme farmers for example those from Etunda can just go to Agribank and say I need to buy seeds, fertilizers, and then a voucher is written so that the farmer can go and buy without any questions asked unlike us (P41, 67:67).* Those who borrow were also asked

Table 3 Loan access distribution

Do you have a loan?	Gender		Type of farmer		Green-scheme or independent	
	Male	Female	Small	Medium	Green-scheme	Independent
Yes	11 (59%)	4 (50%)	16 (79%)	0	15 (83%)	1 (10%)
No	9 (41%)	4 (50%)	6 (21%)	6 (100%)	3 (17%)	9 (90%)
Total	20	8	22	6	18	10

Source Author's data

Table 4 Range of amounts borrowed by farmers interviewed

ID	The amounts of loan received
VF	U$ 3411.18
DC	a
ES	U$ 9575.25
GE	U$ 5984.53
GH	
JS	
BY	U$ 9575.25
CN	U$ 2693.04
GP	
LN	N$ 9575.25
PH	
ZX	U$ 4488.40
MS	U$ 3590.72
OU	U$ 3411.18
PT	U$ 4787.63
KK	
AA	
PM	
SH	
TH	
EE	
AM	U$12,268.29
PN	
KK	U$11,969.06
LS	U$ 3590.72
SP	U$ 4189.17

[a]Blank rows in Table 3 mean the participant did not apply for a loan
Source Authors' data

the amounts that they borrow for agricultural farming purposes. The results are depicted in Table 4.

From Table 4, it is confirmed that indeed agricultural SMEs usually borrow funds that are lower or fall between USD 5000 and USD 500,000 and thus are referred to as the missing middle (Doran et al. 2009). About 80% of farmers indicated that the sources of their funds were from Agribank

Table 5 Gap between demand and supply among green-scheme communal farmers in Namibia

Year	2012	2013	2014	Overall
Number of loan applications received (estimate)	623	316	529	1468
No. of loans approved	436	221	370	1027
Amounts granted (N$)	62,333,436	28 764 407.84	56,828,666.66	147,926,511
% of total amount granted	23	11	19	18
Amount applied for (estimate)	89,068,189.54	41,129,198.54	81,249,634.22	211,447,022
Finance gap (estimate)	26,734,754	12,364,790.70	24,420,967.56	63,520,512

Source Agricultural Bank of Namibia (2012, 2013, 2014) and estimations by the author

16 FINANCE GAP

Using data in the 8th row (green-scheme communal farmers in Table 2) to determine the magnitude of the finance gap in monetary terms for a three-year period between the years 2012 and 2014, there is a clear mismatch between demand and supply (see Table 5). The estimated agricultural finance gap stands at the value of N$ 63 520 512. However, the finance gap has fluctuated falling significantly between 2012 and 2013 and rising again between 2013 and 2014 from N$ 12,364,790 to 24,420,967.56. This means that applicants did not get the amounts they requested because demand was always more than the supply between the three year period.

Similarly in terms of the number of applications, as shown in Table 2, for a three-year period from 2012 to 2014, there is a clear mismatch between demand and supply. The total number of applications received resulted in 2395 applications and number of applications approved was 1677 pointing to a financial gap of 718 unserved farmers (see Table 2). This gap however varies within different loan categories for different types of farmers because the financial performance of Agribank between 2012 and 2014 shows that there is bias toward funding of commercial farmers (who are mainly large and have title to land). Although more communal farmers (appearing under loan type of green-scheme in Table 1) demand more loans (1468 of the total number of applications received for the three-year period) than commercial farmers (533 of the total number of applications received for the three-year period) commercial farmers still get the largest portion of finance (amounts granted column) pointing to a constraint in lending to communal farmers despite a high demand from communal farmers. The gap is therefore larger for small and medium-scale farmers in communal areas (green-scheme loan type) (1468 total number of applications received – 1027 total number of loans approved = 441 unserved farmers) than commercial farmers (533 total number of applications received − 374 total number of loans approved = 159).

16.1 Causes of the Finance Gap

16.1.1 Views from the Supply-Side

Interviews with the xxx at Agribank note the following on why the gap is larger for communal farmers than commercial farmers. He narrated as follows: '*We are saying finance is there, but they don't have the conventional collateral*'[5] (P18, 49:49).[6] This indicates that collateral poses a challenge to agricultural SMEs especially medium-scale farmers who are expected to provide their own collateral. Seibel et al. (2005) dubbed availability but inaccessibility of finance as a lack of qualified demand and Jessop et al. (2012) dubbed it as a lack of viable demand.

Apart from the issue of collateral, Agribank is also reluctant to provide funding because of the difficulty in recovering loans

The manager of xxx at Agribank head office noted: "*The recovery problem is generally a problem especially with the Development Finance Institutions (DFIs) and when the people have got the perception that it is government money so it's always a bit of problem*" (P17, 73:73). This supports previous literature by Singh and Sagar 2004 (as cited in De 2010) who posit that a notion has settled among many rural borrowers that loans taken by them are government support and hence, needn't be repaid.

Figure 3 supports the fact that there is a problem of loan recovery. Amounts in arrears have been on the increase between the years 2012 and 2014 from N$ 224 million reaching 387 million.

Dishonesty among medium-scale farmers toward Agribank is argued to be another issue widening the gap between demand and supply where beautiful business plans are drawn up with promises of qualification in agriculture but when farmers are given funds, the job on the ground does not match the promises on paper. Here the importance of quality of training offered to farmers become important before starting any agricultural work.

16.1.2 Views from the Demand-Side

On the demand-side, two different categories of farmers were recognized.

1. Those who borrow
2. Those who do not borrow.

Both categories share the sentiments that demand mismatches supply because of a lack of requirements that banks are looking for this low-distribution of funds and because of a lack of financial institutions in the country. Two farmers narrated the following:

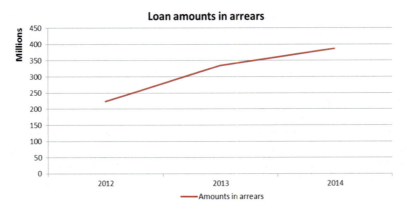

Fig. 3 Loan amounts in arrears (*Source* Agricultural Bank of Namibia 2012, 2013, 2014)

> Money is available but if one does not have the requirements e.g., collateral that the banks are looking for, it becomes a problem to get access to funds. (P35, 57:57)

> I think demand is more than supply because is there any other institution that gives funds to *farmers apart from Agribank?* (P38, 72:72)

For farmers who choose not to borrow, many of whom are operating outside the green-scheme projects, argue that they do not have information on the financing schemes available at Agribank and that is why they do not borrow. This reason was given more than any other. Farmers from Omusati and Hardap regions note the following, respectively:

> I think there is a lack of information on the side of the *farmers on where to get funding that is why they struggle to get funding.* (P15, 107:107)

> Rumours from the community for example from SME funds are spread but because no formal institution is giving awareness so trust is minimal. Information is not very clear about agricultural funds. (P2, 88:88)

Other independent farmers feel they do not need the funds to do their agricultural activities and that is why they do not borrow.

I don't need the funds. It is not like it is expensive to farm, so I do not really need funds from financiers (P1, 67; 67). This is consistent with results found in Ecuador, Guatemala, Nicaragua, Panama, and the Dominican Republic cited in Anand and Rosenberg (2008). They found that 42% of people (among their respondents) who did not apply for loans did not do so because they do not need the loans.

For those who borrow, they are given lower amounts than what they applied for. This means that the government seems to have predetermined amounts on what farmers (employed in green-schemes) should receive and so it is not really up to the applicants to decide on the amounts they should receive.

The amount which I applied for was three hundred and fifty thousand and the one I got was one sixty-one thousand (P9, 159:159).

Another participant noted:

We give our business plans and then Agribank goes with it with our cropping programmes to the extension officer's office, Agribank looks at it and come up with a decision on how much money to give us. (P13, 91:91)

On the issue of loan default as claimed by Agribank, farmers feel the reason for their default on loans (as argued by lenders) is caused by insufficient capital provided by the bank, higher cost of inputs and low selling price. The following quote summarizes:

The requirements are fine, it's just that the loan amount itself is not enough because for anyone to put up collateral at the bank they usually put up a collateral equal to the value of the amount of money they are requesting so when the government decide to put a collateral, we don't get enough money because the value of the collateral is small. It makes it difficult because the costs of inputs nowadays are very high especially considering the fact that most of the inputs such as fertilizers and chemicals are coming from South Africa now you have to buy this product on higher costs and when it comes to the selling price, the selling price is too low because which leads us not to pay back the money from Agribank. (P11, 104:104)

This quote supports the results in Table 2 because although communal farmers who are mainly made up by green-scheme farmers have the highest number of loans approved as compared to commercial farmers, yet they are still granted the lowest amounts than commercial farmers.

According to Riedl (2007), low selling price is caused by overproduction and markets influence on price which leads farmers to reduce their prices in order to sell most of their production.

17 How Can the Finance Gap Be Reduced?

The aim of this paper was to determine the gap between the demand and supply of finance resources and reasons behind this gap. Results confirm that there is a mismatch between demand and supply because of an undersupply of loans. The results are similar to one saying the approval rate (supply) is lower as compared to the number of applications received (demand). The mismatch caused by a lack of qualified demand explains why in spite of the government's support mechanisms' effort, certain segments of the economy continue to lament the lack of access to finance (Amadhila and Ikhide 2016). Constraints to finance are more prevalent among communal farmers as compared to commercial farmers and this suggests an underlying problem of having a fixed asset (such as land) to serve as collateral. Commercial farmers in Namibia are generally differentiated from communal farmers on the basis that the former have title to the land as compared to the latter. This explains why the high amounts of funds reported are disbursed to commercial farmers as compared to communal farmers. Alternative forms of collateral such as group lending and innovative financing mechanisms such as warehouse receipts should be introduced. Alternative forms of collateral could solve the problem of loan default as there will be social pressure for example from other parties in the group to pay back loans (Tschach 2002).

For farmers in communal areas (outside the green-schemes) who do not borrow the problem is not that lending institutions are reluctant to lend them or that there is a gap in funding but rather a lack of information on the availability of financial services. This lack of information on the availability of finance for farmers in the country is pointing also to an indication that the financial gap may be higher than reported in this paper (Karlan 2016).

The loan recovery/low repayment rate problem among contract farmers was mentioned as another cause of the finance gap. This is because borrowers have the perception that is government money and therefore treat loans as grants resulting in non-repayment. Doligez et al. (2010) refer to non-repayment as "culture of credit" making it further difficult for many farmers to get access to finance. This attitude needs constant training for farmers which concentrates on the difference between loans and grants, and the importance of paying back the loans. The low repayment of loans can also compromise the financial position of lending institutions which consequently can have negative impact on the economic performance of the country. Jessop et al. (2012) found that in Tunisia, subsidized credit often fails to consider repayment capacity and this has proven to be true as well in Namibia. In this paper, there is evidence that farmers are rather not willing to pay the back their loans because of subsidized credit. In distinguishing between the role of ability and willingness to pay, Tschach (2002), discuss that ability to pay is influenced by asymmetric information while the willingness to pay is influenced by intrinsic and extrinsic factors. Intrinsic factors are those factors such as attitudes, personal relationships, and ethical considerations that the borrower takes into account in order to come to a decision to pay back their loans. This also includes consideration of the environment in the sense that borrowers are noted by other persons in their social environment and if they fail to pay they must expect social sanctions from society for behavior which does not follow the rules and regulations. Extrinsic factors, on the other hand, are those economic factors that are advantageous to the borrower such as losing his house if he fails to repay the loan. Asymmetric information (which influences ability to pay) leads to a situation where banks raise interest rates above a certain level. Stiglitz and Weiss (1981)argue that when lending interest rates go up, low-risk borrowers do not borrow while risky borrowers continue to borrow and implement their project despite an increase in interest rates. The bank usually bears part of the risk which is reflected in their returns.

Though farmers attribute the loan default problem to factors such as insufficient capital, higher cost of input and low selling price, perhaps in addition to credit extension, agricultural support should put more emphasis on other ways to provide support to farmers such as provision of inputs or machinery for production and savings facilities because one would ask how much money is really "sufficient" to allow purchase of inputs and still be able to repay the loan? Even countries such as Indonesia that have done better in their agricultural sectors, subsidy programs have always provided limited quantities of subsidized credit so that not all farmers had access to this credit, and most farmers who had access could still not obtain all the financing they wished to obtain with subsidy. Instead, there was improved provision of formal sector credit through Bank Rakyat Indonesia (BRI) (Cervantes-Godoy and Dewbre 2010). The sole focus on subsidized emphasis on credit could therefore be doing more harm not only to farmers but also to lenders because of loan default.

Even if the finance gap is larger for communal farmers (where the majority of small and medium-scale farmers are based) as compared to commercial farmers (where large farmers are based), the lack of access to finance is even more pronounced for medium-scale farmers, as they have to borrow on their own without much government support in collateral provisions. Agribank indicates that for many of these medium-scale farmers, access to finance is there but lack of conventional collateral makes it difficult to provide loans to them. The high price of land (Shinovene 2015) in the country could be reduced in order to make land affordable and be used as collateral ultimately promoting agricultural businesses.

Finally, access to information is important were Agribank could implement aggressive marketing to allow farmers in rural communities especially those working outside the green-scheme projects to be aware of the financing schemes available at Agribank. This may allow them to apply for financial assistance and also promote prosperous agricultural activities.

This study has implications for crafting and developing financial services structures that positively contribute to access of finance in agriculture specifically the prosperity of agriculture for smallholder farmers and their access to information.

Acknowledgements The chapter draws insights from the corresponding author's unpublished thesis submitted to the University of Stellenbosch. The helpful comments from the reviewers' that have helped to improve the earlier drafts of the work are also appreciated.

NOTES

1. The ministry has appointed the Agricultural Business Development Agency (AGRIBUSDEV) to oversee the implementation of the green-schemes and achieve the green-scheme policy objectives.
2. The independent farmers were identified by way of snowball sampling.
3. 70% approval rate was information obtained from Agribank's lending department.
4. The loans granted were secondary data obtained from Agribank.
5. Only small-scale farmers are provided collateral by government and not medium-scale farmers.
6. The numbers at the end of the quotes represent the primary document numbers and paragraph numbers in ATLAS.ti. For example 18, 49:49 means that the quote is from primary document 18, starting and ending in paragraph 49.

REFERENCES

Abor, J., & Biekpe, N. (2006). Small business financing initiatives in Ghana. *Problems and Perspectives in Management, 4*(3), 69–77.

Adeleye, N., Osabuohien, E., Bowale, E., Matthew, O., & Oduntan, E. (2018). Financial reforms and credit growth in Nigeria: Empirical insights from ARDL and ECM techniques. *International Review of Applied Economics, 32*(6), 807–820.

Agricultural Bank of Namibia. (2012). *Agribank annual report 2012*.

Agricultural Bank of Namibia. (2013). *Agribank annual report 2013*.

Agricultural Bank of Namibia. (2014). *Agribank annual report 2014*.

Akinyemi, O., Efobi, U., Asongu, S., & Osabuohien, E. (2019). Renewable energy, trade performance and the conditional role of finance and institutional capacity in sub-Sahara African Countries. *Energy Policy, 132*, 490–498.

Allen, F., Carletti, E., Cull, R., Qian, J., Senbert, L., & Valenzuela, P. (2012). *Resolving the African financial development gap: Cross country comparisons and a within-country study of Kenya* (No. 18 013). Retrieved from http://www.nber.org/papers/w18013.

Amadhila, E., & Ikhide, S. (2016). Unfulfilled loan demand among agro SMEs in Namibia. *South African Journal of Economics and Management Sciences, 19*(2), 282–301.

Amiss, B. Y. N. (2012). *Financing of small and medium enterprises (SME's) in Namibia through an investigation of the existence of an "SME financing gap": The case of Bank Windhoek Limited*. Maastricht School of Management.

Anand, M., & Rosenberg, R. (2008). *Are we overestimating demand for microloans?* CGAP Brief. Retrieved from https://www.cgap.org/sites/default/files/CGAP-Brief-Are-We-Overestimating-Demand-for-Microloans-Apr-2008.pdf.

Arshad, J. (2011). *Agricultural credit falling short of demand*. Retrieved October 15, 2015, from The Express Tribune with the International New York Times website http://tribune.com.pk/story/226427/agricultural-credit-falling-short-of-demand/.

Attride-Stirling, J. (2001). Thematic networks: An analytic tool for qualitative research. *Qualitative Research, 1*(3), 385–405. https://doi.org/10.1177/146879410100100307.

Bruck, C. (2006). Millions for millions. *The New York*. Retrieved from http://www.newyorker.com/magazine/2006/10/30/millions-for-millions.

Cervantes-Godoy, D., & Dewbre, J. (2010). *Economic importance of agriculture for sustainable development and poverty reduction: Findings from a case study of Indonesia*. Retrieved from http://www.oecd.org/agriculture/agricultural-policies/46341215.pdf.

Coates, M., & Hofmeister, R. (2012). Financing agriculture: Selected approaches for the engagement of commercial Finance. In T. Beck & S. M. Maimbo (Eds.), *Financial sector development in Africa: Opportunities and challenges* (pp. 83–108). Retrieved from http://dx.doi.org/10.1596/9780821396285_CH03.

Consultative Group to Assist the Poor. (2013). *Advancing financial inclusion to improve the lives of the poor* (Annual Report). Washington, DC. CGAP. License: Creative Commons Attribution CC BY 3.0.

Cooper, D. R., & Schindler, P. S. (2011). *Business research methods* (3rd ed.; N. Jacobs, K. Harlow, & J. Bishop, Eds.). Berkshire: Mc Graw-Hill Education.

Cressy, R. (2002). Funding gaps: A symposium. *The Economic Journal, 112*(477), F1–F16.

De, S. (2010). Agricultural credit in India. *Economic and Political Weekly*. Retrieved from https://www.academia.edu/915389/Agricultural_Credit_in_India_An_Overview.

De la Torre, A., Martínez Pería, M. S., & Schmukler, S. L. (2010). Bank involvement with SMEs: Beyond relationship lending. *Journal of Banking and Finance, 34*(9), 2280–2293.

Doligez, F., Lemelle, J., Lapenu, C., & Wampfler, B. (2010). Financing agricultural and rural transitions. *Challenges for African Agriculture*, 179. Retrieved from http://elibrary.worldbank.org/doi/pdf/10.1596/978-0-8213-8481-6#page=205.

Doran, A., McFadyen, N., & Vogel, R. (2009). *The missing middle in agricultural Finance*. Retrieved from http://scholar.google.com/scholar?hl=en&btnG=\ Search&q=intitle:The+Missing+Middle+in+Agricultural+Finance#3.

Ehrbeck, T. (2006, October). Optimizing capital supply in support of microfinance industry growth (*Working paper*). Washington, DC: Microfinance Investor Roundtable.

Friese, S. (2014). *Qualitative data analysis with Atlas.ti* (2nd ed.; K. Metzler, Ed.). Washington, DC: SAGE.

Guangwen, H. (2008). *An analysis of microfinance demand in China*. World Microfinance Forum Geneva. Retrieved from https://www.microfinancegateway.org/sites/default/files/mfg-en-paper-an-analysis-of-microfinance-demand-in-china-feb-2008_0.pdf.

Hartig, P., Jainzik, M., & Pfeiffer, K. (2014). The potential of structured finance to foster agricultural lending in developing countries. In *Finance for food: Towards new agricultural and rural finance* (pp. 1–295). https://doi.org/10.1007/978-3-642-54034-9.

Hes, T., & Polednáková, A. (2013). Correction of the claim for microfinance market of 1.5 billion clients. *International Letters of Social and Humanistic Sciences, 2*(2013), 18–31. https://doi.org/10.18052/www.scipress.com/ILSHS.2.18.

International Finance Corporation. (2010). *The SME banking knowledge guide*. Retrieved from http://www.ifc.org/wps/wcm/connect/b4f9be0049585ff9a192b519583b6d16/SMEE.pdf?MOD=AJPERES.

International Finance Corporation. (2011). *Scaling up access to finance for agricultural SMEs policy review and recommendations*. Retrieved from http://www.ifc.org/

wps/wcm/connect/04da89804a02e2e19ce0fdd1a5d13d27/G20_Agrifinance_Report.pdf?MOD=AJPERES.

International Finance Corporation. (2012). *Innovative agricultural SME finance models*. Retrieved from http://www.ifc.org/wps/wcm/connect/55301b804eb-c5f379f86bf45b400a808/Innovative+Agricultural+SME+Finance+Models.pdf?MOD=AJPERES.

International Finance Corporation. (2013). *Small and medium enterprises finance: New findings, trends and G-20/Global partnership for financial inclusion progress*. Retrieved from http://www.gpfi.org/sites/default/files/documents/SMEFinanceNewFindings,TrendsandG20GPFIProgress.pdf.

Jessop, R., Boubacar, D., Marjan, D., Abdallah, M., Job, H., & van Bert, M. (2012). *Creating access to agricultural finance creating access: Based on a horizontal study of Cambodia, Mali, Senegal, Tanzania, Thailand and Tunisia*. Retrieved from http://www.reherche/afd.fr.

Karlan, D. (2016). *Finance for the poor: How can financial services work better for low-income consumers?* International Banker 2019.

Karakara, A. A., & Osabuohien, E. (2019). Households' ICT access and bank Patronage in West Africa: Empirical insights from Burkina Faso and Ghana. *Technology in Society, 56*, 116–125.

Koranteng, K. Y. (2010). *Contract farming model of financing smallholder farmers in South Africa: The case of the IDC-KAT river citrus development scheme*. Stellenbosch University.

Lopez de Silanes, F., McCahery, J., Schoenmaker, D., & Stanišić, D. (2015). *Estimating the financing gap of small and medium-sized enterprises*. Retrieved from http://www.voxeu.org/article/estimating-financing-gap-small-and-medium-sized-enterprises.

Milder, B. (2008). Closing the gap: Reaching the missing middle and rural poor through value chain finance. *Enterprise Development and Microfinance, 19*, 301–316. https://doi.org/10.3362/1755-1986.2008.027.

Ministry of Agriculture, Water and Forestry. (2008). *Green scheme policy*. Windhoek: Ministry of Agriculture, Water and Forestry.

Minot, N. W. (1986). *Contract farming and its effect on small farmers in less developed countries, East Lansing*. Retrieved from http://ideas.repec.org/p/ags/midiwp/54740.html.

Navajas, S., & Tejerina, L. (2006, November). *Microfinance in Latin American and the Caribbean: How big Is the Market?* Washington, DC: Inter-American Development Bank.

Osabuohien, E., & Karakara, A. A. (2018). ICT usage, mobile money and financial access of women in Ghana. *Africagrowth Agenda Journal, 15*(1), 14–18.

Organization for Economic Co-operation Development (OECD). (2006). The SME financing gap: Theory and evidence. *Financial Market Trends, 2006*(2), 89–97. https://doi.org/10.1787/fmt-v2006-art11-en.

Padgett, D. K. (1998). *Qualitative methods in social work research: Challenges and rewards* (J. Nageotte & F. Lyons, Eds.). Thousand Oaks: Sage.

Pope, C., Ziebland, S., & Mays, N. (2014). Qualitative research in health care: Analysing qualitative data. *British Medical Journal, 320*(7227), 114–116.

Ramlee, S., & Berma, B. (2013). Financing gap in Malaysian small-medium enterprises: A supply-side perspective. *SAJEMS Special Issue, 16*(16), 115–126.

Reinke, J. (2004). *Demand studies and how not to do them: A story about pancakes (with lessons from microfinance)* (Vol. 2004). Retrieved from http://www.ruralfinanceandinvestment.org/sites/default/files/Demand__studies_pdf.pdf.

Riedl, B. M. (2007). How farm subsidies harm taxpayers, consumers, and farmers, too. Retrieved October 29, 2015, from The Heritage Foundation website http://www.heritage.org/research/reports/2007/06/how-farm-subsidies-harm-taxpayers-consumers-and-farmers-too.

Salami, A., Kamara, A. B., & Brixiova, Z. (2010). Smallholder agriculture in East Africa: Trends, constraints and opportunities (*Working Paper No. 105*). African Development Bank Group.

Samuel, Y., Ernest, K., & Awuah, J. B. (2012). What are small enterprises finance needs? *European Journal of Business and Management [Online], 4*(17), 196–207.

Sarantakos, S. (2005). *Social research* (3rd ed.). New York: Palgrave Macmillan.

Seibel, H. D., Giehler, T., & Karduck, S. (2005). *Reforming agricultural development banks reforming agricultural development banks*. Retrieved from http://www.gtz.de.

Shinovene, I. (2015). Namibia's house prices spark land grab fears. *Mail & Guardian*. Retrieved from https://mg.co.za/article/2015-02-19-namibias-house-prices-spark-land-grab-fears/.

Stiglitz, B. J. E., & Weiss, A. (1981). Credit rationing in markets with imperfect information. *American Economic Review, 71*(3), 393–410.

Stupnytska, A., Koch, K., MacBeath, A., Lawson, S., & Matsui, K. (2014). *Giving credit where it is due how closing the credit gap for women-owned SMEs can drive global growth* (Vol. 81). Retrieved from http://www.goldmansachs.com/our-thinking/public-policy/gmi-folder/gmi-report-pdf.pdf.

Tejerina, L., & Westley, G. D. (2007). *Financial services for the poor household survey sources and gaps in borrowing and saving*. Washington, DC: Inter-American Development Bank. Retrieved from https://www.researchgate.net/publication/254422665_Financial_Services_for_the_Poor_Household_Survey_Sources_and_Gaps_in_Borrowing_and_Saving/citations.

Tschach, I. (2002). *The theory of development finance: How microcredit programmes alleviate credit and labour market segmentation*. Lang. ISBN: 3631392036, 9783631392034.

Underhill Corporate Solutions. (2011). *Literature review on small and medium enterprises' access to credit and support in South Africa*. Retrieved from www.underhillsolutions.co.za.

Vitoria, B., Mudimu, G., & Moyo, T. (2012). Status of agricultural and rural finance in Zimbabwe. In *FinMark Trust*. Retrieved from http://www.finmark.org.za/wp-content/uploads/pubs/Rep_Status_of_RAFin_Zim2.pdf.

Watson, J., Newby, R., & Mahuka, A. (2009). Gender and the SME "finance gap". *International Journal of Gender and Entrepreneurship, 1*(1), 42–56.

World Bank. (2006). *Microfinance in South Asia: Toward financial inclusion for the poor*. Retrieved from http://sitesources.worldbank.org/SOUTHASIAEXT/Resources/Publications/448813-1184080348719/fullreport.pdf.

World Bank. (2008). *World development report 2008: Agriculture for development* (Vol. 54). https://doi.org/10.1596/978-0-8213-7233-3.

Yin, R. (2009). *Case study research: Design and methods* (Fifth). Retrieved from http://books.google.com/books?hl=en&lr=&id=FzawIAdilHkC&oi=fnd&pg=PR1&dq=Case+Study+Research+Design+and+Methods&ots=lX6R-7goWYv&sig=ZgXTX0AHOMZCW1UoGEsHJ0FvDKU.

Access to Land and Food Security: Analysis of 'Priority Crops' Production in Ogun State, Nigeria

Ngozi Adeleye, Evans S. Osabuohien, Samuel Adeogun, Siraj Fashola, Oyinkan Tasie, and Gideon Adeyemi

1   Nigeria's Land Use Policy and Agro-Food Agenda: An Overview

Agriculture is conventionally considered as the 'backbone' of Nigeria's economy with many assigned roles to perform in the course of achieving economic advancement. Among the roles are: the provision of adequate food for the growing population; providing sufficient raw materials to its budding manufacturing sector; constituting the main source of employment; creating

---

N. Adeleye (✉) · E. S. Osabuohien
Department of Economics and Development Studies & Chair, Centre for Economic Policy and Development Research (CEPDeR), Covenant University, Ota, Nigeria
e-mail: ngozi.adeleye@covenantuniversity.edu.ng

E. S. Osabuohien
Alexander von Humboldt Visiting Professor, Witten/Herdecke University, Witten, Germany

S. Adeogun · S. Fashola
Planning, Research and Statistics, Ogun State Ministry of Agriculture, Abeokuta, Nigeria

a major source of foreign exchange earnings; and providing a market for the products of the industrial sector. However, problems in the agricultural sector began to arise about a decade after independence with increasing food supply short-falls, rising food prices and declining foreign exchange earnings from agricultural exports, rising food import bills, and declining labour force required in the sector. The situation was further worsened by the after-effects of the civil war, severe droughts in some parts of the country, government fiscal and monetary policies and above all, an 'oil boom' which created serious distortions in the economy and accelerated the rate of migration of labour from agriculture.

To stem this declining tide, the federal government embarked on several agriculture promotion schemes required to revamp the sector among which is the move from rudimentary farming (small-scale) to commercialized farming in the form of large-scale land investments (Osabuohien 2014; Osabuohien et al. 2019) and a renewed vigour into research, innovation, and development (Federal Ministry of Agriculture 2016). Therefore, it is correct to say that Nigeria is using research into the agricultural sector to drive its food security agenda as obtained in developed countries. For instance, research institutions in developed economies have played extremely important roles by undertaking basic research required to support the strategic goals of promoting food security in their respective countries. They transfer these ideas through the use of adaptive and applied research using various international centres, forums to provide the necessary training for other developing-country researchers (Reeves et al. 1998; Hajirostamlo et al. 2015).

Furthermore, agro-food research in Nigeria is recognized as a critical enabler of economic growth. It is therefore prioritized by the constitution and explicitly assigned as the primary responsibility of the federal government on the concurrent legislative list. Thus, the importance of agro-food research in driving the country's overall food agenda towards national food security, import substitution, and job creation cannot be overemphasized. To this end, concerned stakeholders, institutions, and bodies at different locations in the country are required to conduct research for increased agricultural productivity and to make the research outcomes available to farmers and other actors in the agricultural development of the states. Finally, to boost

---

O. Tasie
Department of Agriculture, Food and Resource Economics,
Michigan State University, East Lansing, MI, USA
e-mail: otasie@anr.msu.edu

G. Adeyemi
Geographic Info. System (GIS) Centre, Department of Civil Engineering,
Covenant University, Ota, Nigeria
e-mail: gideon.adewale@cu.edu.ng

Nigeria's commercialization drive and achieve one of its agenda for Vision 2020, the need for agro-food research is thus summarized herein.

First, investment in agro-food research must be accelerated if the country is to assure future food security for its citizens at reasonable prices and without irreversible degradation of the natural resource base. This is needful as the country will not achieve reasonable economic growth, poverty alleviation, and improvements in food security without productivity increases in agriculture. Also, agro-food research will enable yield-enhancing technology for the majority of crops grown in the country. The production of foundation seeds or improved crop varieties and their subsequent multiplication as commercial seeds; the development of hybrids with less than optimal production conditions reduces risks and uncertainty and enhances sustainability in production through better management of natural resources and reduced environmental risks. In addition, it will lead to the development of risk-averse measures resulting in tolerance or resistance to adverse production factors such as pests and drought, leading to biological and integrated pest control.

In addition, agro-food research will help to ensure sustainability. The international agricultural research centres have recognized the importance and urgency of research to assure sustainability in agricultural intensification through appropriate management of natural resources (CGIAR 2005).[1] In the same vein, accelerated research will prevent land degradation and reduce pressures on fragile lands across the geopolitical zones with particular attention to addressing extensive waterlogging and other forms of land degradation. Lastly, since a large proportion of Nigeria's population reside in the rural areas—characterized by low-incomes and poverty, incentives should be provided to the private sector to undertake biotechnology research using modern science with focus on the problems of local farmers which will assist in reducing poverty in the local communities. Failure to expand agricultural research significantly will make food security, poverty, and environmental goals elusive.

In the same vein, since ensuring food security is one of the main challenges of the twenty-first century in developing countries, the knowledge of land use and the formulation of policies governing its usage is important not just in an agrarian economy like Nigeria, but applies to other developing regions globally, due of its natural connection of land with diverse aspects of human lives (Issa et al. 2019). Likewise, the efficiency of any food security is a function of an effective land management system because land policy determines the frameworks for land ownership and development in any society (Kuma 2017).

Land policy is a significant tool in the determination of rights, protection, and transfer of wealth in addition to ensuring food security. Land policy development is very important in a society in order to ensure a condition of orderliness and a legal framework upon which transfer, acquisition, and uses will take place without certain vices and/or anti-cultural dispositions and conflicts. The formulation of a land policy involves a complex and dynamic process that is influenced by different factors, such as political constraints, rent-seekers, etc. However, there is the dichotomy among scholars, jurists, and stakeholders as to where land ownership lies. Does ownership lie with the State or with individual citizens? The system of land ownership requires a critical review in Nigeria as this will enhance agricultural productivity and promote the mechanized farming that is needed to prevent hunger, ensure food security, and prevent poverty. In Nigeria like most African countries, it is generally accepted that land is the property of the family with the community as a corporate unit. Hence, land is the property of both the living, the dead, and the unborn members of the families and community by virtue of its transferability from generation to generation (Kingston and Oke-Chinda 2016). To achieve Nigeria's agro-food agenda, Akintunde (2015) argues that land should be available for those that are ready to farm and not for speculators.

This study positions on Ogun State and gives a depiction of the synergy between land access and food security for several reasons: (1) it is one of the six states in the South-West geopolitical zones of Nigeria with arable land of 1,204,000 ha and cultivated area of 350,000 ha; (2) it is strategically positioned given its agricultural and location advantages to becoming an *agricultural powerhouse*; (3) proximity to Lagos State and Economic Community of West African States (ECOWAS) markets like Cotonou and Idiroko border towns create a growing demand for its food products and a competitive advantage for export and logistics, and (4) the State is endowed with fertile arable land and significant rainfall for two planting seasons in a year and available water bodies for all year round irrigated farming. Therefore, stemming from the above, this chapter explores the nexus between access to land and food security in Ogun State focusing on the production of crops deemed to be priority. The remainder of the study is structured as follows: Sect. 2 discusses Ogun State's food policy agenda; Sect. 3 details the ecological zoning of crops, Sect. 4 examines pattern of hectarage and output of priority crops; Sect. 5 discusses impact of farmers–herders conflicts on the food security agenda while Sect. 6 concludes with some policy recommendations.

2   Ogun State Food Policy Agenda

Ogun State is one of the 36 States in Nigeria, predominantly a *yoruba-speaking* State was created on 3rd of January 1976 with an approximate population of 5.2 million people.[2] It is located in the South-West geopolitical zone and borders Lagos State to the south, Oyo and Osun States to the north, Ondo State to the east, and the Republic of Benin to the west. Abeokuta is the capital and the largest city in the State (Osabuohien et al. 2018). With respect to agriculture in Ogun State, statistics reveal that about 3 million people live in the rural area which is the mainstay of agricultural engagements. The number of farming households is probably above 360,000 persons, which comprises an average family size of 4.8 persons. Recently, the State acquired over 47,334 ha of agricultural land across 28 communities in different Local Government Areas (LGAs) that are deemed to be suitable for the cultivation of crops such as cassava, rice, cocoa, maize, plantain, and oil palm. The State has a blend of agrarian (Ijebu-Ode, Sagamu, Ijebu Igbo, Ilaro, Ayetoro) and industrial (Abeokuta and Ota) communities.

The total land area is 1,685,100 hectarage with total arable land estimated to be 1,204,000 representing 71.45% of total land area (see Table 3 in Appendix). Out of the above total arable land, about 350,000 hectares is presently cultivated, which constitutes 29.07% of arable land area. The general vegetation cover comprises: rain forest, swamp forest, and derived savannah (Ogun State Government 2016). As of 2015, the State had allocated over 31,000 ha (32.6%) to various agricultural investors implying that there still exist about 67.4% of *un-used* agricultural land sites. The State intends to create clusters of production and value addition, around selected crops and specially targeting increased participation of youth and women. In addition, it will provide enablers around improving access to land and security, roads, inputs, capacity building, among others. Given the above fallouts, this study carries out an empirical investigation of enhanced crop production focusing on the *priority crops* in Ogun State, Nigeria. This is achieved using survey data collected by the Ogun State Agricultural Development Programme in various LGAs, which was analyzed using quantitative techniques.

According to Dada (2017), the land use pattern in Ogun State is described as majorly arable, permanent pastures, permanent crops, forest, and a host of others. Thus, land ownership is still the main asset of the people. However, for the farmers, this asset has not been put to optimal use, partly due to lack of proper registration and titles acceptable for use as collateral to raise capital as well as ascertain ownership. Given that the abilities of both small-landholders and commercial-scale farmers to own arable land (land access) is a pre-cursor to ensuring agro-produce, the Ogun State Government (OSG) put in place several measures towards ensuring that the farmers' agricultural cycle is not threatened. Some of the measures are: (1) that there are secure dealings on land matters, (2) transaction costs are kept low, (3) farmers have credit access, (4) land dealings are transparent, (5) no discrimination on land participations, (6) protection of minority rights, especially women, and (7) environmental sustainability is supported. From the Ogun State Ministry of Agriculture, it takes an average of 3–6 months for an individual to secure land for agricultural purposes (which can be through leasing or borrowing) while it takes an average of 7 months for a corporate body (commercial scale) to obtain the same. Successful individual applicants are entitled to a maximum of 19 hectares of land while that for a corporate body is not specific.[3]

In order to ensure that agriculture in the State is focused on increasing the productivity of smallholder's farmers in a sustainable manner that is market driven, the State Government established the Ogun State Agricultural Development Programme (OGADEP 2017) to provide the necessary technical back-stopping for farmers in areas of crops, livestock, and fisheries through relevant capacity building along the value chain. This is essential as the role of value chain development in enhancing agricultural production cannot be overemphasized (Oyebola et al. 2019). On gender participation, the State Government and other Non-Governmental Organizations (NGOs) recognize the roles played by women in agricultural production and local processing. The current issue in rural women's development is now tending towards, recognizing the possible ways of sustaining all developmental programmes aimed at improving the lives of rural women. Generally, in Nigeria, a number of gender-specific developmental projects like Better Life Programme for Rural Women (BLPRW), Women-In-Agriculture (WIA), the Family Support Programme (FSP), have been introduced to take care of women's needs in the rural areas (Adisa and Okunade 2005).

In Ogun State, the Women-in-Agriculture (WIA), a component of OGADEP Extension Structure is providing technical support to women in form of training to enhance the utilization of major food crop and at the same time influence their nutrition status. For instance, the women are trained in the processing of cassava into chips, floured starch, and its utilization for confectioneries; yam processing into chips and flour and the tuber and flour utilization for porridge, etc.; plantain processing into flour and chips; maize processing into paste and flour, fortification, and utilization as weaning diet; fortification and enhancement of carbohydrate food with soya bean among others (OGADEP 2017). All these measures are to support the food security initiative of the State Government. Specifically, the cassava value chain in Ogun State is a major employer of labour with virtually every household in the rural and semi-urban communities producing one cassava-based product or another plus the cassava processing small and medium scale enterprises (SMEs) engaging between 15 and 25 direct employees each not to mention the indirect employment associated with haulage/carriage of the raw tubers from the farm to the vehicle location, loading and offloading of the vehicles, vehicle hire/transportation, ad-hoc staff, supplier of water for processing. Cassava plays a major role in the livelihoods of women, youth, transporters, and other players in Nigeria. About 90% of cassava farmers are smallholders with 95% women responsible for the processing and marketing of cassava (Sanni et al. 2012; Adeogun et al. 2017).

3 Ecological Clustering in Ogun State

To ensure food security, Ogun State is divided into four ecological zones identified as best suited for the production of certain crops and livestock, in terms of soil properties, relative humidity, rainfall levels, vegetative cover, temperature fluctuations, and day length. The zones are: the guinea savannah area; rain forest area; mid-region of the rain forest area; and freshwater swampy area. The guinea savannah area comprises Egbado North, part of Egbado South and Abeokuta Local Government Areas (LGAs), which is suitable for the production of cassava, maize, melon, cowpea, yams, soyabeans, citrus, and cocoa. The rain forest area is made up of Odeda, Remo, part of Ijebu East, Ijebu-Ode, and Ijebu-North LGAs that is reputed for the

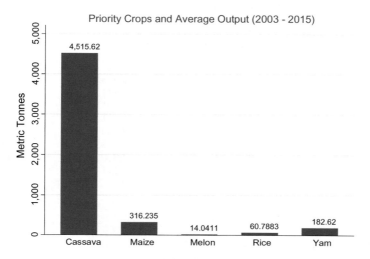

Fig. 1 Ecological clustering of crops in Ogun State (*Source* The Authors')

production of maize, plantain, cassava, kola, cocoa, oil palm, citrus, cowpea, and rubber. The mid-region of the rain forest area is made up of Obafemi/Owode and Ifo/Ota LGAs suitable for the production of rice, maize, cassava, and cowpea. The freshwater swampy area entails mainly Ijebu East, which is well suited for fish and swamp rice production (Awotide 2012; Adeogun et al. 2017).

The map of Ogun State highlighting the ecological zones *vis-à-vis* the crops produced are depicted in Fig. 1, while details on ecological clustering including population density per hectarage as well as major crops produced are presented in Table 3 in the Appendix.

4 Land Access and Food Production of Priority Crops in Ogun State

The data utilized for the descriptive analysis is obtained from the annual surveys conducted by Ogun State Agricultural Development Programme (OGADEP) in the major Local Government Areas (LGAS) where the crops are grown across the State. We build the empirical analyses of the crops that are known as the priority crops due to the volume of production, acreage of cultivation as well as potential for commercial values in the State (Ogun State Government-OSG 2016). The period covered using the State-level data is from 2003 to 2015, which is the survey period covered by OGADEP. The crops listed according to cultivation acreage and output quantity include: cassava, maize, rice, yam, cocoyam, potato, cowpea, and melon. Table 1 shows the average harvested area, output, and yield of each crop.

Table 1 Average values of the crops

S/n	Crop	Cultivated land (Hectares)	Output produced (Metric tonnes)	Yield per hectare
1	Cassava	270,829.00	4,515,615.10	16.408
2	Maize	233,672.38	316,235.23	1.3323
3	Rice	25,156.10	32,256.00	1.249
4	Melon	21,171.10	14,041.10	0.628
5	Yam	20,711.60	182,620.30	8.684
6	Potato	19,331.00	51,831.20	5.744
7	Cocoyam	18,279.60	82,360.80	6.013
8	Cowpea	2126.33	2241.20	0.725

Note The crops are arranged according to size of land cultivated
Source The Authors'

Statistics reveal that cassava is cultivated on a larger farm area of 270, 829 hectares with 4.5 million metric tonnes produced on the average giving a yield of 16.41. Following cassava are maize, yam, cocoyam, potato, rice, melon and cowpea, in that order. The study advanced further by examining the performance of the above crops over the years given the various interventionists programmes of Ogun State Government.

4.1 Hectarage, Output, and Yield Pattern of Priority Crops

Using descriptive statistics, this section examines the pattern of land cultivated, output produced, and yield of five out of the eight priority crops.[4] Statistics in Table 2 details the pattern of these crops using comparative year-bands approach to show if there is an improvement in a measure compared to the previous band which to some extent shows the impact of the State Government's interventionist's policies towards ensuring food security in the State. Each crop is analyzed in turn.

4.1.1 Cassava

Cassava is generally considered the predominant crop in the state by area of hectarage against other crops cultivated in the State. The crop is grown in the guinea savannah area (made up of Egbado North, part of Egbado South, and Abeokuta local government areas), rain forest area (comprising Odeda, Remo, part of Ijebu East, Ijebu-Ode, and Ijebu-North local government areas), and mid-region of the rain forest area (Obafemi/Owode and Ifo/Ota local government areas). A report of the Food and Agriculture Organization (FAO)[5] gives a brief expose on the relevance of cassava both a staple delicacy and as a source of raw materials for industrial production. Cassava is a very versatile commodity with numerous uses and by-products. Each component of the plant is valuable to its cultivator. The leaves are consumed as vegetables, cooked as a soup ingredient, dried, and fed to

Table 2 Hectarage, output and yield pattern of priority crops (2003–2015)

Measures	Crops	2003–2007	2008–2015	% Change
Cultivated land (Hectares)	Cassava	230,365	296,119	28.54
	Maize	200,825	254,202	26.58
	Rice	11,251.80	67,894.75	503.41
	Yam	14,769.20	26,654	80.47
	Melon	16,219	26,123.20	61.07
	All Crops	**94,686.00**	**153,223.90**	**61.82**
Output produced (Metric tonnes, '000)	Cassava	3,594.58	5,091.26	41.64
	Maize	272.14	343.79	26.33
	Rice	13.53	90.33	567.63
	Yam	121.41	243.83	100.83
	Melon	8.38	19.70	135.08
	All Crops	**802.00**	**1,338.85**	**66.94**
Yield per hectare	Cassava	15.48	16.99	9.75
	Maize	1.37	1.31	(4.38)
	Rice	1.19	1.29	8.40
	Yam	8.26	9.11	10.29
	Melon	0.49	0.76	55.10
	All Crops	**5.36**	**6.06**	**13.06**

Note Percentage change is computed as: [(period 2008–2015) − (period 2003–2007)/(period 2003–2007) × 100]; Yield is computed as: Metric Tonnes/Hectares; data for Yam and Melon ends at 2012
Source Authors' Computations from Ogun State Agriculture Data

livestock as a protein feed supplement. The stem is used for plant propagation and grafting. The roots are typically processed for human and industrial consumption.

In Ogun State, just as in other parts of the country, *garri*, a roasted granule is the dominant product and is widely accepted in both rural and urban areas. It can be consumed without any additives or it can be consumed with a variety of additives such as sugar, groundnut, fish, meat, and stew. The fermented wet paste, locally called *fufu* is widely consumed throughout the southern zones. It is known as *akpu* in the South-Eastern and South-Southern regions. On its industrial usage, estimates from the FAO suggest that approximately 16% of cassava root production is utilized as an industrial raw material in 2001 in Nigeria. Ten percent used as chips in animal feeds, 5% processed into a syrup concentrate for soft drinks, and less than one percent processed into high-quality cassava flour used in biscuits and confectionary, dextrin pre-gelled starch for adhesives, starch, and hydrolysates for pharmaceuticals, and seasonings (Kormawa and Akoroda 2003). This estimate leaves 84% or 28.9 million tonnes of production for food consumption, a portion of this of course being lost in post-harvest and waste.

Nevertheless, cassava plays a major role in the livelihoods of women, youth, transporters, and other players in Nigeria. About 90% of cassava farmers are smallholders with 95% women responsible for the processing and marketing of cassava (Sanni et al. 2012). Cassava processing has moved from cottage/small and medium scale enterprises (SMEs) to large scale with most of these large-scale companies situated in Ogun State (Adeogun et al. 2017). Over the last 13 years, the output and yield of cassava have consistently improved. A close look at the statistics reveal that between 2003 and 2007, cassava was planted on 230, 365 hectares of land which as a result of more land farming land acquisition by the government, increased to 296,119 hectares representing an increase of 28.54%. The effect of the increase in average land cultivated can be observed from the pattern of output produced which increased on average by 41.64% from 3.59 million metric tonnes to 5.09 million metric tonnes. As expected, the average yield also grew by 9.75% from 15.48 to 16.99%. Some of the measures introduced in boosting the production of agriculture in the state are provision of more arable lands for cultivation,[6] use of hybrid cassava seeds which reduces planting and harvesting periods, use of fertilizers, educating farmers on embracing new planting techniques, improved value-added chain that allows off-takers to be available to pick up the products, availability of microscale finance, and so on. These measures have been successful in ensuring that cassava maintains its status as the State's main priority crop.

4.1.2 Maize

This is the commonest grain produced in Ogun State and adjudged to be the second priority crop in terms of hectarage, output, and yield. The crop is also grown in the guinea savannah area, rain forest area, and mid-region of the rain forest in the State and produced within two seasons, namely, early and late maize. Its major economic importance is hinged on human consumption, livestock feeds, and industrial processes including breweries and confectionaries. For the records, the demand for maize is very high within the State and across neighbouring towns and States. Maize is a cereal plant that produces grains that can be cooked, roasted, fried, ground, pounded, or crushed to prepare various food delicacies like pap (called *ogi*), '*tuwo*', '*gwate*', '*donkunu*', and host of others. All these food types are readily available in various parts of Nigeria among different ethnic groups, notably among which are the Yorubas, Hausas, Igbos, Ibiras, Ishas, Binis, Efiks, Yalas, among others. According to Abdurahaman and Kolawole (2006) maize is known and called by different vernacular names depending on locality like '*agbado*', '*igbado*', or '*yangan*' (Yoruba); '*masara*' or '*dawar masara*' (Hausa); '*ogbado*' or '*oka*' (Ibo); '*apaapa*' (Ibira); '*oka*' (Bini and Isha); '*ibokpot*' or '*ibokpot* union' (Efik), and '*igumapa*' (Yala). The maize meal is also used as a replacement for wheat flour, to make cornbread and other baked products.

In addition, since Ogun State has one of the largest concentration of industries in the country, maize has become a source of raw materials for most of the agro-based industries located in Ota and Agbara industrial areas of the State. It is used most especially in the production of pharmaceutical drugs, ethanol, confectionaries, beverages, and other manufactured goods. Hence, the crop maintains its status as the second priority crop and to further boost all the indices of maize production, the State Government is proposing the establishment of additional 7000 hectares of maize farms.[7] As a result of more allocated farming lands, the cultivation of maize increased on average from 200,825 hectares of land to 254,202 hectares representing an increase of 26.58% (see Table 2). The impact of more cultivated lands led to an average increase of 26.33% in productivity from 272,140 metric tonnes to 373,970 metric tonnes. However, this did not transmit to an increase in yield which declined from 1.37 yield per hectare to 1.31 yield per hectare representing a decline of 4.38%. This decline is not unconnected to inadequate rainfall, poor seedlings (non-treated seedlings), old rudimentary ways of farming, poor farming techniques, inadequate fertilizers, pests' (termites, ants, and millipedes) and birds invasion, etc.

4.1.3 Rice
This is third priority (mandate) crop in terms of area harvested and sixth in terms of output. Like other rice producing states, Ogun State, is the foremost producer of rice in the South-western part of the country and is billed to become one of the expected exporters of rice. Indeed, the State is popular for its production of brown rice popularly referred to as *Ofada* rice. The crop is grown the swampy area of Ijebu East and in the rain forest area of Obafemi/Owode and Ifo/Ota local government areas and according to Osabuohien et al. (2016), eight out of the 20 LGAs in Ogun State, representing 40%, are involved in rice production. These LGAs include: Abeokuta North, Egbado North, Ewekoro, Ifo, Ijebu-North, Ikenne, Obafemi Owode, and Ogun Waterside. The produce is predominantly cultivated by rice farmers in the agrarian town of Eegua, in Yewa North Local Government Area of the state who have vowed to make the produce in abundant supply provided they get the required assistance from government at all levels.[8] As expected, these have made Ogun State become a major player in rice sector revolution in Nigeria. Rice possesses both local and industrial values. It can be cooked from its raw form into several local delicacies like 'white rice', '*jollof* rice', 'fried rice' 'coconut rice', etc. Its blended and fermented form is processed to make "*tuwo*" which is eaten with different varieties of soups. Industrially, rice oil is processed from the bran for both food and industrial uses. Broken rice is used in brewing, distilling, and in the manufacture of starch and rice flour. Hulls are used for fuel, packing material, industrial grinding, fertilizer manufacture, and in the manufacture of an industrial chemical called furfural.[9]

From Table 2, the cultivation and production of rice have consistently witnessed an upswing across all parameters. As a result of the State government's drive to increase rice productivity, the size of land cultivated increased on average from 11,251.80 hectares to 67,874.75 hectares representing 503.41%. Not surprising, a similar impact is seen on the output which showed an average increase of 567.63% signalling an increase in output produced from 13,530 metric tonnes to 90,330 metric tonnes. In the same vein, the yield per hectare increased by 8.40% from 1.19 yield per hectare to 1.29. It is noteworthy to mention that, the success recorded in the production of rice is directly connected to the initiatives of the incumbent governor who invested in heavy land-clearing equipment on a scale never witnessed in the annals of the state in 2013. Just recently, another investment was made on farm machinery. Hundreds of acres of land have been cultivated. More hectares are being cleared for rice production after the successful launch of MITROS (Mission to Rebuild Ogun State) Rice in December 2018. This marked a positive turning point for Ogun State making it a prime rice-producer in the country.[10]

4.1.4 Melon

Melon, known locally as *egusi* is a type of melon that is very popular in South-western, Eastern Nigeria, and other parts of the country. *Egusi* melon seeds are popular condiments in Nigerian local soups. It resembles small-size watermelon with only edible seeds while its flesh is bitter and inedible. The crop is a good source of oil, protein, minerals, vitamins, and energy in form of carbohydrates. This is also one of the priority crops grown in the guinea savannah area of the State. It is predominantly farmed in Egbado North, Egbado South, Abeokuta North, and Abeokuta South Local Government Areas. Due to its domestic and industrial values, the crop benefited from more arable land for planting by the State Government. As a result of more allocated farming lands, the cultivation of melon increased on average from 16,219 hectares of land to 26,123.20 hectares representing an increase of 61.07% (see Table 2). The effect of more cultivated areas led to an average increase of 135.08% in productivity from 8.38 metric tonnes to 19.70 metric tonnes translating to an increase in yield per hectare of 0.76 from 0.49 representing a percentage change increase of 55.10%. A cursory look at the data revealed that the crop witnessed a rising trend from 2003 till 2011 from where it experienced a negative shock whose reversal cannot be confirmed due to lack of data. Also, relative to the land area harvested, the trend analysis of the yield curve is on the rise.

4.1.5 Yam

Nigeria is adjudged to be the world's largest producer of yams, accounting for over 70–76% of the world production.[11] The country produces 18.3 million tonnes of yam from 1.5 million hectares, representing 73.8% of total yam production in Africa. Several States in the country contribute to the national production of the crop of which Ogun State is one. The crop is also grown in the guinea savannah area of the State, is the fifth crop in terms of area harvested and third in output and predominantly farmed in Egbado North, Egbado South, Abeokuta North, and Abeokuta South Local Government Areas. Yam has both domestic and industrial uses. The production process of yam is summarized this: yam selection: fresh harvested yam gotten from the farm are sorted to select whole-some tubers that are suitable for the production of instant pounded yam flour; milling: the dried yam slices are milled directly into flour of uniform particle size. Domestically, it can be processed into several forms to make different delicacies such as pounded yam, locally called *iyan*, yam pottage called *asaro*, fried yam known as *dundu*. It can also be roasted. Industrially, it is used in production of all-purpose-adhesives. The adhesives are used by producers of cartons, packaging companies, and lather and shoe producers. The all-purpose adhesives are produced with yam or cassava starch. The State Government's pro-poor programmes to stimulate agro-production and ensure food security led more cultivated lands for yam. This increased on average from 14,769.20 hectares to 26,654 hectares representing an increase of 80.47% (see Table 2). The outcome of more cultivated areas led to an average increase of 100.83% in productivity from 121.41 metric tonnes to 243.83 metric tonnes which further translates to an increase in yield per hectare of 9.11 from 8.26 representing a percentage change increase of 10.29%. Yam production has consistently witnessed an upswing from 2003 to date perhaps because yam is a staple meal across all households in the country.

4.2   Other Crops

Other crops, namely: cocoyam, potato, and cowpea[12] have also shown relative improvements. Cocoyam is grown in the guinea savannah and cultivated on 18,279.60 hectares of land. Output produced is about 82,360 metric tonnes with 6.013 yield per hectare. Potato is cultivated in the rain forest region of the State on 19,331 hectares of land producing a yield of 5.74 from an output of 51,831.20 metric tonnes. Lastly, cowpea is the least cultivated. It is grown in the mid-region of the rain forest on a sparse 2126.33 hectares of land with an average output of 2241.20 metric tonnes and 0.73 yields per hectare.

4.3   Comparative Advantage

From the eight crops presented in Table 1, the study further examined those with comparative advantage by matching their respective average area harvested with average output and yield per hectare from 2000 to 2015.[13] These statistics are depicted in Figs. 2 and 3 of the Appendix. As shown in Fig. 2, the cultivation of cassava gives the highest average output of 4,515,620 metric tonnes relative to other produce. Likewise, the crop produced the highest yield per hectare of 16.41 relative to other crops as shown in Fig. 2 which confirms that Ogun State has the highest comparative advantage in the cultivation of cassava. The statistics suggest that more returns for food production and processing can be derived from the cultivation of cassava compared to the other seven crops. This is essential as the agricultural transformation processes taking place in the State and the country in general has led to the enhancement of value chains. For instance, there has been an increase in the availability of off-takers, out-grower schemes as well as the emergence of mechanized cassava processing plants in many parts of Nigeria.[14]

5 Challenges to Ogun State Food Security Agenda

5.1 Farmers–Herders Conflicts

A major challenge to the food security agenda of the State Government is the recurring farmers–herders clashes which are mainly attributable to resource control and divergent value systems in the country. The movement of pastoralists from one area of the country to another is usually caused by the increasing demand for fresh grazing grounds (Alawode 2013; Adelakun et al. 2015). From the Focus Group Discussions (FGDs) in Imeko/Afon, Yewa, and Ewekoro Local Governments with the representatives of farmers, herders, religious leaders, security apparatus, women society, and the youths, the persistent conflicts between farmers and pastoralists have threatened both the food security agenda of the State in addition to the security of lives and properties of the people. Some recent incidences are those recorded in Iwoye-Ketu (located in Imeko/Afon axis) in 2017; Oja-Odan, Igbogila, Owunbe, Egua (in Yewa axis) in 2016; and Afamu, Onigbegu, and Kajola (in Ewekoro axis), among others. These sporadic invasions of pastoralists on farmlands have led to the abandonment of farms with grave multiplier effects on agro-produce and farmers' living conditions. Information gathered from the FGDs reveals that the conflicts are rampant in dry seasons than in rainy seasons when grazers seek greener pastures for their herds and in all cases, the pastoralists do encounter problems with the local people because farmers' crops were being destroyed. Evidences reveal the destructive nature of the menace. Across all ecological zones of the State, the cost of these crises is mounting. From loss of farmlands, crops, incomes, livelihoods, and lives these conflicts have grave multiplier effects on the economy (Adisa 2012; Adelakun et al. 2015; MercyCorps 2015).

As a resolution, both the Federal and State Government are working harmoniously to put an end to these menace by proposing grazing reserves, ranching, and carving out new stock routes for the herdsmen. For instance, Nigeria has 415 government-designated grazing reserves throughout the country, while farmer-herdsmen reconciliatory committees in most conflict-prone states have been set up to control resource-based conflicts among farmers and pastoralists (Adisa and Adekunle 2010; Adelakun et al. 2015). These proposed measures have been received with mixed reactions from the concerned parties. The farmers oppose grazing but support ranching while the herders oppose ranching while supporting the idea of grazing reserves. The grazing reserve is not wholly supported due to insufficient lands available for crop production while the herders want unrestricted movement for their cattle. A case in point is that in Imeko/Afon, Yewa, and Ewekoro the farmers did not support the idea of grazing zones because the farmlands are open areas, unfenced with likely encroachment on farmlands since the herders are not likely to hold up their own end of the agreement.[15] The herdsmen, on the other hand, prefer open areas. Overall, the lack of trust between both parties is a huge problem, which has become a major challenge to Ogun State's food security agenda.

5.2 The Need for Information Technology in Agricultural Productivity

The earth furnishes the raw materials that we use in our daily lives, either directly in the manufacturing of the goods we consume or in the formation of the soils upon which we depend on for agriculture (Peters et al. 2010). Land mass arable portion is limited in supply, it is a natural resource that must well be taken care of and its utilization must be well planned. Application of information technology in land management and administration is of significant importance especially in the developing countries where land resources need more digital management. The benefits of integrated remote sensing and Geographic Information Systems (GIS) technique in cadastral mapping and land use zoning cannot be overemphasized. The ability of remote sensing to provide a repetitive look of the earth surface makes it a veritable tool in determining changes over time and space of an area.

Other applications of GIS and remote sensing technologies in agriculture include: pests and disease control, crop yield estimation, afforestation planning, soil suitability mapping, erosion control, wildfire control, and myriads of other benefits. This technology is able to bring orderliness to land management and administration, digital copies of land information could be kept for a longer period of time, land ownership and transfers could easily be managed and tracked and land encroachment could easily be monitored. Information technology in land use and monitoring to favour agricultural development would go a long way in enhancing food security in the state, in addition, effective land administration would need proper monitoring whereby the potency of laws, codes, ordinances, and zoning restrictions must be fully exercised at the federal, state, and local government levels. A zoning classification describes the permitted use of the site. This legal description determines the type of development in a location (Daisy 2006).

5.3 Other Challenges

There are other factors that are capable of reducing total productivity in the agrarian sector culminating into adverse shortage of food supply, loss of income to households, loss of revenue to the State and Federal Governments, loss of foreign revenue and rising food prices. For instance, documentary evidence reveals that even with prohibitive lending rates, commercial banks are still averse to lending to farmers (exposure is about 6%) while the insurance sector's exposure in the sector is less than 3%, measured by farmers enrolled and cropping area covered (CBN 2016; Federal Ministry of Agriculture 2016). The role of financial institutions in the commercialization agenda is paramount to driving agro-exports, enhancing tradability, increasing global competitiveness, and foreign exchange (Osabuohien and Olayiwola

2010; Akinyemi et al. 2019). Also, the allocation of lands from smallholders to large-scale farmers arises the problem of land inequality and in its wake loss of wealth and income inequality of small land farmers (Unal 2007). In addition, majority of the farmers operate largely in local markets due to lack of connectivity to more lucrative markets at local, national, or global levels.

6   Conclusion and Policy Recommendations

The study analyzes the land access and food policy initiatives of the Ogun State government in Nigeria from 1980 to 2015. To drive agro-food production, the State Government divided the 20 LGAs across four ecological zones such that the various pro-poor programmes required to stimulate the agricultural sector saw a reversal of the declining trend and a rise began to occur from 2014. The main reason for zoning into different geographical areas according to their resource endowments, is to identify those areas that have a relative advantage in the production of certain crops and livestock, as well as other nonfarm products, over other areas, with a view to maximally utilizing the areas for the production of the crops/livestock so identified, at the best economic levels. Also, the study shows that to ensure food security, the State is involved in the production of several crops of which eight (cassava, maize, rice, melon, yam, potato, cocoyam, and cowpea) of them are highlighted and given available statistics. Evidence reveals that Ogun State has comparative advantage in the cultivation of cassava in the areas of cultivated land area, productivity, and yield relative to others.

Given the above, in order to ensure food sustainability for the people, the study recommends that:

1. There is the need for the State Government to have a long-term agricultural development plan (e.g. between 20 and 25 years) to ensure consistency and continuity of agricultural policies;
2. The Ogun State should reduce its overdependence on cassava produce while establishing its comparative advantages on related crops such as yam, potato, cocoyam, and rice;
3. A comprehensive agricultural land database with information on cultivated land, ratio of women and youth participations *vis-à-vis* ratio of small—commercial landowners is necessary for planning;
4. Visible presence of the State Government on acquired lands is needed and where there are infractions, the necessary institutions should enforce the law, which will make the land acquisition processes to be less cumbersome and more transparent;
5. Delineation of agricultural land after a comprehensive land mapping of the State and ensure that such land is used for agricultural purposes and not to succumb to pressure to release it for other purposes; and
6. Work out a lasting solution to the persistent farmers–herders clashes in the State.

In conclusion, the desire of the Ogun State Government to become an agricultural *powerhouse* with the capacity not to only feed her residents but supply farm produce outside the State using the platform of crop production can be realized when the needed supports are accorded as enumerated above. This will also involve the private sector engagements that will provide complementary roles through up-takers and out-grower schemes. This is essential as the farmers will have the needed farm inputs as well as the assurance that there are ready-markets for farm produce which adds value to their labour. As suggestions for future studies, and given data availability, the cost of farmers-pastoralists conflicts on food security in Ogun State using both descriptive and econometrics analysis may be taken up.

Appendix

See Table 3 and Figs. 2, 3.

Table 3 Ecological clustering of crop production

S/No.	Ecological zones	LGAs	Population	Area (Hecterage)	Density	Major crops
1	Guinea Savannah	6	1,034,924	587,900	0.568	Cassava, maize, melon, cowpea, yams, soya beans, citrus, cocoa
2	Rain Forest	9	1,284,828	656,900	0.511	Maize, plantain, cassava, kola-nut, coca, oil-palm, citrus, cowpea
3	Mid-region (Rain Forest)	4	1,335,409	340,300	0.254	Rice, maize, cassava, cowpea
4	Swampy area	1	72,935	100,000	1.371	Rice
	Total	20	3,728,096	1,685,100	2.705	

Notes **LGAs**: Local Government Areas; **Density**: Area/Population; **Guinea Savannah**: Egbado North, Egbado South, Abeokuta North, Abeokuta South; **Rain Forest**: Odeda, Ijebu East (part), Ijebu Ode, Ijebu North; **Mid-Region (Rain Forest)**: Obafemi/Owode, Ifo, Ado-Odo Otta; **Swampy Area**: Ijebu East (part), Ogun Waterside
Source The Authors'

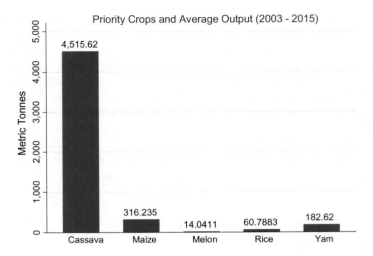

Fig. 2 Output of selected priority crops in Ogun State, Nigeria (*Source* The Authors')

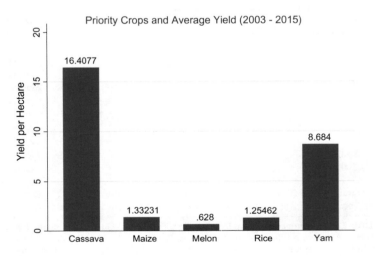

Fig. 3 Yield per hectare of selected priority crops in Ogun State, Nigeria (*Source* The Authors')

Notes

1. CGIAR is a consortium of agricultural research centres, which was formerly called Consultative Group on International Agricultural Research. For details, see www.cgiar.org.
2. Ogun State at a Glance, Government of Ogun State Website available at http://ogunstate.gov.ng/ogun-state/ last accessed September 25, 2018.
3. In this case, the intended size of land by the potential corporate applicant is negotiated with the State Government in conjunction with the LGA as well as the leaders of the community where such land is to be acquired.
4. Due to the very low indices of cocoyam, potato, and cowpea, they are excluded from these descriptive analyses.
5. http://www.fao.org/3/y5548e/y5548e08.htm.
6. https://www.vanguardngr.com/2018/04/boosting-rural-agriculture-ogun/.
7. http://ogunstate.gov.ng/ministry-of-agriculture/.
8. https://www.tribuneonlineng.com/112615/.
9. https://www.britannica.com/plant/rice.
10. https://www.vanguardngr.com/2018/04/boosting-rural-agriculture-ogun/.
11. https://www.pulse.ng/lifestyle/food-travel/yams-nigeria-is-the-highest-producer-of-this-crop-thanks-to-these-states/478clck.
12. For space consideration and to avoid having to many Figures, we did not present their graphs. However, they can be made available upon request. More so, cocoyam, potato, and cowpea are not part of priority crops. While other priority crops (cocoa, plantain, and oil palm) were not covered in the survey due to the fact that the survey mainly focused on annual crops.
13. Data for melon and yam is from 2003 to 2012.
14. As in some States like Kwara located in North-Central Nigeria, there are a number of large-scale cassava processing machines in Ogun State.
15. There are also speculations that there is more to the issue of herders–farmers conflict in terms of the possibility of having religious and political undertone; however, this is outside the focus of this present study.

References

Abdurahaman, A. A., & Kolawole, O. M. (2006). Traditional preparations and uses of maize in Nigeria. *Ethnobotanical Leaflets, 10*, 219–227.

Adelakun, O. E., Adurogbangba, B., & Akinbile, L. A. (2015). Socioeconomic effects of farmer-pastoralist conflict on agricultural extension service delivery in Oyo state, Nigeria. *Journal of Agricultural Extension, 19*(2), 1–12. https://doi.org/10.4314/jae.v19i2.5.

Adeogun, S., Adeleye, N., Fashola, S., & Osabuohien, E. (2017). *Promoting cassava productivity in Ogun State: Linking data and policy* (State Policy Note 6). Nigeria Agricultural Policy Project (Feed the Future).

Adisa, R. S. (2012). *Land use conflict between farmers and herdsmen – Implications for agricultural and rural development in Nigeria, rural development—Contemporary issues and practices*. IntechOpen. https://doi.org/10.5772/45787. Retrieved from https://www.intechopen.com/books/rural-development-contemporary-issuesand-practices/land-use-conflict-between-famers-and-herdsmen-implications-for-agricultural-and-rural-development-in.

Adisa, R. S., & Adekunle, O. A. (2010). Farmer-Herdsmen conflicts: A factor analysis of socio-economic conflict variables among arable crop farmers in North Central Nigeria. *Journal of Human Ecology, 30*(1), 1–9.

Adisa, B. O., & Okunade, A. (2005). Assessment of rural youth participation in community based rural development projects in Osun state, Nigeria. *Internal Journal of Biological and Physical Sciences, 10*(1), 18–25.

Akintunde, K. O. (2015). The land use act and land ownership debate in Nigeria: Resolving the impasse. *SSRN Electronic Journal.* https://doi.org/10.2139/ssrn.2564539.

Akinyemi, O., Efobi, U., Asongu, S., & Osabuohien, E. (2019). Renewable energy, trade performance and the conditional role of finance and institutional capacity in sub-Sahara African countries. *Energy Policy, 132,* 490–498.

Alawode, O. O. (2013). Determinants of land use conflicts among farmers in Southwestern Nigeria. *Journal Research in Peace, Gender and Development, 3*(4), 58–67.

Awotide, D. O. (2012). Assessment of women's participation in cooperative societies and its determinants in Yewa North Local Government Area of Ogun State, Nigeria. *Asian Journal of Agriculture and Rural Development, 2*(3), 344–350.

CBN. (2016). *Central bank of Nigeria Communiqué No. 105 of the monetary policy committee meeting of Monday and Tuesday, January 25 and 26, 2016.* Abuja: Central Bank of Nigeria.

CGIAR. (2005). *Science for agric development.* Rome, Italy. Retrieved from www.cgiar.org/enews/december2005/scienceforagrdev.pdf.

Dada, S. (2017). *Public-private dialogue report on land administration, registration and acquisition in Ogun State.* Nigeria: Deutsche Gesellschaft für Internationale Zusammenarbeit (GIZ).

Daisy, L. K. (2006). *Land development* (10th ed.). Washington, DC: National Association of Home Builders. ISBN-13: 9780867186093.

Federal Ministry of Agriculture. (2016). *The agricultural promotion policy (2016–2020).* Abuja: Federal Government of Nigeria.

Hajirostamlo, B., Mirsaeedghazi, N., Arefnia, M., Shariati, M. A., & Fard, E. A. (2015). The role of research and development in agriculture and its dependent concepts in agriculture. *Asian Journal of Applied Science and Engineering, 4*(10), 79–83.

Issa, I. B., Nei, A. N., Wellyngton, S. A., Gabriel, A. A., Franciani Rodrigues, S. V., Haendchen, F., et al. (2019). The contributions of public policies for strengthening family farming and increasing food security: The case of Brazil. *Land Use Policy, 82,* 573–584.

Kingston, K. G., & Oke-Chinda, M. (2016). The Nigerian land use act: A curse or a blessing to the Anglican Church and the Ikwerre ethnic people of Rivers State. *AJLC, 6*(1), 147–158.

Kormawa, P., & Akoroda, M. O. (2003). *Cassava supply chain arrangements for industrial utilization in Nigeria.* Ibadan: IITA.

Kuma, S. S. (2017). Land policy and land delivery system in Nigeria. *Emerging Issues in Urban Land Use and Development.*

MercyCorps. (2015). *The economic costs of conflicts and the benefits of peace: Effects of farmer-Pastorist conflict in Nigeria's Middle Belt on State, Sector and National Economies.* Portland, Oregon. Retrieved from https://www.mercycorps.org/.../Mercy%20Corps%20Nigeria%20Household%20Costs.

Ogun State Agricultural Development Programme (OGADEP). (2017, April 25–28). *Work/Plan Budget 2017*. Paper presented at the 30th Refils Workshop on OXFAR/EXTENSION Proposals Year 2017, Institute of Agricultural Research and Training, Near Gate House, Ibadan.

Ogun State Government. (2016). *Ogun State—Nigeria investors' forum*. Retrieved from Retrieved June 30, 2016, from http://ogunstateinvestorsforum.ng/agriculture/.

Osabuohien, E. S. (2014). Large-scale agricultural land investments and local institutions in Africa: The Nigerian case. *Land Use Policy, 39*(July), 155–165. https://doi.org/10.1016/j.landusepol.2014.02.019.

Osabuohien, E. S., Osabohien, R., & Okorie, U. (2016). *Putting rice on our tables: Boosting production, processing and marketing of rice in Ogun state, Nigeria* (pp. 1–25).

Osabuohien, E., Efobi, U. R., Herrmann, R., & Gitau, C. M. (2019). Female labor outcomes and large-scale agricultural land investments: Macro-micro evidence from Tanzania. *Land Use Policy, 82*, 716–728.

Osabuohien, E., & Olayiwola, W. (2010). *Enhancing tradability of SSA's agricutural exports: What can institutions offer?* 1–25.

Osabuohien, E. S., Osabohien, R., & Okorie, U. (2018). Rice production and processing in Ogun State, Nigeria: Qualitative insights from farmers' association. In Obayelu, E. (Eds.), *Food systems sustainability and environmental policies in modern economics* (pp. 188–216). Hershey, PA: IGI Global. https://doi.org/10.4018/978-1-5225-3631-4.ch009.

Oyebola, P. O., Osabuohien, E., & Obasaju, B. (2019). Employment and income effects of Nigeria's agricultural transformation agenda. *African Journal of Economic and Management Studies*. https://doi.org/10.1108/AJEMS-12-2018-0402.

Peters, S. W., Ekpo I. J., & Bisong, F. E. (2010). *Environmental education (Module 1) for Nigerian conservation foundation*.

Reeves, T., Pinstrup-Andersen, P., & Pandya-Lorch, R. (1998). Food security and the role of agricultural research. *Resource Management in Challenged Environments*, 97–102.

Sanni, L. O., Siwoku, B. O., & Adebowale, A. A. (2012). *Baseline survey report of cassava value-chain in Ogun State*.

Unal, F. G. (2007). *The impact of land ownership inequality on rural factor markets*. Policy Innovations.

Rural Transformation Through Savings and Credit Cooperative Societies in Moshi District, Tanzania

Neema P. Kumburu and Vincent Pande

1 INTRODUCTION AND BACKGROUND

Tanzania, like many developing countries, has its share of problems associated with developing its rural sector where the majority of its population lives. Since independence, the government of Tanzania has proclaimed the development of the rural sector to be the cornerstone of the country's development strategy (Aman and Mkumbo 2012). A number of approaches had been initiated in Tanzania to that respect. Some of them have been abolished and then re-established in an effort to pave a smooth road toward rural development through improved agricultural performance and provision of essential social services (Chirwa 1985).

These approaches have had different entry points of foci. There were those that have taken a macro or nationwide coverage while others taking meso level down to micro level focus (Aman and Mkumbo 2012). These attempts included, inter alia, programs to increase access to education, health care

---

N. P. Kumburu (✉)
Department of Business Management, Moshi Co-operative University, Moshi, Tanzania
e-mail: neema.kumburu@mocu.ac.tz

V. Pande
Department of Community and Rural Development,
Moshi Co-operative University, Moshi, Tanzania
e-mail: vincent.pande@mocu.ac.tz

services and water supply and improvement of physical infrastructure supportive for rural, agriculture and industrial development (Mohammed and Lee 2015). These attempts included, inter alia, programs to increase access to education, health care services and water supply and improvement of physical infrastructure supportive for rural, agriculture and industrial development.

In all these programs, more emphasis was given to the improvement of farmers' productivity, food security and stabilization of farm income and markets (Aman and Mkumbo 2012). At all levels, the initiatives which were taken include the provision of rural roads, water master plans, regional integrated development plans, universal primary education, and provision of adult education. Others include rural electrification programs; establishment of a number of industrial estates; industrial research, and folk development institutions throughout the country. The focus was to promote and ensure adaptability of rural-friendly technologies. Further, regional cooperative unions and crop marketing authorities were established in order to allow farmers to easily access credits and export markets.

Despite these approaches, the overall proportion of Tanzanian households below the basic needs poverty line fell slightly from 34.4% in 2006 to 28.2% by 2012 and extreme poverty declined from 11.7 to 9.7% (Belghith et al. 2019). Given that the incidence of poverty declined only slightly, while the population continued to grow, around 12 million Tanzanians continue to live below the poverty line. Poverty remains an overwhelmingly rural and basically an agricultural phenomenon, and particularly among households whose major source of income is from crop production (Aman and Mkumbo 2012). The majority of Tanzanians are still smallholder farmers, but agriculture is the least remunerative sector in the economy (Osabuohien et al. 2019). Records show that the household poverty rate in rural areas is 33%, compared with 21.7% in other urban areas and 4.2% in Dar es Salaam (Household Budget Survey, 2016/2017). The large proportion of the population engaged in agriculture and high rural poverty rates combine to explain why three-quarters of the poor are dependent on agriculture. Generally, rural areas experience variety of social, economic, political, and moral problems such as lower per capita income, lower educational level, fewer employment opportunities, limited educational and cultural facilities, out-migration, less developed health and transport services, fewer commercial facilities, declining small towns, and less confidence in the future prospects (Aman and Mkumbo 2012). The challenge remains to link poor rural households, particularly smallholder farming households, to the national growth story by enhancing their capabilities and accessibility to inputs and technological improvements for increased productivity (Karakara and Osabuohien 2019).

Despite the fact that many people wish to invest in agriculture and other economic activities, however, accessibility to initial capital becomes a challenge to them (Karlsson 2014). SACCOS being one of the microfinance institutions have been seen as having a potential to provide initial capital. SACCOS are considered to be more important in the rural area of Tanzania because they are semiformal financial institutions which serve many inhabitants in rural areas (Wangwe and Lwakatare 2004). SACCOS also operate by focusing not only on the profit but also the welfare of members. SACCOS like any other cooperative work to maximize the welfare of members. In SACCOS members participate in setting the interest rates for loans in which members receive back later as dividends. SACCOS in Tanzania are not only important for providing the capital to rural dwellers who were not previously served by the formal financial institutions but also contribute to overall economy of the country. Bwana and Mwakujonga (2013) stressed that SACCOS contribute to about 40% of the Tanzania's GDP, act as employer for secondary school and college leavers and play important roles for financing small and medium enterprises in the rural areas. Hence many small and medium entrepreneurs are self-employed in the rural areas because they have access to capital from the rural SACCOS. Likewise, SACCOS provide an opportunity to their clients both in rural and urban areas to save their money and hence work as rural banks (Qin and Ndiege 2013).

The government of Tanzania continues to promote SACCOS to enable them to perform their essential roles in Tanzania. The government has formulated various policies which help to sensitize the formation of many SACCOS in Tanzania especially in rural areas (Magali 2014). Statistics show that about 1,153,248 members joined 5559 SACCOS in 2013 (MOFT 2013). This reveals that there is favorable environment for establishment and joining of SACCOS. The government is of the view that SACCOS are an important agency of change especially in its efforts to alleviate poverty and hence the campaign throughout the country encouraging people to form or join SACCOS (Magali 2013; Kumburu et al. 2014). SACCOS are also perceived as an appropriate and microfinancing outlet for rural and poor people. This is because SACCOS are seen as simple form of financial institutions which are well suited to the socio-economic milieu of the rural setting and poor communities.

Over the years, political leaders, policymakers and advocates as well as researchers have come to place more emphasis on rural transformation as one veritable way out of continued impoverishment, moral and social decay precipitated partially by mass inequality, unemployment and poverty in the country (Coker and Obu 2011). It is assumed that rural transformation is a prerequisite for the overall national development of Tanzania (Agwanda and Amani 2014). The government is of the view that SACCOS are an important agency of change especially in its efforts to alleviate poverty.

It therefore becomes imperative to evaluate the operations of existing SACCOS to ascertain their functions in rural areas. One of the questions that still demand answers is whether proper handling of SACCOS can facilitate genuine rural transformation. This study bridges this knowledge gap by analyzing and documenting the contribution of SACCOS in facilitating rural transformation in Moshi district, Tanzania.

This study serves as a guide toward improving knowledge about the contribution of SACCOS on rural transformation. For policymakers this research will be useful because it highlights on how best to use SACCOS loans to finance rural projects. It also gives the government an overview of constraint of rural financing and how best to manage SACCOS' loan in order to yield output. Moreover, the study shows how to use SACCOS to increase rural financing for economic growth.

2 Insights from Previous Studies

2.1 Transformation Paradigm

Paradigms are modalities or path to follow to achieve development, based on a codified set of activities or based on a vision regarding the functioning and evolution of a socio-economic system. Bellu (2011) and Obetta and Okide (2011) identified various transformation paradigm to include the growth pole theory, big push policy, selective approach, the protectionist, top-down, key settlement strategy, bottom-up approach, decentralized territorial approach, adaptive approach, laissez-faire (Magali 2014). The approaches to transformation differ from the above-stated strategies, for instance, the growth pole theory, top-down, trickle-down talk about a centralized, monolithic model of development where economic growth is achieved through the spread of economic growth from urban to rural areas as the government of developing countries induce economic growth and welfare by investing heavily in capital intensive industries in large urban centers or regional capitals (Obetta and Okide 2011). This growth is supposed to spread to the rural areas in a process of regional transformation.

A centralized, monolithic model has been criticized for its failure to meet the need of the rural dweller; the top-down model failed because the institutions created to foster development from the top had themselves become the greatest hindrance to development. The trickle-down model is inappropriate, irrelevant to the environment and needs of the people, it is always a misdirected and misplaced concept when passing down to the poor certain policies and directives from the governing bureaucracy (Joseph 2014). In contrast to the top-down models' central objectives of industrialization and economic growth, the bottom-up model advocates rural transformation and distributional issues. Instead of the state-administered, large scale infrastructure projects that were central to the employment generation strategy of the top-down model, it proposed small-scale, bottom-up projects that directly involved the urban and rural poor in income generating schemes. From the down-up models the community is empowered and mobilized to implement sustainable transformation projects, this implies that transformation starts with the people free from foreign ideology and infections and promotes self-reliance and self-consciousness.

In relation to the transformation initiative undertaken by the Tanzanian government, the term connotes the rapid and fundamental changes to be pursued by the government and other organization, SACCOS inclusive to achieve certain goals within the predetermined framework. Transformation focuses on changes that are material in nature, in particular the transformation of the economic activities (Coker and Obo 2012; Ngah 2012). Transformation permits an improvement in the overall welfare and quality of life of the rural people. It is a trade-off between economic growth and environmental conservation, introducing modern technology yet preserving the traditional culture or reconciling growth with improved social equity.

2.2 Rural Transformation

In the context of this chapter, rural is defined as areas that have a relatively low population density compared to cities, areas where agriculture and related activities usually dominate the landscape and economy. It also includes the towns that are located in these areas and which are linked to them culturally and economically by acting as a focal point for people living in the surrounding areas—places where they can meet, exchange goods and services, and find transport to larger urban centers (Coburn et al. 2007). Rural transformation is a synchronized, complex, four-fold transition of economy, politics, administration, and society. Rural transformation promotes opportunity for synergy in decision-making and practice, requires adequate understanding or appreciation of the rural conditions and meets the vision for rural development (Aman and Mkumbo 2012). Rural development is a process of social and economic change; it is a complex phenomenon and is defined as the outcome of a series of qualitative and quantitative intervention measures occurring in a rural area for the purpose of raising the standard of living and improving livelihoods amid favorable changes in the way of life of the majority of population residing in rural areas (Hodge and Midmore 2008; Osabuohien et al. 2015). Rural development must be sustainable and be self-sustaining.

This study adopts the definition of Mabogunje (1980) who defined rural transformation as improvement of the living standards of the low-income population living in the rural areas on a self-sustaining basis through transforming the socio-spatial structure of their productive activities. This definition is comprehensive and reflects this study as it embraces the changes in rural settings and changes to systems that impact rural people's standard of living particularly low-income people. Further Adedayo (1983) described rural transformation as the improvement and transformation of the rural space with a view to enhancing the quality of life of the inhabitants.

2.3 Theory of Change and Rural Transformation

The theory of change captures the community aspects of rural transformation as well as the economic aspects and identifies potential synergies among economic development and social capital formation. It takes into account both the contributions that community-building can make to rural transformation and the contributions that rural transformation can make to community-building, and treats community as both subject and object of the action (Cordero-Guzmán and Auspos 2006). This theory assumes a direct and linear relationship between community development and economic development inputs. In order to suit the objectives of the study, more variables were added such as government policies, community willingness to participate in community development and community culture. These variables were added in order to portray that community economic development is a result of integrative factors which when combined lead to economic and development outcomes.

The theory proposes a sequential pathway of change in community economic development projects and identifies possible outcomes that include community-building outcomes as well as economic ones (Vidal 1992; and Bendick and Egan 1993). Vidal (1995) article provides additional evidence about long-terms pathways of change and potential spillover effects in revitalization efforts that combine business development with infrastructure improvements and commercial real estate development. Grogan et al. (2001) noted the interconnections among commercial revitalization, housing reinvestment, and efforts to restore public order without elaborating specific pathways of change. Bendick and Egan (1991) looked at the interconnections between rural transformation strategies and business development strategies, the ways progress in one area can stimulate progress in the other, and the potentially synergistic effects of pursuing both types of activities simultaneously. The above literature shows how rural transformation can potentially create business opportunities by creating new markets and reducing operating costs; and how business development can potentially contribute to rural transformation by expanding employment, improving consumer services, creating business markets, rehabilitating real estate, and fostering role models and community leaders.

The overview theory of change shown in Fig. 1 shows that economic development in a rural community can include both targeted economic development strategies and rural transformation strategies such as efforts to promote asset accumulation and access to capital among community residents, projects to improve a neighborhood's physical appearance or the safety of its commercial or residential areas, efforts to organize community groups around economic development projects or to connect local residents or organizations to outside networks or institutions important to the process (Cordero-Guzmán and Auspos (2006). The outcomes that will result from the successful implementation of these projects can include a range of economic outcomes, such as, increased asset accumulation, increased community access to sources of capital, improvements in the general business climate, an increase in the number of healthy businesses (as measured by increased sales, increased number of new and repeat customers, and increased income)

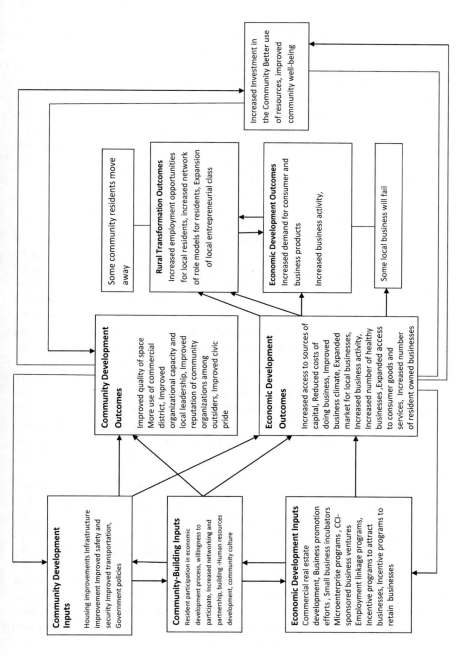

Fig. 1 Overview of theory of change for rural transformation (*Source* Modified from Cordero-Guzmán and Auspos [2006])

an increase in the number of healthy businesses owned by local residents, increased employment opportunities for residents, increased entry into the economic mainstream for some residents, improvements in the price, quality, or mix of goods and services that are available locally to community residents and growth in the size of the local entrepreneurial class.

Cumulatively, these economic outcomes will help plug leaks from the local economy and increase local tax revenues. In addition, rural transformation and business development strategies can produce positive outcomes on the physical infrastructure of the neighborhood. Such outcomes benefit residents directly by improving the quality of space in which they live, and indirectly by encouraging more people to come into the commercial area to spend or invest, and by sending a more positive signal to outsiders about the neighborhood. They also help business by creating new markets and reducing operating costs.

2.4 The Role of SACCOS in Rural Transformation

SACCOS have had a substantial role in the mobilization and allocation of otherwise untapped resources from members. These societies are willing to offer even small sized loans to members which are something that the formal financial institutions will not do in view of the high costs of administration, and lengthy procedures involved in processing information before a decision is made to give out a loan (Wangwe et al. 2004). The high transaction costs, inadequate information and the perception of high risk associated with small scale financing have limited the growth and development of financial services to the low-income people in the country. Financial institutions that have utilized the knowledge and proximity of established institutions have tended to do better (Aryeetey 1998). Unlike banks that experience low loan repayment rates from peasant borrowers, SACCOS' loans have a tendency toward lower default rates. Borrowers know that the loans come from savings of the community. Community pressure, access to information and close follow up have been combined to enhance access even without having to use conventional forms of collateral (Wangwe and Lwakatare 2004).

SACCOS, like every cooperative financial institution, are institutions that present eminent advantages over other types of financial intermediaries, but also weakness which if ignored often lead to failures. On the advantage side, the most important is that SACCOS provide a solution to the problem of market failure by the investor-owned formal banking system which tend to exclude micro and small enterprises, poor individuals and small farmers. The primary objective of SACCOS is to ensure that the rural population has access to fund for microenterprises. SACCOS have impacted the rural communities in such a way that it has transformed the economic, social and political life of the people. In that regard, SACCOS can focus on aiding the creation or expansion of small businesses in rural areas in Moshi District Tanzania by attracting established businesses; or retaining existing businesses that could expand their markets and improve production and reduce costs by relocating.

Based on the above explanation, SACCOS can focus on aiding the creation or expansion of small businesses in rural areas by attracting established businesses into the area; or retaining existing businesses that could expand their markets and improve production and reduce costs by relocating. Frequently, these business development efforts are undertaken in tandem with physical revitalization efforts, especially with commercial and agricultural activities. The theory of change discussed here and shown in Fig. 2 is derived from a number of studies and what they suggest about the outcomes that might result from the various strategies. In the short term, business stimulation strategies might result in several direct economic benefits for Moshi District residents. Specifically, they could help to:

- Increase the overall level of business activity or the number of healthy businesses
- Increase employment opportunities for local residents
- Increase the number of resident entrepreneurs
- Expand, diversify or improve the supply of goods and services available to residents
- Stem leakages from the local neighborhood economy.

Each of these outcomes could also be a step along a pathway of longer term economic change. For example, achieving an overall increase in the level of local business activity, agricultural activities or the number of healthy companies, and/or improving the local shopping options might encourage more residents to shop locally. This increased demand could, in turn, help promote additional investment, which could lead to more jobs and more business development, a phenomenon known as economic multiplier effects. Business stimulation strategies can also produce important community building outcomes by

- developing human resources that have been under-utilized;
- increasing the supply and capacity of local leadership;
- developing local role models who can provide mentorship, guidance, and resources for young residents; and
- building networks and social connections among residents, local organizations, and outside groups.

In the longer term, these community-building effects can help improve the capacity of the community to solve its own problems and enhance its reputation with external groups, as well as reinforcing and contributing to economic growth. The added community capacity can be used to bring additional resources into the community and to make better use of what is available.

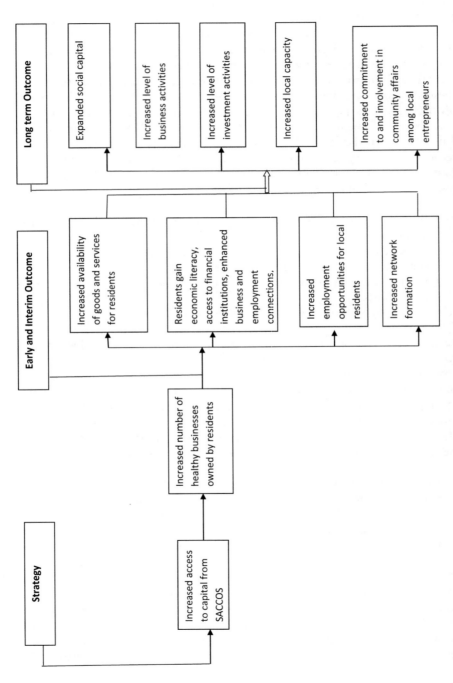

Fig. 2 Role of SACCOS in rural transformation (*Source* Modified from Cordero-Guzmán and Auspos [2006])

2.5 Issues in Empirical Literature Review

Many have subscribed to the belief that microfinance is an effective and powerful tool for poverty reduction. To affirm the above statement, Amin et al. (2003) focused on the ability of microfinance to reach the poor and concluded that microfinance has served people below and above the poverty line. The result of empirical evidence indicates that the poorest can benefit from microfinance both on economic and social well-being point of views, and that this can be done without jeopardizing the financial sustainability of the micro financial institutions (Dahiru and Zubair 2008; Nwankwo 2007).

Taiwo (2012) in another study of the impact of microfinance banks on welfare and poverty alleviation in South West States in Nigeria using regression analysis indicates that microfinance banks in Ogun and Lagos States of Nigeria shows that microfinancing had improved the welfare of the enterprises and the individuals in terms of improved savings, earning (both for individual wage earners and the self-employed), facilitated access to loan facilities, improved sales revenue as well as the level of employment and growth in the microenterprises examined. The study recommended that since higher education has been found to increase the income of the microfinance institutions (MFIs) clients; the MFIs clients should be encouraged by the MFIs to improve on their current level of education by engaging in adult education or lifelong learning.

Girabi and Mwakaje (2013) applied the descriptive and multivariate regression model to investigate the impacts of microfinance (SACCOS) on agricultural productivity of smallholder farmers in Tanzania specifically in Iramba District (Singidaregion). The study found out that majority of the beneficiaries invested only 26.5% of the total credit received for agricultural production. However, the credits beneficiaries realized high agricultural productivity compared to the non-credits because they were relatively better in accessing markets for agricultural commodities, use of inputs and adoption of improved farming technologies.

Babajide (2011) studied the effects of microfinancing on micro and small enterprises (SMEs) in South West Nigeria using Diagnostic Test Kaplan–Meier Estimate, Hazard Model and Multiple Regression Analysis. The study indicated that microfinance enhances survival of small businesses but does not enhance growth and expansion capacity of MSEs although they impact significantly on the level of productivity of MSEs operators. Further it was reported that the provision of non-financial service by microfinance institutions enhances the performance of micro and small enterprises (MSEs).

Olaitan (2006) observed that microfinance banks have disbursed more than 800 million micro credits to over 13,000 farmers across Nigeria to empower their productive capacities. As such, it was expected that agricultural output will increase with the increase in funding. Kato and Kratzer (2013) examined how microfinance empowered women in Tanzania by using Mann–Whitney U test. The study noted a significant difference between the women members and non-members of the MFIs. The women members had more control over savings and income and were empowered in decision-making. Nwanko and Okeke (2017) asserted that microfinance has impacted positively on the rural poor by providing loans and advances for agriculture, investment opportunities, savings mobilization and credit delivery; asset financing and community development financing. Further, he observed that despite the achievements of microfinance in transforming the rural areas, they have been met with stiff difficulties like repayment problem, illiteracy among the poor and inadequate or non-monitoring of micro and small enterprises by the micro financial institutions. Ravikumar (2016), in his study on contribution of microfinance in empowering the women entrepreneurs in Gulbarga city concluded that women entrepreneurs have been empowered in the different sections of their business operations and social status under the dynamic guidance and support of microfinance institutions. This shows that microfinance institutions have played a crucial role in improving the status of people.

Ndiege et al. (2014) noted that failure of formal financial institutions to serve properly the rural financial markets has been the strengths of the less-formal financial institutions which appear to have the ability to reach many people at one time (Kaleshu and Temu 2012) although their main challenge is inadequate finance. SACCOS which are cooperative-based microfinance institutions are the most useful less-formal institutions in Tanzania (Bee 2009; Maghimbi 2010) and were principally developed to meet financial services particularly savings and credit to support the lower and middle-class income earners so as to improve their living (McKillop and Wilson 2011). Due to their deep ability to reach the poor majority that formal institutions have failed to serve, SACCOS have proved to be superior as they can work without physical collateral through using other means which reduce financial risks (Okura and Zhang 2012). The Report on the Survey of Rural Savings and Credit Cooperative Societies in Tanzania revealed that the SACCOS are the most significant forms of participation in financial markets available to the rural Tanzanians aiming at improving rural livelihood (Mwelukilwa 2001). Thus, to facilitate easy access to financing social and economic needs, Tanzania encouraged the establishment and use of SACCOS.

Kushoka (2013) argued that employee-based SACCOS are essential for economic development of its members in Tanzania because they provide capital. Maghimbi (2010) noted that some SACCOS in Tanzania expressed their sympathy to the surrounding communities as a way of sharing their impacts. Example UruNjari Co-operative Society in Kilimanjaro region in Tanzania, built schools and also donated money for the construction of water scheme, gave aids to the dispensary and supported the caring of orphans. Moreover, some primary cooperatives facilitated the construction of a water scheme for their members. Similarly, Nelson (2012) reported that Lulu SACCOS donated 25 matrices and 60 school benches worth 3.4 million Tshs (about 2100 $) to Luanda ward health center in Mbeya city.

On the other side, there have been conflicting ideas about the impact of microfinance in the transformation of rural dwellers. The objective of microfinance system in Tanzania is to serve low-income segment of the society and contribute to economic growth and reduction of poverty (URT 2012), few studies have revealed little contribution of SACCOS in poverty reduction. A study by Churk (2015) revealed that SACCOS have little contribution in supporting business, agriculture and education sectors in the study area. She further noted that SACCOS in the study area have been providing a minimal financial support in agriculture sector, a feature that prevents rural people to access important agricultural inputs that could help them to improve production and ultimately contribute to alleviate poverty. Similarly, Chambo (2003) noted that in rural areas, SACCOS were not seen as providing alternative financial mechanisms for the agricultural economy, but centers for storing money, separated from investment activities in agriculture. On the contrary, Islam (2006) stated that the poorest can benefit from microfinance from both a material and social well-being as studies have proof of impact of microfinance on health, nutrition, and school supporting.

Based on the above empirical studies, it can be established that SACCOS can facilitate rural transformation. However, the extent to which SACCOS can facilitate rural transformation is yet to be quantified. This study makes a contribution to knowledge by bridging this observed gap.

3 Methodology

This study was carried out in Moshi rural District in Kilimanjaro Region in 2016. The study focused on cross-case variations with consideration within-case variation. The total number of Savings and Credit Co-operatives (SACCOS) in Moshi rural District was 56. Two SACCOS, Umoja, and Mruwia formed a potential case. Official statistics from the Co-operative office in Kilimanjaro shows that in Moshi rural there were 32,106 members. Out of the total number, 150 members were selected, which is equivalent to 10% of the total population. According to Mugenda and Mugenda (2003), a sample size of 10% of the total population is considered adequate for a descriptive study.

The survey method was applied with the use of structured pre-tested questionnaires. To identify and document SACCOS' practical contribution on rural transformation, a 5-point Likert scale was used. The points were distributed into five responses; 5 points for strongly agree, 4 points for agree, 3 points for neutral, 2 points for disagree and 1 point for strongly disagree. The scoring technique was revised for negatively worded items. This is designed to solicit more definitive responses from respondents, rather than eliciting muted, unvarying responses (DeVellis 2003; Roberts, et al. 1999), and in order to reduce bias response (Churchill 1979). In that regard, a decision range was set at mean rating of 3.0 and above, accepted as positive contribution, and mean rating below 3.0, regarded as not significant and hence negative contribution.

Note that the declarative statement typically expresses a clearly positive or negative opinion and not a neutral one. Furthermore, some argue that a well-designed questionnaire should have some of the items reversed so that response bias in the form of acquiescence is reduced. To examine the impact of rural transformation contributed by SACCOS with a view to measure the weight of contribution, multiple regression analysis was used. Past studies of similar nature were consulted in the selection of which variables that would come into the model. The multiple regression equation is thus written as:

$$Y = \alpha + \beta_1 x_1 + \beta_2 x_2 + \beta_3 x_3 + \beta_p x_p + \varepsilon \qquad (1)$$

where;

Y = Dependent variable representing annual turnover and expenditures.

$x_1 - x_p$ = Independent variables which includes, asset, annual profit, liabilities, rural customer size, rural investment rural income generation and loan and advances.

$\beta_1 - \beta_p$ = Regression coefficients.

α = Intercept.

ε_i = Error term.

When X and Y variables mentioned above are substituted into Eq. 1 above the following model was obtained:

$$Y = \alpha + \beta_1 ASS + \beta_2 ANPR + \beta_3 LIA + \beta_4 RCSIZ + \beta_5 RI + \beta_6 RIG + \beta_7 LA + \varepsilon \qquad (2)$$

For details see Table 1.

Table 1 Explanatory variables and the hypotheses included in regression analysis

Variables	Definition of variable	Unit	Hypotheses
x_1 = Assets	An asset is a resource with economic value that an individual owns and controls with the expectation that it will provide a future benefit	Value of asset in Tsh (USD)	+
x_2 = Annual Profit	Difference between the amount earned and the amount spent in buying, operating, or producing something	Amount of money in Tsh (USD)	+
x_3 = Liabilities	Debts or obligations that arise during the course of business operations	Amount of money in Tsh (USD)	−
x_4 = Rural Customer Size	Number of people who repeatedly purchase the goods or services of a business	Number of people	+
x_5 = Rural Investment	The act of putting money, effort, time, etc. into something to make a profit or get an advantage in rural area	Amount of money in Tsh (USD)	+
x_6 = Rural income	Per capital rural income of residents	Amount of money in Tsh (USD)	
x_7 = Loans and Advances	Debt that one is obligated to repay according to the loan's terms and conditions	Amount of money in Tsh (USD)	+

3.1 Social Economic Characteristics of Studied SACCOS

The findings show that the studied SACCOS had been in operation for more than ten years with total number of 1405 members and capital of 300 million Tsh (157,894.7 USD) for Mruwia and 620 and capital of 600 million Tsh (315,789.4 USD) for Umoja SACCOS. The results further indicate that loans issued to members were at the edge of 1.2 billion Tsh (equivalent to 657,894.7 USD) and 900 million Tsh (equivalent to 473,682.2 USD) for Mruwia and Umoja SACCOS, respectively. The findings reveal that both SACCOS had been providing loan to the members. This implies that members have been engaging in social economic activities. This concurs with the study done by Cheruiyot et al. (2012) and Diagne and Zeller (2001) which purport that the primary role of SACCOS is. to promote economy among its members by providing loans at fair and reasonable interest rate for provident and productivity purpose. SACCOS are geared toward providing opportunities for improved incomes to members and protecting them from risk (ILO 2003). This is to say that SACCOS have been successful in partaking in rural community development issues. For details see Table 2.

3.2 SACCOS Practical Contribution on Rural Transformation

The analysis revealed that each of the 9 items processed had a mean score greater than the accepted mean score of 3.00. This depicts that the respondents (community members) do agree that SACCOS in the study area do transform rural sector. SACCOS as member-owned and controlled business distributes benefits based on use, and the distribution of net income based on patronage rather than investment (Zeuli and Cropp 2004). Similarly, SACCOS provide its members with means where by significant proportion of the people are able to take into its own hands the tasks of creating productive employment, overcoming poverty and achieving social integration and continue to be an important means, common to all are the cooperative values of safe-help, self-responsibility, democracy, equality equity, and solidarity (Ezekiel 2014). For details see Table 3.

In this study cooperatives capture three contemporary development paradigms: self-help, asset-base, and self-development for transforming rural communities (Zeuli and Radel 2005). SACCOS create a model of self-help community development where members are at the core of the process

Table 2 Socio-economic characteristics of studied SACCOS

Variables	Mruwia SACCOS	Umoja SACCOS
Established	2003	2006
Membership	1405	620
Loan Issued	1,250,000,000	900,000,000
Capital	300,000,000	600,000,000

Table 3 Members transformation through SACCOS

Variable	Avarage	SD
Self-help: (Members)		
Improved quality of life;	4.754	0.90
Increased internal capacity	4.467	0.77
gainful employment,	4.725	0.90
guaranteed income,	4.371	0.87
Community asset: (Members and community)		
Human capital—education, skills, and training;	4.719	0.93
Social capital—increased political knowledge; greater network opportunities and community cohesion;	4.060	1.02
Financial capital—increase in income via employment and return on investment, equity building and easier access to fund	4.808	0.82
Self-development: (community)		
Leadership and governance skills;	4.234	0.96
Improved knowledge—administrative, technical and financial	4.826	0.81

Decision range: *Is that, mean rating of 3.0 and above was accepted as SACCOS transform rural rector, while a mean rating below 3.0 was regarded as not significant*

with the goals of improving the quality of life and increasing the internal capacity of the community to create change by institutionalizing the community development process (Flora et al. 2004; Green et al. 2002; Zeuli and Radel 2005). This reveals that SACCOS members in Umoja and Mruwia SACCOS used local financial resources to create businesses that in turn provide income to the owner and also provide employment opportunity even to other community members who were not members of the SACCOS and thus leads to rural transformation.

Furthermore, a community's assets include the human, social, physical, financial, and environmental. By virtue of being locally developed, locally owned, and locally controlled, cooperatives clearly build on a community's human capital, social capital, and financial capital. The cooperative contribution to human capital development (education, skills, and experience) is reasoned as the most substantial community transformation impact (Zeuli and Radel 2005). Cooperatives build local human capital through member education and leadership opportunities by holding a position in SACCOS, for instance, be among the board of directors. It was reported that though education given members were able to make analysis concerning price of their produce and finally they managed to sell at a higher price. Thus, cooperatives play an important role in developing local leadership (Green et al. 2002; Zeuli and Radel 2005).

On the aspect of the role of SACCOS in transforming rural areas, three variables were studied. These includedemployment opportunities, cash flow and rural investment as well as community development programs. Concerning employment opportunities, findings indicate that for the past five years a total of 50 members were employed in the SACCOS at different levels and functions. This reveals that that in term of employment opportunities, substantial members of the rural communities were employed. This is a form of transformation that is capable of enhancing proper grass-root development.

Concerning community development programs, findings show that 60% of selected SACCOS participated in rural transformation directly in community-based programs. Such programs included direct financial support to some projects like repair roads, hospitals, and schools. This is a boost to rural transformation because without SACCOS contributions to these development projects it would take a longer time for the government either central or local to fund those projects.

Other areas on which SACCOS contribute to rural transformation is on cash flow and rural investment. Since SACCOS are owned and controlled by their members. The members typically have some connection with each other. SACCOS provide low-cost financial services. They charge lower rates for fees and services, and pay higher interest rates on savings. In Mruwia and Umoja, SACCOS help members move into the economic mainstream by providing loan, education, and counseling which enable them to effectively invest the funds in agricultural. For example, for the past five years a total of 1.2 billion Tsh (equivalent to 657,894.7 USD) and 900 million Tsh (equivalent to 473,682.2 USD) were issued to the members as loans in Mruwia and Umoja SACCOS and thus contribute to cash flow and rural investment.

3.3 Effects of SACCOS on Rural Transformation

Table 4 summarizes the multiple regression estimates of effects of SACCOS on rural transformation. The F-value was 23.3, with a p-value 0.001, indicating that the model was statistically significant. The coefficient of determination (R^2) was 0.523, meaning that approximately 52% of variability of the dependent variable (Annual turnover) was accounted for by the explanatory variables in the model. Thus, the regression model was adequate. Gujarati and Porter (2004) states that in determining model adequacy, we look at some broad features of the results, such as the R^2 value and F-value, which were both statistically significant in this study.

Table 4 Multiple regression on the effects of SACCOS to rural transformation

Variables	B	Std. Error	Beta	T	P-value
Constant	−8,439,417	2,431,803		−3.47	0.000
Assets	32,386	29,564	0.060	1.10	0.280
Annual profit	915,591	950,532	0.060	.963	0.340
Liabilities	618,620	680,032	0.060	.910	0.360
Rural customer size	27,046	15,009	0.110	1.80	0.046
Rural investment	2,064,320	718,437	0.170	2.87	0.010
Rural income generation	710756	64,898	0.630	11.0	0.000
Loans and advances	−1,839,085	440,337	0.240	4.18	0.000

Dependent Variable: Annual turnover and expenditures on development issues $R^2 = 0.523$ F = 23.3 Significant at $P < 0.05$

The results (Table 4) show that asset (P-value = 0.280), annual profit (P-value = 0.340) and liabilities (P-value = .0.360) were positively correlated though not statistically significant with rural transformation. This means rural transformation does not depend on asset, annual profit and liabilities of the SACCOS, respectively. This implies although SACCOS members do get benefit from loans obtained from SACCOS but not all the time have direct impact to community. Similarly, Amin et al. (2003) noted that, microfinance is not considered by beneficiaries to be an effective and powerful tool for rural transformation perhaps due to low circulation of money in the study area as a result members fail to meet their economic goals and at the same time fail to repay their loan on time. Indeed this is obvious to SACCOS whose members perceive that cooperative society benefited more than its members through interest rates, forfeited shares and other penalties upon default of the debts.

The findings further imply that not all the time members are able to meet their liabilities. This can be attributed by poor participation of members in decision-making and inability of members to repay loans due to poor yield from their economic activities. On some occasions, members are forced to repay some amount of their loan before investing for fear of losing their assets guaranteed as collateral security for the loan. Similarly, Komba (2005) noted that low repayment rate of loans among majority of rural SACCOS is due to the fact that most of the members depend on agriculture activities to earn income on which agriculture is seasonal and hence lead to high loan delinquency (Wangwe and Lwakatare 2004). This was also supported by Wangwe and Lwakatare (2004) who reported that poor loan repayment and high loan delinquency is among the major challenges facing Tanzania's SACCOS. This is apparent that poor governance in some SACCOS leads to inadequate planning and management henceforth poor participation in decision-making and poor members' empowerment in all aspects of money management and entrepreneurship. This is supported by Chambo (2003) who noted that lack of participatory planning, poor management and poor SACCOS' leaders who do not have member empowerment strategies have therefore prevented members' prosperity in terms of living standards.

Rural Customer size was observed to be a very important measure of rural transformation involving SACCOS in the study area. A correlation (R) of 27,046 was obtained. This indicates that a unit increase in customer size will lead to an increase in SACCOS profit by Tsh 27,046 (equivalent to USD 11.75). This suggests that as SACCOS' membership increases it will lead to increase in SACCOS' capital. This implies that many people in rural areas depend much on SACCOS for their financial services. In turn this enables them to access loan from the SACCOS and perform their social economic activities. Kessy and Urio (2006) noted that poor majority who are residing in rural settings are the most excluded in formal financial system and thus credit unions become the solution to many rural people (Bee 2009; Maghimbi

2010). One could therefore infer that the rural customer size facilitates SACCOS' financial sustainability through their savings which in return enable members to obtain financial resources hence leading to rural transformation. Similarly, Kumburu et al. (2014) found that rural settings provide customer base to SACCOS who repetitively purchase the goods or services of a business and thus appear to be very important measure of rural transformation in the rural areas. On the contrary, a study by Kaleshu and Temu (2012) portrayed that although SACCOS have the ability to reach many people at one time in rural areas, they have less to give to meet the real demand for financial services especially loans hence (Churk 2015) promotion of rural livelihood becomes insignificant. This means not all SACCOS have been able to satisfy their members through provision of loans that enable them to meet social economic requirements.

Rural investment was statistically significant (0.10) and had a positive value. Rural investment contributes to the pace of rural transformation with a correlation R of 0.2064320. This reveals that rural investment contributes to Tsh 2,064,320 (equivalent to USD 897.5). The possible explanation is that SACCOS facilitate their members to engage in rural investment through providing development loans. This concurs with the study done by Ahimbisibwe (2009) who asserted that SACCOS have enabled the savers to put their loans in agricultural development thereby increasing the productivity in the agricultural sector and enhancing food security. Nuwagaba (2012) also found that loan provided to members by SACCOS in rural settings enabled them to purchase agricultural inputs in order to enhance their productivity. Similarly, Christiaensen et al. (2009) noted that loans given by SACCOS to members help create conditions that, in the long run, encourage enterprise development, enable them to remain economically viable, and stimulate additional investment in the community. Sizya (2001) in similar case found that cooperative societies play a significant role in efficient marketing and distribution of goods and services especially for small-scale farmers and the rural poor people. However, a study by Churk (2015)revealed that SACCOS have been providing a minimal financial support in agriculture sector, a situation that inhibits rural dwellers to access important agricultural inputs that could help them to improve production and ultimately contribute to rural transformation. The same case was supported by Chambo (2003) who noted that in rural areas, SACCOS were not seen as providing alternative financial mechanisms for the agricultural economy, but centers for storing money, separated from investment activities in agriculture. This is to say that not all SACCOS in a rural setting provide adequate services to members that result in their economic change and community transformation in general.

The coefficient of rural income was statistically significant ($P=0.000$) and positive meaning that a unit increase in the capital resulted in the increase to the total variance in rural transformation across the rural communities by Tsh 710,756 (equivalent to USD 309). This implies that SACCOS enable members to engage in economic activities that facilitate increase of income.

That is to say, rural dwellers who are traditionally farmers, fishermen or petty traders get access to financial services from the SACCOS which enable them to raise their income. Credits and savings facilities enable farmers to invest in land improvements or agricultural technology such as high-yielding seeds and mineral fertilizers that increase incomes (IFPRI 1998).The same is supported by Sizya (2001) who noted that the benefits of SACCOS, among others, include improvement in member's income earned and other economic benefits.

Loan and advances were found to be statistically significant and positively correlated with rural transformation. This suggests that a unit increase in loan and advances will lead to increase in rural turnover and expenditure by Tsh 1,839,085 (equivalent to USD 799.6), This implied that the studied SACCOS do provide loans to members which in return are used to meet socio-economic needs of members thus create benefits not only to members but also to community. It further indicates that the SACCOS do get reasonable profit as a result of interest repaid by members from their loans which some of it might be used to spearhead rural socio-economic development. Similarly, Gachara (1990) noted that cooperatives are seen as vehicles for resource mobilization and gateways to economic prosperity for families and communities hence they play an important role in members' wealth and employment creation thus facilitating in poverty alleviation. A study by Mbagga (2013) in Tanzania found that SACCOS act as a good predictor of long run rates of economic growth, capital accumulation and productivity improvement due to provision of loan to members. Martin et al. (2001) on the study of analysis of customer disequilibrium preferences also revealed that the majority of loans from credit and cooperative unions were used by members for housing and real estate related developments. Also, Isote (2007) found that through loans from the SACCOS, rural people had managed to pay tuition fees of their children hence contributed to rural transformation. The Report on the Survey of Rural Savings and Credit Co-operative Societies in Tanzania revealed that the SACCOS are the most significant forms of participation in financial markets available to the rural Tanzanians aiming at improving rural livelihood (Mwelukilwa 2001).

Likewise, Churk (2015) noted that cooperatives have been playing a role in the construction and improvement of various basic rural infrastructures such as school classrooms, school desks, and other rural infrastructure. Islam (2006) supported this when he stated that the poorest can benefit from microfinance from both a material and social well-being as studies have proof of impact of microfinance on health, nutrition and school supporting. It is apparent that, SACCOS are a leading source of the cooperative credit for socio-economic development in rural areas as a result of provision of credit for a wide range of purposes and the relatively very easy and friendly loaning terms.

4 Conclusion and Recommendation

The overall objective of the study was to analyzing and documenting contribution of SACCOS in facilitating rural transformation in Moshi District, Tanzania. Specifically, the study identifies and documents SACCOS practical contribution on rural transformation. It can be concluded that in the study areas, SACCOS have considerable potential to transform rural areas through the provision of goods, services and employment, which are needed in rural communities. SACCOS play very important roles in increasing the material welfare of their members in terms of living standards, income, enhancement of skills and knowledge as well as leadership and governance. Further, it can be concluded that SACCOS enabled the rural communities to generate their own financial and physical capital within the rural environment thus giving them ownership and hence a stronger interest in the project and its outcome. However, it should be noted that inadequate SACCOS management, poor leadership and participation of members can make the SACCOS become insolvent hence inadequate financial services.

In this light, it can be said that more campaigns should be made to educate rural people on the purpose and benefits of SACCOS as a driver of the socio-economic transformation of rural communities, emphasizing the need for synergy and the economic efficiency gains to be derived from SACCOS endeavors. In the same line, good governance should be promoted in SACCOS to make them sustainable and stronger organizations. Through practicing (the pillars of) good governance, the SACCOS leaders can be accountable and responsible with the capacity to formulate and implement good strategic, business and succession plans as well as adequate organizational setup and transparent operational system. For these suggestions, therefore, more studies are required to determine governance practices and sustainability of SACCOS in rural areas.

References

Adedayo, A. F. (1983). Spatial dimensions of rural development projects in Kwara state. In *Proceedings of the 26th Annual Conference of NGA*. Ilorin.

Agwanda, A., & Amani, H. (2014). *Population growth, structure and momentum in Tanzania*. Economic and Social Research Foundation.

Ahimbisibwe, F. (2009). *The effects of Savings and Credit Co-operative (SACCOS) on members saving culture case study: Ntungamo District*. Cooperatives Development Department, Ministry of Tourism, Trade and Industry.

Aman, H., & Mkumbo, E. (2012). *Strategic research on the extent to which Tanzania has transformed its rural sector for economic growth and poverty reduction*. REPOA 17th Annual Research Workshop, White sands Hotel, Dar es Salaam.

Amin, S., Rai, A. S., & Topa, G. (2003). Does Microcredit Reach the poor and Vulnerable? Evidence from Northern Bangladesh. *Journal of Development Economics, 70*(1), 59–82.

Aryeetey, E. (1998). *Informal finance for private sector development in Africa*. CIRAD, Montpelie: Finance and Rural Development in West Africa.

Babajide, A. (2011). Impact analysis of microfinance in Nigeria. *International Journal of Economics and Finance, 3*(4).

Bee, F. K. (2009). *Rural financial markets in Tanzania: An analysis of access to financial services in Babati district, Manyara region*. Doctoral dissertation.

Belghith, N. B. H., Karamba, R. W., Talbert, E. A., & De Boisseson, P. M. A. (2019). *Tanzania - Mainland poverty assessment 2019 (Vol. 2): Part 2: Structural Transformation and Firms Performance* (English). Washington, DC: World Bank Group.

Bellu, L. G. (2011). *Development and development paradigms*. Accessed February 14, 2018, from http://www.fao.org/easypol2011.

Bendick, M., & Egan, M. L. (1991). *Business development in the inner-city: Enterprise with community links*. Community Development Research Center, Graduate School of Management and Urban Policy, New School for Social Research.

Bendick, M., & Egan, M. L. (1993). Linking business development and community development in inner cities. *Journal of Planning Literature, 8*(1), 3–19.

Bwana, K. M., & Mwakujonga, J. (2013). Issues in SACCOS development in Kenya and Tanzania: The historical and development perspectives. *Developing Country Studies, 3*(5), 114–121.

Chambo, S. A. (2003). *What is micro credit?* Paper Presented to the East African Regional Block, Assembly and Conference, Dar es salaam, Tanzania 14th–15th July.

Cheruiyot, T. K., Kimeli, C. M., & Ogendo, S. M. (2012). Effect of savings and credit co-operative societies strategies on member's savings mobilization in Nairobi, Kenya. *International Journal of Business and Commerce, 1*(11), 40–63.

Chirwa, W. C. (1985). Malawian migrant labour and the politics of HIV. *Aids*, 1993.

Christiaensen, L. J. M., & Todo, Y. (2009, August 16–22). *Poverty reduction during the rural-urban transformation: The role of the missing middle*. Paper presented at the 2009 Conference of the International Association of Agricultural Economists, Beijing, China.

Churchill, G. A. (1979). A paradigm for developing better measures of marketing constructs. *Journal of Marketing Research, 16*(2), 64–73.

Churk, J. P. (2015, July). Contributions of savings and credit cooperative society on improving rural livelihood in Makungu ward Iringa, Tanzania. In *Proceedings of the Second European Academic Research Conference on Global Business, Economics, Finance and Banking (EAR15Swiss Conference), Zurich, Switzerland* (pp. 1–14).

Coburn, A. F., MacKinney, A. C., McBride, T. D., Mueller, K. J., Slifkin, R. T., & Wakefield, M. K. (2007). Choosing rural definitions: Implications for health policy. *Issue Brief, 2*, 1–8.

Coker, M. A., & Obo, U. B. (2011). *Problems and prospects of implementing rural transformation programmes in Odukpan Local Government Area of Cross River State, Nigeria*.

Coker, M. A., & Obo, U. B. (2012). *Problems and prospect of implementing rural transformation programmes*. Accessed March 25, 2015, from http://www.rrpjournals.com/.

Cordero-Guzmán, H., & Auspos, P. (2006). *Community economic development and community change* (pp. 195–265). Community change: Theories, practice and evidence.

Dahiru, M. A., & Zubair, H. (2008). *Microfinance in Nigeria and the prospects of introducing its Islamic version there in the light of the selected Muslim countries experience* (Munich Personal REPEC Archive. Paper, 8287, 68–86).

DeVellis, R. F. (2003). *Scale development: Theory and applications* (2nd ed.). Thousand Oaks: Sage.

Diagne, A., & M. Zeller. (2001). *Access to credit and its impact on welfare in Malawi* (Research Report 116). International Food Policy Research Institute, p. 153.

Ezekiel, P. O. (2014). A study on co-operative societies, poverty reduction and sustainable development in Nigeria. *IOSR Journal of Business and Management, 16*(6), 132–140.

Flora, C. B., Flora, J. L., & Fey, S. (2004). *Rural communities: Legacy and change* (2-rd ed.). Boulder: Westview.

Gachara, D. (1990). A study of co-operative sector in Kenya. *Co-operatives as Means of Economic Recovery and Poverty Reduction* (1st Ed.). Macmillian.

Girabi, F., & Mwakaje, A. E. G. (2013). Impact of microfinance on smallholder farm productivity in Tanzania: The case of Iramba district. *Asian Economic and Financial Review, 3*(2), 227–242.

Green, G. P., Haines, A., Dunn, A., & Sullivan, D. M. (2002). The role of local development organizations in rural America. *Rural Sociology, 67*(3), 394–415.

Grogan, P., Grogan, P. S., & Proscio, T. (2001). *Comeback cities: A blueprint for urban neighborhood revival*. Westview Press.

Gujarati, D. N., & Porter, D. C. (2004). *Basic econometrics* (ed.). McGraw-Hill. Irwin, a business.

Hodge, I., & Midmore, P. (2008). Models of rural development and approaches to analysis evaluation and decision-making. *Économierurale Agricultures, Alimentations, Territories, 307,* 23–38.

ILO. (2003). *The role of co-operatives in designing and implementing poverty reduction strategies*.

International Food Policy Research Institute. (1998). *Food policy report on rural finance and poverty alleviation*. Washington, DC: Urban Institute Press.

Islam, S. (2006). Can microfinance 'Halve' poverty by 2015: Review of theories and explanations. In L. Kushnick & J. Jennings (Eds.), *A new introduction to poverty: The role of race, power, and politics*. New York: New York University Press.

Isote, L. G. (2007). *An assessment of the performance of savings and credit cooperative societies in delivering services to rural primary school teachers*. Unpublished Advances Diploma in Rural Development Planning Dissertation Dodoma.

Kaleshu, J. T., & Temu, S. (2012). Expansion of rural financial services through linkage banking in Tanzania: Is joint action between savings and credit co-operative societies (SACCOS) a promising approach? *Journal of Enterprise Development and Microfinance, 23*(2), 146–160.

Karakara, A. A., & Osabuohien, E. (2019). Households' ICT access and bank patronage in West Africa: Empirical insights from Burkina Faso and Ghana. *Technology in Society, 56,* 116–125. https://doi.org/10.1016/j.techsoc.2018.09.010.

Karlsson, J. (2014). *Challenges and opportunities of foreign investment in developing country agriculture for sustainable development* (FAO Commodity and Trade Policy Research Working Paper, 48).

Kato, M. P., & Kratzer, J. (2013, February). Empowering women through microfinance: Evidence from Tanzania. *ACRN Journal of Entrepreneurship Perspectives, 2*(1), 31–59.

Kessy, S. S., & Urio, F. M. (2006). *The contribution of microfinance institutions to poverty reduction in Tanzania* (No. 6). Mkuki and Nyota Publishers.

Komba, L. C. (2005). *Report of the special presidential committee on reviving, strengthening and developing cooperatives in Tanzania*, Government Printer, Dar es salaam, Tanzania.

Kumburu, N., Pande, V., & Buberwa, E. (2014). Agency theory and performance of savings and credit co-operative societies (SACCOS) in Kilimanjaro region: The case of selected SACCOS in Moshi municipality. *Journal of Co-Operative and Business Studies (JCBS)*, *1*(1), 2014.

Kushoka, I. (2013). Sustainability of an employee based savings and credit co-operative society: A case of Dar Es Salaam City Council SACCOs Tanzania. *American Based Research Journal*, *2*(7).

Mabogunje, A. L. (1980). *The development process: A spatial perspective*. London: Hutchinson.

Magali, J. (2013). *Impacts of rural savings and credits cooperative societies (SACCOS') loans on borrowers in Tanzania*.

Magali, J. J. (2014). Effectiveness of loan portfolio management in rural SACCOS: Evidence from Tanzania. *Business and Economic Research*, *4*(1), 299–318.

Maghimbi, S. (2010). *Issues in subsides and sustainability of microfinance: An empirical investigation* (Working papers CEB, 10).

Martin, L., Menold, M. M., & Donnelly S. L. (2001). Analysis of customer disequilibrium preferences. Ravan SA. *Effects of Promoting Longer-Term Financing*, *9*(6), 43–48.

Mbagga, A. P. (2013). *The role of saving and credit cooperative societies (SACCOS) in poverty reduction: Evidence from same district*. Doctoral dissertation.

McKillop, D., & Wilson, J. O. (2011). Credit unions: A theoretical and empirical overview. *Financial Markets, Institutions & Instruments*, *20*(3), 79–123.

Ministry of Finance, Tanzania (MOFT). (2013). *Speech by the Minister for Finance Hon. Dr. William AugustaoMgimwa (Mp)*. The Estimates of Government Revenue and Expenditure for the Fiscal Year 2013/14.

Mohammed, N., & Lee, B. W. (2015). Role of cooperatives in rural development, the case of south nations nationalities and people region, Ethiopia. *Science Journal of Business and Management*, *3*(4), 102–108.

Mugenda, O. M., & Mugenda, A. G. (2003). *Research Methods: Quantitative and Qualitative Approaches*. Nairobi: African Centre Technology Studies press (ACTS).

Mwelukilwa, J. S. (2001). *The role co-operatives play in poverty reduction in Tanzania*. Paper Presented at the United Nations in observance of the International Day for the Eradication of Poverty on 17 October 2001.

Ndiege, B. O., Qin, X., Kazungu, I., & Moshi, J. (2014). The impacts of financial linkage on sustainability of less-formal financial institutions: Experience of savings and credit co-operative societies in Tanzania. *Journal of Co-operative Organization and Management*, *2*(2), 65–71.

Nelson, B. (2012). *SACCOS Yatoa Msaada wa Madawati, Magodoro*. Mwananchi News paper, Thursday November 1, 2012. Retrieved December 20, 2013, from http://www.mwananchi.co.tz/-/1597570/1609504/-/xh4aof/-/index.html.

Ngah, L. (2012). *Rural transformation development*. Accessed March 23, 2018, from http://www.academia.edu/2300538/rural_transformation_development.

Nuwagaba, A. (2012). Savings and credit co-operative societies (SACCOS) as a source of financing agriculture: Challenges and lessons learnt. *Journal of Environment and Earth Science, 2911*, 109–114.

Nwankwo, O. (2007). Micro credit finance and poverty reduction: Challenges and prospects. *Journal of Banking, Finance and Development, 1*(1), 66–70.

Nwankwo, F. O., & Okeke, C. S. (2017). Rural entrepreneurship and rural development in Nigeria. *Africa's Public Service Delivery and Performance Review, 5*(1), 1–7.

Obetta, K. C., & Okide, C. C. (2011). *Rural development trends in Nigeria: Problems and prospect.* Accessed August 15, 2013, from http://www.academicexcellencesociety.com.

Okura, M., & Zhang, W. (2012). Group Lending Model under Sequential Moves. *International Journal of Economics and Finance, 4*(5), 146–155.

Olaitan, M. A. (2006). Finance for small and medium scale Enterprise in Nigeria Journal of international Scale Enterprises in Nigeria. *Journal of International Farm Management, 3*(2), 7–12.

Olawepo, R. A., & Ariyo, B. (2011). Facilitating rural transformation through community banking: An example from Kogi State, Nigeria. *International Journal of Business and Social Science, 2*(5), 55–61.

Onyeagocha, S. U. O., Chidebelu, A. N. D., Okorji, E. C., Ukoha, A. H., Osuji, M. N., & Korie, O. C. (2012). Determinants of loan repayment of microfinance banks in Southeast of Nigeria. *International Journal of Social Sciences and Humanities, 1*(1), 4–9.

Osabuohien, E. S., Gitau, C. M., Efobi, U. R., & Bruentrup, M. (2015). Agents and implications of foreign land deals in East African community: The case of Uganda. In E. Osabuohien (Ed.), *Handbook of research on in-country determinants and implications of foreign land acquisitions* (pp. 263–286). Hershey, PA: Business Science Reference. https://doi.org/10.4018/978-1-4666-7405-9.ch013.

Osabuohien, E., Efobi, U. R., Herrmann, R., & Gitau, C. M. (2019). Female labor outcomes and large-scale agricultural land investments: Macro-micro evidence from Tanzania. *Land Use Policy, 82*, 716–728. https://doi.org/10.1016/j.landusepol.2019.01.005.

Qin, X., & Ndiege, B. O. (2013). Role of financial development in economic growth: Evidence from savings and credits cooperative societies in Tanzania. *International Journal of Financial Research, 4*(2), 115–125. https://doi.org/10.5430/ijfr.v4n2p115.

Ravikumar. (2016), Contribution of Microfinance in empowering the women entrepreneurs in Gulbarga city. *International Journal of Business Quantitative Economics and Applied Management Research, 2*(8).

Roberts, J. S., Laughlin, J. E., & Wedell, D. H. (1999). Validity issues in the Likert and Thurstone approaches to attitude measurement. *Emotional and Psychological Measurement, 59*(2), 211–233.

Sizya, M. J. (2001). *The role cooperatives play in poverty reduction in Tanzania.* Paper Presented at the United Nations International Day for the Eradication of Poverty.

Taiwo, J. N. (2012). *The Impact of Micro finance on Welfare and Poverty Alleviation in Southwest Nigeria.* Doctoral dissertation, Covenant University.

Thomas, J. (1985). Force field analysis: A new way to evaluate your strategy. *Long Range Planning, 18*(6), 54–59.

URT. (2012). *Poverty and human development report 2011*. Ministry of Finance: Research and Analysis Working Group. Mkukuta Monitoring System.

Vidal, A. (1992). *Rebuilding communities: A national study of urban community development corporations*. Community Development Research Center, Graduate School of Management and Urban Policy, New School for Social Research.

Vidal, A. C. (1995). Reintegrating disadvantaged communities into the fabric of urban life: The role of community development. *Housing Policy Debate*, 6(1), 169–230.

Wangwe, S., & Lwakatare, M. (2004, March). Innovation in rural finance in Tanzania. *Third Annual Conference on Microfinance held from 15th to 17th March* (pp. 1–18). Arusha: AICC.

Zeuli, K., & Cropp, R. (2004). *Cooperative principals and practices*. Madison, WI: University of Wisconsin Extension.

Zeuli, K. A., & Radel, J. (2005). Cooperatives as a community development strategy: Linking theory and practice. *Journal of Regional Analysis and Policy*, 35(1), 43–54.

Zeuli, K. (2002). The role of cooperatives in community development. *University of Wisconsin Center for Cooperatives Bulletin*, 3, 1–4.

Employment, Migration and Transformation Nexus

ns and Yo# Rural–Urban Labor Migration and Youth Employment: Investigating the Relevance of Nigeria's Agricultural Sector in Employment Generation

Abiodun Elijah Obayelu, Oluwakemi Adeola Obayelu, and Esther Toluwatope Tolorunju

1 Introduction

There has been a rapid increase of youths' movement from rural areas to urban centers (Ajaero and Onokala 2013). Rural–urban migration constitutes a key component of human population movement (Qin 2010). The rural areas contain most of the world's natural resources such as land and forests and rural households rely on agriculture for most of their livelihood (Njeru 2017). Agriculture is recognized as the single largest source of employment in rural areas where most rural workers are self-employed, whether it be on their own farms or in the small, often very small, enterprises typical of rural non-farm activities (Overseas Development Institute 2007). New and good jobs in agriculture can be generated through demand for aggregation, storage, processing, logistics, food preparation, restaurants, and other related services which are becoming increasingly important in the larger agri-food

---

A. E. Obayelu (✉) · E. T. Tolorunju
Department of Agricultural Economics and Farm Management,
Federal University of Agriculture Abeokuta, Abeokuta, Nigeria

O. A. Obayelu
Department of Agricultural Economics, University of Ibadan, Ibadan, Nigeria

© The Author(s) 2020
E. S. Osabuohien (ed.), *The Palgrave Handbook of Agricultural and Rural Development in Africa*, https://doi.org/10.1007/978-3-030-41513-6_16

systems (Christiaensen 2017). However, a key impediment to the involvement of youth in agriculture has been the lack of national efforts to make agriculture attractive to them (World Bank 2014). People move from one area of a country (or from one country) to another area of the same country (or to another country) for a number of reasons such as to establish a new residence (International Organization for Migration 2011). This movement may also be to search for employment, market, natural disaster, armed conflict, education, health, and other means of livelihood.

Migration is therefore the movement of people over defined space and time (Ikwuyatum 2016). It is a change of residence either permanently or temporarily. Migration can be defined in terms of spatial boundaries as internal and international. It means the crossing of the boundary of a pre-defined spatial unit by persons involved in a change of residence (Henderson 2002). Internal migration is the movement of individuals within a country whereas international migration involves the movement of individuals across international boundaries. It is internal migration if the change of residence is within national boundaries, such as between states, provinces, cities, or municipalities, rural to urban. For instance, movement from Abeokuta in Ogun State to Ibadan in Oyo State either to settle there permanently or temporarily. In Nigeria, the issue of rural–urban migration is quite disturbing owing to the unfair centralization of facilities in the urban areas as well as widening income gap between the urban and rural areas (Osita-Njoku and Chikere 2005). It is international migration if the change of residence is over national boundaries such as Nigeria to the United States of America. Rural–urban youth migration is the physical movement of young individuals or group of young people from rural areas to urban centers (Mbah et al. 2016). It is the most important aspect of labor migration because it affects the organizations and arrangement of the population.

The important feature of migration is that it involves a change in place of abode, or place of "usual" residence and a taking up of life in a new or different place. Statistically, this is often captured in terms of duration of stay at the destination. The movement can be temporary or permanent (European Migration Network 2011). Migration is a major factor that affects the size of labor force as well as its distribution by skill, education, industry, and occupation (Fadayomi and Olurinola 2014). It is also a factor that has social and economic consequences on both the area of origin and destination (Future Directions International 2014). Global estimates showed 258 million international migrants in 2017, representing 3.4% of global population and one-third of all international migrants from developing countries are 12–24 years old (United Nations 2017).

Migration can be termed a labor migration if the purpose of the cross-border movement is for employment. Nigeria is facing a major youth unemployment challenge despite a large uncultivated land that can create jobs through agricultural production. Millions of youth are migrating from rural to urban areas, from agriculture to non-agricultural jobs in Nigeria owing to political, security, socioeconomic, and demographic factors. Migration is a universal phenomenon and people move from rural areas to urban areas, from developing countries to developed countries, and from societies with stagnant economic conditions to societies with better-off economic conditions to address their economic and social needs (Imran et al. 2013; Zafar et al. 2013). The growing gap between the haves and the have-nots, and relative deprivation prompts people to migrate abroad (Stark 2006). Findings from a recent study has shown that the strength of Nigeria's democracy is most strongly associated with Nigerian youths' desire to migrate abroad, in addition to low levels of trust in local security institutions (Kirwin and Anderson 2018).

The definition of "youth" on the other hand varies across societies, cultures, and tribes. For instance, International organizations such as the United Nations and the World Bank define youth as all those aged 15–24 years (UN 2005; UNECA 2009); Ghana, Tanzania and South Africa and the African Youth Charter define youth population as those between the ages of 15–35 years (African Union Commission 2006); Swaziland define it as those between 12 and 30 years (Alliance for a Green Revolution in Africa 2015). The Nigerian National Youth Policy (2009) describes youths as those between the ages of 18 and 35 years. The age range is necessitated in Nigeria because between ages 12 and 35 years, a lot of individuals, though still live under the roofs of their parents, take decision of what they want to do in most cases. Availability of information on youth employment and rural–urban migration is critical to the identification of key challenges, and to shaping policies and programs to address them. This study is premised on the general assumption that youths migrate from rural areas (whose predominant occupation is agriculture) to urban in search for better job. This study sought to understand the phenomenon of rural–urban youth migration and employment generation in agricultural sector; present the theoretical background and approaches used to explain issues relating to rural migration; provide new understanding of the drivers of youth labor migration, rural–urban youth migration and migration from agriculture to non-agricultural sectors; assess the consequences of rural–urban youth migration and migration from agriculture to non-agricultural on agricultural production; and investigate the potential of employment generation from agricultural sector and reduction of rural–urban youth migration.

The most prominent contribution of this chapter to knowledge is to provide recent and systematic data on the driving forces of youths' labor and rural–urban migration. The findings from the study will serve as guiding documents for policy makers for the adoption, formulation, and implementation of a genuine rural development strategies and migration policy. In addition, the chapter would contribute to the growing body of knowledge on youth employment in agriculture.

The organization of this chapter takes us first to a discussion of the introductory background of rural–urban labor migration and youth employment. Second section presents the conceptual framework on rural–urban migration and youth employment, an overview of the theories of migration that have appeared in the mainstream literature and early contributions made by scholars on migrations and employment. The third section presents the data sources, methods of data collection together with the approaches adopted in analyzing the data. The fourth section presents the results and discussion of the analyses for the study, while the final section concludes and identifies some key policy implications emanating from the study.

2   Literature Review and Conceptual Framework on Migration and Youth Employment

This section reviews theoretical and empirical literature on migration. The literature on rural to urban migration is vast (Massey et al. 1993; Todaro and Steven 2006; Faist 2000; Portes 1999). The literature reviewed in this section provides significant evidence and conceptual framework on the rural–urban labor migration. Conceptually, and consistent with the position of Ikwuyatum (2016), several migration theories and models were examined in the literature on migration in Nigeria; however, there is no precise model or theory developed for studying migration and youth employment in Nigeria. Varied factors are responsible for the pattern and characteristics of migrations in Nigeria. These are both exogenous and endogenous factors that predispose the migration and youth employment processes. Exogenous factors responsible for migration include economic differentials, decision-making process of individuals that shape their aspiration and perception of potential places to move to, and social-economic networks that affect the migration dynamics.

Rural–urban migration is viewed by Okereke (2003) to be associated to what is termed "ghost" rural villages as most rural communities are disserted due to the mass influx of youths and able bodied individuals to cities leaving the elderly and children thereby making social life dull and unattractive in the rural communities. The departure of youths in the rural areas reduced their availability to provide assistance in the daily functioning of their parents' households who are basically farmers (Knodel and Saengtienchac 2005). Rural youths are more likely to be in temporary jobs and more likely to be in jobs without promotion prospects compared to urban youth (AfDB/OECD//UNDP/UNECA 2012). They are more likely to be in manual occupations, and receive lower pay, despite rural earnings overall (for all ages) being higher.

Todaro (1969) in his labor migration and employment model stated that the decision to migrate from the rural to the urban area is to achieve high urban pay as compared to the low rural pay. People migrate to cities in search of better job opportunities that will enhance their standard of living.

Decisions to migrate could be spontaneous and strongly related to the disruption of the rural economy. Such spontaneous decisions could be as a result of natural disaster like flood, drought, land slide, erosion, earthquake, insect and pest infestation, escape from political instability, rights abuses, communal clashes, family disputes, outbreak of war, and other adversities (Nwanna 2004; Adewale 2005). People also migrate in search of a "safe heaven" where their safety is significantly assured (Adepoju 2008; Bakewell and de Haas 2007; Afolayan and Ikwuyatum 2011). To Bradshaw (1987), underdeveloped nations are experiencing a gradual transition from an agrarian to a service and informal economy, a transformation that impedes economic expansion and agricultural conditions alone will not push rural citizens to urban areas.

Agesa and Sunwoong (2001) conducted a study in Kenya focusing on the household unit maximizing its utility through various forms of migration. They observed that because of large households, including numerous dependents, the majority of rural-to-urban migrants engage in split migration where the household head typically moves to an urban area initially without his family and the family follows later after sufficient income has been generated to stay in an urban area.

Other literature on migration (such as Macharia 2003) also pointed out that lack of jobs, famine, drought, various kinds of poverty for example landlessness, the hope to find a job, increase one's income, educational opportunities, in search of better service (economic welfare) influence the tendency of individuals to migrate to urban areas. Migrating from rural area to urban is seen as an alternative to get out from poverty trap and one of the factors that influence population growth in the urban areas (Yunita 2009).

3 Theoretical Framework and Migration Models

The core principle of migration theories is rationality (de Haas 2014). The migration theories imply that more people will migrate from poor areas that have relatively low return to labor and more exposure to risks and shocks (de Haas 2010). This section reviews various approaches to migration studies, starting from Ravenstein (1885) laws' of migration to the Todaro model, and the "new economics" of migration. These theories and models (push–pull theory, the quantitative theory, the urban-biased theory, human capital theory, dual-labor market theory, historical-structural theory, the world system theory, social capital theory, neoclassical economics theory, the new economics of migration theory, the Harris and Todaro model) are put forward to explain why rural to urban migration occurs. Discussing all of them would be too wide; a little overview is done in this study to provide us with a general knowledge.

Ravenstein laws of migration still forms the basis for modern migration theory (Ravenstein 1885). The laws are as follows: (i) Every migration flow generates a return or counter-migration. In other words, the major cause of voluntary migration is economic. (ii) There is a process of absorption, whereby people immediately surrounding a rapidly growing town move into it and the gaps they leave are filled by migrants from more distant areas, and so on until the attractive force is spent and there is also a process of dispersion, which is the inverse of absorption. That is, most migrants advance step-by-step. (iii) Migration increases in volume as industries and commerce develop and transport improves. (iv) The majority of migrants move a short distance. (v) Migrants who move longer distances tend to choose big city destinations and major sources of economic activity. (vi) Urban residents are often less migratory than inhabitants of rural areas. (vii) Families are less likely to make international moves than young adults. That is, most international migrants are young adults. (vii) Most migrants are adults, natives of towns are less migratory than those from rural areas and large towns grow by migration rather than natural population growth. (viii) Longer distance migrants are male and are adult individuals rather than families with children. (ix) Females are more migratory than males. (x) Females are more migratory than males within their country of birth, but males frequently venture beyond. (xi) The usual direction of migration is from agricultural areas to centers of industry and commerce.

Push–pull theory, built on the Ravenstein laws, states that migrants are forced to leave rural areas because of push or repulsive forces (such as poverty, unemployment, dearth of basic socio-economic infrastructure, and generally lack of economic opportunities/economic hardships) and are pulled by the higher opportunities or attraction of urban life. The decision to move out of rural areas is often based on the socio-economic inadequacies that exists in the source region (rural); this sets up a trajectory or pattern of movement from places (rural) with "push" endogenous factors (unemployment, dearth of socioeconomic, poverty, etc.) to destinations with attractive exogenous factors (pull) of employment opportunities, accessibility and availability of socio-economic facilities, and better life generally (Castles 2012). Several scholars such as Udo (1975), Afolayan (1976) have criticized the "push-pull" theory as being mechanical in nature, with a proposal for a behavioral the theory of spatial behavior which postulates that migration decision-making process, is based on an evaluation of the exogenous factors. According to the International Organization of Migration (IOM 2010), unemployment is one of the main push factors driving international migration. Thus, it is expected to see that there is a positive relationship between the unemployment and migration.

Urban-biased theory advanced by Lipton (1977) explains the complex interaction that exists between urban and rural populations and development/underdevelopment. The theory posits that the disparity in welfare between rural and urban increases rural-to-urban migration and thereby expands both urbanization and service/informal employment. Lipton applied this theory to explain that helplessness to famine during the 1970s in developing countries was often due to biased government policies, which favored urban elites and consequently discriminated against those living in the rural areas. This shows the level of structured imbalance of power, away from rural areas, toward urban political and commercial centers which consequently leads to an explicit imbalance in resource allocation, and drive people away from rural areas to urban centers.

Human capital theory introduced by Sjaastad (1962) relates to voluntary job mobility or quits. The theory predicts that: mobility will be higher among the youths, because there is a greater potential return from any investment in the youths than the aged. Youths have a longer period for benefits to realize; unmarried people are more likely than the married to migrate and among married ones, those without children are more likely to move; within the same age group, the more educated are likely to move. As migration costs rise, flow of migration will fall; and community level factors which influence the individual's stream of returns such as pressure of population results in low rate of investment in agriculture, fragmentation of land ownership, inequalities in the distribution of land and productive assets, institutional mechanisms. In addition, the human capital theory on labor migration predicts that a worker will have a higher probability of quitting a low-wage job than a higher paying one, all things being equal; workers will have a higher probability of quitting if it is relatively easy for them to obtain a better job quickly. That is, when labor markets are tight; workers will flow from low-wage jobs to higher wage jobs; and incomes of people who migrate are higher than they would have been in the absence of migration.

Human investment model of migration by Sjaastad (1962) was the first model of migration. This model connects migration and investment in human capital. It treats the decision to migrate as an investment. A migrant calculates the value of the opportunity available in the market at each alternative destination relative to the value of the opportunity available in the market at the point of origin, subtracts away the costs of moving, and chooses the destination which maximizes the present value of lifetime earnings. This means that the decision of an individual to migrate is based on the expected stream of earnings which also depends on both the prevailing urban wage and a subjective estimate of the probability of obtaining employment in the urban modern job. This model explains how high rates of urban unemployment can discourage rural–urban migration. Inversely, the theory shows how high rates of migration can remain rational even in the face of urban unemployment, provided that urban real wages are attached sufficiently high relative to rural wages. Sjaadstad used distance as a proxy for migration costs. He justified this by pointing out that the greater is distance traveled, the greater are the monetary costs of migration such as transportation expenses, food, and lodging costs for oneself and one's family during the move, and interruptions in income while between jobs. The migration decision is also very dependent on available information about job vacancies which can both be formal (advertisements in publications and employment agencies) and informal (by friends and relatives). According to the theory, if a husband and wife both work, then the husband's decision to migrate is likely to depend upon his wife's career prospects at the destination, and vice versa. Migrants with more children tend to have a lower likelihood of migrating than those with fewer children.

Labor-flow model posits that migration is a response for spatial differences in the returns to labor supply. At the micro level, this model implies that the migrant's goal is to maximize utility by choosing the location which offers the highest net income (Bodvarsson and Van den Berg 2013). Hence, users of this model implicitly assume that utility maximization is achieved through the maximization of income. These models, ignore the obvious fact that people migrate for reasons other than income maximization, e.g., family reunification, seeking refuge or political asylum, a more attractive culture, and religious beliefs.

Dual (segmented) labor market theory posits that there is surplus labor in the subsistence economy leading to marginal product of labor being zero, with a relatively low subsistence wage. The modern industrial wage is higher than the subsistence wage because of continuous investment, higher profits, and pressure from unionized labor. This wage differential will motivate people to move from rural to urban areas. In this theory, the pull factor of these societies cause migration, instead of the push factors of unemployment and poverty in the "periphery" (Van der Kruk 2009). The rural–urban wage differentials serve as both push and pull factors for migration. The wage differential is the main factor for rural–urban migration which leads to urbanization.

Neoclassical economics theory of labor migration by Stark (1991) assumes that migration decision-making process, is a collative issue, carried out by the household which bears both the cost and benefits of migration. The concept is based on the world systems theory which states that international migration is a by-product of global capitalism. In contrast to neoclassical migration theories, in which the migrant is considered to be a rational agent seeking to maximize her utility, migration systems theory considers the migrant in her social, political, historical, and economic context (Rajendra 2014). When a specific place has a higher "potential advantage" in comparison with the current place, the individual decides to migrate (Van der Kruk 2009). The theories state that developed countries created more opportunities due to its industrialization, and this has encouraged the developing and less developed nations to migrate to the core nations and migration can lead to development as it redistributes resources through remittances and moves labor to places where it is needed (Mafukidze 2006). The important assumption underlying this theory is that in a case of equal wages, migration will no longer take place.

New Economics of Migration is a theoretical model that has arisen in response to the neoclassical theory (Stark and Boom 1985). According to that model: (i) families, households, and other culturally defined units of production and consumption are those who count in analysis for migration research (not individuals) (ii) A wage differential is not a necessary condition for making a decision about migration to other country (iii) International migration does not necessarily stop when differences in wages disappear. Conviction of migration rightness will exist if other markets in the country of origin such as: insurance market, capital market, consumer credit markets are absent or imperfect (iv) governments are able to change the size of migration flows through regulating labor markets.

Network (social capital) theory perceives networks as a form of social capital. That is, sets of interpersonal ties that connect migrants, former migrants, and non-migrants in origin and destination areas through ties of kinship, friendship, and shared community origin (Massey et al. 1993). The fundamental assumption of this theory is that migration alters the social, cultural, economic, and institutional conditions at both the sending and receiving ends. The network theory mainly focuses on the vital role of personal relations between migrants and non-migrants, and the way this social capital facilitates, perpetuates, and transforms migration processes. The migration systems theory goes beyond this point, stressing that migration not only affects or is affected by the direct social environment of migrants, but restructures the entire societal context in which migration takes place, both at the receiving and sending end (de Haas 2010). The basic principle of migration systems theory is that migration flows are the result of interacting macrostructures of geopolitical relationships often rooted in history, and meso-structures of informal social networks that migrants have with one another (Faist 2000).

The **cumulative causation theory** refers to the process by which migration sustains itself. In this case, each act of migration alters the social context within which subsequent migration decisions are made (Massey et al. 1993).

Harris and Todaro model considered migration to be influenced by the wage differential between rural and urban areas (Harris and Todaro 1970). They also viewed the decision to migrate as an individual decision. Improvements on this model have been suggested, which consider migration to be a family decision rather than an individual decision.

Dependency model took into account structural and institutional elements which are shortcomings of the neoclassical theories. The dependency theorist argued that migration result from economic forces of a western-dominated world system characterized by structural inequalities, including the continued underdevelopment in the excluded periphery (Mafukidze 2006). This approach explains rural–urban migration as a function of a complex web of interacting elements concerned not only with why people migrate but also with all the implications and ramifications of the process. Migration, according to this approach, results from a series of adjustments between rural control sub-systems based on kinship, overpopulation, and environmental deterioration and one connected to residential and occupational incentives. The stimulus to migrate varies according to dynamic factors such as skill differentiation and status advancement.

Alternative models of migration concept are the Historical–Structural and the World System theories. The Historical–Structural theorists claim that international migration is caused by unequal distribution of political and economic power in the world economy (Castles and Miller 2009), while the Worlds System theorists argue that penetration of capitalist economic relations into non-capitalist or pre-capitalist societies creates a mobile population that can easily trigger a decision to migrate (Massey 2014).

In summary, there is no single theory/model widely accepted by social scientists when it comes to migration phenomenon as research of migration is intrinsically interdisciplinary (Tomanek 2011). Common to all these approaches on migration is the fact that migration to urban areas occurs as a result of changes in the demand for amenities. However, the demand for amenities may change as a person moves from one phase of his/her life cycle to another or change as culture changes or as economic growth changes incomes and the mix of products available. Based on the various theoretical models of migration, this study adopts the push and pull model combined with urban-based theories as the theoretical framework for this study owing to varying factors that make youths migrate from rural to urban areas, where they foresee higher opportunities probably as a result of the government policies in favor of urban areas in Nigeria.

4 Methodological Issues on Youth Employment and Rural–Urban Migration

Several methodological issues arise when working on youth employment and rural–urban migration. Finding a definition for "youth" "rural", even by those sources that report something on labor force, rural–urban youth migration or rural–urban migration statistics, remains elusive. The International Labor Organization website has a list of countries across the globe and their various definitions of what constitute rural or youth. In many instances, the methodological sections of surveys do not define these concepts. Because of the methodological challenges, there is a lack of urban–rural information and often times rural is determined by the total population minus the urban populace. Where data are reported by urban–rural, the main measure used is usually of population density (Rajack-Talley 2016). Most studies often report urban or rural populations and only few report urban–rural populations as distinct categories. Similarly, for types of youth employment, assumptions and inferences are made about sources of employment known to be located in rural settings (e.g., farm work and casual labor).

5 Materials and Methods

Census data in Nigeria does not provide a suitable basis for determining the causes and consequences of youth labor migration. We used to purpose-make migration surveys and interviews to get an understanding of why youths move from rural to urban areas, from agriculture to non-agricultural jobs. Qualitative research was conducted between August 15 and September 13, 2018, and it aimed at generating information and perceptions in a comprehensive and participatory way. A specific participatory tool (Focused Group Discussion) was used in order to assess the voice of migrant youths on specific issues in relation to the migratory phenomenon. The questionnaire includes questions pertaining to interest in rural–urban and labor migration as well as questions on perceptions of the relevance of agricultural sector to solve youth unemployment challenge in Nigeria (see Appendix 1). The existing literature and theories on labor migration (such as push–pull theory, dual labor market theory, neoclassical theories, the quantitative theory, the human capital theory, dependency approach) were critically reviewed through available information obtained mainly from secondary sources (relevant books, internet search and journals) and analyzed. Rural–urban labor migration by youth in Nigeria is often informal and undocumented leading to the problem of unavailability of data. To generate data on youth labor migration, a mixed method (combination of quantitative and qualitative) approach was used.

Focus group discussion guide (Appendix 1) was used for data collection. The sampling process involved non-probability purposive sampling technique. Data were collected from 10 Focus Group Discussion (FGDs) of selected migrant youths of between eight to ten participants who were into "motorcycle riding" livelihood activity in the city of Abeokuta, Ogun State and Ibadan, Oyo States per group after ensuring that selected participants were those who migrated from rural areas (where farming is the most predominant occupation) to urban areas. The motorcyclists (Okada Riders) were purposively selected because the percentage of youth in the occupation in urban areas were found to be very high probably because of the ease of doing the job, economic benefits or due to lack of other government or private jobs. Information and data collected were analyzed using a push–pull model combined with an actor-oriented approach.

The study analyzed the extent of youth engagement in agriculture in Nigeria using data from the Living Standards Measurement Study-Integrated Surveys on Agriculture (LSMS-ISA). The survey is an integration of longitudinal panel survey into General Household Survey (GHS) (Osabohien 2018). The GHS sample comprised of 60 Enumeration Areas (EAs) chosen from each of the 36 states and the Federal Capital Territory, Abuja in Nigeria (or 2220 EAs nationally). Each EA constitutes 10 households in the GHS sample, resulting in a sample size of 22,200 households. The LSMS-ISA data for Nigeria specifically covers 500 EAs (5000 households) from all the Local Government Areas (LGAs). It also covers the urban and rural areas. The data were collected in three Waves (Wave 1, 2011/2012 sessions; Wave 2, 2013/2014 session; and Wave 3, 2015/2016 session).[1]

The GHS-Panel (especially wave 3) comprises three questionnaires for the two different visits (post-planting and post-harvesting seasons) and on three different levels (households, agriculture, and on the community) (World Bank 2016). While the survey on agriculture involves questionnaire which was given to individuals who are farmers and engages in agricultural activities like crop farming, rearing of livestock, and other similar activities to solicit information on the ownership of land and its uses such as farm labor; inputs use; Global Positioning System (GPS) measuring area of land and management of household farmland; machinery used for farming; irrigation; harvesting and crop utilization; animal holdings and fishing; the survey for the community involves questionnaire containing necessary information on socio-economic indicators of the enumeration areas where the sample households live. The household questionnaire contains information on socioeconomics; characteristics, food consumption and expenditure, non-food expenditure, health, well-being (counting anthropometric estimation for kids and kid vaccination); work and work information accumulation alternatives; nourishment and non-sustenance use; remittances; food security, safety nets; lodging conditions; resources; data economic shocks and death; non-farm enterprises and income generating activities, household income (Osabohien 2018; Osabuohien et al. 2018, 2019; Oyebola et al. 2019).

We also used the "yes" or "no" debate on whether "agriculture is (un) likely to be the main answer" to youth employment. Recognizing the challenges and without grossly overselling the idea that agriculture is the solution to youth unemployment, we discussed what can be done to make agriculture more attractive and demand-driven to young people. The strength of this method is on its capacity to generate and trigger discussions within heterogeneous groups of youths.

6 Results and Discussion

6.1 Status of Migration in Nigeria

In 2015, net migration rate for Nigeria was −0.35 migrants per thousand populations. Though Nigeria net migration rate fluctuated substantially in recent years, it tended to decrease through 1970–2015 period ending at −0.35 migrants per thousand populations in 2015 (Pew Research Center 2018). This figure indicates that more people are moving out of the country as emigrants than those coming in as immigrants. There has been an increase in youth migration from rural to urban areas in Nigeria in search of a livelihood. Urban unemployment can be attributed to the influx of migrants from the rural to urban areas.

6.2 Causes of Rural–Urban Youth Migration

People migrate based on the prevailing conditions and the reasons for it vary from one person to another depending on the situation that brought about the decision. Migration is often analyzed in terms of the "push–pull model". Push factors look at those things which drive people to leave their residence (such as lack of services, lack of safety, high crime, crop failure, drought, flooding, poverty, war) and the pull factors (such as higher employment, more wealth, better services, good climate, safer, less crime, political stability, more fertile land, lower risk from natural hazard) are those attracting them to the new destination (Deotti and Estruch 2016). Migration literature has shown that migration is welfare improving for the migrant (Bezu and Holden 2014).

The migrants' youths were primarily into farming before migration. Youth rural–urban migration was also found to be largely induced by the expectation of higher wages in the urban area, job livelihood, higher education, search for quality education for children, wealth displays by friends living in urban areas, provision of food for family members left behind.

The following excerpts from FGDs confirmed the reasons youths migrate from rural areas (villages) to urban (cities) in the study areas.

> *"It is more dignify leaving in the urban areas."* Ibadan 10 FGDs; Abeokuta 10 FGDs.
>
> *"We left our various villages which are rural in nature with no social amenities for this city to enjoy such facilities like medical centers, good schools for our children and road."* Ibadan FGDs-1, 2, 4, 5, 6, 8, 9 & 10; Abeokuta FGDs- 2, 3, 6,7, 8, 9.
>
> *"We move from rural area to search for jobs in order to be able to feed members of our family with us and those we left behind in the village".* Ibadan 10 FGDs; Abeokuta 10 FGDs.
>
> *"We migrate to urban area from rural areas where we were before because we want to enjoy access to more social amenities such as good drinking water, electricity, medical care facilities, education and entertainment".* Ibadan FGDs-1, 2, 4, 5, 6, 8, 9 & 10.
>
> *"We moved out from our village to stay in Abeokuta in search for job and for the future education of our children".* Abeokuta 10 FGDs.
>
> *"We moved from village where we were before to this city of Ibadan in order to free themselves from traditional family systems and restrictions in the rural areas, provision food for members of their families they left behind".* Ibadan FGDs-1, 2, 3, 6, 7, 8, 9 & 10.
>
> *"We migrated to urban areas as a result of the absence of higher education in our village for our children".* Ibadan FGDs-1, 2, 5, 6, 9 & 10; Abeokuta FGDs -3, 4, 6, 8 &10.
>
> *"We migrated from the village to the city because of the future education of our children. The quality of education in our village is poor with the existing schools having no teachers".* Ibadan FGDs- 3, 2, 5, 6, 7 & 9; Abeokuta FGDs -1,2, 3, 4, 6, 7, 8 & 10.
>
> *"We want to enjoy urban livelihood and make money because our friends, relatives and colleagues who have left us in the village often display wealth whenever they come home during festive period such as Easter, Sallah and Christmas".* Ibadan FGDs-1, 2, 3, 4, 5, 6, 9 & 10; Abeokuta FGDs -2, 3, 4, 5, 6, 7, 8 & 10.

The FGDs excerpts from both Ibadan and Abeokuta were remarkably similar and some were consistent with the findings of Van der Geest (2011) that people leave their places of origin to accumulate more food for their families back home.

6.3 Youth Labor Migration from Agricultural to Non-Agricultural Sector

The causes of rural youth migration are context-specific. Rural youths are increasingly likely to migrate to urban areas because the prospects for gainful employment in urban centers. We found that youth in the study areas still equated agriculture with farming, but had no connection with the technical or research-intensive aspects of agriculture. The youths were afraid of practicing agriculture because they perceived the occupation to be hard and stressful and gives low income. Some youths knew some farmers who were not doing well despite their hard labor in agriculture. These findings agreed with those of Njeru et al. (2015) and Noorani (2015) that lack of incentives and drudgery are some of the reasons why youths are disinterested in agriculture; and in most parts of the world, agriculture is seen as a less worthwhile subject or as a last resort for underachievers. To compound the situation, youths often lack access to land, credit, and high cost of labor to start their own farms. Many young people in rural areas are unwilling to remain there to practice farming after graduating from basic education and high schools, the big wage gap between urban and rural agricultural activities. Further, owing to the difficulties young people face in obtaining land tenure and overall lack of physical assets, few youths could offer the collateral that banks seek. Loans from financial institutions often have interest rates in the range of 25–30%, which make repayment very difficult. The youths thus move to the urban areas in search of non-existent white-collar jobs. Some youths were also enticed to migrate to urban centers by the wealth displayed by friends and relatives who returned from the urban areas during social events and during festivals. The desire to acquire such wealth lures them to the urban areas.

The following excerpts from the FGDs corroborate the above findings on why youths migrate from agricultural works to non-agricultural works in the study areas.

"We cannot afford to continue to farm like our parent because agriculture is a difficult task and not meant for people who are not strong with money in it after paying for inputs especially labour. People who works in banks, oil companies have a very fat salary when compare to those farming earns with a lot of efforts and money invested". Ibadan FGDs-1, 2, 5, 6, 9 & 10; Abeokuta FGDs -3, 4, 6, 8, 10.

"We move out from village so that we would not be like our parents who farms all their years to look for white collar jobs in urban areas". Ibadan FGDs-1, 2, 5, 6, 9 & 10; Abeokuta FGDs -3, 4, 6, 8, 10.

"We cannot be spending our money and energy for cattle to graze upon free of charge with no justice or compensation from the Fulani herdsmen caught in this very act in Nigeria." Ibadan FGDs-1, 2, 5, 6, 9 & 10; Abeokuta FGDs -3, 4, 6, 8, 10.

"There is no incentive or motivation by the government that can encourage those of us who are interested to go into agriculture by the government. Some of the programmes initiated to provide these incentives are often hijacked by the politician who put those in the government there, corruption by those in charge seeking for kick back before actions are taken." Ibadan FGDs-1, 2, 5, 6, 9 & 10; Abeokuta FGDs -3, 4, 6, 8, 10.

"When considered the effort involve in agriculture with the price of the produce, it is not a profitable venture. If one is not careful, it will be very difficult to be able to pay for the cost invested." Ibadan FGDs-1, 2, 5, 6, 9 & 10; Abeokuta FGDs -3, 4, 6, 8, 10.

"We need to move out from rural area to cities to struggle like others before we get old and can no longer do anything. Those who have gone out of the village for cities often comes home during festive period like new year celebration to display wealth in the village and we look on them as if we are nothing with all efforts at farming." Ibadan FGDs-1, 2, 5, 6, 9 & 10; Abeokuta FGDs -3, 4, 6, 8, 10.

Every land you see in the rural areas are not free but own by one family or the others and the limit by which one can farm as a youth on commercial level is determine by available land due to the land tenure system. Ibadan FGDs-1, 2, 5, 6, 9 & 10; Abeokuta FGDs -3, 4, 6, 8, 10.

"Cost of taking loan in bank to embark on agriculture is too high for some lenders given out their money as high as 25% contrary to the single digit on paper. A lot of the banks are not even ready to give for agricultural purpose possibly because of fear of default and they place difficult conditions to secure the loan" Ibadan FGDs-1, 2, 5, 6, 9 & 10; Abeokuta FGDs -3, 4, 6, 8, 10.

6.4 Youths' Perceptions of Agriculture as Provider of Employment, and Extent of Engagement in Agriculture

Perception refers to consciousness of a particular objects and events by means of sense (Narain et al. 2015). Based on the results from a series of focus groups, all the youths viewed agriculture as the major source of employment, while some agreed that agriculture also provides jobs in other variety of ways through formal and informal wage work, unpaid family labor, self-employment, and cooperative membership across all levels of the value chain.

The following FGDs excerpts confirm the above findings on the perceptions of youths about the potentials of employment generation through agriculture.

> *"Agricultural production has a lot of potentials of generating employments to the teeming youth population of Nigeria"*. Ibadan 10 FGDs; Abeokuta 10 FGDs.
>
> *"Employment opportunities in agriculture exists in storage"*. Abeokuta FGDs -3, 8.
>
> *"Agriculture can provide employment through supply of production inputs and in the provision of services such as extension, processing and distribution of agro-based products"*. Ibadan FGDs-1, 2, 5, 6, 9 & 10; Abeokuta FGDs -3, 4, 6, 7 & 9.
>
> *"Agriculture creates employment through marketing or sale of agricultural products"*. Ibadan FGDs-1, 3, 5, 6, 7 & 9; Abeokuta FGDs -2, 3, 4, 6, 7, 8, 9, 10.
>
> *Agriculture is capable of creating job through farm labour*. Ibadan 10 FDGs; Abeokuta FGDs-1, 3, 4, 5, 6, 7, 8, 9 & 10.

These results are in contrast with the findings of Brooks et al. (2013) that agriculture is not perceived as a viable source of employment as it remains highly unattractive to the youth.

Further results on the extent of youths' engagement in agriculture in Nigeria using data from the LSMS-ISA were presented in Table 1. The proportions of youths or adults in a household who were engaged in agriculture in rural areas (69.2 and 71.3% in 2011/2012 and 2015/2016, respectively) was higher than in urban areas (30.8 and 28.7% in 2011/2012 and 2015/2016, respectively). However, youths worked fewer hours per week in agriculture in rural area than urban in 2011/12 and 2014/15, while more hours per weeks were spent by both youths and those of older age group (>35 years) in 2015/16 probably because agriculture was viewed as being more productive in 2015/16 than in the previous wave. The findings were in line with the structural transformation theory which states that people switch out of low productivity sectors when structural transformation occurs. The results also corroborated empirical results of Maïga et al. (2015) that youths work less hours per week on agriculture than those of older age group. The productivity differences between agricultural sector in the rural areas and the non-agricultural sector in the urban areas gives rise to better wages in the latter and labor is progressively moving out of agriculture (Timmer 1988).

Table 1 Rural–urban migration and engagement of youths in agriculture

Period	Average number of youth engagement in agriculture (12–35 years)						Average number older age group (35+ years)					
Post-planting	Wave 1 (2011/12)		Wave 2 (2014/15)		Wave 3 (2015/16)		Wave 1 (2011/12)		Wave 2 (2014/15)		Wave 3 (2015/16)	
Location	Rural	Urban	Rural	Urban	Rural	Urban	Rural	Urban	Rural	Urban	Rural	Urban
Youth/older age group in household engaged in agric. sector	7425 (69.2)	3310 (30.8)	7582 (71.2)	3066 (28.8)	7800 (71.3)	3144 (28.7)	4727 (69.9)	2035 (30.1)	4896 (71.3)	1975 (28.7)	4875 (69.7)	2115 (30.3)
Average hours spent in agric activities per week	36.99	43.68	34.68	41.79	30.45	21.70	40.71	46.49	37.69	43.32	32.26	25.02
Post-harvesting												
Youth/older age group in household engaged in agric. sector	7447 (69.8)	3215 (30.2)	7730 (70.7)	3210 (29.3)	7481 (71.1)	3037 (28.9)	4662 (70.4)	1958 (29.6)	5546 (69.8)	2396 (30.1)	9410 (69.2)	4183 (30.8)
Average hours spent in agric activities per week	37.10	45.27	39.46	44.65	23.75	19.33	40.19	46.78	40.97	45.97	27.14	24.62

Note Values in parentheses are in percentage
Sources Computed from LSMS-ISA Data, 2012, 2015, 2016

6.5 Consequences of Youth Migration from Rural to Urban and Agricultural to Non-Agricultural Sectors on Food Production in Nigeria

Rural–urban migration and movement from agriculture to non-agriculture such as manufacturing, artisan, trading, and provision of services of all kinds have significant effect on both rural and urban areas and agricultural production. The major consequence of rural–urban youth migration was excessive urbanization, which conforms with the findings of Abedi-Lartey (2016) that migration from rural to urban areas is the major cause of urbanization. In addition, youths' rural–urban migration creates more income to the migrants. This buttresses the economic theory of migration, which states that people migrate because of the benefits which may be economic or non-economic in nature (International Labor Organization-ILO 2010). However, due to the movement of consumption expenditure of the migrants to urban centers, youths' rural–urban migration leads to a poor standard of living in rural area resulting from a reduction in rural households' income. The finding also revealed that rural–urban migration of youths leads to a rise in wage rate due to scarcity of labor for agricultural works in rural areas. This buttresses the findings of de Haas (2010) that migration will cause labor to become less scarce at the destination and scarcer at the sending end. FAO (2016) further stated that migration may reduce pressure on local labor markets and raise a more efficient allocation of labor and higher wages in agriculture while rural areas of origin risk losing the younger, most vital, and dynamic share of their workforce. Migration of the youths from rural areas to urban towns also had a negative effect on the agricultural sector through low production. This may not be unconnected with the fact that through migration able-bodied young people leave rural areas for cities leading to a lack of enough labor force to cater for agricultural production and sometimes abandonment of many farmlands. As more youths migrate into urban areas to earn a living, more aged people are also left to accomplish the tasks associated with farming, especially the tasks which are reserved for the youths. Therefore, the added responsibilities are capable of reducing the agricultural production.

The excerpts from FGDs presented below illustrate the perceived consequences of youth rural–urban migration to corroborate the above findings.

Youth rural-urban migration is capable of creating rapid population growth in the urban areas. Ibadan FGDs-1, 2, 3, 4, 5, 6, 7, 8 & 9; Abeokuta FGDs -1, 2, 3, 4, 6, 7 & 8.

Youth rural-urban movement leads to reduction in rural household income. Ibadan FGDs-1, 3, 4, 7, 8 & 9; Abeokuta FGDs -2, 9 & 10.

Youth migration creates low rate of rural development. Ibadan FGDs-1, 3, 4, 5, 6, 7, 8 & 9; Abeokuta FGDs -1, 2, 3, 8, 9 & 10.

Youth rural-urban migration leads to poor standard of living in rural area. Ibadan FGDs-1, & 9; Abeokuta FGDs -1, 3, 4, 6, & 8.

"Youth moves from rural to urban provides more employment." Ibadan FGDs-1, 3, 5, 7 & 9; Abeokuta FGDs -2, 3, 5, 6, 7, & 10.

"Youth rural-urban migration provides more income to the migrants' part of which they can send back to take care of their family." Ibadan FGDs-1, 2, 5, 6, 8 & 9; Abeokuta FGDs -1, 2, 3, 4, 6, 7, 8, & 10.

On the other hands, the below excerpts from the FDGs were some of the consequences of migration from agricultural to non-agricultural activities in the study area.

> *"Migration from agricultural to non-agricultural provides more income to the migrants' youths"*. Ibadan FGDs-1, 2, 3, 4, 5, 6, 7, 8 & 9; Abeokuta FGDs -1, 2, 3, 4, 6, 7, 8, 9 & 10.
>
> *"Youth migration from agriculture to non-agriculture raise agricultural wage rate in rural areas"*. Ibadan FGDs-1, 3, 4, 5, 6, 8 & 9; Abeokuta FGDs -2, 3, 4, 6, 7 & 8.
>
> *"Migration agriculture to non-agriculture is a mean of escaping from poverty trap"*. Ibadan FGDs-1, 8 & 9; Abeokuta FGDs - 2, 3, 4, 8, & 10.
>
> *"Migrating from agriculture to non-agriculture by youth is seen as a way of elongation of life"*. Ibadan FGDs-1, 5, 6, & 9; Abeokuta FGDs -1, 2, 3, 5, 6, 7, & 8.
>
> *"Youth migration from agriculture to non-agriculture reduces agricultural labor force in rural area"*. Ibadan- all the 10 FGDs; Abeokuta FGDs -1, 2, 3, 4, 6, 7, 8, 9, & 10.
>
> *"Leaving agriculture by youths for non-agricultural activities bring more food on the table"*. Ibadan FGDs-1, & 9; Abeokuta FGDs -2, 3, & 7.
>
> *"Migrating of the youth from agriculture to non-agricultural activities will lead to a reduction in agricultural productivity."* Ibadan FGDs-1, 2, 5, 6, 7, 8 & 9; Abeokuta FGDs -1, 2, 3, 4, 6, 7, 8, & 10.

From the FGDs excerpts above, migration generates a considerable employment for a number of young people entering labor markets and remittances to the sending areas in line with ILO (2004) report.

7 Conclusion and Recommendations

In order to make appropriate policy, this chapter discussed theories of why youths migrate from rural to urban, agriculture to non-agriculture works, and the consequences of such youth labor migration. The study revealed that youth are less engaged in agriculture than the aging population suggesting that they are leaving agriculture for non-agricultural jobs, especially those from poorer households and villages with less agricultural potential are more likely to migrate to urban areas. Educated youths with prospect of better employment in urban areas are more likely to migrate to urban areas. They migrate from rural to urban areas because they viewed agriculture as a hard and tough job, thereby diminishing the labor force in the agricultural sector and consequently hindering agricultural productivity and rural development. Notably, most youths migrated with the consent of their parents, who in most cases covered the costs of their migration.

The high level of rural–urban migration and migration from agriculture to non-agriculture works are probably responsible for the high unemployment rates in Nigeria. Thus, migration is an important component of the livelihood strategies. Youths in rural area move out of agriculture in order to find jobs in urban centers although not all such migration decisions lead to the expected success. This is shown in the results of this study as the perception of the migrant youths were not all met.

In view of these findings, local and state government should make the rural areas attractive enough to retain the restless youths, through the provision of basic agricultural inputs (land and credit/capital) and infrastructure (electricity, good road and rail networks, water supply, higher learning institutions, access to market, and telecoms base stations). Further, at all levels of education, students must be trained in agriculture and agribusiness with necessary modern techniques that will make them see agriculture as an enterprise and not just a mean of pulling people out of poverty. There is the need to modernize agriculture by mechanizing the farming process and making it attractive to the youths.

8 Suggestions for Further Studies

Opportunities for progress are abundant for anyone willing to think beyond the work presented in this chapter. Based on research gaps in the literature, we suggest the following:

i. Decomposition of rural–urban or urban–rural migration flows in relation to migrants' demographic and economic characteristics.
ii. A comprehensive mapping of youths' labor migration and economic participation of the different types of migrants.
iii. Impact of rural–urban migration on expenditure patterns and savings of remittances among the receiving households.
iv. Impact of finding better urban employment on rural households' well-being.

Appendix 1: Sample of the FGD Questions

Rural–Urban Labor Migration and Youth Employment: Investigating the Relevance of Nigeria's Agricultural Sector in Employment Generation

Focus Group Discussion (FGD) Protocol

Based on the increasing rate of youth unemployment as well as rural-urban migration despite the existence of large areas of un-utilized agricultural land in Nigeria, this study attempts to assess rural-urban labor migration and youth employment looking at the relevance of agricultural sector in employment generation with sample respondents from Abeokuta in Ogun State and Ibadan in Oyo State.

This FGD protocol elicits information/data from you and the information/data obtained through this FGD would strictly be kept confidential and use only for this research purpose. Your participation in answering these questions is very much appreciated.

CONSENT
Before I start, do you have any questions or is there anything which I have said on which you would like any further clarification? May I proceed with interviewing you?
Yes □ No □
If answer is no, please state the reason for refusal
_____
_____
_____

INSTRUCTIONS
1. The target respondents for the FGD are motorcyclists (Okada Riders) in Abeokuta/Ibadan.
2. Eight to ten participants are expected to participate in each FGD.
3. Consent of every participant in the FGDs would be obtained before admission to participate.

Questions

1. State the main reasons for migrating from rural to urban areas.
2. State the main reasons for migrating from agricultural works to non-agricultural works.
3. What is your perception on the capability of Agriculture at generating employment through each of the following: (i) Agricultural production (ii) Harvesting of crops and livestock (iii) Transportation of agricultural products (iv) Storage (v) Food and livestock processing (vi) Sales or marketing of Agricultural products (vii) Sale of agricultural inputs such as seeds and agrochemicals (viii) Making money through sale of information to farmers (ix) Creation of on-farm labor (x) Aquaculture production.
4. What do you think are the consequences of labor migration from agricultural to non-agricultural sectors on food production in Nigeria?

Note

1. Details are freely available online at: http://microdata.worldbank.org/index.php/catalog/2734.

References

Abedi-Lartey, J. (2016). *Causes of rural-urban migration on Sankana in the Nadowli-Kalio District of Ghana and its effects on community development.* Unpublished projected for Bachelor in Natural Resource Management Nonia University of Applied Sciences, Nonia.

Adepoju, A. (2008). *Migration and social policy in Sub-Saharan Africa February 2008 prepared for the UNRISD-IOM-IFS project on social policy and migration in developing countries*.

Adewale, J. G. (2005). Socio-economic factors associated with urban-rural migration in Nigeria: A case study of Oyo State, Nigeria. *Journal of Human Ecology (JHE), 17*(1), 14–15.

AfDB, OECD, UNDP, UNECA. (2012). *African economic outlook*. (pp. 125–156). Retrieved online August 3, 2018, from http://www.cpahq.org/cpahq/cpadocs/The%20Employment%20Outlook%20for%20Young%20People.pdf.

Afolayan, A. A. (1976). *Behavioural approach to the study of migration into, and mobility within the metropolitan Lagos*. Unpublished PhD Thesis, Department of Geography, University of Ibadan, Nigeria.

Afolayan, A. A., & Ikwuyatum, G. O. (2011). *Dynamics of internal and international iobility of traders in Nigeria*. Nigeria: University of Ibadan Press.

African Union Commission. (2006). *Strategic framework for youth empowerment and development at continental, regional and national levels*. African Youth Charter. Retrieved online December 21, 2018 at https://www.africa-youth.org/frameworks/african-youth-charter/.

Agesa, R. U., & Sunwoong, K. (2001). Rural to urban migration as a household decision: Evidence from Kenya. *Review of Development Economics, 5*(1), 60–75.

Ajaero, C. K., & Onokala, P. C. (2013). The effects of rural-urban migration on rural communities of Southeastern Nigeria. *International Journal of Population Research, 1*(2013), 1–10.

Alliance for a Green Revolution in Africa (AGRA). (2015). *Africa agriculture status report: Youth in agriculture in Sub-Saharan Africa*. Nairobi, Kenya. Issue No. 3.

Bakewell, O., & de Haas, H. (2007). African migrations: Continuities, discontinuities and recent transformations. In L. De Haan, U. Engel, & P. Chabal (Eds.), *African Alternatives*. Leiden: Brill.

Bezu, S., & Holden, S. T. (2014). *Rural-urban youth migration and informal self-employment in Ethiopia*. Centre for Land Tenure Studies/School of Economics and Business Norwegian University of Life Sciences.

Bodvarsson, Ö. B., & Van den Berg, H. (2013). *The economics of immigration*. New York: Springer.

Bradshaw, Y. W. (1987). Urbanization and underdevelopment: A global study of modernization, urban bias and economic dependency. *American Sociological Review, 52*(2), 224–239.

Brooks, K., Amy, G., Goyal, A., & Zorya, S. (2013). *Agriculture as a sector of opportunity for young people in Africa* (Policy research working papers). Washington, DC: The World Bank.

Castles, S. (2012). Methodology and methods-conceptual issues. In M. Berriane & H. de Haas (Eds.), *African migrations research innovative methods and methodologies* (pp. 31–70). Trenton: African World Press.

Castles, S., & Miller, M. J. (2009). *The age of migration: international population movements in the modern world* (4th ed.). Basingstoke: Palgrave Macmillan.

Christiaensen, I. (2017). *Can agriculture create job opportunities for youth?* Retrieved online August 3, 2018, from http://includeplatform.net/knowledge-portal/can-agriculture-create-job-opportunities-for-youth/.

de Haas, H. (2010). Migration and development: A theoretical perspective. *International Migration Review (IMR), 44*(1), 227–264.

de Haas, H. (2014). *Migration theory: Quo Vadis?* (DEMIG project paper 24) Published by the International Migration Institute (IMI), Oxford Department of International Development (QEH), University of Oxford. Retrieved online January 14, 2019, from https://heindehaas.files.wordpress.com/2015/05/de-haas-2014-imi-wp100-migration-theory-quo-vadis.pdf.

Deotti, L., & Estruch, E. (2016). *Addressing rural youth migration at its root causes: A conceptual framework.* Rome, FAO: Social Policies and Rural Institutions Division.

European Migration Network. (2011). *Circular and temporary migration empirical evidence, current policy practice and future options in Luxembourg.* Available online at https://ec.europa.eu/home-affairs/sites/homeaffairs/files/what-wedo/networks/european_migration_network/reports/docs/emn-studies/circularmigration/lu_20111012_fv_circular_and_temporary_migration_en.pdf.

Fadayomi, T. O., & Olurinola, I. O. (2014). Determinants of labour force participation in Nigeria: The influence of household structure. *Journal of Economics and Development Studies, 2*(2), 169–190.

Faist, T. (2000). *The volumes and dynamics of international migration and transnational social spaces.* Oxford: Oxford University Press.

FAO. (2016). *Migration, agriculture and rural development: Addressing the root causes of migration and harnessing its potential for development.* FAO, Rome. Retrieved online October 2, 2018, from http://www.fao.org/3/a-i6064e.pdf.

Future Directions International. (2014). *Factors influencing migration and population movements–Part 1.* Retrieved online November 1, 2018, from http://futuredirections.org.au/wp-content/uploads/2014/10/FDI_Strategic_Analysis_Paper_Migration_and_Population_Movements_Part_1.pdf.

Harris, J. R., & Todaro, M. P. (1970). Migration, unemployment and development: A two sector analysis. *American Economic Review, 60*(1), 126–142.

Henderson, V. (2002). Urbanization in developing countries. *World Bank Research Observer, 17*(1), 89–112.

Ikwuyatum, G. O. (2016). The pattern and characteristics of inter and intra regional migration in Nigeria. *International Journal of Humanities and Social Science, 6*(7), 114–124.

ILO. (2010). *International labour migration: A rights-based approach* (p. 304p). Geneva: ILO.

Imran, F., Nawaz, Y., Asim, M., & Hashmi, A. H. (2013). Socio-economic determinants of rural migrants in urban setting: A study conducted at city Sargodha Pakistan. *Academic Journal of Interdisciplinary Studies, 1*(2), 71–76.

International Labour Organization (ILO). (2004). *Towards a fair deal for migrant workers in the global economy* (p. 216). Geneva: ILO.

International Organization for Migration. (2010). *Labour migration from Indonesia.*

International Organization for Migration (IOM). (2011). *Glossary on migration* (2nd ed.). Geneva: IOM. Available from https://publications.iom.int/books/international-migration-law-ndeg25-glossary-migration.

Kirwin, M., & Anderson, J. (2018). *Identifying the factors driving West African migration* (West African Papers, No. 17). Paris: OECD Publishing.

Knodel, J., & Saengtienchac, C. (2005). *Rural parents with urban children: Social and economic implications of migration on the rural elderly in Thailand* (Population Study Center Research Report. 05–574). University of Michigan Institute for Social Research.

Lipton, M. (1977). *Why poor people stay poor: Urban bias in developing countries.* London: Templesmith London.

Macharia, K. (2003). *Migration in Kenya and its impact on the labor market.* Paper prepared for the Conference on African Migration in Comparative Perspective, Johannesburg, South Africa, 4–7 June.

Mafukidze, J. (2006). A discussion of migration and migration patterns and flows in Africa. In C. Cross, D. Gelderblom, N. Roux, & J. Mafukidze (Eds.), *Views on migration in Sub Saharan Africa* (pp. 103–129). Cape Town, South Africa: HSRC Press.

Maïga, E., Christiaensen, L., & Palacios-Lopez, A. (2015). *Are youths exiting agriculture en-masse?* Paper presented at the 2016 Center for the Study of African Economies Conference, Oxford, UK.

Massey, D. S. (2014, September). *Criminalizing immigration in post 9/11 era.* Point of Migration, Centre for Migration and Development, Research Brief, Princeton, University.

Massey, D. S., Arango, J., Hugo, G., Kouaochi, A. Pellegrino, & Taylor, J. E. (1993). Theories of international migration: A review and appraisal. *Population and Development Review, 19*(3), 431–466.

Mbah, E. N., Ezeano, C. I., & Agada, M. O. (2016). Effects of rural-urban youth migration on farm families in Benue State, Nigeria. *International Journal of Agricultural Research, Innovation & Technology 6*(1), 14–20.

Narain, S., Singh, A. K., & Singh, S. R. K. (2015). Perception of farming youth towards farming. *The Indian Research Journal of Extension Education, 15*(2), 105–109.

Njeru, L. K. (2017). Youth in agriculture; perceptions and challenges for enhanced participation in Kajiado North Sub-County, Kenya. *Greener Journal of Agricultural Sciences, 7*(8), 203–209.

Njeru, L., Gichimu, B., Lopokoiyit, M., & Mwangi, J. G. (2015). Influence of Kenyan youth's perception towards agriculture and necessary interventions: A review. *Asian Journal of Agricultural Extension, Economics & Sociology, 5*(1), 40–45.

Noorani, M. (2015). *To farm or not to farm? Rural youth perceptions of farming and their decision of whether or not to work as a farmer: A case study of rural youth in Kiambu County, Kenya.* Retrieved online December 30, 2018, from https://ruor.uottawa.ca/handle/10393/31960.

Nwanna, C. (2004). Rural-urban migration and population problems in Nigeria Cities. In M. O. A. Adejugbe (Ed.), *Industrialization, urbanization and development in Nigeria 1950–1999* (p. 58). Lagos-Nigeria: Concept Publication.

NYPD. (2009). *Second national youth policy document of the Federal Republic of Nigeria.* Retrieved October 10, 2019, from www.youthpolicy.org/natioanl/Nigeria.

Okereke, C. (2003). *Urbanization.* Nigeria: Skilmark Media LTD Owerri.

Osabohien, R. (2018). Contributing to agricultural mix: Analysis of the living standard measurement study-integrated survey on agriculture dataset. *Data in Brief, 20,* 96–100.

Osabuohien, E., Efobi, U. R., Herrmann, R., & Gitau, C. M. (2019). Female labor outcomes and large-scale agricultural land investments: Macro-micro evidence from Tanzania. *Land Use Policy, 82,* 716–728. https://doi.org/10.1016/j.landusepol.2019.01.005.

Osabuohien, E., Okorie, U., & Osabohien, R. (2018). Rice production and processing in Ogun State, Nigeria: Qualitative insights from farmers' association. In E. Obayelu (Ed.), *Food systems sustainability and environmental policies in modern economics* (pp. 188–216). Hershey, PA: IGI Global.

Osita-Njoku, A., & Chikere, P. (2005). Rural-urban mmigration and the underdevelopment in selected rural communities in Imo State, Nigeria. *British Journal of Education, Society & Behavioural Science, 10*(1), 1–10.

Overseas Development Institute (ODI). (2007). *Rural employment and migration: In search of decent work new thinking on rural employment is needed to create more and better rural jobs.* Retrieved online January 10, 2019, from https://www.odi.org/sites/odi.org.uk/files/odi-assets/publications-opinion-files/6.pdf.

Oyebola, P. O., Osabuohien, E., & Obasaju, B. (2019). Employment and income effects of Nigeria's agricultural transformation Agenda. *African Journal of Economic and Management Studies.* https://doi.org/10.1108/AJEMS-12-2018-0402.

Pew Research Center. (2018, February). *International migration from sub-Saharan Africa has grown dramatically since 2010.* Accessed September 27, 2018, from www.pewresearch.org/fact-tank/2018/02/28/international-migration-from-sub-saharanafrica-has-grown-dramatically-since-2010/.

Portes, A. (1999). Immigration theory for a new century: Some problems and opportunities. In: C. Hirschman et al. (Eds.), *The handbook of international migration.* New York: The Russell Sage Foundation.

Qin, H. (2010). Rural-to-urban labor migration, household livelihoods and the rural environment in Chongqing Municipality, Southwest China. *Hum Ecology Interdisciplinary Journal, 38*(5), 675–690.

Rajack-Talley, T. A. (2016). *Rural employment and rural development in the Caribbean. International Labour Organization, ILO Decent Work Team and Office for the Caribbean.* Port of Spain: ILO.

Rajendra, T. (2014). The rational agent or the relational agent: Moving from freedom to justice in migration systems ethics. *Ethical Theory and Moral Practice, 18*(2), 355–369. Retrieved from Loyola eCommons, Theology: Faculty Publications and Other Works, January 10, 2019, from http://dx.doi.org/10.1007/s10677-014-9522-z.

Ravenstein, E. G. (1885). The laws of migration. *Journal of Statistical Society of London, 48*(2), 167–235.

Sjaastad, A. H. (1962). The cost and return of human migration. *The Journal of Political Economy, 70*(5), 80–93.

Stark, O. (1991). Migration in LDCs: Risk, remittances and the family. *Finance and Development, 28*(4), 39–41.

Stark, O. (2006). Inequality and migration: A behavioral link. *Economics Letters, 91,* 146–152.

Stark, O., & Bloom, D. E. (1985). The new economics of labour migration. *American Economics Review, 75,* 173–178.

Timmer, C. P. (1988). The agricultural transformation. In H. Chenery & T. N. Srinivasan (Eds.), *Handbook of development economics* (Vol. 1, pp. 275–331). Amsterdam: North-Holland.

Todaro, M. P. (1969). A model of labor migration and urban unemployment in less developed countries. *The American Economic Review, 59*(1), 138–148.

Todaro, M. P., & Steven, S. (2006). *Economic development*. Boston: Addison Wesley.
Tomanek, A. (2011). *Understanding migration*. Retrieved online January 3, 2019, from http://understandingmigration.blogspot.com/2011/03/international-migration-theories.html.
Udo, R. K. (1975). *Migrant Tenant farmers of Nigeria: A geographical study of rural migrations in Nigeria*. Lagos: African University Press.
United Nations. (2005). *Definition of youth*. Retrieved September 25, 2018, from https://www.un.org/esa/socdev/documents/youth/fact-sheets/youth-definition.pdf.
United Nations. (2017). *Population facts*. United Nations, Department of Economic and Social Affairs Population Division. Available online at http://www.un.org/en/development/desa/population/publications/pdf/popfacts/PopFacts_2017-5.pdf.
United Nations Economic Commission for Africa (UNECA). (2009). *African youth report 2009: Expanding opportunities for and with young people in Africa*. Addis Ababa.
Van der Geest, K. (2011). *The Dagara Farmer at home and away: Migration, environment and development in Ghana*. Unpublished PhD Dissertation, University of Amsterdam. Leiden: African Studies Centre.
Van der Kruk, M. (2009). *Towards places of opportunity? A literature study into rural-urban migration among young people in Tanzania* (Extended Essay: RSO-80912). Wageningen University.
World Bank. (2014). *Agriculture overview*. Retrieved October 1, 2018, from http://www.worldbank.org/en/topic/agriculture/overview#1.
World Bank. (2016). *Nigeria—General household survey, panel 2015–2016, Wave 3*. Retrieved January 5, 2019, from http://microdata.worldbank.org/index.php/catalog/2734/study-description.
Yunita, S. (2009). Perkembangan Migrasi Di Pulau Sumatera. *Wahana, 1*(1), 1–10.
Zafar, M. I., Siddique, S., Zafa, M. U., Azim, M., & Batool, Z. (2013). Migration behavior within socio-cultural and demographic context: A case study of Faisalabad City, Pakistan. *Academic Journal of Interdisciplinary Studies, 2*(2), 29–35.

Fostering Rural Development and Social Inclusion in East Africa: Interrogating the Role of Cooperatives

Mangasini Katundu

1 Introduction

Rural development is ranked high in both developing and developed country development agenda. There are three important reasons that make rural development an important development activity. First, most poor people in the world today live in rural areas. For instance, the World Bank in 2003 estimated that, three out of every four of the world's poor live in rural areas and depend on agriculture for their livelihood (World Bank 2003, 2005). Second, there is an increase in rural to urban migration, which threatens development activities in the rural areas (see WHO 2010; Tefera 2014; Tacoli et al. 2015). Third, rural areas are sources of food and therefore they cannot be abandoned. A study by Owuor (2003) confirms that majority of the urban dwellers in Kenya, Botswana, Zimbabwe, and Nigeria depend on food produced in the rural areas.

This chapter presents a review of key literature on the role of cooperatives as grassroot organizations in reducing rural poverty and enhancing social inclusion in East Africa, using Tanzania, Kenya, and Uganda as case studies. The three countries present good cases because, despite having a large rural population and cooperatives, their people still suffer from abject poverty. The chapter promotes the use of the Integrated Co-operative Model (ICM) that has proved to be effective in linking the rural poor in terms of production, marketing support, and financial services. The sections in this chapter include,

---

M. Katundu (✉)
Moshi Cooperative University, Moshi, Tanzania

introduction, which is followed by the section on contextualization of rural development and the one on poverty and inequality in the three East African countries. The next section is on theoretical framework of cooperatives. Within this section we have reviewed three vital theories of cooperation which are important for African smallholder farmers and other small-scale producers. The theories include the Marxist Theory, the Theory of Economies of Scale, and the Amartya Sen's Theory of Human Development. The next parts tackle the cooperative movement in East Africa, the post-colonial cooperative movement in the three countries, and the integrated cooperative development model and its usefulness to rural development. The chapter ends by the analysis of the government–cooperative relationships in East Africa and conclusions which is followed by recommendations.

2 Contextualization of Rural Development

Rural development has been conceptualized differently as a result of continuous evolution in the perceived mechanisms and goals of development. This necessitates a clear definition of the term in order to guide the discussion afterward. van der Ploeg (1998), Adisa (2012) argue that, the definition of rural development has always been characterized by "continuity and change" i.e., "changing and stable elements." The author argues further that, the term must be conceptualized in both contexts in order to have a "balanced" and practical definition. According to Anríquez and Stamoulis (2007), during 1960s and early 1970s, rural development was conceptualized within the context of intensive industrialization, which characterized many development initiatives at that time. Hence, it was a consensus to define rural development as a part of structural transformation characterized by diversification of the economy away from agriculture (Osabuohien et al. 2015, 2019). Johnston (1970) emphasizes that, rural development process is initially facilitated by a rapid agricultural growth, but in the long run it leads ultimately to a significant decline in the share of agriculture to total employment and output and in the proportion of rural population to total population. Toward the end of 1970s, development was conceptualized in terms of "equity," as a result the definition of rural development changed to emphasize provision of social services to the rural poor. Ruttan (1984) argues that the changes were partly attributed to the recognition of the fact that, even under rapid growth of income in rural areas, the availability or equitable access to social services and amenities was not guaranteed. Since then, rural development has been highly associated with improving standards of living as a precondition for rural poverty alleviation (Anríquez and Stamoulis 2007).

On the other hand, economists championed by International organizations such as the World Bank and the International Monetary Fund (IMF) for long time have defined rural development as the process of improving the economic and social life of the rural poor such as small-scale farmers, tenants and the landless[1] (Adisa 2012). Other definitions include that of the United

States Department of Agriculture (USDA) which defined rural development as 'improvement in the overall rural community conditions, including economic and other quality of life considerations such as environment, health, infrastructure, and housing' (USDA 2006). Today rural development is generally conceptualized as the "the actions and initiatives taken by governments and their respective development partners to improve livelihood conditions in non-urban areas, countryside, and villages" (Obadire et al. 2013). Rural development in most cases aim at achieving social and economic development of the targeted population. In its nutshell, rural development entails both the economic improvement of people as well as greater social transformation.

Three things emerge from these definitions; first, they all suggest that rural development is a process of change and not an overnight activity. Second, the definition entails that goal for rural development is to empower the rural poor; and third, rural development is a multi-stakeholder and a multi-institutions process. This means institutions such as cooperatives which are found in the rural areas have a significant role to play in the process. Cooperatives fits well in the definition of rural development as advocated by the world bank which centers on improving the economic and social life of the rural poor such as small-scale farmers, tenants, and the landless. Emphasis on cooperatives is based on the current conceptualization of development which has put "the role of institutions" at its center. Cooperatives as member-based institutions have the potential of reducing poverty and inequality and hence, fostering rural development and social inclusion. Altman (2010) defines cooperative as a voluntary network of individuals who own or control a business that distributes benefits on the basis of use or ownership where ownership is largely weighted equally across individual members. Moreover, the International Cooperative Alliance defines cooperatives as autonomous associations of persons united voluntarily to meet their common economic, social, and cultural needs and aspirations through a jointly owned and democratically controlled enterprise.[2]

Cooperatives have existed for a long time in East Africa as in other parts of the world. They are found in different forms and sizes and are scattered in almost all sectors of the economy. They range from, Snake catchers in India, prisoners in Ethiopia and taxi drivers in Tanzania and Rwanda to Housing cooperatives in Kenya (Alldred 2013). They are regarded as unique forms of member organizations because they operate in accordance with the pre-set principles and core values which are open and voluntary membership, democratic member control, members' economic participation, and autonomy and independence. Other principles include: education, training, and information, cooperation among cooperatives as well as concern for the community (NRECA 2016). Besides, cooperatives are based on the values of self-help, self-responsibility, democracy, equality, equity, and solidarity. The modern cooperative principles originate from the first cooperatives founded in Rochdale, England in 1844.

To this end a cooperative works to ensure the socio-economic development of the members, community, and the nation at large. One can say in general terms, cooperatives bring people together. Cooperatives create links between people in a specific community or a social environment, whose interests are common, enabling activities that alone would be very difficult or impossible to accomplish. Such partnerships are guided by democratic choices, through assemblies, where there is solidarity among participants and each member has the right of vote (Coutinho et al. 2015). To what extent do these principles make cooperatives a strong engine for rural development and social inclusion in East Africa is the question to be answered. The theoretical framework on why do people cooperate and a history of cooperatives in East Africa are presented in the subsequent section.

It is necessary to note as well that, the basic organic parts of the cooperative enterprises or organization are the connectivity of people, the association of those people, and the cooperative business enterprise. By people we mean ownership of a cooperative starts naturally at the family level. It is also important to take recognition of the fact that the type of cooperatives popular in East Africa and Africa at large, are "the ancillary" type meaning they are formed to address a few but critical problems or just one major problem, affecting all the would-be members. The identified problem, the geographical location, and the main economic activities, are providing the identity for the *would-be* members, known as the common bond. By definition the common bond links all the members into a network known as the association of members. A common bond in cooperatives could be an occupation or association of groups of the *would-be* members within a well-defined neighborhood, community, or geographical area.[3] After the association of members has realized their main problem, they agree to form the cooperative business enterprise which will address their main problem established voluntarily and ran democratically, by the members. This chapter explores the pathways which cooperatives can utilize to promote rural development and social inclusion in East Africa. It also seeks to propose mitigations for the challenges facing cooperatives in the region in order to enhance their capacity as engines of rural development. The following section presents an assessment of the poverty and inequality levels in East Africa. It is argued that poverty and inequality in the region have remained high despite several governments' attempts. The section finishes by assessing the position of cooperatives in reducing poverty and inequality.

3   Poverty and Inequality in East Africa

An individual is considered to live in absolute poverty when his/her income is equal or less than 1.90 US dollars per day (World Bank 2018). Researchers have revealed that poverty is gender, age, and location specific. Women face potentially life-threatening risks from early pregnancy and frequent pregnancies, among other factors. This can result in lost hope for education and a better income. Poverty affects age groups differently, with the most devastating effects experienced by children (Aber et al. 1997). It affects their education, health, nutrition, and security, impacting emotional and spiritual development. Likewise, many poor people today are found in rural than in urban areas and they suffer from social and economic exclusion. Mood and Jonsson (2016) argue that, being poor is about being unable to partake in society on equal terms with others, and therefore in the long run being excluded by fellow citizens or withdrawing from social and civic life because of a lack of economic resources, typically in combination with the concomitant shame of not being able to live a life like them. Citing Callan et al. (1993) Mood and Jonsson (2016) further report that, economic hardship affects the standard of life, consumption patterns, and leisure time activities, and this is directly or indirectly related to the possibility of making or maintaining friends or acquaintances; poverty is revealed by not only lacking appropriate clothes, or a car; but also by not being able to afford vacation trips, visits to the restaurant, or hosting dinner parties. In short, low incomes prevent the poor from living a life in "decency."[4]

Africa and more specifically Sub-Saharan Africa have the greatest share of the world's poor people. Gumede (2016) presented an extensive outline of the state of poverty and inequality in Africa. According to the author, notwithstanding relatively impressive rates of economic growth in Africa in the past ten years or so, poverty and inequality, however measured, have remained stubbornly high. The author further argues that poverty is bad, and there is no debate about that. Interestingly, some scholars argue that inequality at some point is inevitable as it is the character of inequality that matters and that at early stages of socio-economic development certain levels of inequality are required. Fascinatingly, Wilkinson and Pickett (2010), argue that inequality in itself, not the character of it per se, is bad for any society. On the other side, Stiglitz (2012) demonstrates in the case of United States that inequality slows economic growth and can result to economic instability, and that it is hazardous for political stability.

Data on economic dimensions of poverty and inequalities in East Africa are disturbing. Even if poverty in Africa is said to be declining, the rate at which poverty is declining in East Africa is not convincing. The United Nation's 2014 Human Development report indicates that East African countries had a very low human development and are still trapped in serious poverty. In its report the United Nations (UN) placed the East African states in the last category of countries with very low human development, which implies that these countries rank worst on major development indicators such as, life expectancy, education, and income. Kenya, the region's largest economy, was ranked 147, Rwanda 151, Tanzania 159, Uganda 164, and Burundi pulls in at 180 out of a total of 187 countries which were surveyed.[5] It is important to note that, within East African countries, poverty levels are higher in rural areas rather than it is for urban areas which could translate that many poor people in this region live in rural rather than urban areas.[6] The poverty levels in rural and urban areas of selected African countries including

Tanzania, Kenya, and Uganda, which shows that among countries south of Sahara, only Mozambique and Zambia have higher poverty levels than East African countries (World Bank 2016).

Concerning inequality, statistics released by the Society for International Development (SID) in 2018 indicated that in 2011 Rwanda was the East Africa's most unequal country. In this country, the richest 10% of Rwandese earned 3.2 times the income of the poorest 40% of their compatriots. These statistics further show that, income inequality rose between 1985 and 2006, taking Rwanda from the most equal to the most unequal country in the region. After 2006, inequality is trending downwards.[7] During the same time, the richest 10% of Kenyans were earning 2.8 times more than the poorest 40% while Uganda's richest 10% earned 2.3 times more than the poorest 40% of their compatriots. Interestingly, notwithstanding the variations, the level of Uganda's income inequality in 2009 was almost identical to that of two decades earlier. Using data from the World Bank, Development Research Group, SID (2018) further, establishes that Burundi was the least unequal country in the region. During that time, the richest 10% of Burundi's citizens earned 1.35 times the income of the poorest 40%. The trend shows that Burundi's income inequality was rising from 1992 to 1998, after which it returned back to its level of a decade earlier.[8]

A study by Fanta and Upadhyay (2009) confirms that growth helps poverty alleviation. In addition, we find that the attainment of a higher level of development allows a country to translate a given growth into greater poverty reduction. An unequal income distribution, on the other hand, works as an impediment to effective poverty alleviation. In this paper, I argue that economic growth is a function of many factors including strengthening business networks among which one is through cooperatives.

4 Theoretical Framework of Cooperatives

There are three critical theories of cooperation which are important for African small holder farmers and other small-scale producers in Africa. The theories, respond to the basic question as to why should people cooperate. To start with is the Marxist Theory of economic classes which assume that there are two principal classes in any society, i.e., the *bourgeoisie* and proletariat (Hoffman 1986). *The bourgeoisie* is the upper class *consisting* of the rulers while *proletariatis lowerclass which consists of* the workers. The theory assumes further that, factors of production are owned by the *bourgeoisie and that* wages of the workers are determined at subsistence level of living. The theory holds further that, labor is homogenous and perfectly mobile and is the main source of value generation. The *bourgeoisie* or capitalists mercilessly exploit the *proletariat because; they* own capital, purchase, and exploit labor power and in turn use the surplus value from employment of this labor power to accumulate or expand their capital.[9] The *proletariats* have no other resources except their labor power which they use to work for the *bourgeoisie* in an exploitative social relationship in order to feed themselves and their families.[10]

According to the Marxist theory the cooperative enterprise is very important for the *proletariats or* the workers. The *bourgeoisie* or capitalists may not need to unit because they are already powerful. It is important for the lower class to unit in form of a cooperative enterprise because they are exploited classes of society. The cooperative could be their only arsenal to fight the *bourgeoisie*. Jossa (2005) argues that, Karl Marx was a strong believer of the power of cooperative firms in empowering the poor and the marginalized, he maintained that introduction of cooperative firms would result in a new production mode which would eventually supplant capitalistic firms altogether. The author further holds that, even Lenin endorsed the cooperative movement and, in a 1923 work (entirely devoted to this subject), he went so far as to equate cooperation with socialism at large (Jossa 2005, p. 1). Therefore, cooperation is seen here as a process of class struggle for the economic and social emancipation of the exploited.

Second is the Theory of Economies of Scale. Economies of scale is an economics term that describes a competitive advantage that large entities have over smaller entities (Silberston 1972; Celli 2013). In simple language it means the larger the business, non-profit or government, the lower its costs.[11] Two types of economies of scale do exist, namely the internal and external.[12] Internal economies are internal to the firm and are controllable by management whereas, external economies are supported by external factors such as industry, geographic location, or government. Economists believe that small firms don't have the leverage to take advantage of external economies of scale. But, they can join together and take advantage of geographic economies of scale by clustering similar businesses in a small area; as Dollery and Fleming (2005) proclaimed, "bigger is better."

The Theory of Economies of Scale presupposes that small producers need collective action in order to reduce their costs but also increase their bargaining power. In this paper, it is argued that small-scale producers organized through cooperative can advance their scale of production and produce large quantities of commodities at a lower cost. Such collection of large-scale quantities of commodities gives small producers the opportunity for collective power of bargaining and negotiation for better prices than if they operated individually. For example, smallholder cashew nut farmers in Mtwara and Lindi Tanzania are using effectively the theory of economies of scale. Farmers in these two regions are marketing their cashew nuts though cooperatives linked to the warehouse system where they express collective bargaining power with large international buyers.

Third is, the Amartya Sen's (1999) Theory of Human Development, Education and Political Freedom. In his theory, Sen argues that human development is about the expansion of citizens capabilities.[13] Sen views freedom as a process of increasing citizens access and opportunities to the things they have reason to value, hence challenges the mainstream concept of measuring development by economic growth[14]; to him development means freedom (Evans 2002). Sen's argument supports that of Mwalimu Julius Nyerere who emphasized that government officials, academicians and policy makers should understand the connection between freedom, development, and discipline, because the national policy of creating socialist villages throughout the rural areas depended upon it. According to him, freedom and development are as completely linked together as are chickens and eggs! Without chickens you get no eggs; and without eggs you soon have no chickens. Similarly, without freedom you get no development, and without development you very soon lose your freedom.[15] In this paper it is argued that, the main agenda for the operationalization of co-operative business is education, training and information. According to Sen, education and training will free the cooperative members to widen their choices and opportunities for their social and economic freedom.

5 The Cooperative Movement in East Africa

Cooperatives for many years have been used as a vehicle for rural development and social inclusion in East Africa. Mindful of its importance, governments within East African countries have been supporting the cooperative movement since 1960s when these countries gained political independence. This subsection provides the historical perspective and structural arrangement of the co-operative movement in East Africa; using three countries Tanzania, Kenya, and Uganda as case studies.

5.1 The Cooperative Movement in Tanzania

Tanganyika gained its political independence in December 9, 1961 and on April 26, 1964; it joined with Zanzibar to form the United Republic of Tanzania.[16] Since then, the Agricultural Marketing Co-operatives (AMCOS) have dominated the cooperative movement in the country. Besides, by the year 1966 they were 857 well performing cooperatives and 1533 moderately operating ones; such that, the cooperative movement of Tanzania was known as "the cooperative giant of Africa."[17] Chambo (2018) reports that, the cooperative movement in East Africa Tanzania inclusive was established as a result of external demand of export crops such as coffee, cotton, cashew nuts, and tobacco; and that, the strength of the movement have to a larger extent depend on the external demand and price of the listed cash crops. In most cases, a decline of external demand and a fall in prices resulted to the failure of the cooperative organization. Regarding the structure of the cooperative movement, the British introduced the unified structure of the cooperative movement which linked primary societies with second tier cooperative unions; which in turn formed national apex for all specialized commodities and activities (ibid.). However, the situation changed; cooperatives started performing poorly due to corruption, mismanagement, inefficiency, and limited internal democracy which prompted the government to take control of the cooperatives in 1980s and started financing import substitution industrialization through agricultural capital accumulation.[18] This was the first time government of Tanzania is using the cooperative model in its industrialization process.

Major changes within the Tanzania's cooperative movement happened during "villagilization" period (1973–1976) when cooperative unions were removed and villages became the primary cooperative societies. During this time, individuals who were aged 18 years and above were granted automatic membership of the village-based primary cooperatives contrary to the first principles of cooperatives on "open and voluntary membership." Cooperatives are open to all people "free entry" and also members are free to opt out "free exist" (Ashley 2016). Open membership is regarded as key principle of cooperative. In a cooperative, membership is open to all individuals who are willing and ready to use its services and are also ready to accept the responsibilities of membership, regardless of race, religion, gender, or economic condition. Similarly, cooperatives are democratically governed organizations controlled by their members, who actively participate in setting policies and making decisions.

Members execute their mandate during the Annual General Meeting (AGM), and decision is normally based on majority votes. Elected representatives (board members) are elected from among the membership and are accountable to the membership via the general meeting. Shareholders have the right to vote, on matters of policy changes, including decisions on the makeup of the board of directors, issuing securities, initiating corporate actions, and making substantial changes in the cooperative operations. In cooperatives, members have equal voting rights, that is, one member one vote. This principle ensures that no one dominates in decision-making both minority and majority shareholders have equal right when it comes to voting, and every shareholder has only one vote. Unlike the single vote right that individuals commonly possess in cooperative societies, the number of votes a shareholder has in privately owned companies corresponds to the number of shares he or she owns.[19] Individuals with many shares have the supreme say when it comes to matters of the company.

Concerning the domination of AMCOS in East Africa, currently, we are witnessing a reverse, where the financial cooperatives especially Savings and Credit Cooperative Societies (SACCOS) are now becoming dominant form of cooperatives in Tanzania and they account for more than 56% of the total members (Sumelius et al. 2013). Data from the Tanzania Cooperative Development Commission (TCDC) indicates that in 2017 there were a total of 5918 SACCOS compared to only 3413 AMCOS countrywide.[20] Similarly, there are 217 livestock, 208 mining, and 217 consumer cooperatives in the country (TCDC 2017). There is also an ongoing process to establish the National Cooperative Bank and Cooperative Insurance Company spearheaded by the cooperative umbrella organization in the country, the Tanzania Federation of Cooperatives (TFC). Other forms of cooperatives include consumer, fisheries, livestock, mining, irrigation, industrial, housing, and services. The growth of SACCOS can be a blessing to rural poor, because they are the only financial institutions able to penetrate the rural areas of Tanzania and have branches in nearly every village. SACCOS if well managed and utilized can be an important vehicle for financial inclusion.

5.2 The Cooperative Movement in Kenya

Cooperatives in Kenya dates back to 1908 when the Lumbwa Cooperative was formed by white settlers to develop their agriculture (see Imungi 2016; Zeleza 1990). Imungi (2016) further reports that by early 1960s, cooperatives had already shown signs of becoming dominant rural institutions in economy and by the end of 1963, about 1000 cooperatives were already registered in Kenya; such that by 1970s cooperative activities were evident in almost all sectors of the economy. Besides, Zeleza (1990) reports that, cooperative movement in Kenya grew very rapidly to the extent that in 1982 registered cooperative societies had reached 2652. Mumanyi (2014) estimated that by the end of 2005 there were over 11,200 registered Cooperative Societies in Kenya, out of this, 38% are Agricultural, 46% Financial-based that is SACCOS and 16% are others. During this time, the main activities of cooperatives were to mobilize marketing of agricultural produce, engage in agro-processing, ensure property ownership and investments, and involve in banking and insurance. Gweyi et al. (2013) report different observation, that, SACCOS as savings associations in Africa did not come with the establishment of colonialism, they have been evident in African continent using different names even before the advent of colonialism; examples of such pre-colonial SACCOS are "*sanduk*" in Sudan, "*esusu*" in Nigeria, "*chilimba*" in Zambia, and "*ekub*" in Ethiopia. The reasons why these first forms of SACCOS faded out during the colonial times is because the colonial government favored AMCOS than SACCOS due to the nature of colonial crop production which was meant to produce raw materials for industries in Europe.

It is important to note as well that colonial government in Kenya did not favor Black African Cooperatives; as a result by the end of 1940s there were very few African-owned cooperatives which were mainly formed without government support. Among early African-owned AMCOs in Kenya were the Taita Vegetable Cooperative and the Kisii Coffee Growers' Association as well as the Kenya African Traders and Farmers Association, which had over 200 members and a share capital of KShs. 4000.10 (Zeleza 1990). The main objective of these cooperatives was to improve members' economic conditions in the colonial capitalist environment. Africans saw establishment of these cooperatives as one of the means to reduce Indian monopoly of rural trade. It is further argued that, the government opposition to African owned cooperatives was founded on uncertainties the colonial government had, that, African cooperatives could strengthen the economic position of peasants, which plight make it more difficult for settler farmers to get labor, and that increased peasant economic power would provide Africans with the political muscle to overturn the settler-dominated colonial regime and hence would threaten the stability of the colonial authority (Seimu 2015; Okello and Ahikire 2013).

Today, the cooperative movement of Kenya is regarded as the strongest in East Africa boosting the Kenyan economy with more than 45% of gross domestic product (GDP), the highest proportion in percentage points of GDP attributed to cooperatives in the world followed by New Zealand in the second place with 22%.[21] More than 63% of the Kenyan population earns a living from cooperatives with over 250,000 benefiting through direct employment, such that one out of every five Kenyans is a member of a cooperative; which means at least eight million Kenyans are members of cooperatives while 20 million depend on the movement indirectly (Mumanyi 2014; Imungi 2016). There are 3280 SACCOS, and considered the fastest growing sub-sector in the cooperative movement, this sub-sector is the fastest growing in Africa. It accounts for about 60, 64, and 63% of the country's savings, loans, and assets, respectively.[22] This is not accidental, unlike in Tanzania Chambo (2018) argues that in Kenya and Uganda, there was more observation of the operation of the cooperative principles through the complementary relationship between the government and the cooperative movement and as a result cooperatives maintained stability in the years after political independence. Imungi (2016) reports further that, because the cooperative sector is very important for Kenyans' development it is the most regulated in Africa and the best in East Africa. However, this is not to say that cooperatives in Kenya are free from government interventions.

Kenya has a four-tier vertical structure of the cooperative movement which starts with the primary cooperative societies, cooperative unions, national cooperative organizations, and one apex (Wanyama 2007). According to Wanyama et al. (2008) the apex (the Kenya National Federation of Co-operatives [KNFC]) is the organization of cooperatives at the national level which represent all cooperatives in the country. Membership of KNFC includes national co-operative organizations as well as co-operative unions. The KNFC further links the Kenyan co-operative movement to the world cooperatives movement (Gweyi et al. 2013). Though linkages with the global cooperative movement; KNFC fulfills its main policy objective which is to spur sustainable economic growth by focusing on achievement of desired outcomes through strengthening of the movement, improving cooperative extension service delivery, corporate governance, access to markets, and marketing efficiency (Gunga 2013).

5.3 The Cooperative Movement in Uganda

The first forms of cooperatives was established in 1913, by a group of peasants mainly cotton growers from Kiboga in Mubende District (Kyamulesire 1988). The Colonial government tried to control the cooperative movement in Uganda right at its early stage. Following the racial clashes and peasant protests of 1940s, the government ratified the first Cooperative Societies Act in 1946 as a strategy of the colonial government to "co-opt" local leaders among the African peasantry (Flygare 2006). During this period, cash crops such as cotton and coffee were given priority by the colonial administrators (Okello and Ahikire 2013). Mwejune (1993) argues that, African peasants were forced into the production of cash crops and the direct encouragement was in the form of distribution of free seeds and technical advice by the colonial administration. Distribution of seeds was done through chiefs and traditional elders who could also benefit economically by levying a small charge. They also took advantage of this to exercise their powers on their subjects. Indirectly it was done through the imposition of taxes (head tax, hut tax). Also, a Registrar for cooperatives was appointed and a Department for Cooperative Development created (Kyamulesire 1988). Many cooperative groups saw this as a means of increasing government control in their business and they refused to register under it.

The colonial cash economy was exploitative in nature and many African farmers were dissatisfied. The colonial economic policy favored European and Asian business owners than Africans; as a result, the European and Asian monopolized domestic and export marketing of cotton and coffee (Okello and Ahikire 2013). The dissatisfaction was manifested in the form of boycotts (Kyamulesire 1988). The exploitation was in form of "the business arrangement" where, the native farmers (Africans) were allowed only to engage in the production of cash crops, while the Europeans and Asians were permitted to concentrate with processing and marketing of such produce which gave them an upper hand against Africans. Africans then realized that forming cooperatives would give them a common voice, purpose, and strong bargain power (Kyazze 2010).

Following Uganda's political independence in 1962, government favored cooperatives as policy instruments for rural development. During this time, literature shows that cooperative movement in Uganda continued to grow especially those involved in cash crops; they successfully provided agricultural-related services to farmers until the mid-1980s. At that time, as Kwapong and Korugyendo (2010) noted, due to increased political instability, liberalization of markets, and mismanagement, cooperatives failed. According to Flygare (2006), democracy in Uganda is still not well established to permit revitalization of cooperatives as strong people-centered institutions. He further argues that, there are still question marks in regard to the development of the Ugandan civil society and democratic rule that may affect the cooperative movement. However, there are some encouraging developments; the government has embarked on restructuring and reorganizing post-liberalization cooperatives. The developments include the establishment of the Uganda Cooperative Alliance (UCA), which is as an apex body, supported by the cooperative unions (Kwapong and Korugyendo 2010). Efforts are also underway to transform the old Unified Co-operative Model

(UCM) into a new ICM. The old model as discussed was exploitative and farmers were severely impoverished.

A critical look at the cooperative movement in the three selected countries in East Africa, four things emerge. First, it is clear that cooperatives in these countries were established strategically to aid the colonial economy, especially in the production and semi-processing of raw cash crops such as, tobacco, cotton, coffee, cashew nut, and tea. Second, it is also evident that AMCOS dominated early cooperative movement in Tanzania, Kenya, and Uganda due partly to the nature of colonial economy which preferred cash crops than food crops. Third, is the fact that governments (colonial or post-colonial) tried to control cooperatives right at its infancy. The colonial authorities feared that if cooperatives become so strong they will empower smallholders and make labour mobilization very difficult. Also, the post-colonial governments feared stronger cooperatives will dominate politics and hence threaten the survival of the regimes. The fourth point to note is that, there is a shift from AMCOS dominated cooperative movement to financial cooperative dominated one. SACCOS and other forms of financial cooperatives such as Village Community Banks (VICoBA) are on increase.

6 Post-Colonial Cooperative Development in East Africa

Cooperative-led development is not a new concept. Cooperatives have been around for more than 200 years; I trace the formation of cooperatives globally from Robert Owen who proposed the introduction of "villages of cooperation" as a response to the economic crisis in 1815 the idea which was adapted globally and attracted about 1 billion members (Alldred 2013). He further argued that, cooperatives are stronger than trade unions which are found in over 100 countries, being second most common institutions in rural areas especially of Africa after faith groups.

Cooperative-led development as a people-centered business model has a particularly vital role in rural areas as they mobilize self-help mechanisms through a common purpose covering a wide range of economic sectors and social needs; including access to housing, energy, markets, decent work, financial services, water, or fresh and quality food, to name a few (Mendoza 2016). The versatility of the cooperative model permits the creation of innovative initiatives capable of addressing unmet needs in case of natural disasters, or disasters caused by national or regional conflict. The potential of the cooperative model to generate and provide sustainability to social and economic enterprises capable of addressing the new needs of modern societies is huge. This is the case, for example, of some social care cooperatives that are being formed in responding to the care needs of ageing populations (Mendoza 2016). Cooperatives in Africa were very strong between the year 1950s and 60s, and thereafter they faced serious government interference hence, many of them failed, and were written off by most development agencies (Alldred 2013). In this sub-section, I am discussing the government–cooperative relations in East Africa by assessing critically various models which were developed and applied to strengthen the cooperatives.

According to the Alliance Africa (2017), cooperative movement in Africa passed through four main stages of its evolution the first stage being Colonial Period. During this stage, Africa experienced a Top-down Approach Co-operative Movement. The development of cooperatives based largely on colonial legacies and hence followed the British, French, and Belgian Cooperative traditions. (i) The British promoted a UCM which saw cooperatives grow into powerful business ventures that, through vertical structures, controlled much of agricultural production, marketing, and processing in rural areas, in particular with regard to export crops. (ii) The French introduced the so-called "*Sociétes Indigènes (which became Africaines) de Prévoyance*" in the early 1920s as semi-public organizations officially formed to foster rural development, but in practice used to dominate the rural populations and collect taxes, with little economic and societal importance. (iii) The Belgian and Portuguese Africa did not experience Co-operative development activities during the colonial period (ibid.).

The second stage was the Post-Independence Era (1960–1985) which Schwettmann (2014) called the Era of "Cooperativism." This stage witnessed the newly independent African governments employing cooperatives as a means to promote the concept of African socialism as a "third way" between capitalism and communism. During this period cooperatives in East Africa were mainly established to market strategic crops such as coffee, tobacco, cashew nut, and cotton.[23] In some East African countries such as Tanzania, cooperatives were given enormous government support, both financial and technical; they were also given marketing and supply monopolies for agricultural inputs and produce, carrying out government functions such as the management of the strategic grain reserve. The third stage was the Era of Trade Liberalization which started in the mid-1980s. Alliance Africa (2017) further report that, during this stage, Africa experienced an era of structural adjustment, democratization, and commercialization, marking the end of government hold on and control of the cooperative movement. The state assumed facilitative role instead, restructuring the cooperative legal framework, and opening up cooperative dominated sectors to other actors. During this stage cooperatives were required to compete in the market.

Besides, most AMCOS in the region were caught off guard as they were unable to compete with private companies in the market. During this period many cooperatives lost their members as some cooperative societies stopped operations, due to farmers' selling their crop to private companies; while others had a lot of debts and had to sell some of their properties to make them debt-free. Some cooperatives such as AMCOS (Agricultural and Marketing Cooperative Societies) had to re-visit their structures in order to be able to compete with private buyers a good example is Mamsera in Rombo district, Tanzania. Other examples of cooperatives which survived the challenges of economic liberalization are the Nyakatonzi Cooperative Union (NCU) in Kasese, which deals with cotton and the Bugisu Cooperative Union (BSU) that deals with coffee (Okello and Ahikire 2013). The author further argues that the NCU and the BSU unlike the traditional cooperatives adopted the culture of quick cash which attracted more coffee farmers and hence increased membership.

The fourth stage comprised of the so called the "Fourth Generation Co-operative Movement." This stage saw the pulling out of the state support and state control over cooperatives; this led to the weakening of the position of cooperative registrars and as a result, causing the unavailability of reliable statistics on cooperatives and their members in Africa (Schwettmann 2014). A study conducted by the International Labour Organization (ILO) in 2006 and 2007 concluded that out of 100 African citizens, including children and the elderly, only seven were members of cooperatives exactly the same rate as in the early 1990s. This could imply that, the whole African continent host only 70 million cooperative members the figure which do not include membership in less formal types of cooperation and mutuality in the wider social economy. It is further argued that, until the 1990s, AMCOS were by far the largest group.[24] According to Mumanyi (2014) this position today is taken by savings and credit cooperatives. In 2013, a total of 22.385 credit unions existed in 25 African countries, representing 17 million individual members and 7.2 billion US-$ in assets (Schwettmann 2014).

This growth could be attributed to the implementation of liberal policies during the structural adjustment era. Kwapong (2013) reports that, the "unified cooperative model" promoted by the British administration lost ground and gave way to more heterogeneous, less structured cooperative movements. Due to the stained image of "state-owned" cooperatives in the past, many countries experimented with more holistic social economy models that cater for diverse organizational manifestations of self-help, including community-based organizations, farmers groups, and mutual benefit groups. This led to the slowdecline of the unified model and paved the way for the emergence of a myriad of "non-traditional" types of cooperatives, such as housing, handicraft, cultural, transport, mining, and social services cooperatives, as well as informal sector associations.

Alliance Africa (2017) reports that cooperatives in Africa face three main challenges; first is the crisis of identity: Most cooperatives exist in names only, not by nature. The various country cooperative registries are yet to clean out this mess; also there is a crisis of environment: the legal, institutional, and administrative context continuous to prevent, not support, the emergence of genuine, self-managed growth-oriented Cooperatives; and finally is a crisis of management: Most of the existing cooperatives are unable to survive without subsidies, state protection, and government intervention. Another main challenge faced by many cooperatives is over-control and regulation by government. Cooperatives are often subject to more burdensome regulations than other private sector players with high cost and time burdens associated with setting up a cooperative. A robust legal environment with prudential regulation needs to protect democratic member control, autonomy and independence, and voluntary membership (Alldred 2013).

7 Integrated Cooperative Model as a Tool for Rural Development and Social Inclusion

The unified model is the traditional model which was introduced and promoted by British colonial administrators within British colonies, to support its "indirect rule" approach (Schwettmann 2014; Kwapong and Hanisch 2013). The model was characterized by a multi-stage system with primary cooperatives at the bottom and a single apex body at the top. In between are secondary societies in the form of regional chapters, federations, and unions that provide for the horizontal and vertical integration of the movement (Develtere et al. 2008). Additionally, the unified model was a "top-down approach" which aimed at exploiting cooperative members. This model turned cooperatives into agents as Braverman et al. (1991) noted, most cooperatives ended up as mere collecting agents of agricultural produce for public marketing boards; distribution channels for agricultural inputs; or as lending agencies for government- or donor-provided resources. Wanyama (2013) found that liberalization has also triggered the diversification of cooperative ventures to enable them survive market forces and offer competitive services to the members. The loss of monopoly status, coupled with the business-oriented demands of the market, is increasingly seeing cooperatives redesign their activities competitively. This calls for an introduction of a new cooperative development model.

Research carried out by Moshi Cooperative University (MoCU), Tanzania, Makerere University Uganda, the University of Lay Adventists of Kigali (UNILAK) of Rwanda, and the University of Saskatchewan in Canada, added value to the current debate, on the collapse of the unified model and a gradual shift to the ICM which establishes a more proactive linkage with rural development.[25] In the ICM perspective, the current shift to SACCOS domination for example, is not static, but a dynamic reflection of moving toward the ICM which links multi-commodity agricultural cooperatives with financial cooperatives at the local level. The study assessed the ICM's ability to reduce poverty as compared to locations where only a single cooperative or a cluster of less integrated co-ops existed. Findings revealed positive results of link between rural poverty reduction and cooperative enterprises. Similarly, a study by Rutaremara et al. (2016) in Rwanda found that the ICM had positive impact to rural development and poverty reduction. For instance, with access to financial services; the study showed that integrated cooperatives accessed easily financial services such as savings and credit than less integrated ones. ICM integrates production, marketing support, and financial services for agricultural producers. These three pillars of sustainable cooperative development

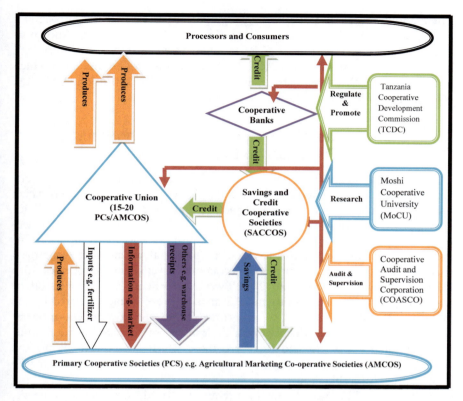

Fig. 1 The integrated co-operative Model (ICM) as modified from Joint Acholi Sub-Regional Leaders' Forum and Trócaire (JASLF) (2017)

aim at improving the livelihoods of rural farmers through access to production, marketing, and financial services.[26] A typical ICM is presented in Fig. 1.

The ICM model presented in Fig. 1 summarizes the role of various actors including institutions in cooperative development. The model is a modification of the one presented by the Joint Acholi Sub-Regional Leaders' Forum and Trócaire in short JASLF in 2017. Modification was necessitated by the fact that, the model presented by JASLF specifically targeted the Acholi in Uganda and did not include the role of cooperative development institutions such as the TCDC in Tanzania and The UCA in Uganda which regulate and promote the cooperatives, the auditing, and supervision institutions such as COASCO in Tanzania as well as the research institutions such as MoCU. The earlier model also ignored the fact that Banks offer credits to both SACCOS and the processors and consumers. The proposed model is a self-sufficient one which indicates that primary cooperative societies form the base of the model. First, 20–30 members of a community in a given geographical area form a primary cooperative society (PCS) for purposes of improving their farming activities and collective marketing.

Then, about 15–30 PCS in a larger geographical area known as a Sub-county in Uganda or district in Tanzania form a secondary cooperative known as Area Cooperative Enterprise (ACE) in Uganda and Unions in Tanzania.[27] The Primary Societies plus the ACE/Unions then form one SACCOS which is shared by all the three categories as their financial institution. SACCOS offer credit facilities to the ACE/Union and or PCs.

8 Government–Cooperative Relationships and Its Impact to Rural Development

Theoretically, as Bee (2016) pointed out, cooperatives are supposed to be private self-help organizations that are free from government interventions which uphold the fundamental human rights and principles of equality and equity. They are supposed to promote social integration and inclusion which create a society that is safer, more stable, and more just. As a result, scholars have been recommending a use of cooperative development model as an alternative approach to deal with the contemporary socio-economic development challenges (Bee 2016; Ashley 2016; Dondo 2012). However, experience has revealed otherwise. Cooperatives in East Africa and Africa at large are being interfered by the governments either for good or for worse. There are government–cooperatives relationship models which weaken the capacity of cooperatives to contribute to rural development and there are those which are positive. While the ICM is positive to rural development, they need the appropriate government–cooperative relationship model.

Nkhoma (2011) argued that in attempting to address consumer needs, some African governments have come up with policies that may harm cooperatives. These policies include the price ceiling, pan-territorial or uniform pricing, pan-seasonal pricing, marketing margin control, high import and export taxes, and parastatal marketing monopolies. The author further establishes that the implementation of these polices have to some extent lead to a failure of cooperatives to realize the benefits of competition since they meant to reward the inefficient operation. For example, White (1985) claimed that uniform pricing for all economic regions would increase regional income differentials, by disadvantaging those areas with less favorable natural and infrastructural conditions and rewarding better endowed areas.

Arguing in a similar line, Seimu (2015) pointed out that the cooperative laws, policies, and legislations enacted in Tanganyika by the British Colonial Government and even the new post-colonial government was meant to control the cooperative movement in Tanganyika now Tanzania. For instance, Section 36 of the 1932 cooperative legislation which was further reinforced by three policies, the 1934 Chagga Rule, the 1937 Native (control and marketing) Ordinance and the Defence Ordinance, Orders of 1939 and 1940; and the African Agricultural Products (Control and Marketing) Ordinance, 1949. The author further argues that the post-colonial authority perpetuated the colonial policies in promoting cooperatives and the control of agricultural export revenues provided under the 1962 by the National Agricultural Products Board (Control and Marketing) Act by intensifying the intervention, effectively strangling and restructuring them to provide for effective control. Likewise, there was an increased politization of the movement's function as they became an integral part of the propagation of the socialist/ujamaa ideology and the national development plan as the 1976 villagization policy.

Due to frequent harmful government interference, cooperatives in Africa have been weakened; and as such, they cannot be trusted as they are to be vehicles for rural development and social transformation unless they are left free to be regulated by the forces of free market (see Seimu 2015; Nkhoma 2011; White 1985; Sumelius et al. 2013). Nkhoma (2011) noted that weak legal and regulatory frameworks, which rarely enforce contracts or push those who breach contracts, affects the farmers' cooperatives. This according to the author has opened up avenues for corruption and manipulative behaviors, and a weaker regulatory environment also makes cooperatives vulnerable to exploitation by deceitful businessmen. Referring to Nkhoma (2011) also added that, due to weak formal contract enforcement mechanisms, there is a great deal of mistrust among the players. This in turn may increase the transaction costs, since, business firms deals are tempted to screen every single firm or individual with whom the deal is with.

Tentatively, there are four models which can be applied to explain the government–co-operative relational models; the conflictive, the administrative, the complementary, and the educational development models. Tanzania as an example has gone through the first three models which were responsible for the cooperative organizational evolutionary process over the years. The first model is based on the use of cooperatives as policy implementation institutions including rural development. The model is conflictive because the government does not recognize the democratic, equity, equality, and self-responsibility values and principles. Second model is the administrative model where the government respects the democratic principles of cooperatives and values, but takes the cooperative movement as an extension of the Ministry of Agriculture. It is almost similar to the first one because cooperatives are taken as conduits of policy implementation. The complementary model is where the government takes cooperatives as partners in development. The model makes government see the cooperative movement as a genuine democratic system through which it can give limited and promotional support to co-operatives as long as they demonstrate successful business operations. However, if they fail, they should reorganize themselves. This is the current model being implemented by the government. The educational development model is said to be the best where the government supports the implementation of principle no. 5 of the provision of education, training, and information and let it go and compete in the market (Chambo 2018).

If we analyze the implications of the ICM, we see that the model is based at the primary society level where natural members are connected to markets more directly. At this level, the discussion about the fostering of rural development can be more focused as a push or pull outcome. It is considered a push outcome because rural development will be a result of the integrated cooperative development processes. As more people join cooperatives though this model, and government fulfills its responsibilities, such cooperatives will definitely push rural development as a positive outcome. It is also a pull outcome if members of the integrated cooperative movement are running an efficient business system and the government does not fulfill its designated responsibilities, cooperative members through their federation will put pressure on the government to carry out its designated responsibilities in infrastructure, basic health, and educational services. In this analysis, the cooperative movement should be considered as an organic link to rural development than a substitute (Alldred 2013; Chambo 2018).

However, in order to have an efficient link between cooperatives and rural development, cooperatives need to have the following interventions; First is the legal recognition of the primary society as the anchor of cooperative development, because that is where members as natural persons are connected with cooperative business and impact can easily be traced. Second intervention, is the enhancement of problem-solving member education and training. The stock of knowledge of members, leaders, and management should also be improved through the continuous assimilation of external knowledge and experience in an absorption capacity process. Third, is the institutional intervention of pluralistic governance through the provision of leadership education and training to the members, so that they are in a position to run the cooperative business (Alliance Africa 2017). Fourth, is raising the business skills of all members through practical entrepreneurial practices. Entrepreneurship development need can be implemented through processes of planned change based on strategic planning, innovation, and change. Finally the institutionalization of the warehouse receipt mechanism and the international commodity exchange system.

9 Conclusion and Recommendations

Given the current organizational, structural, resources, legal, political, and economic milieu in which cooperatives operate in East Africa, one is bound to agree that cooperatives in this region have been weakened and as such struggle to compete in the current liberalized environment. The broader discussion on the role of cooperatives in promoting rural development which have been presented above, have demonstrated that: Early forms of cooperatives were exploitative and did not benefit the poor. They were mainly established to assist the colonial rulers. It has also shown that, cooperatives are an organ of rural development in whichever form and model and can contribute to rural development whether they are weak or strong. Similarly, cooperative formation is a design issue which will always respond to the needs of the members and rural development is always related to push or pull outcomes depending on the policy environment that exists at the time. In this way, at the formation, cooperatives have a particular purpose to address members' economic and social objectives as a priority. Government intervention on cooperatives can be more positive by strengthening the integrated cooperative organization at the primary society levels. Finally, the ICM offers the best alternative approach to achieve cooperative-rural development objectives.

In order for cooperatives to contribute meaningfully to rural development and social inclusion in Africa, the following need to be done: First, I encourage the use of ICM which has proved to be effective in linking the rural poor in terms of production, marketing support, and financial services. Second, member education should be given priority; East African cooperatives should invest more in training their members especially on how they can work in an ICM. Training is also needed on member's roles and responsibilities, knowledge of production, marketing, and management. This may in turn increase the success rate of cooperatives in reducing poverty and ensuring social inclusion. Third, positive government intervention is needed especially on areas related to punishing the criminals in the cooperative industry. People who misused the cooperative funds and properties need to be brought to justice immediately. However, I recommend further studies on the role of government in cooperative development because there are scholars who believe that too much interference into the cooperative movement will kill cooperatives while others still maintain that the government should interfere in all matters related to cooperatives.

Acknowledgements I am grateful to Prof. Suleman Chambo, Dr. Nyanjige Mayalla, Dr. Neema Kumburu, Dr. Lukas Mataba and Dr. Benson Ndiege from the Moshi Cooperative University (MoCU) for their useful inputs during early stages of this Chapter. I also wish to thank independent reviewers for their useful inputs.

Notes

1. The World Bank, 2018. Rural development, http://documents.worldbank.org/curated/en/522641468766236215/Rural-development.
2. http://learningstore.uwex.edu/assets/pdfs/A1457.pdf and https://www.gov.mb.ca/jec/coop/pdf/rib01s01.pdf.
3. William R. Emmons and Frank A. Schmid (1998), https://www.ifkcfs.de/fileadmin/downloads/publications/wp/99_01.pdf.
4. Galbraith J. The affluent society. Boston: Houghton-Mifflin; 1958.
5. Kenneth Agutamba (2014). UN report exposes poverty among East Africans, http://www.newtimes.co.rw/section/read/125/.
6. Moyombuya Ngubula (2017). Africa in Focus Figure of the week: Urbanization, poverty, and social protection in East Africa, https://www.brookings.edu/

blog/africa-in-focus/2017/09/01/figure-of-the-week-urbanization-poverty-and-social-protection-in-east-africa/.
 7. Dicta Asiimwe (2017). East Africa: Rwanda Has Region's Highest Inequality Rate, http://www.theeastafrican.co.ke/business/Rwanda-has-regions-highest-inequality-rate-/2560-3908112-t4t51ez/index.html.
 8. SID (2018). Economic Dimensions of Inequalities in East Africa, http://inequalities.sidint.net/soear/data/one-people-one-destiny/economic-dimensions-of-inequalities.
 9. The Communist Manifesto—Bourgeoisie and Proletariat. The British Library Board, http://www.bl.uk/learning/histcitizen/21cc/utopia/methods1/bourgeoisie1/bourgeoisie.html.
 10. http://uregina.ca/~gingrich/s28f99.htm.
 11. https://en.wikipedia.org/wiki/Economies_of_scale.
 12. https://www.thebalance.com/economies-of-scale-3305926.
 13. Sen, A. 1999. *Development as Freedom*. Oxford: Oxford University Press.
 14. Denis O'Hearn, 2009. Amartya Sen's *Development as Freedom*: Ten Years Later.
 15. Nyerere, J. K. Freedom and Development, 1973.
 16. Encyclopedia Britannica, https://www.britannica.com/place/Tanganyika.
 17. A speech delivered by Prof. Suleiman Chambo during the seminar to prepare a concept note for 2017, Cooperative day at the Moshi Cooperative University.
 18. A speech delivered by Prof. Suleiman Chambo during the seminar to prepare a concept note for 2017, Cooperative day at the Moshi Cooperative University.
 19. Investopedia. Voting Right, https://www.investopedia.com/terms/v/votingright.asp.
 20. Tanzania Cooperative Development Commission (TCDC) (2017), https://www.ushirika.go.tz/statistics/.
 21. Article by Amina Mbuthia, Cooperative Movement Shifting Economic Potential, by Soko Directory Team/May 24, 2016.
 22. Article by Amina Mbuthia, Cooperative Movement Shifting Economic Potential, by Soko Directory Team/May 24, 2016.
 23. A speech delivered by Prof. Suleiman Chambo during the seminar to prepare a concept note for 2017, Cooperative day at the Moshi Cooperative University.
 24. A speech delivered by Prof. Suleiman Chambo during the seminar to prepare a concept note for 2017, Cooperative day at the Moshi Cooperative University.
 25. http://usaskstudies.coop/documents/pdfs/Lou%20JoAnn%20Cindy%20poster%20January%202017.pdf.
 26. https://words.usask.ca/thinkingaboutcoops/tag/integrated-co-operative-model/.
 27. https://www.trocaire.org/sites/default/files/resources/policy/180215_final_inclusive_business_models_ibm_user_guide.pdf.

REFERENCES

Aber, J. L., Bennett, N. G., Conley, D. C., & Li, J. (1997). The effects of poverty on child health and development. *Annual Review of Public Health, 18,* 463–483.

Adisa, R. S. (2012). *Rural development in the twenty-first century as a global necessity.* Accessed September 11, 2018, from https://www.intechopen.com/books/rural-development-contemporary-issues-and-practices/introductory_chapter_rural_development_in_the_twenty_first_century_as_a_global_necessity.

Alldred, S. (2013). *Cooperatives can play a key role in development.* Accessed August 14, 2018, from https://www.theguardian.com/global-development-professionalsnetwork/2013/jul/06/international-day-of-cooperatives.

Alliance Africa. (2017). *Africa co-operative development strategy 2017–2020.* Accessed August 14, 2018, from https://icaafrica.coop/sites/default/files/basic-page-attachments/africa-cooperative-development-strategy-2017-2020-859927886.pdf.

Altman, M. (2010). *History and theory of cooperatives.* Accessed August 10, 2018, from https://www.researchgate.net/publication/228272144_History_and_Theory_of_Cooperatives.

Anríquez, G., & Stamoulis, K. (2007). Rural development and poverty reduction: Is agriculture still the key? (ESA Working Paper No. 07-02). Accessed September 12, 2018, from http://www.fao.org/3/a-ah885e.pdf.

Ashley, N. T. (2016). *The role of agricultural cooperatives in poverty reduction: A case study of selected cooperatives in the four local municipalities of Vhembe district municipality, Limpopo Province, South Africa.* A Dissertation Submitted in Fulfillment of the Requirements for the Master of Science Degree in Agriculture (Agricultural Economics). School of Agriculture, University of Venda, Thohoyandou, Limpopo, South Africa.

Bee, F. K. (2016). Mobilizing co-operatives for a higher regional development impact: A paper presented to the First East African Co-operative Conference on Harnessing East Africa's Industrial Potential, organized at the Intercontinental Hotel, Nairobi Kenya from 29 February to 2 March 2016.

Braverman, A., Guasch, L., Huppi, M., & Pohlmeier, L. (1991). *Promoting rural cooperatives in developing countries: The case of sub-Saharan Africa.* Washington, DC: World Bank.

Callan, T., Nolan, B., & Whelan, C. T. (1993). Resources, deprivation, and the measurement of poverty. *Journal of Social Policy, 22,* 141–172. https://doi.org/10.1017/S0047279400019280.

Celli, M. (2013). Determinants of economies of scale in large businesses—A survey on UE listed firms. *American Journal of Industrial and Business Management, 3,* 255–261.

Chambo. (2018). *Keynote address to the conference on innovations for sustainable co-operative development.* CO-operative Training Retreat Center, Co-operative University of Kenya (CUK), 26–27 March 2018.

Coutinho, D., Moreno, A. S., & Matsuzawa, V. R. O. (2015). *Cooperatives: An important tool for economic and social inclusion.* Accessed July 8, 2018, from http://www.admpg.com.br/2015/down.php?id=1906&q=1.

Develtere, P., Pollet, I., & Wanyama, F. (2008). *Cooperating out of poverty: The renaissance of the African cooperative movement.* Accessed July 3, 2018, from https://www.ilo.org/public/english/employment/ent/coop/africa/download/coop_out_of_poverty.pdf.

Dollery, B., & Fleming, E. (2005). *A conceptual note on scale economies, size economies and scope economies in Australian local government.* Accessed August 9, 2018, from https://www.une.edu.au/__data/assets/pdf_file/0005/67964/econ-2005-6.pdf.

Dondo, A. M. (2012). *The cooperative model as an alternative strategy for rural development: A policy analysis case study of Kenya and Tanzania 1960–2009* (ETD Collection for AUC Robert W. Woodruff Library, Paper 283).

Evans, P. (2002). Collective capabilities, culture, and Amartya Sen's development as freedom. *Studies in Comparative International Development, 37*(2), 54–60.

Fanta, F., & Upadhyay, M. P. (2009). Poverty reduction, economic growth and inequality in Africa. *Applied Economics Letters, 16*(18), 1791–1794. https://doi.org/10.1080/13504850701719587.

Flygare, S. (2006). *The cooperative challenge farmer cooperation and the politics of agricultural modernisation in 21st century Uganda*. Accessed August 29, 2018, from http://www.divaportal.org/smash/get/diva2:169231/FULLTEXT01.pdf.

Gumede, V. (2016). *Poverty and inequality in Africa: Towards the post-2015 development agenda for sub-Saharan Africa*. Accessed June 10, 2018, from www.vusigumede.com/content/…/Poverty%20and%20Inequality%20in%20Africa.pdf.

Gunga, S. O. (2013). *The cooperative movement in Kenya and its potential for enhancement of ICT livelihoods*. Accessed August 29, 2018, from http://erepository.uonbi.ac.ke/bitstream/handle/11295/45953/Samson%20O.%20Gunga.pdf?sequence=1.

Gweyi, M. O., Ndwiga, P. M., & Karagu, J. M. (2013). An investigation of the impact of co-operative movement in rural development in Kenya. *International Journal of Business and Commerce, 3*(2), 1–13.

Hoffman, J. (1986). The problem of the ruling class in classical marxist theory: Some conceptual preliminaries. *Science & Society, 50*(3), 342–363.

Imungi, J. K. (2016). *Synergy between the cooperative sector and the academia in promoting research and innovation to enhance industrial and socio-economic development in east Africa*. Paper for presentation in the First East African Co-operative Conference on 29 February to 2 March 2016, Nairobi, Kenya. Accessed August 18, 2018, from http://www.industrialization.go.ke/images/downloads/feacc-materials/synergy-between-the-cooperative-sector-and-the-academia.pdf.

Johnston, B. F. (1970). Agriculture and structural transformations in developing countries: A survey of the research. *Journal of Economic Literature, 8*(2), 369–404.

Joint Acholi Sub-Regional Leaders' Forum and Trócaire (JASLF). (2017). Development of Inclusive Business Model (IBM) for leveraging investments and development in Acholi sub-region. *User Guide*. https://www.trocaire.org/sites/default/files/resources/policy/180215_final_inclusive_business_models_ibm_user_guide.pdf.

Jossa, B. (2005). Marx, Marxism and the cooperative movement. *Cambridge Journal of Economics, 29*, 3–18. https://doi.org/10.1093/cje/bei012.

Kwapong, N. A. (2013). *Restructured agricultural cooperative marketing system in Uganda: Study of the "Tripartite Cooperative Model"* (Euricse Working Paper No. 57 | 13).

Kwapong, N. A., & Hanisch, M. (2013). Cooperatives and poverty reduction: A literature review. *Journal of Rural Cooperation, 41*(2), 114–146.

Kwapong, N. A., & Korugyendo, P. L. (2010). *Revival of agricultural cooperatives in Uganda*. Accessed August 29, 2018, from http://citeseerx.ist.psu.edu/viewdoc/download?doi=10.1.1.227.1042&rep=rep1&type=pdf.

Kyamulesire, A. R. (1988). *A history of the Uganda cooperative movement, 1913–1988* (207 pp). Kampala: Uganda Cooperative Alliance.

Kyazze, L. M. (2010). *Cooperatives: The sleeping economic and social giants in Uganda* (Coop AFRICA Working Paper No. 15). Accessed August 29, 2018, from http://ilo.org/public/english/employment/ent/coop/Africa/download/wpno15cooperativesinuganda.pdf.

Mendoza, I. V. (2016). *The role of cooperatives in empowering indigenous people and older persons*. The United Nations for the Expert Group Meeting:

"Ensuring That No One Is Left Behind: The Cooperative Sector as a Partner in the Implementation of the United Nations 2030 Agenda for Sustainable Development" New York, November 2016. Accessed August 18, 2018, from www.un.org/esa/socdev/egms/docs/2016/Coops-2030Agenda/Mendoza.pdf.

Mood, C., & Jonsson, J. O. (2016). The social consequences of poverty: An empirical test on longitudinal data. *Social Indicators Research, 127,* 633–652. https://doi.org/10.1007/s11205-015-0983-9.

Mumanyi, E. A. L. (2014). Challenges and opportunities facing SACCOS in the current devolved system of government of Kenya: A case study of Mombasa County. *International Journal of Social Sciences and Entrepreneurship, 1*(9), 1–26.

Mwejune, N. N. (1993). *Problems of the cooperative movement in Uganda: A case study of Banyankore Kweterana Cooperative Union Limited.* A Dissertation Submitted in Partial Fulfilment of the Degree of Masters of Arts (DS) University of Dar-Es-Salaam, Tanzania. Accessed August 18, 2018, from https://www.codesria.org/IMG/pdf/m_mwejune_nuwagira_naboth-3.pdf?7785/0706bf001ba7f31528b1dbb8d52e0e2ca5f3eef.

National Rural Electric Cooperative Association (NRECA). (2016). *Understanding the seven cooperative principles.* Accessed June 20, 2018, from http://www.westerncoop.com/content/seven-cooperative-principles.

Nkhoma, A. T. (2011). Factors affecting sustainability of agricultural cooperatives: Lessons from Malawi: A thesis presented in partial fulfillment of Master of AgriCommerce at Massey University, New Zealand.

Obadire, O. S., Mudau, M. J., Sarfo-Mensah, P., & Zuwarimwe, J. (2013). Active role of stakeholders in the implementation of comprehensive rural development programme in South Africa. *International Journal of Humanities and Social Science, 3*(13), 273–280.

Okello, L., & Ahikire, J. (2013). *The cooperative movement and the challenge of development: A search for alternative wealth creation and citizen vitality approaches in Uganda.* Accessed August 29, 2018, http://www.actionaid.org/sites/files/actionaid/cooperatives_report.pdf.

Osabuohien, E., Efobi, U. R., Herrmann, R., & Gitau, C. M. (2019). Female labor outcomes and large-scale agricultural land investments: Macro-micro evidence from Tanzania. *Land Use Policy, 82,* 716–728.

Osabuohien, E. S., Gitau, C. M., Efobi, U. R., & Bruentrup, M. (2015). Agents and implications of foreign land deals in east african community: The case of Uganda. In E. Osabuohien (Ed.), *Handbook of research on in-country determinants and implications of foreign land acquisitions* (pp. 263–286). Hershey, PA: Business Science Reference.

Owuor, S. O. (2003). *Rural livelihood sources for urban households: A study of Nakuru town, Kenya.* Accessed September 12, 2018, from https://www.ascleiden.nl/pdf/workingpaper51.pdf.

Rutaremara, V., Jean, N., Tumusabyimana, V., Semana, J., Habiyaremye, G., Hakizimana, E., & Butera, A. (2016). *Examining success factors for sustainable rural development through the integrated co-operative model.* Accessed September 1, 2018, from http://usaskstudies.coop/documents/pdfs/Africa%20Project_Sec%205_Rwanda%20report%20FINAL.pdf.

Ruttan, V. W. (1984). Integrated rural development programmes: A historical perspective world-development. *World Development, 12*(4), 393–401.

Schwettmann, J. (2014, September 2). Cooperatives in Africa: Success and challenges. In *A Contribution to the International Symposium on Cooperatives and Sustainable Development Goals: The Case of Africa Berlin*. Accessed August 14, 2018, from https://www.dgrv.de/webde.nsf/7d5e59ec98e72 442c1256e5200432395/0773f60d3d0e5ab8c1257d4f003fa05e/$FILE/ Vortrag_J%C3%BCrgen%20Schwettmann_ILO.pdf.

Seimu, S. M. L. (2015). *The growth and development of coffee and cotton marketing co-operatives in Tanzania, c.1932–1982*. A thesis submitted in partial fulfilment for the requirements for the degree of Doctor of Philosophy at the University of Central Lancashire University, UK.

Silberston, A. (1972). Economies of scale in theory and practice. *The Economic Journal, 82*(325), 369–391.

Stiglitz, J. (2012). *The price of inequality: How today's divided society endangers our future*. New York: Norton and Company.

Sumelius, J., Tenaw, S., Bäckman, S., Bee, F., Chambo, S., Machimu, G., & Kumburu, N. (2013). *Cooperatives as a tool for poverty reduction and promoting business in Tanzania* (University of Helsinki Department of Economics and Management Discussion Papers No. 65). Accessed April 2, 2018, from http://formin.finland.fi/public/download.aspx?ID=128559&GUID=%7BB4BB921C-3E40-4D4B-AD04-EDB2B4A954BE%7D.

Tacoli, C., McGranahan, G., & Satterthwaite, D. (2015). *Urbanization, rural–urban migration and urban poverty*. Accessed September 12, 2018, from pubs.iied.org/pdfs/10725IIED.pdf.

Tefera, A. A. (2014). *Rural-urban migration: Causes, migrants' town livelihood activities and social capital in Berehet District, Ethiopia*. Accessed September 12, 2018, from https://brage.bibsys.no/xmlui/bitstream/handle/11250/2447226/Adefris%20 Tefera%20Abebe.pdf?sequence=1.

USDA. (2006). *United States Department of Agriculture—2007 farm bill theme papers rural development executive summary*. Accessed September 10, 2018, from http://www.usda.gov/documents/Farmbill07ruraldevelopmentsum.pdf.

van der Ploeg, J. (1998). *Continuity and change: The continuous elements of rural development, The Hague (The Netherlands), National Council for Agricultural Research (NRLO)* (NRLO Report 97/42).

Wanyama, F. O. (2007). *The impact of liberalization on the cooperative movement in Kenya*. A paper presented at the First International Ciriec Social Economy Conference on Strengthening and Building Communities: The Social Economy in a Changing World, October 22–25, 2007, Victoria, British Columbia, Canada. Accessed August 29, 2018, from https://www.researchgate.net/profile/fredrick_wanyama/publication/255581291_the_impact_of_liberalization_on_the_cooperative_movement_in_kenya/links/5564af2808ae89e758fd951d/the-impact-of-liberalization-on-the-cooperative-movement-in-kenya.pdf.

Wanyama, F. O. (2013). *Cooperatives for African development: lessons from experience*. Accessed August 2, 2018, from https://social.un.org/coopsyear/documents/wanyamacooperativesforafricandevelopment.pdf.

Wanyama, F. O., Develtere, P., & Pollet, I. (2008). *Encountering the evidence: Cooperatives and poverty reduction in Africa* (Working Papers on Social and Co-operative Entrepreneurship WP-SCE 08-02). Accessed August 29, 2018, from http://dx.doi.org/10.2139/ssrn.1330387.

White, C. (1985). Agricultural planning, pricing policies and cooperative in Vietnam. *World Development, 13*(1), 97–114.
WHO. (2010). *Rural poverty and health systems in the WHO European Region.* Copenhagen: WHO Regional Office for Europe.
Wilkinson, R., & Pickett, K. (2010). *The spirit level: Why greater equality makes societies stronger.* New York: Bloomsburry Press.
World Bank. (2003). *Reaching the rural poor: A renewed strategy for rural development.* Accessed September 13, 2018, from documents.worldbank.org/.../en/.../271450REVISED010WB0Revised01PUBLIC1.pdf.
World Bank. (2005). *Beyond the city, the rural contribution to development.* Accessed September 11, 2018, from https://openknowledge.worldbank.org/bitstream/handle/10986/7328/32333.pdf.
World Bank. (2016). *Poverty in a rising Africa. Africa poverty report overview.* http://documents.worldbank.org/curated/en/994551467989467774/pdf/100260-REVISED-PUBLIC-PovertyInARisingAfrica-Overview.pdf.
World Bank. (2018). *Decline of global extreme poverty continues but has slowed.* Accessed June 7, 2019, from http://www.worldbank.org/en/news/press-release/2018/09/19/decline-of-global-extreme-poverty-continues-but-has-slowed-world-bank.
Zeleza, T. (1990). The development of the cooperative movement in Kenya since independence. *Journal of Eastern African Research & Development, 20,* 68–94.

Impact of Non-agricultural Activities on Farmers' Income: Evidence from the Senegalese Groundnut Area

Amadou Tandjigora

1 Introduction

The Senegalese primary sector is predominantly agrarian, which is the main economic activity of several developing countries. Agriculture[1] lasts up to four months in Senegal with often disturbed rainy seasons. Farm incomes alone do not allow households to escape from precariousness. In addition, households that limit themselves to the sole exercise of agricultural activities encounter a great deal of financial difficulty and ultimately run into debt before the next campaigns (Guèye 2010), because their only agricultural income does not cover their food needs generally. Despite this worrying situation, in the Senegalese rural areas in general and particularly in the groundnut area, the agricultural sector employs the majority of the occupied individuals (66.48% in 2011).

In spite of this, monetary poverty, in other words the significant reduction of financial resources and prevalence of poverty still remains considerable. According to Institut Sénégalais de Recherche Agricole-ISRA (2008), the expansion of this poverty besides the deterioration of the living conditions of the rural populations have been the consequence of several phenomena such as the high demographic pressure, the drought, and the underperformance of groundnuts. Added to this is the fact that young farmers are generally not

---

A. Tandjigora (✉)
Faculty of Economics and Management, Cheikh Anta Diop University, Dakar, Senegal

paid when they participate in the family's farming activities, even if they can receive gifts in kind or in cash (Grain de Sel 2015) they have more and more needs and desires whose satisfaction require monetary incomes. Because of the constraints mentioned above, agriculture will no longer be sufficient for rural people, neither for food consumption nor for monetary income. There is in fact a sufficient reason to believe that rural poverty and the random nature of food consumption throughout the year can be successfully tackled if new risk management opportunities are promoted. Faced with this situation, two alternatives may be submitted to these rural poor. The first is the migration and the second is the engagement in non-farm² activities. This second alternative will be the subject of our present research.

According to "Grain de Sel" (2012), in 1950, 10 producers had to release, in addition to their consumption needs, a surplus for the demand of one non-agricultural consumer. In 2010, this ratio was 1 to 1. In 2030, it will be one producer facing the demand of two non-agricultural consumers. In this situation, should not a rational anticipation of this change? In other words, should we not firmly integrate now this new situation in the process of survival of rural populations? Because of the importance given to these non-agricultural activities in a risk management approach, what would be their contribution to the farmers' income in the Senegalese Groundnut area? Would non-agricultural activities not be a solution for the revival of agriculture in rural areas? These previous research questions are important because a positive contribution from non-agricultural activities would enable rural people, especially young people who were mainly tempted by migration, to stay in their respective lands and develop them. In the same way, agriculture i.e., cropping activities could find rather large sources of financing, which could have a positive impact on food self-sufficiency.

This chapter is composed of four main parts: the first deals with the review of the literature, the second deals with the methodology used, the third is devoted to the discussion of the main results, and the last part is reserved for conclusion.

2 REVIEW OF LITERATURE

2.1 *Generalities*

It is clear that in several countries in Sub-Saharan Africa, population growth is quite significant and the majority of the population lives and works in rural areas with agriculture as the main activity. The latter does not generally meet all the needs of households, and is assisted or even replaced by a multitude of non-agricultural activities, often more remunerative. Madaki and Adefila (2014) posited think that it is a universally accepted fact that agricultural sector is incapable of creating gainful employment opportunities amidst increasing population in the developing countries.

According to "Grain de Sel" magazine (2015), 75% of family farms in Sub-Saharan Africa are less than 2 ha and each average agricultural worker would have non-agricultural asset for its agricultural and food products, which explains the low average agricultural incomes. It proves to be necessary to undertake non-agricultural activities capable to raise the income levels of the farming and to sustain agriculture as well. By definition, non-agricultural activities in rural or non-agricultural rural economy include all activities that are not agricultural activities, i.e., all secondary, tertiary, and non-agricultural primary activities, whatever the place and function of these activities (Losch et al. 2013). However, this sector is long neglected by policymakers even if it has attracted considerable attention in recent years according to Haggblade et al. (2009). Thus, a lot of empirical studies like FAO (1998) revealed the growing importance of the non-agricultural activities in the developing and transition countries.

In this report, a large chapter has been dedicated to the non-agricultural farming incomes in the developing countries. Non-agricultural incomes represent 42% of the total income on the continent which explains the incentives for diversification play a major role. Thus, African households, although poorer, are more likely to diversify their incomes due to the thinness and random nature of their farm income (FAO 1998). Winters et al. (2007) confirmed that incomes from the non-agricultural activities in Africa would surpass at third of total income on the continent. Thus, for the half of the continent, the non-agricultural income is more important than those coming from agriculture, even though a meaningful variability exists across the countries on the importance of agricultural and non-agricultural activities.

According to Fonds International de Développement Agricole (2010, 2015), increased share of rural non-farm income relative to non-farm income is expected to escalate owing to increased demand for goods and services in rural areas that will not be limited to food in the coming decades. There are every indication that the rural non-farm economy, in addition to its major contribution to income diversification and hence risk management, will be particularly important in providing economic opportunities for rural youth in particular.

Specifically, the non-agricultural incomes take up an important place in Senegal according to some studies that have been conducted by Reardon (1997) and Sarah (2014). According to Reardon, non-agricultural incomes (including migration) in the total income rose to 60% in the Northern Senegal, 24% in the Center, and 41% in the southern country. For Sarah, the share of farm income is 51.15% divided between crop production (38.22%), livestock production (10.94%), processing of farm products (0.31%), hunting, fishing and gathering (0.84%), agricultural wage labor (0.74%). Non-agricultural income from diversification of activities was 48.83%, spread between non-farm wage labor (8.11%), self-employment (32.09%), public transfers (0%), remittances (6.82%), and rents (1.81%) (Table 1).

Table 1 Incomes shares from the diversification of activities (%)

Diversification of activities	Percentage
Crop productions	38.32
Livestock production	10.94
Processing of farm products	0.31
Hunting, Fishing, Gathering	0.84
Agricultural wage labor	0.74
Farm income	**51.15**
Non-farm wage labor	8.11
Self-employment	32.09
Public transfers	0.00
Remittances	6.82
Rents	1.81
Part of the non-agricultural income	**48.85**

Source Sarah (2014)

2.2 The Initial Capital of the Participating Households to the Non-agricultural Activities

The initial capital of a household represents the main source of any non-agricultural activity starting. According to the World Bank (2007 cited by Katega 2013), the participating farming households to the non-agricultural activities get the initial capital from a variety of sources. It is therefore necessary to signal that some sources are common and others however, are proper to the activities of the concerned area.

In Senegal in particular, Micro and Small Enterprises, as well as some non-agricultural trades, are generally created with little financial capital and material capital and generally on own funds or by recourse to relatives (République du Sénégal, Ministère de la PME, de l'Entreprenariat Féminin et de la Microfinance 2004). This financial capital, however, can generally cover only a few weeks of activities. Most often, their promoter has a know-how acquired after a few years spent in a workshop as an apprentice. In the same context, Sakho (2009) argues that the decision to engage in nonagricultural diversification requires an initial investment, and physical capital endowment may be a proxy for assessing wealth, she believes that the best-equipped households in physical capital will be more incentivized to engage in non-agricultural activities. The physical capital represents the cultivable area in hectare obtained by inheritance as well as the agricultural equipment.

In other areas, such as Nigeria, where the rural non-farm economy has been extensively studied, start-up sources for non-agricultural activities come from income or savings from agricultural, non-agricultural activities or trade, income or savings from wage labor, money lent by formal lenders or banks, capital from relatives or transfers, sale of land or other family assets (Igwe 2013). According to this author, income used for start-ups and working capital is an important source for both agricultural and non-agricultural activities and that farm income is an important source of start-up for non-farm business. Those from non-agricultural sources also provide additional income for expansion of agricultural production. Elsewhere in Tanzania, agricultural activities provide capital for the start-up and exercise of non-agricultural activities and these provide a source of capital for the purchase of agricultural inputs. As a result, many non-farm households (64.1%) obtain their starting capital from crop sale savings and loans from relatives and friends for 18.5%. Other sources include loans to financial institutions for (3.3%) and transfers from urban migrants (3.9%), loans from traditional lenders (5.8%), and from other sources such as livestock and bee products (Katega 2013).

2.3 Motivations of the Involvement to the Non-agricultural Activities

The motivations to engage in non-agricultural activities are often interpreted through two notions, namely, the factors "pull" and the factors "push." According to Atamanov (2011), a "push" scenario happens when participation in non-farm activities is driven by inability to earn enough from agricultural activities due to the poor asset base or risky agricultural environment. Imperfections in rural institutions, such as access to credit or insurance markets can also stimulate non-farm activities. A "pull" scenario means that participation in non-farm activities is driven by higher payoffs or lower risk in the non-farm sector compared to agriculture. The combined relevance of "push" and "pull" factors suggests that there are two sets of non-farm activities: those who serve as last resort activities for the poor, and those that provide profitable opportunities for those who have access. In addition to push and pull factors, participation in non-farm activities is influenced by various human capital variables and infrastructure development that affect the ability of rural people to deviate from farming activities. Thus, the best educated individuals especially with a higher or professional level are more likely to choose non-agricultural activities or combine agriculture with non-agricultural occupations because they are more qualified for formal non-agricultural work.

2.4 Actors of the Non-agricultural Sector

The rural non-farm sector presents actors that differ in their level of income but also in their individual characteristics that can often influence their decision to participate in rural non-farm activities, their success or failure in this sector.

Households participating in non-farm activities can thus be classified into two categories, according to Conférence des Nations Unies sur le Commerce et le Développement-CNUDED (2015). The most affluent households often become entrepreneurs by choice, taking advantage of opportunities to increase their income. Sarah (2014) confirms this statement and points out, farmers who are able to sell agricultural products or who have large farms have significantly more diversified sources of income suggesting that they are able to access opportunities and engage in non-agricultural activities. Here, the broadest field suggests that wealthier households are more likely to have high sources of diversification income. According to Initiative Prospective Agricole et Rural-IPAR (2015), in the groundnut area, for example, the richest households rely on four to five sources of income (crops, livestock, self-employment, wage labor, and private transfers). The poorest households, however, diversify their sources of income in general by necessity, encouraged to increase their incomes to maintain a minimum level of consumption or to protect themselves from the vagaries of agriculture (Conférence des Nations Unies sur le commerce et le développement 2015). These households rely essentially on up to two main sources of income. Some qualitative variables as the quality of education of the actors, their access to the agricultural capital, to the transportation, to the market of the agricultural products, to the mutual or to the non-gainful work, their access to the opportunities of the migration or to household features as the exploiting size and access to the irrigation are also significant factors in the determination of the level of the diversification among the farming households in Senegal (Sarah 2014).

2.5 Effects of the Rural Non-agricultural Economy on Agriculture

In Africa, several studies show that non-agricultural rural activity tends to be regularly and equitably divided around the trade, industry, and service sectors, to be directly or indirectly related to local agriculture or small towns, and to be informal rather than formal (Reardon 1997). It is a risk management strategy adopted by rural farming households. However, these households rely on non-farm profits to diversify risks, moderate seasonal income swings, and finance purchases of agricultural inputs, while landless and near landless households, everywhere, rely heavily on non-farm income for their survival (Haggblade et al. 2009). In the Groundnut area of Senegal, it has been shown that the resources of non-agricultural activities often refinance agricultural activities (Guèye 2010). The author indicates that it is very common to see that the farmer gets all his work for a year that feeds his family for a month. In such situations, there is a need to rely on non-farm income for the rest of the year and the start of farming activities next season. According to (De Janvry et al. 2005), participation in non-farm activities has huge effects on farm incomes. Thus, the farm incomes of non-agricultural households increase by 195%. If households that participate only in agricultural activities participate in non-agricultural activities, their incomes increase by 52%. Hence, participation in non-farm activities helps to increase total factor productivity in agriculture. According to Conférence des Nations Unies sur le commerce et le développement-CNUCED (2015), they can help modernize agriculture by generating resources that can be invested in it and by providing upstream and downstream services, particularly in higher value crops. According to this institution, as non-agricultural rural activities can significantly contribute to modernizing agriculture, an inadequate or insufficient development of the non-agricultural sector can also hamper agricultural development.

Various studies have also been successful in showing the effects of non-agricultural activities on agriculture at various levels, including agricultural investment, input prices, land factor, and food consumption.

2.5.1 Effect of the Non-agricultural Activities on the Agricultural Investments

According to Food and Agricultural Organization-FAO (1998), non-agricultural activities would affect the availability of funds for the purchase of capital goods and agricultural inputs. In Africa, this availability conditions the adoption of appropriate technologies, and non-farm income is generally the main source of liquidity, which may also be the necessary guarantee for the adoption of credit. In general terms, access to non-farm income can provide to a household the oxygen what he needs to undertake longer-term investments, such as multi-year commercial crops. However, the effects of non-farm income are greater on sustainable investments, especially on livestock and equipment, and an increase in a non-agricultural income unit increases agricultural expenditures and investments by 0.18 and 0.58%, respectively. These results indicate that non-farm income is an important source of financing for investments that have the highest payment and therefore impact on agricultural activities (Mathijs et al. 2011). For Seng (2015), since non-farm employment generates additional income for households, it can provide participants with additional capital for investment in agricultural technology, which is a factor in increasing productivity. Beyond generating income for investments in agricultural technology, engaging farm households in non-farm jobs can reduce the possibility of disguised unemployment as a result of excessive farm labor, improving productivity and thus increase the level of production on the farm.

2.5.2 Effect of Non-agricultural Activities on Prices of Agricultural Inputs

The rural non-farm sector also affects factor and input prices in agricultural activity and hence the profitability of the farm and the composition of its range of crops. The existence of small-scale local manufacturing and service units can help reduce prices and improve the availability of agricultural inputs, while adapting them to the needs of local farmers (FAO 1998). For example, locally produced inputs must cost less than those produced elsewhere in the same country or imported. Agri-food processing and distribution would likewise affect the level and price stability of the products offered. The non-agricultural sector therefore acts upstream and downstream of agricultural production on factor prices.

2.5.3 Effects of the Non-agricultural Activities on the "Land" Factor

Non-agricultural rural employment also affects the land factor. It can reduce the pressure on the land. To the extent that non-farm activities reduce the incidence of poverty and direct dependence on land, they can help to break the vicious circle of poverty-extensification-degradation-poverty and generate the necessary cash for fixed assets to intensify production on a given land (FAO 1998). On the other hand, according to Wang et al. (2011), non-farm income has a positive and significant effect on investment in agricultural capital. A 10% increase in non-farm income boosts by mu, the capital stock of 4.2%. This capital investment positively impacts the total contribution of non-farm activities to the productivity of the land, and as a result, non-farm activities contribute significantly to the growth of agricultural productivity.

2.5.4 Effect of the Non-agricultural Activities on the Households' Food Consumption

The rural non-farm economy can also affect the food consumption of rural households. Thus, Seng (2015) concludes that agricultural households engaging in non-agricultural employment tend to benefit more from household income. They produce agricultural products more efficiently, indicating the vital role of non-agricultural activities in increasing the incomes of farming households and in improving agricultural practice. Therefore, participation of farm households in non-farm activities could most likely increase and stabilize household food consumption over an extended period of time. Following his empirical analyzes, Seng concludes that when they participate in non-agricultural activities, farm households can on average make food consumption gains of 725 riels (110.4 FCFA) per household member. This result reveals that participation in non-agricultural activities can enable rural farming households to increase their per capita food consumption and thus improve their food security. Barret and Reardon (2001) as well as Jatta (2013) also returned to non-agricultural employment action on food security. They argue that the short-term effects of non-farm activities in rural areas on the food security of farm households are clear, and that non-farm income provides the means for farm households to buy food during drought or after a harvest deficit. They further argue that non-farm income is also a source of savings for farm households used to buy food during difficult times.

2.6 Effects of the Non-agricultural Farming Economy on the Income Inequality

De Janvry et al. (2005) found that, without non-farm employment, rural poverty would be higher and deeper and that income inequality would be high on the same basis. Thus, rural non-farm income helps to reduce not only poverty but also inequality. This is because participation in non-farm activities differentially improves the incomes of the poorest households, although the best farmers remain in agriculture. Using the Gini model for this study, the authors showed that the large impact on the intensity of poverty suggests that participation in non-farm activities narrows the income gap among the poor. Thus, the impact of the severity of poverty suggests that participation in non-farm activities not only reduced the income gap among poor rural households but also disproportionately increased the income of the poorest households. Seng (2015), however, concludes that low-profit non-farm work is associated with low income inequality while high-income non-farm activities have an uneven impact on household income distribution, which would mean inequality between household incomes depends on the size of the gain received as a result of non-agricultural activity. Indeed, Jatta (2013) emphasizes that growth in the non-farm sector could reduce income inequality if incomes from such activities disproportionately favor the poor. In addition, participation in high-profit activities has a positive correlation with better household welfare in terms of spending on all necessary goods and services, confirming a positive effect of non-farm jobs on household welfare (Seng 2015). However, after claiming that non-farm activities are a means of reducing income inequality among households that practice it, Furaha et al. (2013) have also shown that non-farm activities can be a source of income inequality between households taken together. According to these authors, inequality can also come from other sources. Thus, in a society where a certain category of households cannot overcome the entry barriers of a non-agricultural activity, in other words, they do not have enough resources to access it, the diversification of the sources would not solve the problem of the poorest and would create a considerable gap and therefore inequality between households.

2.7 Effects of the Non-agricultural Farming Economy on the Income Distribution

According to Seng (2015), the extent to which non-farm employment contributes to improvements in the livelihood s of farm households depends on the benefits of these activities, and that, in addition, these could have an impact on the households' income distribution of farm households, since it is the strategy of farming households to diversify the income portfolio. Ndione (2015) confirms these remarks by stating that the distribution of income in the absence of non-agricultural income is more unequal and that non-agricultural income reduces income inequality among households. Similarly, the growth experiences of East Asian countries such as Japan, Taiwan, and Korea indicate that rural non-farm income has a positive impact on income distribution among rural households (Singh 2011). As the share of non-farm income increases in total income, the distribution of total income will become more uniform (Lachand 1999; Sadoulet 2001, cited by Furaha et al. 2013). These positive effects of the distribution of non-agricultural income cumulated with other factors constraining the agricultural sector to be profitable for the benefit of the households (lack of land, difficulty of access to financing, the problem of moral hazard with external work) lead Ndione (2015) assers that, the choice is on non-agricultural activities and not on increasing production capacities to increase the income of rural households. Nevertheless, the distribution of non-agricultural income can take another turn, that which highlights its negative aspect. Thus, according to Singh (2011), although non-farm income is perceived as being able to reduce income inequality, not all of its components have a favorable impact on income distribution. The distribution of income from non-agricultural sources would, however, be unlikely to be more equal than that from agriculture simply because non-farm businesses are usually small in size and require very little investment capital; therefore, they should not lead to being as optimistic about their ability to improve income distribution. Dirven (2011), returns with more details. According to her, analyzes show that because of the impact of the productive non-farm rural economy, the effects of the rural non-farm economy on the income distribution among rural populations are almost always negative. However, although those working in the rural non-farm economy are on average less poor than others, this does not make them rich or extremely wealthy, so it should not be a result for worries.

2.8 Opportunities of the Rural Non-agricultural Economy

Opportunities in the non-farm sector are numerous and diverse. These are not limited only to rural areas but extend to the national economy as suggested by many authors. According to the African Development Bank-AfDB (2015), many of the farmers are moving partially and gradually. Many of them are already spanning different sectors that help them increase their incomes. This pattern of structural transformation differs within households but will remain an important future for rural people. Participation in the rural non-farm sector thus enables the poor to smooth out or offset farm income fluctuations that may occur on a seasonal basis to supplement or replace farm incomes (Jatta 2013; Haggblade et al. 2010). This is especially the case where savings, credit, and insurance mechanisms are not available as is the case in many rural areas in Africa (Haggblade et al. 2010; Akinyemi et al. 2019; Osabuohien et al. 2019; Oyebola et al. 2019). FAO (1998) made a pertinent point by noting that the poor are looking for opportunities in the rural non-farm economy, not only to raise income levels but also to stabilize household incomes all the time. As a result, non-farm profits serve as an important net security function. They provide a tool to stabilize household incomes during years of drought. There are strong expectations for the dynamism of the rural non-farm economy and its potential to sustain rural populations, attract public and private investment in infrastructure and services, and thus reduce some limitations in rural areas, increasing average incomes and decreasing poverty indicators (Dirven 2011). Beyond the potential for higher gains than agriculture, increased household liquidity, and the distribution of risk strategies, the rural non-farm economy could be a vehicle for rural and economic growth, but also a means of reducing poverty (ILO 2008). For this institution, the increasingly important role played by these non-agricultural activities in many rural societies is that they are not only secondary activities but also a significant source of income and a growth factor employment.

The non-agricultural sector can still play other roles. Thus, well invested, the sector will be very dynamic and will allow residents to no longer depend on income transfers (Sakho 2009).

3 METHODOLOGY

Due to the existence of more than two categories of income, we use a multinomial logit model that is part of the larger family of multinomial models. This model is indeed a simple extension of the binomial logistic regression model. The Multinomial Logit Model is useful analyzing the influence; thus, the effect of the independent variables on the dependent variable, here, the effect of the income from the non-agricultural activities on the improvement of the famers' total income. A positive or negative effect must therefore be established between the independent variables and the dependent variable following the use of this model. The dependent variable for this study is the farmers' total income, which is a quantitative variable. Information about income is obtained and coded as an ordinal variable with 5 levels (income's quintile).

According to Singh et al. (1986) and Zahanogo (2002) cited by Zahanogo (2011), most modern research on farm household's behavior is based on these types of models. The dependent variable is not a continuous variable (the number of variables is limited to five), the application of the Ordinary Least Squares (OLS) model, for example, is not appropriate. We were able to verify this inadequacy through the Skewness/Kurtosis test of normality of residues (sktest) and the test of error's heteroscedasticity (hettest).[3]

Probit multinomial or Multinomial Logit models should be used as an alternative to the Ordinary Least Squares model. Technically, these two models are very similar. They differ only in the distribution of error terms (Kropko 2008) or when the sample size is very large (Kpodar 2007 Tutorial to Stata).

3.1 Evaluation of the Model Quality

To ensure the quality of the multinomial logit model, the Wald, likelihood ratio, and the Independence of Irrelevant Alternative (IIA) tests were carried out, and their satisfactory results allow us to preserve it. Marginal effects were also calculated so that the interpretation of the results is simpler.

3.2 Data Sources

The data used are secondary and come from the Senegalese Poverty Monitoring Survey (ESPS II), carried out in 2011. This survey is essentially based on intelligence monitoring indicators of living conditions and poverty and has unfolded throughout the national territory.

3.3 Framework

The estimation model includes, as a dependent variable, Farmers' Income and as explanatory variables, non-agricultural income. The latter is the interest variable. Some control variables such as age, sex, household size, educational level, experience in agricultural activity, number of days devoted to secondary activity per week (which are some individual characteristics which can also influence the improvement of farm income) were used. They are also widely used in previous research.

3.3.1 Definition of Model Variables

The Dependent Variable

Rv_agr: Farmers' Income
Farmers' income assessed as income quintile is the dependent variable. Each quintile represents a specific income level (0 = Very Low Income, 1 = Low Income, 2 = Average Income, 3 = High Income, 4 = Very High Income). The first is the lowest quintile and the fifth is the highest quintile. Since farmers have different incomes, often because of the size of the farms as stated by Sarah (2014), the subdivision into quintile allows seeing for each category of farmer, i.e., according to the level of income, the influence of non-agricultural income on the corresponding quintile. Among the studies that we have however coveted, the incomes are not categorized as we had to do in this chapter.

Explanatory Variables

Rev_nagr: Non-agricultural Income
These are the income derived from non-agricultural activities practiced by farmers. This variable is the variable of interest of the model. The objective is to analyze its influence on the dependent variable that is farmers' income.

In previous research, such as Wang et al.'s (2011), non-agricultural income has a significant impact on agricultural productivity specifically on agricultural employment, farm capital stock, and farmland productivity. This study has shown that the impact is certainly significant but sometimes negative as for certain modalities, namely, agricultural employment and agricultural land productivity

e8a: Number of Years Spent in Farming
The number of years spent in farming is a no less important variable that can influence the level of income. A long period of time spent in cropping activities may encourage farmers to exercise only these activities to the detriment of non-agricultural activities. Thus, agricultural experience for households that have a non-agricultural secondary activity alternately may have a

significant effect or no on income. A positive influence would mean that the number of years spent in cropping activities is essential to increase farmers' incomes. This individual variable was used in the Sanusi et al.'s article (2016) on "Determinants of Participating in Non-Farm Activities among Rural Households in Osun State" and its effect was significant and negative.

e15: Number of Days Spent on Non-agricultural Activity Per Week
The time spent on non-agricultural activities per week, which varies according to our data from 1 to 7 days, is a key variable that could potentially have an effect on improving farmers' incomes. Thus, a positive influence on income would mean that the more time spent on these types of activities, the higher the income of farm assets.

Niv_inst: Level of Education
Theoretically, the effect of education on income is explained by the fact that by accumulating human capital, agricultural assets increase the gains they can expect. Thus, the relative chances for a farmer to increase his income should go from no level of education to secondary level. The higher level education does not exist among the farmers in our sample. In other words, any increase in the level of education to the secondary level would more likely help to increase income from assets.

a08: Household Size
The size of the household (in which the farmer belongs) is a variable that implies that the household needs to mobilize its members, especially workers, in order to satisfy some of its charges, which affect the possibilities for higher income research. Several authors include this variable in their research. We can mention among others Kumar et al. (2011) and Onya et al. (2016).

b2: Sex
Sex is a characteristic that can affect the level of income. It has been remarked that the number of men with non-agricultural activity (78% of workers) far exceeds that of women, which is estimated at 22% (Tandjigora 2018). The influence of gender on income needs to be studied in order to confirm or disprove the assumption that the farmers' occupation is more male than female, as suggested by Sanusi et al. (2016).

b3: Age
It is an individual characteristic widely used in studies using econometric models of qualitative variables. A positive and significant effect of age on income indicates that the older the farmer, the more important his income will be, and a negative and significant effect would mean that age decreases the potential of farmers to earn more. This variable appears among the explanatory variables of several research models, among which, those of Onya et al. (2016).

3.3.2 Estimate Model

$$AI = F(NAI) \tag{1}$$

AI Agricultural income/Dependent Variable
NAI Non-agricultural Income

$$AI = W\beta + \varepsilon_i \tag{2}$$

where
W Series of explanatory variables

$$AI = X_i\beta_i + \varepsilon_i \tag{3}$$

X_i Independent variable's vector summarizing the variables of interest (Secondary activity income) and Household Control.
β_i Estimation of the parameter for the ith independent variable/Parameters to estimate.
ε_i Error terms

$$AI = \beta_0 + \beta_1 X_1 + \beta_2 X_2 + \cdots + \beta_n X_n + \varepsilon_i \tag{4}$$

3.3.3 Mathematical Specification of the Model

The mathematical specification of the multinomial logit model thus reflecting the probability that a farmer engaged in a secondary non-agricultural activity has income in one of the five quintiles is estimated using the following equation:

$$\text{Prob}(AI = J/X_i) = \frac{\text{Exp}(\beta_j X_i)}{\sum_{k=0}^{4} \text{Exp}(\beta_k X_i)} = \frac{\text{Exp}(\beta_j X_i)}{1 + \sum_{k=1}^{4} \text{Exp}(\beta_k X_i)}$$

where
j Modality and $J = (0, \ldots, j)$

Applying Variables to the Model

3.3.4 Applying the Variables to the Model

By applying all the variables to the model, we obtain the following equation:

$$AI = \beta_0 + \beta_1 \text{Rev\_nagr} + \beta_2 e8a + \beta_3 e15 + \beta_4 a08 + \beta_5 b2 + \beta_6 b3 + \beta_7 \text{Niv\_inst} + \varepsilon_i$$

where

Rev_nagr Non-agricultural secondary activity income
e8a Number of years spent in agriculture
e15 Number of days per week spent on non-agricultural activities
a08 Household size
b2 Sex
b3 Age
Niv_inst Level of education

3.3.5 Descriptive Analysis of Model Variables

Dependent Variable: Farmers' Income

Descriptive statistics on farmers' incomes are mentioned in Table 2. We note that only 7% of farmers are in the lowest income quintile, 11% of farmers have an income in the second quintile, 23% of farmers have an income in the third quintile, 28% for the fourth, and the highest, 31% of farmers have an income in the highest quintile (Table 2). This leads to the conclusion that the higher the income, the greater the number of farmers.

Thus, 7% of farmers have an income on average equal to 93,000 FCFA; 11% of them have an average income equal to 240,000 FCFA. The income of the third quintile, though close to the highest quintiles, does not exceed 458,000 FCFA during the whole year, i.e., an average of 376,000 FCFA. It's only in the last quintile where incomes are more or less higher, and where 31% of farmers have an income on average greater than or equal to 28,527,000 FCFA.

Interest Variable: Non-agricultural Income

Among the farmers in our sample, only 11% practice a non-agricultural secondary activity beyond agriculture; therefore, 89% of them are limited to agriculture as their sole activity throughout the year (Tables 3 and 4).

Table 5 shows that farmers who diversify their activities are more likely to have more income, which verifies the existing literature on the issue. The finding is made by a horizontal reading of the High and Very High Income of the farmers in terms of Non-agricultural Income.

It should be noted that the higher the income of farmers, the greater the number of farmers who diversify their income from non-agricultural sources. On the other hand, we realize that a farmer exercising a non-agricultural activity that provides him a high income cannot have a low total income,

Table 2 Descriptive statistics of farmers' income

Farmers' income	Frequency (%)	Annual amount corresponding to each quintile (CFAF)	Mean (CFAF)
Very low income (Quintile 1)	109 (7.032)	[0–186,000]	93,000
Low income (Quintile 2)	173 (11.16)	[186,001–294,000]	240,000
Average income (Quintile 3)	351 (22.65)	[294,001–458,000]	376,000
High income (Quintile 4)	437 (28.19)	[458,001–855,000]	656,000
Very high income (Quintile 5)	480 (30.97)	[855,001–5.62.10^7]	28,527,000

Author's calculations

Table 3 Descriptive statistics of the non-agricultural activity as a secondary activity

Do you do a secondary activity?	Frequency	Percentage
YES	1550	11.34
NO	12,120	88.66
Total	13,670	100

Author's calculations

Table 4 Farmers' non-farm income

Non-agricultural income (NAI)	Frequency (%)	Annual income	Mean
Very low income	366 (23.61)	[0–216,000]	108,000
Low income	344 (22.19)	[228,000–600,000]	414,000
Average income	452 (29.16)	[612,000–1,440,000]	1,026,000
High income	388 (25.03)	[1,452,000 and +]	1,452,000
Total	1550		

Author's calculations

Table 5 Non-agricultural income in terms of agricultural income

Farmers' income	Very low NAI	Low NAI	Average NAI	High NAI
	Frequency (%)	Frequency (%)	Frequency (%)	Frequency (%)
Very low income	48 (13.11)	41 (11.92)	20 (4.425)	
Low income	62 (16.94)	60 (17.44)	48 (10.62)	3 (0.773)
Average income	117 (31.97)	85 (24.71)	114 (25.22)	35 (9.021)
High income	78 (21.31)	88 (25.58)	140 (30.97)	131 (33.76)
Very high income	61 (16.67)	70 (20.35)	130 (28.76)	219 (56.44)
Total	366	344	452	388

Author's calculations

what is illustrated on the Table by a zero percentage. This means that non-agricultural activities benefit farmers by raising their incomes. Only 1% of farmers with high non-agricultural income are classified among those

Table 6 Descriptive statistics of the number of days devoted to secondary employment

Number of days devoted to secondary employment	Frequency (%)
1	124 (8.026)
2	183 (11.84)
3	232 (15.02)
4	175 (11.33)
5	133 (8.608)
6	698 (45.18)
Total	1545

Author's calculations

who have a low income and 9% of them have an average income. Those with a high and very high total income are more numerous (34 and 56%, respectively).

Number of Days Per Week Devoted to Secondary Employment
Of the agricultural households, 45% of them, i.e., the highest proportion, carry out secondary activities for six days a week, which reveals its importance. Only 8% of farmers spend a single day a week on these non-agricultural secondary activities and less than 1% practices it all week (Table 6). This last share also corresponds to the lowest share because of the need for at least a break day per week. Variations are still noted in the other days devoted to these non-agricultural jobs since the evolution is not in constant growth as shown in Table 6.

Number of Years Spent in Agricultural Activity
The number of farmers, whose experience in agricultural practice is not very high, in this case four years at most, and those whose experience exceeds twenty years have incomes that vary upwards (Table 7). However, those with experience varying between five and twenty years have incomes that vary up to a certain level (Average level for those with five to ten years' experience and High level for those with experience between ten to twenty years) then thereafter, vary downward.

Education Level
The educational level of farm households varies between "without level" and the secondary level. None of the farmers in the sample reached the high

Table 7 Farm experience and farmer income

rv_agr	(1)	(2)	(3)	(4)	(5)
	[0–4 years]	[5–10 years]	[10–20 years]	[20–30 years]	[30 years and +]
	Frequency (%)	Frequency (%)	Frequency (%)	Frequency (%)	Frequency (%)
Very low	13 (11.02)	26 (13.20)	34 (7.623)	18 (5.085)	18 (4.138)
Low	18 (15.25)	31 (15.74)	61 (13.68)	28 (7.910)	35 (8.046)
Average	25 (21.19)	65 (32.99)	106 (23.77)	82 (23.16)	73 (16.78)
High	28 (23.73)	43 (21.83)	131 (29.37)	100 (28.25)	135 (31.03)
Very high	34 (28.81)	32 (16.24)	114 (25.56)	126 (35.59)	174 (40)
Total	118	197	446	354	435

Author's calculations

Table 8 Farmers' education level

niv_inst	Frequency (%)
None	4 (1.575)
Primary	188 (74.02)
Average	47 (18.50)
Secondary	15 (5.906)
Total	254

Author's calculations

level. The level of education is relative to attendance at the French school. Of the 1550 farmers, only 254 attended school, which corresponds to 16.39%. 74.6% of those who attended school were limited to primary level, 18.5% to the average level, and 6% to secondary level. The rest of the farmers who did not go to school however, accounted for 83.61% (Table 8).

Sex
Men are more employed in the agricultural sector than women, 78% versus 22%, respectively (Table 9).

Table 9 Farmers' sex

Sex	Frequency (%)
Male	1205 (77.74)
Female	345 (22.26)
Total	1550

Author's calculations

Table 10 Age and farmers' income

	(1)	(2)	(3)	(4)	(5)
Age	[Under 15 years]	[15–30 years]	[31–50 years]	[51–60 years]	[61 years and more]
rv_agr	Frequency (%)	Frequency (%)	Frequency (%)	Frequency (%)	Frequency (%)
Very low	5 (62.50)	56 (11.18)	37 (5.132)	9 (3.965)	2 (2.151)
Low		86 (17.17)	63 (8.738)	20 (8.811)	4 (4.301)
Average	1 (12.50)	139 (27.74)	163 (22.61)	36 (15.86)	12 (12.90)
High	1 (12.50)	130 (25.95)	208 (28.85)	69 (30.40)	29 (31.18)
Very high	1 (12.50)	90 (17.96)	250 (34.67)	93 (40.97)	46 (49.46)
Total	8	501	721	227	93

Author's calculations

Age
Farmers' ages range from 8 to 85 years old. Those under 15 are the least numerous in the sample and represent less than 1% of the sample. We also note that the size of agricultural workers increases by age group up to a certain period (age group of 31–50 years) and decreases thereafter. For all age groups shown in the table, except for [Under 15], the increase in assets is proportional to that of Income (Table 10).

Household Size
Household size evolves from 1 to 21 individuals. The number of farmers decreases as the size of the household increases. This means that the larger the household, the more sources of income come from sources other than agriculture; all things equal otherwise (Table 11).

Table 11 Farmers' household size

Household size	Frequency (%)
1–5	445 (28.71)
6–10	413 (26.65)
11–15	403 (26)
16–20 and more	289 (18.64)

Author's calculations

4 Results and Discussion

This section presents and discusses the results obtained from the estimation of the model (Table 12).

The results of the logit estimates have showed that "Low" and "Average" non-agricultural income, the number of years spent in agricultural practice, the number of days per week allocated to non-agricultural activities, the sex, the age, as well as the level of education, have a significant influence on the improvement of the farmers' income. However, the last modality of the non-agricultural incomes in the circumstances the "High non-agricultural income" as well as the importance of the housekeeping remain the variables visibly no significant of the estimate.

4.1 The Interest Variables

The results show a positive and significant influence of "Low Non-Agricultural Income" modality at 5, 10, 5, and 10%, respectively, on the farmers' "Low Income," "Average income," "High income," "Very High income" modalities. That means that non-agricultural income, even if it is low, has a positive and significant impact on the improvement of total income of the farmers. However, the positive impact expresses that this income is important for the household and therefore permits it to invest in its activities, agriculture mainly. The chances for farmers to have a Low-income equivalent to 240,000 CFAF rather than a Very Low income which is equivalent on average to 93,000 CFAF increase by 5.4% when Non-Agricultural Income, equal to 414,000 CFAF is Low. They increase by 2% when non-agricultural income is Average, i.e., 1,026,000 CFAF.

"High non-agricultural income," equivalent to 1,452,000 CFAF a year, whose impact on Farmer" income is not significant, means that once farmers find other sources of income giving them much larger incomes than what they hope to gain by practicing agriculture, they can abandon the agricultural

Table 12 Estimations Results

Variables	Low income		Average income			High income			Very high income		
	Logit coeff	dy/dx	Logit coeff		dy/dx	Logit coeff		dy/dx	Logit coeff		dy/dx
2. Low NAI	1.733**	0.054	1.158*		−0.0405	2.000**		0.0984	1.506*		0.0070
	(0.831)	(0.055)	(0.699)		(0.085)	(0.836)		(0.0714)	(0.885)		(0.0752)
3. Average NAI	1.733*	0.0188	1.098		−0.1487	2.920***		0.2123	2.266***		0.0487
	(0.888)	(0.049)	(0.755)		(0.0762)	(0.848)		(0.0677)	(0.860)		(0.0654)
4. High NAI	1.136	−0.090	15.06		−0.2368	17.95		0.3191	17.59		0.1797
	(1.429)	(0.035)	(1.087)		(0.0788)	(1.087)		(0.0757)	(1.087)		(0.0074)
Number of days allowed to	0.0493	0.0012	−0.0573		−0.0354	0.0825		−0.0260	0.501**		0.0656
Non-agricultural activities	(0.198)	(0.0098)	(0.165)		(0.0137)	(0.181)		(0.0141)	(0.197)		(0.0142)
Number of years spent in	−0.190**	0.0065	−0.0942		0.0061	−0.132*		0.0009	−0.173**		−0.0074
agriculture	(0.0872)	(0.0037)	(0.0768)		(0.0053)	(0.0773)		(0.0036)	(0.0781)		(0.0031)
Household size	−0.0444	(−0.003)	−0.0033		0.0011	−0.0029		0.0002	0.00239		0.0012
	(0.0661)	(0.0033)	(0.0560)		(0.0048)	(0.0600)		(0.0047)	(0.0619)		(0.0043)
Sex (Female)	−0.631	0.02046	−0.725		0.04792	−0.752		0.1415	−2.536**		−0.2599
	(0.865)	(0.0450)	(0.740)		(0.0757)	(0.825)		(0.0960)	(1.070)		(0.1152)
Age	0.137*	−0.0010	0.117*		−0.0105	0.230***		0.0060	0.281***		0.0141
	(0.0771)	(0.0025)	(0.0712)		(0.0043)	(0.0734)		(0.0030)	(0.0742)		(0.0025)
Level of education	0.0125	−0.016	0.0477		−0.0455	0.183		0.0642	1.083*		0.1358
	(0.699)	(0.0335)	(0.610)		(0.05065)	(0.652)		(0.0474)	(0.644)		(0.0361)
Constant	−1.265		−0.229			−5.527**			−8.466***		
	(2.604)		(2.221)			(2.479)			(2.673)		
Observations	253		253			253			253		

Standard deviation in parentheses
***p < 0.01, **p < 0.05, *p < 0.1

practice for these incomes' sources, although agriculture also has its part to play mainly in food consumption.

Only, the "Low" non-agricultural income has a positive and significant influence at 10% on the farmers' "Average Income." This is explained by the fact that the "Low" non-agricultural income equivalent to 414,000 CFAF as well as the farmers' "Average" income, equal to 376,000 CFAF are not consistent. Therefore, the non-agricultural income has not reached a level that could discourage farmers to keep on practicing agriculture which is their main activity. "Average" and "High" non-agricultural income are not significant for this modality. However, if the farmers realize that the alternative source of income, i.e., non-agricultural incomes are more profitable than his agricultural incomes, even all his other sources of income, the agricultural practice will be regressed.

The variables "Low non-agricultural income" and "Average non-agricultural income" have a positive and significant influence at 5 and 1%, respectively, on the farmers' High income category. The result of the marginal effects calculation shows that the relative chances for farmers to have a high income, equivalent to 656,000 FCFA rather than a Very Low income, equivalent to 93,000 FCFA, increase by 10% when non-agricultural income is low, i.e., equal to 414,000 CFAF and 21% when Non-agricultural Income is average, i.e., equal to 1,026,000 CFAF. This means that the more non-agricultural income is, the more important is its impact on farmers' resources; except in the case where non-agricultural incomes far exceed agricultural incomes. For this situation agriculture may entirely be given up only because of the non-agricultural activities.

The variables "Low non-agricultural income" and "Average non-agricultural income" have a positive and significant influence at 10 and 1%, respectively, on the farmers' "Very High income" category, which also corresponds to the highest income quintile, an average value of 28,527,000 FCFA. The marginal effects calculated, show that the relative chances for farmers to have a Very High income rather than a Very Low income increase by 1% when non-agricultural income is low and by 5% when non-agricultural income is average. "High non-agricultural incomes" are not yet significant because of its high value, which may jeopardize the main activity of the area. This allows our research to be in phase with previous studies like Wang et al. (2011) who argued that an increase of 10% in rural non-agricultural income reduces the use of farm labor by 0.4% per mu,[4] all things equal otherwise.

Thus, at several levels, non-agricultural income has a positive impact on the farmers' total income. This result is in line with those of De Janvry et al. (2005). According to these authors, participation in non-agricultural activities creates large effects on the agricultural incomes and without non-agricultural employment, rural poverty would be higher and deeper and income inequality would be high in the same way.

4.2 The Control Variables

4.2.1 Number of Days Per Week Spent on Non-agricultural Activities

Regarding the number of days per week devoted to the practice of non-agricultural activities by farmers, we note that this variable is significant and positive at 5% on the Very High income level of farmers. The marginal effect value corresponding to 0.065, means that the relative odds for farmers to have a Very High income increases by 6.5% when the number of days spent on non-agricultural jobs is increasing. This result confirms previous studies, such as Initiative Prospective Agricole et Rurale (IPAR) (2009), that the richest farm households are those who diversify their income the most, especially from non-agricultural sources.

4.3 The Number of Years Spent in Agriculture

As for the number of years spent in agriculture practice, we find that the variable has a significant and negative effect at 5, 10, and 5%, respectively, for the "Low income," "High income," and "Very High income" modalities of farmers and remains no significant for the "Average income" modality. For the Low-income category, the marginal effect value estimated at −0.006 means that the relative odds for farmers to have Low income rather than Very Low income decrease by 1%. In other words, the agricultural experience acquired by farmers in the Groundnut area, does not hardly improve their incomes. In order for farmers to also have higher incomes compared to the reference, the marginal effect calculated and evaluated at 0.001, means that the relative chances of achievement increase by 0.1%. The marginal effect of the variable for the last modality, namely, the Very High income is equal to −0.007. It indicates that the relative odds for farmers to have a Very High income compared to the reference decrease by 1% when the acquired experience in agriculture is becoming more important. In short, the number of years spent on farming practices does not have a positive impact on income improvement; which means that a long period of time spent in agricultural activities may encourage farmers to practice only those farming activities to the detriment of non-agricultural jobs that can improve their income. Sanusi et al. (2016) found a similar result. For their study, years of experience in agriculture havaa negative and significant impact at 10% on non-agricultural self-employment.

4.4 The Household Size

The household size remains however a no significant variable for all the modalities of the dependent variable, which means that the improvement in farmers' income does not depend on the increase of the number of farm workers, but rather on the number of non-agricultural sources. Kumar et al. (2011) found a similar result. For him, the household size variable has a significant and negative impact on the agricultural sector. Zahanogo (2011) also stated that the number of household assets has a positive and significant impact on the diversification strategy by non-agricultural sources.

4.5 The Gender

The farmers' sex is a variable with a negative and not significant coefficient for the first three modalities of the dependent variable, namely, the "Low income," the "Average income," and the "High income" of the farmers. It is negative and significant for the "Very High income" modality at 5%. Therefore, gender is not a determinant factor of income improvement. The negative and significant coefficient at 5% implies that female farmers are more likely to have a "very high" income than men. This may be linked to the fact that they are less engaged in non-agricultural activities than men and are ready to provide the necessary efforts for the positive evolution of their income. The marginal effect calculated and evaluated at −0.26 confirms this. It means that the relative odds for farmers to have a Very High income compared to the reference decrease by 26% when farmers are mostly men.

4.6 The Age

Regarding the age of the farmers, the marginal effects are negative for the first two modalities of the dependent variable even if the values are very low. Thus, the relative odds of farmers to have a Low income rather than a Very Low income decrease by 0.1% when age increases. Those that farmers have an Average income rather than a Very Low income diminish by 1%. These negative values of marginal effects mean that the positive effect of age on income improvement is not constant over time, so income may increase and decrease thereafter, according to age. For the last two remaining modalities, the marginal effects are positive but still remain low, therefore the relative odds for farmers to have High and Very High income increase by 0.6 and 1.4%, respectively, according to age. The results obtained for these last two modalities, however, are not in phase with those of Onya et al. (2016). Their research found that the age of the head of household negatively affects participation in agricultural wage employment. For these authors, the youngest households are more active in agricultural activities. However, they indicate in their comments that, in order to support themselves, these younger households also depend on non-agricultural employment.

4.7 The Level of Education

The level of education has a positive and not significant coefficient for the first three modalities of the dependent variable. In addition, it has a coefficient that is positive and significant at 10% for the last modality, in this case "Very High Income." So, education is not a decisive factor in improving income from the "Very Low" stage to the "High" stage. Its significance at 10% for the most important modality means that as the farmer is educated, he is more likely to have very high incomes. The marginal effect, equal to 0.14 means that the relative odds that farmers' incomes will be Very High increase by 14% if the level of education varies from "uneducated" to secondary level.

Several authors (Barret et al. 2001; Reardon 2006) have also shown that education increases the probability of engaging in non-agricultural activities, especially those that are more remunerative; which is likely to increase household income. Sakho (2009) also addresses this point. For this author, empirical studies carried out in West Africa have concluded a positive relationship between the level of education and the probability of engaging in non-agricultural activities and that an individual who has attended French school will be able to acquire knowledge and value them in other areas. However (Stavkova and Turcinkova 2012) found that households headed by a person with the lowest level of education, reach the highest income and that the households with the lowest income are those headed by someone with the highest level of education.

5 Conclusion

We have been interested in this chapter to find alternatives to rural people, especially those of the Senegalese groundnut area, whose agricultural income cannot satisfy their food and monetary needs. The aim was to assess the impact of non-agricultural income on improving total income for farmers. Non-agricultural activities globally have a positive and significant impact on the farmers' total income. When the incomes generated by these activities are low, the chances for farmers to have an annual amount of 240,000 CFAF increase by 5.4%. However, if the generated revenues are average, the chances for farmers to have an amount of 240,000 CFAF annually, increase by 2%. The independent variables, namely, "low non-agricultural income" and "average non-agricultural income" also have a positive impact on the famers' "High income" category. Thus, chances for farmers to have a high income, on average equal to 656,000 CFAF, increase by 10% when the non-agricultural income is low and by 21% when the non-agricultural income is average. Regarding the highest income quintile, namely, the "Very High Income" category, marginal effects showed that chances for farmers to have an average income equivalent to 28,527,000 FCFA per year, increase by 1% if non-agricultural income is equal to 414,000 CFAF and by 5%, if non-agricultural income is equal to 1,026,000 CFAF. Only one income level of the interest variable, namely, "High non-agricultural income," is not significant.

Other individual variables also have a positive impact on improving farmers' incomes. That's the number of days per week spent on non-agricultural activities, age, and level of education. However, sex has a negative impact on income improvement. It is the same for the experience in agriculture, justifying that the improvement of agricultural income is rather dependent on the different non-agricultural sources than the seniority in the agricultural practice. The different estimates results showed the importance of non-agricultural activities and the need for rural people to engage in this field in order to thwart the unfavorable and frequent agro-ecological conditions in the area.

This research deserved to be spread on the whole agro-ecological areas of the country, namely, the delta, Casamance as well Anambé areas, since the rainfall weakness is a general order remark, which expands on all Senegal. Beyond the extension over the entire Senegalese territory, what is also considered is its extension over a large part of the Sahel countries. These countries are also characterized by a strong reduction in rainfall and this situation deteriorates growing conditions and negatively affects agricultural yields and productivity.

Notes

1. Agriculture is here defined in the strict sense, i.e., it only represents cropping activities
2. Non-farm = Non agricultural
3. We carried out a number of tests to be sure that the results were reliable. The results (not reported) from the Homoscedasticity Error Test; Test of Normality of Residues; Quality Assessment Tests of the Model; Wald Test; Likelihood Ratio Test; and Hausman Test or Independence of Irrelevant Assumption confirm the robustness of the model estimates.
4. The "Mu" is a unit of surface measurement used in the Far East, and especially in China, where it is officially standardized. It corresponds to about 1/15 hectare, or about 666.67 m^2.

References

African Development Bank. (2015). *African development report 2015 on growth, poverty and inequality nexus: Overcoming barriers to sustainable development*. Intrieved from: https://www.afdb.org/en/documents/document/african-development-report-2015-growth-poverty-and-inequality-nexus-overcoming-barriers-to-sustainable-development-89715.

Akinyemi, O., Efobi, U., Asongu, S., & Osabuohien, E. (2019). Renewable energy, trade performance and the conditional role of finance and institutional capacity in sub-Sahara African Countries. *Energy Policy, 132,* 490–498.

Atamanov, A. (2011). *Microeconomic analysis of rural nonfarm activities in the Kyrgyz Republic: What determines participation and returns?* (Maastricht Graduate School of Governance, WP001, 1–35).

Barret, C., Reardon, T., & Webb, P. (2001). Nonfarm income diversification and household livelihood strategies in Rural Africa: Concepts, dynamics, and policy implications. *Development Studies Research, 1,* 77–89.
Bureau International du Travail. (2008). *Rapport IV sur la Promotion de l'emploi rural pour réduire la pauvreté, Suisse.* Récupéré de: https://www.ilo.org/wcmsp5/groups/public/---ed_norm/---relconf/documents/meetingdocument/wcms_092055.pdf.
Conférence des Nations Unies sur le Commerce et le développement. (2015). *Rapport 2015 sur les pays les moins avancés. Transformer l'économie rurale: Aperçu général,* Suisse. Récupéré de: https://unctad.org/fr/PublicationsLibrary/ldc2015_fr.pdf.
Dirven, M. (2011, January 24–25). *Non-farm rural employment and rural poverty reduction: What we know in Latin America in 2010.* Paper presented at the IFAD Conference on New Directions for Smallholder Agriculture, Italia.
Furaha, G., Mastaki, L., & Lebailly, P. (2013). L'impact des activités non agricoles sur la pauvreté et l'inégalité rurales. Cas des groupements Katana et Kavumu (Province du Sud Kivu). In Dans INRA (Ed.), *7èmes Journées de Recherches en Sciences Sociales: actes du colloque* (pp. 1–22). France, Société Française d'Economie Rurale.
Grain de Sel. (2012). Quelles politiques pour les populations rurales pauvres du Sahel? *59* (62), 1–60.
Grain de Sel. (2015). Jeunes ruraux en Afrique de l'Ouest: Quelles réalités et quelles perspectives. *Bulletin de Synthèse Souveraineté Alimentaire, 17,* 1–8.
Guèye, M. (2010). Activités non agricoles et territoires ruraux. *Défis Sud, 97,* 19–21.
Haggblade, S., Hazell, P., & Reardon, T. (2010). The rural non-farm economy: Prospects for growth and poverty reduction. *World Development, 38*(10), 1429–1441.
Haggblade, S., Reardon, T., & Hazell, P. (2009). Transforming the rural non-farm economy: Opportunities and threats in the developing world. *IFPRI, 58,* 1–9.
Igwe, P. (2013). *Rural non-farm livelihood diversification and poverty reduction in Nigeria.* Unpublished PhD thesis, Plymouth Business School, University of Plymouth, United Kingdom.
Initiative Prospective Agricole et Rurale. (2009). *Changements structurels dans l'agriculture et le monde rural au Sénégal. Rapport final de la seconde phase du Programme Ruralstruct: Résumé exécutif,* Sénégal (Rapport no. 1). Récupéré de http://ipar.sn/IMG/pdf/RuralStruc_Resume_Phase_2.pdf.
Institut Sénégalais de Recherche Agricole. (2008). *Caractérisation et typologie des exploitations agricoles familiales du Sénégal.* Dakar, Sénégal: ISRA.
De Janvry, A., Sadoulet, E., & Zhu, N. (2005). *The role of non-farm incomes in reducing rural poverty and inequality in China* (Working Paper No. 051001). Retrieved from https://escholarship.org/uc/item/7ts2z766.
Fonds International de Développement Agricole. (2010). Créer des opportunités dans l'économie rurale non agricole. In *Rapport sur la pauvreté rurale, Synthèse* (pp. 1–15). FIDA: Rome, Italie.
Fonds International de Développement Agricole. (2015). *Jeunes: Investir dans les jeunes ruraux pour favoriser un développement durable et équitable.* Italie. Récupéré de https://www.ifad.org/documents/38714170/39135645/investing_f.pdf/b9b6454a-9379-4bd8-b377-d3311ee17aab.
Initiative Prospective Agricole et Rurale. (2015). *Subventions des intrants agricoles au Sénégal: Controverses et Réalités, Rapport annuel sur l'état de l'agriculture et du monde rural au Sénégal.* Sénégal. Récupéré de https://www.ipar.sn/IMG/pdf/ipar-rapport_agriculture-2015-_p_p_.pdf.

Jatta, S. (2013). Non-farm wages and poverty alleviation in developing countries. *MPRA, 47180*, 1–28.

Katega, I. (2013, April 3–4). *Rural non-farm activities and poverty alleviation in Tanzania: A case of selected villages in Chamwino and Bahi Districts in Dodoma Region*. Presented at REPOA's 18th Annual Research Workshop held at the Kunduchi Beach Hotel, Tanzania.

Kpodar, K. (2007). *Manuel d'initiation à Stata (Version 8)*. Clermont-Auvergne, France, CERDI.

Kropko, J. (2008). *Choosing between multinomial logit and multinomial probit models for analysis of unordered choice data*. Unpublished PhD Thesis, University of North Carolina, Chapel Hill.

Kumar, A., Kumar, S., Singh, D. K., & Shivjee. (2011). Rural employment diversification in India: Trends, determinants and implications on poverty. *Agricultural Economics Research Review, 24*, 361–372.

Losch, B., Fréguin-Gresh, S., & White, T. (2013). *Transformations rurales et Développement: Les défis du changement structurel dans un monde globalisé*. Paris, France: Pearson France.

Madaki, J. U., & Adefila, J. O. (2014). Contributions of rural non-farm economic activities to household income in Lere area, Kaduna State of Nigeria. *International Journal of Asian Social Science, 4*(5), 654–663.

Mathijs, M. and Maertens, M. (2011). *Farm/non-farm linkages in smallholder agriculture: Evidence from Tigray, Northern Ethiopia*. Unpublished Master Memory, Leuven University, Belgium.

Ndione, Y. C. (2015, November 26–27). Analysis of the pluriactivity of Senegalese rural households. In *Second International Conference on Sustainable Development in Africa Dakar*, Senegal.

Onya, S. C., Okezie, C. A., & Ejiba, I. V. (2016). Determinants of participation in non-farm employment among rural farmers in Ebonyi State, Nigeria. *Journal of Scientific Research and Reports, 11*(6), 1–11.

Organisation des Nations Unies pour l'alimentation et l'agriculture. (1998). *Rapport sur la situation mondiale de l'alimentation et de l'agriculture: Les revenus ruraux non agricoles dans les pays en développement*, Italie (Rapport no. 1). Récupéré de: http://www.fao.org/3/w9500e/w9500e.pdf.

Osabuohien, E., Efobi, U. R., Herrmann, R., & Gitau, C. M. (2019). Female labor outcomes and large-scale agricultural land investments: Macro-micro evidence from Tanzania. *Land Use Policy, 82*, 716–728.

Oyebola, P. O., Osabuohien, E., & Obasaju, B. (2019). Employment and income effects of Nigeria's agricultural transformation agenda. *African Journal of Economic and Management Studies*. https://doi.org/10.1108/AJEMS-12-2018-0402.

Reardon, T. (1997). Using evidence of household income diversification to inform study of the rural nonfarm labor market in Africa. *World Development, Elsevier Science Ltd., 25*(5), 135–741.

Reardon, T. (2006). Household income diversification into rural nonfarm activities. In S. Haggblade, P. Hazell, & T. Reardon (Eds.), *Transforming the rural nonfarm economy*. Baltimore: Johns Hopkins University Press.

République du Sénégal, Ministère de la PME, de l'Entreprenariat Féminin et de la Microfinance. (2004). *Rapport Final sur la Microfinance et le Financement des PME et MPE*, Sénégal (Rapport no. 1). Récupéré de: https://www.microfinancegateway.org/sites/default/files/mfg-fr-etudes-de-cas-microfinance-et-financement-des-pme-senegal-08-2004.pdf.

Sakho, M. S. J. (2009). *L'autonomie alimentaire par la diversification des activités: Le cas des ménages agricoles du Bassin arachidier au Sénégal*. Thèse non publiée, Université de Montpellier1, France.

Sanusi, W. A., Dipeolu, A. O., & Momoh, S. (2016). Determinants of participation in non-farm activities among rural households in Osun State: An application of multinomial logit (Mnl) model. *International Journal of African and Asian Studies, 25*, 66–72.

Sarah, A. (2014). Determinants of rural household income diversification in Senegal and Kenya. In *6èmes Journées de recherches en sciences sociales* (pp. 1–22). France: Société Française d'Economie Rurale.

Seng, K. (2015). The effects of nonfarm activities on farm households' food consumption in rural Cambodia. *Development Studies Research, 2*(1), 77–89.

Singh, I. (2011). *Impact of rural non-farm employment on poverty and income inequality*. Unpublished Thesis chapter, Indian University, India.

Singh, I., Squire, L., & Strauss, J. (1986). *Agricultural households models: Extensions, applications and policy*. Baltimore, USA: John Hopkins University Press.

Stavkova, J., & Turcinkova, J. (2012). Does the attained level of education affect the income situation of households? *Social and Behavioral Sciences, 55*, 1036–1042.

Tandjigora, A. (2018). *La Gestion du risque agricole par les activités non agricoles: Evidence de la zone rurale du Bassin arachidier du Sénégal*. Thèse non publiée, Université Cheikh Anta Diop de Dakar (A venir).

Wang, Y., Wang, C., & Pan, S. (2011, July 24–26). *The Impact of nonfarm activities on agricultural productivity in rural China*. Selected Paper prepared for presentation at the Agricultural and Applied Economics Association's, Pennsylvania.

Winters, P., Davis, B., Carletto, G., Stamoulis, K., Covarrubias, K., Krausova, M., & Zezza, A. (2007). Assets, activities and rural poverty alleviation: Evidence from a multicountry analysis. *eJADE electronic Journal of Agricultural and Development Economics Agricultural, 4*(1), 1–18.

Zahanogo, P. (2011). Determinants of non-farm activities participation decisions of farm households in Burkina Faso. *Journal of Development and Agricultural Economics, 3*(4), 174–182.

Zahanogo, P. (2002). *La dynamique des activités non agricoles dans la stratégie de développement en milieu rural: Evidences empiriques du Burkina*. Thèse non publiée. Université de Ouagadougou, Burkina Faso.

Youth (Un)employment and Large-Scale Agricultural Land Investments: Examining the Relevance of Indigenous Institutions and Capacity in Tanzania

Evans S. Osabuohien, Uchenna R. Efobi, Ciliaka M. Gitau, Romanus A. Osabohien, and Oluwasogo S. Adediran

1 Introduction

Youth unemployment level remains high in Africa and the poverty rate among the youths is expected to increase in the continent by 2030 (United Nations 2015). The ratio of youth to adult unemployment rate in Africa is about 2.5; that is, two and half times larger than the adult unemployment rate (Cassim and Oosthuizen 2014; Afolayan et al. 2019) while youths account for 60% of all joblessness in the continent (Ighobor 2017).

E. S. Osabuohien (✉)
Department of Economics and Development Studies & Chair,
Centre for Economic Policy and Development Research (CEPDeR),
Covenant University, Ota, Nigeria
e-mail: evans.osabuohien@covenantuniversity.edu.ng

Alexander von Humboldt Visiting Professor, Witten/Herdecke University, Witten, Germany

U. R. Efobi
College of Business and Social Sciences & Senior Research Fellow,
Centre for Economic Policy and Development
Research (CEPDeR), Covenant University, Ota, Nigeria

© The Author(s) 2020
E. S. Osabuohien (ed.), *The Palgrave Handbook of Agricultural and Rural Development in Africa*, https://doi.org/10.1007/978-3-030-41513-6_19

The challenge of youth unemployment in Africa is a serious and sensitive issue due to several reasons. First, Africa is one of the most youthful regions of the world, with the youth population summing up to 19% of the entire 1.81 billion youth population in the world (United Nations 2015; Central Intelligence Agency [CIA] 2018). The African youth population is expected to be one-quarter of the world's young people by 2025. By 2015, the youth population as a proportion of the total population in Africa exceeded 75% with over 60% of them being younger than 25 years (Anyanwu 2014; Hilson and Osei 2014; African Development Bank [AfDB] 2018). Second, the youthful population is usually subjected to social injustice and they are disgruntled by the lack of opportunities to enjoy the benefits derived from economic and natural/societal resources. Like many civil wars in Africa, the main thrust of the Sierra Leonean decades of the civil war was the disenfranchised youths who would pledge allegiance to rebellious enticement mainly driven by high rate of unemployment and unproductive occupation (Bellows and Miguel 2009). The work by Otchia (2015) has also reiterated that when natural resources are not properly managed it could result in Dutch disease and the attendant structural change.

Before the year 2000, youth-targeted policies targeted were either minimal or non-existent. The lack of youth-targeted policies has been identified as a key contributing factor to a number of catastrophes such as: civil unrest, political upheavals and in some cases, civil war. For instance, the Ugandan and the Sierra Leonean wars were among the prominent in African that witnessed a huge involvement of young combatants. Their involvement can be associated with lack of employment (Bellows and Miguel 2009; Vindevogel et al. 2013). Substantial evidence suggests that a poor or non-engagement of the youths—in the face of rising inflow of foreign investors that engage their natural resources (e.g. land)—can result in violent clashes and in some cases armed rebellion (Ariyo and Mortimore 2012). In 2006, noting this national threat and ticking *time bomb*, the African Union enacted a charter that protects and enumerates the rights and privileges of African youths, termed: African Youth Charter- AYC (African Union 2006). Consequently, some African countries have initiated activities to make the agricultural sector more attractive to reduce unemployment and enhance job creation. This is being realized through the attraction of investments to create opportunities for youth participation through efficient utilization of available lands (Elumelu 2017; Bluwstein et al. 2018). The presence of foreign investment is expected to increase land productivity creating direct and indirect employment opportunities (Engström and Hajdu 2019).

C. M. Gitau
The World Bank Group, Washington, DC, USA

R. A. Osabohien · O. S. Adediran
Department of Economics and Development Studies & Research Fellow,
Centre for Economic Policy and Development Research (CEPDeR),
Covenant University, Ota, Nigeria

According to rational expectations theory in the institutional economic literature (La Porta et al. 1999; Acemoglu and Robinson 2012; Osabuohien et al. 2018), institutions provide a framework that structures the behaviour of economic agents. More so, they ensure a guideline through which contracts are established and enforced (North 1990; Osabuohien and Efobi 2013). In many African countries, the institutional framework has not been effective in the enforcement of contracts because it is weak (Nolte 2014; Osabuohien et al. 2015, 2019). The African weak institutional framework has hindered the overall growth and developmental process despite the presence of foreign capital expected to complement the available resources and stimulate development (Asiedu 2006; Osabohien et al. 2018). Against this backdrop, this study contributes to the extant literature by arguing that that the presence of large-scale agricultural land investments (LALIs) may not really translate to development progress: for example, youth employment—without an effective institutional framework especially at the local level to support it. Inadvertently, this argument has not received much empirical attention in extant studies, which formed one of the motivations for this study.

The study of Anyanwu (2014) provided some insights where the author relates the issue of youth unemployment to intra-African trade. This present study differs from Anyanwu study in many respects. Whereas Anyanwu used a macro approach examining the issue using panel data consisting of 46 African countries (1980–2010), this study focuses on the micro aspect using data from household and community surveys and compares the issue of youth employment in communities with and without LALIs in Tanzania. In addition, a related study was done by Ariyo and Mortimore (2012) where they examined mainly a single case study using popular media reports in Shonga, Kwara State, Nigeria. The present study expands its focus by providing more encompassing cases in Tanzania using a broader dataset- the Living Standards Measurement Study-Integrated Surveys on Agriculture (LSMS_ISA).

Furthermore, both Anyanwu (2014) and Ariyo and Mortimore (2012) did not consider the issue of indigenous institutional framework that is likely to affect the LALIs' outcomes. Tanzania was chosen because it is among the top 20 destinations of global large-scale land deals and top five in Africa (LMGO 2017; Osabuohien et al. 2019) and is covered by LSMS_ISA and Land Matrix Global Observatory (LMGO) datasets, which are the major sources of data for the study. Also, like other African countries, agricultural sector in Tanzania has the potential of transforming local communities, economies and the environment, which is hinged on the fact that the sector employs more than 65% of active labour force (African Development Bank-AfDB 2014). In addition, Tanzania is among the top 20 destinations of global large-scale land deals and top five in Africa (LMGO 2017; Osabuohien et al. 2019).

The study is structured in five sections; following this introduction section is Sect. 2 which provides some background information regarding the incidence of youth unemployment and some emerging issues on land deals. Section 3 presents the empirical model and analytical framework. Section 4 presents and discusses results from estimation process, while Sect. 5 is the conclusion.

2 Youth Unemployment and Agricultural Land Investment: Some Emerging Issues

This section discusses youth unemployment trend and relates it with the increasing LALIs. The availability of arable land in recipient countries—among others—is likely a convincing explanation for the increased flow of land investments (Cotula et al. 2009; Deininger et al. 2011; Arezki et al. 2012; Osabuohien 2014; Sulle 2017).

Figure 1 shows Tanzania is fourth out of the top 10 countries in Africa with the highest number of land deals. This suggests growing interest in LALIs in Tanzania. Literature indicates that LALIs are more rampant in countries with weak institutional settings at the national level (Arezki et al. 2012). Recent evidences also confirm the same applies at the community level, at least for Nigeria, Tanzania and Uganda (George et al. 2015; Osabuohien et al. 2015; Sulle 2017; Bluwstein et al. 2018). LALIs are mainly intended for food crops and biofuels, where the large proportion of the investors are foreign (see Table 1).

In Tanzania, the situation is not too different. Following the increased investments in land and related resources, there have been occurrences of land use conflicts between rural pastoralists and agro-farmers (Massay 2015; Engström and Hajdu 2019). There are conflicts of various forms: arising from encroachments; tenure conflicts between customary and granted land rights; forceful displacement of original landowners by the state and wealthy investors, especially in the Morogoro, Iringa and Pwani Regions of Tanzania (Simbarashe 2012; Mugabi 2013). In some cases, the land-related clashes result in loss of lives, destruction of property and turning land areas into

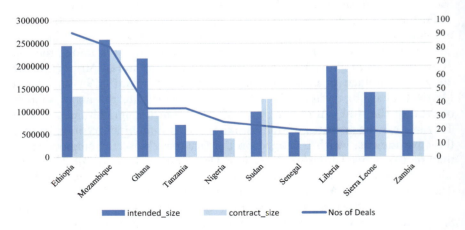

Fig. 1 The top 10 major recipients of land investments in Africa (*Source* Authors' Calculations based on Land Matrix Global Observatory Data)

Table 1 Large-scale land deals in Tanzania (domestic versus foreign)

	Nature		Total	Food crops	Biofuels	Non-Food	Others
Tanzania	Foreign	Number of deals	27.00	13.00	10.00	2.00	2.00
		Intended size in Ha	671,367.00	110,506.00	451,729.00	51,000.00	58,132.00
		Contract size in Ha	291,943.00	106,051.00	101,785.00	50,000.00	34,107.00
	Indigenous	Number of deals	9.00	4.00	4.00	1.00	0.00
		Intended size in Ha	41,114.00	914.00	25,200.00	15,000.00	0.00
		Contract size in Ha	60,389.00	16,189.00	34,200.00	10,000.00	0.00

Source Authors' computation using Land Matrix Global Observatory Data

conflict zones as opposing factions tend to control territories and clinch the right to use land (Simbarashe 2012).

The clashes and violent reactions that are experienced are driven by the disenfranchised youth, who fight to protect their ancestral lands against the 'encroachers' as they demand opportunities to apply themselves productively. Similar incidences have been witnessed in other African countries like Sierra Leone, where the rebel group (Revolutionary United Front), largely championed by disgruntled youths, confronted the government for corruptly enriching self with resources (i.e. diamond) (Bellows and Miguel 2009). The youth forms bulk of the unemployed active population that can easily be lured into violence or other particular cause. The consequences of youth unemployment in most African countries are analogized as a *ticking time bomb* that can undermine social cohesion and political stability (Ncube 2012; Elumelu 2017).

To inform the policy direction in Tanzania, this study presents two main arguments drawn from Hilson and Osei (2014). First, the presence of LALIs leads to the development of an informal sector. Following the rising youth unemployment in most African countries and the resultant effects, there is a need to rethink public policies that address informality. Moving beyond the paradigm, investors can: apart from acquiring land for contingencies or other motives that neglect the interest of the host communities—commit to utilize the services of local labour and invest in local development. Second, the investors should develop infrastructural facilities that can enhance the economic opportunities for the youth. This suggests the need for more emphasis on human capital development, which is crucial for preparing youths for waged employment opportunities (Ejemeyovwi et al. 2018).

The main intuition of this study is that: the presence of LALIs in a community can translate to youth employment if critical policy instruments can be effectively addressed. Some of these policy instruments include an institutional framework that reduces the incidence of corruption, enhances active participation of non-government agencies (Non-State Actors [NSAs]), development of rural infrastructure and creating community structure that enhances proper representation of the interest of community members.

3 Research Method and Analytical Framework

3.1 Data Description

The Living Standard Measurement Study–Integrated Surveys on Agriculture (LSMS_ISA) is the main source of household and community data used in this study, and is complemented by the LMGO dataset on the occurrences of land deals around the world. This study considered the LSMS_ISA for Tanzania (Wave 1, 2010/2011 panel session and Wave 2, 2012/2013 panel session). Wave 1 of the LSMS-ISA data consists of 3265 households, half of which had been surveyed for the 2007 Tanzania Household Budget Survey (THBS). The sample is representative and provides useful information on key socioeconomic variables for mainland rural areas, Dar es Salaam, other mainland urban areas, and Zanzibar. In the second wave (2012/2013), all original households were revisited. The members still residing in their original location were re-interviewed, and all adults who had relocated were tracked and re-interviewed in their new location with their new household members. The sample size for the second wave was expanded to 3924. The size of accessible plots was measured using the Global Positioning System (GPS).

This study empirical analysis used the second wave of the LSMS-ISA data because it provides a well-coordinated survey data on Tanzania and will most likely reflect a most recent situation in Tanzania and it has an expanded representation of Tanzanians, compared to the first wave. The survey focused on youth respondents that are the focus of this study. From the LMGO dataset, communities and locations that have the presence of LALIs were identified. The locations and communities with LALIs in LMGO dataset are matched in the LSMS-ISA dataset and coded as 1.[1] All other locations/communities in the LSMS-ISA dataset, are coded as 0. This means that 1 represents locations/communities where LALIs have occurred and 0 otherwise. It was observed that most of the land investments occurred in the period 2008–2010; the global economic crisis, which fuelled the need for land investment (Abdallah et al. 2014; Osabuohien 2014; Osabuohien et al. 2015, 2019). The analysis considered the year that most of the land investments as reported in the LMGO dataset.

In addition to the location information, the LMGO dataset contains demographic information such as the source of investment (in terms of foreign or domestic investors) and the intended and/or contract sizes (in hectares). The latest version (Beta Version 2) of the LMGO dataset also contains the status of the land deals—whether the contract was finalized/concluded or not. This study considers land deals that have been contracted. the descriptive summary and scope of the dataset is represented in Anseeuw et al. (2013). Osabohien (2018) provides overview for Nigeria, which is similar to other countries where LSMS-ISA is available include Tanzania.

3.2 Formulation of the Empirical Model

In formulating the empirical model for this study, two studies are relevant. The first is Asiedu (2004), where the author examined the determinant of employment status of multinationals affiliates from the US in Africa. The author examined a panel data consisting of 34 African countries (1983–2000). One of the main findings is that the education level of residents, within the location of the Multinational affiliates, is a major determinant of the employment capacity of the affiliates. The second relevant study is

Asiedu et al. (2011) that examined the health situation of 84 different countries and linked it with the status of FDIs located in those countries. Asiedu et al. (2011) stated that the health status of residents within the FDI location area would affect the productivity of FDIs since healthy workers are more productive than sickly ones. Gleaning from these two studies, we present an empirical model that includes the educational attainment and the health status of the respondents as the main covariates.

Given the issue of gender discrimination in Tanzania,[2] two important socioeconomic variables; age and gender of the respondents, are included in the model. Therefore, the empirical model for this study is such that youth unemployment is a function of land deals and other covariates, i.e.:

$$\text{Youth\_employment}_i = \alpha_i + \beta \, \text{Land\_Deal}_i + \alpha' \, \text{Covariates}_i + \varepsilon_i \quad (1)$$

where 'i' is the identifier for the individuals, α, β and α' are the coefficients. The error term is 'ε'. The institutional framework in the LALIs location is vital (Osabuohien 2014) therefore an interactive effect of the institutional framework is included in the model. Thus, Eq. (1) is transformed as:

$$\text{Youth\_employment}_i = \alpha_i + \beta \text{Land\_Deal}_i + \alpha' \, \text{Covariates}_i \\ + \lambda \text{Institutions}_{ci} + \partial \text{Interactive}_{ci} + \varepsilon_i \quad (2)$$

The 'ci' is the community identifier, which defines the institutional framework in community, where the individual 'i' is located. The interactive variable is a multiplicative of the institutions and the land deal occurrence. A positive interactive variable signifies that land deal has a positive effect on the explained variable in a situation where the measure of institutions is improving: thus, both variables are complementary. The negative sign implicates a substitutive effect between land deal and the institutional framework.

3.3 Some Key Definitions

In defining youth employment, we start with the definition of a youth as individuals from 15 to 35 years of age according to the African Union (2006). In the light of the above, employment is measured using the response to these LSMS-ISA questions: 'did you do any work for pay in the last 7 days?'; or 'did you work for pay in the last 12 months?'; or if you work for yourself (self-employment). The use of these three components is essential to capture a broader view of employment, as it is not unusual for people in African communities work on themselves especially within the informal sector.[3] The variables are dichotomous, where 1 represents the affirmative response of yes and 0 otherwise. The variable LALIs variable takes the value of 1 in the presence of land investors in the community where the individual resides and 0 otherwise.

Another important variable is the institutional framework indicator. The classical definition by North (1990) that institutions provide the basic structure to enhance and enforce contracts. It also provides checks against the expropriation of resources by the state/leaders (Acemoglu and Johnson 2005). The study focuses on those institutions that enhance contract enforcement between land investors and the host community. Two measures suffice in this study. They are the presence of NSAs and Legal Tribunals. The choice of these two variables was informed by the works of George et al. (2013), Osabuohien (2014), Massay (2015), Osabuohien et al. (2015), where the studies attributed the presence of NSAs to be a formidable mechanism to pursue contract legal issues and reduce undue advantages that can result from economic relationships. Second, the capacity of traditional leaders is essential. We are interested in the capacity of the community leaders to reduce *predatory* tendencies. Insight was drawn from Jo-Ansie (2007) and Efobi (2015) that established the linkage between political leaders and corrupt practices in African countries and how the capacity of the leaders can reduce the tendency of state capture of public resources. More so, the tendency of expropriation will be reduced by the capacity of the leaders. Thus, the educational qualification and the tenure of the traditional leader are included as a measure of the capacity of the traditional leader. Indicators of institutions considered in the study include; NSA (presence of NSA and number of different groups), indigenous legal framework (presence of ward tribunal and frequency of ward tribunal meetings), social stability (presence of social vigilance groups and number of violent attacks), and capacity of local community leaders (education level of community elders and office tenure of community elders). The data on these indicators is derived from the LMGO dataset.

3.4 Analytical Framework

The conceptual framework represented in Fig. 2, further explains the interactive variables in the empirical model, their interplays and how they could exert possible implications for employment level within the host

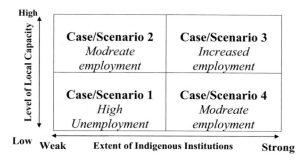

Fig. 2 Analytical framework: Large-scale land deals and employment interaction (*Source* The Authors')

communities. The most ideal scenario is captured in Case 3, with a combination of strong institutional framework and high level of local capacity.

The local capacity in this regard entails, inter alia, the ability of the host community leaders to act on behalf of their community members to review the agreement and negotiate for LALIs expected benefits to the community. It has been noted that in many cases, the community leaders engage in LALIs agreement without a proper grasp of the content implication (Timko 2014; Osabuohien et al. 2015, 2019). This capacity can be enhanced by targeted enlightenment of the community leaders and their members on the many-faceted ramifications of issues shrouding LALIs. Promoting the capacities of local communities is imperative, which include the provision of paralegal, occasional campaign and community meetings, among others (Doss et al. 2014; Osabuohien et al. 2015; Massay 2015).

On the other hand, the extent of the institutional framework in the communities is essential in ensuring that sincerity and integrity principles are upheld. This is an acid test for accountability and transparency for the community leaders not to be lured into the web of corrupt practices as there could be the possibility of being enticed and enthused by the glamour of money from potential investors and government officers (Abdallah et al. 2014; Nolte 2014; Osabuohien 2014). In summary, both enhancement of capacities of community leaders and improvement of institutional framework are essential to ensure that the host communities negotiate for better agreements such as asking to be part owners of the new venture instead of the money illusion of once-off meagre payment as compensation. It will also help to drive the realization of promises made by the investors to the communities during LALIs negotiation.

4 Empirical Results

4.1 Results from Descriptive Statistics

The empirical analysis set out with the discussion of LALIs in Tanzania based on the communities where such land deals have occurred in comparison with those without such land deals. It uses the African Union' definition of youth in the African Youth Charter as individuals between the age group of 15 and 35 years (African Union 2006). Based on this definition, the levels of youth unemployment are compared between communities with LALIs and those without.

Weighted averages are computed for both employed and unemployed youths as indicated in the last row of Table 2. As reflected by the values, on the average, communities that have LALIs had higher lower employment level of 26.21% compared to those communities without the presence of LALIs that had the average value of 34.33%. This finding is quite revealing as it challenges the paradigm that employment generation (particularly for the youth) is one of the benefits that accrue to LALIs host communities. The next sub-section discusses the summary statistics.

Table 2 Locations surveyed, # land deals and youth unemployment using ILO's definition of youth

#	Location	# Land deals	# Youths surveyed	Unemployed (%)	Employed (%)	#	Location	# Land deals	# Youths surveyed	Unemployed (%)	Employed (%)
1	Rufiji River	10	13	100.0	0.0	12	Arusha	0	7	14.29	85.71
2	Dodoma	3	1	100.0	0.0	13	Shinyanga	0	15	100.0	0.0
3	Iringa	4	6	83.33	16.67	14	Ruvuma	0	11	72.7	27.3
4	Kagera	3	9	88.9	11.1	15	Manyara	0	3	33.3	66.7
5	Kigoma	2	18	94.44	5.56	16	Tabora	0	2	50.0	50.0
6	Kilimanjaro	3	6	16.67	83.33	17	Rukwa	0	2	100.0	0.0
7	Lindi	1	3	100.0	0.0	18	Singida	0	2	50.0	50.0
8	Mbeya	1	23	65.22	34.78	19	Magharibi	0	2	100.0	0.0
9	Morogoro	9	5	60.0	40.0	20	Mtwara	0	6	100.0	0.0
10	Pwani	11	7	100.0	0.0	21	Mwanza	0	1	0.0	100.0
11	Tanga	2	2	100.0	0.0	22	Mara	0	1	100.0	0.0
	Weighted average			73.79	26.21		Weighted average			65.67	34.33

Note '#' indicates number of'. The weighted average was computed by examining the number of youths surveyed in accordance to the percentage of the unemployed and employed, respectively
Source Authors'

4.2 Results from Descriptive Statistics

Table 3 presents some important issues on summary statistics of key variables in the empirical model. Examining the main dependent variable, the first row indicates that communities with LALIs had lower youth employment level at 20.40% compared to 26.90% in communities without LALIs. Thus, this finding corroborates the earlier observation refuting that the possibility of LALIs presence in promoting youth employments in host communities.

Regarding the indicators of institutional framework, the statistics suggest that communities without LALIs have relatively better institutional capacity compared to those with LALIs as both values for Institution 1 and Institution 2 are greater. This seems to confirm the argument that LALIs occur in locations (national and local) with weak institutions (Arezki et al. 2012; Osabuohien 2014; Osabuohien et al. 2015; Sulle 2017). On the capacity of the community leaders, the indicators suggest, on an average, that there are not much differences in the capacity of the leaders in communities with LALIs and those without.

4.3 Econometric Results

The econometric results of the baseline regression where four covariates - education, health, sex and age—are examined as major determinants of youth 'employability'. The results in Table 4 are consistent with expectations; showing that these covariates are important determinants of the employability of youths in Tanzania.

4.3.1 Institutions and the Presence of Non-State Actors

We present the effect of institutions on the relationship between the presence of LALIs in a community and youth employment. As earlier discussed, we used the presence of NSA and the indigenous legal framework as indicators for local institutions, the social stability of the community and the capacity of the local/community. Since we have confirmed the consistency of the covariates and at least their signs and significant values remained somewhat steady with the inclusion of land deal, then there is no need to follow a stepwise approach in estimating further regressions. Consequently, variables are plugged into the baseline model (inclusive of LALIs).

To test the effect of institutions on the relationship between LALIs and youth employment in Tanzania, we began by plotting youth unemployment and the presence of NSAs using the presence of farmers association as an indicator. Figure 3 (in the Appendix) shows that there is no explicit difference between unemployment incidences in the communities with NSA and those without. Taking a closer look at this chart, the communities without NSA were experiencing slightly more youth employment than the communities with NSA. Thus, we resolve to consider the reactive effect from the regression analysis presented in Table 4. It is needful to state that we considered

Table 3 Summary statistics of selected variables using ILO's definition of youth

Name/description	All communities		With land deals		Without land deals	
	Mean	Std. Dev	Mean	Std. Dev	Mean	Std. Dev
Employment (Youth Emp): Did Individual do any work for pay 7 days or work for pay in the last 12 months or work for yourself (1=yes, 0=no). The higher, the better	0.228	0.421	0.204	0.405	0.269	0.448
Covariates						
Education (Youth Educ.): Did name ever go to school? 1=yes, 0=no. The higher, the better	0.897	0.306	0.925	0.265	0.846	0.364
Health Condition (Health): Are you physically fit to do a rigorous work? 1=yes, 0=no. The higher, the better	0.938	0.242	0.957	0.204	0.904	0.298
Sex (Sex), 1=male; 2=female	1.524	0.501	1.505	0.503	1.556	0.502
†**Age (Age)**, How old is name on his last birthday (in years)	17.19	5.86	16.67	5.48	18.09	6.41
Non-state actors						
*NSA1 **(NSA1)**: Number of different interest group in the community. The higher, the better	5.647	13.902	4.103	5.192	7.681	20.411
NSA2 (NSA2): Are there any farmers' cooperative group in the community? 1=yes, 0=no. The higher, the better	0.413	0.494	0.387	0.490	0.456	0.504
Institutions to resolve dispute						
Institution1 (Inst1): Is there a ward tribunal in this community? 1=yes, 0=no. The higher, the better	0.918	0.276	0.913	0.283	0.926	0.264
†**Institution2 (Inst2)**: How many times do the ward tribunal meet per month? The higher, the better	7.463	11.623	8.176	14.415	6.224	2.867
Community's social stability and security						
Vigilante (Vlante): Is there any form of citizen's vigilante in this community? 1=yes, 0=no. The higher, the better	0.800	0.402	0.773	0.421	0.850	0.362
†**Violence (Vlence)**: Number of cases of violent attack reported in the last calendar month. The lower, the better	33.483	73.961	35.816	77.745	29.05	66.900
Capacity of community leader						
Tenure in office (Lead1): Tenure of Community Leader. Not clear apriori	6.728	8.790	5.796	3.872	8.333	13.516
Education of leader (Lead3): Education of Community Leader: 1=None; 2=incomplete primary education; 3=primary; 4=secondary; 5=diploma; 6=university. The higher, the better	3.167	0.819	3.242	0.807	3.038	0.831
Observations (# Communities)	392		220		172	

Note # 'indicates number of'. †: These are continuous variables. Since indigenous institutions and local capacity are essentially at the level of the community, we collapsed the data to community analysis using median. Thus, the means are the means of the median

Source Authors'

Table 4 Baseline regression inclusive of presence of NSAs

	1	2	3	4	5	6
Education	1.480***	1.574**	2.160	2.383***	1.542***	2.465*
	(0.054)	(0.045)	(0.122)	(0.094)	(0.055)	(0.100)
Health condition	15.883*	15.505*	16.254*	16.751*	16.524*	16.843*
	(0.000)	(0.000)	(0.000)	(0.000)	(0.000)	(0.000)
Sex	−0.903***	−0.877***	−1.291	−1.320	−0.882***	−1.356
	(0.087)	(0.098)	(0.145)	(0.136)	(0.094)	(0.115)
Age	0.150*	0.151*	0.159**	0.147**	0.144*	0.152**
	(0.000)	(0.000)	(0.014)	(0.024)	(0.000)	(0.020)
Land deal	−0.589		−0.555			
	(0.243)		(0.480)			
NSA1	0.356***	0.338***				
	(0.081)	(0.096)				
NSA2			−0.014	−0.020		
			(0.709)	(0.739)		
NSA1 × Land deal					0.100***	
					(0.085)	
NSA2 × Land deal						−0.036
						(0.723)
Pseudo	0.220	0.210	0.194	0.186	0.207	0.187
Prob. value	0.000	0.000	0.000	0.000	0.000	0.000
Log likelihood	−49.695	−50.357	−21.238	−21.447	−50.554	−21.408

Note *, ** and ***: significant at 1, 5 and 10%, respectively. Constant term was included in all the estimations but not reported for space
Source Authors'

only the indirect effect of the presence of LALIs in communities with NSA on youth employment incidence in such communities. Therefore, we report only the indirect effect of the variable in columns 5 and 6 of Table 4.

For robustness, we used two measures of NSAs. The first measure is the presence of NSAs in the community (NSA1) and the second measure is the number of different farmers groups in the community (NSA2). The number of different groups measures the strength of pressure groups within the community that is groups that can hold the investors and the government accountable. From Table 5, the variable land deal was still consistently not significant in columns 1 and 3. The two NSA variables displayed varying significant behaviour. NSA1 that measures the presence of an NSA (presence of farmers' association) was an important determinant of the incidence of youth employment. Implying that communities with such associations are likely to experience a significant increase in the rate of youth employment between 0.356 and 0.338.

The second measure of NSA (*NSA2*) that captures the number of active groups in the community was not significant in columns 3 and 4. Nevertheless, we infer from the behaviour of the interactive term of NSA1 and land deal that NSA plays an important role in determining the incidences of youth employment in a community that has the presence of land investors. The behaviour of the interactive variable (*NSA1 × Land Deal*) was positive and significant. Therefore, we can infer from column 5 that a community with functional farmers' association and experiences land investment will likely have about 10% improvement in the level of youth employment, other things being equal. A possible explanation for this is that such communities can rely on the combined strength of the association to push their demands as agreed with the land investors. More so, the association can be involved in the negotiation process and will seek to protect the interest of the members of that community; perhaps, even pursue altruistic pacts that enhance the welfare of its members and their households.

4.3.2 Effect of Indigenous Legal Framework
We considered the effect of indigenous institution on the youth employment rate by plotting the rate of youth employment against the response to the question on whether there is a ward tribunal in the community. The presence of a ward tribunal in the community is indicative of the fact that aggrieved individuals can easily be protected by the tribunal through the usual litigation process; at least at the community level. In Fig. 4 (in the Appendix), we observed that in the communities where there are ward tribunal, the rate of youth employment is clearly higher than communities without ward tribunal. However, we are not just interested in the divergence of youth employment in the communities; but in the behaviour of rate of youth (un)employment in the communities with land deal and ward tribunals? Will it significantly reduce?

Table 5 Baseline regression inclusive of local institutions

	1	2	3	4	5	6
Education	1.770**	1.831**	1.846**	1.926**	1.702**	1.817**
	(0.035)	(0.031)	(0.028)	(0.024)	(0.044)	(0.034)
Health condition	16.682*	16.646*	16.755*	16.744*	15.011*	16.789*
	(0.000)	(0.000)	(0.000)	(0.000)	(0.000)	(0.000)
Sex	−0.813***	−0.819***	−0.719	−0.724	−0.786	−0.703
	(0.100)	(0.104)	(0.156)	(0.151)	(0.123)	(0.161)
Age	0.168*	0.169*	0.169*	0.169*	0.167*	0.161*
	(0.000)	(0.000)	(0.000)	(0.000)	(0.000)	(0.000)
Land deal	−0.259		−0.162			
	(0.592)		(0.749)			
Institution1	0.995***	0.986***				
	(0.100)	(0.085)				
Institution2			−0.353**	−0.359**		
			(0.026)	(0.017)		
Institution1 × Land deal					0.049**	
					(0.019)	
Institution2 × Land deal						−0.209**
						(0.043)
Pseudo	0.230	0.228	0.213	0.213	0.221	0.212
Prob. value	0.000	0.000	0.000	0.000	0.000	0.000
Log likelihood	−58.756	−58.901	−56.601	−56.653	−59.426	−56.721

Note The variable Institutions2 is a count variable and was logged. The logarithm value was used in the regression analysis in columns (3, 4 and 6). *, ** and ***: significant at 1, 5 and 10%, respectively
Source Authors'

In clarifying the above, we conducted a logistic regression by including the indicator of indigenous institutions. We used two indicators for robustness checks: the first is the presence of ward tribunal (Institution1) and the second is the frequency of meeting of the ward tribunal (Institution2). We present the result of the logistic regression in Table 6. The column that includes the interactive variables (columns 5 and 6) presents only the indirect effect of the interaction.

The logistic regression results in Table 5 show that the variable 'land deal' is consistently displaying an insignificant relationship with youth employment. Although this is not surprising since the other covariates that were earlier included in Table 4, were still consistently behaving the same way. However, we observed that the measures of institutions were significant in explaining the level of youth employment in the communities. Significantly, the presence of a ward tribunal in the community has a high indicative probability that youth employment will improve in such community. The likelihood is as high as 0.995 and 0.986, respectively. When considering the number of meeting the ward tribunal holds in a month, the value was still significant. Since it is a logarithmic variable, the sign does not raise concerns.

In Table 5, another interesting observation is that the indirect effect of these measures of institutions was essential in enhancing the presence and effect of land deal in the community on youth employment. At least, it can be verified that in communities where there is land deal and ward tribunal, the chances of youth unemployment will be marginally lower. Plausibly, such communities have the chances of enhancing the youth employment by 4.9%. It is important to state that the measure of employment runs from 0 (not worked before) to 1 (worked in the past seven days). Therefore, a positive coefficient indicates that when land deals occur, and the community has a ward tribunal, then the resultant effect on youth will be tending towards more employment.

The mechanism through which this effect happens is that cases of disillusioned indigenous community members will be effectively controlled through the legal framework of lodging complaints and security of rights. More so, in such communities, contracts that bind land investors and the communities can be effectively enforced through the legal process that reduces the incidence of opportunistic behaviour that may likely arise from any of the party. The presence of the ward tribunal will enforce the contractual agreement between the community and the land investors. Acemoglu and Robinson (2012) pointed this out in their text on why nations fail that countries (as well as communities) with an efficient legal system will witness some levels of prosperity and the incidence of poverty will be reduced. More so, such territory will have the power to enforce the system that will create such wealth.

Table 6 Baseline regression inclusive of social stability indicators

	1	2	3	4	5	6
Education	1.967**	2.019**	1.973***	1.990***	2.034**	1.916***
	(0.033)	(0.034)	(0.072)	(0.077)	(0.037)	(0.089)
Health condition	15.694*	15.208*	12.006*	12.879*	15.165*	11.734*
	(0.000)	(0.000)	(0.000)	(0.000)	(0.000)	(0.000)
Sex	−1.122**	−1.084***	−1.117	−1.079	−1.060***	−0.979
	(0.046)	(0.058)	(0.123)	(0.132)	(0.068)	(0.120)
Age	0.174*	0.176*	0.240**	0.237*	0.182*	0.224*
	(0.001)	(0.001)	(0.011)	(0.001)	(0.000)	(0.000)
Land deal	−0.515		−0.449			
	(0.360)		(0.482)			
Vigilante	0.434***	0.444***				
	(0.054)	(0.055)				
Violent attacks			0.213	0.185		
			(0.446)	(0.492)		
Vigilante × Land deal					0.058***	
					(0.090)	
Violent attacks × Land deal						−0.007***
						(0.097)
Pseudo	0.244	0.236	0.288	0.284	0.234	0.277
Prob. value	0.000	0.000	0.000	0.000	0.000	0.000
Log likelihood	−47.001	−47.452	−36.464	−36.718	−47.600	−37.069

Note The variable 'Violent Attacks' is a count variable and was logged. The logarithm value was used in the regression analysis in columns (3, 4 and 6). *, ** and ***: significant at 1, 5 and 10%, respectively
Source Authors'

4.3.3 Social Stability of the Community

The third institutional framework, we consider is the social stability of the community. We included the following variables two variables—presence of social vigilante group and the number of violent attacks in the past month—as a measure of social stability for robustness checks. The main intuition is that a community with social vigilante groups will experience relative stability compared to other communities that only leverage on the police presence. This is tenable especially in African communities where this vigilante group use 'spiritual powers' and instil some *ruthless* judgement on transgressors. The other variable 'number of killings in the community' was included following rational expectation that a community with increased killings is an indicator of some form of social instability.

The pictorial description of the youths' employment situation in communities with and without vigilante groups is described in Fig. 5 (in the Appendix). The Figure shows a marked difference between the rates of youth employment situation in the two groups of communities. The youth in communities with relative social stability will experience better chances of being employed than their contemporaries in other communities. However, we move further to confirm this situation using the output from the logistic regression that is presented in Table 6.

From Table 6, we observed that the variable 'vigilante' was positive and significant in columns 1 and 2, where it was tested in the model that included and excluded the effect of land deals. The sign and significant results of this variable show that in communities with social stability, the chances of youth unemployment reduces; put differently, the chances of youth employment increases in communities where there is likely to be social stability as enforced by the vigilante group. This likelihood is within the range of 0.434 and 0.444 in columns 1 and 2. This is not surprising since such communities will be attractive to investors and their cost of investment will be drastically reduced. By the cost of investment we mean associative cost to investment like insurance premium, output losses, investment damages and security cost (Bandyopadhyay et al. 2014). Thus, in the case of the reduced cost of investment due to social stability, investors can extend their social responsibility benevolence to utilizing the services of some of the indigenous groups—including the youth. This result confirms the findings from the outlook in Fig. 3.

The variable 'violent attacks' was not significant in columns 3 and 4 of Table 6. However, when considering the signs that are displayed by the interactive variable (violent attack and land deal) in column 6, we note that communities with LALIs and for which violent attack is increasing will likely increase the incidence of youth unemployment. The negative sign of the variable suggests that in communities where there are land deals and an increase in violent attacks, the likelihood that the respondent will indicate that they have not worked for pay in the past seven days will increase by 0.007.

Although this magnitude is marginal, the escalating effect will be higher when considering that youths who are not gainfully employed can participate in intensifying the violent attacks.

The interactive variable between the presence of vigilante and land deals (i.e. Vigilante × Land Deal) was positive; this suggest that the chances of youth employment improving will be higher for communities that witness land deals and vigilante group are present to ensure social stability. Apart from the reduction of cost of investment, social instability increases the risk of investment losses, which deters land investors from extending their benevolent social responsibilities to the host communities. In extreme cases, such community ends up losing the land investors and the vicious cycle of unemployment will likely continue.

4.3.4 Local Capacity of Community Leaders

We present the effect of the capacity of the community leader on the rate of youth employment in the respective community. The quality of the community leader was measured using their highest educational qualification and the tenure in office as a community leader. In Fig. 6 (in the Appendix), a pictorial overview was highlighted where the rate of youth employment was matched with the educational qualification of the community leader. This exercise was aimed at understanding if there is a divergence between the educational qualification of the community leader and the rate of youth employment. From the Figure, it is understandable that the community with the highest rate of youth employment is the community with a leader that has a diploma degree as the highest degree obtained. Although, we can also perceive that most of the communities were led by individuals with low educational attainment; the general overview suggests that youth employment will likely improve in communities where the leaders have higher educational attainment. This claim is subsequently examined in the logistic regression and reported in Table 7.

Looking at the variables of interest, we confirmed from column 1 and 2 that the educational attainment of the community leader significantly matters in defining the incidence of youth employment in the particular community with or without LALIs. The literature argues that the educational attainment of the leader matters in defining the quality of their decision in solving confronting problems (Osabuohien and Efobi 2013; Efobi 2015). In the case of an indigenous community—like in our sample—the educational attainment will enhance the negotiation process between the leaders and the land investors, which will be reflected in the benefit derivable by indigenes. Of course, there is a caveat in this case and that is; this claim is only obtainable in communities where individuals are not involved in the sale of land but the community—perhaps represented by the community leaders—are the ones involved in the negotiation process (Nolte 2014; Osabuohien et al. 2015).

Irrespective of the fact that the leader's educational attainment is significant; the tenure of the leader in the position of community leadership matters also. The outlook from Table 8 (columns 3 and 4) suggest that the longer

Table 7 Baseline regression, inclusive of quality of community leader

	1	2	3	4	5	6
Education	1.922*	1.979*	1.810**	1.859**	1.902**	1.850**
	(0.010)	(0.010)	(0.017)	(0.016)	(0.014)	(0.017)
Health condition	16.852*	16.733*	−1.810*	15.343*	15.350*	15.347*
	(0.000)	(0.000)	(0.000)	(0.000)	(0.000)	(0.000)
Sex	−0.881***	−0.871***	−0.844***	−0.845***	−0.900***	−0.843***
	(0.089)	(0.094)	(0.090)	(0.091)	(0.077)	(0.093)
Age	0.176*	0.177*	0.165*	0.166*	0.168*	0.167*
	(0.000)	(0.000)	(0.000)	(0.000)	(0.000)	(0.000)
Land deal	−0.367		−0.226			
	(0.465)		(0.646)			
Education of leader	0.367***	0.338**				
	(0.075)	(0.022)				
Tenure of leader			−0.008***	−0.007***		
			(0.069)	(0.076)		
Education of leader × Land deal					0.005***	
					(0.097)	
Tenure of leader × Land deal						−0.011***
						(0.086)
Pseudo	0.251	0.247	0.233	0.231	0.238	0.231
Prob. value	0.000	0.000	0.000	0.000	0.000	0.000
Log likelihood	−56.784	−57.057	−59.682	−59.792	−57.760	−59.794

Note The superscripts *, ** and *** implies significant at 1, 5 and 10%, respectively
Source Authors'

Table 8. Sensitivity checks (regression inclusive of only rural sample)

	1	2	3	4	5	6	7	8
Education	1.303	2.221	1.488	1.357	1.814	1.454	1.610***	1.511
	(0.249)	(0.341)	(0.146)	(0.175)	(0.187)	(0.421)	(0.100)	(0.144)
Health condition	16.452*	16.840*	15.520*	16.400*	14.835*	12.243*	15.561*	15.518*
	(0.000)	(0.000)	(0.000)	(0.000)	(0.000)	(0.000)	(0.000)	(0.000)
Sex	−0.596	−0.944	−0.264	−0.175	−0.482	−0.460	−0.419	−0.271
	(0.322)	(0.316)	(0.657)	(0.769)	(0.467)	(0.518)	(0.488)	(0.644)
Age	0.130*	0.147**	0.142*	0.129*	0.140*	0.199*	0.134*	0.142*
	(0.006)	(0.034)	(0.002)	(0.007)	(0.007)	(0.003)	(0.005)	(0.003)
NSA1_deal	0.069***							
	(0.092)							
NSA2_deal		0.077						
		(0.461)						
Institution1*Land_Deal			0.074***					
			(0.090)					
Institution2*Land_Deal				−0.177**				
				(0.049)				
Vigilante × Land deal					0.266***			
					(0.067)			
Violent Attacks × Land deal						−0.063***		
						(0.074)		
Education of leader × Land deal							0.020***	
							(0.091)	
Tenure of leader × Land deal								−0.001***
								(0.090)
Pseudo	0.178		0.190	0.171	0.185	0.238	0.188	0.189
Prob. value	0.000		0.000	0.000	0.000	0.000	0.000	0.000
Log likelihood	−34.623	38.436	38.436	−37.029	−30.930	−24.161	−37.091	−38.444

Note The variable 'Violent Attacks' is a count variable and was logged. *, **, and ***: significant at 1, 5 and 10%

Source Authors'

the tenure of a community leader, the lower the chances of youth enjoying the benefits of employment. In this case, we borrow intuition from the political economy literature, which induces that the longer a leader—be it, community or otherwise—stays in office, the more corrupt they become. This is especially the case in the African context, where longer tenure makes the leader become bureaucratically powerful and can expropriate public resources for private gains (Jo-Ansie 2007; Efobi 2015). Therefore, we can infer that the negative relationship between this variable and youth employment implies that the community leader that is in office longer will likely become self-seeking and pursue self-interest goals as against the community goals. This includes accepting resources from the land investors and not focusing on ensuring that the land investors will deliver on the contractual agreement with the community.

In column 6 of Table 8, there are chances of youth employment reducing in communities where there is the incidence of land deals and an increasing tenure of the community leader. Of course, the claim from the political economy literature suffices. In the case of the education of the community leader, the interactive variable (Education of Leader × land Deal) suggest that the chances of improving incidence of youth employment increases in communities where there are land deals and the community leaders have higher educational attainment.

4.4 Some Robustness Checks

To establish the consistency of our results, especially the sign of the variables, we conducted two main robustness checks. The first check was the re-estimation of our model, including the variables that define institution with only rural sample.

Since, this is a check on the consistency of our variables of interest; we will consider only the model that includes the interactive variables. The essence of this robustness is to ensure that our result is not being informed by the mixed locality of the respondents included in the sample. Possibly, the behaviour of the variables may likely differ depending on the locality of the respondents. An urban resident may not be considering the effectiveness of vigilante group or traditional chief; however, a rural dweller does. Therefore, the result of the re-estimated model is presented in Table 8. From Table 8, it can be ascertained that the signs of the variables remained consistent. More so, the significant values were somewhat consistent in most of the columns.

The second robustness check is to re-estimate the baseline model using the TOBIT estimation technique. The Tobit regression is suitable for estimating models with truncated explained variable. In the case of this study, the explained variable is measured between two alternatives: either the respondent has worked for pay in the past seven days (right censored) or not (left censored). Therefore, any response that is not related to any of these

Table 9 Sensitivity checks (regression using TOBIT technique)

	1	2	3	4	5	6	7	8
Education	1.176*	1.619**	1.296*	1.332*	1.183*	0.960*	1.287*	1.286*
	(0.001)	(0.012)	(0.001)	(0.000)	(0.005)	(0.022)	(0.000)	(0.000)
Health condition	0.366	1.077	0.198	0.395	−0.232	−0.937	0.332	0.223
	(0.408)	(0.144)	(0.671)	(0.374)	(0.714)	(0.190)	(0.480)	(0.618)
Sex	−0.760*	−1.021**	−0.713*	−0.669**	−0.702**	−0.422	−0.744**	−0.706*
	(0.004)	(0.013)	(0.008)	(0.014)	(0.022)	(0.138)	(0.004)	(0.007)
Age	0.061*	0.068**	0.073*	0.068*	0.091*	0.107*	0.071*	0.072*
	(0.007)	(0.037)	(0.001)	(0.002)	(0.000)	(0.000)	(0.001)	(0.001)
NSA1_deal	0.063***							
	(0.086)							
NSA2_deal		−0.020						
		(0.728)						
Institution1 × Land_Deal			0.077***					
			(0.083)					
Institution2 × Land_Deal				−0.177				
				(0.475)				
Vigilante × Land deal					0.009			
					(0.979)			
Violent attacks × Land deal						−0.026		
						(0.760)		
Education of Leader × Land deal							0.043***	
							(0.066)	
Tenure of Leader × Land deal								−0.011***
								(0.076)
Pseudo	4.99	2.52	6.140	5.510	4.400	6.440	6.550	6.510
Prob. value	0.000	0.0472	0.000	0.000	0.001	0.000	0.000	0.000

Note The variable 'Violent Attacks' is a count variable and was logged. *, ** and ***: significant at 1, 5 and 10%
Source Authors'

alternatives are entirely omitted and not accounted for and this will lead to possible truncation of the variable. The result of the Tobit model is presented in Table 9 and they are largely consistent with the results discussed above.

5 Conclusion

This study made efforts to explore the role of local capacity and institutions in translating the presence of LALIs in African communities—into employment opportunities for the youth using Tanzania case study. The scope of this study has an important contribution to the current literature due to the fact that; to the best of our knowledge, limited analysis has been done relating youth unemployment to the presence of LALIs with empirical emphasis on local capacity and institutions. This is imperative as the process of strengthening institutions is complementary to the development policy agenda of developing countries.

The findings from this study are summarized as follows: the presence of NSAs, the presence of community tribunals and the frequency of their meetings, the social stability in terms of security and reduction in social violence and the education attainment level of community leaders, are important factors that can enhance the host community benefiting from the presence of land investors through their social responsibility for instance granting employment to the youths. The result from the estimations also discourages longer tenures of the community leaders. This is mainly because the longer they are in power the higher the possibility that they become motivated by self-interest and will likely become corrupt.

The policy implication from this study is that there is a need to strengthen and ensure functional institutions including effective NSAs are present in host communities with land investors. This is because they can propel land investors to extend their responsibilities towards the gainful employment of youths in their host communities. These NSAs can utilize the combined strength of its members in pushing the investors to deliver on the contractual agreement including employment creation. More so, communities should be encouraged to set up tribunals that meet frequently if they must enhance their benefit from the presence of land investors. In addition, social stability and security should be maintained in host communities to attract and maintain LALIs. This is because investors will be expending more resources to maintain and secure their investments in communities where there are occurrences of instability and in doing so, they have limited resources and incentives to extend employment to youths in the host community. Finally, the leadership capacity in the host community is an important factor to consider. The education level of the community leaders is critical and community leaders should be discouraged from occupying power for a long period. If this is not possible due to informal rules that may not easily be altered, then mechanisms should be in place to ensure that the leaders do not become corrupt and pursue self-motivated agendas; rather than ensuring that investors become committed to the welfare of the community members.

For future research in this area, it will be interesting to examine the subject matter using different approach particularly within the framework of impact evaluation to have a deeper and a more comparative influence of LALIs on employment not only in Tanzania and East Africa but in other African countries where the occurrence of LALIs are also notable such as Ethiopia and compare with LALIs outcome in other continents. It is also important to complement this study with some case studies as well as considering time dimensions with a view of capturing deeper realities of LALIs-employment nexus.

Acknowledgements The first author acknowledges the Fellowship Award from Alexander von Humboldt Foundation [Ref: 3.4-NGA/1147508]. The study draws some insights from the research project funded by the African Growth and Development Policy Modelling Consortium (AGRODEP)/International Food Policy Research Institute (IFPRI), under the Innovative Research Grant [Ref: 2015X192. GIT]. The earlier versions of the paper have been presented in conferences, notably: *UNU-WIDER Development Conference on Transforming Economies for Better Jobs*, Bangkok, Thailand, September 2019; and *Conference on Land Policy in Africa* organized by African Union Commission, United Nations Economic Commission for Africa & African Development Bank, Addis Ababa, Ethiopia, November 2017). The views expressed are those of the authors.

Appendix

See Figs. 3, 4, 5, and 6.

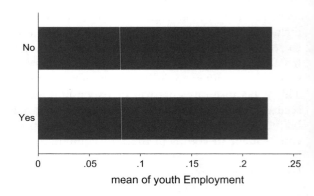

Fig. 3 Farmers' association and youth employment

Fig. 4 Ward tribunal and youth employment

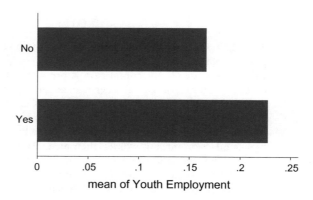

Fig. 5 Civilian vigilante group and youth employment

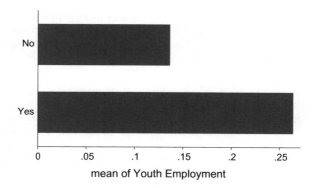

Fig. 6 Educational qualification of community leader and youth employment

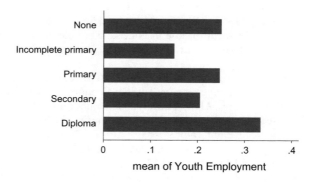

Notes

1. The Table showing the location, names of the investors, country of origin and purpose of the investment is not reported for space.
2. In Tanzania, gender discrimination is prevalent. The country ranks 125th out of 155 countries on the Gender-related Development Index for 2009. While Tanzania is on track to reach the MDG target on gender, high dropout rates for girls and gender parity in secondary and tertiary education remain a concern. Also, maternal mortality remains high and the burden of HIV is still heavy, with higher infection rates in women than men. Women also face challenges in economic empowerment and access to decision-making at all levels (Osabuohien et al. 2019). Women continue to be more likely than men to be poor and illiterate, to be subject to gender-based violence and usually have less access than men to medical care, property ownership, credit, training and employment (United Nations 2011).
3. For the sake of measurement and in congruency with the data in LSMS_ISA, 'youth unemployment' is measured using the mirror image of 'youth employment'. This is not out of context since increasing 'youth employment' means reducing 'youth unemployment' as *they are different sides of the same coin*.

References

Abdallah, J., Engstrom, L., Havnevik, K., & Solomonsson, L. (2014). Large-scale land acquisition in Tanzania: A critical analysis of practices and dynamics. In M. Kaag & N. Zoomers (Eds.), *The global land grab: Beyond the hype* (pp. 36–53). London and New York: Zed Books and Fernwood Publishers.

Acemoglu, D., & Johnson, S. (2005). Unbundling institutions. *Journal of Political Economy, 113*(5), 949–995.

Acemoglu, D., & Robinson, J. A. (2012). *Why nations fail: The origins of power, prosperity and poverty*. New York: Crown Publishers.

Afolayan, O. T., Okodua, H., Matthew, O., & Osabohien, R. (2019). Reducing unemployment malaise in Nigeria: The role of electricity consumption and human capital development. *International Journal of Energy Economics and Policy, 9*(4), 63–73.

African Development Bank-AfDB. (2014). *Gender, poverty and environmental indicators of African countries*. Tunisia: Economic and Social Statistics Division/Statistics Department, ADB. Retrieved September 12, 2018, from http://www.afdb.org/fileadmin/uploads/afdb/Documents/Publications/Gender__Poverty_and_Environmental_Indicators_on_African_Countries_2014.pdf.

African Development Bank-AfDB. (2018). *African economic outlook: Tanzania*. Retrieved March 11, 2018, from http://www.africaneconomicoutlook.org/fileadmin/uploads/aeo/PDF/Tanzania%20Full%20PDF%20Country%20Note.pdf.

African Union. (2006). *African Youth Charter*. Retrieved September 12, 2014, from http://africa-youth.org/sites/default/files/african_youth_charter.pdf.

Anseeuw, W., Lay, J., Messerli, P., Giger, M., & Taylor, M. (2013). Creating a public tool to assess and promote transparency in global land deals: The experience of the Land Matrix. *The Journal of Peasant Studies, 40*(3), 521–530.

Anyanwu, J. C. (2014). Does Intra-African trade reduce youth unemployment in Africa? *African Development Review, 26*(2), 286–309.

Arezki, R., Deininger, K., & Selod, H. (2012). Global land rush. *Finance and Development, 49*(1), 46–49.

Ariyo, J. A., & Mortimore, M. (2012). Youth farming and Nigeria's development dilemma: The Shonga experiment. *IDS Bulletin, 43*(6), 58–66.

Asiedu, E. (2004). The determinants of employment of affiliates of U.S. multinational enterprises in Africa. *Development Policy Review, 22*(4), 371–379.

Asiedu, E. (2006). Foreign direct investment in Africa: The role of natural resources, market size, government policy, institutions and political stability. *World Economy, 29*(1), 63–72.

Asiedu, E., Jin, Y., & Kanyama, I. (2011). *The impact of HIV/AIDS on foreign direct investment in developing countries*. University of Kansas, mimeo. Retrieved September 12, 2014, from http://www.business.uwa.edu.au/__data/assets/pdf_file/0004/1655446/JIN-ADEW2011.pdf.

Bandyopadhyay, S., Sandler, T., & Younas, J. (2014). Foreign direct investment, aid, and terrorism. *Oxford Economic Papers, 66*(1), 25–50.

Bellows, J., & Miguel, E. (2009). War and local collective action in Sierra Leone. *Journal of Public Economics, 93*(11–12), 1144–1157.

Bluwstein, J., Lund, J. F., Askew, K., Stein, H., Noe, C., Odgaard, R., & Engström, L. (2018). Between dependence and deprivation: The interlocking nature of land alienation in Tanzania. *Journal of Agrarian Change, 18*(4), 806–830.

Cassim, A., & Oosthuizen, M. (2014). *The state of youth unemployment in South Africa*. Retrieved November 2, 2018, from https://www.brookings.edu/blog/africa-in-focus/2014/08/15/the-state-of-youth-unemployment-in-south-africa/.

Central Intelligence Agency-CIA. (2018). *The World Factbook: Tanzania*. Retrieved June 21, 2018, from https://www.cia.gov/library/publications/resources/the-world-factbook/geos/tz.html.

Cotula, L., Vermeulen, S., Leonard, R., & Keeley, J. (2009). *Land grab or development opportunity? Agricultural investment and international land deals in Africa*. London/Rome: IIED/FAO/IFAD.

Deininger, K., Byerlee, D., Lindsay, J., Norton, A., Selod, H., & Stickler, M. (2011). *Rising global interest in Farmland*. Washington, DC: The World Bank.

Doss, C., Meinzen-Dick, R., & Bomuhangi, A. (2014). Who owns the land? Perspectives from rural Ugandans and implications for large-scale land acquisitions. *Feminist Economics, 20*(1), 76–100.

Efobi, U. (2015). Politicians' attributes and institutional quality in Africa: A focus on corruption. *Journal of Economic Issues, 49*(3), 787–813.

Ejemeyovwi, J. O., Osabuohien, E. S., & Osabohien, R. (2018). ICT investments, human capital development and institutions in ECOWAS. *International Journal of Economics and Business Research, 15*(4), 463–474.

Elumelu, A. (2017). *Youth unemployment is Africa's greatest challenge*. Retrieved December 21, 2018, from https://africanbusinessmagazine.com/interviews/youth-unemployment-africas-greatest-challenge-says-tony-elumelu/.

Engström, L., & Hajdu, F. (2019). Conjuring 'Win-World'—Resilient development narratives in a large-scale agro-investment in Tanzania. *The Journal of Development Studies, 55*(6), 1201–1220. https://doi.org/10.1080/00220388.2018.1438599.

George, T., Olayiwola, W. K., Adewole, M. A., & Osabouhien, E. S. (2013). Effective service delivery of Nigeria's public primary education: Role of non-state actors. *Journal of African Development, 15*(1), 221–245.

George, T., Olokoyo, F., Osabuohien, E., Efobi, U., & Beecroft, I. (2015). Women's access to land and economic empowerment in selected Nigerian communities. In N. Andrews, E. N. Khalema, & N. T. Assie-Lumumba (Eds.), *Millennium Development Goals (MDGs) in retrospect—Africa's development beyond 2015* (pp. 45–61). Geneva: Springer International Publishing. https://doi.org/10.1007/978-3-319-16166-2_4.

Hilson, G., & Osei, L. (2014). Tackling youth unemployment in sub-Saharan Africa: Is there a role for artisanal and small-scale mining? *Futures, 62,* 83–94.

Ighobor, K. (2017). *Africa's jobless youth cast a shadow over economic growth.* Africa Renewal Special Edition on Youth 2017. Retrieved November 21, from https://www.un.org/africarenewal/magazine/special-edition-youth-2017/africas-jobless-youth-cast-shadow-over-economic-growth.

Jo-Ansie, V. W. (2007). Political leaders in Africa: Presidents, patrons and profiteers? African Centre for the Constructive Resolution of Disputes (ACCORD). *Occasional Paper Series, 2*(1), 1–38.

La Porta, R., Lopez-De-Silanes, F., Shleifer, A., & Vishny, R. (1999). The quality of government. *Journal of Law, Economics and Organisation, 15,* 222–279.

Land Matrix Global Observatory. (2017). *Global map of investments.* Retrieved October 2017, from http://landmatrix.org/en/get-the-idea/global-map-investments/.

Massay, G. E. (2015). Compensating landholders in Tanzania: The law and the practice. In E. Osabuohien (Ed.), *Handbook of research on in-country determinants and implications of foreign land acquisitions* (pp. 374–388). Hershey, PA: Business Science Reference.

Mugabi, C. (2013). *Challenges facing land ownership in rural Tanzania: What needs to be done? Economic and Social Research Foundation (ESRC)* (Policy Paper No. 4/2013).

Ncube, M. (2012). Speech Presented at the African Development Bank's Seminar on Youth Employment, Lusaka, Zambia.

Nolte, K. (2014). Large-scale agricultural investments under poor land governance in Zambia. *Land Use Policy, 38,* 698–706.

North, D. C. (1990). Institutions. *Journal of Economic Perspectives, 5*(1), 97–112.

Osabohien, R. (2018). Contributing to agricultural mix: Analysis of the living standard measurement study—Integrated survey on agriculture dataset. *Data in Brief, 20,* 96–100.

Osabohien, R., Osabuohien, E., & Urhie, E. (2018). Food security, institutional framework and technology: Examining the nexus in Nigeria using ARDL approach. *Current Nutrition & Food Science, 14*(2), 154–163.

Osabuohien, E. S. (2014). Large-scale agricultural land investments and local institutions in Africa: The Nigerian case. *Land Use Policy, 39,* 155–165.

Osabuohien, E. S., & Efobi, U. (2013). Africa's money in Africa. *South African Journal of Economics, 81*(2), 291–306.

Osabuohien, E. S., Efobi, U. R., Herrmann, R., & Gitau, C. M. (2019). Female labor outcomes and large-scale agricultural land investments: Macro-micro evidence from Tanzania. *Land Use Policy, 82,* 716–728. https://doi.org/10.1016/j.landusepol.2019.01.005.

Osabuohien, E. S., Gitau, C. M., Efobi, U., & Bruentrup, M. (2015). Agents and implications of foreign land deals in East African community: The case of Uganda. In E. Osabuohien (Ed.), *Handbook of research on in-country determinants and implications of foreign land acquisitions* (pp. 263–286). Hershey, PA: Business Science Reference.

Osabuohien, E. S., Okorie, U., & Osabohien, R. (2018). Rice production and processing in Ogun State, Nigeria: Qualitative Insights from farmers' association. In E. Obayelu (Ed.), *Food systems sustainability and environmental policies in modern economics* (pp. 188–216). Hershey, PA: IGI Global.

Otchia, C. S. (2015). Mining-based growth and productive transformation in the Democratic Republic of Congo: What can an African lion learn from an Asian tiger? *Resources Policy, 45*(September), 227–238.

Simbarashe, M. (2012, June 3, Sunday). Land: Efforts needed to end conflicts between farmers and Cattle elders.' *Tanzania Daily News.* http://allafrica.com/stories/201206041179.html.

Sulle, E. (2017). Social differentiation and the politics of land: Sugar cane outgrowing in kilombero, Tanzania. *Journal of Southern African Studies, 43*(3), 517–533.

Timko, J. A. (2014). An analytical framework for assessing the impacts of Jatropha curcas on local livelihoods. In M. Bavinck, L. Pellegriniand, & E. Mostertpp (Eds.), *Conflicts over natural resources in the global south conceptual approaches* (pp. 174–191). London: CRC Press.

United Nations. (2011). *Gender.* Retrieved March 11, 2014, from http://tz.one.un.org/index.php/core-commitments/gender.

United Nations. (2015). *Youth population trends and sustainable development* (Population Facts, No. 2015/1).

Vindevogel, S., Coppens, K., De-Schryver, M., Loots, G., Broekaert, E., & Derluyn, I. (2013). Beyond child soldiering: The interference of daily living conditions in former child soldiers' longer term psychosocial well-being in northern Uganda. *Global Public Health: An International Journal for Research, Policy and Practice, 8*(5), 485–503.

Local Politics of Land Acquisitions for Foreign and Domestic Investments in Tanzania

Godfrey Eliseus Massay

1 Introduction

Large-scale land acquisitions have received considerable attention in recent times, especially after the 2007/2008 financial and economic crises when the perception of land regarding its values for growing food crops, feed-stocks, biofuels, and so on had a new and more profound identity (Osabuohien 2015). The scenario was amplified by the increasing oil price that resulted to the search for alternative sources, which lead to the bio-based materials, and the sale of certificates for reducing emissions (Cotula et al. 2009; Deininger and Byerlee 2011). Hence, it was not surprising to see the rising global demand for land in countries where land was perceived to be abundant. Many recipients of countries are in Sub-Saharan Africa and East and South Asia (Deininger and Byerlee 2011; Osabuohien 2014; Osabuohien et al. 2019).

There are a number of studies on the global determinants of large-scale land-based investments (Cotula et al. 2009; Moyo and Yeros 2011; Deininger and Byerlee 2011; Anseeuw et al. 2012; Cotula 2013) and few are those on the in-country determinants (Osabuohien 2015). This chapter contributes to further the discussions on the in-country determinants of the large-scale land-based investments using Tanzania as a case study. For instance, studies show that while most of the biofuels investments in Tanzania have been largely influenced by the global drivers, there were some pushes from within to facilitate such acquisitions (German Technical Cooperation [GTZ] 2005; Kamanga 2008; Sulle and Nelson 2009). Similarly, investments in the agricultural sector have not only been driven by global demands for food security,

---

G. E. Massay (✉)
Landesa, Dar es Salaam, Tanzania

but are also influenced by Tanzania's internal policies for green economy and commercial mechanization of agricultural sector such as the "kilimo kwanza" policy (the United Republic of Tanzania-URT 2009; Sulle 2015; Massay and Talemu 2014; Massay 2015). The kilimo kwanza policy has been the driver for commercial agricultural investments such as the Southern Agricultural Growth Corridor of Tanzania (SAGCOT), a multi-billion dolor project which targets a third of a country's landmass. Similarly, the recent industrialization policy of the current regime of Present Magufuli is also another driver of land acquisition as discussed in this study.

Land acquisition for investments purpose often have clear procedures stipulated by the laws governing land and investment in any country. In Tanzania, there are several laws governing the process of land acquisitions. However, the practice has shown that there are local politics that dominate the process which often varies between local and foreign investments. For instance, land acquisition for foreign investors is often facilitated by the State or its agents. It may also be supported by politicians on behalf of the State. This is what Cotula (2013) described as government facilitated land rush. As for the local investors, they are often on their own or using their connection with the local government to acquire land. This is what Cotula (2013) described as "land grabbing from below." Such politics have differentiated gender approaches and impacts and are viewed differently across communities and geographies.

Using two investments, one foreign and the other domestic, this chapter explores different approaches used in land acquisitions and the perceptions of communities toward such approaches in Chakenge Village of Kisarawe District in the Coastal Region of Tanzania. Although in both cases there is massive involvement of local politicians for the purpose of political rent-seeking, communities have viewed them differently. The involvement of politicians in the foreign investment was perceived negatively than the involvement of the same in the domestic one. Communities trust more, a domestic investor not because he is from their area but because they felt cheated by the foreign investor and thus cannot trust anything foreign.

Food insecurity is one of the impacts of large-scale land-based investments in most developing economies (Othiambo 2011) causing labor movement to non-agrarian activities (Moyo and Yeros 2011). The chapter presents some of the anecdotal evidence of food insecurity and labor movements and how the general national political economy in the last decade has shaped politics of land acquisitions at the local village level. Following this introductory part, the chapter has six other sections. A section on the context of investment is next after detailing the general picture of agricultural investments in Tanzania. It is followed by the methodology section which highlights the procedural approaches employed by the author. This is followed by land acquisition process which gives a general overview of land acquisition in Tanzania. A case of two companies which discusses the profile and land acquisition issues of the two companies comes afterward. Observations and further discussions on key issues are enunciated, while the last part is the conclusion that sums up the discussion and pinpointing some research gaps.

2 Context of Investment

The Government of Tanzania, like many governments, seems to believe that investment could provide solutions to its economic problems. In this regard, the government created a favorable environment for foreign direct investment (FDI) and created institutions to promote, coordinate, and facilitate investment into Tanzania, such as the Tanzania Investment Centre (TIC) and the Export Processing Zones Authority (EPZA). A core function of TIC, for example, includes "to identify investment sites, estates, or land together with associated facilities of any sites, estates, or land for the purposes of investors and investments in general."[1] On the other hand, the EPZA is responsible for land acquisition and putting in place all necessary infrastructure for investors to start business. Such institutions work diligently to ensure investors are attracted to Tanzania. The study briefly discusses the investments in agriculture for food production, agro-fuels, and agro-forestry with a view to providing an understanding of the extent to which land-based investments in Tanzania in the context of the existing policy and legal framework. However, unlike other sectors, the government has allowed investments in biofuels to reduce Emission from Deforestation and Forest Degradation (REDD) schemes without creating a policy and legal framework to guide investment in these sectors.

2.1 Agriculture for Food Security

Investment in agriculture for food production is growing. The Rufiji River Basin, which represents about 20% of all Tanzanian land, and which is under the authority of the Rufiji Basin Development Cooperation (RUBADA),[2] is the area most coveted for investment in the agricultural sector. Tanzanian districts in which many agricultural land acquisitions deals have been reported in the last decade include Kisarawe, Bagamoyo, Rufiji, Morogoro Rural, and Kilombero.

Both internal and external forces drive the quest for food security in Tanzania. Internally, the government has created the Agricultural Sector Development Program (ASDP). Since 2003, this has been an agricultural transformation program from national to district level. Several international development partners joined hands with the government in support of agricultural sector development. Some of them include the Danish International Development Agency (DANIDA), Japanese International Cooperation Agency (JICA), the European Union (EU), and Irish Aid (IA). Others are the International Fund for Agricultural Development (IFAD), and the International Development Association (IDA). This was followed by the Kilimo

Kwanza (Agriculture First) initiative in 2009, which intends to develop large, medium, and small-scale farmers. Funds have been allocated through Tanzania Investment Bank, and farmers can access agricultural inputs. As part of implementing Kilimo Kwanza, Tanzania is developing the SAGCOT, an agricultural partnership investment project with an area amounting to 300,000 km^2, launched at the World Economic Forum Africa meeting in Dar es Salaam, in 2010. SAGCOT aims to increase agricultural productivity and food security and improve livelihoods in Tanzania. Other initiatives include the Alliance for Green Revolution in Africa (AGRA) and the Comprehensive Africa Agriculture Development Program (CAADP), whose stated objective is to emancipate small-scale farmers through research on the best agronomy, seed development, soil fertility, and commercialization of the agricultural sector. In 2011, the government produced a strategic Investment Blueprint for SAGCOT, to promote commercial farming in the areas known to be the granary of food production in Tanzania. Foreign investors are increasing in the country in search of good arable land and have been allocated thousands of hectares (Locher and Sulle 2013; Osabuohien et al. 2019). This might seriously affect small-scale farmers if an alternative strategy for the farmers is not adopted.

While plans such as the SAGCOT may reflect the government's commitment to transform the agricultural sector and, thus, contribute to realizing the National Strategy for Growth and Reduction of Poverty and the National Development Vision 2025, analysts are wondering whether the initiative will meet the objectives and be sustainable, given that many similar previous large-scale investments in groundnuts in Dodoma and wheat plantations in Hanang, or programs such as ASDP and CAADP, have mostly failed to meet the objective of changing the livelihoods of most Tanzanians. Statistics from the 2007 Household Budget Survey show that poverty remains widespread, especially in rural areas. Between 2000/01 and 2007, the proportion of Tanzanians unable to meet basic needs only marginally decreased, from 35.6 to 33.4%. In the same period, the incidence of poverty in rural areas decreased from 38.7 to 37.4, while in urban areas (excluding Dar es Salaam) it decreased from 25.8 to 24.1%.

The failure of the agricultural initiatives to achieve a significant impact on rural livelihoods could be attributed to many factors, but a close look at these initiatives shows that they are top-down projects and devoid of small-scale farmers' consultations (Cooksey 2012; Maghimbi et al. 2010).

2.2 Agriculture for Energy Security

Tanzania, like other countries around the world such as Malawi (Herrmann et al. 2018), ventured into the production of biofuels based on four main assumptions that have driven the global bioenergy industry. The first assumption is that bioenergy is a more economical and renewable alternative source of energy than fossil fuels; the second is that bioenergy can reduce carbon emissions; the third is that bioenergy provides countries with the prospect of being energy independent, by reducing or even cutting out dependence on imported fossil fuels; the forth is that bioenergy offers new avenues to farmers in developing countries to reduce poverty and improve their livelihoods (Sosovele 2010). After a study conducted by German Technical Cooperation (GTZ) in 2005 (GTZ 2005), the doors were opened to biofuel investment in Tanzania. As of 2011, more than 40 companies, mostly with foreign capital, were involved in biofuel development activities in Tanzania, while only a few and small local companies were engaged in such activities (Mshandete 2011). Yet, it has been shown that to realize poverty reduction and sustainable development programs through biofuel investment, engaging and promoting small-scale farmer productivity is indispensable (Arndt et al. 2010).

While investors have acquired, and others seeking to acquire, thousands of hectares of land for biofuels (Veit et al. 2012), and while awaiting a national policy on biofuels, the government formed the National Bioenergy Task Force (NBTF) to prepare biofuels guidelines as an interim measure (ActionAid 2009). The guidelines, released in 2010, provide general statements with no binding force, enforcement mechanism, and legal teeth. The wave of investors in the biofuels sector scared the government and it suspended new biofuel development until appropriate policies, regulatory frameworks, and laws are in place to guide the process (Sulle and Nelson 2009). In September 2012, the government issued the first draft of the National Liquid Biofuel Policy for public comments, but the policy is still in its draft form.

Several studies have explored issues related to biofuel investment in Tanzania. For example, Mshandete (2011) examines players in biofuels projects and their roles, value chains, social-economic and environmental impacts, tenure issues, food security, sustainability, research and development. Evidence shows that the role of the state in facilitating land deals is higher than in enforcing the terms on the deals. For instance, state agencies more often assist investors to obtain land, mobilize villagers to give land to investors, and draft contract terms or Memoranda of Understandings (MoUs) than make public all the contract terms and enforce the obligations made in such deals (Kweka 2012).

Poverty and illiteracy in local communities have been used to the advantage of the local elites, politicians, and investors in negotiating land deals (HAKIARDHI 2011b; ActionAid 2011). In some land deals (for example, Bagamoyo and Rufiji), in the process of the negotiations meals (rice meat) and bribes (giving tips) were reportedly given to the village leaders (Massay 2017). In Songea, an investor offered an allowance of two thousand shillings to any villager to attend the village assembly as a consideration to approve his request for land (HAKIARDHI 2012). This is not surprising, given the high level of poverty in rural areas.

Studies show that politicians and district officials have been instrumental in land acquisitions for biofuels companies such as Sunbiofuels in Kisarawe, African Green Oil in Rufiji, and BioShape in Kilwa, but the same state has given people a cold shoulder when investors fail to deliver the pledged benefits (ActionAid 2011; HAKIARDHI 2011a; Veit et al. 2012). This casts a shadow of doubt as to whether their active participation in the land acquisition process is really for the "public interest." Moreover, government agency interference has created fear among villagers and their leaders, but it has also made villagers and leaders trust the government officials and politicians who they know best when giving land for investment. There is evidence that negotiations for land deals, supervised by government agencies, have been done in a very short period (HAKIARDHI 2012). To date, much less land (641,179 hectares), has already been allocated for biofuel investments. Only 100,000 hectares have been fully secured by biofuel investors following the land acquisition procedures (Sulle and Nelson 2009; Mshandete 2011).

Most companies engaged in biofuel activities in Tanzania are foreign companies and because of the lack of a national policy on biofuels, there are increasing concerns both within and outside the country that the industry may not be of a lot of benefits to local people, or the nation at large. For example, the Evert Vermeer Foundation (van Teeffelen 2013) reveals that European biofuel companies operating in Tanzania have caused problems for rural communities; it calls for a change in EU biofuel policy to ensure that it is commensurate with country development objectives (including those of Tanzania), minimizes the likelihood of food insecurity, and ensures people's land rights. This is especially important as many European companies invest in Tanzania because of EU support for Tanzania's biofuel industry (van Teeffelen 2013).

2.3 *Forest Plantations for Carbon Market*

Forest plantation investments are new in Tanzania, but agro-forestry investors are looking forward to using the opportunities of the Clean Development Mechanism (CDM), as provided in the United Nations Framework for Climate Change Convention (UNFCCC), of 1992.[3] Tanzania is a signatory to the UNFCCC and the Kyoto Protocol—two international legal instruments that provide a framework for industrialized countries to incentivize developing countries to conserve forests to increase carbon stock, which absorbs carbon dioxide and other greenhouse gases (GHG) from the atmosphere.

Tanzania, with over 33.5 million hectares of forestry reserves and a sizable rural land under forest cover, formulated a National Climate Change Strategy in 2012, which delineates strategic interventions to guarantee that the communities and the nation at large benefit from the global initiatives (for example, UNFCCC) to mitigate the effects of climate change (URT 2012). Climate change mitigation and adaptation programs have been encouraged worldwide. More funds are channeled to programs that have climate change adaptation or mitigation objectives, and funding proposals sent to donor agencies or development partners are only accepted if they include climate change adaptation and mitigation objectives. The Carbon Market can now be accessed through REDD projects.[4] In Tanzania, foreign companies have acquired land for agro-forestry projects in Mufindi, Kilombero, and Kilolo districts. Projects are now extending to Muheza, Songea, and Njombe districts (see, Locher and Sulle 2013).

Deals around this kind of investment are hindered with lack of *consensus ad idem* principle in contract law—or "meeting of minds." That is, contracting parties must be on the same level of understanding of the terms of contract before entering into a contract. In Idete village, where a Norwegian based Green Resource Limited (GRL) entered into an agreement with Idete Village, in Mufindi district, Iringa region, the village chairperson, who signed the contract, confessed to the team of researchers that he did not understand the terms of the contract because the whole contract was written in English and not translated for him.

3 Methodology

3.1 Description of the Study Areas

Generally, the study area which is found Kisarawe District in the coastal zone of Tanzania is regarded as the poorest areas in the country (Sulle and Nelson 2009), with low income and low nutritional status. The main source of income for the population is natural resources mostly wood products (Sulle and Nelson 2009) and there is very limited alternative source of livelihood.

3.2 Sample

Interviews were conducted in Chakenge village located in Kisarawe District where two companies, one foreign and the other local have acquired land. The choice of Chakenge village was purposively to include because it has been involved with investment which acquired land. The selection of two companies which are case studies of this chapter is purposive and has been informed by number of factors. First, both companies are located in the same geographical area- in Kisarawe district. Two, although the two companies are different and have started land acquisition at different time, there are similarities to the greater extent on the role played by the local politicians in land acquisition process. Third, the two companies started their operations in response to the priority of the government. The first case study is responding to the Agriculture First "kilimo kwanza" of the former government regime of President Jakaya Kikwete and the other study responding to "industrialization" priority of the current regime of President John Magufuli.

The focus of this study is limited to the land acquisition process by looking at the participation and engagement process only. While the first case study is an old company which has moved further with operations, the second case

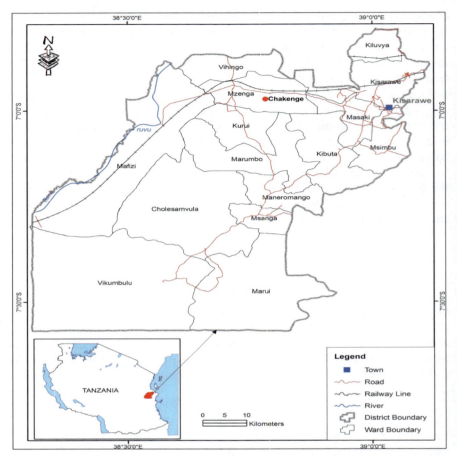

Fig. 1 Map of Tanzania showing the study area (*Source* Author's Construction)

study is fairly new and is in the final stages of land acquisition. Both cases are presenting interesting issues of local tactics used to lure communities to give away their land. The two cases are also validating findings from most literature on land grabs showing the role of state and local elites in facilitating land acquisitions (Fig. 1).

3.3 Analytical Approach

The chapter draws from interviews with villagers- men, women, youth, pastoralists, and officials from government institutions. A total of 6 focus group interviews were conducted with village leaders, women, women heads of households, youth, pastoralists, and district officials. Moreover, 10 interviews with officials in the government institutions and companies were conducted. Review of communications between state officials and villagers was also conducted. Furthermore, the chapter draws from secondary information obtained from the available literature on land acquisitions. Next section is the highlight of the process provided by the laws to acquire land for investment purpose in Tanzania.

4 Land Acquisition Procedure

Tanzania's land laws, the 1999 Land Act, and the 1999 Village Land Act (VLA), primarily govern land rights and land acquisitions. Under these laws, all land is public land vested in the President as trustee. The right to use land is called a right of occupancy. Customary rights of occupancy are recognized, whether or not formally registered and documented with the state, and are classified as Village Land.[5] Individual members or groups within the village may also acquire customary rights of occupancy in their name.[6] Village Land comprises about 70% of land in Tanzania and is managed by village councils, local governance bodies created under local government law,[7] and the village assembly, composed of all members of the community 18 years old and up. The District government and the Commissioner, as well as Minister in charge of land, do oversight.[8]

Under the VLA, any acquisition or allocation of village land to investors must be approved by the village council and village assembly.[9] In the case of foreign investors, the acquisition will involve the reclassification of Village Land to "General Land," which are lands under state control and management.[10] The President has the power to reclassify land from Village Land to General Land for investments of national interest.[11] Upon being reclassified, the government can either give the investor a granted right of occupancy or use rights called a derivative right. Once land is reclassified, it will remain General Land even if the project fails or is terminated for whatever reason, even though the villagers have yet to be fully compensated or are still waiting for benefits promised by the investor.[12] For Tanzanian nationals,[13] the reclassification of land is not necessary. The village council may grant rights of occupancy to non-residents or non-village organizations[14] subject to advise and guidance from the Land Commissioner or district officials, for up to 99 years, upon payment of a premium and annual rent.[15]

The procedural requirements for the transfer of Village Land to General Land include formal notice given by the Minister to the village; village meetings that include representatives of government and the investor to explain the project and its potential benefits; and opportunities to make representations to the Commissioner for any concerns which the village council and affected villagers may have. The village assembly approves the allocation of land to the investors up to 250 hectares, beyond which—as is usually the case—the Minister has final approval. Importantly, the VLA provides that no transfer shall be made until compensation, including type, amount, method and timing, has been agreed upon between the Commissioner and the village council and affected individual or group rights holders.[16] In practice, many foreign investors directly negotiate with the village, typically facilitated by a local broker or politician and the District government. Although the village council and village assembly approval are secured, they are *pro forma* (Sulle and Nelson 2009).

Village land may also be expropriated or compulsorily acquired for future allocation of derivative rights to investors.[17] An old law still in force, the 1967 Land Acquisition Act (LAA), also provides for compulsory acquisition of village land for "public purpose."[18] The LAA requires notice to the affected village and published in the Official Gazette, and payment of compensation to the village and affected residents, or to the court if there is dispute or disagreement. Several sectoral laws permit compulsory acquisition, including the 2010 Public–Private Partnership Act, for purposes of development, including agriculture, infrastructure, mining, natural resources, tourism, and energy; the 2013 Wildlife Act, for the creation of game reserves; and the 2010 Mining Act, for the operation of mining licenses. The provisions of the LAA, the Land Act, and VLA will govern compulsory acquisition under these laws.

5 A Tale of Two Companies

5.1 Company Profiles

Sunbiofuels: A British biodiesel company which acquired 8211 hectares of land from 11 villages[19] in Kisarawe District in 2006. In July 2009, Sunbiofuels started operations on the farms and employed about 750 workers. In July 2011, the company suspended its operation and about 700 workers lost their jobs. Thirty Degree East, a partnership between Mauritians (90% share) and Tanzanians (10% share) bought shares of Sunbiofuels on 5 September 2011, and registered with BRELA as the new owner in October 2011. At the end of 2013, Mtanga Farms Limited, a Tanzanian-owned cattle operation that has overlapping shareholders with Sunbiofuels had taken over the lease (Wise 2014). Communities have some grievances with the company for limiting access to some resources such as herbs, firewood and pasture, lack of transparency on the owner of the company, impact of the investment to the environment especially water sources, and failure to meet the promises.

Gagaja Contactors Limited: This is a local real estate company founded and registered in 1998 with its offices located in Dar es Salaam. It is well known as GI among the villagers in Chakenge village. Although the primary work of the company is construction of real estates and in civil engineering, in the last five years, the company has been acquiring land and develops its own real estates. It has already acquired a 200 acre land in Mhaga Village, surveyed land, sold plots to middle-income people, and constructed a health center for the village. The company is now in the final stages of acquiring 1700 hectares of land in Chakenge Village for the purpose of building medium and large-scale industries and as well as residential apartments for middle-income people. The managing and founding director of the company is now one of the councilors of Kisarawe District. Communities consider this company friendlier because it has met its promises and its owners are from their community, the process of land acquisition is also considered inclusive by the community.

6 Land Acquisitions

Village leaders and villagers in Chakenge village provided narrations of how their land was taken by Sunbiofuels. There were no discrepancies on both narratives. They all said that in the first meeting, it was the Member of Parliament of Kisarawe who came to their village assembly meeting and informed them of the investor and how his investments will help improve their lives. It was also stated that accepting the investor was the only chance left to develop; thus, other villages in Kisarawe have already accepted allocating land to the investor. The community members were told they would benefit from employment, improved roads, health, school, and water services which will all be developed by the investor. From what they perceived, it appeared to them that a decision to allocate land to the investor was already made and that they were obliged to endorse that decision.

The meeting with the Member of Parliament was followed by meetings with government officials from the land department which was mainly on landholders' identification, valuation, and survey of the land. In most of the meetings, villagers attended in numbers but men were the ones who asked questions. Villagers and their leaders did not get feedback on the exact size of their land which was taken by the investor and did not get the opportunity to meet with the investor during the land acquisition process. Only government officials and the Member of Parliament appeared and talked on behalf and for the investor. There was no any recorded memorandum of understanding or formal contract between the village council and the investor.

After being subjected to the process of land acquisition for three years, in January 2009 the village land was gazetted as general land and the title granted to the Tanzania Investment Center (TIC). In May 2009, the TIC issued a leasehold title to Sunbiofuels for 98 years (Tenga and Kironde 2012). The amount in the compensation schedule for the whole land in eleven villages was TZS 838,943,655. Out of this, land claimed by individuals was to the extent of TZS 261,234,785 and was paid in November 2008. The remaining balance TZS 577,708,870 was for bare land which nobody claimed (Massay and Talemu 2014; Bergius 2012). Kisarawe District council claimed the balance for bare land in 2009 but the Commissioner for lands, when contacted by the General Manager for Sunbiofuels for advice, warned Kisarawe District Council from claiming the money and insisted that the due process of law should be followed. The Commissioner for Lands, however, couldn't advise who is entitled to the balance for bare land (Massay 2015).

The information regarding unpaid compensation was made public through the Guardian Newspaper which stated on 15 July 2013, Kisarawe

District Council Officials would meet to receive a cheque for the remaining balance of compensation. It was also noted that the payment would be made in three phases starting on 15 July 2013. Reasons for the delay were noted to be "technical fault from the Ministry of Lands" and the "new investor overlooked the demands of the villagers." Sadly, villagers, not even the leaders of the task force formed to make a follow up of the compensation, were not invited to witness the handover of the cheque on 15 July 2013. The Guardian Newspaper of January 14, 2014 reported that Sunbiofuels had paid all compensation for bare land by December 2013. It further reported that villagers were demanding to be paid cash and not in kind that was proposed by Kisarawe District Council. The company did not pay compensation with interest as required by the law on the ground that "the delay was not caused by the company but the government of Tanzania" (Massay 2015).

Chakenge village received 47 million TZS as the compensation for bare land which was used to construct village office.[20] Still, it was not clear to both village leaders and villagers how the District council arrived at the amount given to them.

Gagaja Construction Limited also fondly known as Gagaja Industries (GI) started the process of land acquisition in Chakenge in 2016. The process started by a councilor for Kibuta Ward[21] who is also the owner of GI asked a councilor for Mzenga Ward where Chakenge village is located to assist in identifying potential land for his investments. Councilor for Mzenga knew that the only village with big size of land for investment in his region is Chakenge and so he discussed the matter the village chairperson for Chakenge. They both agreed to identify some famous and respectable elders in the village and discussed the issue with them. They then invited the councilor for Kibuta to present his company and discuss his business plan with elders. Elders felt honored and respected and they promised to do their best getting the land.

When the village assembly meeting was convened, it was the elders who presented the investor to villagers. Villagers felt respected and they approved elders to lead the process of land acquisition by identifying the land, resolving existing disputes and in negotiating compensation. A forested land which was previously used to gather fire woods, make charcoal, get thatched grasses, gather local fruits, was identified. It is approximately 1700 hector the same as the amount that investor needed. In the beginning, it was proposed that for every acre of land given to the investor, a landholder will be paid 1 million TZS and will retain a quarter of the land while the investor will take three-quarter of the land. This was later changed. It was agreed that one acre of land would be compensated with 1.5 million TZS.

Villagers considered this as the best deal because it was based on negotiation which was led by elders on their behalf. Currently, the District Council is reviewing the land deal and has put on halt next steps including compensation payment. Elders were annoyed by the decision of the district council to put on halt the land acquisition process. In one event, village elders waited for the District Commissioner who was scheduled to visit their village until 9 p.m. They met him and pleaded to make a quick decision on approving the investment.

When land officials and the head of the land department of Kisarawe district were asked about GI, they assured that the District Council was in the final stages of approving the investor. Regarding the conflict of interest, land officials said that the investor who by his political role is supposed to sit in the meetings which approve his request for land, would not be allowed to attend such meetings. They also highlighted that there were other Chinese investors who are in a joint venture with GI.

7 Some Observations and Further Discussions

In both cases, there is the involvement and influence of local politicians. In the case of Sunbiofuels, it was the Member of Parliament whereas in GI it was the councilor. However, the approach used by Sunbiofuel intimidated communities when government officials and a member of parliament dominated negotiation. Communities felt like they have no option but to accept the deal. On the other hand, Gl exuded some level of trust from communities when elders were used.

The local and foreign narratives distinguished both cases. According to communities, the GI is a local investor, someone from their region that they know who speaks their language, who has done good work in the neighboring village, and who appeared in the village assembly meetings and who is endorsed by respectable elders. On the other hand, Sunbiofuels is a foreign investor who failed, delayed their compensation, retrenched employees, never appeared before them, used experts and government officials, and who was defended by the government including their former member of the parliament. However, as shown, the community is unaware of the fact that behind GI there are Chinese investors. Thus, it is clear that the communities have learned from the failure and mistakes of the Sunbiofuel and the GI have also learned from the mistakes of the Sunbiofuels. This has informed the change of approaches and actions used in land acquisition by both communities and investor.

Although there is no evidence obtained from this study to substantiate this, both investments also show the existence of political rent-seeking in land acquisitions. The politicians who were involved have in one way or another gained from their involvement in the land acquisitions either financially or in furtherance of their political interests in their constituencies.

Both investments are also showing how national policies such as those that promote agriculture and industry sector are driving land acquisition. The Sunbiofuels investment is directly likened to the changes in agricultural and energy policy of the fourth phase government under President Jakaya Kikwete and GI is linked to the national industrialization agenda of the fifth phase government under President John Pombe Magufuli.

Moreover, there are two tendencies that are linked to the dominance of the government policies. The first is, the involvement of government officials in the foreign investment such as Sunbiofuels substantiates the role of state in facilitating land acquisition as discussed in many kinds of literature on land grabbing. And the second is strong control from the state in monitoring investment. This is seen in the aspect of compensation and approval in both case studies.

In terms of impacts, according to the study conducted by ActionAid (2009, 2011) and the study conducted by Lawyers' Environmental Action Team (2011), the Sunbiofuel investment has caused food insecurity, drying up of water sources, decreased business in wood products and charcoal and other related health effects. Historically, Kisarawe has been selling food crops to the metropolitan City of Dar es Salaam. However, due to food insecurity caused by the extraction of labor to Sunbiofuel plantation, Kisarawe residents have started getting their food from Dar es Salaam (Lawyers' Environmental Action Team-LEAT 2011). This study has also obtained anecdotal evidence of the movement of labor from Kisarawe to Dar es Salaam as well as youth engagement to motorcycle-ride business. Thus it has been observed that there is an emerging movement of labor from agriculture to non-agricultural activities.

8   CONCLUSION

Throughout this chapter, the practices on the process of land acquisition for foreign and local investments have been highlighted. There have been notable differences and similarities in the way investors and communities have responded and engaged throughout the process. In the two cases discussed, communities have been more forthcoming and trusting to the local investor than to the foreign investor mainly because of the different approaches used by the local investor. Similarly, communities and the local investor have learned from the mistakes and weakness of the process of land acquisition used by foreign investor. However, there is a need to be more cautious in understanding other players behind the company and the powers they have before making a decision on any land deal.

The findings have also shown inadequate transparency and control of the state on land compensation as well as the domineering state facilitation and supportiveness to investments that are in line with policies and plans of the government in power. The influence of the state officials has intimidated communities in making free, prior, and informed decisions on the investment they want. The study did not inquire on whether the GI land acquisition deal was concluded and how it was concluded as well as the gendered implications of both cases and detailed analysis of the labor question. These are research gaps which can be filled by any subsequent study.

NOTES

1. Section 6(c) of the Investment Act of 1997.
2. The RUBADA was established by the The Rufiji Basin Development Authority Act of 1975.
3. According to an anonymous interview, "[a]s far as I know, there is no single CDM project approved yet in Tanzania. As far as I know, GRAS has so far sold carbon certificates on the voluntary market instead. However, I think the company's application for being accepted as CDM project might be pending at the respective Tanzanian government authority" (19 February 2013).
4. REDD is an effort to create a financial value for the carbon stored in forests, offering incentives for developing countries to reduce emissions from forested lands and invest in low-carbon paths to sustainable development. REDD+ goes beyond deforestation and forest degradation, and includes conservation, sustainable forest management and enhanced forest carbon stocks; see http://www.un-redd.org.
5. The two other categories of land are general land and reserved land, both under the control and management of the state directly. General land is defined as land that is not reserved land or village land. In the Land Act (but not the Village Land Act), general land includes unoccupied or unused village land. Reserved land refers to areas set aside for conservation and protection as well as reserved for public utilities, land where water resources for a natural drainage basin originate, and land declared by the State as hazardous land. The land laws also recognize private use rights in general land, called granted right of occupancy.
6. Others, those in urban areas and non-citizens, are granted rights of occupancy.
7. 1982 Local Government (District Authorities) Act, 1982.
8. VLA, Secs. 4 and 8.
9. VLA, Secs. 4 (6), 8 (5).
10. Under the Land Act, General Land includes unoccupied or unused Village Land.
11. Land Act, Sec. 5; 1999 VLA, Secs. 4–5. Note that villages may also choose to transfer Village Land to General Land.
12. Land Act, Sec. 20 (5).
13. Individuals and entities that are majority owned by Tanzanians.
14. VLA, Sec. 22.
15. VLA, Secs. 22–29.
16. VLA, Sec. 4. Note that if no agreement is made, the issue shall be brought to the Tanzanian High Court for final determination, pending which the Commissioner may direct payment of compensation in the amount deemed proper (VLA, Sec. 4 (8)).
17. Land Act, Sec. 20 (2).
18. "Public purpose" includes: (a) exclusive Government or general public use, for any Government scheme or the development of agricultural land or provision of sites for industrial, agricultural or commercial development, social services or housing; (b) for or in connection with sanitary improvement of any kind, including reclamations; (c) for or in connection with the laying out of any new city, municipality, township or minor settlement or the extension or improvement of any existing city, municipality, township or minor settlement; (d) for

or in connection with the development of any airfield, port, or harbor; (e) for or in connection with mining for minerals or oil; and (f) for use by any person or group of persons who, in the opinion of the President, should be granted such land for agricultural development." The law further provides that "[w]here the President is satisfied that a corporation requires any land for the purposes of construction of any work which in his opinion would be of public utility or in the public interest or in the interest of the national economy, he may, with the approval..., declare the purpose for which such land is required to be a public purpose" (LAA, Sec. 4).
19. Name of the 11 villages are; Mtamba, Mhaga, Marumbo, Palaka, Visegese, Vilabwa, Mzenga, Mtakayo, Kidugalo, Kului, and Mitengwe.
20. Interview with Village Chairperson on 25 February 2017.
21. He is also civil engineer by profession and practice.

References

ActionAid. (2009). *Implication of biofuels production on food security in Tanzania.* Available: http://www.actionaidusa.org/sites/files/actionaid/implications_of_biofuels_in_tanzania.pdf.

ActionAid. (2011). *Impact of biofuel investment in Kisarawe district.* Available: http://letstalklandtanzania.com/s/download/case_studies/Impact%20of%20Biofuel%20Investment%20in%20Kisarawe%20July%202011.pdf.

Anseeuw, W., Wily, L., Cotula, L., & Taylor, M. (2012). *Land rights and the rush for land: Findings of the global commercial pressures on land research project.* Rome: International Land Coalition.

Arndt, C., Pauw, K., & Thurlow, J. (2010). *Biofuels and economic development in Tanzania* (IFPRI Discussion Paper 00966). Available: http://www.ifpri.org/sites/default/files/publications/ifpridp00966.pdf.

Bergius, M. (2012). *Large scale agro-industrial for biofuel development in Tanzania.* Impact on Rural Households. Institute of Development Studies. University of Agder.

Cooksey, B. (2012). *Politics, patronage and projects: The political economy of agricultural policy in Tanzania.* Available: http://www.future-agricultures.org/publications/research-and-analysis/working-papers?start=10#.UUlzQhemjoI.

Cotula, L. (2013). *The great African land grab? Agricultural investments and the global food system.* London: Zed Books.

Cotula, L., Vermeulen, S., Leonard, R., & Keeley, J. (2009). *Land grab or development opportunity? Agricultural investment and international land deals in Africa.* London: IIED/FAO/IFAD.

Deininger, K., & Byerlee, D. (2011). *Rising global interest in Farmland: Can it yield sustainable and equitable benefits?* Washington, DC: World Bank.

German Technical Cooperation (GTZ). (2005, August). *A study on liquid biofuels for transportation in Tanzania: Potential and implications for sustainable agriculture and energy in the 21st century.* Tanzania: German Technical Cooperation.

HAKIARDHI. (2011a). *Accumulation by land dispossession and labour devaluation in Tanzania: A case of biofuel and forest investments in Kilwa and Kilolo.* Dar es Salaam: HAKIARDHI.

HAKIARDHI. (2011b). *Land grabbing in a post investment period and popular reactions in the Rufiji River Basin.* Dar es Salaam: HAKIARDHI.

HAKIARDHI. (2012). *Report of the fact finding mission on the conflict between the Lutukira Mixed Farm Limited and Lutukira Villagers in Songea District*. Dar es Salaam: HAKIARDHI.

Herrmann, R., Jumbe, C., Bruentrup, M., & Osabuohien, E. (2018, July). Competition between biofuel feedstock and food production: Empirical evidence from sugarcane outgrower settings in Malawi. *Biomass and Bioenergy, 114,* 100–111.

Kamanga, K. C. (2008). *The agrofuel industry in Tanzania: A critical enquiry into challenges and opportunities*. A research report. Hakiardhi and Oxfam Livelihoods Initiative for Tanzania (JOLIT), Dar es Salaam.

Kweka, O. L. (2012). On whose interest is the state intervention in biofuel investment in Tanzania? *Cross-Cultural Communication, 8,* 80–85.

Lawyers' Environmental Action Team (LEAT). (2011). *Land acquisition for agribusiness in Tanzania: Prospects and challenges*. Dar es Salaam: LEAT.

Locher, M., & Sulle, E. (2013). *Foreign land deals in Tanzania: An update and a critical view on the challenges of data (re)production* (LDPI Working Paper No. 31). Available: http://www.plaas.org.za/sites/default/files/publications-pdf/LDPI31Locher%26Sulle.pdf.

Maghimbi, S., Lokina, R. B., & Senga, M. A. (2010). *The agrarian question in Tanzania: A state of the art paper*. Available: http://nai.diva-portal.org/smash/get/diva2:405966/FULLTEXT01.pdf.

Massay, G. (2015). Compensating landholders in Tanzania: The law and the practice. In E. Osabuohien (Ed.), *Handbook of research on in-country determinants and implications of foreign land acquisitions* (pp. 374–388). Hershey, PA: Business Science Reference. https://doi.org/10.4018/978-1-4666-7405-9.ch019.

Massay, G. E. (2017). Energy and food demands, drivers of land grab: A case of Rufiji River Basin in Tanzania. *Estudos Internacionais: revista de relações internacionais da PUC Minas, 5*(2), 121–131.

Massay, G., & Talemu, K. (2014). *Land-based investments in Tanzania: Legal framework and realities on the Ground* (LDPI Working Paper No. 56). Available: http://www.plaas.org.za/plaas-publication/ldpi56-Massay-Kassile.

Moyo, S., & Yeros, P. (Eds.). (2011). *Reclaiming the nation: The return of the national question in Africa, Asia and Latin America*. New York: Pluto.

Mshandete, A. M. (2011). Biofuels in Tanzania: Status, opportunities and challenges. *Journal of Applied Biosciences, 40,* 2677–2705.

Osabuohien, E. S. (2014). Large-scale agricultural land investments and local institutions in Africa: The Nigerian case. *Land Use Policy, 39,* 155–165.

Osabuohien, E. (2015). *Handbook of research on in-country determinants and implications of foreign land acquisitions* (pp. 1–430). Hershey, PA: IGI Global. https://doi.org/10.4018/978-1-4666-7405-9.

Osabuohien, E., Efobi, U. R., Herrmann, R., & Gitau, C. M. (2019). Female Labor outcomes and large-scale agricultural land investments: Macro-micro evidence from Tanzania. *Land Use Policy, 82,* 716–728.

Othiambo, M. (2011). *Commercial pressure on land in Africa: A regional overview of opportunities, challenges and impacts*. Nakuru: ILC. Available: http://www.landcoalition.org/sites/default/files/documents/resources/Africa%20Overview%20WEB%2014.07.11.pdf.

Sosovele, H. (2010). Policy challenges related to biofuel development in Tanzania. *Africa Spectrum, 45,* 117–129.

Sulle, E. (2015). Land grabbing and agricultural commercialization duality: Insights from Tanzania's transformation agenda. In D. Chinigo (Ed.), *New harvest. Agrarian policies and rural transformation in Southern Africa*. Afriche. Anno XVII Numeno 3/2015.

Sulle, E., & Nelson, F. (2009). *Biofuels, Land access and rural livelihoods in Tanzania*. London: International Institute for Environment and Development.

Tenga, R., & Kironde, J. (2012). *Study of policy, legal and institutional issues related to land in the SAGCOT project area*. Draft Report.

United Republic of Tanzania (URT). (2012). *National climate change strategy*. [online]. Available: http://tanzania.um.dk/en/~/media/Tanzania/Documents/Environment/TANZANIA%20CLIMATE%20CHANGE%20STRATEGY/TANZANIA%20CLIMATE%20CHANGE%20STRATEGY.pdf.

URT. (2009). *Kilimo Kwanza*.

van Teeffelen, J. (2013). *Fuelling progress or poverty? The EU and biofuel in Tanzania policy coherence for development in practice*. Available: http://www.fairpolitics.nl/doc/Impact%20Study%20DEF.pdf.

Veit, P. G., Stickler, M., Schibli, C., & Easton, C. (2012). *Biofuel investments threaten local land rights in Tanzania*. Available: http://www.wri.org/stories/2012/02/biofuel-investments-threaten-local-land-rights-tanzania.

Wise, T. (2014). *Picking up the pieces from the failed land grab project in Tanzania*. Global Post. Available: https://www.pri.org/stories/2014-06-27/picking-piecesfailed-land-grab-project-tanzania.

Agricultural Policy and Food Security in Nigeria: A Rational Choice Analysis

Opeyemi Idowu Aluko

1 Introduction

Agriculture is an important sector in the growth and food sufficiency quest of countries of the world. The agricultural sector is the food hub and a major provider of employment in any country (Moyer and Josling 2017). Some countries have reached food sufficiency level while others are at various level of agricultural development. It is in practice that any state that has a viable agricultural sector has a better ripple effect of development in the other sectors of the economy (Montanarella 2015). This is because when there are available, cheap and high-quality foods for the population, there will be an increment in the productivity level in the country's economy (Udofia and Essang 2015).

Every country of the world has various sectors through which the administrators sharpen the political, economic and social landscape of the country. The methodology adopted to shape such policies gives the specific direction and pattern of development to such country (Daugbjerg 2018). Agriculture is an important sector for the growth and food sufficiency quest of all countries of the world. Some countries of the world have reached the food sufficiency level while others are at various level of agricultural development. The Nigeria state is not left out of this quest of attaining food security (Mgbenka et al. 2015). Several policies were put in place to attain this; some had failed while others have little relevance to the present-day reality (Pinto 1987; Naswem and Ejembi 2017; Gray 2017).

O. I. Aluko (✉)
Political Science Department, Ajayi Crowther University,
Oyo, Oyo State, Nigeria

© The Author(s) 2020
E. S. Osabuohien (ed.), *The Palgrave Handbook of Agricultural and Rural Development in Africa*, https://doi.org/10.1007/978-3-030-41513-6_21

It is important to note that the roles which administrators in Nigeria had played in the agricultural sector date back to the colonial era where some agricultural policies were formulated. These policies were also modified after independence in 1960. Therefore, each successive administration has its modified Agricultural policies which drive the agricultural sector to some extent before they fissured out. The continuity of the viable agricultural policies that gave progressive results in the country is of importance to be sustained while the policies that debar the country from sustainable growth should not be promoted for further implementation in the country.

Nigeria is not left out of this quest of attaining food security and food sufficiency. Several policies from the colonial era, the military interregnum and to the civilian regimes had been rolled out and implemented to various levels of accomplishments (Michael et al. 2018). The Central Bank of Nigeria noted that Nigerian government efforts in ensuring food security in the country amount to about four percent (4%) of the annual budgets in Nigeria invested into the agricultural research, policy formulation, implementation and feedback processes (Central Bank Nigeria 2017). Despite the resources invested in agriculture, there is still a lacuna in the relevance of the policy to the growth and development of the agricultural sector and the country at large. These lacuna prompts the question such as why is poverty, hunger and unemployment on the increase in the country despite the agrarian investments? What can be done to reduce the ineffectiveness in the sector?

The rational choice theory is used to analyse the political economy dimensions of why agricultural policies delivery fall below expectation in Nigeria. This argument is premised on the rational choice, prejudice, whims and caprices of the various actors involved in the policy research, formulation, implementation and evaluation of the policy. Their level of political, economic and social will power to succeed in the development of the agricultural sector and the country at large are critical factors. When Nigeria gets it right in the agricultural sector, it will have ripple effects on other sectors of her political economy and Africa's food insecurity challenges will be effectively solved to a reasonable extent. This is because Nigeria has the largest market in Africa. Also, the country has the population strength that can make agricultural goods and market chain productive and prosperous.

'This chapter investigates the factors inhibiting the development of the agricultural sector in Nigeria' could be an alternative despite the huge resources invested in agriculture. It will unveil why there is a lacuna in the relevance of the policy to the growth and development of the agricultural sector and the country at large. Also, the rationale behind the increasing poverty, hunger, and unemployment in the country despite the agrarian investments will be unravelled. Finally, what to be done to reduce the ineffectiveness in the sector will be analysed. The chapter will be sectionalized to include; the introduction, conceptual clarification, the theoretical framework to discuss the rationales of policy formulators, the overview of the agricultural policies in Nigeria, trends of agricultural policy in Nigeria to show the successful and failed approaches, reason for the failure of agricultural policies in Nigeria, way forward and conclusion.

2 Conceptual Clarification

The following concepts will be clarified in this section of the chapter; policy and Agricultural Policy. The term policy has varied connotations as opined by different scholars. Policies are administrative tools that guide our actions. This implies that policies can be guidelines, rules, regulations, laws, principles, or directions. Buller et al. (2017) further remarked that policies say what is to be done, who is to do it, how it is to be done and to whom it is to be done. Invariably, a policy is a statement of personal or collective administrative intentions to achieve a certain goal(s) by the leader of a local, regional, or national governments of a country. In the view of Etuk et al. (2012) policy could be documented in legislation or other official documents and institutional setup for implementation or enforcement to achieve the goals of the institution or organization.

PerNormak Project (2007, p. 8) and Republic of Macedonia (2007) policy is a 'course of action or inaction chosen by the Government to address a given problem or interrelated set of problems or the way in which the courses of action for achieving the appropriate goals are determined'. The term policy can also be defined as a deliberate action of Government that in some way alters or influences the society or economy outside the government. It includes, but it is not limited to, taxation, regulation, expenditures, information, statements, legal requirements, and legal prohibitions (Pezzini 2012).

Vargas-Hernandez et al. (2011) noted that policy primarily refers to guidelines and interventions for the changing, maintenance or creation of living conditions that are conducive to human welfare. This notion of policy has a sort of social policy orientation. Examples of social policy are education, agricultural, health, housing, employment, and food for all people. Social policy is part of public policy, but public policy is more than that, it is economic policy, industrial policy, and social policy, among others. It is important to note that policy has a pathway or cycle.

Policy cycle is a tool used for the analyzing of the development of a policy item. There are various policy cycles. These can be summarized into the five stages and the eight stage cycles. The five-stage version includes the following stages: (1) Agenda setting (Problem identification), (2) Policy Formulation, (3) Adoption, (4) Implementation, and (5) Evaluation. The eight-step policy cycle version includes the following stages: (1) Problem/Issue identification, (2) Policy analysis, (3) Policy instrument development, (4) Consultation (which permeates the entire process), (5) Coordination, (6) Decision, (7) Implementation and (8) Evaluation.

Agricultural policy, on the other hand, refers to policies that are designed specifically at agricultural course of action with the aim to achieve agricultural set objectives and goals (Gold 2016; DeLonge et al. 2016; Babalola and Salman 2016). Agricultural policies are administrative tools to boost the practice of agriculture in a country. Agricultural policy primarily refers to guidelines and interventions for the changing, maintenance or creation of living conditions that are conducive to supporting agricultural practice to improve human welfare (Adeogun et al. 2017; Oyebola et al. 2019). Agricultural policy could also be a form of documentation in legislation or other official documents and institutional setup for implementation or enforcement to foster agricultural goals of the country.

In the field of agriculture, policies are aimed to maximize agricultural production. To achieve this goal, Parisi et al. (2015) and Buller et al. (2017) opined that there are two general courses of action that the policy plan or statements will entail; (1) to increase the number of acres under crops and (2) to increase the yields per acre. The adoption of one course of action or the other, or both, with their priority, are all policy matters. For instance, the policy to give priority to raising the yields per acre, some of the means will be; (*a*) adequate and regular water supply, (*b*) chemicals fertilizers and farm yard manure, (*c*) better seed, (*d*) better implements, (*e*) better cultural practices, and (*f*) control of pests and diseases among others.

3 Theoretical Framework

3.1 The Rational Choice Theory

> Rational choice theory is an umbrella term for a variety of models explaining social phenomena as outcomes of individual action that can in some way be construed as rational. "Rational behavior" is behavior that is suitable for the realization of specific goals, given the limitations imposed by the situation. (Wittek 2013, p. 623)

The rational choice theory, also known as choice theory or rational action theory is a theory for understanding and often modelling social, political and other individual behaviours. The goal of the rational choice theory is merely to describe choices, to generate predictions, to understand choice behaviour or to provide normative criteria for rationality (Encyclopedia Britannica 2012). This theory originated from the microeconomics school of thought and modern political science, as well as other disciplines such as sociology and philosophy. A pioneering figure in establishing rational choice theory in sociology was George Homans (1961), who set out a basic framework of exchange theory, which he grounded in assumptions drawn from behaviourist psychology.

Becker (1976) recorded that the rational choice theory was early popularized in social sciences by using it to analyse the reason why a decision is taken or a course of action is selected amidst of many other choices by a policy actor be it the judiciary, legislature, or the executive. Elster (1989) stated the essence of rational choice theory when he noted that "when faced with several courses of action, people usually do what they believe is likely to have the best overall outcome". Ogu (2013) aligned with Friedman (1953) opinion that the 'rationality' in the rational choice theory simply means that an individual act by balancing the effect of costs against benefits to arrive at action that maximizes personal advantage and minimizes overall loss. The core of the theory was subsequently anchored on three assumptions: (1) individuals have personal prejudice and agenda, (2) they capitalize on their own strength and gains, and (3) they act in isolation based on full personal digression and available information.

There are many different opinions about rational choice theory. Such opinions create different variations of rational choice theory. This is classified depending on the degree to which they adhere to the assumptions of the classical model, neoclassical model, sociological versions, political science version and the economics variations. Regardless of these variations, the assumptions are premised on three dimensions: (1) the type of rationality, (2) preference, and (3) individualism assumptions. The neoclassical economics and political science versions of rationality have assume full rationality: Individuals are fully informed about all their decision alternatives, the probabilities of their outcomes, and their consequences, and there are no cognitive limitations in the perception or processing of this information (Wittek 2013, p. 689). Individuals base their decisions on minimum loss, zero sum game and cost–benefit analysis. The sociological and psychological models of rational choice theory is specified under the conditions of maximization of benefits or gains and other rationality traits guiding human decision making, learning and or automatic responses (Acheson 2002).

The political variants of the theory assume that social preferences may motivate individual behaviour; that is, they have a concern for the wellbeing of others. The Individualism assumption in the economic version (methodological individualism), social structures are not relevant as constraints on behaviour (since all the necessary information is contained either in the objective prices of goods or in the subjective meanings). Sociological and psychological versions (structural individualism) consider social and institutional incorporation as major conditions affecting individual decisions and behaviour (Wittek 2013).

Rational Choice Theory is an approach that is adopted to show that the actors in the Nigerian agricultural sector have a rational instinct to the current growth and development of the country. There are some certain important steps which the rational choice actor and analyst should follow in making decisions. These include a definition of the problem, identification of decision criteria, weighing the criteria, generation of valid alternatives, rating of each alternative on each criterion and computation of optimal decision.

These steps and other assumptions informed the rational choice of people, individual actors and the state towards other states.

The agricultural sector in Nigeria is saddled with the responsibility of providing food for all members of the political entity—Nigeria. This is also to make sure food is sufficient for all the members of the community so as to ensure an increase in the productivity level of all workers in various sector of the economy and by extension Nigeria at large (Osabuohien et al. 2018).

Agricultural policy formulators as rational actors have the task of ensuring that the best policies are formulated which should benefit all and sundry in the country is delivered on all the cases. Their personal and self-regarding actions and rationalities are essentially channelled to how mutual prosperity, progress, reduced food crises and the sustenance of the democratic process can be ensured by the adequate food production and food security attainment. Their eventual agricultural policy implementations are seen as in the optimum interest of all stakeholders to sustain the level of optimum performance of individuals in their respective endeavours. The rational choice theory is appropriate for this discourse because it points out the actors as a rational, independent being that has the responsibilities of perspectives in policy formulation to all and sundry in utmost good faith.

The theory is criticized on the bases that the individual actor can be compromised and his actions may jeopardize the popular interests in the country. Also at what point can other people rate the actor's action as rational and irrational because he has his self-regarding purpose and decisions. Nevertheless, the rational choice theory holds sway that actors must be physically fit to make a decision at the optimum level in a political system. A rational actor's decisions in a democratic setting are further subjected to further analysis by other actors before it is implemented. Agricultural policy makers as rational actors do not make decisions in isolation but in conjunction with other actors to maintain a rational choice of the best policy for the entire country and to ensure food security and sustainable development.

4   A Discourse on Agricultural Policies in Nigeria

A few of the Agricultural policies in Nigeria include; River Basin Development Authority (1976), Green Revolution (1980), Better life program for rural women (1987), Family support program (FSP) (1994), National Economic and Empowerment Development Strategies (NEEDS) (1999), National Special program on Food Security (2002), Root and Tuber Expansion Program (2003), Specialized Universities for Agriculture, Agriculture and Rural Management Training Institute (ARMTI), FADAMA I (2010), FADAMA II (2017) and FADAMA III (2018), among others.

Nigeria's independence of 1960 makes room for self-governance and policy formulation for all sectors of the country including the agricultural sector. Several policies formulated as at then still had the resemblance of the colonial government outlines. Therefore, the post-colonial agricultural policies are mostly a continuation of the colonial government's strategies. This strategy gives major room for the development of urban areas using the resources of the rural areas. At independence, the agricultural policies have more of exploitative tendencies than the developmental effects. This strategy has an immediate adverse effect on the exploited rural areas and a long time adverse effects on the entire developmental prowess of the country (Tersoo 2014; Ayinde et al. 2017).

The River Basin Development Authority (1976) agricultural policy was formulated to utilize the water resources in the some selected rivers to boost the agricultural process in the locality and as well generate employment for a lot of people. This policy was successful to a little extent because of the relative employment it generated at the respective locations of its operations before it stops been effective (Johnson and Masias 2017). The primary reason for its failure was the localization of the policy in terms of the river selection for the policy implementation. The financial allocation and uptake in the project implementation were saddled with corruption, nepotism, favouritism and politicization of the distribution of the agricultural produce from the venture. The failure of the River Basin Development Authority led to the formulation of another policy—Green Revolution (1980) to complement the process of the quest for food sufficiency.

The Green Revolution (1980) agricultural policy was initiated to cover the whole country as a unit and not selected areas in the country like the River Basin Development Authority policy project. A more radical approach was adopted to 'revolutionized' the country from the use of crude farm implements to mechanized farming, and other farming supplements were provided such as improved seeds and fertilizer provisions so as to increase the extent of yield from the agricultural processes. The policy was effective significantly; however; the rationality and choice of other policy implementers sabotage the policy. The distribution of tractor and other mechanized farm implements were politicized, the distribution of the fertilizers in some quartiles were commercialized also laden with favouritism and nepotism. Therefore, the policy did not survive beyond the political regime of the policy formulators.

Another agricultural policy focus was directed towards the women in the rural community. This was tagged 'better life program for rural women' in 1987. This agricultural policy considered the women as the most vulnerable group of people in the Nigerian communities especially the rural areas. The policy was aimed to empower the women folk alone with farming techniques, agricultural loans, training on other vocations so as to have a better life. This policy worked to a large extent but was not effective and misplaced from the policy formulation stage. The policy failed to analyse who the rural women were, the locations of the rural areas and how to give the rural women the proposed better life The policy failed to proffer solution to conceptualizing who the rural women were, there proportion in the country and the plight of other actors in the agricultural sectors such as the urban women, the rural men and the urban men. The policy implementers diverted the proposed better life resources to 'the urban men' therefore the policy financed private aggrandizements other than national development.

The better life for rural women policy faded off as the regime of the policy actor ended. The new administration formulated the family support program (FSP) (1994). This policy tends to be an improvement from the other earlier 'better life policy'. The entire family structure was targeted in this policy. However, the policy covers the entire country, but it incorporated other policy statements which transcend the agricultural sector focus to mental and health sector, financial management, and family planning strategies. The actors formulating the policy made the policy 'dead on arrival' because of its multi-facet approach. Therefore, the impact analysis on the agricultural sector was meagre. However, the policy environment gave room for unaccountability, nepotism, favouritism, 'prebendalism', backdoor approach in who gets what when and how, therefore, the policy was short lived with poor impacts on the entire target populations.

The poor implementation, general failure and diversion of the policy focus of the FSP to finance a few private hands and the demise of the military interregnum that formulated it makes way for a new democratic, inclusive agricultural policy called the National Economic and Empowerment Development Strategies-NEEDS (1999). The NEEDS strategy was a workout plan to develop the entire part of the national economy whereby the agricultural sector carries a large share of the focus of the developmental plan. The NEEDS make provision for mechanization program, financial provision and post-harvest storage. This policy opened other areas of the agricultural chain of business other than farm tillage. The agro-allied and poultry farms were given more breathing spaces, and it employed more people in the agricultural sector. The shortfalls of the policy were the areas of inefficient management of the funds and the diversion of the resources to private hands instead of national development.

The NEEDS policy gave birth to offshoots of the National Special program on Food Security (2002) and the Root and Tuber Expansion Program (2003). The National Special program on Food Security was a special intervention to aid food security in the country. This was aimed to make good food available for all Nigerians at an affordable price at any point in time or season. This worked out to a large extent in some states in the country. The economies of scale and comparative advantage of each state were considered to provide a kind of food crop peculiar to the area for national and international consumption. The Root and Tuber Expansion Program were also scheduled to work in the same process of comparative advantage and economies of scale of each state. The policy is still relevant, but the major challenge is the limited fund allocated to the project with regards to the extent of food shortage in the country. Also, the management and accountability of the available funds are at debacle to the success of the policy.

Specialized Universities for Agriculture such as ARMTI among others in the country is a vital point in the agricultural think tank for national policies that promoted the culture of agricultural research, training of manpower for the upkeep of new and best practice. However, it is a different point to invent a new product to ease the work of agricultural practice and to invest in the new research on a large scale to benefit the whole country. Majority of the agricultural technologies locally invented are not financed to aid the inventor to produce on a large scale and as well turn out to aid agricultural extension services. Coupled with this, is the general problem of funding to aid the researchers to do more and the research environments are not so conducive to warrant the best of service output for the country.

In recent times, FADAMA I (2010) and FADAMA II (2017) were invented which were the replicas of the river basin development program earlier invented. The FADAMA project is assisted by the World Bank to aid the irrigation process in the upland areas and all year-round farming in the selected region. This program focuses on areas where crops of national values are produced for all-year-round production of food crops to aid national development and food security in the country. The major plague of the project is the localization of the program to favour some regions while the equivalent program is not installed in other regions of the country (Takeshima and Liverpool-Tasie 2015; Adeyemo et al. 2016).

The trend of the policy shows that a few of these policies are moribund even from its inception and it has little or no impact on the citizens. Others have a continuous relevance especially institutionalized policies and academic training related policies. Nigeria is also a partner in the United Nations' Sustainable Development Goals (SDGs) which have food sufficiency as one of its cardinal goals to be achieved within a short period.

5   Trends of Agricultural Policy in Nigeria

The trend of agricultural policy in Nigeria has two major approaches with their respective pathways. These are the successful approach and the failed approach (Figs. 1 and 2). Generally, the policy onset to its fulfilment has five levels or stations of accomplishment for its course of action to be complete. There must not be a point of disconnection from any of the stations in the policy pathway for the fulfilment of the policy lifespan.

The first agricultural policy station is the policy initiators level. The number of initiator collaborations of stakeholders matters a lot to the authenticity and the predictable level of acceptance of the policy. Usually, a large input from the technocrats and the research institutions are needed and a little contribution from the political actors at this first key station. The second station in the pathway of policy trend is the central policy actor. These actors determine the workability of the policy, it's level of contribution to growth and development in the country and the level of its acceptance in the country.

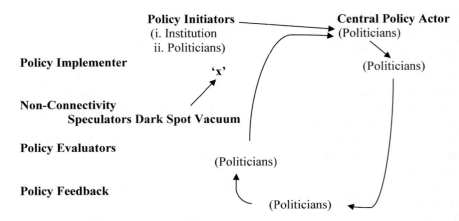

Fig. 1 Failed approach (*Source* The Author's)

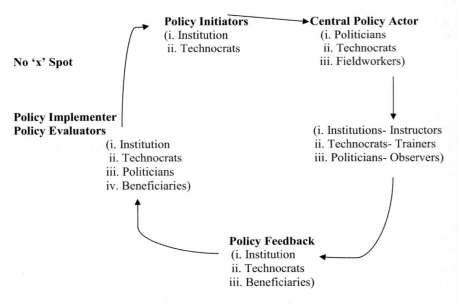

Fig. 2 The successful approach (*Source* The Author's)

The higher the numbers of the policy actors the greater the extent of its performance in the country.

The third station in the pathway of policy trend is the policy implementer. These actors determine how and where the policy works and to what extent it contributes to growth and development in the country and the level of its acceptance in the country. The higher the numbers of the policy implementer the greater the extent of the policy performance in the country. The fourth station in the pathway of policy trend is policy feedback. These station reports back to the policy actors for reviewing their policy workability. They give a rethinking perspective to the policy actor and implementer stations whether to halt the policy or reinvigorate the process so that it can fulfil the purpose of its existence in the country.

The fifth station in the pathway of policy trend is the policy evaluation. These actors determine the level of the policy performance with regards to the extent of its contribution to the growth and development in the country and the level of its acceptance in the country. The higher the level of neutrality in the composition of the policy evaluators, the higher the level of reliability of the policy performance report in the country. The policy evaluators' reports go directly back to the policy initiators and not any other stations in the policy trend pathway so that drastic actions will be made to generate the vicious cycle again.

The failed approach in the agricultural policy trend resulted from a relatively good initiating point with at most two major initiating actors, but the central policy actors' proportion reduces to just only the political class who are mostly unlearned in the technicalities of the policy functions (Fig. 1). The composition of the policy implementers are as well mainly politicians who are mostly unlearned in the technicalities of the policy functionalities. Therefore, the implementations of such policy will not be at par with the general expectations of the entire population. At the policy feedback station, the composition of the policy actors responsible for the feedback are as well mainly politicians who are mostly unlearned in the technicalities of the policy functionalities thus their feedbacks will never correspond to the real event that transpired in the policy circle.

The evaluators' station of the policy pathway composition is as well made up of mostly politicians who are mostly unlearned in the technicalities of the policy functionalities. Therefore, their evaluations will not be as objective as it should be because they are in the pathway to protect a secluded interest contrary to the public interest. The dread point of the failure in the policy pathway is the reportage directly back to the central policy actors who are the politicians instead of the group of the policy initiators. This leaves the policy pathway with an 'x' non-connectivity speculators dark spot vacuum which shows the final missing link resulting in the reason for the outright failure of the public policy. This is political caucus policy ideas which do not reflect the general public acceptability of its occurrence in the country.

The successful approach in the agricultural policy trend resulted from a relatively good initiating point with at most two major initiating actors without the politicians' involvement at this early stage, the central policy actors' proportion increases to more vibrant actors' which include the political class who are to be briefed of the policy initiation, the technocrats and the field workers mostly learned people in the technicalities of the policy functions (Fig. 2). The composition of the policy implementers is as well mainly the institutions concerned who serve as the instructors, the technocrats who serve as the trainers and lastly the politicians who are mostly observers. Therefore, the implementations of such policy will be at par with the general expectations of the entire population because it carries along the set of people that has the technical know-how in the policy pathway. At the policy feedback station, the composition of the policy actors responsible for the feedback is as well mainly the institutions concerned in whose sector domicile the public policy, the technocrats and the direct beneficiaries of the policy. The politicians are not needed at this policy cycle station.

The evaluators' station of the policy pathway composition is as well made up of mainly the institutions concerned in whose sector domicile the public policy, the technocrats, the direct beneficiaries of the policy. At this point, the political class is invited to evaluate the feedback from the beneficiaries and other stakeholders. Such evaluations will be as objective as it should because the stakeholders include the entire concerned representatives in the pathway with interest not contrary to the public interest. There is no dread point leading to failure in the policy pathway because the reportage is directed to the policy initiators which include the institution and the technocrats for reappraisal and reinitiating processes for the central policy actors. Therefore, the policy pathway has no 'x' non-connectivity speculators dark spot vacuum which shows the final missing link resulting in the reason for the outright failure of public policies.

River Basin Development Authority (1976), Green Revolution (1980), Better life program for rural women (1987), Family support program (FSP) (1994), National Economic and Empowerment Development Strategies (NEEDS) (1999), National Special program on Food Security (2002), Root and Tuber Expansion Program (2003), Specialized Universities for Agriculture, ARMTI, FADAMA I (2010) and FADAMA II (2017).

6 Reason for Failure of Agricultural Policies in Nigeria and Way Forward

Many agricultural policies have failed or not worked effectively because of so many reasons. A few of the reasons are as follows; there is a subjective rational choice of the political actors and a lack of political will to fulfil all the tenets of the policies so made. This means that policies are mere political statement to have a means of spending or diverting public monies to private uses. Examples of such policy lacuna are the better life for rural women agricultural policy and National Economic and Empowerment Development Strategies (NEEDS) (1999). Most of the empowerment scheme ended up in the urban areas and much more with men at the helms of political and administrative affairs (Akpan et al. 2015; Aluko 2017).

There are difficulties in getting agricultural loans despite the premium on small scale farmers as seen in the Family Support Agricultural Program and FADAMA I and II. Also, failed mechanization plans and widespread poor infrastructures contributed to the demise of many laudable agricultural policies in Nigeria. Such policies affected include; River Basin Development Authority (1976), Green Revolution (1980) and Root and Tuber Expansion Program (2003) among others. There is also continuous poor interaction between the government and farmers' stakeholders. The government only makes policies, and much effort is not taken to investigate its suitability with the host communities. Example of such is in the FADAMA I and FADAMA II programs.

Another reason for agricultural failure in Nigeria is that there are weak Agricultural policies that cannot stand the test of time. Therefore, policies have short durations of lifespan especially at the expiration of the political administrators' tenure that initiates the policy. Examples of these are the Green Revolution program; Operation Feed the Nation and others. There are also role conflict between two or more policies and projects in such a way that there is duplication of functions, duties and roles (John et al. 2017). Example of these menaces is the River Basin Development Authority, FADAMA projects and ARMTI.

Due to the aforementioned duplication of roles and functions, there are embezzlement of Agricultural funds, inadequate technical services provision and inadequate evaluation programs among others. This is because no agency created with similar functions will like to take full responsibilities of the policy plan and implementations. The political will to execute agricultural projects that will have wide impacts on the country is at alow ebb (Udah et al. 2015). Most policies are regionally sectionalized without its corresponding project in other regions of the country. For instance, the FADAMA I–III program is concentrated in Northern Nigeria without corresponding financial commitment to other agricultural projects in other regions.

The reoccurring farmers-herdsmen crises have made many farm lands to be abandoned and rendering agricultural policies not implementable in such areas. The crises and the destruction of farmland and crops by herdsmen in the middle belt and some Northern, West and Southern part of Nigeria has made farming unsecured and unprofitable venture (Aluko 2017). However, another major reason for the failure of agricultural policies in high premium is layed on crude oil as its main stay of the economy instead of Agricultural sector that has the potential of employing a large percent of the workforce in the rural and urban areas (Aluko and Aremu 2017).

Therefore, to forestall these reasons for agricultural failure in Nigeria from continuous reoccurring, the following steps need urgent attention from all stakeholders; the government, farmers, farming community, and international donors. Stakeholders must be incorporated at the policy formulation stage so that the right policy statements and inputs can be included in the schemes. The government should invest in Agricultural researches and make adequate use of the outcomes. Good infrastructure must be provided for better outcomes to be achieved. As a rider to this, there should be a policy to eradicate the use of hoes as the mainstay agricultural tool so that higher grade farm implements can be invented for local farmers and boost agricultural production. Institutions that perform the same functions must be given specific and general functions.

At the point of institutional overlap, there must be a leading institution that will take responsibilities of the situation. This may be delineated due to the region jurisdiction or specialization of the institution. Also, programs must be monitored and implemented to the letters with a good political will regardless of the political regime that initiated the policy or program. Large plantations of cash crops and plantations of annual crops must be embarked on based on the geographical peculiarities of the regions, and more of the private sector must be involved in the project for effective public–private partnership. This will curb the menace of making political statements without actions.

7 Conclusion

Food security is a major challenge in Nigeria. The extent of food production is very low as compare to the population strength. There are shortages of vital food nutrients and wastage of food due to poor storage or preservative techniques and capacity. This problem has made food prices to be high and food production to be seasonal. High-quality food available for consumption is low and mostly out of reach of the masses. The agricultural machinery and the techniques needed to operate them for easier farm practice is grossly missing. High-quality seedling with the best output is as well not sufficiently available coupled with administrative bureaucracy and corruption. All these and more make food security to be difficult to attain in Nigeria.

Successive government regimes have noticed this problem and had initiated various agricultural policies. The policies are initiated to enhance Agricultural development at the grass root and at the commercial scale. Yet many of these policies have failed due to their inappropriateness to the environment, poor implementation and execution coupled with financial embezzlement, diversion of farm inputs (fertilizer, seedling and machinery), diversion of farm produce in such a way that the masses in the local markets are not benefiting from the farm produce. Another cogent reason for the failure of Agricultural policies is the poor political will to make the lives of the people more comfortable.

In other to forestall this, policy makers must engage the farmers directly not through proxy or contractor to know the peculiar need of the farmers at a given area and time. The rate of agricultural turn over must be enhanced through the conversion of agricultural produce to finished goods which should be packaged primarily for domestic consumption, and the excess can be exported for international consumption which serves as a source of foreign exchange.

The use of crude implements such as hoes, mattocks, and cutlass must be minimized, and the state should encourage farmers to go into large scale production using the expanse of land available all over the country. The training and retraining of farmers on how to use and take care of advance farm machinery such as tractors and its coupling implements must be regular. In this vein, for food production to be sustainable and food security to be attained to, the lingered farmers' herdsmen crises across the country must be resolved by providing a geographical, social, economic and political solution. This can be achieved by legislating policies to ensure all cattle, sheep and goat farmers provides privately adequate ranches for their livestock and enacting laws prohibiting open field migratory grazing.

No doubt, the agricultural sector has the capacity to employ about 65% of the unemployed people and ensure food security in Nigeria. Also, a few mechanized farmers can as well solve the food insufficiency in Nigeria if the socio-economic and political atmospheres are conducive. This will create more employments in the agricultural value chain production and packaging of finished goods. Other countries in Africa will be a major beneficiary if the government–private partnership scheme is initiated and efforts are channelled into large scale production, processing, packaging and marketing of the finished goods.

The rational choice and decision making of the political leaders are expected to be at par with the yearning of the general populace. Also, their political will must be backed up with practical relevant and sustainable actions. Such actions include the distribution and monitoring of farm inputs to make sure it gets to the targeted farmers. The mete out of adequate punishment for any government official that prebend, divert and usurp agricultural public goods for his personal or unofficial uses. Also, adequate punishments must be measured out for farmers that divert farm produce away from the local market. When these are done, there will be food security and sustainable agricultural policies in the country which will benefit the whole country and the rest of the world.

References

Acheson, J. (2002). Rational choice, culture change, and fisheries management in the Gulf of Maine. *Research in Economic Anthropology, 21,* 6.

Adeogun, S., Adeleye, N., Fashola, S., & Osabuohien, E. (2017). *Promoting cassava production in Ogun State: Linking data and policy* (State Policy Note, No. 6).

Adeyemo, T. A., Amaza, P., Okoruw, V., & Abass, A. (2016, September). The food security effect of a biomass value web concept among smallholder cassava households in Edo State Nigeria. In *2016 AAAE Fifth International Conference, September 23–26, 2016, Addis Ababa Ethiopia (No. 249319)*. African Association of Agricultural Economists (AAAE).

Akpan, S. B., Udoh, E. J., & Patrick, I. V. (2015). Assessment of economic policy variables that modeled agricultural intensification in Nigeria. *Russian Journal of Agricultural and Socio-economic Sciences, 41*(5), 47.

Aluko, O. I. (2017). Urban violence dimension in Nigeria: Farmer and herders onslaught. *AGATHOS, 8*(1), 33.

Aluko, O. I., & Aremu, F. A. (2017). Tension in the paradise: A paradigm shift in urban violence in Nigeria. *Silpakorn University Journal of Social Sciences, Humanities, and Arts, 17*(1), 75.

Ayinde, O. E., Aina, I. V., & Babarinde, S. O. (2017). Effect of agricultural growth on unemployment and poverty in Nigeria (1980–2012): A co-integration approach. *Tropical Agriculture, 41,* 3216.

Babalola, I. A., & Salman, K. K. (2016). Impact of agricultural policy on relative price variability of food crops and inflation in Nigeria. *Tropical and Subtropical Agroecosystems, 19*(2), 46.

Becker, G. S. (1976). *The economic approach to human behaviour.* Chicago: University of Chicago Press.

Buller, H., Wilson, G. A., & Holl, A. (2017). *Agri-environmental policy in the European Union.* New York: Routledge.

Central Bank Nigeria. (2017). *Special report on Nigeria economy.* Abuja: Central Bank Nigeria.

Daugbjerg, C. (2018). *Policy networks under pressure: Pollution control, policy reform and the power of farmers.* New York: Routledge.

DeLonge, M. S., Miles, A., & Carlisle, L. (2016). Investing in the transition to sustainable agriculture. *Environmental Science & Policy, 55,* 266–273.

Elster, J. (1989). Social norms and economic theory. *Journal of Economic Perspectives, American Economic Association, 3*(4), 11–17.

Encyclopedia Britannica. (2012). *Political science encyclopedia Britannica ultimate reference suite.* Chicago: Encyclopedia Britannica.

Etuk, G., Ering, S., & Ajake, U. (2012). Nigeria's Universal Basic Education (U.B.E.) policy: A sociological analysis. *American International Journal of Contemporary Research, 2*(7), 39.

Friedman, M. (1953). *Essays in positive economics.* Chicago: University of Chicago Press.

Gold, M. V. (2016). *Sustainable agriculture: The basics* (p. 1). Boca Raton: CRC Press.

Gray, C. S. (2017). *Inside independent Nigeria: Diaries of Wolfgang Stolper, 1960–1962.* Routledge: CRC Press Book.

Homans, G. (1961). *Social behaviour: Its elementary forms.* London: Routledge and Kegan Paul.

John, O. A., Adelani, B. S., Abolade, J., Opeyemi, A. A., Adeyemi, B. I., Bolanle, S., et al. (2017). Challenges of Oyo state agricultural development program (OYSADEP) for rural farmers in Oyo state, southwestern Nigeria. *Science Letters, 5*(1), 8–12.

Johnson, M. E., & Masias, I. (2017). *Assessing the state of the rice milling sector in Nigeria: The role of policy for growth and modernization* (Vol. 40, pp. 20–22). Washington, DC: International Food Policy Research Institute.

Mgbenka, R., Bah, E., & Ezeano, C. (2015). The role of local government council in agricultural transformation in Nigeria: Need for review of policy. *Agricultural Engineering Research Journal, 5*(2), 27–32.

Michael, A., Tashikalma, A. K., & Maurice, D. C. (2018). Agricultural inputs subsidy in Nigeria: An overview of the growth enhancement support scheme (GESS). *Acta Universitatis Agriculturae et Silviculturae Mendelianae Brunensis, 66*(3), 781–789.

Montanarella, L. (2015). Agricultural policy: Govern our soils. *Nature News, 528*(7580), 32.

Moyer, W., & Josling, T. (2017). *Agricultural policy reform: Politics and process in the EU and US in the 1990s.* Routledge: CRC Press.

Naswem, A. A., & Ejembi, S. A. (2017). Reviving agricultural extension for effective transition from subsistence to commercial agriculture in Nigeria. *Journal of Rural Social Sciences, 32*(1), 12.

Normak Project. (2007). *Policy development handbook Norwegian Assistance to the Republic of Macedonia.* SIGMA and Skopje. http://www.vlada.mk/.

Ogu, M. I. (2013). Rational choice theory: Assumptions, strengths, and greatest weaknesses in application outside the western milieu context. *Arabian Journal of Business and Management Review (Nigerian Chapter), 1*(3), 90–99.

Osabuohien, E., Okorie, U., & Osabohien, R. (2018). Rice Production and Processing in Ogun State, Nigeria: Qualitative insights from farmers' association. In Obayelu, E. (Ed.), *Food systems sustainability and environmental policies in modern economics* (pp. 188–216). Hershey, PA: IGI Global. https://doi.org/10.4018/978-1-5225-3631-4.ch009.

Oyebola, P. O., Osabuohien, E., & Obasaju, B. (2019). Employment and income effects of Nigeria's agricultural transformation agenda. *African Journal of Economic and Management Studies.* https://doi.org/10.1108/AJEMS-12-2018-0402.

Parisi, C., Vigani, M., & Rodríguez-Cerezo, E. (2015). Agricultural nanotechnologies: What are the current possibilities? *Nano Today, 10*(2), 124–127.

Pezzini, M. (2012). *Industrial policy and territorial development lessons from Korea Development Centre Studies Development Centre of the Organisation for Economic Co-operation and Development.* www.oecd.org/dev.

Pinto, B. (1987). Nigeria during and after the oil boom: A policy comparison with Indonesia. *The World Bank Economic Review, 1*(3), 419–445.

Republic of Macedonia. (2007). *Methodology for policy analysis and coordination* (Official Gazette of the Republic of Macedonia No. 52/06).

Takeshima, H., & Liverpool-Tasie, L. S. O. (2015). Fertilizer subsidies, political influence and local food prices in sub-Saharan Africa: Evidence from Nigeria. *Food Policy, 54,* 11–24.

Tersoo, P. (2014). Agribusiness as a veritable tool for rural development in Nigeria. *International Letters of Social and Humanistic Sciences, 3,* 26–36.

Udah, S. C., Nwachukwu, I. N., Nwosu, A. C., & Mbanasor, J. A. (2015). Assessment of various policy regimes towards agricultural export growth in Nigeria. *Asian Journal of Agricultural Extension Economics and Sociology, 6*(2), 94–101.

Udofia, L., & Essang, N. (2015). Agricultural expenditure and poverty alleviation in Nigeria. *Development, 7*(21), 29–44.

Vargas-Hernandez, J., Noruzi, M. R., & Irani, F. N. H. A. (2011). What is policy, social policy and social policy changing? *International Journal of Business and Social Science, 2*(10), 287–291.

Wittek, R. (2013). Rational choice theory. In R. L. Warms & R. Jon McGee (Eds.), *Theory in social and cultural anthropology: An encyclopedia.* London: Sage.

Processing, Value Chain and Food Security

Socio-Cultural Factors and Performance of Small-Scale Enterprise in Agro-Allied Manufacturing Firms in Nigeria

Alidu O. Kareem, Temitope F. Jiboye, Oluwabunmi O. Adejumo, and Michael O. Akinyosoye

1 Introduction

The Nigerian economy witnessed a dramatic increase in the incidence of poverty and unemployment during the collapse of oil boom of the 1970s (Onuoha and Elegbede 2018). This brought about the resurgence of the need for agriculture given the ease of the sector to create employment and mitigate food insecurity. Despite this resurgence, majority of the sub-sectors within the agricultural sector have not fared so well, among which is the small-scale agro-allied manufacturing firms (Central Bank of Nigeria—CBN Report 2016).

The agro-allied manufacturing sector is generally believed to be a major panacea for sustainable development of any nation. This is because of the value addition that these industries contribute to raw agricultural output. The steady increase in the number of small-scale agro-allied manufacturing enterprises (SSAME) in the world stems from its growing importance.

T. F. Jiboye · O. O. Adejumo (✉) · M. O. Akinyosoye
Institute for Entrepreneurship and Development Studies,
Obafemi Awolowo University, Ile-Ife, Nigeria

A. O. Kareem
Osun State University, Okuku, Nigeria
e-mail: alidu.kareem@uniosun.edu.ng

This importance is reflected in issues such as being a source of employment, wealth creation, foreign earnings, poverty alleviation, and socio-cultural transformation. Statistics from the Small and Medium Enterprises Development Agency of Nigeria (SMEDAN) (2003) showed that significant number of private sector operators are made up of small-scale agro-allied manufacturing businesses. Among 85 million in labor force, this sector employs over 32 million people representing three-quarters of all jobs in Nigeria and they account for a considerable amount of the total Gross Domestic products (National Bureau of Statistics-NBS 2016).

Agro-Allied Manufacturing Enterprises refer to small-scale enterprises (SSEs) that engage in all economic activities that process agricultural products into finished goods for human and animal consumptions. They include such firms that involve in transformation of raw materials that are from agricultural and nonagricultural sectors whose final products could be used for agricultural purposes (Osabuohien et al. 2018; Oyebola et al. 2019). Included in these categories are enterprises that process rice, corn, peanuts, cocoa, coffee, millet, soybeans, palm produce, rubber, cotton, livestock feeds, fishery feeds, biscuits, bread, sweets, cornflakes, chocolate, cake, furniture making, hides, and skins, among others.

In Nigeria, small-scale industries, particularly those in the manufacturing sector, plays significant roles in the utilization of indigenous technologies and technological upgrading in agro-industrial sub-sector (Adeoti and Olubamiwa 2009; Vaarst 2010; Oyesola and Obabire 2011; United Nation Development Program [UNDP] 2012; Olajide et al. 2012; Egbouna et al. 2013). From previous studies, the importance of SMEs for the Nigerian agro-allied manufacturing businesses has been well espoused. The agro-processing sector is by far the most significant components in the agro-food industry and covers a broad area of post-harvest activities, packaged agricultural raw materials, industrial and technology intensive processing of immediate goods, and the fabrication of final products derived from agriculture. Also, agro-allied manufacturing businesses often provide crucial inputs and services to the farm sector—fertilizers, insecticides, herbicides, for those with no access to such inputs thereby inducing productivity and stimulating market induced innovations through chains and networks; facilitating linkages and allowing domestic and export markets to become mutually supportive. Moreover, SSEs remain key actors in the largely informal trading and processing networks which dominate food procurement in most urban Africa, and this has proved remarkably adaptive and resilient in the face of a range of economic, institutional, and infrastructural challenges.

In addition to the importance of small-scale agro-allied industries, specific areas of relevant for developmental purposes which have also been identified by previous articles include labor-intensive content; local capital (finance) involvement instead of foreign exchange expenditure; relatively high level of use of locally serviced raw materials; relatively cheap and standard quality products that are within the purchasing power of most consumers; ease of entrance into production by new comers; simpler infrastructure requirements; stimulation of economic growth; and possession of potential ability to substantially reduce poverty, and improved social outcomes. Indeed, some evidences on the link between growth and poverty reduction have revealed that agro-allied industry is also among the most accessible of industrial activities; and that agro-allied manufacturing and processing activity in Africa is distinguished by a high percentage of female employment ranging from 50 to 90% Food and Agriculture Organization of the United Nations (FAO) (2011).

Despite the benefits of SSAME, its potential for contributing to economic growth is far from being adequately exploited. It has been observed that the sector's importance has fluctuated with the rise and fall of oil revenue. Specifically, previous studies revealed that the Nigerian agro-allied manufacturing sector has remained stagnant while its contribution to the GDP has declined significantly (Olaoye 2014). Also, it is evident from extant literature that SSEs in Nigeria is passing through turbulent period resulting into decline in performance (Ucha 2010; Aworemi et al. 2010; Bowale and Akinlo 2012; Salami 2013; Sumberg and Okali 2013).

Poor performances of these enterprises have implications for critical shareholders such as owner/managers, employees, customers, suppliers, and government and its agencies. Poor performance will not give the owners the expected profit, and the employees will not get salaries and wages as of when due or may even experience retrenchment from their jobs; moreover, customers (both buyers and suppliers) will not be able to relate profitably with firms while government will not get the desired taxes. Incidentally, these challenges to SSAMEs may have social dimension to it where attitudes, beliefs, and culture constituting a barrier to these enterprises. Therefore, in order to further address these challenges, a socio-cultural dimension is introduced for analytical purpose. Hence, the aim of this study is to integrate, from a theoretical perspective, the socio-cultural factors involved in SSAMEs performance.

The rest of the chapter is structured as follows. The review of empirical literature is covered in Sect. 2; while Sects. 3 and 4 discusses theoretical constructs related to the study and methodology, respectively. The empirical findings from the analysis are disclosed in Sects. 5 and 6 concludes with implications and future research directions.

2 Literature Review

As noted in extant literature, SSAME have been underperforming in Nigeria. These small firms are operating below their capacity utilization while sizeable number moribund as a result of constraints emanating from the business environment (Ajani and Igbokwe 2014; Igudia 2017). Factors constraining agro-allied manufacturing enterprises in Nigeria include those relating to technical constraints, resource constraints, socio-cultural constraints, socio-economic constraints and organizational constraints. These constraints are caused by narrow-based policy formulation, policy instability, poor policy implementations, and weak institutional framework for policy co-ordination. These factors also include insecurity, poor or absence of infrastructure, unstable power supply, corruption and insufficient capital, poor managerial experience, high level of illiteracy, lack of relevant skills, and motivation of owner/manager.

Also identified, as contributing factors to the poor performance of these firms are socio-cultural variables such as shared norms, values, attitudes, beliefs, education, occupation, and experience of the owner/manager (Olagunju 2004; Olawale 2010). Among the plausible benefits of SSAME identified by extant literature include reduction in unemployment, rural–urban drift, poverty, deprivation, and economic instability (Okafor 2011; Kormawa 2011; Adesina 2013). However, despite these benefits, some indicators such as high unemployment rate of about 14% in 2016 showed that SSAME have not yielded desired results (NBS 2017). Incidentally, high level of unemployment has been linked to many social problems such as armed robbery, kidnapping, insurgency, suicide, and general insecurity of lives and property (Duhu 2015; Itumo 2016).

Furthermore, performance indicators from the small-scale agro-allied sub-sector revealed persisting negative cash flow; declining profit; uncompetitive products or services; declining working capital; declining physical facilities; and mismanagement. Other observable trends in SSAMEs performance include high debt rate, sales of goods and services at cost price, shortage of stock and inventories, high level of unserviceable assets, large-scale retirement of staff, premature resignation of key staff, and persisting difficulty in securing new funds from banks and creditors (Kormawa 2011; Adesina 2013).

Studies carried out by Ekpenyong and Nyong (1992), Aworemi et al. (2010), Yusuff et al. (2012), Bowale and Akinlo (2012) have consistently shown the relationship between demographic variables and SSEs performance, but the influence of socio-cultural factors on the SSEs performance is still shrouded in controversy (Van der Sluis et al. 2005; Egwuonwu 2012).

Evidence from previous studies on the effects of socio-cultural factors on SSEs performance is inconclusive. Scholars within scientific management school of thought represented by Taylor and behavioral theorists such as Mayo and Fayol and other universal theorists emphasize the insignificant influence of socio-cultural factors on organizational performance. Other scholars are of the view that socio-cultural factors such as education, gender, extended family, owners/managers experience, beliefs, religion, values, attitude, language, and artifacts do influence the performance of organization (Dore 1973; Ahiauzu 1986; Hofstede 1991; Iguisi 1994; Sorensen and Chang 2006; Woldie et al. 2008; Zhou and de Wit 2009; Thornton et al. 2011). Although there has been considerable research on the influence of socio-demographic variables on the performance of SSEs, the influence of socio-cultural factors on SSEs performance remains understudied.

3 Theoretical Reviews on Socio-Culture and Enterprise Development

The socio-cultural environment consists of the components that make up the social systems and the way of life of the people in a particular environment. Anthropologist has submitted that socio-cultural factors such as social networks, social capital, histories, norms, values, beliefs, and attitudes of a particular locality or environment goes a long way in determining the success or otherwise of an enterprise (Akhter and Sumi 2014). Following the ideas of Hofstede (1984), anthropologist view entrepreneurial setup as part of a cultural process since it involves fitting knowledge, skills, and resources that are available in a particular locality or environment for productive purposes (Hayton et al. 2011).

Unlike Karl Marx, Weber's approach to social groups and classes was defined and determined by whether or not they bourgeoisies owned their production means. Basically, Weber's theory stems from the socio-cultural systems in which individuals live and their decisions whether or not to be entrepreneurs. These socio-cultural contents that therefore shape the activities of an enterprise have been identified to birth different theories. For instance, the family orientation theory opines that family background and orientation shape entrepreneurial activities (Kuratko and Hodgetts 1998). Also the education incubation theory asserts that education assists entrepreneurial development as it assists to create new knowledge and build on existing knowledge. Meanwhile, some other factors that explain entrepreneurship and small business development within the socio-cultural context also include institutional setups which may be formal or informal as the case may be (Thornton et al. 2011; Urbano et al. 2011); as well as behavioral patterns often referred to as cognitive skills (Finke et al. 1992).

The Contingency theory argues for appropriate managerial action to tackling issues within a socio-cultural context. Thus, rather than seeking universal principles that apply to every situation, contingency theory attempts to identify possible principles that prescribe actions to take depending on the characteristics of the situation. Therefore, the contingency theory identified elements of organization that shape a successful firm such as technology, which are the tools and devices that are used in effecting transformation of raw material into finished products (Oyebola et al. 2019). The technological elements also include stock of knowledge and skills available for actualizing entrepreneurial success. Other elements are structure or the arrangement of relationship of power, authority, and communication within the organization; as well as the sentiments of participants within a venture—where sentiment include satisfaction, senses of commitments, feelings of alienation, and feeling of identification.

According to Hunger and Wheelen (2003), the concept of contingency implies that there is no one absolute "right" design, rather, there is a multitude of possibilities and the best or preferred choice will be contingent on the situation being analyzed. The contingency theories also suggest that universal theory cannot be applied to organizations because each organization is unique. The approach emphasize appropriate managerial action depends on the particular parameters of the situation.

The work of Woodward (1980) is most often referred in the study of contingency model of organization. According to her, the most effective form of organization tends to vary with types of technology. The relevance of her theory lies in the position of technology in production process at any level; be it small-scale production or large organization.

4 Methodology

4.1 Area of Study

The study was carried out in the Southwest geo-political zones of Nigeria. The choice of this geographical area was due to the largest concentration of SSEs. The presence of the sizeable proportion of small businesses in this zone might be attributed to its proximity to the seaports and the fact that the zone is the most industrialized zone in the country. Also, the influx of people from other regions to this zone in search of job and income-generation ventures corroborates this assertion. Besides, there is dearth of information on the influence of socio-cultural factors on performance of small-scale agro-allied manufacturing firms in the southwestern Nigeria. The south western Nigeria is made up of six states; Ekiti, Ogun, Ondo, Oyo, Osun and Lagos state. The study was conducted on Ondo, Osun, and Oyo state because agro-allied activities are more predominant in these states compared to Ogun and Lagos states, while Ekiti state was recently carved out of Ondo state and therefore, could be regarded as part of Ondo state. The south-west geopolitical zone is bounded in the west by Republic of Benin; in the south by the Gulf of Guinea; in the east by Edo and Delta state; and in the north by Kwara and Kogi state. The area lies between longitude 20,421 and 60,031 east of Greenwich and latitude 50,491 and 90,171 north of the equators.

4.2 Research Design

Descriptive survey design was employed for the study. Primary and secondary data were collected using qualitative and quantitative methodologies through the use of questionnaire and publications reports and records of National Association of Small-Scale Industrialists (NASSI). Questionnaires were purposely administered on the 438 respondents (owners/managers) from the three States of Ondo, Osun, and Oyo, while qualitative data were gathered using in-depth interview techniques, from nine members of executive of NASSI from the study area. The data were analyzed using simple percentage, cross tabulation, and ranking as well as logistic regression because some of the variables are dichotomous in nature. The inclusion criteria were: small scale firms in agro-allied manufacturing sub-sector that have been in existence for at least three years; with a total of capital equipment employed including working capital but excluding cost of land being N2 million but not exceeding N50 million (as categorized by the Company and Allied Matters Decree, 1990, amended by the Company Allied Matters Act, 2004) and having a workforce of at least 10 staff.

The total population of 438 agro-allied firms that met the above criteria were listed from the membership register of NASSI during pre-field survey exercise carried out in the three states where the study was conducted. The total population of 438 owners/managers was selected as sample size in order to have adequate data, geographical spread of respondents, and fair representation of arrays of products classified as agro-allied firms. The distribution of firms in each of the state were Ondo state (156), Osun state (93), and Oyo state (189). This distribution was based on the number of firms in each state.

The dependent variables employed in explaining the performance of SSAMEs in south western Nigeria include efficiency, market coverage, and staff expansion. Rust et al. (2002) identified efficiency especially in terms of cost and increasing revenue as indices for measuring good performance as far as organizations setups are concerned. Also, Ward (1993) shed light on how firm expansion through entrepreneurial strides can bring about reduction in unemployment, which is evident in staff, market, and even goods expansion. While there are several variables that can explain firm performances as it were; for this chapter, the selected independent variables that are based on previous empirical studies to include religion, values, attitude, education, gender, manager's experience. Craig and Dibrell (2006) referred to value and culture as an intangible phenomenon that is consistent with high as far as business performance especially as families are concerned; this is also consistent with the thoughts of Tseng (2010).

Religion could contribute to firm performance; as a matter of fact, studies have shown that where there are deep religious inclinations, entrepreneurs will tend to use religious positions to inform their decision-making, even when they are inconsistent with business interests in the short-run (Dana 2010). Meanwhile, Dodd and Gotsis (2007) suggested that religious groups can also provide a resource for the generation of entrepreneurial social capital and business development. Other cultural dimensions are seen it the works of Stoyanovska (2001) that opines that attitude and gender has strategic influences in accounting for entrepreneurial success, Johnsen and McMahon (2005) were of the opinion that gender has no sufficient dimensions in dictating the pace of a successful enterprise. While Kuratko and Hornsby (1999) emphasized on skills in terms of leadership as a key performance indicator of entrepreneurial ventures; the education incubation theory posits that high level of education tend to produce more entrepreneurs than societies with less educated people (Akhter and Sumi 2014). However, Van der Sluis et al. (2008) in an account of samples drawn from hundred firms found five different positions on the education–enterprise nexus which include the insignificance of education on entrepreneurship; the significant positive effect of education on performance; the returns to a marginal year of schooling are 6.1% for an entrepreneur; the effect of education on earnings is smaller for entrepreneurs than for employees in Europe, but larger in the USA; and the returns to schooling in entrepreneurship are higher in the USA than in Europe, higher for females than for males, and lower for non-whites or immigrants. This goes to explain the conflicting perception of the education–entrepreneurship nexus given the peculiarities and design of different organizations.

4.3   Validations of Research Instrument and Testing

The level of instrument reliability is dependent on its ability to produce the same score when used repeatedly (Babble and Monton 1998). Five academics who are expert in methodology and questionnaire design from different departments: Sociology, Demography and Social Statistics, Psychology, Management, and Accounting were asked to evaluate the questionnaire and examine the reasonableness and accuracy of the questionnaire in measuring what it is supposed to measure.

Also, a pretest of the questionnaire was carried out using related companies to the ones under review. Five of such companies were selected in each of the three states on owners/managers that were not among the selected respondent for the main study. For the purpose of analysis, the reliability test was conducted for each of the socio-cultural factors and small-scale agro-allied manufacturing firms' performance indices. The reliability of the measuring instrument was conducted by means of Cronbach's Alpha test; the results were shown in Table 1.

All of the research questions have been answered based on the data of the pre test study sample except the question of measuring the performance indicator. Initially, the researcher suggested the use of profit, productivity, market shares, and firm sales as measure of performance; however, it was observed that any performance indicator that entailed enquiring about exact monetary values was completely rejected by the managers/owners. A monetary measure was not possible either due to the respondents' inability or to unwillingness to offer such data. In general, the pretest phase proved satisfying in terms of the ways to improve upon the questionnaire and interview guide and in terms of asking the appropriate questions on the way to test the hypotheses and reflecting upon the research question.

4.4   Hypothesis

Emanating from the objective of the study is the hypothesis which centers on the extent to which socio-cultural factors influence the performance of SSAME in the south western Nigeria. The hypotheses are stated as follows:

Table 1 Result of reliability test

	Reliability	Unreliability
Independent variables		
Religious	0.997	0.003
Values	0.995	0.005
Attitude	0.982	0.018
Education	0.988	0.012
Gender	0.995	0.005
Owners/managers experience	0.993	0.007
Dependent variables		
Efficiency	0.998	0.002
Market coverage	0.999	0.001
Staff expansion	0.998	0.002

Source Authors' field survey

H_0 There is no significant relationship between socio-cultural factors and performance of small-scale agro-allied manufacturing enterprises in south western Nigeria

H_1 There is a significant relationship between socio-cultural factors and performance of small-scale agro-allied manufacturing enterprises in south western Nigeria

4.5 Model Specification

In this sub-section, all the selected explanatory variables are expressed as a function of the response variables, which are efficiency, market coverage, and staff expansion.

$$\text{Efficiency} = f(X_1, X_2, X_3, X_4, X_5, X_6) \tag{1}$$

$$\text{Market Coverage} = f(X_1, X_2, X_3, X_4, X_5, X_6) \tag{2}$$

$$\text{Staff Expansion} = f(X_1, X_2, X_3, X_4, X_5, X_6) \tag{3}$$

where

X_1 Gender
X_2 Religious Belief
X_3 Dependency of Extended Family
X_4 Ostentatious Life Style
X_5 Education
X_6 Experience of Managers

5 Findings

5.1 Socio-Cultural Factors Capable of Influencing Performance of Small-Scale Agro-Allied Manufacturing Enterprises

In order to achieve the objective, both respondents of the questionnaire and in-depth interview were asked to mention the socio-cultural factors they knew in their areas that are capable of influencing SSAMEs performance. Table 2 revealed the various factors mentioned by the respondents of the in-depth interview and the responses of the owners/mangers of the investigated firms as factors capable of influencing performance of Small-Scale and Agro-allied Manufacturing Firms in the South Western Nigeria. Religious beliefs was the most often quoted socio-cultural factor with 20.1%, followed by corruption (14.6%), ostentatious life-style (11.0%), nepotism (8.7%), spirituality with 9.8% each, illiteracy 10.7%, extended family (8.9%), commitments to wealth with 8.9% while time factor was with 7.3%. These findings revealed the significant roles of religious beliefs, corruption, ostentatious lifestyle, and illiteracy on the social structure of Nigerian society, which in a way affected other social institutions and organizations within the social system. These four factors accounted for 56.4% of the total socio-cultural factors influence while the remaining six factors accounted for 43.7%. In order to achieve significant growth in SSAMEs contribution to the national economy, the government needs to address the problems of corruption, illiteracy, ostentatious lifestyle and religious bigotry.

These findings confirmed the evidence from the previous studies (Dore 1973; Hofstede 1991; Iguisi 1994; Aluko 2001, 2004) that socio-cultural factors—beliefs, education, gender, extended family, corruption, norms, values, and attitude of the people have significant influence on the organization (SSEs inclusive) performance. Studies by,

Table 2 Socio-cultural factors influencing performance of SSAMEs in South-western Nigeria

Socio-cultural	Frequency distribution	Valid percentages (%)	Cumulative (%)
Religious beliefs	88	20.1	20.1
Spiritual problem	43	9.8	29.9
Extended family	39	8.9	38.8
Ostentatious life style	48	11.0	49.8
Corruption	64	14.6	64.4
Commitments to wealth	39	8.9	73.3
Time factor	32	7.3	80.6
Nepotism	38	8.7	89.3
Illiteracy	47	10.7	100
Total	438	100	100

Source Authors' field survey

Blunt (1973), Blunt and Jones (2011) produced similar results. In addition, Leonard's (1987) discussion of the difference between Western World and Africa confirmed that socio-cultural factors do influence performance of.

5.2 Multiple Regression Analysis Linking Socio-Cultural Factors to Small-Scale Agro-Allied Manufacturing Enterprises Performance

In the actual measure of the performance of SSAMEs, the indices employed included efficiency, market coverage, and staff expansion. Table 3 shows the mechanism linking social-cultural factors and SSAMEs performance. The explanatory variables accounted for approximately 50% of the variation in the SSAMEs performance measured by efficiency in Model 1. Gender is found to be positive and significantly related to efficiency of SSAMEs ($\beta=0.367$, $t=15.56$) at 0.5 level. The result indicated a direct relationship between gender and efficiency, implying that gender was found to be significantly influencing the level of efficiency of SSAMEs. This view is in line with the general observation and findings of Bamiduro (2001), Yusuff et al. (2012) that the gender of the owner/managers significantly has influence on the performance of SSAMEs.

Religious belief is also found to be positively and significantly ($\beta=0.39$, $t=15.79$) related to efficiency of SSAMEs. Dependency of extended family members is also found to be positively and significantly ($\beta=0.075$, $t=3.277$) related to efficiency of SSAMEs these findings imply that religious beliefs and

Table 3 Mechanism linking socio-cultural factors to SSAMFs performance

Explanatory variables	Model 1 (efficiency)		Model 2 (market coverage)		Model 3 (staff expansion)	
	Coefficient β	t-stat	Coefficient β	t-stat	Coefficient β	t-stat
Gender	0.367	15.56*	−0.161	−6.07*	0.184	7.006*
Religious belief	0.349	15.79*	0.133	5.361*	0.382	15.59*
Dependency of extended family	0.075	3.277*	0.074	2.876*	0.139	5.422*
Ostentations life-style	0.142	6.313*	0.258	10.21*	0.009	0.372
Education	0.055	2.223*	0.099	3.587*	−0.104	−3.83*
Experience owners/managers	0.118	5.547*	0.055	2.299*	0.035	1.469
Constant	−0.006	−0.086	0.864	11.29	0.514	6.936*
R^2	0.5004		0.250		0.379	
F-stat	171.072*		56.064*		102.669*	

Note *Depicts significance of the estimate at 5% level of significance
Source Authors' data analysis

burden of extended family exert influence on the performance of SSAMEs. Similarly, ostentatious lifestyle of the owners/managers is found to be positive and significantly related to efficiency of SSAMEs ($\beta=0.142$, $t=6.313$). The average Nigerian entrepreneur is found to be engage in ostentations life styles—during, expensive clothe pleasurable and expensive cars completed with excessive spending on social ceremony such as chieftaincy tittles, naming, burial and funeral, birthday, house warming among others. The implication of this is low level of savings, which made it difficult for many of the SSAMEs to raise needed working capital for their operations (AbdulRasaq 2014; Babagana 2010).

The findings also found education to be positively and significantly related to efficiency of SSAMEs ($\beta=0.055$, $t=2.223$) the distribution of the educational attachment of owners/manager revealed that majority of the owners/manager (90.7%) had acquired secondary and tertiary education (Table 3) these findings confirmed the assertion by Bowale and Akinlo (2012) that there was significant relationship between level of education of owners/managers and SSEs performance. Previous experience of the owners/managers is found to be positive and significantly related to efficiency of SSAMEs ($\beta=0.118$, $t=5.547$), it is evident from the literature that previous experience from the literature that previous experience (administrative, occupational, industry, and managers) impact significantly on the performance of SSAMEs (Hamilton 2000; Bosma et al. 2004; Woldie et al. 2008).

In the market coverage of model 2 of Table 3, all explanatory variables accounted for 25% of the variation in SSAMEs performance measured by market coverage. Religious beliefs ($\beta=0.133$, $t=5.361$) extended family dependency ($\beta=0.074$, $t=2.876$) ostentatious lifestyles ($\beta=0.142$, $t=313$) education ($\beta=0.099$, $t=3.587$) experience of owner/managers ($\beta=0.55$, $t=2299$) are found to be positively and significantly influenced by market coverage at 0.05 significant level. This implies that religious beliefs, dependency of extended family, ostentatious lifestyle, education and experience of owners/managers, impact directly on the market coverage of these firms. On the contrary, gender ($\beta=-0.161$, $t=-6.07$) have negative but significant effect influence on market coverage of SSAMEs, implying that the gender of the owners and managers do not have influence on market coverage.

In the staff expansion model of model 3, all explanation variables accounted for 38% of the variation in SSAMEs performance measured by staff expansion. Gender inclusive had a positive significant influence on ($\beta=0.184$, $t=7.006$) on SSAMEs performance.

From the logistic regression above, the Analysis of Variance (ANOVA) is presented in Table 4. The results of the test indicated a rejection of the null hypothesis at 0.05; level implying that socio-cultural factors do have a significant influence on SSAMEs performance ($F=102.669$; $p=0.000$).

From the analysis, gender is seen to have a mixed effect on the performance of SSAMEs. While gender had a positive effect on efficiency and staff expansion, it is seen to have a negative effect on market coverage. This

Table 4 ANOVA results for test of the hypotheses

Model	Sum of squares	Df	Mean square	F	p-value
Regression	540.462	9	60.051	102.669*	0.000
Residual	886.125	1515	0.585		
Total	14,265.588	1524			

Note *Indicate significant at 1%
Source Authors' data analysis

mixed position is consistent with the findings in literature; while the positive effects are consistent with the findings of Stoyanovska (2001), Johnsen and McMahon (2005) did not find enough evidence for the gender–enterprise performance nexus. This is unlike religious belief and ostentatious lifestyle which had an overall positive effect on SSAME performance; thus, indicating that just like Dana (2010), Dodd and Gotsis (2007), Craig and Dibrell (2006) that affirmed that culture which includes religious beliefs and life styles indeed have significant effects as far as firm performances are concerned. Similarly, from this study and in consonance with the position of Kuratko and Hornsby (1999) on skills and leadership style and experience, managers/owners experience that has been identified as an important determinant of entrepreneurial outcomes, had an overriding influence on SSAME performance in Nigeria. Meanwhile, unlike the education incubation theory proposes, education had a mixed effect on firm performance. Just like Van der Sluis et al. (2008), education had significant positive effects on efficiency and market coverage of SSAMEs; however, a negative relation was spotted on staff expansion as far as this study is concerned for the Nigerian case. Therefore, it can be deduced that societal and cultural structures like beliefs, religion, and lifestyle are more contingent for firm performances than formal educational structures especially as regards SSAMEs in Nigeria.

6 Conclusion

Central to the hypothesis, is the assumption that "socio-cultural factors" are capable of influencing small-scale agro-allied enterprise performance, and as such every small-scale business is subject to the dictates of its socio-cultural environments. From the study, a significant relationship is therefore expected between performances on one hand and socio-cultural factors on the other hand. Thus, from the analysis, SSAMEs that are performing well or optimally are linked to the socio-cultural environment that is suitable for their operations. This implicates that is performance are strongly related and adaptable to the dominant values, norms, and belief in society. On the whole, these findings lend credence to the contingency proposition that no single factor determines the performance of small-scale business (French and Bell 1978; Oribabor 2012).

Meanwhile, from the findings, the significant roles of religious beliefs, corruption, ostentatious lifestyle, and illiteracy on the social structure of Nigerian society does a long way in determining social institutions and organizations within the social system. Thus, to achieve significant growth of SSAMEs' contribution to the national economy in Nigeria, the government needs to among others address the problems of gender limitations, corruption, illiteracy, ostentatious lifestyle, and religious bigotry. While at individual levels, for owners/managers of SSAMEs to achieve maximum result, adequate attention must be paid to the socio-cultural environment, which researches have shown to play significant roles in the overall performance of business. This is further strengthened by the findings of this study that revealed the strength of each socio-cultural variable being significant in determining the SSAME's performance as it relates to efficiency, market coverage, and staff expansion. While this study has concentrated on SSAMEs, it can be extended to other sectors in Nigeria and the indices of assessment can be expanded to give more insights on developmental strides in Nigeria.

References

AbdulRasaq, M. (2014, December). SMES owners perception on the value of accounting information for economic decision making in Ilorin metropolis. *Ilorin Journal of Management Sciences,* 1(2), 16–28.

Adeoti, J. O., & Olubamiwa, O. (2009). Towards an innovation system in the traditional sector: The case of the Nigerian cocoa industry. *Science and Public Policy,* 36(1), 15–31.

Adesina, A. (2013). Unemployment and security challenges in Nigeria. *International Journal of Humanities and Social Sciences,* 3, 107.

Ahiauzu, A. I. (1986). The African thought system and the work behaviour of the African industrial man. *International Studies of Management and Organization,* 16(2), 37–58.

Ajani, E. N., & Igbokwe, E. M. (2014). A review of agricultural transformation agenda in Nigeria: The case of public and private sector participation. *Research Journal of Agriculture and Environmental Management,* 3(5), 238–245.

Akhter, R., & Sumi, F. R. (2014). Socio-cultural factors influencing entrepreneurial activities: A study on Bangladesh. *IOSR Journal of Business and Management,* 16(9), 1–10.

Aluko, M. A. O. (2001). *The impact of culture on organizational performance in selected textile firms in Nigeria.* Unpublished Ph.D. Thesis Submitted to the Department of Sociology and Anthropology, O.A.U., Ile-If, Nigeria.

Aluko, M. A. O. (2004). The impact of culture on organizational performance in selected textile firms in Nigeria. *Global Environment Journal of Social Science.*

Aworemi, J. R., Abdul-Azeez, I. A., & Opoola, N. A. (2010). Impact of socio-economic factors on the performance of small-scale enterprises in Osun State, Nigeria. *International Business Research,* 3(2), 92.

Babagana, S. A. (2010). Impact assessment of the role of micro finance banks in promoting small and medium enterprises growth in Nigeria. *International Journal of Economic Development Research and Investment,* 1(1), 42–53.

Babble, E., & Monton, J. (1998). *The practice of social research.* Cape Town: Oxford University Press.
Bamiduro, A. A. (2001). Factors influencing small scale business start-ups: A comparison with previous research. In *Advances in management*, Journal of Department of Business Administration, University of Ilorin, Ilorin, Nigeria.
Blunt, P. (1973). Cultural and situational determinant of job satisfaction amongst management in South Africa: A research note. *Journal of Management Studies, 10,* 133–140.
Blunt, P., & Jones, M. L. (2011). *Managing organisations in Africa* (Vol. 40). Berlin: Walter de Gruyter.
Bosma, N., van Praag, C. M., Thurik, R., & de Wit, G. (2004). The value of human and social capital investments for the business performance of startups. *Small Business Economics, 23,* 227–236.
Bowale, K., & Akinlo, A. (2012). Determinant of small and medium enterprises and poverty alleviation in developing countries: Evidence from South-Western Nigeria. *European Journal of Humanities and Social Sciences, 17*(2), 848–863.
Central Bank of Nigeria. (2016). Statistical Bulletin. *Central Bank of Nigeria,* P. M. B. 0187, Garki, Abuja.
Craig, J., & Dibrell, C. (2006). The natural environment, innovation, and firm performance: A comparative study. *Family Business Review, 19*(4), 275–288.
Dana, L. P. (Ed.). (2010). *Entrepreneurship and religion.* Cheltenham: Edward Elgar Publishing.
Dodd, S. D., & Gotsis, G. (2007). The interrelationships between entrepreneurship and religion. *The International Journal of Entrepreneurship and Innovation, 8*(2), 93–104.
Dore, R. (1973). *British factory—Japanese factory.* London: George Allen and Unwin.
Duhu, J. O. (2015). *Political economy of Nigeria–China relations (1999–2013).* Doctoral dissertation.
Egbouna, C. K., Aiyewalehinmi, E. O., Louis, I. A., & Agali, I. (2013). The role of engineering in agro-industrial development in Nigeria. *Educational Research, 4,* 340–344.
Egwuonwu, U. I. (2012). The impact of education in the use of ICT by small and medium scale entrepreneurs in Zaria and Kaduna. *The Pacific Journal of Science and Technology, 13,* 418–423. Retrieved from http://www.akamainuniversity.us/PJST.htm.
Ekpenyong, D. B., & Nyong, M. O. (1992). *Small and medium scale enterprises in Nigeria: Their characteristics, problems and sources of finance* (AERC Research Paper 18).
FAO. (2011, March). *The role of women in agriculture* (ESA Working Paper No. 11-02). As Prepared by SOFA Team and Cheryl Doss, Agricultural Development Economics Division, The Food and Agriculture Organization of the United Nations. Online: www.fao.org/economic/esa.
Finke, R. A., Ward, T. B., & Smith, S. M. (1992). *Creative cognition: Theory, research, and applications.* Cambridge, MA: MIT Press.
French, W. L., & Bell, C. H. (1978). *Organization development: Behavioural science interventions for organization improvement* (2nd ed.). Eaglewood Chiffs, NJ: Prentice-Hall.
Hamilton, B. H. (2000). Does entrepreneurship pay? An empirical analysis of the returns to self-employment. *Journal of Political Economy, 108,* 604–631.

Hayton, J., Chandler, G. N., & DeTienne, D. R. (2011). Entrepreneurial opportunity identification and new firm development processes: A comparison of family and non-family new ventures. *International Journal of Entrepreneurship and Innovation Management, 13*(1), 12–31.

Hofstede, G. (1984). *Cultur's consequences.* Beverly Hills, CA: Sage.

Hofstede, G. (1991). *Culture and organizations: Structure of the mind.* London: McGraw–Hill.

Hunger, J. D., & Wheelen, T. l. (2003). *Essentials of strategic management* (3rd ed.). Upper Saddle River, NJ: Prentice Hall.

Igudia, P. O. (2017). A qualitative analysis of the agricultural policy dynamics and the Nigerian economy: 1960–2015. *European Scientific Journal, ESJ, 13*(34), 284–312.

Iguisi, O. (1994, January–March). *Appropriate management in an Africa culture in management in Nigeria.* Published by the Nigeria Institute of Management, Vol. 30, No. 1, Inquiry, *Economic Inquiry* 35.

Itumo, V. N. (2016). Nigeria's mono-cultural economy: Impact assessment and prospects. *European Journal of Interdisciplinary Studies, 8*(2), 20–35.

Johnsen, G. J., & McMahon, R. G. (2005). Owner-manager gender, financial performance and business growth amongst SMEs from Australia's business longitudinal survey. *International Small Business Journal, 23*(2), 115–142.

Kormawa, P. M. (2011, June 2). *Nigeria industrialization: Unlocking the potential.* A Paper presented at the Quarterly Business Luncheons Organized by Lagos Chamber of Commerce and Industry, LCCI Conference and Exhibit Centre.

Kuratko, D. F., & Hodgetts, R. N. (1998). *Entrepreneurship: A contemporary approach.* Orlando, USA: The Dryden Press, Harcourt Brace College Publisher.

Kuratko, D. F., & Hornsby, J. S. (1999). Corporate entrepreneurial leadership for the 21st century. *Journal of Leadership Studies, 5*(2), 27–39.

Leonard, D. K. (1987). The political realities of African management. *Word Development, 15,* 899–910.

National Bureau of Statistics (NBS). (2016). *Nigerian gross domestic product report.* Quarter four 2016. www.nigeranstat.gov.ng.

National Bureau of Statistics (NBS). (2017). *Nigerian gross domestic product report.* www.nigeranstat.gov.ng.

Okafor, E. E. (2011). Youth unemployment and implications for stability of democracy in Nigeria. *Journal of Sustainable Development in Africa, 13*(1), 358–373.

Olagunju, Y. A. (2004). *Entrepreneurship and small scale business enterprises development in Nigeria.* Ibadan: University Press PLC.

Olajide, O. T., Akinlabi, B. H., & Tjani, A. A. (2012). Agriculture resource and economic growth in Nigeria. *European Scientific Journal, 8*(22), 103–115.

Olaoye, O. A. (2014). Potentials of the agro industry towards achieving food security in Nigeria and Other Sub-Saharan African Countries. *Journal of Food Security, 2*(1), 33–41.

Olawale, A. (2010). *Entrepreneurship development* (5th ed.). Lagos: Gilgal Creations and Publications.

Onuoha, M. E., & Elegbede, I. O. (2018). The oil boom era: Socio-political and economic consequences. In *The political ecology of oil and gas activities in the Nigerian aquatic ecosystem* (pp. 83–99). London: Elsevier.

Oribabor, E. P. (2012). Approaches to organization theory: New-classical management theory. In A. O. Ogunbameruand & E. P. Oribabor (Eds.), *Industrial sociology.* Ibadan: Penthouse Publications (Nig).

Osabuohien, E., Okorie, U., & Osabohien, R. (2018). Rice production and processing in Ogun State, Nigeria: Qualitative insights from farmers' association. In E. Obayelu (Ed.), *Food systems sustainability and environmental policies in modern economics* (pp. 188–216). Hershey, PA: IGI Global. https://doi.org/10.4018/978-1-5225-3631-4.ch009.

Oyebola, P. O., Osabuohien, E., & Obasaju, B. (2019). Employment and income effects of Nigeria's agricultural transformation agenda. *African Journal of Economic and Management Studies*. https://doi.org/10.1108/AJEMS-12-2018-0402.

Oyesola, O. B., & Obabire, I. E. (2011). Farmer's perceptions of organic farming in selected local government areas of Ekiti State, Nigeria. *Journal of Organic Systems, 6*(1), 20–26.

Rust, R. T., Moorman, C., & Dickson, P. R. (2002). Getting return on quality: Revenue expansion, cost reduction, or both? *Journal of Marketing, 66*(4), 7–24.

Salami, C. G. E. (2013). Youth unemployment in Nigeria: A time for creative intervention. *International Journal of Business and Marketing Management, 1*(2), 18–26. www.Resjournalsorg/IJBMM.

Small and Medium Enterprises Development Agency of Nigeria (SMEDAN). (2003). *Who we are.* Retrieved from http://www.smedan.gov.ng.

Sorensen, J. B., & Chang, P. M. Y. (2006, February). *Determinants of successful entrepreneurship: A review of the recent literature* (Report Prepared for the Ewing Marion Kanffman Foundation).

Stoyanovska, A. (2001). *Jobs, gender and small enterprises in Bulgaria* (No. 993510263402676). International Labor Organization.

Sumberg, J., & Okali, C. (2013). Young people agriculture and transformation in rural Africa: An "opportunity space" approach. *Innovations*, A quarterly Journal published by MLT Press. *Global Youth Economic Opportunities Conference.*

Thornton, P. H., Ribeiro-Soriano, D., & Urbano, D. (2011). Socio-cultural factors and entrepreneurial activity: An overview. *International Small Business Journal, 29*(2), 105–118.

Tseng, S. M. (2010). The correlation between organizational culture and knowledge conversion on corporate performance. *Journal of Knowledge Management, 14*(2), 269–284.

Ucha, U. (2010). Poverty in Nigeria: Some dimensions and contributing factors. *Global Majority E. Journal, 1,* 46–56.

UNDP, A. (2012). *Africa human development report 2012 towards a food secure future* (No. 267636). United Nations Development Programme (UNDP).

Urbano, D., Toledano, N., & Ribeiro-Soriano, D. (2011). Socio-cultural factors and transnational entrepreneurship: A multiple case study in Spain. *International Small Business Journal, 29*(2), 119–134.

Vaarst, M. (2010). Organic farming as a development strategy: Who are interested and who are not? *Journal of Sustainable Development, 3*(1), 38–50.

Van der Sluis, J., Van Praag, M., & Vijverberg, W. (2005). Entrepreneurship selection and performance: A meta-analysis of the impact of education in developing economies. *The World Bank Economic Review, 19*(2), 225–261.

Van der Sluis, J., Van Praag, M., & Vijverberg, W. (2008). Education and entrepreneurship selection and performance: A review of the empirical literature. *Journal of Economic Surveys, 22*(5), 795–841.

Ward, N. (1993). The agricultural treadmill and the rural environment in the post-productivist era. *Sociologia Ruralis, 33*(3–4), 348–364.

Woldie, A., Leighton, P., & Adesua, A. (2008). Factors influences small and medium scale enterprises (SMEs): An explanatory study of owner/manager and firm characteristics. *Banks and Bank System, 3*(3), 5–13.

Woodward, J. (1980). *Industrial organization: Theory and practice* (No. 04; HD38, W6 1980).

Yusuff, S. O., Olagbemi, A. A., & Atere, A. A. (2012). *Factors affecting small scale business performance in informal economy in Lagos State Nigeria: A gendered base analysis*.

Zhou, H., & de Wit, G. (2009). *Determinants and dimensions of firm growth* (SCALES EIM Research Reports (H200903)).

Labor Processes in Large-Scale Land Investments: The Case of Sugar Estates in South-Eastern Zimbabwe

Patience Mutopo

1 Introduction

The land question remains a key issue of academic and policy enquiry in Zimbabwe since the 1980s. Events that happened with the advent of the fast track land reform in Zimbabwe on the 15th of July 2000 have; however, altered the geopolitical and physical landscape. This has created four systems of landholding thus the fast track farms that are characterized by smallholding of land that is now being owned by the black majority, medium-scale farms that are modeled on the former large-scale farms, the estates (i.e., plantations) and the former large-scale white farms still exist (Mutopo 2015; Mutopo et al. 2015). Zimbabwe has also been rezoned into farming units that (Moyo 2011), have proffered as referring to the trimodal system of land use. However, an important narrative in the land debate is that within these new farming systems labor issues have unequivocally become an important issue of consideration. Since the large estates still exist and now in tandem with the small-scale and medium-scale farms it becomes imperative to understand how labor arrangements are modeled in the sugar estates in the South Eastern Lowveld. Sugar production remains one of the critical crops that is dominated by the large-scale acquisitions of land with the aim of trebling the

---

P. Mutopo (✉)
Centre for Development Studies, Chinhoyi University of Technology, Chinhoyi, Zimbabwe

© The Author(s) 2020
E. S. Osabuohien (ed.), *The Palgrave Handbook of Agricultural and Rural Development in Africa*, https://doi.org/10.1007/978-3-030-41513-6_23

sugar production. In this process, the large-scale sugar estates exist side by side with the new fast track farmers who are also squeezing themselves for space in the production of sugar cane.

These developments tend to alter the sugarcane labor matrix, as the producers are all sourcing labor. The important aspect which becomes quite critical to understand is how the labor is sourced, an understanding of at what levels of the crop production is the labor sourced by whom and where. Teasing out these questions gives one glimpse into the everyday forms of labor arrangements and how they can be understood. An important aspect that the author also demonstrates is how new fast track farmers find themselves entangled in a well-established industry that carries a white face and is highly organized in terms of labor processes.

2 Issues from Extant Studies

2.1 Theoretical Framework

Theorizing large-scale land investments locally and internationally has witnessed controversies. The disagreements emanate from the different discourses permeating academia, civic, and international organizations working on the importance of land-based foreign direct investment growth in rural areas. However, in order to employ a middle of the road approach in this debate, I adopted the political economy approach to labor trade in the sugarcane plantations and the fast track farms. The literature on the political economy of trade policy was transformed by Grossman and Helpman (1994) who developed a formal model on it. It opines that special interest groups make political contributions in order to influence a government's choice of trade policy. Chambati and Moyo (2013) posit that, the interest groups bid for government protection by providing political campaign support. These contributions are assumed to be "truthful" in the sense that each interest group's contribution function varies with tariffs in the same way that their profit function varies. Politicians determine the optimal policy by maximizing their own utility, which is a weighted function of political contributions collected and social welfare. In equilibrium, interest groups pay contributions in accordance with the political strength of their rivals. An interest group that faces no competition from other groups captures the entire surplus from lobbying, whereas if all voters are represented and all sectors are organized, then free trade prevails and the government captures the entire surplus from the political relationships.

The study has decided to theorize with the angle of taking trade and labor in tandem because the sugar industry in Zimbabwe is largely dominated by white conglomerates, and therefore, the bigger actors in the process. For example, Tongaat Hullets, Chiredzi Estates, and others due to their control of the agenda setting process tend to control the labor prices as well as the commodity prices. This argument evokes the notion that the political economy approach to labor brings to the fore the interplay of race and class interest as forming the formidable attributes of how the sugarcane industry operates and how the labor processes are modeled.

3   Method of Analysis

It is also important to note that methodological considerations of studying large-scale land acquisitions have also been recently contested (Moyo 2009). It is important, therefore, to create systematized data that has roots in original research work. However, in this section, the study presents the importance of how empirical validations create a good basis for analyzing the impacts of large-scale land acquisitions on women's livelihoods. Data collection modes of study were qualitative in nature, in Chiredzi sugar estates and the surrounding fast track farms of Dangasaruri. Since this is a study that raises emotional overtones form the different respondents due to land questions, preference was made to use qualitative methodological approach. This differs from the quantitative technique used for sugarcane estates in Malawi as employed by Herrmann et al. (2018).

The above is with a view to glimpsing into the lives of the new fast track farmers and understanding how they accessed labor since they were surrounded by the triangle sugar estates. This, therefore, led the researcher to engage in, in-depth interviews, focus group discussions and administered participatory games to the respondents. The *mono-methodims* of the study enabled the researcher to get experiences of the landowners, the people who provided the labor and how labor was construed and understood by the Chiredzi Estates as opposed to the fast track farmers. The data analysis was done thematically and this helped in understanding how studies on large-scale land investments ought to have coordinated reflective methodologies especially with regards to livelihoods. It is important therefore to create systematized data that has roots in original research work.

4   Evidences of Labor Processes in Zimbabwe's Large-Scale Land Investments

4.1   *Labor Evolvement in the Sugarcane Fast Track Farms*

Land tenure and labor regimes are interdependent in their contribution to livelihood activities and outcomes, however, because they have often been analyzed separately, their interconnections are often missed (Tsikata 2009). Studies on land tenure have demonstrated how inequalities between men and women in ownership and control of—and access to—land have resulted in gender inequalities in livelihood outcomes (Matondi 2012; Goebel 2005; Chingarande 2004; Moyo and Chambati 2004). Labor use Dangasaruri is regulated by different household regimes depending on the nature of the farming activities undertaken by each family. The new sugarcane farmers used either family-based labor or labor hired from the surrounding communal areas. If a household has a number of fields under cultivation, labor is hired from places as far away as Chivi District, because the people from Chivi who are involved in *maricho* (labor in exchange for either cash or food) require lower payment than people from other districts.

In some cases, the laborers were new in the area or came from other areas such as Birchenough in Chipinge District. Cattle-herders, in particular, came from homes that are more distant and pointed out that it was better to work in Chiredzi than in their original home area because the income was much better in Chiredzi. FTLR has led to new labor dynamics and a shift in livelihoods for the seasonal laborers, who also at times are given portions of land to plant either groundnuts or maize. The new configuration of agricultural space in Zimbabwe has led to the altering of the labor regime that existed in the commercial farms before the FTLRP. These changes are based on the duration of working time that a person invests in a particular plot. Chambati (2009, p. 1) states that "much of the debate on the effects of redistributive land reform has been narrowly focused on job losses ignoring the other opportunities created for labor to reproduce themselves among the beneficiaries of new workers." Labor recruitment is still on going, albeit on a shorter timescale than the commercial farms; but labor viability and hiring proved to be important considerations for most households, especially those growing highly labor-intensive cotton.

4.2 Labor Dimensions Within Dangasaruri Households

Some households had fulltime laborers who helped look after cattle. Cattle-herders were all men; there was no household with a female cattle-herder, except when the wife of the plot holder would look after the cattle, or a widow would look after her cattle and those of her daughter/s. Five percent of the laborers at Dangasaruri Village came from the surrounding communal areas of Chiredzi, Neshuro, Lundi, Ngundu, and Gold Star, and 30% came from communal areas in Gutu, Zaka, and Chivi; the remaining 65% came from other provinces, such as Midlands and Manicaland communal areas. Increasingly, there is a move toward the commercialization of agricultural labor in these new settlements (Mutopo 2015; Chambati 2018). On a micro-scale, additional employment opportunities are created by the FTLRP, although the former farm workers at Dangasaruri might have incurred losses. Chambati and Moyo (2013) note that the extensive redistribution of land has opened up a new framework for land and labor relations. This should be understood within the ambit of a new political, economic, and social structure with regards to land ownership patterns. Before they existed clear demarcations of land between the white commercial farming areas, the medium small-scale farms, and the communal farming areas. After a decade, new entrants have entered the terrain with smallholder farmers mainly the A1 farms emanating from the often-controversial fast track land reform.

4.3 Gendered Dimensions of Labor

Women are the main food producers worldwide, and they contribute more than 70% of the total labor force employed in the agriculture sector (Jirira and Halimana 2008; Osabuohien et al. 2019). Tsikata (2009, p. 23) says that feminist anthropologists have made invaluable contributions to livelihoods analysis by "emphasizing the importance of intra-household divisions of labor and resources such as land, as well as women's unpaid work." Their analysis has drawn attention to women's roles in the everyday and long-term reproduction of the labor force. Women's labor contributions lead to a need to rethink how agricultural labor should be critically analyzed and how women's roles, rather than those of men, should be codified as instrumental in production activities (Osabuohien et al. 2019).

In Zimbabwe, women provide most of the farm labor and in any case constitute 52% of the population (Mutopo 2015). This makes them a key resource in farm production activities. Labor use in Dangasaruri sugar farms was regulated according to the socioeconomic status of the household. Those employed were both men and women from the communal areas, with women constituting slightly less than half and men slightly more than half of the total employed. Most of the households that I observed and the household heads I interviewed pointed out that women from Chivi communal lands, were the best short-term laborers as they worked hard and demanded only food, in the form of maize, or clothes for their families, compared to their male counterparts, who required money and who would sometimes disappear on beer-drinking sprees. This proved to be viable options of labor endowment since the farmers would not provide a monetary benefit. The monetary payment that women usually asked for was for their bus fare back home, after staying at a homestead until the harvesting period ended. Most of the employed had also been involved with providing labor for these households when they were still based in the communal areas, and they had a long labor connection tie. The importance of female laborers at Dangasaruri Village is demonstrated in the case history provided herein.

Narrative 1: Female laborer at Dangasaruri Village
I am aged 25 and I come from Chivi communal lands. I am the first child in my family, and my parents both died and I look after my brothers and sisters. I started working permanently at Mrs. M's plot in 2003; before, I had been her casual laborer in Neshuro communal lands. When they moved here in 2000, I continued working in their communal home, until they asked me to come here. I do the household chores, work in the fields, and sometimes if the cattle herder does not come I also herd cattle. I enjoy working here, as I am paid most of my money, they provide food, accommodation, and sometimes my family visits me here. I enjoy picking cotton mostly, and I am now able to cultivate using the harrow and can make ridges on my own. I am even better than the other male laborers here as they ask for my help on how to use the ox-drawn plough and herd the

cattle. I have contributed to the progress of the plot, and I still want to continue working here. (Source: Author's fieldwork)

In terms of the labor on the plots in Tavaka Village, wives of the plot holders were a rich source of labor. Their husbands would be involved with ox-ploughing (*kusunga mombe*) and inspecting whether the farming business was being done properly. Children, both boys and girls, within these families worked alongside their mothers, especially at weekends when they were not at school. In some households, the children would help with weeding or planting before they left for school to contribute to productive time.

The findings about the division of labor are supported by Jirira and Halimana (2008), who say that there are clear differences between women and men in rural areas when it comes to issues relating to the gender division of labor. The definition of domestic chores and care-work as women's tasks stems not only from patriarchal domination and socialization but also from customary laws and practices on the ground. The same applies to agricultural labor within households. In terms of planting the sugarcane men took center stage as the sugarcane suckers to be planted had to be handled with care and transported to the fields either in scotch carts or wheelbarrows. Some of the farmers had irrigation at their plots and the watering of the sugarcane was done by both male and women; thus, demonstrating how sugarcane production was now a *genderized* crop in which both women and men played a 50–50% role in its total production.

The tasks they were involved in included ploughing (*kurima negejo*), planting, weeding, and harvesting, involved men, women, and children. They would wake early in the morning, at 4 a.m., to fetch water if it was time for planting the sugarcane seedbeds. When it was time for applying herbicides the sugarcane farmers ensured that the process was done by male children and their fathers since the farmers believed that the herbicides had health-related hazards that affected the health of women, young children, and girls mainly.

During the harvesting period this was supposed to be done before mid-day in the afternoon, since the harvesting procedure required the sugarcane to be stored in highly cool places to avoid loss of the sucrose content. This information is based on observational diaries and seasonal calendars that I kept for each homestead for 16 months. In terms of harvesting the sugarcane women played a critical role as sugarcane was a highly sensitive crop that required sensitivity in its harvesting which was done by the big knives known as machetes or hoes, so women were deemed to have the patience to deal with this agricultural harvesting procedure.

Community interactions with the villagers revealed that, although women are considered farm hands, they serve as primary producers who play both specialized and general roles in farm production processes. Their obligations went beyond functions, such as cooking for male farm hands (both members of the household and hired labor), that support men's primary roles.

In addition, they performed the following activities: working in hand-irrigated gardens, weeding fields, collecting firewood, collecting both drinking and bathing water, feeding their families and households, childcare activities, family/household laundry, and food preparation. Men featured mostly in wood collection, taking cows to look for drinking water, stacking cotton bales, ploughing, brickmaking, and giving instructions to women. Most men used scotch carts or wheelbarrows when collecting firewood, whereas women collected firewood in bundles that they carried on their heads. The fact that the men use technologies to alleviate drudgery is seldom mentioned in discussion of production systems in resettlement areas. It is therefore important to develop a sound infrastructure base in resettlement areas so that women's practical needs are taken into consideration.

Both labor and land tenure studies suffer from the weakness of failing to fully integrate reproductive work in their analysis of livelihoods. Thus, although the burden of unpaid reproductive work and its implications for women's livelihoods are increasingly becoming topical, these themes have yet to be fully integrated into studies of labor and land relations (Tsikata 2009). Often, they are discussed in terms of their contribution to production and their costs to women's productive work. In their wider ramifications, as taken up in the literature on intra-household gender and inter-generational relations, questions of sexuality open a large arena of contestations and insights that have the potential to transform our understanding of land-based livelihoods. From a political economy analytical angle gender dimensions of labor tend to stratify the role that women play in the production sphere. Women emerge as belonging to the class that is seen as the providers of labor due to the stratification that exist in African societies due to the patriarchal form social organization.

4.4   Polygyny as a Labor Enclave

Polygyny, "*kuroora vakadzi vazhinji*," is a social practice whereby a man has more than one wife; it is common practice in many parts of Africa and Asia. In Dangasaruri village, five of the families were polygynous. Some of the men had been in monogamous unions at their communal homes, but as soon as they moved to the new plots, they quickly married more wives. The men argued that they married more wives because they required more labor at the farms, as there was a lot of work to be accomplished. The children born of these unions were an excellent source of labor as they could look after cattle, help in the sugarcane fields, particularly during the planting, weeding, and harvesting processes. The children would also help with tasks such as cooking, fetching water, and help look after other younger children while the parents worked in the sugarcane fields. Polygyny has existed between the Karanga and the Shangaan since the precolonial period and is seen as a prestigious way of life.

Polygyny was traditionally associated with wealth, and men who married more than one wife were known as *hurudza* (a man who is a good farmer and has plenty of livestock to feed himself and the community, as well as to sell); in the new plots, men are still thinking along those lines as they want to be considered *hurudza*. Men would always want to prove that they were the best in a particular village, and so most families would want their daughters to marry these men for security stemming from the men's wealth and the fact that they would also be looked after. The man becomes the manager of the farm and the wives and the children are the workers. If there are three wives, the first wife does the ploughing with oxen, the second drives the cattle, the third drops the seed, and the children close the seed holes. I argue that polygyny made men drivers of the farm operations, and women and children became the workers who had to produce in order to fulfill men's aspirations to be the best farmers. The polygynous families in Dangasaruri, were doing well agriculturally; for instance, Mr. Ndeya had totally revamped his homestead and, from the wealth-ranking criteria, which was one of the methodologies employed in the study, he was rated as the best farmer and the richest in the village.

4.5 Labor Arrangements at Chiredzi Sugar Estates

Chiredzi state employed a myriad of labor practices for its sugarcane estates. An important point to note is that the labor in the estate is highly mechanized with the planting, application of herbicides, and weeding mainly done by machines. However, the labor pool for these tasks involved skilled labor that was recruited from the people who had completed agricultural diplomas from agricultural universities such as Chibero and Kushinga Phikelela. The management of the sugarcane estates echoed the sentiments. In terms of harvesting the crop labor was mainly drawn from men and women from the surrounding communal areas of Mwarura, Mwenezana, and Chiredzi villages who had to pick the sugarcane when the combine harvesting machinery cut it. In some fields the sugarcane was harvested using manual methods such as hands due to the highly specialized nature of the crop.

Interestingly some farmers from the fast track farms of Dangasaruri would also go to the estates and provide their labor as a way of cushioning themselves against different forms of shocks such as droughts, which would have affected their sugarcane crop. This demonstrates that large-scale land investments also rely on labor pools of the smallholder farmers thereby leading to the notion that there is a symbiotic interdependence between large-scale sugar production and fast track sugar production since both entities rely on each other in terms of labor provision and financial boost due to labor provision. An analysis of the large-scale land investments and high-value crop production therefore leads to the notion that labor as an enclave alternates in both large-scale and small-scale farms.

It is important to note that, the political economy of large-scale land investments therefore lies on the bedrock of acquisition of large tracts of land that belong to the smallholder farmers' communities due to the issue of class interests. The class dynamics emanate from the way the capitalist mode of agricultural production is organized. Those who have a lot of agricultural financing for agriculture and also for paying labor as the Chiredzi sugar estates can hire labor from any corner of the society. Hence the mode of labor provided on the sugar estate straddles the boundaries of skilled, semi-skilled, and also the fast track farmers due to the nature of the power vested in finances and control over the sugar estates that the Chiredzi management has over the sugarcane value chain production in Chiredzi.

4.6 Policy Analysis and Sugarcane Production in Zimbabwe

Policy analysis involves the searching of the best alternative among a set of competing public choices in dealing with an issue of public concern. Gleanings into the Zimbabwean agricultural sphere indicate that the absence of a codified land law hampers the production of sugarcane in fast track farms since the farmers lose land grudgingly since they are no clear-cut landholding tenure systems. The fast track farmers reported that, they also lived in fear since they feared encroachment into their plots of land by the Chiredzi estate. A review of the policy arena revealed that the sugarcane industry had a codified wage labor bill that corporations could use for paying the laborers. However, the fast track framers did not adhere to the wage bill due to the nature of the Zimbabwean economy which is fluid, and had many other politico-economic challenges such that the farmers used different modes of payment which comprised of cash and payments in kind.

It will be credible to craft a sugarcane production-based policy that curtails the fears of both the fast track farmers and also the monolithic corporations such as the Chiredzi estate. This policy should also have detailed sections on land tenure regimes as this helps to allay fears form the sugarcane producers and ensure sound agricultural sugar production. This is connected to the labor question because once the fast track farmers and the Chiredzi estate have tenure regimes that are solid it also ensures that the laborers work in a secure environment. The crafting of the policies should also involve the Sugarcane Association; so that labor issues are dissected and an equal level playing field is created that does not compromise the developmental needs of the laborers.

5   Conclusion

Glimpses into the sugarcane production in the face of large-scale land investments reveal that the labor processes are rooted in class dynamics and self-interest sharing modes of production that are a characteristic feature of capitalist agricultural modes of production. The fast track farmers had a myriad of labor arrangements that permeated the social fabric that involved sharing labor among the farmers, labor pool exchanges; family-based labor, polygamy labor societies. The labor facets also involved gendered aspects with women, men, and children all involved in the sugarcane value chain. Notably the labor enclaves within the Chiredzi estate involved skilled, semi-skilled, and unskilled laborers that were also compartmentalized into gendered segments.

In both fast track farms and the Chiredzi sugar estate management, it emerged that women played a pivotal process in the planting and harvesting of the sugarcane production. A credible and equal level policy field should be created that addresses the needs of the sugarcane laborers so that in the face of large-scale land investments and the changes in the geophysical landscape, policy regimes are created that lead to equity in terms of how sugarcane laborers are treated in fast track and large sugarcane states such as Chiredzi in Zimbabwe.

References

Chambati, W. (2009). *Emergent agrarian labor relations in Zimbabwe's new resettlement areas*. Mimeograph Series. Harare: African Institute for Agrarian Studies.

Chambati, W. (2018). *Changing agrarian labor relations in Zimbabwe in the context of the 'fast track' land reform*. John Hopkins School of Arts and Social Sciences.

Chambati, W., & Moyo, S. (2013). *Land and agrarian reform: Beyond white settler capitalism*. Dakar: Codesria.

Chingarande, S. (2004). *Review of the Zimbabwean agricultural sector following implementation of land reform: Gender and the fast track land reform in Zimbabwe*. Monograph. Harare: African Institute of Agrarian Studies.

Goebel, A. (2005). *Gender and land reform: The Zimbabwean experience*. Quebec: McGill-Queen's University Press.

Grossman, H., & Helpman, W. (1994). Agricultural trade policies and labor. *Journal of Economic Perspectives, 8*(1), 23–44.

Herrmann, R., Jumbe, C., Bruentrup, M. & Osabuohien, E. (2018). Competition between biofuel feedstock and food production: Empirical evidence from sugarcane outgrower settings in malawi. *Biomass and Bioenergy, 114*(July), 100–111. https://doi.org/10.1016/j.biombioe.2017.09.002.

Jirira, O. K., & Halimana, C. (2008). *A gender audit of women and land rights in Zimbabwe* (Desk Review Final Report). Harare: Prepared for the Zimbabwe Women Resource Centre Network, Institute of Development Studies, University of Zimbabwe.

Matondi, P. B. (2012). *Zimbabwe's fast track land reform*. London: Zed Books.

Moyo, S. (2009, August 22–24). *Zimbabwe's land reform and agricultural production in Zimbabwe: Emerging trends*. Paper Presented at Round Table Conference on Land and Poverty Reduction in Zimbabwe in Collaboration with the University of Zimbabwe and University of Manchester, Harare, Zimbabwe.

Moyo, S. (2011). Three decades of Zimbabwe's land reform. *Journal of Peasant Studies, 1*(38), 1123.

Moyo, S., & Chambati, W. (2004). *Emerging agrarian labor structure in new resettlement areas*. Monograph Series. Harare: African Institute of Agrarian Studies.

Mutopo, P. (2015). *Fast track land reform: Experiences from Zimbabwe*. Leiden: Brill Publishers.

Mutopo, P., Chiweshe, M. K., & Mubaya, C. P. (2015). Large-scale land acquisitions, livelihoods, and gender configurations in Zimbabwe. In E. Osabuohien (Ed.), *Handbook of research on in-country determinants and implications of foreign land acquisitions* (pp. 130–144). Hershey, PA: Business Science Reference.

Osabuohien, E., Efobi, U. R., Herrmann, R., & Gitau, C. M. (2019). Female labor outcomes and large-scale agricultural land investments: Macro-micro evidence from Tanzania. *Land Use Policy, 82*, 716–728. https://doi.org/10.1016/j.landusepol.2019.01.005.

Tsikata, D. (2009). Gender, land and labor relations and livelihoods in Sub-Saharan Africa in the era of economic liberalization: Towards a research agenda. *Feminist Africa, 12*, 11–30.

Poverty Reduction, Sustainable Agricultural Development, and the Cassava Value Chain in Nigeria

Waidi Gbenro Adebayo and Magdalene Silberberger

1 Introduction

A high poverty rate bedevils the Nigerian state. While there has been some progress in poverty reduction in the past, Nigeria is now being considered the country with the most people living in poverty worldwide. Currently, the percentage of Nigeria's population living in extreme poverty[1] stands at about 45%. Despite a global decline in poverty rates, the country's prospects are weak, and the share of people living under $1.90 per day is expected to increase in the next decade (World Poverty Clock 2019).

According to the government in its National Economic Empowerment and Development Strategic (NEEDS) document, "poverty reduction is the most difficult challenge facing Nigeria and its people, and the greatest obstacle to the pursuit of socioeconomic growth" (NNPC 2004, p. 24). Successive governments, since 1986, have embarked on different forms of poverty alleviation strategies to reduce the incidence of poverty in the country. However, while many countries of the world have made headways in poverty reduction, the continuing rise in poverty incidence in Nigeria is a serious cause

---

W. G. Adebayo (✉) · M. Silberberger
Witten/Herdecke University, Witten, Germany
e-mail: waidi.Adebayo@uni-wh.de

M. Silberberger
e-mail: Magdalene.Silberberger@uni-wh.de

© The Author(s) 2020
E. S. Osabuohien (ed.), *The Palgrave Handbook of Agricultural and Rural Development in Africa*, https://doi.org/10.1007/978-3-030-41513-6_24

for concern. Agriculture and particularly cassava cultivation, processing, and marketing, which continues to provide a means of livelihood and income generation to hundreds of millions of Africans and tens of millions of Nigerians, is an agricultural subsector that could be exploited in Nigeria's fight against poverty.

Dr. Nkosazana Dlamini Zuma, the chairperson of the African Union, explained that the agricultural sector is a critical sector in African countries: it holds the potential to support the quest for sustainable development, economic diversification, industrialization, generation of employment opportunities, and in the struggle against inequality, poverty, and hunger (Zuma 2013). In the same vein, the Chief Executive Officer of the "New Partnership for Africa's Development" (NEPAD), Ibrahim Mayaki, explained that compared to other sectors in Africa the agricultural sector provides a better opportunity for job creation and poverty reduction especially for the disadvantaged poor and susceptible people both in the cities and rural areas. He further stated that on the continent in 2016, the agricultural sector contributed 32% of the continent's GDP and continues to employ around 65% of its labor force. Also, economic growth in the agricultural sector is projected to be eleven times more effective in reducing poverty than growth in other sectors (Mayaki 2016). The consensus is that extreme poverty and hunger continue to be a largely rural phenomenon and the majority of people that fall under this category are smallholder farmers and their dependents (Anríquez and Stamoulis 2007; Schultz 1980; Cervantes-Godoy and Dewbre 2010; Mehta and Shah 2003; United Nations 2015). Consequently, solving these problems is intertwined with boosting "food production, agricultural productivity, and rural incomes" (United Nations 2015, para. 7).

Cassava is an essential crop in Sub-Saharan Africa as it thrives on marginal soils and can withstand adverse weather conditions and survive where other crops do not (Howeler et al. 2013; FAO 2003; Bellù and Liberati 2005). According to Hahn et al. (1992), it is an invaluable crop in "tropical Africa" due to "its efficient production of cheap food energy, year-round availability, tolerance to extreme ecological stress conditions, and suitability to present farming and food systems in Africa, it plays a major role in efforts to alleviate the African food crisis" (p. 3). Abass et al. (2013) posited that it forms a significant proportion of the food intake of 500 million people across Africa. Every part of the crop is useful: the leaves are rich in protein, minerals, and vitamins and consumed as vegetables by humans and also feed to farm animals, the stem is used for vegetative propagation of the crop, and the roots which are rich in carbohydrate is a source of energy to humans and animals and can be processed into several industrial derivatives that are raw materials for industry. It is estimated that around 450 million poor African farmers grow cassava as a means of sustenance, and for generating revenue, of these many, are women farming on degraded lands. The crop holds the potential to feed much of Africa's rising population and to provide a means for changing the fortune of many rural and urban poor by helping to "increase farm income" and "close the food gap" (Nweke 2005, p. 4). "The capacity of the crop to provide income, and thereby alleviate poverty, is the principal attribute allowing cassava to function as a catalyst for development" (Hershey et al. 2001, p. 5). Dr. Martin Fregene, the Director for Agriculture of the African Development Bank (AFDB) at the fourth international conference on cassava in Cotonou in 2018, asserted that the development of the cassava value chain in Africa holds the potential to help reduce imports and save $1.2 bn that could be put to use on the continent (AllAfrica 2018; CGIAR 2018). The Nigeria Cassava Growers Association believes that using cassava flour to replace wheat flour in breadmaking at a ratio of 20% will save the country 250 billion Naira in wheat imports. Also, the boosting of local starch and ethanol production from cassava could save 800 billion and 500 billion, respectively, that would be spent to import these items (*The Punch Newspaper* 2019).

Thus, this chapter explores how improving the cassava crop value chain can support poverty alleviation in Nigeria. It argues that investments in activities that enhance the cassava value chain would ultimately have the effect of reducing poverty. The value-added from the totality of a value chain is known to produce value-added that is more than the addition of the specific value-added at each disjointed stage (Meridian Institute 2010). A functional cassava value chain would lead to an efficient network among the relevant stakeholders, contribute to mechanization and innovation, as well as a reduction in the importation of certain raw materials. It would also create business opportunities, generate employment, reduce waste, drive down the price to the final consumer and lead to increases in profitability, which would ultimately increase farmers' incomes. The cassava value chain in Sub-Saharan Africa and Nigeria remain underdeveloped due to neglect, and it is not until recently that the crop is being studied in-depth and efforts are being made to harness its potentials. Cassava research in the past three decades has led to two sets of significant breakthroughs. The first is the production of new varieties of cassava that are high yield, pest, disease, and drought-resistant (Balagopalan 2002; Nweke 2003, 2005; Cock 1985; FAO 2013). The second is the discovery of several industrial uses for processed cassava tuber, which has helped to debunk its "poor man's crop" tag (FAO and IFAD 2005; Phillips et al. 2004; Akoroda et al. 2004; Abass et al. 2013; IITA 2015; Dziedzoave et al. 2006). Both occurrences have given life to two sets of possibilities: the first is the opportunity of improving cassava yield per hectare from planting new high yield, pest, disease, and drought-resistant varieties of cassava combined with the use of proper agronomy practices. The second is the creation of new markets and new demand for cassava for the production of newly found derivatives like High-Quality Cassava Flour (HQCF), ethanol, industrial starch, glucose syrup, sweeteners, and so on. However, cassava production has continued to increase in Nigeria but not as a result of increasing yield per hectare but as a result of an expansion of cultivated land. Farmers continue to complain of the lack of a market for their harvests and low prices, a situation that is further exacerbated by the bulkiness of the cassava tuber and the fact that it starts to deteriorate 48 hours after harvest. Also, the prime time for cassava tuber harvest to get a high starch content is between 8 and 12 months after planting.

Furthermore, there is still a weak link between farmers, processors, and the end users of cassava products. On their part, potential end users of cassava derivatives are wary of stock out due to unstable supply of raw material for their production, while processors face the challenge of having to source cassava tuber from numerous sources to make up a sizeable production. In Nigeria, there have been attempts to boost cassava production and create a linkage between cassava growers, mechanized processors, and industrial-scale end users. One of these was the Presidential Cassava Initiative (PCI) between 2002 and 2010. The program was thought to have expanded cassava production by 25% (Abass et al. 2011, 2013). There was also the "Cassava Bread Initiative" between 2012 and 2015. The program aimed at 20% substitution of cassava flour for wheat in breadmaking in the country as a means of reducing the country's wheat import bill that averages $4 m annually (FMARD 2014). In spite of government's huge investments in the program, Oluwale et al. (2018) found that there was low usage of cassava flour in breadmaking in southwestern Nigeria due to the cost of modification of oven, and operations and raw material costs. At present, cassava production is still predominantly carried out by smallholder farmers farming on marginal lands and expectedly with low yields.

The chapter proceeds as follows: Section two deals with conceptual analysis and explores the definition of sustainable agricultural development and poverty. Section three discusses the poverty situation in Nigeria and efforts that have been made to combat the worsening poverty situation in the country since 1986. Section four looks at the place of agriculture in Nigeria's economy from independence, and documents how it became relegated to the background. Section five discusses the cassava crop and its value chain. Section six looks at the ways forward, and section seven concludes the essay.

2 Conceptual Analysis

2.1 Sustainable Agricultural Development

Sustainable agricultural development is described by the High-Level Panel of Experts for Food Security and Nutrition (HLPE) of the Committee on World Food Security (CFS) as "agricultural development that contributes to improving resource efficiency, strengthening resilience and securing social equity/responsibility of agriculture and food systems in order to ensure food security and nutrition for all, now and in the future"

(HLPE 2016, p. 13). Also, the United Nations Food and Agricultural Organization (FAO) describes sustainable agricultural development as:

> The management and conservation of the natural resource base, and the orientation of technological and institutional change in such a manner as to ensure the attainment and continued satisfaction of human needs for present and future generations. Such sustainable development (in the agriculture, forestry and fisheries sectors) conserves land, water, plant and animal genetic resources, is environmentally non-degrading, technically appropriate, economically viable and socially acceptable. (FAO Council 1989, p. 65)

Agriculture provides a pathway for self-sufficiency and food security. In 2014, 37.5% of the world's land area had been used for agricultural purposes (World Bank 2019a). The need to feed an increasing population of people and the modernization of agriculture has led to the additional acquisition of land and its intensified use for agricultural purposes, which has grave environmental consequences (Mateo-Sagasta et al. 2017).

According to FAO (2011), the contemporary usage of global freshwater resources for agricultural purposes is unsustainable. Ineffective water usage for crop production is leading to loss of underground water reserves, diminishing river flows, destroying biodiversity, and has also greatly contributed to the salination of the soil in 20% of the irrigated land area worldwide. In the same vein, the misuse of fertilizers and pesticides has resulted in water pollution—affecting groundwater, rivers, streams, ponds, lakes, and wetlands. Apart from this, poverty is also a driver of environmental degradation and poor conservation practices. The neglect of rural areas in developing countries is considered a major obstacle to conservation. Poor rural dwellers in a desperate bid to feed themselves and their families continue to clear up forest areas, leading to deforestation and soil erosion (IUCN 1980). These "rural people often know best how to conserve their environment, but they may need to overexploit resources in order to survive." In contrast, large scale profit-oriented mechanized farming usually leads to degradation of resources due to overuse (FAO 1995, p. 109).

Adams (2009) argued that the poor are more severely affected by environmental degradation, as they usually only have access to cheap degraded lands. Regarding sustainable agricultural development, agriculture must seek to conserve the environment throughout its value chain. Farmers, farm produce processors, distributors/wholesalers, retailers, consumers, and so on have a role in sustainable agricultural development and, consequently, sustainable development.

2.2 Poverty: Definitions and Its Dimensions

There are different definitions of poverty; each looks at the phenomenon from a different perspective. According to Laderchi et al. (2003, p. 10), "there is now worldwide agreement on poverty reduction as an overriding goal of development policy, but not on the definition of poverty." Reference to food poverty, absolute poverty, and relative poverty are some of the most important metrics of poverty. According to Bellù and Liberati (2005), "It is important to tailor the concept of poverty on the appropriate context, as there is not a general concept that we can safely assume to hold for all countries at all times" (p. 3).

Dowler et al. (2001) posited that food poverty could be viewed "as the inability to acquire or consume an adequate quality or sufficient quantity of food in socially acceptable ways, or the uncertainty that one will be able to do so" (p. 3). According to the Copenhagen Declaration on Social Development, absolute poverty describes "a condition characterized by severe deprivation of basic human needs, including food, safe drinking water, sanitation facilities, health, shelter, education, and information. It depends not only on income but also on access to services" (United Nations 1995). Todaro and Smith (2015) describe absolute poverty as the number of people who are incapable of meeting their basic needs due to lack of resources, measured as the number of people living below a certain threshold of real income, usually a specific international poverty line. There are three international poverty lines in use by the World Bank. The first is the international poverty line (extreme poverty) specified at less than $1.90 a day using the 2011 Dollar (World Bank 2015a, b). The other two are the ones for lower-middle-income countries specified at $3.20/day and that for upper-middle-income countries, which is pegged at $5.50/day (Ferreira and Sánchez-Páramo 2017). These new poverty lines are important as the lower $1.90/day poverty line is not able to capture poverty situations in lower-middle-income and upper-middle-income countries. Relative poverty is contextual and is usually defined in relation to the economic status of other members of a society or community. Relative poverty occurs when people are considered poor after dropping below the predominant standard of living in a particular society (UNESCO 2017).

The definitions of absolute and relative poverty receive knock for what is considered a narrow focus on "income and consumption" (UNESCO 2017). In recent times, the international community has become aware that poverty is multidimensional, recognizing that poverty situation could result in being affected by a multiple of the above poverty dimensions at the same time. One of the most popular definitions capturing the multidimensional nature of poverty is the one contained in the statement of commitment of the Administrative Committee on Coordination (ACC) for action to eradicate poverty by the United Nations (UN), signed by the heads of all UN agencies on 22 June 1998. It states that:

Fundamentally, poverty is a denial of choices and opportunities, a violation of human dignity. It means lack of basic capacity to participate effectively in society. It means not having enough to feed and clothe a family, not having a school or clinic to go to, not having the land on which to grow one's food or a job to earn one's living, not having access to credit. It means insecurity, powerlessness and exclusion of individuals, households and communities. It means susceptibility to violence, and it often implies living in marginal or fragile environments, without access to clean water or sanitation. (United Nations 1998, p. 1)

Per FAO (2017b, p. 4), "Poverty is one of the biggest obstacles to human development and economic growth." The last three decades have, however, witnessed a significant fall in the world poverty level. The world poverty headcount ratio at $1.90 a day (2011 US$ PPP) stands at 10% in 2015 compared to 35.9% it was in 1990. In East and South Asia, it dropped from 61.6 to 47.3%, respectively, in 1990 to 2.3% in 2015 for East Asia in 2015 and 16.2% for South Asia in 2013. Sub-Saharan Africa is the region of the world lagging in the fight against poverty. The poverty headcount in the region, which was estimated at 54.3% in 1990, stood at 41.1% in 2015 (World Bank 2017). Notwithstanding the worldwide drop in poverty incidence, close to a billion people are still thought to be living in extreme poverty worldwide, and a further billion are considered poor (FAO 2015).

3 THE POVERTY SITUATION IN NIGERIA AND POVERTY REDUCTION EFFORTS

3.1 *The Poverty Situation in Nigeria*

According to Bello et al. (2009), the incidence of poverty only became an issue of concern in the country in the early 1980s; this was due in large part to the economic instability brought about by the second international oil shock and the fall in oil prices. With the increase in the international prices of crude oil from 1973 through to January 1981, revenue from crude oil sales had become the mainstay of Nigeria's economy. The price of Bonny Light, the type of crude oil exported by the country, rose from $2.00 per barrel in 1973 to $14.33 per barrel in 1978, to $29.27 in 1979 by January 1981 it was $40.00 per barrel. The same started tumbling by mid-1981, reaching $18.00 per barrel by 1983, $10.00 in 1985, and was hovering around $16.00 and $18.00 per barrel in 1989 (Olowu et al. 1991). The sudden fall in oil prices starting from 1981 plunged the country into an economic crisis with far-reaching consequences, including the rising incidence of poverty (Table 1).

The above shows that from a 27.2% poverty level in 1980, except for 1992 (42.7%) and 2004 (54.4%), where the incidence of poverty abated temporarily, the poverty situation in the country continued to worsen. Rising from 27.2% in 1980 to 46.3% in 1985, to 65.6% in 1996, and it stood at 69%, representing 112.47 million of the country's estimated population of 163 million in 2010.

Table 1 Nigeria—relative poverty headcount (1980–2010)

Year	Poverty incidence (%)	Estimated population (million)	Population in poverty (million)
1980	27.2	65	17.1
1985	46.3	75	34.7
1992	42.7	91.5	39.2
1996	65.6	102.3	67.1
2004	54.4	126.3	68.7
2010	69	163	112.47

Source NBS (2012)—Nigerian Poverty Profile 2010

Table 2 Nigeria—urban/rural incidence of poverty by different measures in 2010

Sector	Food poor	Absolute poverty	Relative poverty	Dollar per day
Urban	26.7	52	61.8	52.4
Rural	48.3	66.1	73.2	66.3

Source NBS (2012)—Nigerian Poverty Profile 2010

Table 3 Nigeria—Gini index (inequality index) Nigeria (1985–2010)

Year	Gini index (%)	Source
1985	38.5	(World Bank 2019b)
1992	45	(World Bank 2019b)
1996	51.9	(World Bank 2019b)
2003	40.1	(World Bank 2019b)
2004	43	(NBS 2012)
2009	43	(World Bank 2019b)
2010	44.7	(NBS 2012)

Data source World Bank (2019b), NBS (2012), Table authors construction

Additionally, the incidence of poverty is more severe in rural areas in the country compared to urban areas (Table 2).

Using any of the different measures of poverty above, the poverty situation in rural areas is worse compared to what is obtainable in urban areas.

The country's Gini Index (Inequality Index) shows that the inequality level in the country never fell below 40% from 1992 to 2010 (Table 3).

3.2 Efforts Aimed at Poverty Reduction in Nigeria

In 1980, the country had an estimated 17.1 million people living in poverty. This figure represented 27.2% of its estimated population of 65 million people. By 1985, the poverty situation had worsened, and the share of the poor stood at 34.7 million people representing 46.3% of its estimated population of 75 million people. The General Ibrahim Babangida military regime

(1985–1993) instituted several programs to check the poverty situation in the country; some of these include:

1. Directorate for Food, Roads and Rural Infrastructure (DFRRI): This was established in 1986 and aimed at improving the quality of life of the rural dwellers by the construction of new roads and the repair of old ones, the provision of rural electricity, pipe-borne water, and other essential amenities.
2. Better Life for Rural Dwellers Program (BLP): The program was established in September 1986 and aimed to better the lives of rural dwellers, especially women. Another goal of the program was to integrate "rural women into the mainstream of national development by creating greater awareness" about the problems they face (Gabriel 1994, pp. 198–199).
3. National Directorate of Employment (NDE): The Directorate was established in November 1986 to create and execute programs aimed at reducing unemployment. Its founding was a direct response to the massive job losses experienced in the country in the mid-1980s due to the economic instability prevalent at that time, which led to the closure of many businesses (NDE 2019).
4. People's Bank of Nigeria (PBN): The PBN was established by the People's Bank of Nigeria act of 1990. It has the mandate to provide credit facilities to, "underprivileged Nigerians who are involved in legitimate economic activities in both urban and rural areas and who cannot normally benefit from the services of the orthodox banking system due to their inability to provide collateral security" (FGN 1990, 2:(1)a).
5. Community of Bank Nigeria (CBN): The CBN was also established in 1990, the enabling decree provided that a community bank can be set up by a community or group of communities to provide banking and financial services, especially in rural areas. These activities were to be geared toward improving productive capacity, especially in rural areas, and to the facilitation of the activities of small businesses in rural and urban areas (FGN 1992).

General Sani Abacha became the head state of the country in November 1993, in 1994 the first lady of the country instituted the Family Support Program (FSP). It was aimed at assisting families in dire situations, with emphasis on maternal health, children's welfare and youth development. Its backbone was the Family Support Trust Fund decree No. 10 of 1995. The next important poverty alleviation program was instituted in 2000 by the Olusegun Obasanjo led government. The program was christened Poverty Alleviation Program (PAP), the program aimed at reducing the poverty incidence in the country. It was replaced by the National Poverty Eradication Program (NAPEP) in 2001. NAPEP was designed to fight poverty, especially absolute poverty and focused on four major areas these are: Youth

Empowerment Scheme (YES), Rural Infrastructure Development Scheme (RIDS), Social Welfare Service Scheme (SOWESS), and Natural Resource Development and Conservation Scheme (NRDCS). It is under the control of the National Poverty Eradication Council (NAPEC) which coordinates its activities and the poverty alleviation activities of other government ministries and parastatals, so a to synchronize their effort for greater impact and efficiency. The NEEDS was introduced in 2005 under President Olusegun Obasanjo's government. It embodied new policies, legislation, and development programs designed to reduce poverty. It attempts to address the principal causes of poverty like weak governance, social conflict, limited technological innovations that have hindered productivity, and reducing environmental degradation that aggravates poverty by reducing the natural resource base. Most of the above poverty programs were especially focused on rural dwellers. While some of the programs may have had some impact in their area of focus, the continuing rise in poverty incidence all through the period overshadowed their modest achievements.

4 The Nigerian Economy and Agriculture

Before independence in 1960 and until the late 1960s, agriculture was the mainstay of the Nigerian economy. At independence, each region of the country had a main crop it produced and exported; for the north, it was groundnut, the south-west; cocoa and for the south-east, it was palm oil. Crude oil was discovered in commercial quantity in 1956 at Oloibiri, in present Bayelsa state. However, it was increased oil production output after the Nigerian civil war (1967–1970) and the oil boom of the early 1970s that drove agriculture to the background. Revenue from crude oil sales continues to account for around 90% of the country's annual income since the 1970s (Wrights 2017). A famous quote credited to General Yakubu Gowon, Nigeria's military head of state between 1966 and 1975, that, "Nigeria has become so rich her problem was not money but how to spend it" (Okoro 2009, p. 125) captures the mood in the country at the start of the oil boom in the early 1970s. According to Olowu et al. (1991, p. 4), the oil booms of the 1970s, brought about a "false sense of economic self-sufficiency," which "led to the neglect of the agricultural sector since the nation had access to cheap money to import all sorts of things: foodstuffs, raw materials, and manufactured goods."

By the mid-1970s, it has become clear that the country was no longer self-reliant in food production. Kirk-Greene et al. (2019) posited that faced with a scarcity of basic food items due to falling domestic production, the country started importing foods like rice and cassava in 1975. This led to the launching of a national agricultural program by the General Olusegun Obasanjo led Military government on 21 May 1976. The program was called Operation Feed the Nation (OFN) and aimed at national self-sufficiency in basic food production (Associated Press 2015). It ran from 1976 to 1980. The Alhaji Shehu Shagari led government (1979–1983), after just over a year in government was faced with an economic downturn and increasing poverty incidence caused by the continuing crash of global oil prices starting in 1981. The government put in place austerity measures to curtail economic instability and instituted an agricultural program called Green Revolution program (1980–1983) to boost the local production of food as a means of reducing the over-reliant of the country on imported agricultural products with little success. There have been other efforts aimed at reviving interest in agricultural activities and increasing agricultural output in the country, but till present, the country has been unable to replicate its pre-1970s agricultural production successes.

5 The Cassava Crop and Its Value Chain

5.1 The Cassava Crop

Manihot Esculenta Crantz, popularly called Cassava in Africa, is an annual tuberous crop belonging to the (Euphorbiaceae) of plants. It is native to Brazil and was introduced to Africa, Asia, and the Caribbean by the Portuguese in the sixteenth century. Due to its ability to withstand drought and grow on poor soil, and survive under conditions where other crops might not thrive, it soon became a staple crop in many of these places (Howeler et al. 2013; Hershey et al. 2001; FAO 2003; Bellù and Liberati 2005). Cassava thrives "best on light sandy loams or on loamy sands which are moist, fertile and deep" (Grace 1977). It has a high proficiency in carbohydrate production and can be planted and harvesting at flexible periods compared to some other crops (FAO 2003). For example, even after maturity, the plant can be left unharvested (Nweke 2003), usually as a means of storage till when it is needed, or until there is an appropriate price for it. As such, "cassava plays an essential role in food security, especially in those regions prone to drought and with poor soils." It forms a vital part of the diet of more than one billion people in the world, and after rice, wheat, and maize, it ranks as the world's fourth most significant staple crop (FAO 2000, p. 5). It is the third major calorie source in the tropics after rice and maize (FAO 2000). It is the second major staple food in Africa after maize and an essential source of calories for an estimated two out of five Africans, and a significant part of the daily diet in some countries and consumed up to twice a day in some cases (Nweke 2003).

According to Nang'ayo et al. (2005), major cassava-related research in the latter part of the last century attested to the increasing importance of the crop to the economic development in Africa. Also, studies with regards to "root and tuber crops have stressed the great potential of cassava to spur rural industrial development, raise rural incomes, and contribute to food security" (p. 1). Sub-Saharan Africa is the world's largest producer of cassava, followed

Table 4 Production share of cassava by region average (1990–2017)

Production share of cassava by region		
Average 1990–2017		
Region	Cassava produced (tones)	% Share of world cassava production
Asia	63,985,545.86	30.39
Africa	114,903,601.96	54.57
Oceania	210,081.29	0.10
Americas	31,460,700.57	14.94
Total	210,559,929.68	100.00

Source FAO (2019). FAOSTAT: Data, Table authors construction

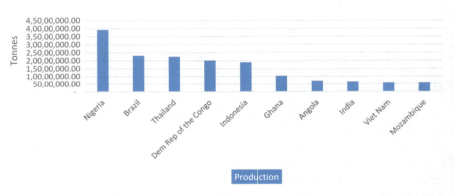

Fig. 1 World cassava production: top 10 producers average 1990–2017 (*Source* FAO [2019]. FAOSTAT: Data, Table authors construction)

by Asia, and the Americas and Oceania in third and fourth positions, respectively (FAO 2019). Table 4 summarizes global and regional total annual average cassava production between 1990 and 2017 and the percentage share of the relevant continents to world cassava production.

Nigeria produced an annual average of 39,327,834.29 tonnes of cassava yearly from 1990 to 2017, making it the largest producer of the crop. The next four top world cassava producers are Brazil averaging 23,088,097.43 tonnes per year within the same period, followed by Thailand in third place with 22,482,792.75 tonnes, and there is the Democratic Republic of the Congo and Indonesia in fourth and fifth places, respectively, with 20,115,599.39 and 19,002,311.29 tonnes (FAO 2019). Other African countries like Ghana, Angola, and Mozambique are among the top ten producers of cassava in the world (Fig. 1). As shown in Table 5, Nigeria's cassava

Table 5 Nigeria's cassava production, share of world production and gross production value (current million US$)—(1961–2017)

Year	Cassava produced (tones)	% Share of world cassava production	Gross production value (current million US$)
1961	7,384,000	10	
1965	8,182,000	10	
1970	10,206,000	10	
1975	10,500,000	10	
1980	11,500,000	9	
1985	12,090,000	9	
1990	19,043,008	12	
1995	31,404,000	19	3080.281257
2000	32,010,000	18	4506.383353
2005	41,565,000	20	6940.464117
2010	42,533,180	18	6058.864605
2015	57,643,271	20	6636.096093
2017	59,485,947	20	

Source FAO (2019). FAOSTAT: Data, Table authors construction

production, its share of world production and the gross production value has continued to increase annually between 1961 and 2017.

5.2 The Cassava Value Chain

The cassava value chain refers to the important stages after harvest where the farm produce is processed, and as a result, gain added value. According to the Meridian Institute (2010), "a value chain can be described as a series of sequential activities where at each step in the process, the product passing through this chain of activities gains some value" (p. 1). They explained further that the value-added derivable from the whole chain far outweighs the value-added by adding together the values obtained at the individual stage of the value chain (Fig. 2).

Cassava is consumed in different forms and used for various purposes, including uses as industrial raw material. For example, the leaves are consumed as a vegetable in certain quarters; the tuber is consumed after boiling like other tuberous crops like yam and potatoes. Also, it has traditional local derivatives like toasted granules (gari), local flour (elubo-lafun), unsteamed paste (fufu), and chips. Its contemporary derivatives are HQCF, starch, ethanol, glucose syrup, sweeteners, chips/pellets, animal feeds, and so on. As crucial as cassava is, there are two major drawbacks to its consumption and processing: the quick perishability of its roots within a short period after harvest (usually 48 hours) and its high cyanogenic content which makes it harmful to consume it without proper processing (Nhassico et al. 2008).

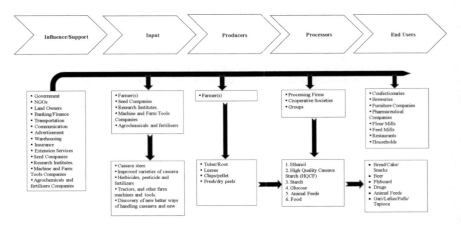

Fig. 2 A cassava value chain map (*Source* Authors construction)

The different uses and derivatives for the cassava crop leaves and tubers are discussed in detail below.

5.2.1 Direct Cassava Consumption

Direct consumption of cassava include the following

i. Cassava Leaves—these are edible and eaten as food in many of the African countries where cassava is grown (Lancaster and Brooks 1983; Latif and Müller 2015), including in Nigeria where it is considered a vegetable. The leaves fresh and dry are feed to farm animals like cattle, pigs, sheep, and goats. It is estimated that fresh cassava leaves contain around 7% protein (Cock 1985; Dziedzoave et al. 2006), while dry matter cassava leaves contain between 20 and 30% protein (Cock 1985). It also contains minerals like calcium, phosphorus, and iron and vitamins A, B1, B2, B3, and C (Bokanga 1994; Lancaster and Brooks 1983) and amino acids apart from methionine and phenylalanine (Dziedzoave et al. 2006). Dr. Adeola Bankole, a Nutritional Biochemist and Food Technologist at the Federal Institute of Industrial Research (FIIRO) in Nigeria, explained that "the amino acid profile of cassava leaf protein compares favorably well with those of milk, cheese, soybeans, fish and egg" (Bankole 2017). The quality of the protein content of cassava leaves are at par with soybeans, and the lysine content of the leaves is higher than that of soybeans (Cock 1985). On their part, Awoyinka and Abegunde (1995) found that cassava leaves contained far higher crude protein between (29.3–32.3% dry matter) than the widely eating vegetable Amaranthus (19.6% dry matter). The consumption of the leaves holds the potential to help bridge the vitamin A, iron, and protein intake deficiency gap in areas with high consumption of foods lacking these nutrients (Aregheore 2012). Also, it is acknowledged that a combination of cassava leaves and tubers can be used to a certain percentage to replace the maize content in animal feeds. The United States Department of Agriculture—GAIN report 2018 estimates that the animal feed sector in Nigeria is worth around $2 billion annually and remains unexploited (USDA 2018).

ii. Cassava Tuber—the roots of the crop contain an estimated 60% starch content; as such, it is an inexpensive source of dietetic carbohydrate. It also contains nutrients like calcium, thiamine, niacin, and riboflavin (Dziedzoave et al. 2006). In the same vein, Balagopalan et al. (1988) explained that the starch content of the cassava tuber on a fresh matter basis is between 25 and 35% and up to 85% on a dry matter basis. The cassava root contains more dry matter and carbohydrate compared to the Irish potato, sweet potato, yams, or taro; however, each has higher protein content than the cassava root. The dry matter in the cassava root is estimated to be between 30 and 40%. The tubers are consumed after boiling, roasting, pounding, frying, or after been parboiled and allowed to ferment in water overnight in certain parts of the country; the boiling is believed to remove the toxic (cyanogenic glucosides) content of the tuber thereby making it fit for consumption. Also, whole, peeled, chipped, or pelleted tubers are feeds to farm animals.

5.2.2 Major Traditional Derivatives of Cassava

i. Gari—is an important staple food in several West African countries and one of the most important derivatives of the cassava tuber in Nigeria as close to 75% of the cassava roots produced in Nigeria is used to make gari (Abass et al. 2012). Also, gari produced in Nigeria and Ghana is available in many African shops in Europe and the United States, although the extent of the market is still unknown. The popularity of gari could be attributed to the ease with which it could be prepared and the many ways in which it can be consumed. Gari could be soaked in water and consumed as a flake; it can also be poured into boiling water and steered to make a thick paste called eba.

The product is made by peeling the cassava roots, after which they are washed, and grated using a mechanized grater. The grated roots (wet paste) are then collected into water-permeable white sacks, placed on wooden racks where it is allowed to ferment depending on the kind of gari to be made and then pressed using a hydraulic jack to let out the water. The molded dry cake is then broken into small bits and sieved, afterward toasted on the fire to make the gari.

ii Lafun—local flour, popularly called elubo-lafun, is produced either by first peeling the cassava roots or soaking them for about 4–6 days without peeling to allow for fermentation. After this, if the roots were initially peeled, the fermented paste is dried, and where they were not peeled, the covering for the roots is removed at this stage, and the fermented roots are dried to produce lafun.

iii. Fufu—this is another very important traditional derivative of the cassava roots. It is produced in much the same way as the lafun discussed above, the difference being that the roots here are left until they breakdown completely. After that, the fermented roots are squeezed by hand to get an unsteamed paste (fufu) that can be cooked for immediate consumption or dried to allow for longer shelf life.
iv. Cassava Starch—this is consumed directly as food in the south-south geopolitical zone (Niger Delta part) of the southern region of the country. Also, it is used in making tapioca and for straightening clothes.

5.2.3 The Major Contemporary Derivatives of Cassava

i. High-Quality Cassava Flour (HQCF)—this is produced by peeling, watching, grating, dewatering, sifting, drying, and milling of the cassava roots to produce HQCF. The product is useful as a raw material for the manufacturing of textiles, plywood, paper, packaged food, and some other items. Also, it is used in the preparation of a range of pastries products like bread, biscuit, cake, and so on. This cassava derivative has higher market prices and, therefore, leads to an increase in the value of cassava and, consequently, to an increase in farmers' income (Dziedzoave et al. 2006).

ii. Cassava Starch—is a very important value-added product in the cassava value chain. It can be consumed directly as food (tapioca, custard, and so on). It also can be used as a food processing additive for a wide range of products (pastries, ice cream, noodles, soft drinks, beer, sweets, and so on), and as a nonfood industrial raw material in the making of paper, cardboard, plywood, glue, paints, and others (Henry et al. 1998). Local cassava starch products can replace imports such as glucose and dextrose in cassava producing countries (Phillips et al. 2004).

iii. Cassava Ethanol—this is another important contemporary product extracted from cassava. It can be used as an additive in food, for pharmaceutical uses, and as biofuel. A good example is the Green Ethanol Micro Distillery in Ogbomosho, Nigeria, which produces clean and renewable energy (bioethanol) from cassava tuber (Green Social Bioethanol 2015). Under this system, dry cassava peels can be used as biofuel to power burners, while the peeled cassava tubers are processed into ethanol, and the ethanol as in the case of green bioethanol mentioned above can also be used to power its electric generators.

iv. Chips/Pellets—this is produced by peeling the cassava roots, although in some cases, the outer covering of the cassava root is not removed, washing and afterward slicing them into small chips and dried to get the final product. According to the International Livestock Research Institute, the use of cassava as animal feeds have gained traction in Nigeria (ILRI 2015). The chips are used as animal feeds traditionally, but, in recent times, have found a foothold as an income-generating export to China for the same purpose.

v. Animal Feeds: The processing of cassava tuber for use as animal feed and, in some cases, a mixture of cassava leaves and tuber to produce high-quality animal feed is gaining ground in Nigeria. According to Balagopalan (2002), "various parts of the cassava plant, including tubers, stems, and leaves are used for animal feeding." Also, feeds made from cassava parts have been successful feed to farm animals (p. 305). Presently, a large percentage of animal feed used in the country is made from imported maize. Also, millions of tonnes of cassava peelings that are lying about as waste that is contaminating the environment could have been processed and added as raw material to make animal feeds (ILRI 2015). The use of cassava as animal feed locally will go a long way in reducing the importation of maize for animal feeds.

6   The Way Forward

The need for sustainability in development and agriculture cannot be over-emphasized, and in this regard, cassava cultivation and its value chain. It is through sustainability practices that the eternal existence of resources for developmental and other purposes, including poverty alleviation, can be ensured. Poor farmers usually only have access to marginal lands due to its cheapness (Adams 2009), and in other cases, the soil has become poor due to over-farming that leads to soil erosion (IUCN 1980). Also, many poor farmers continue to plant low yield varieties of cassava and use traditional methods with poor results compared to farms where improved varieties of cassava are planted, and modern methods of farming are implemented (Channels Television 2016a, b). Per FAO (2017a, para. 4), "the national average yield of cassava is estimated at 13.63 MT per ha, as against potential yield of up to 40 metric tons per ha." Potential yield describes yields that could be attained when new high yield, pest, disease, and drought-resistant varieties of cassava are planted combined with proper agronomy practices.

While it is easy to blame poor farmers for continuing to grow low yield varieties of cassava, a critical analysis of their situation gives an insight into their decision-making process. Wossen et al. (2017) found that some Nigeria farmers disadopted certain new varieties of cassava for the following reasons: low selling prices, not good for processing, no funds to buy stems, requires a lot of effort to grow, inability to withstand pest or disease, not good for making traditional local derivatives, cannot stay in the ground for long after maturity, and possibly higher cost for loss of crop from activities of herdsmen. The above points to smallholder cassava farmers as rational and risk-averse beings making planting decisions under uncertain conditions. The decision to plant new or old varieties of cassava is purely a business decision made under conditions of uncertainty due to a lack of steady market and low prices for cassava tubers. Based on a cost–benefit analysis and fear of a loss of income, the cassava farmer would most likely cultivate old varieties of cassava.

Stems for the propagation of old varieties of cassava could be gotten for free or at low cost, the plant requires little effort to grow, they could stay in the ground for up to a year after maturity and the farmer can leave them in the ground until prices are favorable; also they are suitable for processing into local derivatives by the farmers themselves. These local derivatives could be stored for long periods and sold in the local market when prices are reasonable. The planting of new high yield varieties of cassava is mostly viable to smallholder farmers where there is a ready market, and reasonable prices are assured if not the risk of a loss of income is high due to risk versus yield tradeoff.

A kind of sustainable cassava farming system has been tagged "Save and Grow" by the FAO, it is hinged on three essential principles. The first is the protection of the soil structure and organic matter through minimal or zero tillage or what is called the inverted tilling system that is only used to turn grasses covering the soil upside down. The second is the preservation of the soil cover through mulching or the planting of cover crops (creeping crops). The third is the cultivation of a variety of crops together and in succession to help mitigate risks from changing climatic patterns and demand (FAO 2013). Also, farmers need to be taught agronomy practices that would help them incorporates scientific methods, modern technology, innovation, sustainability, high standards, and proper crop management into their work. Furthermore, other aspects of the cassava value chain are not left out, machine fabricators, farm produce processors, distributors/wholesalers, retailers, consumers, and so on all have a role in sustainable agriculture development and consequently sustainable development. Each member of the value chain will need to incorporate sustainability practices into their work by striving for innovations that reduce the adverse effect of their activities on the environment.

For cassava to be useful in the fight against poverty in Nigeria, relevant stakeholders like the government, researchers, farmers, private businesses, and consumers need to play their part and collaborate in certain areas. Top on the agenda for the government and private sector should be the funding of research into the production of new, improved high yield, pest, disease, and drought-resistant varieties of cassava: the development of potentially high value and higher income-generating uses/derivatives of cassava; and the production of new technologies and machinery that can transform cassava cultivation, processing, and marketing into modern automated ones just like has been done for a similar crop like rice (Osabuohien et al. 2018). Apart from new approaches to their work, loan facilities or loan guarantees that allow cassava farmers or potential cassava farmers to procure land for cassava cultivation purposes will be a move in the right direction. Also, assistance in the form of farm input like improve yield and disease resistance cassava stem/seeds to farmers at subsidized prices, offering farm machines for use during the clearing of farmland, plowing, planting, weeding, and harvesting of the crop would lead to an improvement in output.

Another significant problem that needs to be overcome for a cassava poverty reduction project to work is the "Chicken and Egg problem." This phrase describes a disconnect between parties that should be in a circular, mutually beneficial relationship. In this case, there are cassava farmers on the one hand that are unable to venture into large scale cassava farming and the planting of high yield varieties due to the lack of a steady market for cassava tubers and consequently low prices. While on the other hand, there are large cassava processors/industrial end users. The processors require large quantities of cassava tubers to produce industrial derivatives for industrial end users but are mostly unable to meet end-user demand due to the scarcity of cassava tubers at their factory location. Consequently, industrial end users for fear of stock out have continued to import those derivatives from abroad. The disconnect between these major stakeholders along the cassava value chain has left the Nigerian cassava subsector operating at far below its potentials. The situation is indicative of a serious coordination problem due to the long neglect of cassava in favor of crops like rice and maize until the early 2000s by the government. There is currently a weak linkage between the different actors in the cassava value chain, thus causing a disincentive for demand and supply. For example, in many communities' huge piles of cassava waste are lying fallow (Channels Television 2015a, b, c); these can potentially be further processed to animal feeds (ILRI 2015) or used for electricity generation (Ajima Farms 2017). There are several imported industrial raw materials at the present that products from processed cassava can successfully replace, but due to the Chicken and Egg problem, there has been no incentive to either produce because of fear of the possible lack of demand or for fear of disruption in supply along the line. An example of a successful linkage is the Nigerian Breweries and Heineken partnership with Psaltry limited—a cassava offtake company processing cassava tubers into HQCF, which is enabling both breweries to source their starch-based raw materials (sugar and lactose) from processed cassava locally in Nigeria (ICRA 2016).

According to Sachs (2015), "agriculture is the mainstay of rural areas, whereas industry and services are the mainstays of urban areas" (p. 52). Lack of/inadequate infrastructural facilities in rural areas where the bulk of agricultural activities take place continues to pose a great challenge to the growth of agriculture in Nigeria. Poor roads continue to make the transportation of farm produce to the cities exorbitant. Also, the lack of electricity or unstable power supply makes it difficult to store farm produces. There should be a deliberate effort to provide infrastructural facilities in rural areas to make life in these regions meaningful and promote agriculture.

7 Conclusion

Nigeria finds herself in a difficult situation, a high poverty rate both in the rural and urban areas with a slightly more severe situation in the rural areas. Also, since 1986, and several poverty alleviation programs afterward, some still running, the poverty rate remains high. Oil export continues to be the country's primary source of foreign exchange, while the agricultural sector, which is the largest sector of the country's economy, employing two-thirds of the country's labor force remains largely underdeveloped. The value-added per capita in the agricultural sector in the preceding twenty years have been less the 1% yearly (FAO 2017a). The rural areas where most farm produce is cultivated remain mostly underdeveloped. Most rural towns and villages lack basic amenities like stable electric power, pipe-borne water, motorable roads, and so on. Inducing a situation where a significant portion of farm products, including cassava, end up in the local market, fetching very little prices or go to waste due to a lack of access to markets. This creates a disincentive for large scale production on the part of the farmers, and on the other side of the coin are the cassava processors and end users. Many major cassava processors in Nigeria from fear of unavailability of cassava tubers for their processing plant grow cassava that is used when there is a scarcity of cassava roots. Also, potential end users of cassava derivatives like starch, ethanol, sweeteners, and so on continue to import these raw materials due to low local production that is unable to meet their raw material needs. Evident from the before mentioned is a coordination problem. The absence of a sustainable cassava value chain is hampering the production, processing, and marketing of cassava and its derivatives. The government needs to step into help create the necessary linkages among stakeholders in the cassava value chain to help develop a sustainable value chain for the long run. Previous intervention by the government in the same direction has shown promises and should serve as a pointer to the potentials of a sustainable cassava value chain.

An example is a government implemented linkage between cassava farmers and commercial users of cassava between 2002 and 2008 that led to a demand-pull expansion in cassava production in the country by 25% (Abass et al. 2011, 2013). Also, the cassava bread initiative between 2012 and 2015 raised much awareness on the use of cassava flour as a substitute for wheat flour in breadmaking, although the extent of its impact on cassava production and utilization has not been evaluated. Transforming cassava production, processing, and marketing and creating a linkage between cassava producers, processors, and end users have the potential to transform the cassava subsector in Nigeria, which is part of the country's agricultural transformation (Oyebola et al. 2019). One way to go about this would be through a simultaneous intervention across the whole value chain. Assistance/support should get across to all stakeholders in the value chain simultaneously, such that increasing farmers' productive capacity can be readily absolved by the processors and the end users.

Finally, a possible further research path could be an in-depth study of a successful micro cassava linkage story in Nigeria to understand its successes, challenges, and the potential for scale-up and replication across the country and beyond. One such successful linkage in South West Nigeria that brought together input suppliers, farmers (around 5000), a cassava processor, transporters, and several end users is believed to have created over 300 jobs and saved the country at least $7 m in foreign exchange in two years. The cassava subsector, with its many uses and derivatives, provides an opportunity to foster sustainable development and alleviate poverty. Investments in the development of cassava production and its value chain can open a world of opportunity to the country. It would be useful in the country's bid for self-sufficiency in food production and the reduction of its over-dependence on imported essential commodities. There are lots of business opportunities in the value chain, and it holds the potential to employ hundreds of thousands of people across the different strata of society living in the cities and the countryside. It is also potentially helpful in improving the earning of farmers and opening several budding markets for derivatives.

Acknowledgements The first author appreciates the Visiting Doctoral Fellowship at The Centre for Economic Policy and Development Research (CEPDeR), Covenant University, Ota, Nigeria, during which period the chapter was completed.

Note

1. "Extreme poverty" refers to the World Bank definition of an income below the international poverty line of $1.90 per day (in $ 2011).

References

Abass, A. B., Bokanga, M., Dixon, A., & Bramel, P. (2011). Transiting cassava into an urban food and industrial commodity through agro-processing and market-driven approaches: Lessons from Africa. In Carlos A. Da Silva & Nomathemba Mhlanga (Eds.), *Innovative policies and institutions in support of agro-industries development*. Urbana-Champaign, IL: University of Illinois.

Abass, A. B., Dziedzoave, N. T., Alenkhe, B. E., & James, B. (2012). *Quality management manual for the production of gari*. Ibadan: International Institute for Tropical Agriculture.

Abass, A. B., Mlingi, N., Ranaivoson, R., Zulu, M., Mukuka, I., Abele, S., et al. (2013). *Potential for commercial production and marketing of cassava: Experiences from the small-scale cassava processing project in East and Southern Africa*. Ibadan, Nigeria: IITA.

Adams, B. (2009). *Green development: Environment and sustainability in a developing world* (3rd ed.). London, England: Routledge.

Ajima Farms. (2017). Waste- 2- Watt Launch in Rije Community [Video file]. Kuje, FCT, Nigeria. Retrieved from https://www.youtube.com/watch?v=RfBsS7qSA88&feature=youtu.be.

Akoroda, M. O., Sanni, L., Taylor, D. S., & Phillips, T. P. (2004). *A cassava industrial revolution in Nigeria: The potential for a new industrial crop.* Rome: Food and Agricultural Organisation. Retrieved from http://www.fao.org/docrep/fao/007/y5548e/y5548e00.pdf.

AllAfrica. (2018, June 13). *Nigeria: AfDB to invest $120 million to boost cassava, others.* Retrieved from all Africa. https://allafrica.com/stories/201806130166.html.

Anríquez, G., & Stamoulis, K. G. (2007). Rural development and poverty reduction: Is agriculture still the key? *eJADE: Electronic Journal of Agricultural and Development Economics, Food and Agriculture Organization, Agricultural and Development Economics Division, 4*(1), 42. Retrieved from https://ideas.repec.org/a/ags/ejadef/112591.html.

Aregheore, E. M. (2012). Nutritive value and inherent anti-nutritive factors in four indigenous edible leafy vegetables in human nutrition in Nigeria. *Journal of Food Resource Science, 1*(1), 1–14.

Associated Press. (2015). *SYND 23 5 76 Head of the State Lieutenant General Obasanjo in Operation Feed the Nation in Lagos.* Associated Press. Retrieved March 11, 2019, from https://www.youtube.com/watch?v=XM-Q6tLu4FM.

Awoyinka, F. A., & Abegunde, V. O. (1995). Nutrient content of young cassava leaves and assessment of their acceptance as a green vegetable in Nigeria. *Plant Foods for Human Nutrition, 47*(1), 21–28. https://doi.org/10.1007/BF01088163.

Balagopalan, C. (2002). Cassava utilization in food, feed and industry. In A. Bellotti (Ed.), *Cassava: Biology, production and utilization.* Wallingford, UK: CABI Pub.

Balagopalan, C., Padmaja, G., Nanda, S., & Moorthy, S. (1988). *Cassava in food, feed and industry* (1st ed.). Boca Raton, FL: Taylor & Francis Group.

Bankole, A. (2017). *Researcher exposes nutritional values of cassava leaves.* "Nutritional insight into cassava and its commercialization potentials," at the Town and Gown Seminar of the Department of Biological Sciences on February 14, 2017. Ota, Ogun State: Covenant University. Retrieved from https://covenantuniversity.edu.ng/News/Researcher-Exposes-Nutritional-Values-of-Cassava-Leaves.

Bello, R., Toyebi, G., Balogun, I., & Akanbi, S. (2009). Poverty alleviation programmes and economic development in Nigeria: A comparative assessment of Asa and Ilorin West Local Govt. Areas of Kwara State, Nigeria. *African Research Review, 3*(4), 283–297.

Bellù, L. G., & Liberati, P. (2005). Impacts of policies on poverty: The definition of poverty. *EASYPol, 4.* Retrieved from http://www.fao.org/docs/up/easypol/312/povanlys_defpov_004EN.pdf.

Bokanga, M. (1994). Processing of cassava leaves for human consumption. *Acta Horticultura, 375*, 203–207.

Cervantes-Godoy, D., & Dewbre, J. (2010). *Economic importance of agriculture for poverty reduction* (OECD Food, Agriculture and Fisheries Working Papers, No. 23). Paris: OECD.

CGIAR. (2018, June 21). *AfDB to invest $120 million to boost cassava and others.* Retrieved from CGIAR. https://www.cgiar.org/news-events/news/afdb-invest-120-million-boost-cassava-others/.

Channels Television. (2015a). Earthfile focuses on making better use of cassava waste (PT1) 03/07/15 [Video file]. *Earthfile.* Channels Television. Retrieved from https://www.youtube.com/watch?v=OunLjhlFObk.

Channels Television. (2015b). Earthfile focuses on making better use of cassava waste (PT2) 03/07/15 [Video file]. *Earthfile*. Channels Television. Retrieved from https://www.youtube.com/watch?v=FkMimHhv9ck.

Channels Television. (2015c). Earthfile focuses on making better use of cassava waste (PT3) 03/07/15 [Video file]. *Earthfile*. Retrieved from https://www.youtube.com/watch?v=azx8nG6eseU.

Channels Television. (2016a). Earth file: Getting more yields from cassava plantation in Nigeria (PT1) 29/01/16 [Video file]. *Earth File*. Channels Television. Retrieved from https://www.youtube.com/watch?v=RvI01uSXZWA.

Channels Television. (2016b). Earth file: Getting more yields from cassava plantation in Nigeria (PT2) 29/01/16 [Video file]. *Earth File*. Channels Television. Retrieved from https://www.youtube.com/watch?v=7aIjdPFcbQo.

Cock, J. H. (1985). *Cassava new potential for a neglected crop*. New York: Avalon Publishing.

Dowler, E., Turner, S. A., & Dobson, B. (2001). *Poverty bites: Food, health and poor families*. London: Child Poverty Action Group.

Dziedzoave, N., Abass, A. B., Amoa-Awua, W., & Sablah, M. (2006). *Quality management manual for production of high-quality cassava flour* (G. Adegoke & L. Brimer, Eds.). Ibadan: International Institute of Tropical Agriculture. Retrieved from http://hqcf.iita.org/wp-content/uploads/2016/04/6_quality-control-manual-for-hqcfproduction.pdf.

FAO. (1995). *Dimensions of need: An atlas of food and agriculture*. Rome, Italy: Food & Agriculture Organization.

FAO. (2000). *Medium-term prospects for agricultural commodities: Projections to the year 2005*. Rome: Food and Agricultural Organization of the United Nations.

FAO. (2003). *Agricultural commodities: Profiles and relevant WTO negotiating issues*. Commodities and Trade Division. Rome, Italy: Food and Agriculture Organization of the United Nations.

FAO. (2011). *The state of the world's land and water resources for food and agriculture: Managing systems at risk*. New York: The Food and Agriculture Organization of the United Nations and Earthscan. Retrieved from http://www.fao.org/3/i1688e/i1688e.pdf.

FAO. (2013). *Save and grow: Cassava: A guide to sustainable production intensification*. Rome: Food and Agriculture Organization.

FAO. (2015). *The state of food and agriculture (SOFA) 2015: Social protection and agriculture: Breaking the cycle of rural poverty*. Food and Agriculture Organization of the United Nations. Retrieved from http://www.fao.org/fileadmin/user_upload/newsroom/docs/SOFA-in-Brief2015.pdf.

FAO. (2017a). *Nigeria at a glance|FAO*. Food and Agriculture Organization of the United Nations. Retrieved from http://www.fao.org/nigeria/fao-in-nigeria/nigeria-at-a-glance/en/.

FAO. (2017b). *Strategic work of FAO to reduce rural poverty*. Food and Agricultural Organization of the United Nations. Retrieved from http://www.fao.org/3/a-i6835e.pdf.

FAO. (2019). *FAOSTAT (Crops)*. Food and Agricultural Organization of the United Nations. Retrieved from http://www.fao.org/faostat/en/#data/QC/visualize.

FAO Council. (1989). Sustainable development. In FAO's, *The state of food and agriculture 1989* (Vol. FAO Agriculture Series). Rome: FAO. Retrieved from http://www.fao.org/3/a-t0162e.pdf.

Ferreira, F., & Sánchez-Páramo, C. (2017, October 14). *A richer array of international poverty lines.* Retrieved from The World Bank. https://blogs.worldbank.org/developmenttalk/richer-array-international-poverty-lines.

FGN. (1990). *Laws of the federation of Nigeria-people's bank of Nigeria act.* Retrieved March 11, 2019, from LawNigeria. http://www.lawnigeria.com/LawsoftheFederation/PEOPLE'S-BANK-OF-NIGERIA-ACT.html.

FGN. (1992). *Community banks decree NO. 46 1992 ACT CAP. C18 L.F.N. 2004.* Retrieved March 11, 2019, from Laws of the Federal Republic of Nigeria. http://resources.lawscopeonline.com/LFN/COMMUNITY_BANKS_DECREE_NO._46_1992_ACT_CAP._C18_L.F.N._2004.htm.

FMARD. (2014). *Agricultural transformation agenda 2013 report—January–December, 2013 score card.* Abuja: Federal Ministry of Agriculture and Rural Development—Nigeria. Retrieved from https://www.fepsannigeria.com/fepsan2/files/FMARD%20ATA%20Scorcar.

Gabriel, A. (1994). A better life program for rural women in a developing nation. In V. U. James (Ed.), *Environmental and economic dilemmas of developing countries: Africa in the twenty-first century* (p. 264). Westport, CT: Praeger.

Grace, M. R. (1977). *Cassava processing—Cassava cultivation* (Vol. FAO Plant Production and Protection). Rome: Food and Agricultural Organization of the United Nations. Retrieved from http://www.fao.org/docrep/x5032e/x5032e01.htm.

Green Social Bioethanol. (2015). Green Social Bioethanol—Ogbomosho Project. *Ethanol Micro Distillery (EMD) to Produce 1,000 Liters Per Day of Ethanol from Cassava Starch.* Ogbomosho, Oyo, Nigeria. Retrieved from https://www.youtube.com/watch?v=poETylmMlGI.

Hahn, S. K., Reynolds, L., & Egbunike, G. N. (1992). Cassava as livestock feed in Africa. In *Proceedings of the IITA/ILCA/University of Ibadan Workshop on the Potential Utilization of Cassava as Livestock Feed in Africa.* International Institute for Tropical Agriculture.

Henry, G., Westby, A., & Collinson, C. (1998). *Global cassava end-uses and markets: Current situation and recommendations for further study: Report of a FAO consultancy by the European group on root, tuber & plantain co-ordinated by Dr. Guy Henry.* CIRAD. Retrieved from http://www.hubrural.org/IMG/pdf/global_cassava_end_use_study.pdf.

Hershey, C., Henry, G., Best, R., Kawano, K., Howeler, R. H., & Iglesias, C. (2001). Cassava in Asia: Expanding the competitive edge in diversified markets. In *FAO, A review of cassava in Asia with country case studies on Thailand and Viet Nam* (Vol. 3). Food and Agricultural Organization of the United Nations.

HLPE. (2016). Sustainable agricultural development for food security and nutrition: What roles for livestock? *A report by the high-level panel of experts on food security and nutrition of the Committee on World Food Security.* Rome.

Howeler, R., Lutaladio, N., & Thomas, G. (2013). *Save and grow: Cassava: A guide to sustainable production intensification* (Vol. No. FAO 633.6828 S266). Rome, Italy: Food and Agricultural Organization of the United Nations. Retrieved from http://www.fao.org/3/a-i3278e.pdf.

ICRA. (2016). From cassava to beer: Roots to empowerment [Video file]. International Centre for Development Oriented Research in Agriculture. Retrieved from https://www.youtube.com/watch?v=Cwq-ns04SRA.

IITA. (2015). Growing cassava for optimum profitability to sustain HQCF factories [Video file]. International Institute for Tropical Agriculture (IITA). Retrieved from https://www.youtube.com/watch?v=whoEB28kHrQ.

ILRI. (2015). Transforming cassava peels into animal feed [Video file]. International Livestock Research Institute (ILRI). Retrieved from https://www.youtube.com/watch?v=jkvHYqPLvyc&t=240s.

IUCN. (1980). *World conservation strategy: Living resource conservation for sustainable development*. Gland, Switzerland: International Union for Conservation of Nature, & World Wildlife Fund. Retrieved from https://portals.iucn.org/library/sites/library/files/documents/WCS-004.pdf.

Kirk-Greene, A. M., Ajayi, J. A., Udo, K. R., & Falola, T. O. (2019, February 27). *Nigeria*. Retrieved from Enclyclopaedia Britannica. https://www.britannica.com/place/Nigeria.

Laderchi, C. R., Saith, R., & Stewart, F. (2003). Does it matter that we do not agree on the definition of poverty? A comparison of four approaches. *Oxford Development Studies, 31*(3), 243–274.

Lancaster, P. A., & Brooks, J. E. (1983). Cassava leaves as human food. *Economic Botany, 37*(3), 331–348.

Latif, S., & Müller, J. (2015). Potential of cassava leaves in human nutrition: A review. *Trends in Food Science & Technology*. https://doi.org/10.1016/j.tifs.2015.04.006.

Mateo-Sagasta, J., Zadeh, S. M., Turral, H., & Burke, J. (2017). *Water pollution from agriculture: A global review*. Rome: Food and Agriculture Organization of the United Nations and the International Water Management Institute.

Mayaki, I. (2016, May 11). *3 ways to transform agriculture in Africa* (World Economic Forum). Retrieved from World Economic Forum. https://www.weforum.org/agenda/2016/05/3-ways-to-transform-agriculture-in-africa/.

Mehta, A. K., & Shah, A. (2003). Chronic poverty in India: Incidence, causes and policies. *World Development, 31*(3), 491–511.

Meridian Institute. (2010). A cassava value chain overview. In *Innovations for agricultural value chains in Africa: Applying science and technology to enhance cassava, dairy, and maize value chains* (p. 16). Meridian Institute. Retrieved from http://www.merid.org/~/media/Files/Projects/Value%20Chains%20Microsite/Cassava_Value_Chain_Overview_090527FINAL.pdf.

Nang'ayo, F., Omanya, G., Bokanga, M., Odera, M., Muchiri, N., Ali, Z., & Werehire, P. (2005, November 14–18). A strategy for industrialisation of cassava in Africa. *In Proceedings of a Small Group Meeting*. Ibadan, Nigeria and Nairobi, Kenya: African Agricultural Technology Foundation.

NBS. (2012). *Nigeria poverty profile 2010*. Abuja: National Bureau of Statistics. Retrieved from http://www.nigerianstat.gov.ng/pdfuploads/Nigeria%20Poverty%20Profile%202010.pdf.

NDE. (2019). *About NDE*. Retrieved March 11, 2019, from The National Directorate of Employment Website. https://nde.gov.ng/about-nde/.

Nhassico, D., Muquingue, H., Cliff, J., Cumbana, A., & Bradbury, J. H. (2008). Rising African cassava production, diseases due to high cyanide intake and control measures. *Journal of the Science of Food and Agriculture, 88*(12), 2043–2049. https://doi.org/10.1002/jsfa.

NNPC. (2004). *Meeting everyone's needs: National economic empowerment and development strategy*. Abuja: Nigerian National Planning Commission. Retrieved from https://www.imf.org/external/pubs/ft/scr/2005/cr05433.pdf.

Nweke, F. I. (2003, December 1 and 3). *New challenges in the cassava transformation in Nigeria and Ghana* (Conference Paper No. 8). Paper presented at the INVENT, IFPRI, NEPAD, CTA Conference. Successes in African Agriculture, Pretoria.

Nweke, F. I. (2005). The cassava transformation in Africa. *IFAD, & FAO, A review of cassava in Africa with country case studies on Nigeria, Ghana, the United Republic of Tanzania, Uganda and Benin* (pp. 1–66). Rome: FAO and IFAD.

Okoro, O. C. (2009). *NIGERIA: Her woes and their true remedies*. Bloomington: iUniverse.

Olowu, D., Laleye, M., & Victor, A. (1991). *Monograph series on administrative responses to the African economic crisis: The case of Nigeria*. African Association for Public Administration and Management (Nairobi, Kenya), & Workshop of African Public Administration Experts.

Oluwale, B. A., Ilori, M. O., Ayeni, Y., & Ogunjemilua, E. M. (2018). Assessment of cassava composite flour inclusion in bread production in southwestern Nigeria. *Journal of Food Processing & Technology, 9*, 760. https://doi.org/10.4172/2157-7110.1000760.

Osabuohien, E., Okorie, U., & Osabohien, R. (2018). Rice production and processing in Ogun State, Nigeria: Qualitative insights from farmers' association. In E. Obayelu (Ed.), *Food systems sustainability and environmental policies in modern economics* (pp. 188–216). Hershey, PA: IGI Global. https://doi.org/10.4018/978-1-5225-3631-4.ch009.

Oyebola, P. O., Osabuohien, E., & Obasaju, B. (2019). Employment and income effects of Nigeria's agricultural transformation agenda. *African Journal of Economic and Management Studies*. https://doi.org/10.1108/AJEMS-12-2018-0402.

Phillips, P. P., Henry, G., Graffham, A., Vilpoux, O., Titapiwatanakun, B., & Taylor, D. S. (2004). Global cassava market study: Business opportunities for the use of cassava. In *Proceedings of the Validation Forum on the Global Cassava Development Strategy, 6*. Rome: IFAD and FAO. Retrieved from http://www.fao.org/3/y5287e/y5287e00.htm.

Sachs, J. (2015). *The age of sustainable development* (1st ed.). New York: Columbia University Press.

Schultz, T. W. (1980). The economics of being poor—Nobel lecture. *Journal of Political Economy, 88*(4), 639–651.

The Punch Newspaper. (2019, February 17). *Nigeria can save N250bn through cassava bread Nigeria Cassava Growers Association*. Retrieved from Punchng. https://punchng.com/nigeria-can-save-n250bn-through-cassava-bread-ncga/.

Todaro, M., & Smith, S. (2015). *Economic development* (12th ed.). Harlow: Pearson.

UNESCO. (2017). *Poverty|United Nations educational, scientific and cultural organization*. Retrieved from http://www.unesco.org/new/en/social-and-human-sciences/themes/international-migration/glossary/poverty/.

United Nations. (1995). *Agreements of the world summit for social development, Copenhagen 1995*. Retrieved from http://www.un.org/esa/socdev/wssd/text-version/agreements/poach2.htm.

United Nations. (1998, July 6–31). *Statement of commitment of the administrative committee on coordination for action to eradicate poverty*. New York: United Nations. Retrieved from https://www.unsceb.org/CEBPublicFiles/press/981815le.pdf.

United Nations. (2015). *Food security and nutrition and sustainable agriculture.* Retrieved February 6, 2019, from United Nation's Sustainable Development Goals Knowledge Platform. https://sustainabledevelopment.un.org/topics/foodagriculture.

USDA. (2018). *2018 grain and feed annual Nigeria—USDA GAIN reports.* United States Department of Agriculture. Retrieved from https://gain.fas.usda.gov/Recent%20GAIN%20Publications/Grain%20and%20Feed%20Annual_Lagos_Nigeria_4-12-2018.pdf.

World Bank. (2015a, press release). *World Bank forecasts global poverty to fall below 10% for first time; major hurdles remain in goal to end poverty by 2030.* The World Bank.

World Bank. (2015b). *FAQs: Global poverty line update: Poverty brief.* Retrieved from http://www.worldbank.org/en/topic/poverty/brief/global-poverty-line-faq.

World Bank. (2017). *Poverty headcount ratio|Data world.* Retrieved from The World Bank Data. https://data.worldbank.org/indicator/SI.POV.DDAY?locations=1W.

World Bank. (2019a). *Agricultural land (% of land area).* Retrieved from Data.worldbank.org. https://data.worldbank.org/indicator/AG.LND.AGRI.ZS.

World Bank. (2019b). *GINI index (World Bank estimate).* Retrieved from World Bank. https://data.worldbank.org/indicator/SI.POV.GINI?locations=NG.

World Poverty Clock. (2019). *World poverty clock.* Retrieved February 9, 2019, from https://worldpoverty.io/.

Wossen, T., Girma, G., Abdoulaye, T., Rabbi, I., Olanrewaju, A., Alene, A., et al. (2017). *The cassava monitoring survey in Nigeria.* Ibadan: International Institute of Tropical Agriculture.

Wrights, S. (2017). Nigeria: Human rights, development and democracy. In P. J. Burnell, V. Randall, & L. Rakner (Eds.), *In politics in the developing world* (4th ed., pp. 359–367). Oxford: Oxford University Press.

Zuma, N. D. (2013). Feeding Africa and the world. In NEPAD, *Agriculture in Africa: Transformation and outlook* (p. 72). Johannesburg: NEPAD.

Micro-determinants of Women's Participation in Agricultural Value Chain: Evidence from Rural Households in Nigeria

Kehinde Oluwole Ola

1 Introduction

Agriculture plays a dominant role in Nigeria and has been seen as a means for economic diversification by the current dispensation. This has led to substantive commitment of the Federal Government to the agricultural sector. Government in its effort has created policies such as Growth Enhancement Support (GES) Scheme, Commercial Agricultural Credit Scheme (CACS), the Anchor Borrowers Program, the Nigeria Incentive-based Risk-sharing System for Agricultural Lending (NIRSAL), the Green Alternative and the Presidential Initiative on Fertilizer (Ministry of Budget and National Planning 2017). All these efforts tend toward increasing annual average growth rate of contribution of agriculture to the Gross Domestic Products to the tune of 6.92% (Ministry of Budget and National Planning 2017). The success of the efforts and meeting the target set depend on stakeholders in agricultural sector, which includes Nigerian women farmers especially women farmers in the rural areas.

The agricultural sector presently accounts for over 21% of the nominal Gross Domestic Products (Central Bank of Nigeria 2017) and over 38% of the working population (Ministry of Budget and National Planning 2017). It should be noted that women in agriculture account for significant percentage of the statistics. According to the statistics provided by AgroNigeria,

K. O. Ola (✉)
Department of Economics, College of Management and Social Sciences, Samuel Adegboyega University, Ogwa, Edo State, Nigeria
e-mail: kola@sau.edu.ng

a non-governmental agency, women supply 80% of workforce in food production and 10% of the workforce in basic food processing. In addition, women make the largest part of small farmers in the rural communities, where 80% of the agricultural production emerged from; apart from dominating rural marketing to the rate of 60–90% depending on the cultural structures of the region involved (AgroNigeria 2016). In all, women account for over 43% of the agricultural labor force in Nigeria (Roberts-Agbaje 2017).

The high presence of women in rural marketing where agricultural products are the major items of trade showed that women cannot be set aside in production, processing, and marketing of agricultural product. In Nigeria, the major problem in the agricultural sector is the lack of market links between the producers of agricultural products and the end-users (Echono 2015; Roberts-Agbaje 2017). This has great impact on women farmers who are active in agricultural production. Ejike et al. (2018) citing Gurung (2006) note that women tends to play less roles as agricultural products move from the farm to market in terms of income and control. Women's visibility in the agricultural value chain can only be perceived in the retail business of agricultural products and the open-air markets where they transact such products (Sahel 2014; Adam et al. 2018; Oyebola et al. 2019). Thus, women are active at the lowest level and this is where women accounted for over 79.3% compared to 36.7% of men (Adam et al. 2018 citing Apata 2013). Going with Adam et al. (2018), women are rarely placed as middle women across the value chain.

There are reasons for difficulty of women to participate across agricultural value chain call for investigation. Authors such as Ahmadu and Idisi (2014), Aliyu (2015), Onuekwusi et al. (2017), Chete (2018), Ejike et al. (2018), Adam et al. (2018), Apata (2013) have conceptually or empirically investigated the likely factors that might have limited women farmers' participation in agricultural value chain. Cursory look at their studies have shown that they have examined factors, which include education, farm experience, farm size, cassava farms, access to market, and information about the market, female extension workers, technical knowhow, labor saving devices and equipment, membership of cooperative society, family size, availability of capital, processing skill centers, capacity building, and mobility. Nevertheless, there is still lacuna in this area which call for further studies.

None of the above previous studies known to the author have considered the role of distance and time use for community responsibilities play in agricultural value chain, thus this fills this gap by making improvement to previous studies. The nature of rural settings showed that women may be hindered from effectively participating in agricultural value chain when it takes them relatively long distance to reach the market or transport their farm produce to the big markets. In addition, women as they grow old tend to be committed to well-being of their immediate household, extended family, and even others in the community. Distance and community responsibility are two among the key factors identified by International Finance Corporation in 2016.

As known to the author, these two factors have not been empirically investigated in literature in studies relating to women and agricultural value chain. The impact of these two variables-distance travelled and community responsibility should be considered in terms of signs and magnitudes. This is because the signs and magnitudes will show the extent of impact on women participation in agricultural value chain and as such, concrete policy can be formulated to enhance the effective participation of women in agricultural value chain.

This study has the objective of investigating micro-determinants of women participation in agricultural value chain in Nigerian rural communities. The specific objectives are to: (i) identify the determinants; and (ii) examine the influence of those determinants on women's participation in agricultural value chain. The paper is divided into five sections—introduction, literature review, methodology, empirical evidence and discussion, and conclusion and recommendations.

2 Literature Review

The concept of agricultural value chain has become of the highly popularized in the literature in the recent times because it has been seen as a key factor in promoting jobs, household incomes, and economic growth in the developing countries (Vroegindewey and Hodbod 2018). Ejike et al. (2018) citing FAO (2005) describe value chain as "a tool that facilitates investigation of business activities in terms of new value- adding opportunities in relation to existing values with regards to sourcing of factors of inputs, production, processing and delivery of the finished product." Ejike et al. (2018) see agricultural value chain as a mean of stimulating agricultural investment in Nigeria. Agricultural production in Nigeria is characterized by small farm holders and the sustained productivity of these small farm holders are necessary for meeting the growing agricultural demand worldwide (International Finance Corporation 2016). There is therefore the need to have proper linkage between the small farmers and the markets.

Women involvement in agriculture could be dated back to the informal system of education, in which adult members of the society inculcate the cultural practices into younger ones. Since farming is the main occupation of many of the traditional African societies, female members formed part of the household farm workers. Through this means, they imbibe farming as vocations except in households where there are some forms of household trades. Even in those households, farming is still taking as part time occupation. There are some families in rural African society where trades or artisans such as blacksmith, cloth weaving are practiced. Despite practicing these trades or artisans, they involve in subsistence farming. Women from these households also learn how to participate in every stage of agricultural production (Roberts-Agbaje 2017).

In the contemporary times, the roles of women in agriculture has not gone beyond that of small-scale farmers whose primary functions are to sell agricultural produce; act as retailers; and serve as hired extension workers and rural agro-agents (International Finance Corporation 2016). According to Roberts-Agbaje (2017), despite these functions women's contributions are unrecognized and invisible in the agricultural value chain because when it comes to the point of moving the goods to the markets, women are not cut off. Thus, women play active roles in agricultural value chain at the lowest level (see Sahel 2014; Adam et al. 2018; Chete 2018) but at the level where it should have been of economic advantage to them they are rarely noticeable (Chete 2018).

Studies (e.g., Ahmadu and Idisi 2014; Aliyu 2015; Onuekwusi et al. 2017; Chete 2018) have shown that women's ineffectiveness in agricultural value chain arise from certain factors. Sahel (2014), International Finance Corporation (2016), and Roberts-Agbaje (2017) identify limited access to hired labor, equipment, technology, training, finance, and markets; restrictions on land ownership and tenure; sexual harassment and violence; and household, community, and care responsibilities, and certification process.

Some of these factors which are education, farm experience, farm size, cassava farms, access to market, and information about the market, female extension workers, technical knowhow, labor saving devices and equipment, membership of cooperative society, family size, availability of capital have been empirically investigated by authors which include Aliyu (2015), Onuekwusi et al. (2017), Chete (2018), Ejike et al. (2018), Adam et al. (2018), and Apata (2013). One of the studies that focused on Niger Delta comes from Ahmadu and Idisi (2014). Ahmadu and Idisi examined the participation of men and women in cassava value chain in Niger Delta and Southwestern Nigeria. The authors conceptually examined strategies and opportunities for increasing participation of cassava farmers especially women in agricultural value chain. The authors narrated how agricultural value chain could be used as instrument to understand gender inequalities and how gender could be integrated into value chain analysis.

Aliyu (2015) examined the role of women in groundnut value chain in Kano State. Using three local governments and randomly selecting 149 respondents with the aid of well-structured questionnaire, Aliyu made use of variables such as age, education, marital status, and membership of a cooperative society significantly affect women's participation in groundnut value chain. The findings of Aliyu showed that age and membership of a cooperative society were the only factors affecting women's profitability in the groundnut value chain in Kano State. The study by Afolabi et al. (2016) examined the level of women's participation in agricultural value chain utilization in Nigeria and focused on 420 women farmers in Jigawa State. The authors found out that few women did not involve in agricultural value chain. The authors' findings further showed that lack of awareness, lack of knowledge about the agricultural initiatives and marginalization were the basic factors affecting the level of women involvement.

Onuekwusi et al. (2017) examined the impact of cocoyam value added technologies on rural women farmers in Umudike. Using 120 women farmers in Ohafia and Umuahia, Onuekwusi, Odoemelam, and Kanu collected data on the level of awareness of cocoyam technologies. The authors made use of linear regression model and findings showed that out of five technologies available for processing cocoyam into cake, bread, chin-chin, biscuits, and chips only three were efficiently used by the women. The authors further showed that there was improvement in the livelihood of the women after receiving training on use of the technologies. The study by Chete (2018) was on the factor that influenced gender involvement in rice enterprises in Southwestern Nigeria. The author made use of multi-stage sampling method to draw 254 respondents. The author divided the respondents into adult male, adult female, young male, and young female. Though the study did not focus on female farmers, the author's findings showed that women farmers were considerably affected by factors such as years of experience in rice farming, production, processing, and marketing. The above is related to the findings of Osabuohien et al. (2018) with respect to rice farming in Ogun State, Nigeria.

Based on the review of empirical literature, Ejike et al. (2018) investigated the place of women in agricultural value chain and revealed that women presently accounted for 43% of the agricultural labor force globally and their participation has increased in agricultural food value chain. In the authors' review, they found out that mobility, training, market and information, productive resources, and labor saving technologies were basic factors limiting women's participation in agricultural value chain. Another study from the Northern part of Nigeria is that of Adam et al. (2018, which investigated men and women's participation in rice processing activities in Kebbi and Sokoto States. Using purposive sampling to select 152 beneficiaries of the Agricultural Transformation Agenda Support Progam-1 (ATASP-1), Adam et al. (2018) investigated the socio-economic characteristics of the farmers. The findings of the authors showed that 42.2% of the 55.3% of the farmers without education were women. The authors also found out that women ranked rice husking machines, rice de-stoned machines and false bottom machines as the most helpful to them in rice processing value chain. The authors found out that availability of female extension workers, technical knowhow, labor saving devices and equipment, availability of capital, processing skill centers, capacity building, and mobility were significant factors influencing gender's participation in rice value chain.

In the study by Apata (2013), 300 cassava farmers in Southwestern Nigeria were selected using multi-stage sampling method. The author collected the information needed with the aid of questionnaire and analyzed the data using factor analysis and poisson model. Apata found out that women's participation in agricultural value chain were determined by control of productive resources and household level decisions. Apata's finding further showed that women farmers' participation in agricultural value chain were influenced by the status in family and size of land owned. In conclusion, Apata's findings showed that gender, education, farm experience, farm size, cassava farms, access to market, and information about the market play significant roles in participation in agricultural value chain by farmers in Southwestern Nigeria.

The literature reviewed on the issues under discussion showed that the previous studies have gone far in investigating the likely determinants of women participation in agricultural value chain (see Adam et al. 2018; Ejike et al. 2018). For instance, Aliyu (2015) was able to detect the role played by age and membership of a cooperative society while Afolabi et al. (2016) was able to identify the significance of awareness of agricultural initiatives. Studies such as Onuekwusi et al. (2017), Ejike et al. (2018) and Adam et al. (2018) brought years of experience, mobility, and labor saving device into limelight. Nevertheless, these previous studies have not fully captured all the likely determinants of women participation in agricultural value chain, women's functions in the community possessed two distinctive features-productive and reproductive. The reproductive function of women in the community entails some form of communal responsibility, which may demand time. In addition, haulage of farm produce to home or markets are done by means of head carriage, which showed that the quantity of farm produce to be hauled at a particular time is a function of distance. These two determinants are imperative in assessing the likely determinants of women participation in agricultural value chain.

3 Methodology

The study use econometric in analyzing the micro-determinants of women participation in Agricultural Value Chain in some selected farm communities in Esan West Local Government Area (LGA) of Edo State, Nigeria. The population of the study was drawn from all women farmers in the communities. Owing to time and resources available, the purposive sampling method was used to select the 162 women selected for the study. A simple questionnaire was designed to elicit information from the respondents. The questionnaire was structured in nature as to provide the ground for conversion of the variables of interest into nominal scales. The study made use of Probit Regression technique to analyze the categorical variables and scores of the variables were either 1 or 0 since they were all dummy variables.

The study adopts the model of Chete (2018) with slight modification, which is specified as follows:

$$Y_i = \beta_0 + \beta_1 X_{1i} + \beta_2 X_{2i} + \beta_{i3} X_{3i} + \beta_4 X_{4i} + \beta_5 X_{5i} + \beta_6 X_{6i} + \beta_7 X_{7i} + \beta_8 X_{8i} + \beta_9 X_{9i} + \mu_i \qquad (1)$$

where Y=Involvement, X_1=Farm size, X_2=Years of experience, X_3=Type of enterprise (Production), X_4=Type of enterprise (Processing), X_5=Type of enterprise (Marketing), X_6=Self-labor, X_7=Hired labor, X_8=Rented land, X_9 = Inherited land, $\beta_0 \ldots \beta_9$ = Coefficients, μ = Random error term and i = number of observations.

The author dropped the following variables-Type of enterprise (Production), Type of enterprise (Processing), Type of enterprise (Marketing), Self-labor, and Hired labor. The author further added the age of the women farmer, education of the women farmer, distance from farm to house, distance from house to market, time used for household chores, mobility, family size and marital status. The modified model is given as follows:

$$Y_i = \beta_0 + \beta_1 X_{1i} + \beta_2 X_{2i} + \beta_{i3} X_{3i} + \beta_4 X_{4i} + \beta_5 X_{5i} + \beta_6 X_{6i} + \beta_7 X_{7i} + \beta_8 X_{8i} + \beta_9 X_{9i} + \beta_{10} X_{10i} + \beta_{11} X_{11i} + \beta_{12} X_{12i} + \mu_i \quad (2)$$

where Y = Involvement, X_1 = Farm size, X_2 = Years of experience, X_3 = Size of Households, X_4 = Age of women, X_5 = Marital status, X_6 = education of the women, X_7 = distance from farm to house, X_8 = Rented land, X_9 = Inherited land, X_{10} = Distance from house to market centers, X_{11} = Source of mobility, X_{12} = Time spent on household and community responsibilities, $\beta_0 \ldots \beta_{12}$ = Coefficients, μ = Random error term and i = number of observations.

The descriptions and expected signs were given as follows:

Involvement (Y): This is the dependent variable and a categorical variable. It describes the level of involvement of rural women in agricultural value chain. Women that are involving in higher stage of agricultural value chain are assigned 1, otherwise 0. Those women must involve in four stage of agricultural value chain described by International Finance Corporation (2016) which are (1) input provision and use, (2) production, (3) post-harvesting processing, and (4) storage, and transportation, marketing and sales.

Farm Size (X_1): It is assumed that a large farm size may influence the need to participate fully in every stage of agricultural value chain described by International Finance Corporation (2016). Women with relatively large farm size are assigned 1, otherwise 0. The expected sign is positive because it is assumed that the larger the size of the farms, the higher the tendency to involve in the five stages of agricultural value chain described by International Finance Corporation (2016).

Years of Experience (X_2): This is the length of time the women have started farming until the time of this study. According to Chete (2018), this is the exact years of farming experience. It is assumed that women who have involved in farming more than 5 years should have had adequate knowledge of farming business and thereby be able to involve in (1) input provision and use, (2) production, (3) post-harvesting processing, and (4) storage, and transportation, marketing and sales. Women with more than five years of farming experiences are assigned 1, otherwise 0. The expected sign is positive.

Size of the Households (X_3): Studies showed that women play significant roles in household finance (Ogunlela and Mukhtar 2005). Large part of their farm produce may end up as household consumption and income earned spent on children's education and welfare except in case of large farms. This may mop up saving they may likely use as plough-back capital. It is therefore assumed that large households likely reduce women's active participation in agricultural value chain. A value of 0 is assigned to women with large family size; otherwise 1 and the expected sign is negative.

Age of Women (X_4): In this study, the author considered age brackets and two main categories are assumed-women between 35 and 60; and women below 35 or older than 60 years. The author assumed that women in the first category may likely have passed child-bearing age since women in rural communities tend to marry earlier and before 35 they may have stopped bearing. Therefore, they have tendency to have ample time for farming activities and hence, can involve actively in agricultural value chain. The other categories may be taken over by children bearing and rearing or helping their children to nurture their babies. They may even consider themselves too young or old for such activities because of the risk involved. The author therefore assigned 1 for women in the first category and 0 for second category. The expected value is positive for women in the first category.

Marital Status (X_5): The author categorized marital status into married and single women which include widow, single but married, and separated. The author wants to know if this has impact in participating in agricultural value chain. The author assigned 1 to women who are single, widow, single but married, and separated and 0 to married women. The expected sign is positive for women in the category of being single in any form.

Level of Education of the Women (X_6): Women who can read and write have some edges over those who cannot. They can easily involve official transaction and even take advantage of market information, which those with low level of education may be constraint of. The author therefore assigned 1 to women who have at least Secondary School education while those below it are assigned 0. The expected sign for women who have at least Secondary School education is positive.

Distance from Farm to House (X_7): Poor road infrastructure is common in the rural communities, as well as, poor transportation system. In many of rural communities in Esan West Local Government, women wake up as early as 5 a.m. to begin long trek to the farms (Ola 2014). This has effect on amount of land cultivated because long trek weakens the tendency to work for long hours. The author assumed that trekking long distances reduce farm produce, which likely weakens involvement in agricultural value chain. The author assigned 0 to women who trek more than two hours to get to farm and less than 1. The expected sign is negative.

Rented Land (X_8): The patrilineal nature of land ownership in many rural communities does not allow women to own land (Iruonagbe 2009). Many of them resorted to renting of land and this may constraint their ability to do large-scale farming. It is therefore assumed that this likely reduces participation in agricultural value chain. Women that rent land are assigned 0 and other 1. The author therefore assigned negative sign.

Inherited land (X_9): Women who are opportune to have land assigned to them by their parents will likely involve in large-scale farming. In some communities in Esan West Local Government Area, spouses give their wives some parts of their land for farming. This may not be sufficient for them except they inherit or rent it. The author assigned 1 for women who inherit land and 0 for those who do not. The expected sign for women who do not inherit land is negative.

Distance from House to Market Centers (X_{10}): Market centers seem far from many of the rural communities. This likely reduces capacity of the women to take their produce to markets. The produce ends in the hands of the middle men. The author therefore assigned 0 to women who live far from market centers and 1 to those who are not. The negative sign is expected.

Source of Mobility (X_{11}): Women who have means of mobility such as lorry can easily move their produce to market centers or have access to haulage companies. Such women are assigned 1, otherwise 0. The expected sign is negative for women without any source of mobility.

Community Responsibilities (X_{12}): According to International Finance Corporation (2016), this promotes the wellbeing of the community but affect time used for agricultural production. Women in this category are assigned 0, otherwise 1. The expected value is negative. This is essential as the community responsibilities could function like non-state actors (NSAs), which are essential for the development of the community (Osabuohien et al. 2015, 2019).

4 Empirical Results and Discussion

This section provides the summary of statistics of selected variables, as well as, Probit regression results.

The statistics in Table 1 showed the mean and standard deviation (SD) of the variables employed in the study. The mean obtained for the dependent variable 'level of involvement in agricultural value chain'. The value is 0.358 and it reveals that in the communities selected women were less involved in agricultural value. Explanation on statistics of the determinants showed the reason for this. The statistic on farm size showed that large number of women have small size. The mean value is 0.370 and thus, it can be concluded that the women were mainly peasant farmers. They operate farm basically to meet household need. One factor that may have explained operation of small farm may have come from usage of crude farm implements (Sahel 2014).

In terms of years of experience in farming, it can be seen that the mean is 0.920, which showed that large number of the women have been in farming for long. Women at the region became farmers through their mothers or mothers in law. Since many of them enter marriage at tender age, before getting to 30 years of age (Ola 2014). They should have had more than 10 year experience in farming. Considering the age category of 35–59 years

Table 1 Summary of statistics of selected variables

Variables	Description	FRQC	PCTG	Statistics	
				Mean	SD
Involvement (Y)	Involvement at lower stage	105	64.8	0.358	0.493
	Involvement in the 5 stages	57	35.2		
Farm size (X_1)	Small farm	102	63.0	0.370	0.484
	Large farm	60	37.0		
Years of experience (X_2)	Less than 10 years	13	8.0	0.920	0.273
	10 years or more	149	92.0		
Size of the households (X_3)	Less than 6	89	54.9	0.451	0.499
	6 or more	73	45.1		
Age of women (X_4)	Below 35 or older than 59	62	38.3	0.617	0.488
	35–59 years	100	61.7		
Marital status (X_5)	Married women	128	79.0	0.210	0.409
	Single women of any form	34	21.0		
Level of education of the women (X_6)	Below NCE	140	86.4	0.136	0.344
	NCE and above	22	13.6		
Distance from farm to house (X_7)	Less than 1 hour	92	56.8	0.567	0.497
	1 hour or more	70	43.2		
Rented land (X_8)	Rented	10	6.2	0.938	0.241
	Inherited or other forms	152	93.8		
Inherited land (X_9)	Inherited land	47	29.0	0.290	0.455
	Rented or other forms	115	71.0		
Distance from House to Market centers (X_{10})	Less than 1 hour	123	75.9	0.759	0.429
	1 hour or more	39	24.1		
Source of mobility (X_{11})	No access to means of haulage	146	90.1	0.098	0.299
	Access to means of haulage	16	9.9		
Community responsibilities (X_{12})	Less involvement	142	87.7	0.876	0.333
	Total involvement	20	12.3		

FRQC = Frequency, PCTG = Percentage
Source Computed by the author using IBM SPSS 21/EViews9

of age. It can be seen that the mean value is 0.617 which indicates that there is possibility of more women actively involving in Agricultural Value Chain in the communities. These women have matured enough to own and manage agricultural enterprises. Combined with the statistic on average years in farming business, women in these communities can benefit from Agricultural Value Chain.

Their participation may have been reduced by the statistic obtained from marital status. The mean value is 0.210 and this indicates that few women are not in marriage relationships. Since many of the women were full time housewives. They may not be able to go into large-scale farming owing to marriage commitment. It is clearly seen that many of the women did not go beyond Secondary schools. The mean obtained for level of education attained is 0.136. This has implication on the women's participation in agricultural value chain. One, it may be difficult for them to use and apply innovations in agriculture without the help of extension workers. Two, communication may not be easy and as such constraint them from going beyond the four corners of their communities in transacting their farm produce. The table also showed the statistic obtained for size of households. The mean value is 0.451. Relatively, the size of the households is small. It means the majority has on average number of household members less than six. The statistic is based on number available home; it excluded those who have left home in search of livelihood.

The mean obtained for time spent in commuting from farm to house is 0.567 and this shows that many of the women trek on average 1 hour. Since many of them operate small farms, the distance may not totally be a constraint except in hauling farm produce home. Table 1 further showed that the mean value for women obtained land from other source apart from renting is 0.938. Compare this statistic with that obtained for those who inherited land, which is 0.290, it can be seen that the land used by these women for farming may have come from their spouses or relatives. This in addition, may have explained the operation of small farms by these women. From the findings of Ola (2014), it can be concluded that the women do not have access to their own land and they made use of whatever available after their spouses have completed planting.

The nearest market to the women's residences is less than one-hour trek. The mean value of 0.759 reflects this. This provides ample opportunity for the women to take advantage of Agricultural Value but this is constraint by small farm size, and low level of education. Very few women have access to mobility. The mean value is 0.098. Therefore, they may not be able to transport farm produce to large market where they can take advantage of economies of scale. Many of the women spent less time on household or community responsibilities. The mean value obtained is 0.876. From this statistic, it can be seen that few women were held down by household or community responsibilities.

Table 2 gives the probit regression of the micro-determinants of women participation in Agricultural Value Chain. Farm size has positive coefficient has expected but it is not significant at 5% level of significant. This showed that large farm size can stimulate participation in Agricultural Value Chain among women in rural communities. That the coefficient is not significant may have come from few women who have large farm. It is only 37.0% of the women that have farms of relatively big size (see Table 1), which can serve as impetus to have desired for Agricultural Value Chain. The findings of the study are in tandem with Umuhoza (2012) in Rwanda and Apata (2013) in Southwestern Nigeria. Umuhoza and Apata's results showed that farm size

Table 2 Probit regression dependent variable: level of involvement

Variables	Column I	Column II	Column III
Constant	1.692**	0.474	1.243
	(2.240)	(1.380)	(3.040)
Farm size (X_1)	0.250		
	(0.996)		
Years of experience (X_2)	0.222		
	(0.510)		
Size of the households (X_3)	−0.341		
	(−1.373)		
Age of women (X_4)	−0.752**		−0.778*
	(−2.841)		(−3.565)
Marital status (X_5)	−0.313		
	(−1.047)		
Level of education of the women (X_6)	−0.893**		−0.742**
	(−2.202)		(−2.011)
Distance from farm to house (X_7)	−0.349		
	(−1.391)		
Rented land (X_8)	−0.400		
	(−0.785)		
Inherited land (X_9)	0.991*		
	(3.644)		
Distance from house to market centers (X_{10})	−0.687**	−0.511**	−0.535**
	(−2.445)	(−2.151)	(−2.184)
Source of mobility (X_{11})	−0.520	−0.745***	
	(−1.092)	(−1.738)	
Community responsibilities (X_{12})	−0.930*	−0.497***	−0.807**
	(−2.653)	(−1.649)	(−2.463)
Pseudo R squared	0.236	0.051	0.116
LR statistic	49.160	10.583	24.218
Prob (LR)	0.000	0.014	0.000
Observation	162	162	162

The values in parenthesis are z-statistics. Level of significance is *1%, **5% or ***10%
Source Computed by the Author using EView 9

positively influenced in women's participation in coffee and cassava value chain, respectively.

The coefficient of year of experience in farming business also has positive sign as expected but it is not significant at 5% level of significant, despite over 92.0% of the women who have been in farming business for more than ten years (see Table 1). The direct relationship is an indication that the experience counts for participation in Agricultural Value Chain. It is not significant because large number of the women have small farms (see Table 1). Since there is possibility of having large quantity of farm produce from the farms going into household consumption, the women have few left for sale. This result supported the findings of Umuhoza (2012), Apata (2013), and Chete (2018). This made Umuhoza to proffer that the women who have spent years in farming would have the tendency to continue because years should have taught the best technological practices to adopt.

The coefficient of size of the households also has negative sign as expected. This showed that large household can be a constraint to participation in Agricultural Value Chain in the contemporary Nigeria where there is rural–urban migration which leads to reduce farm-hands in rural communities. This also confirmed the study by Umuhoza (2012) who found out that the size of the households has significant impact on participation in coffee production in Rwanda.

The sign expected for coefficient of age of women is positive. Since it is assumed that women of ages 35–59 years in rural community should have passed children bearing age and therefore have less commitment at home. On the contrary, the coefficient is negative but it is significant at 5% level of significance. This showed that the assumptions may be right. This age category has significant impact on women participation in Agricultural Value Chain. This finding agreed with Jeckoniah (2017) who found out that the age of the women at first marriage has significant impact on women involvement in agricultural value chain. The contradictory sign may have come from the fact that: (1) these women may still be nurturing children; (2) there is possibility of large number of them with small farm size; or (3) women do not have the necessary education to launch them out for task as Agricultural Value Chain.

The coefficient of marital status for women in single category is negative contrary to expectation. One should have expected that these women would be available to take active part in Agricultural Value Chain. An explanation for this is that responsibilities of women are relatively the same whether married or unmarried in African societies. Unmarried women have more responsibilities than the married ones because they are saddles with the responsibilities of baby-sitting, cooking, farming, and so on. The coefficient is not significant also. The household commitment may have reduced the time available for large-scale farm business. This conformed to Jeckoniah's (2017) study in Tanzania. Jeckoniah's result showed that marital status was negative and significant.

In the same vein, the coefficient of women with at least NCE certificate is negative contrary to expectation, though it is significant at 5% level of significance. This means women who have at least NCE will have tendency to benefit from agricultural value chain. The negative may have from the fact that only 13.6% of the women acquired at least NCE certificates (see Table 1). This means they may not be able to take advantage of market information available around them. This finding goes in line with Apata (2013) and Jeckoniah (2017) who found out that education of women played significant role in agricultural value chain.

The coefficient of distance traveled from farm to house has the expected sign but it is not significant. An explanation for this is that women are able to cope because they operate small farms and the quantity of farm produce hauled by them is not beyond their capacity. The sign of the coefficient has shown that there is inverse relationship between distance traveled to farms and level of involvement in agricultural value chain. Similar result was obtained by Umuhoza (2012) in Rwanda and Rubin et al. (2018) in Bangladesh. The same can be said of the coefficient of rented land. Though only 6.2% of the women rented their land (see Table 1), but the renting of land reduces active participation of women in agricultural value chain. The coefficient is not significant at 5% level of significance and this may have come from few women who depended on renting. This is in tandem with the findings of Chete (2018).

The coefficient of inherited land has positive sign as expected and significant at 5% level of significance. This showed that as previous studies such as International Financial Corporation (2017) noted land inheritance by women increases their capacity to engage in large-scale farming. This finding also goes in agreement with the findings of Chete (2018). From the table, it can be seen that the coefficient of distance traveled from home to the nearest market as negative sign as expected and is significant at 5% level of significance. This showed that distance traveled by women from home to market play crucial role in their level of involvement in agricultural value chain. The result was similar to the findings of Umuhoza (2012) in Rwanda and Rubin et al. (2018) in Bangladesh.

Looking at the source of mobility, it can be seen that the coefficient is negative as expected but it is not significant. An explanation for this is that the sizes of the farms are small and many women may not be in need of means of haulage. This finding toils in line with the result obtained by Adam, Bidoli, Ammani and Oduehie (2018). Lastly, the coefficient of community responsibilities is negative as expected and significant at 5% level of significance. This showed that women are affected their commitments to their communities and as such they play less role in Agricultural Value Chain. This finding empirically supports the conceptual studies of Bolzani, de Villard and de Prick (2010), Poulson (2016), African Development Bank (2015), and International Finance Corporation (2016).

In Column II, the author considered three determinants—Distance from House to Market centers, Source of Mobility, and Community Responsibilities. The coefficients of the three determinants have the expected sign and significant at 5 and 10% level of significant, respectively. The coefficient of Source of Mobility becomes significant at 10% level of significance when the variable is combined with Distance from House to Market centers, and Community Responsibilities. One explanation for this is that there is possibility for women who are committed to the community duties to have large farm size because of their wealth holdings and possess haulage vehicles, and thereby have the tendency to involve in Agricultural Value Chain.

In Column III, the author included Level of Education and Age of Women to the determinants in Column II excluding Source of Mobility. It can be seen that all the coefficients of the determinants are significant at 5% level of significance and signs do not change. It is therefore assumed that together with inherited land, these determinants may be the principal factors limiting women participation in Agricultural Value Chain in Esan West Local Government.

5 Conclusion and Recommendations

This study has attempted to examine the likely micro-determinants of women participation in Agricultural Value Chain in Nigeria. The study was descriptive in nature using a simple questionnaire to draw information from 162 women farmers purposively selected in some communities in Edo West Local Government, Edo State, Nigeria. All the variables were converted into categorical variables and Probit Regression was used to estimate the model. The findings have shown that level of education, age of women, land inheritance, distance from house to market centers, and community responsibilities are significant. One fact to be drawn from this study is the relevance of women education. From this study, it should be seen that engagement of women in agricultural value chain is constrained on the level of education attained. Without concrete education policy for women in the form of adult literacy, distance learning and nomadic education, women cannot reap the benefits of agricultural value chain. In the contemporary world, with large number of sophisticated technologies, rural women would continue to experience marginalization without ability to read and write.

Another fact drawn from this study is that age of women contributes to participation in agricultural value chain. It is clearly seen that rural women begin child bearing at early age and by the time they are entering 35 years of age some of them may have stopped bearing. Thus, the age bracket 35–60, in which rural women are out child bearing age can be targeted by the government in any agricultural policy to be formulated for rural women. The government can initiate policy in which the women of this category can have access to land, capital, improved seedlings, adult literacy, cooperative, agricultural extension officers, and other forms of aids that gear up their interest in agricultural production.

In addition, the study has shown that access to land is a necessity for women participation in agricultural value chain. The land ownership system in African societies does not uplift the right of the women. Since there is availability of land in every community for farming, government can empower women farmer through zero-interest loan, which they can use to hire land for farming or government can set aside land through land acquisition purposely for women farmers to lease at moderate price. There can also be initiative such as cooperative farms in which women farmers can come together to use their resources in gaining the advantage of economies of scale. Through such initiative, women in collective effort can be encouraged to hire a single large plot of land instead of varieties of small farms insufficient to attract loans from financial institutions or grant from donor agencies. The government to be flexible in the issue of land inheritance can call upon community leaders. If the possibility of women inheriting land is impossible, there should be standing laws in which women by marriage should have access to certain quantity of land from her husband during her lifetime and not transferrable to her offspring or siblings except to her spouse.

In the same vein, the finding of the study has shown that distance to market centers is a determinant of women participation in agricultural value chain. As such there is need to proffer likely way out for this gap, as mentioned earlier, women can be encouraged to form cooperative societies and government should empower them with credit facilities to acquire haulage vehicles. The acquisition of haulage vehicles will enable women to collectively transport their goods to market. This will have the advantage of reducing cost of transportation; increasing the quantity of farm produce taking to market; increasing farm output since the women know that there is access to big market; and making the women to have market power over their produce. Similar to this, government can incorporate women farmers into its transportation policy. Government can commission haulage vehicles to operate along farm communities in order to help women farmers to transport their produce to market. Furthermore, on the need to ensure that distance is not a problem to women farmers, government should improve road networks in the rural communities. Private haulage companies can be encouraged through such efforts to patronize rural communities; as such, women farmers have access to haul their produce to big markets.

Lastly, the finding of the study revealed that community responsibilities influence women participation in agricultural value chain. Women cannot be detached from being responsible in the community but government can initiate policies, which can complement the time women sacrifice for community responsibilities. For instance, handy agricultural tractors and other farm implements can be supplied to women farmers at affordable prices or with high subsidies. The use of modern farm implements can reduce the time women spent at farm and have ample time for community assignment. Large number of women in the community depends on crude farm implements that consume time and energy. When women have access to modern facilities that they can use for land cultivation, harvesting, processing, and marketing, they will be able to balance their commitment between agricultural production and community responsibilities.

From the above discussion, the study therefore recommends that (1) there is need for adult literacy classes among women farmers in this region, (2) women of ages 35–59 years are crucial to agricultural production and therefore, (3) government continue its efforts in ensuring that women are treated evenly in the matter of land inheritance and there should be land allocation policy for women, (4) there should be good roads in many of the farm communities to encourage haulage companies to be available for engagement during marketing exercise, and (5) women should not be over attached community responsibilities as to deny them the right to engage in agricultural production.

REFERENCES

Adam, A. G., Bidoli, T. D., Ammani, A. A., & Oduehie, T. C. (2018). Gender participation in rice processing value chain in Kebbi and Sokoto States, Nigeria. *Agriculture and Veterinary, 18*(2), 57–60.

Afolabi, E. A., Ismail, F. O., Tenuche, S. S., Yerima, O. O., & Izumah, G. D. (2016). Agricultural value chain among women farmers in Nigeria: A veritable tool for increase productivity and sustainable development. *International Journal of Innovative Research in Education, Technology and Social Sciences, 3*(1), 46–63.

African Development Bank. (2015). *Economic empowerment of African women through equitable participation in agricultural value chains*. Abidjan: African Development Bank.

AgroNigeria. (2016). *The role of women in agriculture*. Retrieved from https://agronigeria.com.ng/role-women-agriculture/.

Ahmadu, J., & Idisi, P. O. (2014). Gendered participation in cassava value chain in Nigeria. *Merit Research Journal, 2*(11), 147–153.

Aliyu, N. (2015). *The roles of women in groundnut value chain in Kano State, Nigeria* (Unpublished Master's Thesis). Ahmadu Bello University, Zaria.

Apata, T. G. (2013). *Analysis of cassava value chain in Nigeria, from a pro-poor and gender perspective of farming households in Southwest, Nigeria*. Retrieved from www.agrodep.org/sites/default/files/annualmeeting/RV_Apata_T_final.pd.

Bolzani, D., de Villard, S., & de Prick, J. (2010). *Agricultural value chain development: Threat or opportunity for women's employment?* (Gender and Rural Employment Policy Brief No. 4).

CBN. (2017). *CBN statistical bulletin*. Abuja: CBN.

Chete, O. B. (2018). Enterprise factors influencing gender involvement in rice enterprises in Southwestern Nigeria. *Asian Journal of Agricultural and Horticultural Research, 1*(1), 1–12.

Echono, S. (2015, October 20). *Women are the cornerstone of agricultural production, processing, marketing and utilization in the country*. Paper presented at Economic empowerment of African Women through Equitable Participation in Agricultural Value Chain, Abuja.

Ejike, R. D., Osuji, E. E., Effiong, J. A. L., & Agu, C. G. (2018). Gender dimension in agricultural food value chain development in Nigeria: The women perspective. *International Journal of Agriculture and Earth Science, 4*(3), 37–45.

FAO. (2005). *A value chain analysis of international fish trade and food security*. Retrieved from http://www.fao.org/in-action/globefish/fishery-information/resource-detail/en/c/338795/.

Gurung, C. (2006). *The role of women in the fruit and vegetable supply chain in Maharashtra and Tamil Nadu India: The new and expanded social and economic opportunities for vulnerable groups task order under the women in development IQC*. Washington, DC: U.S. Agency for International Development.

International Finance Corporation. (2016). *Investing in women along agricultural value chains*. Washington, DC: IFC Communication.

Iruonagbe, C. T. (2009). Patriarchy and women's agricultural production in rural Nigeria. *Journal of Cultural Studies, 2*, 207–222.

Jeckoniah, J. N. (2017). Women collective actions and empowerment in agricultural value chains in Simanjiro District Tanzania. *International Journal of Gender and Women's Studies, 5*(2), 51–57.

Ministry of Budget and National Planning. (2017). *Nigeria economic recovery and growth plan 2017–2020*. Abuja: Ministry of Budget and National Planning.

Ogunlela, Y. I., & Mukhtar, A. I. (2005). Gender issues in agriculture and rural development in Nigeria: The role of women. *Humanities and Social Science Journal*, 4(1), 19–30.

Ola, K. O. (2014). Enhancing the productivity of rural women farmers in Ogwa, Edo State. *Redeemer's University Journal of Management and Social Sciences*, 2(1), 186–197.

Onuekwusi, G. C., Odoemelam, I. E., & Kanu, R. I. (2017). Improving rural women income through cocoyam value addition technologies in Abia State Nigeria. *Journal of Agricultural Extension*, 21(3), 116–125.

Osabuohien, E. S., Gitau, C. M., Efobi, U. R., & Bruentrup, M. (2015). Agents and implications of foreign land deals in East African community: The case of Uganda. In E. Osabuohien (Ed.), *Handbook of research on in-country determinants and implications of foreign land acquisitions* (pp. 263–286). Hershey, PA: Business Science Reference.

Osabuohien, E., Efobi, U. R., Herrmann, R., & Gitau, C. M. (2019). Female labor outcomes and large-scale agricultural land investments: Macro–micro evidence from Tanzania. *Land Use Policy, 82*, 716–728.

Osabuohien, E., Okorie, U., & Osabohien, R. (2018). Rice production and processing in Ogun State, Nigeria: Qualitative insights from Farmers' Association. In E. Obayelu (Ed.), *Food systems sustainability and environmental policies in modern economics* (pp. 188–216). Hershey, PA: IGI Global.

Oyebola, P. O., Osabuohien, E., & Obasaju, B. (2019). Employment and income effects of Nigeria's agricultural transformation agenda. *African Journal of Economic and Management Studies*. https://doi.org/10.1108/AJEMS-12-2018-.

Poulson, E. (2016). *Gender mainstreaming in agricultural value chains: Promising experiences and the role of rural advisory services*. Lausanne, Switzerland: GFRAS.

Roberts-Agbaje, C. T. (2017). *Women's empowerment and the success of the agro value chain in Nigeria*. Retrieved from https://etimes.com.ng/womens-empowerment-and-the-success-of-the-agro-value-chain-in-nig/.

Rubin, D., et al. (2018). *Qualitative research on women's empowerment and participation in agricultural value chains in Bangladesh*. Dhaka, Bangladesh: International Food Policy Research Institute Policy Research and Strategy.

Sahel. (2014). The role of women in Nigerian agriculture. *Sahel, 7,* 1–3.

Umuhoza, G. (2012). *Analysis of factors influencing women participation in coffee value chain in Huye District, Rwanda* (Unpublished Master's Thesis). University of Nairobi, Nairobi, Kenya.

Vroegindewey, R., & Hodbod, J. (2018). Concept paper resilience of agricultural value chains in developing country contexts: A framework and assessment approach. *Sustainability, 10*(916), 1–18.

Job Creation and Social Conditions of Labor in the Forestry Agro-Industry in Mozambique

Rosimina Ali

1 Introduction

Many African countries including Mozambique have experienced a growth of foreign direct investment, as from the mid-1990s there was a penetration of capital interested in accessing, exploiting, and controlling natural resources and export-oriented agriculture, on a large scale in the country (Castel-Branco 2010; Herrmann et al. 2018; Osabuohien et al. 2019). From the mid-2000s there has been a growing interest in establishing forest plantations of fast-growing species (e.g., pine and eucalyptus), mostly aimed for export (Ministry of Agriculture—MINAG 2009). Job creation was one of the promises made by foreign investments. The current five-year Government plan and the Employment Policy in Mozambique focus on job creation to enhance living conditions (GdM 2015; MITESS 2016b). Yet, there have been questions about the quality of the employment created in the large agro-industrial plantations (Ali 2017; O'Laughlin 2013; Wuyts 2011).

Economic growth has not been accompanied by socioeconomic transformation and development of people and there has been a contradiction between job creation and better social conditions of work and of life that is generated by the current pattern of growth and accumulation. The extractive

---

This article is part of a broader research on employment dynamics in the agro-industries of Mozambique conducting by the Institute for Social and Economic Studies (IESE) in which the chapter's author is a collaborator.

R. Ali (✉)
Institute for Social and Economic Studies (IESE), Maputo, Mozambique

nature of the pattern of growth in Mozambique was strengthened in a context of exporting primary commodities with low processing (such as timber, coal, ginned cotton, sisal, natural gas, leaf tea, unrefined sugar, tobacco, unprocessed cashew nuts, prawns, hydroelectric power, and aluminum), with narrowed linkages in the economy and lack of linkages with the productive and fiscal base, and a high dependence on the consumption of imported processed goods (Castel-Branco 2010).

The forestry agro-industry in Niassa province, one of the provinces of Mozambique that had the greatest demand for areas on which to set up these plantations provides an interesting case study to explore labor patterns and dynamics in the current pattern of growth. Hence, this chapter is centered on analyzing the type of employment created with particular interest in understanding the relationship between employment patterns, the productive organization of labor and working conditions (including the recruitment and payment system), and how the jobs created connect (or not) with other general forms of work that the workers and households are involved. Also, the study looks at the experience and situation of work besides the companies, the social organization, health and environmental conditions, as well as the implications of these aspects taken together for the welfare of the workers and their families. This is crucial insofar aswell-being is not limited to job creation and obtaining the corresponding remuneration, or to consumption and the possession of goods. Even though these are important, they are just some of the determinant factors.

The research methodology drawn on a triangulation between the qualitative[1] and quantitative information from workers or ex-workers in the forestry companies is currently operating in Niassa and combined with information from official statistics. The field research was held in some areas exploited by the existing forestry companies, namely the districts of Sanga, Chimbonila, Muembe, Lago, and Lichinga. The research period was between 2014 and 2016. Taking a political economy perspective and in the light of the study of the social system of accumulation in Mozambique, this research aims to understand the organization of wage labor in the current productive structures, its tensions and linkages besides the workplace, and how it is embedded in workers' lives.

The study argues that the type of employment created in the forestry agro-industries in Niassa reflects the prevailing productive mode of organization, in which the basis of the profitability of the companies lies in paying low wages in insecure social conditions of labor, and where the workers are responsible for their own social reproduction. The social reproduction of the labor force, given the prevailing productive structures, is guaranteed by the interdependence of diversified forms of labor, paid and/or unpaid, whether agricultural or not. In the current forms of the organization of production and labor, ruptures mark work and employment on the forestry plantations is mostly casual, unstable, and insecure, and develops in a context of tensions and contradictions in productive social relations. The ruptures on the structure of work and the unstable and insecure labor conditions have implications for the type of labor force and productive structure generated, calling into question their reproduction and sustainability for the entire society and country.

This chapter is organized into five sections. The second section is centered on the analysis of the link between wage labor, household agriculture, and the economic crisis in Niassa province, and succinctly frames the development of the forestry industries in connection with the labor situation. The third section considers the productive organization of labor, and the patterns and conditions of employment in the forestry agro-industries. The fourth section looks at the labor experience and analyzes its impact on the welfare of the workers and their families. The final section concludes by reflecting on the need for transformation in the current forms of the productive and social organization of labor.

2 Labor Markets, the Forestry Agro-Industry and the Economic Crisis in Niassa

This section analyzes the general dynamics of labor in Niassa province, focusing in particular on two districts where the forestry companies operate, namely Sanga and Chimbonila. According to the General Population and Housing Census (henceforth, referred to as the census or GPHC), Niassa is one of the Mozambican provinces with the lowest incidence of worker's dependent on an employer. However, it is explained why there is a demand for wage labor in a province where most of the inhabitants are small-scale agricultural producers.

2.1 Labor: The Interdependence of Family Production and Wage Labor

The General Population and Household Censuses data held in 1997 and 2007, being the latter currently the only updated demographic census available[2] and which coincides with the period of establishing the forestry plantations (from the mid-2000s), shows that in Niassa the main work is in agriculture, mostly in family production. Table 1 shows the percentage of the occupied population aged 15 and above (henceforth, referred to as Occ Pop.), whose main work is mostly in agriculture, forestry, and fisheries. It also shows the percentage of the population aged 15 and above who gave their main occupation as "peasant," in Niassa province in general, and in Chimbonila and Sanga districts,[3] the two areas studied, in particular.

Almost a decade later after the establishment of the forestry companies a similar picture is given by the Household Budget Survey (henceforth, referred as HBS) held in 2014 and 2015 as seen in Graph 1 (National Statistics Institute—INE 2010, 2016) which still shows that in Niassa the main work is in agriculture, mostly in family production. The rest of the Occ Pop (a minority) is shown as linked to another called "main activity" such as

Table 1 Percentage of the Occ Pop. in Agriculture, Forestry and Fisheries (AFF) and proportion of the Occ Pop. who gave "peasant" as their main occupation, Sanga and Chimbonila Districts in Niassa Province, 1997 and 2007

Year		Sanga	Chimbonila	Niassa total
1997	Total Occ Pop. (inhabitants.)	4.310	22.551	260.481
	AFF (inhabitants.)	4.146	21.202	229.030
	% of Occ Pop. in AFF (%)	96	94	88
	Peasants (inhabitants)	4.143	21.033	226.923
	% Occ Pop. as peasants (%)	96	94	87
2007	Total Occ Pop. (inhabitants.)	5.490	35.446	405.603
	AFF (inhabitants.)	5.054	32.589	337.235
	% of Occ Pop. in AFF (%)	92	92	83
	Peasants (inhabitants)	4.977	31.516	326.975
	% Occ Pop. as peasants (%)	91	89	81

Source The author's estimates based on the GPHC 1997 and 2007 (INE 1999, 2009)

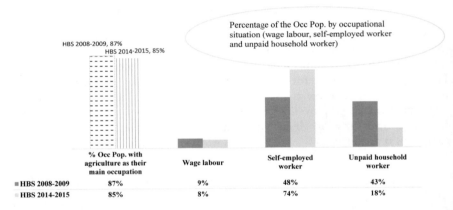

Graph 1 Percentage distribution of Occ Pop. with agriculture as their main occupation and by occupational situation, Niassa province, Mozambique, 2008–2009 and 2014–2015 (*Source* The author's estimates based on HBS 2008–2009 and HBS 2014–2015 [INE 2010, 2016])

services, industry, transport, construction, trade, or others. The occupational situation shows that the incidence of wage labor is minimal while other forms of work such as self-employment (including in agriculture) and unpaid household labor are estimated as dominant.

However, a question that arises is how were promises of jobs based on consultations with the "communities" around the appropriation of land by the forestry companies?[4] And how do accusations of favoritism in recruitment arise against some "*régulos*" (chiefs) who recruited the workers? This leads us to understand that wage labor is important for household reproduction.

Part of the problem is methodological. The census merely records the main activity of the worker in the week in question, which makes wage labor invisible, particularly in the rural areas (Ali 2017; Oya et al. 2009). Other official surveys follow this practice, as is the case of the survey HBS and the recently published Labor Market Information Bulletin which is based on the HBS, among others (MITESS 2016a). For example, the short modules on employment and labor, when asking about the "main activity" of the workers in the reference week, which means the last seven days, instead of questioning more broadly (as over the last 12 months), may imply an inadequate interpretation of the question and that the respondent reports only the activity of long duration he remembers he worked in the reference week, for example "work on the farm," since it is the most regular work although it may not be the only work, and may not have been done in isolation (Ali 2017). This may lead to overlooking many wage workers, who are likely to be classified as "household workers without remuneration" or "self-employed workers." Casual workers who have their own farm generally do not appear in the official statistics because they tend to be classified as peasants since work on their farm is normally declared as their "main activity," since they were working on it more frequently during the reference week. Hence, paid activities undertaken "outside of their farm" are difficult to capture.

Furthermore, the existence of exclusive categories (instead of multiple choices) treats self-employed workers, peasants, and wage workers, for example, as if they were mutually exclusive, hiding the interdependence between these activities, which predominate in the framework of productive structures prevailing in Mozambique (Ali 2017; Bardasi et al. 2010; Oya et al. 2017; Standing et al. 1996). Thus, the statistics do not capture information about the diversity of labor markets and working conditions. These can be poorly reported, leading to under-estimation and negligence of the heterogeneous forms of rural wage labor developed in irregular forms such as casual labor, called in certain cases "ganho-ganho" and "biscatos" (odd-jobs, usually of short duration) (Cramer et al. 2008; Oya 2010). In addition, the central focus on the question of the "main activity" and the lack of a question about secondary activity or work means there is no recognition of the importance of *ganho-ganho*, a term which arose constantly during the interviews held in this research, with women and men, in Sanga, Chimbonila, and Lichinga, both to explain the various sources of household income and to explain how the recruitment of casual labor made it possible to combine cultivating a farm with work on a forestry company.

The other part of the problem derives from theoretical preconceptions, in which draws the idea that insists that Niassa peasants are not integrated into the market, but survive only on their peasant farms. These theoretical preconceptions in analyzing employment and labor markets in Mozambique have been dominant and are based on a dualist method of analysis (GdM 2015; World Bank 2019). This method of analysis separates the various forms of labor (paid and unpaid) within the economy, where paid labor is considered as integrated into the labor markets, while household and unpaid labor is not included. Under this approach, the economy is seen as characterized by two different sectors, one modern (capitalist) and the other traditional (pre-capitalist), regarded as separate from each other. It is assumed that there is only a "formal" subordination of the workforce to capital, which only happens in the capitalist sector, with no linkages to other forms of labor, particularly with unpaid household agricultural production, which are assumed to be characterized by productive processes without accumulation and belonging to the traditional sector. In reality, the population of Niassa has resorted for generations to wage labor, informal trade, and sometimes even to migration with their household production to establish the household and the separate production of the parents, to open and maintain vegetable production in humid areas, to pay for the education and health of children and relatives, and to survive both health and climatic crises. Thus, there is an interdependence between various forms of labor, which is fundamental for the survival and reproduction of the workforce (Castel-Branco 1995; Massingarela et al. 2005; O'Laughlin and Wuyts 2012; Sender et al. 2007). Wage labor and household agriculture finance each other mutually. The workforce is migrant, switching between wage labor and other forms of labor, particularly household production. The income from wage labor, in addition to meeting consumption needs and other obligations is destined to financing household production—for example, by acquiring means of production necessary for the reproduction of household agriculture. In this case, the migrant nature of the workforce ensures work on the land that allows the sustenance of households and their reproduction, particularly in a context of unstable and irregular employment and working conditions in the province.

Signs of wage labor can be seen in the same statistics that show the centrality of household production. In Table 1 and Graph 1, one notes that dependence on agriculture was higher in 1997 than in 2007 and in 2008 than in 2014. In addition, the proportion of the occupied population who called themselves "peasants" was also higher as seen in Table 1. This latter aspect is more visible in the male population (In Sanga, Chimbonila, and in the whole province, a decrease in 2007 of male Occ Pop. considered "peasants" in around 8, 7, and 6%, respectively) (INE 1999, 2009). This does not mean that this non-peasant male population never becomes peasants, nor does it mean that they are not linked to other forms of labor. For young people, it is not easy to establish their own farm and house. A youth may work with his parents but also *ganho-ganho* and/or petty trade to accumulate the money necessary to establish his own farm. Furthermore, many youths undertake wage labor in the hope that they will save enough to become traders on bicycles or motorcycles, carrying charcoal or firewood to the city and returning with consumer or wage goods.

In Niassa, opening a new farm is becoming even more difficult because of population growth (around 50% in the entire province and Chimbonila district and around 30% in Sanga district, between 1997 and 2007 (INE 1999,

2009). However, in areas such as Chimbonila district pressure on the land has increased not only because of population growth but also because of the density of occupation by the new forestry companies.

2.2 Wage Labor and Differentiation of the Peasantry

Three groups of authors have analyzed the differentiation among the peasants who live around the forestry companies as part of studies on the social impact of the forestry industries in Niassa: Landry and Chirwa (2011), Nube (2013), Bleyer et al. (2016). They all distinguish between three different strata, but also agree that the differentiation was not very significant before the companies entered the scene. Using data based on a method of recollection of the facts of the socioeconomic situation, by the interviewees,[5] Nube (2013) concluded that before the entry of the forestry companies, in rural Lichinga (today, Chimbonila district) there was a small middle peasantry (2%), a large poor peasantry (58%), and 41% were living in extreme poverty. In Sanga, this study also shows a small middle peasantry (3%), a sizeable poor peasantry (45%), and slightly more than 50% of the peasantry as a very poor social stratum. Focusing on a household survey in Sanga, Landry and Chirwa (2011)[6] concluded that the majority (82%) of the households were in a socioeconomic condition characterized as medium, 10% as high, and 9% as low.

Although in their surveys, the three studies (i.e., Bleyer et al. 2016; Landry and Chirwa 2011; Nube 2013) focused only on ownership of assets and not on income. They also excluded control of land. Some of the goods included in the various lists of assets, such as bicycles, were common before the entry of the forestry companies, while others, such as motorcycles and cell phones were almost nonexistent. The problem of excluding income from the analysis of socioeconomic differentiation is that it tells us nothing about how households acquired these assets. How much was acquired from selling the harvest, how much from trade, and how much from wage labor for others? What makes some households poor and others better-off, if not rich? The analysis of the differentiation of the peasantry and the formation of classes within it requires an analysis of the structure of the peasant economy and its formation. According to information from the qualitative interviews with various types of workers and members of their households, the research undertaken by IESE shows that having a job with a regular income was an important way of becoming a peasant with better socioeconomic conditions, and that dependency on casual wage labor or *ganho-ganho* to guarantee the subsistence of the household strengthened the descending spiral of poor households, in the prevailing forms of productive organization and of life, where wage labor, household agriculture, and other forms of labor are structurally interlinked and finance each other mutually. For both groups of workers, the promise of employment by the forestry companies was received enthusiastically because it was hoped that these jobs would maintain or improve the modes and conditions of life, including their agricultural production (the crops produced include, for example, beans, maize, potatoes, groundnuts, cassava, tomatoes, onions, garlic, and fruit trees, among others).

Small-scale household production is the fundamental basis of life for the great majority of households in Niassa, but this does not mean that it does not also include wage labor. Wage labor, just like small-scale trading, is a means to accumulate the necessary funds to embark upon small mercantile production, and wage labor is also a safety mechanism making it possible to face periods of crisis (illness, drought, and pests) which are part of agricultural production. Thus, a regular job in a forestry company is something desirable for many groups of workers without implying that it is seen as a career. For example, as one worker in Mapaco locality, in Lichinga district said, work in the company can serve to accumulate the money needed to buy a bicycle, which can then be used to go and buy firewood in distant areas and take it to the market in Lichinga. The income from this activity allows his children to attend school and makes it possible to pay for other consumption expenses (food and health). The prolonged crisis of regional rural unemployment, not only in Mozambique, but also in Malawi, Tanzania, and Zimbabwe, creates more competition in the labor markets and provides few jobs and work opportunities either locally or through the mobility of the labor force (O'Laughlin 2001, 2013).

2.3 Development of the Forestry Agro-Industry in Niassa: Labor Opportunities (or Crisis)?

Forest plantations have been encouraged by the Government but faced different dynamics throughout Mozambican economic history. In the colonial and post-independence time, the State sustained the plantation of forestry to reduce the pressure over the native forest that was emerging. In the early 1990s, some of the productive units such as IFLOMA were privatized, which led to a decline in the plantation activity (Ministry of Agriculture—MINAG 2009). With the growth of foreign direct investment in Mozambique, as from the mid-1990s, there was a penetration of capital interested in accessing, exploiting, and controlling natural resources (land, forests, mineral, and energy resources), on a large scale (Castel-Branco 2010). From the mid-2000s there has been a growing interest in establishing forest plantations of fast-growing species (pine and eucalyptus) particularly in the central and northern regions of Mozambique, mostly for the export of wood and its derivatives. Given the favorable agroecological conditions,[7] Niassa and Zambezia are the provinces with the greatest demand for areas on which to set up these plantations (MINAG 2015). Job creation was one of the promises made by the companies during community consultations, to justify the expropriation of land. At present, around half a dozen large-scale forestry companies are operating in the country, namely: (i) Green Resources (GR) (operating through Niassa GR, Lúrio GR, Chikweti, Companhia Florestal de Massangulo, Tectona Forest of Zambezia and Ntacua), (ii) Portucel, (iii) Florestas de Niassa, (iv) New Forests, (v) Moflor, and (vi) IFLOMA. The Norwegian Green Resources and the Portuguese Portucel have the biggest land concession, although plantation covers only a small part of the concession area (MINAG 2015). Important questions on the impacts on the resident population remain unaddressed.

Niassa province had concentrated almost half of the planted forests in 2012–2013 as part of the government's strategy to address poverty (MINAG 2015). The Government encouraged investment in forestry plantations on a large scale in Niassa, the largest province in the country with the lowest population density,[8] alleging concern with poverty (a poverty rate,[9] according to the HBS, of about 48% in 2002–2003 and 33% in 2008–2009), deforestation and degradation of the fragile miombo soils by intensive agriculture in some areas. However, it should be noted that, according to the recent official estimates of the HBS 2014–2015, Niassa has recorded an increase in poverty compared with the levels of the past decade (when the forest companies were established) and it is currently the poorest province in the country (with a poverty rate of about 61%) (INE 2016).

The Lichinga Plateau (specifically, Lichinga, Sanga, Ngaúma, and Muembe districts) is the region with the greatest potential for the development of forestry plantations (MINAG 2009). But it should be noted that this area of the Lichinga Plateau is the area most densely occupied by small agricultural producers, and where the forestry plantations have been established, facilitated by the Malonda Foundation (henceforth referred to as Malonda). The Malonda Foundation is a private institution of public utility that was set up in the context of cooperation between the Governments of Mozambique and Sweden to promote private investment in Niassa province in various areas. This foundation facilitated the establishment of six forestry companies which were set up in Mozambique in the middle of the last decade, namely: Chikweti Forests of Niassa, Companhia Florestal de Massangulo, Niassa Green Resources, Florestas de Niassa, New Forests, and Florestas do Planalto (UPM). As well as promoting and facilitating the installation of forestry companies, Malonda was also an investor, with a right to use of land or a land-use title (in Mozambique, referred as DUAT) of about 90,000 hectares for forestry investment, which was later transferred to the forestry companies, as they were being set up. This made Malonda part of the shareholding structure of the forestry companies (FIAN 2012).

Moreover, since 2014 the forestry companies entered a phase of crisis due to financial difficulties, limited prospects for expansion, and uncertainty over the installation of a factory to produce paper pulp. In an effort to cut labor costs, the companies implemented a significant reduction in labor recruitment, lowered working conditions, turned to outsourcing or subcontracting of services, and dismissed workers. More than half of the forestry companies in Niassa disappeared. Currently, of the six companies established,[10] only three are operational, namely Niassa Green Resources (NGR), Florestas de Niassa (FdN), and New Forests. The financial crisis faced by NGR and FdN peaked in 2016. The British New Forest (NF) closed down its activities in plantations (set up in Muembe district) in the end of 2014, although recently it was taken over operations by Servir Moçambique. The company Florestas do Planalto (UPM), of Finnish capital, closed its activities and had plans to invest in a paper pulp factory which would make its pine and eucalyptus production profitable. Chikweti Forests of Niassa (CFN), with plantations in Chimbonila, Sanga, and Lago districts, and the Companhia Florestal de Massangulo (CFM), with plantations in Ngaúma district, belong to the *Global Solidarity Forest Fund* (GSFF), a Swedish and Norwegian investment fund, which also has Dutch capital. Chikweti was the most established forestry company in Niassa, before the merger (in 2014) of GSFF with the Norwegian company Green Resources, the company currently operating in Niassa.

Green Resources is one of the largest forestry companies operating in Africa, and it is present in Uganda, Tanzania, and Mozambique.[11] In Niassa, it has plantations in Chimbonila, Sanga, Lago, Ngaúma, and Muembe districts, with an area authorized and exploited summarized in Table 2. These figures according to MINAG estimates up to 2015, show that the company had planted about 27% of the authorized area. Green Resources has plans to expand the forestry plantations, if it can do on a sufficient scale to justify interest is supplying timber and its derivatives to the international market, including the production of cellulose to supply industries on a world scale. The operations of NGR are certified by the *Forest Stewardship Council* (FSC). Green Resources is a company focused on planting, forestry products, carbon compensation, and renewable energy. Its carbon credit projects, linked to forestry plantations, mean that this company is recognized internationally as a leader in the reduction of greenhouse gas emissions derived from forestry (Green Resources 2011). However, despite this certification, there are various questions by the local population and other organizations about the impact

Table 2 Areas occupied by the forestry companies, Niassa province

Company	Area with DUAT (ha)	Area planted (ha)
Green resources (before the merger with GSFF-Chikweti)	7.880	2.250
Green resources (after the merger with c/ GSFF-Chikweti)*	76.252	20.878
Chikweti	63.040	14.250
Companhia Florestal de Massangulo	5.332	4.378
Florestas de Niassa*	42.102	5.770
New forests	33.040	3.400

Source MINAG (2015)
*Companies currently operating in Niassa

of the forestry plantations on the way of life of the population. They suggest greater monitoring of the impact on the population's welfare.

The company Florestas de Niassa (FdN) is operating in the country. Formerly belonging to Rift Valley group and recently bought by Construa Build It. FdN owns pine and eucalyptus plantations in Chimbonila, Majune, and Muembe districts. Its objectives while belonging to Rift Valley group were to produce posts, sawn timber, and wood for cellulose or paper pulp for sale on the local, regional, and international markets, counting on the geographical location of the country, and particularly the port of Nacala. It intended to use the port to move the produce to the Indian, Chinese, and Middle Eastern markets as well as to the south of Africa. According to the Ministry of Agriculture estimates in 2015, this company had planted about 14% of the authorized area, as shown in Table 2.

The companies began their activities in areas that had access to infrastructure and commercial linkages—the same areas where the smallholder farmers are also most densely established. The smallholder farmers in these areas are interested in using wages to invest in establishing their household production (for their own consumption and for sale), and are not "mere" subsistence farmers. They also need land with commercial potential, often desiring to keep access to land within the plantation areas. These concerns have been followed by some environmental Non-Governmental Organizations (NGOs) who have indicated that the companies were planting trees of low value that did not allow recovery of the forest.

The local population has also been disappointed with the scale and type of employment offered by the forestry companies (shown in the following section). In the initial planting of saplings, a substantial amount of labor is needed during the rainy season; However, this work ends as soon as a forest is planted and is left to grow. Furthermore, planting is a seasonal activity which competes with working on household agriculture. Mechanized cutting of the trees is planned for the phase that begins the logging of the forest, and then there is possibly no need for labor. In the case of skilled jobs, such as machine operators, these workers have, in general, been contracted from elsewhere.

Faced with discontent from the population and NGOs over land and jobs, the government has become cautious in approving new DUATs for the companies. This has created uncertainties—many companies withdrew (alleging that production cannot be profitable if new areas cannot be planted) with implications for prospects of employment in the forestry industry. The large operators of heavy machinery moved to Zambezia and small operators went bankrupt.

Forestry production in Niassa faces a crisis of profitability, reflected in financial difficulties and prospects for expansion of the areas under plantation and for the installation of a factory to produce paper pulp, which is not guaranteed, and in an effort to cut labor costs through a massive reduction in labor recruitment, poorer working conditions, the subcontracting of services (which implies reducing labor costs), the intensification of labor, and the disappearance of more than half of the forestry companies that existed in Niassa. The companies in operation although have asked for more land to expand production, they are not yet occupying all the land already allocated to them, as can be seen in Table 2, which raises questions about their expansion plans. Furthermore, there is subcontracting or outsourcing to companies or individual agents of services to the operational forestry companies (also known as workforce subcontractors). The jobs outsourced include, for example, logging trees, preparing the soils, planting, and clearing the fields. Some of these companies providing services are Nomix, SMOPS, Niassa Petróleo, Kukamushissa, and other individual agents. These companies or individual agents are responsible for the instruments and organization of work processes since the workers hired this way are not part of the permanent staff of the forestry companies. This implies that, in this way, the forestry companies hand over payment and other working conditions (which tend to become more vulnerable) to the contracted agents. When some of these subcontractors were interviewed, they showed that they are facing a crisis, stating that there were cases of forestry companies who have not paid the debts incurred to them for the services provided. When the profitability of companies is threatened, they normally restructure the costs of production, including changes in the productive organization, which take on different forms in productive and labor relations.

The National Union of Agricultural and Forestry Workers (henceforth, referred to as SINTAF), at the time of this research, was concerned at the casualization of rural agricultural work, particularly with the labor conditions of casual work. The union suggested the transformation of casual labor into permanent jobs with regular income. But faced with the current trends in the sector, the unions are facing an unemployment crisis, the loss of permanent jobs by skilled workers and a decline in the recruitment of casual labor. The limitations of this union strategy are clear when we consider how workers are recruited and organized on the forestry plantations, as will be discussed and explained in the following section.

3 Current Patterns of Employment and Social Conditions of Labor in the Forestry Agro-Industry

This section analyzes the organization of employment and labor in the productive forms that prevail in the forestry agro-industries. It explains how the productive structures structure (and are structured by) employment and the labor conditions and also shows the profile of employment in the forestry industry in Niassa, including recruitment and payment patterns.

The type of employment being created is mostly casual, poorly paid, and developed under unstable and insecure social labor conditions. This is shown by looking at the organization of the productive and labor system, the structure of employment, the recruitment and payment system, the social conditions of labor in the forestry plantations as well as for the integration of employment in the social organization of labor more broadly. The patterns of labor and employment in the agro-industries reflect the dominant extractive productive structures (Castel-Branco 2010). The productive organization of the forestry plantations exemplifies the extractive pattern of the agro-industries in Mozambique, focused on the production of primary products for export through obtaining huge areas of land and other resources such as water at low cost, as well as access to and control over a reserve labor force, recruited in an unstable manner and mostly seasonally, poorly paid and with precarious social labor conditions. The basis of the profitability of the forestry companies rests on these conditions, and the workers are responsible for their own social reproduction. The focus of the forestry companies is the planting of eucalyptus and pine for producing wood and its derivatives (mostly to supply the international market) and particularly to produce paper pulp for export. Forward linkages in the economy are limited, with the exception of wages, and the existing backward linkages (for example, subcontracting companies to provide some services: preparing the land, cutting trees, and planting) are also restricted and are not well established.

3.1 Organization of the Labor System in Forestry Production in Niassa

The way in which production is organized determines the mode of organization of labor as well as the integration of the workforce in the production of value for capital. Agro-industrial production involves two main activities, namely agricultural and processing. However, in the case of forestry production in Niassa, only the first is being developed. This is because, on the one hand, the plantations have been established recently, and need a growth period of between 10 and 25 years before logging, depending on the species and the development of the trees, as well as on the final use of the raw wood. Furthermore, the operational forestry companies do not possess (and have no clear prospects of setting up) processing factories, faced with the uncertainties associated with profitability that depends on a scale of production, which would make it viable to build them. Also, the form of processing will have an impact on profitability. No construction of sawmills is envisaged because pine and eucalyptus will have more value as pulp than as planks. Currently, it seems that the forestry companies are concerned to expand the plantation areas (which requires the occupation of land on a large scale) with implications for the development of forms of labor directly linked to the land. However, the production process does not end with silviculture and premature logging greatly reduces the final value of the production. At least five years of growth is needed before starting logging.

The labor system in forestry production is complex and involves various stages, labor processes, and types of workers. Table 4 shows the labor processes during the main stages of production in the forestry agro-industries in Niassa. The activities in the forestry sector are generally conditioned by the seasons: rainy and dry. The labor processes are mostly based on manual labor although the processes in some activities are increasingly semi-mechanized and mechanized. During the field research, investment in greater mechanization of some activities was found, as in the case of preparing the land, as shown in Table 3.

The demand for workers during the forestry cycle depends on how the production and labor processes are organized in the plantations and may differ from company to company. The need for labor, apart from depending on the cycle and the various phases of forestry production (such as opening and preparing the land, producing the seedlings, planting, clearing and maintaining the fields, fertilization, pruning, protecting against and fighting fires as well as, possibly, activities of thinning, transport, and perhaps processing), is conditional on the type of investment made by the companies, which may, or may not be mechanized.

Throughout the production process, different types of workers interact. In practically all stages of the productive process, there is a field supervisor who, generally, is a qualified forestry technician or engineer and is responsible for managing work in the field, and to whom the group heads are accountable for the activity undertaken by the field workers (known locally as "forestry auxiliaries") in various areas such as opening and preparing the fields, applying herbicides and fertilizer, planting in the nurseries and in the definitive fields, clearing and maintaining the fields, firebreaks, among others. In the case of the firebreaks, which is one of the most demanding stages in the cycle of forestry operations in terms of monitoring and control, there is a team of workers who, for better protection of the forest, have to coordinate among themselves—namely: the guards, the vigilance team or the communicators (who stay on the watchtowers), and the teams that fight bush fires. Furthermore, with the mechanization of some processes (through which the companies claim better development and quality in forestry production), the demand for labor for such activities has declined. One such case is preparation of the land. In the case of applying herbicides through mechanized processes, there is only a need for a few staff to mix the chemicals as well as a tractor operator.

The labor system on the forestry plantations is based on piecework. That is, it is determined in accordance with a stipulated target on a daily basis, on which the payment system rests. Compliance with this target is equivalent to an effective day of work, but noncompliance can be expressed as absence from work or as half a day's work (implying nonpayment or partial payment). The targets are determined by the labor process, varying according to activity and between companies, depending on management conditions and business profitability. For example, in opening the fields, the needs for labor, to remove the native vegetation (avoiding competition for water and nutrients with the plants that are of interest) vary according to the size of the area. In the clearing and maintenance of the fields, the target can vary, depending on the size of the grass, from an area of 40 m × 40 m or 60 m × 60 m per day.

Table 3 Labor processes in forestry production in Niassa

Stages of forestry production	Labor processes	Season
Opening and clearing the fields	Clearing the area is done by semi-mechanized means (resorting to chainsaws, machetes, and slash) This is generally the first stage, depending on the area to be exploited. In the case of a clean area, for example, former farms, or areas without much vegetation, forestry production begins with preparing the soil	This occurs in the dry season, generally in the June–October months
Preparing the land	Preparing the terrain in Niassa tends to be increasingly mechanized, with the use of machinery and tractors. But there are still cases of the manual preparation of the land, involving use of the workforce, depending on the area it is intended to plant	Preparation of the soil takes place in the dry period, between August and October (or early November, preferably before the onset of the rains). This activity is done after opening and clearing the fields
Application of herbicide	Herbicides are applied manually (with back pumps or sprayers) or mechanically, depending on the company After preparing the land, some companies have opted to apply herbicides before beginning planting, seeking to control competitors such as some grasses and shrubs	This occurs after preparing the terrain, but some weeks before definitive planting. Generally, it occurs between November and December
Initial planting—nurseries	Many of the nursery activities are manual except for the irrigation system which is done with sprinklers (but, whenever necessary, complemented with manual labor to correct failings). It is gravity fed irrigation, using water from the river and, with the help of electric pumps, the water is pushed with pressure to the nurseries, where there are sprinklers to distribute the water to the boxes which contain the seedlings planted in "little vases" held in the boxes. The manual work requires a great deal of attention so as to guarantee the quality of the seedlings (for example, the work of separating duplicate seedlings which can have an impact on the development of the plants)	The seeds are sown in the nurseries to produce the seedlings between May and June Pines can stay 5 months in the nursery and eucalyptus can stay between 2 and 3 months, but as soon as the rains begin they should be outside the nurseries and transplanted to the definitive fields
"Definitive" planting	This activity is undertaken manually. The plants are transplanted to the definitive fields. This stage is the peak period in forestry production, with the greatest demand for labor, and the planting ends in late March or in April	This takes place in the rainy season (November–March). However, depending on the onset of the rains, in certain years the planting period begins in December and lasts until April

(continued)

Table 3 (continued)

Stages of forestry production	Labor processes	Season
Fertilization	Work undertaken manually, In the initial planting, in the nurseries, there is fertilization with water soluble fertilizers, where fertilization coincides with irrigation to make the best use of the fertilizers	The fertilization follows the planting
Maintenance of the field	This is a manual process to remove competitors such as grass and combustible material (reducing the risk of forest fires) Because of the rains, there will be grass which must be removed. The grass should be removed until 3 months after its inception, because it competes for nutrients (e.g., water, light) with other species/trees and after 3 months the grass tends to drop seeds to the ground for the reproduction of new grass)	Generally, between March and June, after the planting phase
Controlling and fighting pests	Done manually. In this period insecticides have been used to control pests, using sprayers or back pumps	Between March and June
Pruning	Pruning (in the case of species where branches do not drop off by themselves) refers to cutting off dead or living branches along the trunk This work of artificial pruning is done manually and so needs labor. Pruning seeks, on the one hand, to attain a better quality of wood, since the branches (dead or living) may prejudice the production of good quality wood. Furthermore, it seeks to protect against fires, since, as the plantations grow, the risk of fire passes from fire in the grass to the risk of fire at the top of the tree	Pruning is done before the rainy season, to avoid the appearance of fungi that can affect the growth of the plant and the quality of the wood
Protection against and fighting fires	Manual process which requires seeking a workforce to prepare the firebreaks or protection against fire and to control the bush fires. In the hunting season, during the period of preparing land for planting in the family farms, there has been a greater possibility of bush fires. There is one group of workers dealing with clearing and firebreaks and another working on the "watchtower" in controlling and communicating cases of bush fires	June (preparation of firebreaks) As from September (control of bush fires) Firebreaks are prepared after the end of clearing and removal of the grass. After maintaining the firebreaks, the land is prepared for the new campaign

Source The author's based on information from the field research

The target for pruning is about 445 plants, per person per day. Processes to intensify labor occur, seeking to reduce workforce costs, which are expressed in increased daily tasks per worker. For example, at the time of the field research, the planting target for one of the forestry companies was 300 basins (or demarcations), 300 holes (size 50 cm × 30 cm), and 300 seedlings to be planted per person per day. This daily piecework used to be done by three workers, but with the intensification of labor, these tasks came to be undertaken, on a daily basis, by just one worker. In general, work begins at around 06.00 or 07.00 in the morning, and the time to leave, to mark a full day of work, depends on meeting the target. After completing the target, the worker can go home or to the camp. In the nurseries, there is no system of targets as such: working hours are from 07.00 to 17.00 with an interval of one hour for meals. However, since the target is defined in accordance with "optimum conditions of the best worker," there are processes of intensification of labor, where the experience of some workers shows that many have difficulty in pausing for meals. Faced with this scenario, the workers step up the pace of work in an attempt to guarantee meeting the daily targets and obtaining the corresponding payment.

Targets, payment, and social conditions of labor are the questions that most concern the agricultural forestry workers and it is around these questions that the workers' struggle should be concentrated in particular. The system of targets is a fundamental point in the forestry plantations. The daily work targets laid down by the forestry companies for the various activities, even if some workers meet them, seem excessive from the point of view of the workers' capacity. Furthermore, it has implications for working conditions and the health of the workers. The effort to meet the targets requires arduous work, affecting the capacity of the workers to meet the targets or even to be available for work on the following days. Furthermore, whether the targets are met or not has consequences in terms of the income earned by the workers, since they may receive less than they envisaged per day of work. The work is undertaken in a context of tensions and contradictions in the social relations of production, and it is crucial to analyze the type of employment and the social conditions of labor in the framework of the current mode of social organization of production and labor.

3.2 Employment Structure and Patterns of Recruitment

The recruitment of the workforce is unstable over the agricultural season, as shown by the information on the total records for recruitment of workers in 2012, by one of the forestry companies (Company A) in Niassa, in Graph 2.

The labor force on the plantations consists of casual and permanent workers. The work is mostly seasonal. Most of the workers are recruited at the peak period, in the planting phase, from November to April. The recruitment of the permanent workforce is stable over the year but in this case there was an

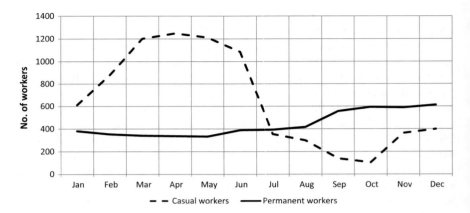

Graph 2 Recruitment of the workforce on the forestry plantations, Niassa province, Company A, 2012 (*Source* The author's estimate based on the statistical information of Forestry Company A, 2012)

increase at the start of the planting season. After the planting season, there is a reduction in the recruitment of casual labor. The profile of employment varies during the agricultural year and with the growth of the forest. The field workers have employment particularly in the November–April months (when there is new planting). They are the bulk of the labor force. The guards and the staff who clean the trees work all year but more intensively in the period of fires. The amount of labor required for the nurseries is more regular, but relatively minor, and seeks to meet the number of seedlings needed to plant in the new planting fields.

Work is not continuous over the agricultural season, not only for the casual workers but also for the permanent ones. This is because a permanent worker on the plantations does not necessarily have work during twelve months. In the hiring system on the plantations, most of the workers have a seasonal labor contract (generally for three months), although there are field workers with contracts for an indeterminate period. However, although it is undoubtedly important to have a work contract, this does not guarantee full days of work, under the current forms of organization of production and labor in the forestry companies. On the one hand, the work contract allows only the opportunity to work when there is a demand, and on the other, the contract does not guarantee that the days worked are really registered, under the current system of productive organization based on targets, where one full day of work implies complying with the stipulated daily piecework.

The workforce consists of men and women, but a great part of the workforce in the forestry companies is male,[12] which is shown in Table 4, calculated on the basis of a subsample extracted[13] from the total records of one of the forestry companies. Men and women workers perform practically the same type of work, with the exception of some activities such as opening

Table 4 Structure of the workforce, Forestry Company A, Niassa, in 2012

No. months Sex		1	2	3	4	5	6	7	8	9	10	11	12	Total
Women (W)	N° W	5	6	6	13	10	10	1	1	1	1	2	26	82
	% W	6	7	7	16	12	12	1	1	1	1	2	32	100
Men (M)	N° M	55	71	45	75	49	32	18	11	10	9	15	128	518
	% M	11	14	9	14	9	6	3	2	2	2	3	25	100
Total	N°	60	77	51	88	59	42	19	12	11	10	17	154	600
Total	%	10	13	9	15	10	7	3	2	2	2	3	26	100

Source Author in accordance with the database of Forestry Company A

No. of months—Number of months worked in Forestry Company A in the year in question; N° (W)—Number of women; N° (M)—Number of men; % (W)—Percentage of women; and % (M)—Percentage of men

and clearing the fields or cutting down trees, which have been done by men. Table 4 shows that about a quarter of the workers have permanent work that 23% work only for one or two months and that about 64% work for 6 months or less.

The structure of employment is polarized, with a small number of relatively well-paid skilled workers and a large mass of unskilled seasonal workers with low wages. That is, employment is mostly seasonal, while there are some unskilled, poorly paid permanent workers, and a minority of well-paid skilled permanent workers. The first group includes "forestry auxiliaries" (workers who undertake activities in the nurseries, in clearing and preparing the fields, planting, firebreaks and pruning, among others), guards, group chiefs, and field supervisors. The last group includes a small number of skilled forestry technicians and engineers. The structure of the workforce changes over the year. In 2012, the subsample taken from the total records of the company showed that in April, the peak month, 74% of the workers were casual, forestry auxiliaries and guards. In October, the month of lowest employment, casual workers formed only 16% of the workforce.

The structure of the workforce, apart from mirroring the seasonal nature of production, also reflects the type of investment made by the forestry companies in agricultural processes and in the organization of production and labor. There has been some investment in the mechanization of some productive processes, with implications for the demand for labor, although there still prevail activities which require manual labor, such as planting, fertilization, in the nurseries, in clearing the areas, and in firebreaks, among others. Investment in mechanization for preparing the land for planting, for example, reduced the demand for labor and the difficulties in expanding the planting area does not allow increases in employment. For example, in a recent interview, one of the operational companies said it is not opening nor preparing the land for new fields, and that it is currently concentrating on using the areas that had already been prepared. In addition, the patterns of employment vary in accordance withthe phase of development of the plantation and not solely along the agricultural year. Manual work is most intensive during the establishment of the forest and clearing in the first years. From the fifth year until the start of logging, the amount of work in the forests is reduced.

As for recruitment, initially the workforce was recruited locally, in the areas where the companies were operating, coordinated by community leaders (or chiefs) who controlled the selection of workers locally, particularly for work which did not require qualifications, such as forestry auxiliaries and guards. The population queried this form of recruitment, alleging the people selected for jobs were those who were related to the chiefs. However, even though the recruitment policy might stress the recruitment of local people for the forestry exploitation areas, it was found that there were groups of workers from other areas (localities, districts, or even provinces) who live in camps close to the production fields. Furthermore, the fact that someone initially enrolled as a worker in a company does not guarantee that he will have a continued job.

A further aspect that should be mentioned is the reduction in direct recruitment of workers in the forestry plantations, where the companies have resorted to subcontracting labor through companies or individual service providers. The workforce recruited by the subcontractors is generally very heterogeneous. Some of the subcontractors operate as outgrowers or integrated producers responsible both for the opening and preparation of land and for planting, often working in less populated peripheral areas. These subcontractors recruit their workers in two different ways: (i) recruiting some workers from other localities and districts in Niassa (for example, from Cuamba and the districts in eastern Niassa) and from other countries such as Malawi, accommodating them in camps during the planting season and (ii) hiring local families in a system of "labor tasks" based on a complete plantation of a specific area over several weeks instead of a single day of work. In this case, the workers generally include members of their family, even children. These companies and individuals are responsible for a significant number of casual workers in the forestry plantations (who, in general, do not have work contracts), which implies that the number of these casual workers has been underestimated in the records of the forestry companies.

There is a sharp crisis of job opportunities in Niassa and when the companies do not expand into new areas this raises questions about the current and future possibilities of employment in forestry production. Currently, the concern goes beyond the precarious nature of employment, as will be shown below, to consider the social conditions of labor including payment conditions.

3.3   *The Payment System*

The wages pattern varies, but work on the plantations is poorly paid. The irregularity of forestry work and the targets system explain the low wages earned by the workers on the plantations. The wages are paid by target or daily task but are received monthly. The determination of the wage paid per target/task, according to the forestry companies, is calculated on the basis of the minimum wage stipulated for the agricultural sector (where it would be expected that the daily remuneration would be equivalent to the monthly minimum wage divided by 30 days). However, the payment system is not as linear as it may appear. The amount to be received in a month depends on meeting the daily target. If the targets are met every day, the monthly wage approximates (or is equivalent to) the value of the monthly wage for the sector. The experience of various workers, both men and women, shows that it is difficult or almost impossible to meet the targets, for several reasons, mostly associated with the excessive nature of the targets because of the intensification of labor in the forestry plantations. For example, there is a range of activities that used to be carried out by more than one worker and then came to be done by a single worker. In these and in other cases linked to noncompliance with the targets due to the working conditions (such as difficulties with the organization of transport, food, instruments, and work equipment), the workers only receive partial payment (equivalent to the piecework done) or they are not paid at all (they are considered as absent). These factors make the standard of wages variable and with amounts that do not reach the minimum wage stipulated by law for the agricultural sector. The minimum wage considered is that for 2012, that is 2300 Meticais (henceforth, referred to as MT) which is also the year referred to in the database used from the forestry company A.

As a worker from the Niassa forestry plantations said in an interview:

> ...This work here is very tough; it even seems that we're in the colonial period (...). The wages aren't enough for anything... it's difficult to meet the target...it's hard to use a pickaxe... This is suffering, it's not a job, it even seems like Xibalo! (translator's note: term for forced labor under colonial rule) (...). When I tried to complain about the pickaxe, boss X replied « I don't talk with material » (...) There are others who also don't like the conditions, but because of life's suffering, we have to accept...when I and other colleagues went to tell the trade union (about the problems), they told us to speak on our own with the production technician]. (Interview with a casual worker, 30-year-old Mr A, Chimbonila, Mussa, 13/12/2014)

The forestry auxiliaries and the guards receive a wage determined by task, and the permanent workers (except the forestry auxiliaries) receive a monthly wage. Table 5, based on the total records of wages paid in 2012, in Forestry Company A, shows the variability in the workers' wages, particularly for the permanent workers who include unskilled field workers, forestry auxiliaries, supervisors, and field technicians, where the wages and duties of the workers in this category are much more variable. This can be seen from the standard deviation and the lowest and highest wages recorded in both categories of workers. In the case of the permanent workers, the value of the lowest wage reflects the payment by task which characterizes the forestry auxiliaries with the status of permanent staff. The same is true for the lowest wages among the casual workers. The low wages reflect discounts from the wages, either because of part payments or because workdays were recorded as absences (where this does not necessarily mean absence from work but can result from failure to meet a defined target, particularly in the current scenario of intensification of work tasks). The median and the average wage of the casual workers in 2010 were lower than the minimum wage stipulated for agricultural activities that year (2300 MT). In the case of the permanent workers, the median wage is slightly above the minimum wage and the average wage is also higher. However, given the great variability between the wages in this group of workers, the average wage may reflect this great variability, as shown in Table 5.

Table 5, also shows the percentage of workers, casual and permanent, whose wages were below the minimum wage stipulated for agricultural activity. Many of the casual workers, who dominate the structure of the workforce

Table 5 Monthly wage[a] (in Meticais—MT) and percentage of workers paid below the minimum wage, Forestry Company A, Niassa, 2012

Type of worker	Average	Median	Standard deviation	Lowest (wage)	Highest (wage)	% of workers paid wages below the stipulated minimum (%)
Casual	1.884	1.945	622	90	6.530	79
Permanent	3.225	2.595	2.438	120	30.603	21

Source Author in accordance with the wages data base of Forestry Company A, Niassa, 2012

[a]This data refers to wages net of discounts for the INSS and union fees as well as of absences. The sample used is of 13,883 observations of workers, in 2012. Note that this does not refer to 13,883 workers but to observations of payments made to the same worker or to several workers monthly, during the period for which he was recruited

on the plantations, are those who earn wages below the minimum stipulated by law for the agricultural sector.

Here a caveat is necessary. The nominal minimum wage, stipulated by law, is worth less in real terms, particularly if we consider inflation in prices of basic consumer goods (Castel-Branco 2017). Given the pattern of wages in the forestry agro-industry, one question that emerges is, if the "minimum" wage is lower in real terms than that stipulated, then the real wages received by the workers (which are already less than the nominal minimum wage) tend to be still lower, in real terms, providing the workers with less purchasing power. Thus, the minimum wage for agriculture (2300 MT, in 2012, and 3642 MT, currently) is lower in real terms, weakening the purchasing power of the workers who earn it. In the case of those agricultural workers who earn below this "minimum wage," who are the majority of the workers (particularly the casual workers), their situation is, in real terms, even more serious. Under these conditions, the satisfaction of basic needs for food, health, accommodation, and transport, among others, is limited, constraining the standard of living and the social reproduction of the labor force. Given the interdependence between wage income and other forms of labor, particularly agricultural production, the low remuneration will have repercussions in limiting other forms of labor complementary to wage labor. Such forms of labor are mutually related to wage income, depending on its financing to establish its activity (for example, household production) and subsidizing the low wage income.

Furthermore, the payment of the wages of the subcontracted casual workers (who are not part of the staff table of the forestry companies) is the responsibility of the subcontractors who tend to pay lower wages. The wage analysis of this group of workers is very limited due to their scattered organization. This fact also puts a block on the possible organization of these workers in the fight for better wage and working conditions.

Workers ask several questions about how their wages are determined under the dominant work and payment systems, based on targets. This question stood out in the interviews with several casual and some permanent agricultural workers (forestry auxiliaries), who said they do not understand how their wages are calculated and expressed uncertainty (for lack of information and knowledge) about how much they would earn at the end of each month of work. Some examples of these questions raised by forestry auxiliaries are:

> ...even when I wake up and go to the field every day, I never receive wages of 2,000 meticais...but I go to the field every day even when my back hurts, but later the wages are little. (Interview with a permanent worker, 27-year-old Ms B, Chimbonila, Naconda, 01/12/2014)

> ...I came in as a casual worker, and now I have become permanent (...) At the start, I was working for targets, but with a timetable, and my presence was marked, but later when the heavy and tight targets began, I wasn't able to finish the work (...) to finish, I have to stay until it is dark in the forest (...) Several times I couldn't dig 300 holes with the pickaxe, and so I don't know whether I will receive any wages; they mark me absent and I don't know how to calculate the wages... one month I receive 1,300 MT, another 1,600 MT and in another I may receive less, but I'm going to work, and I do the same job... I don't know why ... the most I received was 2,200 MT (...) I would like to know how much I should receive for each hole I open!? (...). (Interview with a permanent worker, 31-year-old Mr C, Litunde locality, 11/12/2014)

It is also worth noting that the trade union seems to have a similar concern and lack of information about how the companies determine the wages the workers receive, affecting their possible area for monitoring and, faced with the wage conditions in the current work system. However, a question and possibly a space for negotiation which emerged is, for example, how can the trade union SINTAF guarantee that a day of work undertaken is in fact recorded as an effective day of work?

It should be noted that the basis of profitability of capital at the cost of paying low wages (among other precarious labor conditions in general), is not only a noteworthy concern for the workers but could also call into question the sustainability of the productive system itself. The workers are looking for decent real wages, in the context of inflation in the prices of basic goods and services, weakening their purchasing power. Hence their struggles for higher wages in the forestry plantations could be expressed through: (i) absenteeism, for example, in search for better options to generate income and livelihood, either locally or through migration, (ii) strikes in pursuit of higher nominal wages, and (iii) acts of sabotage, for example, double or triple planting of seedlings, to speed up the work, and meet the daily target fixed, in the attempt to guarantee corresponding remuneration, and blocking the productive process in activities dependent on labor.

Working-class struggles over wages, among other questions linked to the prevailing target-based labor system, are made more difficult in a context where there is poor organization of the working class and weak power of negotiation between the workers and the employers, between the union and the employers, and between the union and the workers.

Faced with this scenario, there is intensification of work by the workers to comply with the piecework task in the attempt to ensure a registered day of work and the equivalent monthly wages, subjecting themselves to vulnerable social conditions, as shown in the following section.

3.4 Social Conditions of Labor: Health and Productivity Questions

Work on the forestry plantations takes place under precarious social conditions that, under the current forms of organization of production and labor, sustain the basis of the profitability of capital. The current mode of the productive organization of labor, based on the piecework system and resting on the intensification of labor, could endanger safety at work and the health of the workers with implications in putting limits on a decent standard of living, on productivity and on the social reproduction of the workforce. This fact is shown by the organization of food, accommodation, transport, and labor and social security conditions; by the day-to-day experience of work, under conditions of the provision (or not) and use (or not) of work equipment and tools; apart from other broader and more diverse forms of social and life organization.

The organization of food, accommodation, and transport, among other conditions, are the responsibility of the workers and are precarious. Under the current target-based system of work, the workers are subjected to intensification of work, with long working days, limiting their time for preparing food and for meals (they take rapid meals which are all much the same) as well as time for rest. This is linked to the effort to speed up their work to meet the targets, due to the direct consequences for registering an effective day of work and for their wages. It was found that the workers' meals were not varied and they opted for cheap food that is easy to prepare, such as maize porridge with fish (dried or fresh) or beans. There are several cases of workers who organized themselves into groups so as to prepare food rapidly, making a sort of "food xitique", or rotation in preparing the food, which also allows them to minimize the costs of food by sharing them.

Furthermore, in the context of a defective transport system (both in terms of access and its conditions), to guarantee the opportunity to work, various workers (men and women—some accompanied by small children) with the status of permanent or casual workers have to live in camps near the forestry production fields. Several of those interviewed complained of the accommodation conditions: they were sleeping on the floor, in a camp with roof problems—a situation that became worse in the rainy season—vulnerable to snake bites, without a medical post nearby or speedy medical assistance, without lighting or clean drinking water, under vulnerable and uncomfortable transport conditions (from the camps to the production fields vice versa mid-week, and from the camps to their houses and vice versa, at weekends). The means of transport was an open truck (commonly known as "my-love") with the capacity to hold 60 people but which usually carried 90–100. It should be noted that all the transport costs are imputed to the workers. The precarious accommodation conditions, living far from their home area (in some cases, far from their children—some of whom are minors with nobody to care for them), and having to abandon some supplementary activities, such as agricultural production, are among the problems identified. According to the interviewees, both the camps and the production fields lack health facilities. This is most problematic for women and could put their safety at risk, in terms of their health and of the risk of aggression and physical abuse. This calls into question hygiene and safety at work.

Various groups of workers have expressed their discontent at the social conditions of labor. Some groups, mainly the workers belonging to a poorer socioeconomic category, tried to tolerate the labor conditions, on the grounds that they had a vital need for a job. Others, even though facing socioeconomic difficulties, were already showing signs of resistance to the current forms and conditions of work. For example, some took time off from the plantations to work on their own household production or on somebody else's farm, for payment. A further example is those who committed sabotage, by planting several seedlings in the same hole, so as to claim they had completed a daily task, which would have implications for productivity and the quality of forest production. There were some workers who were involved in an unorganized demonstration, blocking roads to demand better wages and social conditions, as well as a reduction in the daily work targets. However, even though the workers had their reasons and their rights since the strike was not organized, the police detained some, and others were fired. When interviewed, many of these workers said they felt they had nothing to lose, because they thought that the forestry companies only "brought them misfortune". Several workers said they were only working because of "suffering" and because they had no other way to obtain money to satisfy their basic needs and establish their household and household production. Below we see some experience of workers who started with the category of casual and after three renewals became permanent workers but did not feel any changes in their social conditions.

> ... *I can't manage to buy anything [food, exercise books for the children] ... my wife works on the family farm...I take maize and stew to the camp where I have a food group... each of us brings a little flour and cooks stew to divide among ourselves, there's no transport ... I leave early and I go on foot from home to there... We complained and went on strike but there's no work here in this area. (Interview with permanent worker, 48 year old Mr D, Chimbonila, Mussa, 04/12/2014)*

They call us but we don't want to go there anymore. Almost all of us have left the job because of the poverty there. It's tough, others were even fired because they complained. (Interview with former permanent worker, Mr E, Mapaco, 08/12/2014)

...Our government said it wants to bring a company here for us to have jobs... But these companies come with their directors... Even people with 10th grade here are given hoes; if you're a guard, you're lucky. But someone from outside with 10th grade is immediately put on top.... (Interview with former permanent worker, Mr F, Mussa, 08//12/2014)

The forestry companies have difficulties in providing work equipment (such as raincoats, gloves, and boots) in good time. For example, the provision of raincoats and boots in the rainy season has been late, after the planting. But even in the cases where work equipment is provided hygiene and safety at work can be placed at risk due to the organization of the system of piecework, based on the intensification of labor. In addition, several groups of workers have complained about the use of work instruments, regarding them as "heavy" and hard for their jobs (such as the case of the change from using hoes to pickaxes), putting their health at risk (for example, back pains) and their ability to meet targets, with effects on productivity. The precarious conditions of the social organization of work, on which the productive system rests, puts at risk the workers' health, and the reproduction, availability, and productivity of the workforce in the medium and long term.

It was found that the right to protest about labor conditions is limited due to the weak organization of the workers and the poor relations between the workers and the union and between the union and the company.

Furthermore, to ensure the observance of workers' rights, the labor legislation in Mozambique (Law no. 23/2007, of 1 August), states that, in a piecework-based labor system, the work contract must be in written form (República de Moçambique 2007). However, although this is extremely important for, for example, access to possible social benefits, under the current form of the productive organization of labor, labor practices violate the labor law and call into question the right to stability of labor during the period established under the work contract, envisioned in the labor law. The conditions of hiring the workforce are unstable and, in some cases, the work contracts are not written down. The evidence shows that the workers who are subcontracted by individual agents providing services to the forestry companies (many of whom are not formally registered) do not possess written work contracts. Even so, there is always labor available for the forestry plantations, given the shortage of alternative employment, and given the reduction in the direct demand for labor by the forestry companies, who are the main employers in Niassa. The work contracts give the employers the right to recruit labor when they need it, but they do not guarantee that the worker will have a day's work. Hence having a written work contract, although important, does not guarantee and does not mean that there will be work for every day stipulated in the contract.

As for social security, the workers are concerned that monthly contributions to the INSS are discounted from their wages, but they do not enjoy any social benefits, leading to a question: is social security a contribution without benefits in this labor system? Given the current mode of labor organization, the possible benefits linked to social security are limited. Formally the social security system is obligatory for all wage workers. The formal companies have the responsibility and are obliged to enroll their workers in the social security system, which covers benefits in the event of illness, invalidity, maternity, old age, and death. The National Social Security Institute (hereafter, referred to as INSS) is taking measures that seek to expand coverage of the system to casual and self-employed workers. This process covers the casual workers of the forestry plantations. But there is a lack of coverage by social security, even with contributions from the enrolled workers (contribution without benefit).

Workers must reach a minimum of 20 days' work a month before they can benefit from the social security system. However, casual workers generally have contracts of short duration that are not continual and are unregistered (for example, not longer than 3 months, weekly, or even for one day). The noncontinual registration is explained by the piecework system whereby the worker, even with a work contract for a longer duration than 20 days, may appear and just undertake one task. But in the case of failing to meet the target, this may mean he is marked as working for just half a day or considered as absent, varying from company to company. In this case, the workers have no information and no control over the number of days of work effectively counted. Thus not all the casual workers enrolled and contributing record an effective 20 days of work a month, given that the current work system does not guarantee that a day of work is registered as such by the company and by the INSS. This fact calls into question the right to social security, so the worker makes contributions without a right to social benefits. Even if casual workers are enrolled in the INSS, if the current forms of organization of production and labor in the agro-industrial companies remain and if the necessary conditions for registration and drawing benefits from the formal social security system also remain unaltered, then the possibility of casual workers benefitting from social security is small, even if they do make regular contributions.

It should be stressed that in the current forms of production and of the social organization of labor, the sustainability of the base of profitability of the agro-industrial companies may be threatened. While the workers manage to ensure their social reproduction, through other forms of work, indirectly or informally subordinate to capital, particularly household production, the basis for profitability may be maintained, but that will depend on a complex of factors associated with the social organization of labor and, more generally, of life. Given the interrelationship between the income from wage labor and from other forms of work, any instability or irregularity in either of the activities will influence the other. This balance may be critical since the workers may make calculations on their options and their response depends on how the context in which they operate is organized. For example, during the field research, the companies complained of the absenteeism of the workers, and alleged that they "lack a culture of work" in Niassa. This was given as a justification for the absences from work registered and for failure to meet the targets. Some members of the government and the trade unions, in certain cases, expressed a similar approach. But it can be asked whether the workers did not meet the targets because they were absent in all cases? Is it true that the workers abandon their work out of a mere lack of discipline or a "lack of culture of work", in a scenario of precarious wage and working conditions?

The experience of work in the current context of production and social organization (discussed in more detail in the following section) explains why the argument of "lack of a culture of work" is an illusion (O'Laughlin 2016). On the one hand, it was found that particular groups of workers were marked absent because they did not meet their targets and not because they were physically absent from the workplace. On the contrary, they remained late in the fields attempting to complete their targets in order for a full day of work to be recorded, as discussed above. On the other hand, heterogeneous groups of workers made a judgment between working on the plantations (and subcontracting casual workers in a *ganho-ganho* system to work on the family farm and/or obtain help from household members) or work directly on their own farm or that of someone else, in a context of (i) an overlap between wage labor and household agriculture, particularly in the rainy season, which is the peak planting period for the seedlings but also that for sowing on the family farms and (ii) in a context of precarious working conditions. Nonetheless, despite the arduous working conditions, many continued to work due to the limited job opportunities.

Broadly speaking, the interdependence between household production and wage labor remains dominant, in the current mode of organization of the productive structure. This shows the relation of dependence between the reproduction of the labor force and capital, since the social conditions of labor are important for the reproduction of the system, since they determine what happens with household production which ensures the possibility of keeping the workforce available and cheap. Furthermore, what happens in the productive and social organization of labor and in determining wages has implications for the productivity of the workforce and the reproduction of the base of profitability of the companies. The social conditions of labor do not merely affect the way in which people live, but also how they work, which has implications for the reproduction and productivity of the workforce as well as of the systems of socioeconomic reproduction and of the productive and accumulation structure prevalent in the companies. It is thus crucial to rethink broadly the current systems of the organization of production and labor on the forestry plantations, where it seems important that job creation and increases in productivity should be accompanied by growth in wage income and improved living conditions. From this perspective, some questions arise: how to ensure the profitability of the companies, on the one hand,

and decent working conditions, on the other? What space is there to organize differently in the context of economic crisis and the crisis of the forestry companies in Niassa?

The IESE research took place in a period of crisis in the sector, but the information presented on the structure of the workforce dates from the previous period and shows that the centrality of casual labor and precarious wages precedes the current difficulties of the sector. However, the extension of the targets, the elimination of jobs, and the withdrawal of some companies have led to tougher working conditions and have increased the precarious environment for workers, their families, and the population living around the forestry plantations. This latter aspect is the focus of the next section.

4 Impact of the Current Employment and Work Patterns on the Welfare of the Workers and Their Households

This section looks at the experience of work and discusses the impact of employment patterns on the way of life and well-being of the workers and their families. This experience partly explains both the workers' discontent at the jobs created and the complaints of the companies about the availability and quality of labor. Similarly, questions are raised about the concerns of workers in the current context of a crisis in employment, including temporary employment, and of economic crisis in general in Niassa.

The current patterns and social conditions of labor should be seen in an integrated and broader way, including the situation of labor inside and outside the forestry plantations. It is crucial to look at the organization of labor and the way of life of the workers and their families, before and after they take up forestry jobs.

In the current productive forms, the type of employment created in the plantations, dominated by instability and insecurity in jobs that are mostly casual, poorly paid and precarious, has implications for the way of life and welfare of the workers and their households. There is a differentiated impact of the current employment patterns, reflecting separate forms of social organization of labor and of households' ways of life. How do the workers organize, and how they used to organize their way of life before they took up forestry jobs? How do they divide their time in allocating their labor power to the forestry plantations or to other forms of waged or unwaged work (agricultural or nonagricultural)?

Previous studies of the socioeconomic impact of the forestry plantations in Niassa (Landry and Chirwa 2011; Nube 2013; Bleyer et al. 2016) stressed positive impacts such as the increase in employment, and increased commercial activities and social projects, such as the building of roads, schools, and health facilities. The disadvantages were the reduction in the availability of land and access to forestry resources, particularly firewood, but also other forestry products. Landry and Chirwa (2011) also mentioned the diversity of work outside the family farm. All the studies showed that the forestry jobs generally reduced poverty but that inequality increased. Those who obtained permanent skilled jobs managed to attain a better situation than those who obtained unskilled jobs. Bleyer et al. (2016), Nube (2013) pointed to the latter as a major result of educational differences, although Nube (2013) also mentioned that a dominant aspect has been the knowledge or ignorance of workers' rights.

However, the research undertaken by the author of this article and by the IESE research team, in late 2014, confirmed the importance of the forestry jobs for ways of life. The former workers on the forestry plantations, even with the difficulties inherent to the prevalent working conditions (including wages) felt very unhappy about the loss of employment resulting from the withdrawal of some companies and the reduced scale of planting by others. This fact, as shown in the previous sections, derives from the importance that the wages play in establishing the household. This situation is explained by the fact that the wage income allows the workers: (i) to finance food and nonfood consumption (education, health, housing, and transport); (ii) to invest in household production which, apart from helping develop this activity (through using the money to buy inputs, to pay for labor, and to grow food for the market instead of depending on current consumption), helps subsidize the low and irregular wages they receive from forestry work. This second aspect proves vital in moments of breakdown in agricultural employment (given the irregularity of employment throughout the agricultural year, and particularly the precarious nature of wages and working conditions on the plantations) or facing the crisis of job and work opportunities in the province and country. Furthermore, the wage funds can be (iii) a basis of accumulation to prevent shocks such as breaks in household sustenance (caused by funerals, illness, school fees, and other unexpected consumption expenditure), market falls, increased prices of inputs or transport, sources of investment in alternative activities, adjustment to local crises, or conflicts over resources such as land, among other shocks. One interesting aspect is the wage dynamic, which has a structure similar to an onion, in the sense that some may be receiving wages, for example in forestry employment (and/or in *ganho-ganho*), at the same time that they with their own wages and/or via payment in kind can pay wages to others on their own "machambas" (farms).

But, despite recognizing the importance of forestry jobs for ways of life, our research showed a more complex picture of the nature of the inequality between the workers, its causes and implications. First, inequality between the workers has to do with the organization of labor in itself, both the form of recruitment and the working conditions (including the wages), as shown throughout this article. Secondly, the unequal results of wage labor are explained by the preexisting inequalities in the organization of households which has affected the capacity to recruit labor in *ganho-ganho* in order, for example, to ensure maintenance and expansion of agricultural production.

The divergent experience of two women from Sanga, both agricultural auxiliaries of ex-Chikweti, with permanent contracts, shows how preexisting forms of differentiation, particularly access to income outside of household production, affect the impact of wage labor. The first woman, 50 years old, belongs to a large household. One of her sons is a successful trader. With various sources of income, they can easily buy food to cover shortfalls from their own agricultural production, but this woman also used the wage income earned from ex-Chikweti to hire workers on a *ganho-ganho* system to keep her own plots in good condition and expand her cultivated area. The other woman, 30 years old, has six small children. Her husband is also an agricultural auxiliary, with a contract at Green Resources. When both were working, they had to spend their entire wages on food, clothing, and school fees. There was not enough money left over to hire workers on *ganho-ganho* to help them plant, weed, or harvest on their own family farm. They left the farm without investment and without maintenance. Now the wages are not enough to meet the financial needs of the family, and so the wife had to take on *ganho-ganho* work to cover daily food expenses, leaving her little time to work on her own farm. Both women would like to have permanent contracts again, but in the first case it would be a way of supporting a prosperous and diversified livelihood basis. In the second, it would make the difference between being poor and being desperately impoverished.

4.1 Changes in the Socioeconomic Patterns

The research by Nube (2013) showed that, with the entry of the forestry companies, there was a growth in the middle class (the richest) and a decline in impoverishment as can be seen in Table 6.

This pattern is reflected in the increase in the number of people with mobile phones, bank accounts, and improved houses. Table 6, based on the research by Nube (2013), shows that the main acquisitions were a better house, a cell phone, and a bank account. The goods which most affect the economic capacity of households such as ownership of bicycles or of motorcycles (used for taxis and for trade, as well as for personal transport) and of livestock did not increase much.

One of the gaps of this research seems to be the lack of registration of the increase or decline in cultivated land (probably one of the most important indicators of agricultural capacity). If we analyze the research based on income, we may expect that the withdrawal of companies had some effect since without wage income people will not be able to replace or maintain luxury goods or maintain their improved houses. Our interviews in Chimbonila and Sanga suggest, however, that the interconnection between jobs and the organization of agricultural production is more lasting than the index based on "possession of goods" suggests, both because of differences between permanent and casual workers, and because of existing differentiation in households' means of livelihood. Some experiences of the organization of labor express this relationship:

Table 6 Change in social strata (Part 1) and change in possession of particular goods (Part 2), before and after the entry of the forestry companies, Chimbonila e Sanga districts, Niassa province

Part 1

	Chimbonila		Sanga	
Classes	Before (%)	After (%)	Before (%)	After (%)
Extremely poor	40.6	12.3	51.7	24.2
Poor	57.5	67.9	45	57.5
Middle	1.9	19.8	3.3	18.3

Part 2

Household goods	Before (%)	After (%)	Before (%)	After (%)
Improved house	7.5	33.0	12.5	45.0
Motor-cycle	0.0	1.9	3.3	4.2
Livestock	16.0	18.9	5.0	6.7
Bicycle	80.2	86.8	52.5	55.8
Radio	28.3	32.1	79.2	90.0
Cell phone	1.9	39.6	1.7	26.7
Bank account	0.0	23.6	0.8	30.8
Poultry	24.5	36.8	7.5	18.3

Source Nube (2013)

> (...I come from Mavago, I have two wives and five children, each one living in their own house, here in Mussa (...) Before the forests, I used to work on my own farm which helped me eat and sell... and have money ... I had a charcoal business [I bought in Mussa and sold in Lichinga] ... I stopped the charcoal business in 2005, when I began to work as a forestry auxiliary...I needed the job for the family.... Sometimes I help my mother with money to buy soap, I get food from her farm... I work in the forest for 3 months and then I stop and I go to work on the farm. Later I go back to the forest, and the women cultivate. One of them helps sell in the city. With the money of the wages, I pay for casual wage labor on the farm ... Thus I manage to arrange my affairs and live. (Interview with a permanent worker, Mussa, 06/12/2014)

Another worker reveals a different experience:

> [This ex-worker describes that during his forestry employment he had to sell some of his goods, such as his bicycle, which he owned before working on the plantations, in order to buy food and clothing for himself and his family because the wages he earned were not enough to cover the expenditure. He also did not have enough money to pay people to work on his family field on a *ganho-ganho* system; his production declined, with not enough to sell, only for consumption. Even so, the farm did not produce enough for consumption during the entire year. This ex-worker regrets that he interrupted the activities he was doing

before forestry employment: he is fearful about becoming involved in forestry work, preferring to spend his time on the family farm. He says: *"I am tired of working to pay debts"*. (Permanent Worker, Naconda, 11/12/2014)

However, the overlap of activities and the possible conflict that has emerged between working on the plantations and working on household agricultural production, particularly in the peak or planting periods, ensures that various workers, at this period, face time pressure and have to decide between the options of either work on the plantations, where the work does not offer regularity and stability of employment and income (depending on the socioeconomic conditions and organization of the household, hiring or not *ganho-ganho* for the family farm), or work at household production on the farm (owned by the worker or someone else, in the form of *ganho-ganho*). Their choices depend on the organization of their households, on their means of livelihood, and on the socioeconomic conditions of the workers and of their households, which are not homogenous. This, given the strong interdependence between household production and wage labor, some opt to continue working on the plantations, hiring casual labor to support household production, and/or relying on the support of some members of their household on the farm. Others opt to absent themselves from the plantations to work on the family farm. But the research showed this does not mean that these workers do not depend on wage income to establish their household but that, depending on the case, this often happens because they do not have enough money to sub-contract other workers for their farms in a *ganho-ganho* system. In certain cases, the workers weigh up between the cost of working on the plantations in the current labor system (unstable and insecure) or investing their time in their family farms, where they can control possible income in kind or cash. However, despite this conflict, there is a trend for the workers to continue undertaking activities on the plantations, given the limited job opportunities and the role that wage labor plays in establishing household agriculture and in the social organization of households. Not all the agricultural workers in Niassa want a permanent, full-time job, and some are looking for forms of work that allow them to combine casual wage labor with household production. But these workers, like the permanent workers, are concerned about having employment and better working conditions, in this context of an economic and employment crisis in the province. The problem of absenteeism for the companies seems to decline as a result of the non-expansion of forestry activity, and the mechanization of some processes.

Finally, a further aspect concerns the changes in the ways of life of the population, including certain workers who live in the areas surrounding those occupied by the companies. A generalized implication for various people affected by this situation was the loss of areas for agricultural production or family farms, as well as orchards and pasture for livestock, and the need to travel to more distant, and in certain cases, less productive, areas, in a context of limited conditions of access to and quality of transport. In some cases, they have to walk to reestablish their farms and to obtain resources and consumer products indispensable for their way of life, such as firewood, charcoal, food, and medicinal products obtained from native trees, as mentioned in interviews with some workers and their households.

Currently, the instability of forestry production in Niassa is expressed in the high frequency of bush fires in the forest, including the newly planted area. There was a "community" management committee which handled funds given by the companies on the condition of not burning the plantations. This was called the "social responsibility fund," intended to build social facilities, but the population was unhappy about the management and allocation of these funds and benefits. Mbanze et al. (2013) suggest that 90% of the fires are of human origin—to clear lands, for hunting, through carelessness, and as a form of protest. Right now, the causes of the protests include the exclusion of the livestock of local small traders, the lack of access to firewood and charcoal in the company areas, the sackings of workers, the reduction in the number of jobs, and the tightening of targets and work routines. The discontent unites a range of different interests but is not a solution for anybody, but a challenge to be faced. What options exist?

5   Conclusions

The analysis of the current patterns of employment and work and their impact on well-being requires an understanding of how the productive and accumulation system functions and of the complexity of the labor markets, as a whole and in an integrated manner, in which employment and work are related, and are structured.

This chapter has argued that the structures of employment and work on the forestry plantations in Niassa reflect the more general organization of productive agro-industrial structures of an extractive nature. The prevalent productive structure is centered on the production of primary products for export, through obtaining vast areas of land and access to water at low cost, and a poorly paid workforce, mostly casual and under precarious conditions. In the current mode of organization of production and labor, where the basis of the profitability of the companies depends on low wages and precarious labor conditions, the workers are responsible for the social costs of their reproduction. The social reproduction of the labor force is guaranteed by the interdependence and mutual financing of varied forms of labor, paid and/or unpaid, agricultural or not. Not all the agricultural workers in Niassa want a permanent and full-time job. Some are looking for forms of work that combine a seasonal job with household production. But these workers, as well as the permanent workers, are concerned about having employment and better working conditions, in the context of an economic and employment crisis in the province. The well-being of the workers is not limited to having a job and remuneration, or to consumption and ownership of goods. Although important, these are just some of the determinants of well-being. Social organization and the experience of work, the interconnection between diverse forms of work and life, and health conditions, affect the welfare of workers and their families. Given the strong interdependence between wage labor and household agriculture, which have a historically long-lasting relationship in Niassa, any crisis in one of these forms of labor will affect the other, calling into question people's standard of living and well-being.

The type of employment and work that emerges from the dominant extractive structure has implications on the reproduction and type of workforce that is created, on productivity, on the type (and sustainability) of the future economic structure, in that work is structured by (and structures) the prevailing productive structures. If the objective is to improve the living conditions of Mozambicans, in which the creation of employment for this end stands out, as expressed in the current five-year Government program (PQG 2015–2019) (GdM 2015), it is necessary to reflect on the type of jobs that are being created in the dominant productive structure. Does job creation in itself guarantee improvements in living conditions, under the current forms of productive organization? The present research has shown that it does not. So should we only create jobs that may destroy the existing modes of livelihoods without providing enhanced social conditions? Employment that may reproduce poverty instead of reducing it? If the current forms of productive and labor organization are maintained, this will continue to generate jobs that are not very productive, unskilled, uncompetitive and without quality, and a differentiated workforce with limited employment opportunities and scant social options, reflecting an economy that is not productive. It is thus fundamental to think about alternatives for transforming the current productive structures and the socioeconomic conditions of labor that emerge from them.

A question that is posed to all the social actors, including the trade unions, the government, the companies, NGOs, academics, and the workers themselves, is how can the productive and labor structure be organized differently? What options exist in a context of complex labor markets? What is the space for changing the current patterns of productive organization? Any option involves understanding how the system functions in an integrated way and organizing the working class, which is not homogenous, but notoriously differentiated, in accordance with the real specificities of the organization of its labor and its livelihoods, in connection with the nature of the dominant productive mode, which should be faced and transformed. How can the patterns of development of the forestry industry be linked to the welfare of the workers and the population in the areas surrounding the forestry operations? How can the current system be transformed and the forms of work be organized differently without endangering the profitability of the companies, and at the same time guaranteeing decent living conditions to the workers and their households? How to guarantee that when a day of work is undertaken it is really registered and paid? How to ensure that the workers are enrolled in social security and that those enrolled have a right to, and enjoy, social benefits? In what way can the trade unions and the Ministry of Labour,

Employment and Social Security, for example, help in these questions in coordination with other social actors, including the workers themselves? How can all types of workers be organized, regardless of their status and categories, without privileging some and neglecting others?—for, although they are heterogeneous, with a differentiated social organization, they are all workers with a common concern that unites them: improvements in working conditions and in wages, and the creation of a new, more decent labor and social life.

What productive options in Niassa make it possible to drive the dynamics of labor markets? For each socioeconomic stratum options are necessary consistency with their specific problems. The development of a broad, diversified, and articulated productive structure of the Mozambican economy, and with strong productive linkages, may be crucial for driving the dynamics of the labor markets and job opportunities, as well as activating a space for changing the current patterns of the organization of production and labor, in favor of decent employment. Making available basic consumer goods and services (food, good quality health services, public transport, and education), which are indispensable for the sustenance and social reproduction of the workforce, may make it possible to maintain an available, cheap, and competitive workforce but with improvements in the quality of life and labor productivity.

Notes

1. The workers interviewed will be identified by letters, for example: worker A or B or Z.
2. The demographic data is collected by the General Population and Housing Survey every 10 years, the last one was done in 2017 although as it usually takes two years more to be published, it will only be launched and available in April 2019.
3. Sanga District, Unango Administrative Post.
4. Although the question of land acquisition is not the focus of analysis, since the community consultations involved undertakings about job creation, relevant for this study, an attempt was made to understand the process.
5. The socioeconomic situation of people was analyzed by a definition of three social classes, namely: middle, poor, and extremely poor, depending on the possession of goods (Nube 2013).
6. The data analysis methodology was based on three social categories: low, medium, and high (Landry and Chirwa 2011).
7. Good conditions of rainfall and water capacity, altitude and soil depth (MINAG 2009).
8. Niassa province covers an area of about 129,000 km^2. According to the GPHC in 2007 and 2017 (preliminary estimates), the estimated population in this province was about 1,213,398 inhabitants and 1,865,976, respectively (INE 2009, 2019).
9. Official estimate of monetary poverty based on a consumption-focused approach.

10. There is no uniformity in the Government and the companies' data about the areas authorized and exploited.
11. Besides Niassa Green Resources (NGR) the company operates in Nampula province through Lurio Green Resources.
12. Although the company Chikweti, when operational, employed more women than the other companies.
13. The number of workers considered in this subsample is 600.

References

Ali, R. (2017). Mercados de Trabalho Rurais: Porque são negligenciados nas políticas de emprego, pobreza e desenvolvimento em Moçambique? In R. Ali, C. N. Castel-Branco, & C. Muianga (Eds.), *Emprego e Transformação Económica e Social em Moçambique*. Maputo: Institute for Social and Economic Studies (IESE).

Bardasi, E., Beegle, K., & Dillon, A. (2010). *Do labor statistics depend on how and to whom the questions are asked? Results from a survey experiment in Tanzania* (No. Policy Research Working Paper n. 5192). Washington, DC: World Bank.

Bleyer, M., Kniivilä, M., Horne, P., Sitoe, A., & Falcão, M. P. (2016). Socio-economic impacts of private land use investment on rural communities: Industrial forest plantations in Niassa, Mozambique. *Land Use Policy, 51*, 281–289.

Castel-Branco, C. N. (1995). Opções Económicas de Moçambique 1975–95: Problemas, Lições e Ideias Alternativas. In B. Mazula (Ed.), *Moçambique Eleições, Democracia e Desenvolvimento* (pp. 581–636). Maputo: Brazão Mazula.

Castel-Branco, C. N. (2010). Economia Extractiva e Desafios de Industrialização em Moçambique. In L. de Brito, C. N. Castel-Branco, S. Chichava, & A. Francisco (Eds.), *Economia Extractiva e Desafios de Industrialização em Moçambique*. Maputo: Institute for Social and Economic Studies (IESE).

Castel-Branco, C. N. (2017). Crises Económicas e Estruturas de Acumulação de Capital em Moçambique. In L. de Brito, C. N. Castel-Branco, S. Chichava, S. Forquila, & A. Francisco (Eds.), *Desafios para Moçambique 2017*. Maputo: Institute for Social and Economic Studies (IESE).

Cramer, C., Oya, C., & Sender, J. (2008). *Rural labour markets in sub-Saharan Africa: A new view of poverty, power and policy* (Policy Brief N. 1). London: Centre for Development Policy and Research.

FIAN. (2012). *The human rights impacts of the tree plantations in Niassa Province, Mozambique*. Amsterdam, Netherlands: FIAN.

GdM. (2015, April 14). *Programa Quinquenal do Governo 2015–2019*. Maputo: Boletim da República. Imprensa Nacional de Moçambique.

Green Resources. (2011, Outubro 3). *Niassa Green Resources achieves first FSC certification in Mozambique*.

Herrmann, R., Jumbe, C., Bruentrup, M., & Osabuohien, E. (2018, July). Competition between biofuel feedstock and food production: Empirical evidence from sugarcane outgrower settings in Malawi. *Biomass and Bioenergy, 114*, 100–111.

INE. (1999). *II Recenseamento Geral da População e Habitação de 1997*. Maputo: National Statistics Institute (INE).

INE. (2009). *III Recenseamento Geral da População e Habitação de 2007*. Maputo: National Statistics Institute (INE).

INE. (2010). *Inquérito ao Orçamento Familiar - IOF-2008-09*. National Statistics Institute (INE): Relatório Final.
INE. (2016). *Inquérito ao Orçamento Familiar - IOF-2014/15. Relatório Final*. Maputo: National Statistics Institute (INE).
INE. (2019). *Censo 2017. IV Recenseamento Geral da População e Habitação. Divulgação dos Resultados Preliminares. GPHC.* Maputo: National Statistics Institute.
Landry, J., & Chirwa, P. (2011). Analysis of the potential socio-economic impact of establishing plantation forestry on rural communities in Sanga district, Niassa province, Mozambique. *Land Use Policy, 28*(3), 542–551.
Massingarela, C., Nhate, V., & Oya, C. (2005). *Mercados Rurais de Emprego em Moçambique. Um estudo sobre o trabalho assalariado temporário e informal nas zonas rurais de Manica, Nampula e Zambézia* (Relatório do estudo No. 31P). Maputo: Ministry of Plan and Development.
Mbanze, A., Romero, A., Batista, A., Ramos-Rodriguez, M., Guacha, L., Martinho, C., et al. (2013). Assessment of causes that contribute to the occurrence of plantations forests fires in Niassa Province, North of Mozambique. *African Journal of Agriculture, 8*(45), 5684–5691.
MINAG. (2009). *Estratégia de Reflorestamento*. Maputo: Ministry of Agriculture (MINAG).
MINAG. (2015). *Plantações florestais em Moçambique: Desafios*. Maputo: Ministério da Agricultura.
MITESS. (2016a). *Boletim Informativo do Mercado do Trabalho 2015/2016 – N° 1. Moçambique*. Maputo: Ministério do Trabalho, Emprego e Segurança Social (MITESS). National Directorate of Observation of Labour Market.
MITESS. (2016b). *Proposta de Política de Emprego «Promovendo mais e melhores empregos em Moçambique»*. Maputo: Ministry of Labour, Employment and Social Security—MITESS.
Nube, T. (2013). Impactos socioeconómicos das plantações florestais em Moçambique: Um estudo de caso na Província do Niassa. *Universidade Federal do Paraná*.
O'Laughlin, B. (2001). Proletarianisation, agency and changing rural livelihoods: Forced labour and resistance in colonial Mozambique. *Journal of Southern African Studies, 28*(3), 511–530. https://doi.org/10.1080/03057070220000006495.
O'Laughlin, B. (2013). Land, labour and the production of affliction in rural southern Africa: Land, labour and the production of affliction. *Journal of Agrarian Change, 13*(1), 175–196. https://doi.org/10.1111/j.1471-0366.2012.00381.x.
O'Laughlin, B., & Wuyts, M. (2012). The Agrarian question then and now. Apresentado na III Conferência Internacional do IESE: Moçambique: Acumulação e Transformação em Contexto de Crise Internacional, Maputo: Institute for Social and Economic Studies (IESE).
O'Laughlin, B. (2016). Produtividade Agrícola, Planeamento e Cultura de Trabalho em Moçambique. In *Desafios para Moçambique 2016* (pp. 225–253). Maputo: Institute for Social and Economic Studies (IESE).
Osabuohien, E., Efobi, U. R., Herrmann, R., & Gitau, C. M. (2019). Female labor outcomes and large-scale agricultural land investments: Macro–micro evidence from Tanzania. *Land Use Policy, 82,* 716–728.
Oya, C. (2010). *Rural labour markets in Africa: The unreported source of inequality and poverty*. London: Centre for Development Policy and Research.

Oya, C., Cramer, C., & Sender, J. (2009). Discrection and heterogeneity in Mozambican rural labor markets. In L. de Brito, C. N. Castel-Branco, S. Chichava, & A. Francisco (Eds.), *Reflecting on economic questions* (pp. 50–71). Maputo: Institute for Social and Economic Studies (IESE).

Oya, C., Cramer, C., & Sender, J. (2017). Discrição e heterogeneidade nos mercados de trabalho rurais em Moçambique. In R. Ali, C. N. Castel-Branco, & C. Muianga (Eds.), *Emprego e transformação económica e social em Moçambique* (pp. 89–112). Maputo: IESE.

República de Moçambique. (2007, August 1). *Lei nº 23/007*. Maputo: Boletim da República. Imprensa Nacional de Moçambique.

Sender, J., Oya, C., & Cramer, C. (2007). Lifting the blinkers: A new view of power, diversity and poverty in Mozambican rural labour markets. In *Conference Paper n. 36*. Maputo: IESE.

Standing, G., Sender, J., & Weeks, J. (1996). *Restructuring the labour market: The South African challenge: An ILO country review*. Geneva: ILO.

World Bank. (2019). *World development report 2019: The changing nature of work*. World Development Report.

Wuyts, M. (2011). *Does economic growth always reduce poverty? Reflections on the mozambican experience*. Maputo: IESE.

Boosting Non-oil Export Revenue in Nigeria Through Non-traditional Agricultural Export Commodities: How Feasible?

Grace O. Evbuomwan, Felicia O. Olokoyo, Tolulope Adesina, and Lawrence U. Okoye

1 Introduction

The consensus in literature is that increased agricultural productivity is a vital pre-requisite for rapid economic growth and development (Adubi 1996; Evbuomwan 2004; Anyanwu et al. 2010). Economic development is a process whereby an economy's real national income increases over a long period of time. Among the roles conventionally ascribed to the agricultural sector in a growing economy are those of: (i) providing adequate food for an increasing population; (ii) supplying raw materials to a growing industrial sector; (iii) constituting the major source of employment; (iv) earning foreign exchange through commodity export; and (v) providing a market for the products of the industrial sector (Federal Ministry of Agriculture Water Resources and Rural Development 1988).

G. O. Evbuomwan (✉)
Department of Accounting and Finance, Augustine University, Epe, Nigeria

F. O. Olokoyo · T. Adesina · L. U. Okoye
Department of Banking and Finance, Covenant University, Ota, Nigeria
e-mail: felicia.olokoyo@covenantuniversity.edu.ng

T. Adesina
e-mail: tolulope.oladeji@covenantuniversity.edu.ng

L. U. Okoye
e-mail: lawrence.okoye@covenantuniversity.edu.ng

In Nigeria, agriculture has traditionally been described as the mainstay of the economy. Nigeria's agriculture is diverse, presenting various opportunities. It includes four sub-sectors, namely; crop, livestock, fishery, and forestry. The crop sub-sector is the largest. Available statistics from the National Bureau of Statistics (NBS), revealed that the crop sub-sector accounted for 21.93% of the real national gross domestic products (GDP) in 2016. The livestock sub-sector followed with 1.74% and the fishery sub-sector contributed 0.52%. The forestry sub-sector contributed the least at 0.25%. Thus, these four sub-sectors of the agricultural sector together contributed a total of 24.44% to total real GDP in Nigeria in 2016 as against the 21.96% contribution by the industrial sector and the services sector's contribution of 53.59% (NBS 2017). Interestingly also, the quarterly real GDP growth rate by sector year on year as reported by the NBS revealed that the Nigerian agricultural sector grew by 4.11% in 2016 relative to 2015, whereas; the industrial sector and the services sector declined by 8.85 and 0.82%, respectively, in the spate of recession.

The Nigerian economy can be more clearly understood when classified into oil and non-oil sectors. Available statistics indicated that crude oil exports fetched Nigeria only N8.8 million (about US$17.6 million) at independence in 1960 and this constituted just 2.7% of total export earnings, while non-oil exports amounted to N321.2 million (about US$642.4 million), constituting 97.3% of total exports in the same period. But by 1976, the table turned, and the value of oil exports increased astronomically to N6321.6 million (about US$12,643.2 million), constituting 93.6% of total exports, while the proportion of non-oil exports in Nigeria's foreign earnings had declined substantially to 6.4% at N429.5 million (about US$859.0 million) (Evbuomwan 1996). This was a result of the neglect of the other sectors of the economy including agriculture after the discovery of oil in commercial quantities in the early 1970s in Nigeria.

Even though oil exports constitute a substantial proportion of Nigeria's export earnings, its importance in the GDP is lower than that of the non-oil sector as indicated earlier. Particularly worrisome is the fact that its fortunes have been on the downward trend in recent years with dire consequences for the Nigerian economy. For instance, from an average of US$ 113.77 a barrel in 2011, the price of Bonny Light crude declined to US$53.07 per barrel in 2015. Also, the average price of Forcados crude declined from US$114.52 to US$47.40 in the respective periods. Consequently, Nigeria's goods account in the Balance of Payments (BOP), declined persistently from 8.5% in 2012 to a negative 1.3% in 2015 (CBN 2015). Similarly, the current account balance as a percent of GDP declined to minus 3.79% in 2015 from 4.34% in 2012 while the overall balance as a percent of GDP declined to minus 1.44% from 2.78% in the respective periods.

It is also pertinent to note that, the bulk of the Nigerian population earn their living from the non-oil sector with the agricultural sector alone providing employment for over 50.0% of the populace (NBS 2018), while agricultural produce and semi-processed agricultural commodities have constituted over 70% of non-oil export earnings over the years (Evbuomwan 2016). It is against this backdrop that the feasibility of boosting non-oil revenue through non-traditional agricultural export commodities is being thought of since; Nigeria is endowed with large agricultural land. In this study, an attempt was made to properly situate the contributions of both the traditional and non-traditional agricultural export commodities to the non-oil export sector and highlight the problems that have been militating against their effective performance so that adequate steps can be taken to eradicate them in order to boost their contribution to non-oil export revenue in Nigeria and the development of the Nigerian economy in general. Both descriptive and econometric procedures are employed to achieve this objective. The analysis covered years 2001 to 2015, being the period consistent data were available for both traditional and non-traditional agricultural export commodities.

The rest of this chapter is divided into four sections including this introductory section. The next section titled Literature Review provides some theoretical and conceptual background to the paper. It also highlights the United Nations Industrial Development Organizations report on world agro-industrial imports from Africa as a basis for subsequent analysis carried out in this paper. The third section reviews in detail the performance of the traditional and non-traditional agricultural export commodities in Nigeria. The chapter concludes and put forward suggestions necessary for better performance of the agricultural export commodities in boosting Nigeria's non-oil revenue to assure economic growth and development in the last section.

2 Literature Review

2.1 *Theoretical and Conceptual Issues on Balance of Payments and Trade Policy Reforms*

2.1.1 *Balance of Payments*

A country's balance of payments (BOP) as elucidated by (Ogiogio 1996; Rudiger et al. 2001; Englama et al. 2010) is a financial account of all the external transactions which pass through its official channels of international trade and payments. These transactions occur between the domestic economy and the rest of the world. The BOP has basically two main accounts, namely, the current account (which summarizes the state of the trade flows and unrequited transfers) and the capital account (which presents the position of capital flows). The sum of the balances of both accounts yields three possible positions for the overall BOP. These are a balance (equilibrium state), a surplus and a deficit. When a surplus or deficit occurs, it is then financed through the reserves account. A surplus will require a country to invest its reserves wisely in the international financial market to earn investment incomes. It can also be used to accelerate real investment in the domestic economy to promote growth and raise the standard of living. A consistent BOP surplus improves a country's credit-worthiness rating in the international community and thus, its credibility in international trade and payments.

A BOP deficit, on the other hand, must be addressed by drawing down the reserves of foreign exchange, special drawing rights, gold and other assets acceptable for international payments. A deficit indicates that a country invests more than it saves, consumes more than it produces, and/or exports more capital than it receives. Chronic deficits are an indication of an unhealthy domestic economy and/or growing unfavorable nature of the international economic environment. Such deficits, when they become persistent, erode a country's credit-wordiness and thus, its credibility in trade and payments. Both surplus and deficit positions in the BOP are of considerable concern to macroeconomic policy management. A surplus, if not properly managed, could lead to significant appreciation in the nominal and real exchange rates thereby creating a trade bias against exports while protecting imports. This erodes competitiveness and the level of tariff protection for domestic industries and could possibly create forces that can turn a surplus into deficit in the BOP (Ogiogio 1996; Rudiger et al. 2001; Englama et al. 2010; Akinyemi et al. 2019). A deficit is already a precarious position, which requires adjustments in macroeconomic policies and incentive structures in order to secure a change or switch in expenditure pattern.

2.1.2 Trade Policy Reforms

A country's trade policy refers to the set of measures that direct the flow of its external trade (Ogiogio 1996). These include tariffs and non-tariff control measures (e.g. import licenses, import approvals, import, and export bans). Trade policy works effectively to protect the BOP position when a country has an appropriate exchange rate policy. For instance, high tariffs which are meant to protect import-competing industries and relieve pressure on the BOP could be severely undermined if there is substantial exchange rate appreciation arising from increased (unsterilized) capital inflow or the fixing of an exchange rate below the equilibrium level. In order words, a country whose BOP position is protected under a high tariff wall could suffer severe deficit if its exchange rate is grossly overvalued. The impact of trade policy is conceptually straightforward. Under any set of trade policies, the economy has a set of relative prices and profitability from various activities. These prices act as incentives to determine the structure of production and consumption of goods, which in turn determines the amount and composition of imports and exports. New trade policies therefore change relative prices, either implicitly or explicitly, and these affect production and consumption decisions. Trade reform policies must contribute to an increase in exports; both for growth and for BOP support. An overvalued currency is a primary obstacle to exports, while exchange rate reform is a major part of the cure (Osabuohien et al. 2019; Beecroft et al. 2020).

The National Bureau of Statistics (NBS), the Central bank of Nigeria (CBN), the Federal Ministry of Agriculture and Rural Development (FMA&RD) and the Federal Ministry of Trade and Investment (FMT&I), in 2013, carried out a collaborative survey on the following exportable commodities in Nigeria; cashew, cocoa, cotton, coffee, palm oil, rubber, kola nut, tea, sugarcane, gum arabic, shea nut, ginger, garlic, and sesame seed. The survey brought to the fore some stylized facts that are of particular interest to this study. Among them is the fact that less than 1% of the respondents have access to formal credit, only 14.01% planted improved seeds, 39.4% used fertilizers, and 41.68% used pesticides. Furthermore, majority of the farmers 72.08% rely on hoe and cutlass, over 80% use traditional processing and preservation methods and less than a quarter of them use trucks/pick up vans to transport their commodities. All these have implication for productivity and output of these farmers and subsequently on their income and welfare and finally on the country's gross domestic products and trade volumes as well as balance of payments.

2.2 Agro-Industrial Imports from Africa

According to the United Nations Industrial Development Organization (UNIDO), world agro-industrial imports from Africa are still dominated by unprocessed and horticultural commodities, in sharp contrast with the commodity composition of global agro-industrial exports, which has shifted toward processed and semi-processed commodities. An examination of the Trade Performance Index—a sectoral benchmarking tool of export performance and competition developed by the International Trade Centre (ITC)—for African countries and the products considered in the UNIDO (2011) report, shows that the inability of many African countries to tap into the most dynamic market segments of the global agro-industrial products trade is partly due to lack of competitiveness and partly as a result of inability to adapt export supply to changes in world demand (UNIDO 2011).

3   Performance of the Traditional and Non-traditional Agricultural Export Commodities in Nigeria's Non-oil Revenue

3.1 Oil and Non-oil Exports in Nigeria (2001–2015)

Available data from the Central Bank of Nigeria (CBN 2001–2015), indicated that total export revenue in Nigeria was N1867.95 billion (US$16.69 billion) in 2001 out of which oil export revenue constituted 98.50%, while non-oil export revenue constituted the balance of 1.50%. Oil export earnings declined by 10.06% from N1839.95 billion (US$16.44 billion) in 2001 to N1654.92 (US$13.68 billion) in 2002, thereby constituting 94.57% of total export revenue, while, non-oil exports took a quantum leap of 238.38% from N28.01 billion (US$0.25 billion) in 2001 to N94.78 billion (US$0.78 billion) in 2002, and its proportion of total export revenue increased to 5.43%. However, from 2003, oil export revenue assumed an upward trend until 2009 when it declined again. It picked up in 2010 and 2011, but since 2012 it has assumed a downward trend until 2015 when it constituted 92.49% of total export revenue. Non-oil export revenue on the other hand has been on the increase since 2001 and reached a peak of N1130.23 billion (US$7.18 billion) in 2013 when it constituted 7.41% of total export revenue. Though it has assumed a downward trend since 2014, it still constituted 7.51% of total export revenue in 2015 (see Figs. 1 and 2).

3.2   Non-oil Exports in Nigeria by Products

What constitutes non-oil exports in Nigeria are; agricultural produce, minerals, semi-manufactured products, manufactured products, and others. As contained in the CBN Annual Report, 2015:

- Agricultural Produce captured were; cashew nuts, cocoa beans, coffee, cotton, cow horn/bones, fish and crustaceans, ginger, groundnuts, gum Arabic, rubber, sesame seeds, and other agricultural products;

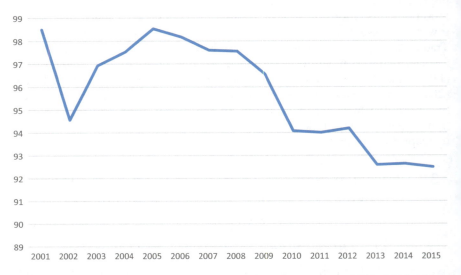

Fig. 1 Oil export revenue as percent of total export revenue, 2001–2015 (*Source* Central Bank of Nigerian annual report and statement of accounts, various issues)

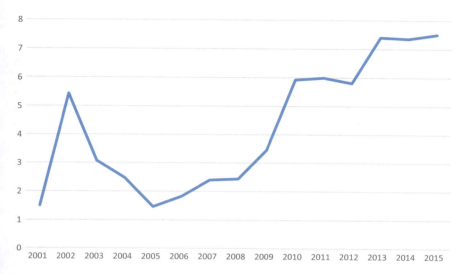

Fig. 2 Non-oil export revenue as percent of total export revenue, 2001–2015 (*Source* Central Bank of Nigerian annual report and statement of accounts, various issues)

- Minerals include; copper, lead, manganese, quartz, zinc, zirconium, and other minerals;
- Semi-manufactured are; aluminum, cocoa products, copper, cotton products, furniture/processed wood, lead, leather and processed skins, palm products, poly products, steel/iron, textured yarn/polyester, tin wheat bran pellets, zinc, and other semi-manufactured products;
- Manufactured products are; aluminum products, asbestos products, beer/beverages, carpet/rug, copper, confectionary, electrical, empty bottles, furniture, glass, insecticide, milk products, paper products, pharmaceuticals, plastic, plastic footwear, soap and detergents, steel/iron products, textiles, tobacco, vehicles, and other manufactured products; and
- Other exports comprise; cement/lime products, charcoal, fertilizer, petroleum products, urea, used/re-exported machinery, electricity, and other products.

Between 2004 and 2015 for which data was available, revenue from agricultural produce contributed 44.09% to total non-oil export revenue, followed by semi-manufactured which contributed 34.07%. Manufactured products contributed 11.95% while minerals contributed 3.16% to total non-oil export revenue in the period under review. The balance of about 6.7% was contributed by other exports (CBN 2015). Further analysis revealed that agricultural produce and semi-manufactured agricultural products alone contributed to the bulk of non-oil revenue in Nigeria between 2004 and 2015. The proportions ranged from 77.97% in 2004 to 59.4% in 2013 (CBN 2015).

3.3 Agricultural Produce Exports in Nigeria by Commodities

The main agricultural produce exported from Nigeria include; cashew nuts, cocoa beans, coffee, cotton, cow horn/bones, fish and crustaceans, ginger, groundnuts, gum Arabic, rubber, sesame seeds, and other agricultural products. However, cocoa, rubber, cotton, and groundnuts can be referred to as the traditional agricultural exports as they had featured in Nigeria's non-oil export account prior to Nigeria's independence in 1960, while crops such as cashew nuts, ginger, gum Arabic, and sesame seed are new entrants as they started featuring from late 1990s and early 2000s, and as such are referred to in this paper as non-traditional agricultural produce (Central Bank of Nigeria Annual Report and Statement of Accounts, 1981–2015, and Evbuomwan 1996).

Analysis of available data from various issues of CBN Annual Reports indicated that cocoa, which is a traditional agricultural export produce contributed most to total agricultural produce earnings in Nigeria between 2004 and 2015 (46.04%). Sesame seed which is a non-traditional agricultural export produce followed with 23.84% contribution to total agricultural produce export earnings. Contributions of other non-traditional agricultural produce such as cashew nuts (5.56%), fish and crustaceans (4.60%) and gum Arabic (2.12%) were more than the traditional ones like coffee (0.001%), groundnuts (0.16%), and cotton (4.20%).

3.4 Econometric Analysis

Taking a cue from the theoretical and conceptual framework on responses of agricultural export commodities production to their producer prices, exchange rate, interest rate and inflation rate, least square regression analysis was carried out with the available data for Nigeria's traditional and non-traditional agricultural export commodities.

The producer prices determine the income of the farmer while the exchange rate determine the competitiveness of the agricultural commodities in the world market (Adubi 1996; Evbuomwan 1996).

3.4.1 Model Specification

The model specified in its implicit form is as follows:

$$Y_t = f(INT_t, INF_t, EXR_t, PY_t) \tag{1}$$

Where Y_t represents the output of the selected agricultural crops in Nigeria, INT_t represents the interest rate, INF_t is the inflation rate, EXR_t is the exchange rate, and PY_t represents the prices of the selected cash crops. The *apriori* expectation is that the producer price and exchange rate will exact positive influences on agricultural output being incentives to farmers, while interest rate and inflation rate will exact negative influences on agricultural output in view of their cost implications.

Assuming that a non-linear relationship between the dependent variable and the independent variables, the model is expressed in the explicit form as:

$$Y_t = A INT_t^{\alpha 1} INF_t^{\alpha 2} EXR_t^{\alpha 3} PY_t^{\alpha 4} \mu_t \qquad (2)$$

In order to carry out the various estimation tests, the model is linearized by taking the double log of both sides which is represented as:

$$\text{Ln}Y_t = \alpha_0 + \alpha_1 \text{Ln}INT_t + \alpha_2 \text{Ln}INF_t + \alpha_3 \text{Ln}EXR_t + \alpha_3 \text{Ln}PY_t + \mu_t \qquad (3)$$

Where $\text{Ln}Y_t$ is the logarithm function of the output of the selected agricultural crops in Nigeria, $\text{Ln}INT_t$ is the logarithm function of interest rate, $\text{Ln}INF_t$ is the logarithm function of inflation rate, $\text{Ln}EXR_t$ is the logarithm function of exchange rate and $\text{Ln}PY_t$ represents the logarithmic function of prices of the selected cash crops. The inflation rate is the 12-month average change in prices for all items year on year, while the prices of the selected cash crops is their annual average price in Naira per ton.

Equation (3) is restarted for the panel estimation as:

$$\text{Ln}Y_{it} = \alpha_i + \delta_t + \alpha_2 \text{Ln}INT_{it} + \alpha_3 \text{Ln}INF_{it} + \alpha_4 \text{Ln}EXR_{it} + \alpha_4 \text{Ln}PY_{it} + \mu_{it} \qquad (4)$$

Where i denotes country and t denotes time, α_i represents the country-specific effects, δ_t is the deterministic time trend and μ_{it} is the estimated residual.

Toward estimating the model in panel data approach, the Hausman test is used to determine whether the fixed effects or random effects regression result is much more appropriate. The fixed effects treat both α_i and δ_t as regression equation parameters, whereas random-effects treat them as components of the error term.

3.4.2 Presentation of Econometric Results

Fixed Effect Regression Results

In Table 1, the coefficients of all the independent variables for cocoa were appropriately signed and an adjusted R-squared of 0.9210 was obtained, indicating that more than 92% of the variation in the dependent variable (cocoa output) was explained by the independent variables (cocoa producer price, exchange rate, interest rate, and inflation rate). The exchange rate coefficient was positive as expected (0.9778) and significant at 1% level, while the interest and inflation rates coefficients (−0.5883) and (−0.1398), respectively, were negative as expected and significant at 5% levels, respectively. The producer price coefficient was positive (0.1311) as expected and significant at the 10% level.

Also, for rubber, all the variables as shown in Table 1 met a priori expectations and the adjusted R-squared was 0.8937 indicating that over 89% of the variation in the production of rubber was explained by the independent

Table 1 Fixed effect results by commodity

Variable	Cocoa	Rubber	Groundnut	Cotton	Sesame	Ginger	Cashew
LnPY	0.1311[c]	0.1051	0.0099	−0.0111	0.0268	0.1809[a]	0.0013
	(0.098)	(0.527)	(0.776)	(0.816)	(0.765)	(0.003)	(0.978)
LnEXR	0.9778[a]	1.0958[a]	−0.1106	1.0288[a]	1.2066[a]	0.7030[a]	1.3068[a]
	(0.003)	(0.000)	(0.170)	(000)	(0.003)	(0.001)	(0.000)
LnINF	−0.1398[b]	−0.1025	−0.7675[a]	−0.1162	−0.1068	−0.0515	−0.1137
	(0.067)	(0.203)	(0.004)	(0.152)	(0.242)	(0.295)	(0.187)
LnINT	−0.5883[b]	−0.7399[a]	1.0714[a]	−0.7046[a]	−0.8107[a]	−0.4391[a]	−0.7791[a]
	(0.019)	(0.006)	(0.000)	(0.006)	(0.006)	(0.013)	(0.005)
C	1.1263	1.3927	5.4178[a]	3.8722[a]	1.2932	0.3736	−0.7392
	(0.315)	(0.488)	(0.000)	(0.006)	(0.329)	(0.608)	(0.559)
R-squared	0.9436	0.9241	0.9167	0.9051	0.9177	0.9721	0.92,340
Adjusted R-squared	0.9210	0.8937	0.8834	0.8672	0.8849	0.9610	0.8936
F-statistics	41.8166[a]	30.4190[a]	27.5118[a]	23.8489[a]	27.905[a]	87.2041[a]	30.3865[a]
	(0.000)	(0.000)	(0.000)	(0.000)	(0.000)	(0.000)	(0.000)
Durbin Watson	1.7060	1.4436	1.6433	1.5475	1.3132	1.9624	1.5277

Note Probability values are in bracket; [a], [b], [c] represents significant at 1, 5, and 10%, respectively
Source Authors' computation

variables in the equation. The exchange rate coefficient was positive (1.0958) and significant at 1% as well as the interest rate coefficient at −0.7399. The inflation rate coefficient at −0.1025 was appropriately signed and significant at the 10% level. The producer price coefficient though appropriately signed was however not significant.

All the independent variables for groundnut carried the appropriate signs and the Adjusted R-squared was 0.8833 which means over 88% of the variation in the output of groundnut was explained by the independent variables that entered the equation. The exchange rate and interest rate coefficients were appropriately signed and very significant, the inflation rate coefficient was also appropriately signed and partially significant, but the producer price coefficient through correctly signed was not significant as can be seen in Table 1.

The adjusted R-squared for cotton was 0.8672, indicating that over 86% of the variations in the output of cotton was explained by the independent variables in the equation. The exchange rate and interest rate coefficients (1.0288 and −0.7046) were appropriately signed and significant at 1%. The inflation rate coefficient was correctly signed (−0.1162) and significant at 10%, while the producer price of cotton coefficient was negative but not significant.

Similarly, all the variable for sesame seed met a priori expectations and the adjusted R-squared was 0.8849 indicating that over 88% of the variations in the output of sesame seed was explained by the independent variables in the equation. The exchange rate coefficient was 1.2066 and significant at 1% level, interest rate coefficient was −0.8107 and was also significant at 1% level. Both the inflation rate coefficient at −0.1068 and producer price for sesame seed coefficient at 0.0268 though correctly signed were; however, not very significant.

All the independent variables for ginger also met a priori expectations and the adjusted R-squared was very high at 0.9610, which means that over 96% of the variations in the output of ginger was explained by the independent variables. The exchange rate, producer price and interest rate coefficients (0.7030, 0.1809, and −0.4391) were correctly signed and very at 1%. The inflation rate coefficient (−0.0515) was correctly signed but not significant.

Finally, for cashew nuts, the independent variables carried the expected signs and the adjusted R-squared was 0.8936, which means over 89% of the variations in the output of cashew nuts was explained by the independent variables in the equation. The exchange rate coefficient and the interest rate coefficients (1.3068 and −0.7791) were correctly signed and significant at 1%, while the inflation rate coefficient was correctly signed (−0.1137) but not significant. The producer price coefficient (0.0013) though positive was not also significant.

Table 2 Random-effects regression result

Variable	Coefficient	Standard error	T-statistics	Probability
LnPY	0.0488439	0.0164774	2.96	0.003
LnEXR	1.129334	0.0640493	17.63	0.000
LnINF	−0.1056888	0.0215913	−4.89	0.000
LnINT	−0.756511	0.0604549	−12.51	0.000
C	1.548245	0.6824575	2.27	0.000
R-squared	0.0165			
Wald Chi2	1579.04			
Prob (Chi2)	0.0000			
Hausman Test (Prob)	1.0000			
Breusch–Pagan LM test (Prob)	0.0000			

The Random Effect Regression Result

The null hypothesis of the Hausman test is that the random-effects model is preferred as against the alternative that the fixed effects model is preferred. From Table 2, the Hausman test probability value is greater than 0.05 indicating that it is not significant, therefore, we accept the null hypothesis that the random effect model is preferred. The Breusch–Pagan Lagrange Multiplier test is then used to ascertain whether the random effects regression is appropriate or the simple OLS regression. The probability value is 0.000; therefore, we can conclude that the random effect regression is more appropriate for the study. In terms of the regression result, the coefficient value of prices of the selected crops is less than one indicating an inelastic relationship. Therefore, a 1% increase in prices of selected cash crops in Nigeria will induce about 0.0488 percentage increase in output of the cash crops. Furthermore, the result is statistically significant at the 5% level. This finding follows the theoretical underpinnings of the supply theory, such that an increase in price will lead to an increase in the quantity of goods produced.

Exchange rate also has a positive, but elastic relationship with output of cash crops in Nigeria. This is consistent with the study of Adesoji and Sotubo (2013) though contrary to the findings of Eyo (2008) that found a negative relationship between exchange rate and agricultural production. In particular, the coefficient value is 1.129 reflecting that a percentage increase in the exchange rate will induce about 1.129 percentage increase in output of selected cash crops. This suggests that the devaluation of the Naira has a positive impact on output of cash crops in the economy as exports become relatively cheaper in the international market for these commodities. In addition to this, the result is statistically significant at the level of 1%.

As expected, inflation rate and the interest rate both have a negative, inelastic relationship and statistically significant relationship with output of cash crops in Nigeria. A percentage increase in the inflation rate leads to a 0.1056 percentage decrease in the output of cash crops in Nigeria. This supports the position of the Phillips curve in which an inverse relationship is expected to exist between output and the inflation rate. The negative relationship between inflation rate and output of cash crop is in line with the empirical work of Eyo (2008). This finding is also not surprising as an increase in the inflation rate indicates that the general price level of goods and services are increasing. In Nigeria, this is usually reflected in transportation costs. This has a negative impact on farmers that have to move these commodities to the local market across states. The interest rate result is not surprising as interest rate is the cost of borrowing; therefore, as the cost of borrowing increases, farmers have less access to funds which could slow down farming activities, hence output of commodities produced. The negative inelastic relationship between output of cash crops and interest rate is also consistent with findings of Othuon and Oyugi (2017) for the Kenyan economy.

4 Conclusion

Concerned with the persistent decline in the export price of crude oil in recent years, and its impact on the Nigerian economy, this chapter examined the performance of both the traditional and non-traditional agricultural export commodities against the backdrop of the resilience of the agricultural sector. As a result of the decline in crude oil prices, Nigeria's goods account in the Balance of Payments (BOP), declined persistently from 8.5% in 2012 to a negative 1.3% in 2015 (Central Bank of Nigeria—CBN 2015). Similarly, the current account balance as a percent of gross domestic products (GDP) declined to minus 3.79% in 2015 from 4.34% in 2012 while the overall balance as a percent of GDP declined to minus 1.44% from 2.78% in the respective periods. Thus, the literature review covered theoretical and conceptual issues in balance of payments and trade policy reforms.

From theory, it is inferred that trade policy works effectively to protect the BOP position when a country has an appropriate exchange rate policy, and for non-traditional exports, a major policy change which can provide a boost is the depreciation of the real exchange rate. Hence, the study employed both descriptive and econometric procedures to analyze the available data obtained from the Central Bank of Nigeria and the National Bureau of Statistics on both the traditional and non-traditional agricultural export commodities which have been the major source of non-oil export earnings in Nigeria.

Available data indicated that, some traditional agricultural export commodities like cocoa and rubber have remained on the export list, while others like groundnut and coffee have almost disappeared from the export list. In the same vein, non-traditional agricultural export commodities like sesame seed and cashew nuts have started featuring prominently on the export list. In line with theory, the econometric analysis carried out confirmed that a major policy change which can provide a boost for agricultural exports is the depreciation of the real exchange rate. For all the agricultural export commodities analyzed in the study, the coefficient of the exchange rate was positive and highly significant. Similarly, the coefficient of the interest rate was negative and very significant for all the commodities, confirming the fact that high interest rate prevalent in the country discourages agricultural production. The results obtained in the study also, confirmed that the inflation rate was affecting agricultural production negatively, though not as significant as the interest rate.

The study therefore recommends that government should evolve policies that are targeted at depreciation of the real exchange rate so that production of agricultural export commodities can remain attractive thereby promoting economic development. Furthermore, the constraints limiting agricultural productivity in Nigeria as gleaned from the report of the survey conducted by the NBS, the CBN, the FMA&RD, and the FMT&I should be addressed by all stakeholders (see the details in the last paragraph of Sect. 2.1.2). Finally, more emphasis should now be placed on export of processed and semi-processed agricultural export commodities as pointed out by UNIDO for African countries, in order to maximize returns in Nigeria.

References

Adesoji, A. A., & Sotubo, O. D. (2013). Non-oil exports in the economic growth of Nigeria: A study of agricultural and mineral resources. *Journal of Educational and Social Research, 3*(2), 403–418.

Adubi, A. A. (1996). The design and management of sectoral policies in Nigeria: Agriculture and economic reform programme. In M. I. Obadan & M. A. Iyoha (Eds.), *Macroeconomic policy analysis: Tools, techniques and applications to Nigeria* (pp. 361–385). Ibadan: National Centre for Economic Management.

Anyanwu, C. M., Ukeje, E. O., Amoo, B. A. G., Igwe, N. N., & Eluemunor, C. A. (2010). The agricultural sector. In C. N. O. Mordi, A. Englama, & B. S. Adebusuyi (Eds.), *The changing structure of the Nigerian economy* (pp. 109–178). Abuja, Nigeria: Published by the Central Bank of Nigeria.

Akinyemi, O., Efobi, U., Asongu, S., & Osabuohien, E. (2019). Renewable energy, trade performance and the conditional role of finance and institutional capacity in sub-Sahara African countries. *Energy Policy, 132*, 490–498. https://doi.org/10.1016/j.enpol.2019.06.012.

Beecroft, I., Osabuohien, E., Efobi, U., Olurinola, I., & Osabohien, R. (2020). Manufacturing export and ICT infrastructure in West Africa: Investigating the roles of economic and political institutions. *Institutions and Economies, 12*(1), 1–37.

Central Bank of Nigeria. (2001–2015). *Annual report and statement of accounts*, Various Issues, 2001–2015.

Central Bank of Nigeria. (2015). *Annual report and statement of accounts for 2015*. Abuja, Nigeria.

Englama, A., Oputa, N. C., Duke, O. O., Sanni, G. K., Yakub, M. U., & Ogunleye, T. S. (2010). The external sector. In C. N. O. Mordi, A. Englama, & B. S. Adebusuyi (Eds.), *The changing structure of the Nigerian economy* (pp. 535–577). Abuja: Central Bank of Nigeria.

Evbuomwan, G. O. (1996). Strategies for revitalizing the export crop sub-sector of the Nigerian agricultural economy. In *Selected Papers of the 1996 Annual Conference*. Ibadan, Nigeria: The Nigerian Economic Society.

Evbuomwan, G. O. (2004). Financing agri-business in Nigeria: Challenges and prospects. In P. B. Okuneye & G. O. Evbuomwan (Eds.), *Proceedings of the 7th African Farm Management Association (AFMA), Conference, Abuja* (pp. 272–297). Ibadan: Daily Graphics Nig. Ltd.

Evbuomwan, G. O. (2016). Diversification of the Nigerian economy: Agriculture and solid minerals as panacea. *Bullion, 40th Anniversary, 1976–2016, 1*(40), 50–62.

Eyo, E. O. (2008). Macroeconomic environment and agricultural sector growth in Nigeria. *World Journal of Agricultural Sciences, 4*(6), 781–786.

Federal Ministry of Agriculture Water Resources and Rural Development. (1988). *Agricultural policy for Nigeria: Strategies for implementation*. Lagos, Nigeria.

National Bureau of Statistics. (2017, May). *Nigeria's gross domestic product, 1st Quarter, 2017*. Abuja, Nigeria.

National Bureau of Statistics. (2018, February). *Nigeria's labour force statistics*. Abuja, Nigeria.

National Bureau of Statistics, Central Bank of Nigeria, Federal Ministry of Agriculture and Rural Development, & Federal Ministry of Trade and Investment. (2013, May). *National survey on agricultural exportable commodities*. Abuja, Nigeria.

Ogiogio, G. O. (1996). Exchange rate policy, trade policy reform and the balance of payments. In M. I. Obadan & M. A. Iyoha (Eds.), *Macroeconomic policy analysis: Tools, techniques and applications to Nigeria* (pp. 103–135). National Centre for Economic Management: Ibadan.

Othuon, V. O., & Oyugi, M. A. (2017). The impact of key macroeconomic variables on agricultural infrastructure investment and output in Kenya. *Journal of Economics and Sustainable Development, 8*(22), 188–191.

Osabuohien, E., Efobi, U., Odebiyi, J., Fayomi, F., & Salami, A. (2019). Bilateral trade performance in West Africa: Gravity model estimation. *African Development Review, 31*(1), 1–14. https://doi.org/10.1111/1467-8268.12359.

Rudiger, D., Stanley, F., & Richard, S. (2001). *Macroeconomics* (8th ed.). New York: McGraw Hill/Irwin.

United Nations Industrial Development Organization. (2011). *Agribusiness for Africa's prosperity* (Kandeh K. Yumkella, Patrick M. Kormawa, Torben M. Roepstorff, & Anthony M. Hawkins, Eds.). UNIDO.

Conclusion: Agricultural Investments and Rural Development in Africa—Salient Issues and Imperatives

Evans S. Osabuohien and Alhassan A. Karakara

1 Introduction

Agriculture remains the sector where the majority of Africans engaged in, with over 60% of the population, especially in the rural areas has agriculture as their main source of income and livelihood. Also, large-scale agricultural land investments (LALIs) and land "transactions" in African countries raise concerns about the impacts on the households and the livelihood of smallholders in locations where they are situated. The implications of these LALIs' presence are numerous and can be far-reaching in terms of dispossession of ancestral lands, reduction in households' livelihood, displacement in household agricultural activities, (un)employment concerns arising from the loss of agricultural engagements, poverty and food security, poor compensations,

---

E. S. Osabuohien (✉)
Department of Economics and Development Studies & Chair,
Centre for Economic Policy and Development Research (CEPDeR),
Covenant University, Ota, Nigeria
e-mail: evans.osabuohien@covenantuniversity.edu.ng

Alexander von Humboldt Visiting Professor, Witten/Herdecke University, Witten, Germany

A. A. Karakara
School of Economics, University of Cape Coast, Cape Coast, Ghana

© The Author(s) 2020
E. S. Osabuohien (ed.), *The Palgrave Handbook of Agricultural and Rural Development in Africa*, https://doi.org/10.1007/978-3-030-41513-6_28

ecological and environmental issues emanating from the use of chemicals (such as herbicides, fertilizers), among others (Osabuohien 2014; Osabuohien et al. 2019).

A number of researchers have opined that LALIs, a typology of agricultural development, have a positive effect on the livelihood of the people where such LALIs are located. The implications of LALIs on water rights and livelihoods have been explored and the conclusion is that it leads to improvement in the livelihood of the people (Smaller and Mann 2009; Williams et al. 2012). Cotula et al. (2009) have acknowledged the potentials of land investments, though warned that these might not be possible if the government in the host countries did not build adequate capacities to negotiate better terms for their people and the host communities. Thus, LALIs could lead to the improvement in the livelihood of communities by encouraging the inflow of land investments (capital and resource inflow) as a veritable tool for the development of the area based on agreed terms between the investors and the landowners in the host communities (Haberl et al. 2009).

Other researchers have indicated that LALIs can jeopardize the welfare of the people living where such LALIs are located. For instance, Schoneveld et al. (2011) studied the acquisition of land used for a plantation for biofuel production in Ghana, and found the occurrence of LALIs increased rural poverty—especially affecting women and migrants—as land acquisitions were focused on customary land and, therefore, deprived the households of their livelihood resources. Similarly, Okuro (2015) noted that large-scale land acquisition might further threaten the welfare of the poor by depriving them of the "safety net" function that this type of land and water use provides. Aigbokhan and Ola (2015) further concluded that a particular LALI deal in Nigeria (that is, Presco Industries in Edo State) was not able to improve the livelihood of the people of the community where they are located as the employment provided was below expectations.

From the foregoing, there is a lack of consensus on the possible effects of LALIs on communities where they are located. While some noted positive effects, others concluded that it has rather reduced the welfare of the communities. As a key fallout from the issues articulated by many authors in this book, it can be maintained that LALIs could be better managed and help to achieve welfare if some frantic efforts are made. Such steps could result to LALIs having the development drive to achieve better livelihood for the communities where they are located. Modernizing and mechanizing the agricultural sector as well as engaging in LALIs can help in transforming agriculture, on one the hand, and the rural areas (where most of the investments take place), on the other. This is so because, with LALIs coupled with agricultural technology and improved access to agricultural finance could help in achieving high yields, improve nutrition, and employment offered by agriculture.

On the above backdrops, this concluding chapter makes an effort in summarizing the key points raised in this book. It also teases out the possible ways on how the negotiations and management of LALIs could be handled to better achieve the welfare of smallholders, create employment, among others. The rest of the chapter is organized as follows. The second section discusses the development and other issues such as employment, agricultural finance, industrialization and technology, land access and livelihood, agricultural value chain and food security and the politics of land acquisition in Africa. The last section concludes by giving policy recommendations and agenda for future research.

2 Development and Employment Issues

Employment, in terms of job offers, could lead to economic growth and development through the creation of wealth and improvement of livelihood opportunities. Little wonder the reason why many African countries have initiated plans and policies that focused on job creation with a view to enhancing the living conditions of their populace. Some examples of these efforts include: The Youth Employment Agency in Ghana; Mozambique Government Plan and Employment Policy; and the Youth Enterprise with Innovation in Nigeria (YouWin). In addition, job creation is most often one of the promises made by LALIs investors. Hence, it is not very surprising why issues relating to employment in developing countries, especially those connected to agricultural development policies in Africa have been researched into in the last decades (Headey et al. 2010; Collier and Dercon 2014). However, the quality of employment created by agricultural investments has raised much concern (Ali 2017). Some studies (Bleyer et al. 2016) looked at the socioeconomic impact of agricultural investments and concluded that positive impacts such as: increase employment, increase commercial activities, and social projects like roads, schools, health facilities, and water exist which leads to the issue of development. While others indicated that it has disadvantaged communities where they are located. Such disadvantages (and challenges) ranges from a reduction in access to land of the members of the host communities, tensions, reduction in welfare to job losses due to smallholder farmers competing with the companies (Ali 2020; Ude 2020).

The structure of the employment and work in the LALIs will determine how jobs created could lead to development. If the LALIs' productive structure is centered on the production of primary products for export, which has poorly paid workforce, mostly casuals who work under difficult conditions, such job offers might not lead to the employment-development drive that LALIs could offer. Such employment could turn out to be vulnerable employment that may "reproduce" poverty instead of reducing it. The wellbeing of the workers is not limited to having a job and remuneration, or to consumption and ownership of goods. Although important, these are just some of the determinants of the wellbeing of households. Social organization and the experience of work, the inter-connection between diverse forms of work and life, and health conditions, affect the welfare of workers and their families.

3 Development and Agricultural Finance

Agriculture is the main occupation of majority of the households in many African countries (Osabuohien 2015; Osabuohien et al. 2019; World Bank 2019). It contributed an average of 15% of gross domestic products (GDP) in 2014 in SSA (Organization for Economic Cooperation and Development/Food and Agricultural Organization—OECD/FAO 2016). However, the current form of agricultural practice in most African countries is mainly subsistence with finance and technology constituting the main constraints to the development process. Agricultural finance refers to finance which is used for crop and livestock production (Amadhila and Ikhide 2020; Montfaucon 2020; Vitoria et al. 2012). There is evidence that finance and technology in the agriculture sector could be the main boost to transforming it and increase in its performance in Africa (International Finance Corporation—IFC 2012). Better access to finance may result in higher yields, more diverse production and fewer losses and, thus, achieving development in the agricultural sector. Increased access to credit can help farmers overcome short-run liquidity challenges and potentially increase the adoption of more efficient and/or more effective agricultural technologies. George et al. (2011) suggest that farmers often need credit for working capital at the beginning of the growing season to purchase inputs and prepare the land as well as to invest in equipment such as tractors and irrigation facilities. Masawe (1994) indicated that agricultural credit is considered an important factor in stimulating agricultural production, particularly among smallholder farmers in Tanzania. By removing credit constraints, the income of farmers would improve considerably (Feder et al. 1990) leading to development.

The issue of access to agricultural finance can also be related to migrant remittance given the growing relevance of remittance in many aspects such as developmental projects in Africa (Osabuohien and Efobi 2013; Efobi et al. 2015). As the fallout from "Impact of Remittances on Agricultural Labor Productivity in Sub-Saharan Africa," Wonyra and Ametoglo (2020) indicated that remittances sent by migrants could be used to increase the land, livestock, as well as the human capital of rural household members. This is crucial as the majority of the people in Sub-Saharan Africa (SSA) are working in the primary sector, funds (remittances) sent to households, especially in rural areas, could serve as finance and stimulate the productivity of labor in the agricultural sector (McCullough 2017).

Agricultural finance could also be achieved if policies are in place that allows borrowers to use a wide range of assets as collateral, including warehouse receipts and movable property such as machinery, equipment, and receivables that remain in the hands of the debtor. Leasing also offers young farmers some relief, as it requires either no or less collateral than typically required by loans. A case in point is the Development Finance Company of Uganda (DFCU) Leasing in Uganda established in 1994, which gave more than US$4 million in farm equipment leases in 2002 for items such as rice hullers, dairy processing equipment, and maize milling equipment. Some out-grower arrangements pre-finance inputs and assure marketing channels (Nair et al. 2004). In Mozambique, Rwanda, Tanzania, and Zambia, Rabo Development (a subsidiary of Rabobank) offers management services and technical assistance to financial institutions, which, in turn, finance supply chains with a range of agricultural clients (Rabo Development 2016).

In addition to the practice of providing farmers with inputs as it is in many African countries, farmers should be afforded credit facilities that are linked to the purchase of agricultural inputs. Thus, it could be understood that improved financial inclusion for smallholder households can be achieved through the improvements in technology (Montfaucon 2020). Also, impact of remittance on agricultural labor productivity needs to be properly targeted in order to ensure that an increase in remittance inflows in SSA can result in desirable agricultural development (productivity). This is because remittances that are received by households can be often used for consumption more than for capital accumulation. Thus, the recipients could have the tendency to substitute remittances to their own income, and thereby decreasing their labor participation rate in the agricultural sector, if not properly guided (Efobi et al. 2015; Wonyra and Ametoglo 2020).

4 Development, Industrialization, and Technology

Agricultural research and technological improvements are seen as the vehicles through which agricultural productivity can be increased. Technological improvements in agriculture are therefore believed to be the most important pathway for reducing rural poverty in many agrarian economies such as those in SSA (Bourdillon et al. 2002; Kijima et al. 2006). The international agricultural research centers have recognized the importance and urgency of research to assure sustainability in agricultural intensification through appropriate management of natural resources (Consultative Group for International Agriculture Research—CGIAR 2005). Hagos et al. (2010), Abro et al. (2014) emphasize the role of investment in irrigation and or improved water management technologies in increasing the income of farmers. Information and Communication Technology (ICT), mechanical, biotechnological, and chemical innovations that help the farmer to optimize input and maximize output at the farm gate are necessary to achieve development and industrialization in Africa. Kolade et al. (2020) indicated that research into the agricultural sector could drive food security agenda in Africa through the use of technology in enhancing the value chain as well as the returns from the agricultural sector. Thus, it is noted that within agriculture, growth is driven by the exodus of less efficient labor, abetted by technical innovation, scale economies, shifts to higher value commodities (driven, in turn, by the changing demands of urbanizing populations) and improving market infrastructure and supporting services. What is vital to note is that achieving agricultural productivity growth will not be possible without developing and disseminating yield-enhancing technologies since it is no longer feasible to meet the needs of the increasing population through the expansion of cultivable area (Asfaw et al. 2012). The role of the development of the agro-allied industries in this process cannot be overemphasized (Kareem et al. 2020).

Furthermore, examining the performance of small-scale enterprise in agro-allied manufacturing firms in Nigeria, Kareem et al. (2020) brought to the fore that "socio-cultural factors" are capable of influencing small-scale agro-allied enterprise performance, and as such every small-scale business is subject to the dictates of its socio-cultural environments. Performance is strongly related and adaptable to the dominant values, norms, and belief in society. According to them, to achieve significant growth of Micro Small and Medium Enterprises (MSMEs) and make MSMEs contribute to the national economy in Nigeria, the government needs to among others address the problems of gender limitations, corruption, illiteracy, ostentatious lifestyle and religious bigotry.

5   Access to Land and Household Livelihood

LALIs could help spur good welfare outcomes in communities where they are located. LALIs activities could help smallholders in terms of knowledge spill over, employment, social amenities, and farm demonstration. Increasing the productivity of farmers is key to improving household welfare, to achieve the desired development in Africa. Improving the productivity, profitability, and sustainability of smallholder farming is, therefore, one critical pathway for improved welfare for the majority of the region's population (World Bank 2008). Kijima et al. (2006), Kassie et al. (2011) found that adoption of upland rice and modern groundnut varieties were crucial for increasing agricultural income and therefore poverty reduction among rural households in Uganda.

Focusing on LALIs and household livelihood, Osabuohien et al. (2020) underscored that on the average, the total consumption of households in communities with LALIs increased by 4.18% compared to those in communities without LALIs. And that household in communities with LALIs spends less amount of their money on consumption, as measured using the three outcome variables. In addition, on household welfare outcomes, an average household in communities with LALIs has consumption higher than their counterparts in communities without LALI and change in period has no effect on the consumption pattern of households. There is a significant improvement in the level of the households' welfare in communities with LALIs. Thus, the results of this study offer policy recommendations that will be useful in addressing the issue of LALIs. Government and policymakers should look at land rights and household access to land and offer regulations that will offer more benefits to the households and the host communities. This will help reduce rural poverty and enhance consumption by households. On the households' welfare outcomes, an average household in communities with LALIs has consumption higher than their counterparts in communities without LALIs. There is a significant improvement in the level of household welfare in communities with LALIs. Regulated land rights and household access to land could help households to enhance welfare as it could help reduce rural poverty and enhance consumption by the households. The aforementioned is germane, as it will build capacities at the host communities and thereby foster sense of belonging, which is sine qua non for sustainability.

Land access by individuals and household mostly in farming settings could help smallholders increase welfare. Land policy development is very important in a society in order to ensure a condition of orderliness and a legal framework upon which transfer, acquisition and uses will take place without certain vices and/or anti-cultural dispositions and conflicts. Akintunde (2015) argues that land should be available for those that are ready to farm and not for speculators. The literature on the direct benefits of improved agricultural technologies points to the importance of such interventions in improving the welfare outcomes of the majority population that live off agriculture in many of the developing countries. The above is best achieved when the community members have access to land that will enable them to engage in agricultural activities. Irz et al. (2001) detail the associated welfare gains from improved technology uptake such as raising incomes of especially the farm households and the indirect benefits of raising employment, wage rates and by the reduced prices of food (Asfaw et al. 2012).

6 Agricultural Value Chain and Food Security

Agricultural context Value chain can be understood to be "the sequence of interlinked agents and markets that transforms inputs and services into products with attributes that consumers are prepared to purchase" (Devaux et al. 2018). A good and efficient Agricultural value chain could lead to the drive in achieving food security. Inadequate market linkage between the producers of agricultural products and the end-users (Echono 2015) has inhibited the efforts to achieve food security and the low returns for farmers. Inefficiencies in the agricultural value chain have led to shortage of food supply in many instances. Lack of knowledge on farm practices including storage facilities, inaccessible roads, and paucity of information by farmers can jeopardize the effort to achieve food security.

The growing food demand in Africa is a major avenue for agro-processing, which can easily be developed using small and medium-sized enterprises (MSMEs). This option requires less capital, is more labor-intensive and facilitates the proliferation of units in rural boroughs and small towns, offering employment and entrepreneurial opportunities, local value-added, and new incomes. Agro-processing MSMEs can also facilitate the resolution of post-harvest problems, which are a significant issue in SSA resulting in a loss of revenue for farmers. This could help to achieve a vibrant agricultural value chain to ensure food security.

Women participation in the agricultural value chain could also salvage the situation. The high presence of women in rural marketing where agricultural products are the major items of trade showed that women could not be set-aside in production, processing, and marketing of agricultural product. Some scholars have studied the likely factors that might have limited female farmers' participation in the agricultural value chain (Ahmadu and Idisi 2014; Ejike et al. 2018). The authors concluded that the factors such as: education, farm experience, farm size, access to market, and information about the market, female extension workers, technical knowhow, family size, and availability of capital could influence agricultural value chain development. On a related note, unraveling the "Micro-determinants of Women Participation in Agricultural Value Chain," Ola (2020) using the case of Nigeria added that the distance to market and community responsibility of women constitute the major factors that influence their participation in the agricultural value chain.

Furthermore, Adeleye et al. (2020) using the case of Ogun State, established that a component of extension structure in providing technical support to women in form of training to enhance the utilization of major food crop ("priority crops" and at the same time influence their nutrition status. For instance, the women are trained in the processing of cassava into chips, floured starch and its utilization for confectioneries; yam processing into chips and flour and the tuber and flour utilization for porridge, etc.; plantain processing into flour and chips; maize processing into paste and flour, fortification and utilization as weaning diet; fortification and enhancement of carbohydrate food with soya bean among others (Ogun State Agricultural Development Program—OGADEP 2017).

7   Large-Scale Land Acquisition and Agricultural Productivity: Policy Issues

Every country of the world has various sectors through which the administrators sharpen the political, economic, and social landscape of the country. The nature of policy gives specific direction and pattern of development to such country (Daugbjerg 2018). To achieve agricultural development to a large extend dwells on a good agricultural policy that includes a policy on land acquisition. Generally, there are two courses of action that agricultural policy plan or statements will entail; to increase the number of acres under crops and to increase the yields per acre (Parisi et al. 2015; Buller et al. 2017). For instance, the policy to give priority to raising the yields per acre, some of the means will be; (*a*) adequate and regular water supply, (*b*) chemical fertilizers and farm yard manure, (*c*) better seed, (*d*) better implements, (*e*) better cultural practices, and (*f*) control of pests and diseases among others. However, from the submission of Aluko (2020) when connecting agricultural policy and food security issues, it is understandable that in achieving food sufficiency based on rolling out agricultural policies should be formulated large input from the technocrats and the research institutions are needed and a little contribution from the political actors. It was also re-echoed that agricultural policies are likely to fail in achieving food security if the composition of the policy implementers are mainly political actors who are mostly *unlearned* in the technicalities of the policy functionalities.

Land policy development is very important in a society in order to ensure a condition of orderliness and a legal framework upon which transfer, acquisition and uses will take place without certain vices and/or anti-cultural dispositions and conflicts. Land ownership in most African countries is generally accepted as the property of the family with the community as a corporate unit. Hence, land is the property of both the living, the dead and the unborn members of the families and community by virtue of its transferability from generation to generation (Kingston and Oke-Chinda 2016).

Similar to the above, Massay (2020) using the case of Tanzania, argued that there are local politics that dominate the process, which often varies between local and foreign investments in land acquisitions. For instance, land acquisitions by foreign investors are often facilitated by the State or its agencies, which at times are supported by politicians on behalf of the State. This is what Cotula (2013) described as government facilitated land rush. There were two different cases of land acquisitions narrated by the chapter. The authors indicated that the Sunbiofuel land acquisition deal that was facilitated by the politicians (the Members of Parliament—MPs and government officials from the Lands Department) turns out to be abhorred by the villagers (land owners). However, for the land acquisition by the Gagaja Industries (GI), which was facilitated by local authorities (community elders) was well received by the members of the community. Thus, in some cases, the politics of land acquisition could best be done directly with the local elders as the people will see the deal as one of their own and welcome such deal.

The two aspects of land administration that matter most to young entrants to the labor force are the need to improve the security of tenure and the need to relax controls on rental. Land redistribution will also enhance young people's access to land. In general, policies and measures that help the poor to gain access to land will also help young people. Thus, land policies must be well designed to entice young people to enter into agriculture and for landowners to benefit greatly from giving out their lands.

8   Concluding Remarks

The rural transformation and development agenda is about improving the overall quality of life in rural areas. This entails promoting investments in health, education, and rural infrastructure; having in place efficient rural financial markets; designing policies that promote greater gender equity and the empowerment of rural people, especially the most vulnerable through designing and implementing effective safety-net programs; improving market access of small-scale farmers in innovative markets and strengthen their involvement in the whole value chain. Empirical evidence already shows that the adoption of improved agricultural technologies enhances household well-being in developing countries (Abro et al. 2014; Ali and Abdulai 2010; Kassie et al. 2011). ICT in land use and monitoring to favor agricultural development would go a long way in enhancing food security.

From this volume, it is noted and argued that agricultural finance is paramount to achieving transformation and development of the African agricultural sector. Inadequacy of finance in the agricultural sector is identified as major obstacle to agricultural development. Thus, in addition to the current practice of providing farmers with inputs, farmers should be afforded credit facilities that are linked to the purchase of agricultural inputs. Also, the adoption of improved agricultural technologies as a key mechanism for enhancing agricultural income and general welfare of rural households could be strengthened to help as some form of finance to farmers.

Land management policies are also found to be a major booster for achieving development (agricultural and rural). The efficiency of any food security is a function of an effective land management system because land policy determines the frameworks for land ownership and development in any society (Kuma 2017). With better land policy, smallholders or landowners could benefit more upon giving out their land for LALIs, leading to enhancement of the welfare of the smallholders and landowners. On a final note, it is essential to underscore that there is yet no uniform model and approach with respect to the best practice of agricultural and rural development in Africa due to the fact that "one cap cannot fit all" as the related issues differ across countries and even across localities in the same countries. Also, future research could examine other issues such as the roles of agricultural extension services, agricultural research and development, climate change and the environment, which could have some interactions with agricultural and rural development.

References

Abro, A. Z., Alemu, B. A., & Hajra, A. M. (2014). Policies for agricultural productivity growth and poverty reduction in rural Ethiopia. *World Development, 59,* 461–474.

Adeleye, N., Osabuohien, E. S., Adeogun, S., Fashola, S., Tasie, O., & Adeyemi, G. (2020). Access to land and agricultural production: Analysis of 'priority crops' in Ogun state, Nigeria. In E. Osabuohien (Ed.), *The Palgrave Handbook of*

Agricultural and Rural Development in Africa. Geneva: Palgrave Macmillan. https://doi.org/10.1007/978-3-030-41513-6_14.
Ahmadu, J., & Idisi, P. O. (2014). Gendered participation in cassava value chain in Nigeria. *Merit Research Journal, 2*(11), 147–153.
Aigbokhan, B., & Ola, K. (2015). Foreign land acquisitions, households' livelihood with some evidence on Nigeria. In E. Osabuohien (Ed.), *Handbook of research on in-country determinants and implications of foreign land acquisitions* (pp. 287–305). Hershey, PA: Business Science Reference.
Akintunde, O. K. (2015). Determinants of poultry farmers' participation in livestock insurance in Southwest Nigeria. *Asian Journal of Poultry Science, 9*, 233–241.
Ali, R. (2017). Mercados de Trabalho Rurais: Porque são negligenciados nas políticas de emprego, pobreza e desenvolvimento em Moçambique? In R. Ali, C. N. Castel-Branco, & C. Muianga (Eds.), *Emprego e Transformação Económica e Social em Moçambique*. Maputo: Institute for Social and Economic Studies (IESE).
Ali, R. (2020). Job Creation and Social Conditions of Labor in the Forestry Agro-Industry in Mozambique. In E. Osabuohien (Ed.), *The Palgrave Handbook of Agricultural and Rural Development in Africa*. Geneva: Palgrave Macmillan. https://doi.org/10.1007/978-3-030-41513-6_26.
Ali, A., & Abdulai, A. (2010). The adoption of genetically modified cotton and poverty reduction in Pakistan. *Journal of Agricultural Economics, 61*, 175–192.
Aluko, O. (2020). Agricultural policy and food security in Nigeria: A rational choice analysis. In E. Osabuohien (Ed.), *The Palgrave Handbook of Agricultural and Rural Development in Africa*. Geneva: Palgrave Macmillan. https://doi.org/10.1007/978-3-030-41513-6_21.
Amadhila, E., & Ikhide, S. (2020). Identifying the gap between the demand and supply of agricultural finance among irrigation farmers in Namibia. In E. Osabuohien (Ed.), *The Palgrave Handbook of Agricultural and Rural Development in Africa*. Geneva: Palgrave Macmillan. https://doi.org/10.1007/978-3-030-41513-6_13.
Asfaw, S., Shiferaw, B., Simtowe, F., & Lipper, L. (2012). Impact of modern agricultural technologies on smallholder welfare: Evidence from Tanzania and Ethiopia. *Food Policy, 37*, 283–295.
Bleyer, M., Kniivilä, M., Horne, P., Sitoe, A., & Falcão, M. P. (2016). Socio-economic impacts of private land use investment on rural communities: Industrial forest plantations in Niassa, Mozambique. *Land Use Policy, 51*, 281–289.
Bourdillon, M., Hebinck, P., Hoddinott, J., Kinsey, B., Marondo, J., Mudege, N., et al. (2002). *Assessing the impact of HYV Maize in resettlement areas of Zimbabwe* (2002, Discussion Paper No. 161). Washington, DC: International Food Policy Research Institute.
Buller, H., Wilson, G. A., & Holl, A. (2017). *Agri-environmental policy in the European Union*. Abingdon: Routledge.
CGIAR. (2005). *Science for agric development*. Rome, Italy. Retrieved from www.cgiar.org/enews/december2005/scienceforagrdev.pdf.
Collier, P., & Dercon, S. (2014). African agriculture in 50 years: Smallholders in a rapidly changing world? *World Development, 63*, 92–101.
Cotula, L. (2013). *The great African land grab? Agricultural investments and the global food system*. London: Zed Books.
Cotula, L., Vermeulen, S., Leonard, R., & Keeley, J. (2009). *Land grab or development opportunity? Agricultural investment and international land deals in Africa*. London/Rome: IIED/FAO/IFAD.

Daugbjerg, C. (2018). *Policy networks under pressure: Pollution control, policy reform and the power of farmers*. Abingdon: Routledge.

Devaux, A., Torero, M., Donovan, J., & Horton, D. (2018). Agricultural innovation and inclusive value-chain development: A review. *Journal of Agribusiness in Developing and Emerging Economies*. Available at https://doi.org/10.1108/JADEE-06-2017-0065.

Echono, S. (2015, October 20). *Women are the cornerstone of agricultural production, processing, marketing and utilization in the country*. Address delivered by Permanent Secretary, Federal Ministry of Agriculture and Rural Development at the Launch of 'Economic empowerment of African Women through Equitable Participation in Agricultural Value Chain'. Abuja.

Efobi, U. R, Osabuohien, E. S., & Oluwatobi, S. (2015). One dollar, one bank account: Remittance and bank breadth in Nigeria. *Journal of International Migration and Integration, 16*(3), 761–781.

Ejike, R. D., Osuji, E. E., Effiong, J. A. L., & Agu, C. G. (2018). Gender dimension in agricultural food value chain development in Nigeria: The women perspective. *International Journal of Agriculture and Earth Science, 4*(3), 37–45.

Feder, G., Lau, I., Lin, J., & Luo, X. (1990). The relationship between credit and productivity in Chinese agriculture: A microeconomic model of disequilibrium. *American Journal Agricultural Economics, 72*(5), 1151–1157.

George, T., Bagazonzya, H., Ballantyne, P., Belden, C., Birner, R., Castello, R. d., et al. (2011). *ICT in agriculture: Connecting smallholders to knowledge, networks, and institutions*. The World Bank Group. Retrieved from http://documents.worldbank.org/.

Haberl, H., Erb, K.-H., Krausmann, F., Berecz, S., Ludwiczek, N., Martínez-Alier, J., et al. (2009). Using embodied HANPP to analyze teleconnections in the global land system: Conceptual considerations. *Journal of Geography, 109*(2), 119–130.

Hagos, F., Awulachew, S. B., Loulseged, M., & Yilma, A. D. (2010). *Poverty impacts of agricultural water management technologies in Ethiopia*. Addis Ababa, Ethiopia: International Water Management Institute (IWMI), East Africa and Nile Basin Office.

Headey, D., Bezemer, D., & Hazell, P. B. (2010). Agricultural employment trends in Asia and Africa: Too fast or too slow? *The World Bank Research Observer, 25*(1), 57–89.

International Finance Corporation. (2012). *Innovative agricultural SME finance models*. Retrieved from http://www.ifc.org/wps/wcm/connect/55301b804eb-c5f379f86bf45b400a808/Innovative+Agricultural+SME+Finance+Models.pdf?MOD=AJPERES.

Irz, X., Thirtle, C., Lin, L., & Wiggins, S. (2001). Agricultural productivity growth and poverty alleviation. *Development Policy Review, 19*(4), 449–466.

Kareem, K. O, Jiboye, T. F, Adejumo, O. O., & Akinyosoye, M. O. (2020). Socio-cultural factors and performance of small-scale enterprise in agro-allied manufacturing firms in Nigeria. In E. Osabuohien (Ed.), *The Palgrave Handbook of Agricultural and Rural Development in Africa*. Geneva: Palgrave Macmillan. https://doi.org/10.1007/978-3-030-41513-6_22.

Kassie, M., Shiferaw, B., & Muricho, G. (2011). Agricultural technology, crop income, and poverty alleviation in Uganda. *World Development, 39*(10), 1784–1795. https://doi.org/10.1016/j.worlddev.2011.04.023.

Kijima, Y., Matsumoto, T., & Yamano, T. (2006). Nonfarm employment, agricultural shocks, and poverty dynamics: Evidence from rural Uganda. *Agricultural Economics, 35*(3), 459–467.

Kingston, K. G., & Oke-Chinda, M. (2016). The Nigerian land use act: A curse or a blessing to the Anglican Church and the Ikwerre ethnic people of rivers state. *AJLC, 6*(1), 147–158.

Kolade, O., Mafimisebi, O., & Aluko, O. (2020). Beyond the farmgate: Can social capital help smallholders to overcome constraints in the agricultural value chain in Africa? In E. Osabuohien (Ed.), *The Palgrave Handbook of Agricultural and Rural Development in Africa.* Geneva: Palgrave Macmillan. https://doi.org/10.1007/978-3-030-41513-6_6.

Kuma, S. S. (2017). Land Policy and Land Delivery System in Nigeria: Emerging Issues in Urban Land Use and Development.

Montfaucon, A. F. (2020). Increasing Agricultural Income and Access to Financial Services through Mobile Technology in Africa: Evidence from Malawi. In E. Osabuohien (Ed.), *The Palgrave Handbook of Agricultural and Rural Development in Africa.* Geneva: Palgrave Macmillan. https://doi.org/10.1007/978-3-030-41513-6_12.

Masawe, J. (1994). Agricultural credit as an instrument of rural development in Tanzania: A case study on the credit programme for tractorization of small-scale agriculture in Morogoro region. *African Study Monographs, 15*(4), 211–226.

Massay, G. E. (2020). Local politics of land acquisitions for foreign and domestic investments in Tanzania. In E. Osabuohien (Ed.), *The Palgrave Handbook of Agricultural and Rural Development in Africa.* Geneva: Palgrave Macmillan. https://doi.org/10.1007/978-3-030-41513-6_20.

McCullough, E. B. (2017). Labor productivity and employment gaps in sub-Saharan Africa. *Food Policy, 67,* 133–152.

Nair, A., Kloeppinger-Todd, R., & Mulder, A. (2004). *Leasing: An underutilized tool in rural finance* (Agriculture and Rural Development Discussion Paper 7). Washington, DC, USA: The World Bank.

OECD/FAO. (2016). Agriculture in sub-Sahara Africa: Prospects and challenges for the next decade. In *OECD-FAO agriculture outlook* (pp. 2016–2025). Paris: OECD Publishing.

Ogun State Agricultural Development Programme (OGADEP). (2017, April 25–28). *Work/plan budget 2017.* Paper presented at the 30th Refils Workshop on OXFAR/EXTENSION Proposals Year 2017, Institute of Agricultural Research and Training, Near Gate House, Ibadan.

Okuro, S. O. (2015). Land grab in Kenya: Risk and opportunities. In *Environment, agriculture and cross-border migrations* (pp. 105–120). CODESRIA Publication.

Ola, K. O. (2020). Micro-determinants of women participation in agricultural value chain: Evidences from rural households in Nigeria. In E. Osabuohien (Ed.), *The Palgrave Handbook of Agricultural and Rural Development in Africa.* Geneva: Palgrave Macmillan. https://doi.org/10.1007/978-3-030-41513-6_25.

Osabuohien, E. S. (2014, July). Large-scale agricultural land investments and local institutions in Africa: The Nigerian case. *Land Use Policy, 39,* 155–165.

Osabuohien, E. S. (2015). *Handbook of research on in-country determinants and implications of foreign land acquisitions* (pp. 1–430). Hershey, PA: IGI Global. https://doi.org/10.4018/978-1-4666-7405-9.

Osabuohien, E. S., Efobi, U. R., Herrmann, R., & Gitau, C. M. (2019). Female labor outcomes and large-scale agricultural land investments: Macro–micro evidence from Tanzania. *Land Use Policy, 82,* 716–728.

Osabuohien, E. S., & Efobi, U. R. (2013). Africa's money in Africa. *South African Journal of Economics, 81*(2), 292–306.

Osabuohien, E., Olokoyo, F., Efobi, U., Karakara, A., & Beecroft, I. (2020). Large-scale land investments and households' livelihood in Nigeria: Empirical insights from quantitative analysis. In E. Osabuohien (Ed.) *The Palgrave Handbook of Agricultural and Rural Development in Africa.* Geneva: Palgrave Macmillan. https://doi.org/10.1007/978-3-030-41513-6_7.

Parisi, C., Vigani, M., & Rodríguez-Cerezo, E. (2015). Agricultural nanotechnologies: What are the current possibilities? *Nano Today, 10*(2), 124–127.

Rabo Development. (2016). *Financial inclusion and rural development.* Utrecht, Netherlands: Rabobank, Rabotoren.

Schoneveld, G. C., German, L. A., & Nutakor, E. (2011). Land-based investments for rural development? A grounded analysis of the local impacts of biofuel feedstock plantations in Ghana. *Ecology and Society, 16*(4), 10. https://doi.org/10.5751/ES-04424-160410.

Smaller, C., & Mann, H. (2009). *A thirst for distant lands: Foreign investment in agricultural land and water.* International Institute for Sustainable Development. Foreign Investment for Sustainable Development Program, Canada. Available from http://www.iisd.org/pdf/2009/thirst_for_distant_lands.pdf.

Ude, D. K (2020). Youth employment challenge and rural transformation in Africa. In E. Osabuohien (Ed.), *The Palgrave Handbook of Agricultural and Rural Development in Africa.* Geneva: Palgrave Macmillan. https://doi.org/10.1007/978-3-030-41513-6_3.

Vitoria, B., Mudimu, G., & Moyo, T. (2012). Status of agricultural and rural finance in Zimbabwe. In *FinMark Trust.* Retrieved from http://www.finmark.org.za/wp-content/uploads/pubs/Rep_Status_of_RAFin_Zim2.pdf.

Williams, T. O., Gyampoh, B., Kizito, F., & Namara, R. (2012). Water implications of large-scale land acquisitions in Ghana. *Water Alternatives, 5*(2), 243–265.

Wonyra, K. O., & Ametoglo, M. E. S. (2020). Impact of remittances on agricultural labour productivity in sub-Saharan Africa. In E. Osabuohien (Ed.), *The Palgrave Handbook of Agricultural and Rural Development in Africa.* Geneva: Palgrave Macmillan. https://doi.org/10.1007/978-3-030-41513-6_4.

World Bank. (2008). *World development report 2008: Agriculture for development.* Washington, DC: World Bank.

World Bank. (2019). *World development indicators (online database).* Washington, DC: The World Bank.

Correction to: Increasing Agricultural Income and Access to Financial Services through Mobile Technology in Africa: Evidence from Malawi

Angella Faith Montfaucon

Correction to:
Chapter 12 in: E. S. Osabuohien (ed.), *The Palgrave Handbook of Agricultural and Rural Development in Africa,*
https://doi.org/10.1007/978-3-030-41513-6_12

In the original version of this chapter, an disclaimer note has been added which reads: "The findings, interpretations, and conclusions expressed in this chapter are those of the author(s) and do not necessarily reflect the views of the World Bank or any of my current nor former affiliations." The correction to the chapter has been updated with the changes.

The updated version of this chapter can be found at
https://doi.org/10.1007/978-3-030-41513-6_12

Index

A

Access to land, 3, 7, 47, 49, 58, 148, 294, 295, 354, 567, 581, 629, 632, 633, 635

Administration, 25, 27, 58, 139, 204, 205, 305, 317, 320, 378, 381, 476, 482, 635

Adult, 5, 8, 12, 42, 43, 73, 165, 180, 224, 250–252, 314, 323, 346, 355, 425, 431, 555, 557, 567, 568

Africa, 1–3, 6, 8, 11, 18, 22, 25, 26, 30, 36, 41, 42, 44, 45, 47–53, 55, 57–61, 72, 92, 112, 133, 134, 136, 137, 147, 149, 156, 166, 202, 247–250, 252, 264, 265, 370–372, 376, 377, 379–381, 384, 385, 387, 397, 400, 401, 404, 425–428, 431, 476, 489, 496, 497, 505, 519, 526, 535, 580, 581, 613, 615, 629–633, 636

Agenda 2063, 2, 21, 22, 31

Agricultural export, 12, 292, 385, 613, 618, 623, 624

Agricultural finance, 7, 253, 263, 265–267, 280, 628–630, 636

Agricultural households, 5, 155, 176, 177, 184, 186–188, 192, 193, 400, 402, 411

Agricultural incomes, 9, 155, 170, 249, 252, 253, 255, 257–260, 397, 416, 632, 636

Agricultural labor productivity, 27, 68–71, 74–79, 81, 82, 631

Agricultural Marketing Co-operatives (AMCOS), 374–376, 379, 380

Agricultural markets, 70, 117, 119

Agricultural policy, 8, 10, 29, 82, 90, 120, 206, 476–478, 480–483, 485–489, 567, 634, 635

Agricultural productivity, 3–6, 28–30, 33, 34, 36, 48, 72, 74, 75, 90–101, 112, 153, 155, 156, 163, 165, 167, 168, 170, 248, 292, 294, 323, 358, 402, 406, 460, 526, 611, 624, 631, 632

Agricultural SMEs, 249, 251, 263–265, 267, 268, 279, 281

Agricultural transformation, 1, 2, 11, 28, 29, 45, 303, 459, 544

Agricultural value chain, 4, 12, 47, 101, 110, 113, 114, 116, 118, 122, 123, 269, 489, 554–568, 629, 633, 634

Agriculture, 1, 8–10, 24, 28–31, 33, 43, 47–50, 52, 53, 57–60, 62, 68, 72, 76, 81, 82, 89–93, 100, 101, 109, 112, 116, 118, 120, 122, 136, 138, 141, 153–155, 157, 168, 170, 175, 179, 204, 247–249, 251, 253, 263, 267, 270, 281, 285, 291–295, 300, 305, 314, 317, 324, 325, 330, 331, 341, 343, 347, 351–353, 355,

357–359, 367, 368, 376, 395–397, 399, 400, 402, 404, 409, 413–417, 420, 459, 469, 470, 475, 476, 478, 495, 521, 526, 528, 529, 534, 541, 553, 555, 573, 576, 579, 581, 593, 599, 604, 606, 612, 627, 628, 630, 632, 633, 635
Agro-Allied, 92, 482, 495, 497, 501, 632
Agro-food, 117, 292–294, 306, 496
Agro-industrial development, 496, 578, 583, 613, 615
Arable land, 49, 136, 180, 294, 295, 300, 302, 428, 460

C
Capacity building, 23, 32–34, 295, 554, 557
Cassava, 7, 11, 203, 207, 295–300, 303, 306, 526–528, 534–545, 554, 556–558, 564, 578, 634
Challenges, 4, 19, 20, 22, 24, 26, 28, 34, 35, 41–44, 51, 53, 57, 59, 62, 101, 110, 114, 115, 123, 142, 162, 168, 205, 211, 220, 249, 251, 264, 267, 281, 293, 304, 305, 314, 324, 330, 342, 343, 350–352, 370, 374, 381, 384, 426, 434, 452, 476, 482, 488, 496, 497, 521, 525, 528, 543, 545, 605, 629, 630
Chicken and Egg problem, 543
Cocoyam, 7, 8, 182, 297, 298, 303, 306, 557
Communities, 4, 5, 10, 12, 23, 24, 27, 31, 34, 74, 120, 122, 134–142, 144–148, 157, 176, 207–210, 221, 222, 224, 225, 230, 237, 242, 270, 285, 293–296, 315–318, 320, 321, 324, 327–333, 344, 347, 349, 351, 352, 369, 370, 383, 427, 428, 430–434, 436, 439, 441, 443, 444, 447, 449, 450, 458, 461, 462, 464–467, 469, 470, 480, 481, 487, 518, 520, 521, 530, 543, 554–556, 558, 560–563, 565–568, 574, 578, 590, 605, 614, 628, 629, 632–635
Commuting, 563

Consumption, 4, 5, 69–72, 75, 79, 81, 83, 91, 92, 134, 135, 145, 146, 148, 158, 160, 165, 166, 179, 226, 227, 230, 231, 235, 248, 299, 300, 348, 352, 357, 371, 396, 400–402, 416, 488, 496, 537–540, 559, 564, 572, 576, 578, 581, 601, 605, 614, 629, 631–633
Cooperatives, 9, 60, 110, 121, 122, 168, 170, 175, 180, 355, 367–370, 372–387, 567, 568
Cooperative society, 330, 554, 556, 558
Cooperativism, 380
Corruption, 26, 137, 204, 205, 375, 385, 430, 481, 488, 498, 504, 508, 632
Cowpea, 7, 296–298, 303, 306
Crop production, 92, 164, 169, 180–182, 251, 270, 278, 295, 304, 307, 314, 376, 397, 398, 514, 520, 529

D
Decentralization, 25–28
Determinants, 6, 7, 23, 24, 135, 143, 160, 177, 181, 182, 185, 186, 223–225, 242, 418, 431, 436, 439, 457, 507, 555, 558, 561, 566–568, 572, 605, 629
Development measurement, 18
Devolution, 3, 25–28, 30–32, 34, 35
Digital finance, 251
Distance, 6, 12, 119, 165, 169, 224, 225, 237, 240–242, 267, 346, 347, 554, 555, 558–560, 563, 565–568, 634
Distance to health care facility, 230, 240
Domestication, 3, 17, 18, 22–25, 28, 29, 31, 32, 34, 35
Drudgery, 47, 354, 519

E
East Africa, 22, 30, 367–371, 374, 375, 377, 379, 380, 384, 386, 450
Ecological clustering, 297

Economic development, 4, 18, 19, 21, 25, 27, 77, 83, 101, 118, 179, 202, 270, 318, 324, 332, 369, 370, 535, 611, 624
Economic resources, 6, 203, 371
Economy, 27, 30, 48, 49, 52, 59, 62, 70, 75, 81, 92, 111, 120, 175, 179, 202–206, 219, 220, 248, 249, 284, 291–293, 304, 314, 315, 317, 320, 321, 325, 327, 331, 345, 348, 349, 368, 369, 371, 376–379, 381, 397, 402, 404, 458, 475, 477, 480, 482, 487, 495, 504, 508, 521, 531, 534, 544, 572, 575, 583, 606, 607, 611–614, 622, 623, 632
Efficiency, 5, 20, 26, 27, 48, 93, 111, 112, 155, 159–161, 163, 166, 179–182, 252, 253, 293, 333, 377, 501, 505–508, 528, 534, 636
Electricity access, 3, 4, 91–93, 95–102
Employment, 1, 4, 8–10, 12, 28, 29, 33, 41–44, 48–50, 55–59, 61, 73, 75, 89, 90, 114, 134, 136, 140, 146–148, 154, 170, 175, 176, 201–203, 205, 206, 247, 291, 296, 314, 316, 318, 320, 321, 323, 327, 328, 332, 333, 341–344, 346, 347, 350, 352, 353, 355, 358, 359, 368, 372, 377, 396, 401, 402, 404, 426, 430–434, 441, 443, 447, 449, 450, 452, 467, 475, 477, 481, 495–497, 516, 526, 527, 571–577, 581–583, 587, 588, 590, 591, 597, 600, 601, 603–607, 611, 613, 628, 629, 632–634
Empowerment, 2, 23, 24, 45, 330, 636
Enterprise, 33, 59, 60, 140, 156, 182, 253, 264, 271, 315, 320, 323, 352, 359, 369, 370, 373, 379, 398, 496–502, 505, 507, 557, 562, 632
Esan, 558, 560, 561, 567
Estates, 11, 137, 140, 314, 459, 466, 513–515, 520, 521
Expenditure, 4, 5, 70, 71, 83, 101, 134, 135, 142–147, 149, 200, 219, 221, 222, 225, 228, 229, 231, 332, 352, 357, 401, 477, 496, 601, 603, 614
Experience, 9, 34, 44, 70, 90, 169, 181–184, 208, 225, 230, 314, 320, 328, 380, 384, 386, 403, 406, 411, 417, 420, 439, 443, 497, 498, 501, 506, 507, 515, 554, 556–559, 561, 564, 567, 572, 573, 587, 591, 595, 596, 599, 600, 602, 603, 606, 630, 634

F
Farm, 6, 7, 11, 12, 28, 42, 43, 48–51, 58, 62, 72, 74, 98, 109–116, 118, 121, 123, 144, 154, 155, 157, 160–164, 167–170, 175, 176, 180–183, 209, 248, 252, 253, 271, 294, 296, 298, 302, 307, 314, 350, 351, 395, 397–404, 418, 481, 482, 487–489, 496, 516–518, 520, 526, 529, 537–539, 542–544, 554–556, 558–561, 563–566, 568, 575, 576, 596, 599, 600, 602, 604, 631–634
Farmers, 3–5, 7, 9, 11, 12, 28, 30–34, 45, 46, 48, 50, 58, 70, 76, 82, 93, 100, 109–123, 136–138, 154–157, 159, 161, 162, 164, 166–170, 179–183, 204, 205, 247–255, 263–272, 275, 278–286, 292, 293, 295, 296, 299–301, 304–307, 309, 314, 320, 323, 331, 332, 344, 351, 353, 368, 369, 372, 373, 377–381, 383, 385, 395, 396, 399, 400, 402, 404–407, 409–411, 413, 414, 416–420, 428, 436, 439, 460, 461, 486–489, 514–518, 520–522, 526–528, 540–545, 553–559, 561, 567, 568, 581, 615, 618, 623, 629–634, 636
Farming households, 49, 157, 160, 164, 294, 314, 398, 400, 402, 403
Fast track, 513–516, 520–522
Female-headed households, 6, 187–189, 192, 193, 258
Financial inclusion, 7, 60, 249–253, 259, 260, 376, 631
Financial institutions, 8, 58, 250, 263, 266–269, 281, 305, 315, 320, 323, 324, 354, 376, 567, 631
Food research, 292
Food security, 3, 4, 7, 8, 10, 11, 30, 33, 46, 47, 57, 89, 119, 134, 136, 137, 153, 170, 292–294, 296, 298,

303–307, 314, 331, 352, 402, 457, 459–461, 475, 476, 480, 482, 483, 488, 489, 528, 529, 535, 627, 629, 631, 633–636
Forestry, 12, 76, 90, 248, 462, 529, 572–575, 577–585, 587, 588, 590–606, 612

G

Generalized Method of Moments (GMM), 77, 81, 82, 101
Governance, 3, 17, 18, 21, 23–25, 27, 29, 32, 33, 35, 90, 117, 137, 199, 330, 333, 377, 386, 465, 534
Growth, 5, 21, 25, 27, 29–32, 34, 41–45, 48–51, 68, 70–72, 76, 81, 83, 91–93, 96, 112, 114, 119, 153–156, 160, 162–164, 170, 175, 202, 206, 207, 248, 265, 270, 292, 293, 314, 316, 317, 320, 321, 323, 325, 332, 345, 346, 350, 368, 371, 372, 374, 376, 377, 381, 403, 404, 411, 427, 475, 476, 479, 483–485, 497, 504, 508, 514, 525, 526, 531, 543, 553, 555, 571, 572, 576–578, 583, 588, 599, 602, 611–615, 629, 632

H

Haulage, 296, 558, 561, 566, 568
Health care demand, 220, 223
Hectarage, 294, 295, 297, 298, 300
High-Quality Cassava Flour (HQCF), 527, 537, 540, 543
Host communities, 10, 135, 137, 139, 148, 430, 433, 434, 436, 444, 449, 487, 628, 629, 633
Households, 1, 4–7, 9, 49, 68, 70, 72–75, 79, 81, 82, 92, 100, 133–141, 143–149, 154–157, 159, 164, 165, 168–170, 180, 181, 183, 184, 186, 187, 189, 190, 192, 202, 219, 220, 222–224, 230, 231, 233, 235, 236, 240–242, 248, 249, 251, 253, 254, 256–260, 303, 305, 314, 344, 345, 348, 351, 352, 358, 395–401, 403, 404, 406, 407, 413, 414, 417–419, 430, 431, 439, 464, 516–519, 555, 560, 563, 565, 569, 572, 576–578, 600–602, 604–606, 627–633
Households demand, 220, 224
Household survey, 93, 165, 231, 253, 577
Household welfare, 5, 91, 142, 145, 146, 148, 149, 155, 156, 158, 160, 165, 166, 168, 170, 403, 632, 633
Hunger, 19, 21, 28, 30, 207, 294, 476, 526

I

Income, 4, 6–9, 11, 18, 33, 42, 43, 47, 48, 58, 68–70, 72–75, 77, 79, 82, 92, 109, 112, 114–116, 119, 135, 137, 138, 142, 153, 154, 156, 164, 168–170, 176, 182, 199–201, 203, 205, 206, 209, 220, 223–226, 228, 229, 231, 232, 235–242, 248–253, 255, 257, 266, 270, 305, 306, 314, 316–318, 323, 324, 327, 328, 330–333, 342, 345, 347, 348, 352, 353, 357, 368, 370–372, 384, 397–400, 402–405, 407–409, 411, 414, 416, 417, 419, 420, 463, 500, 516, 526, 527, 530, 534, 541, 542, 545, 554, 559, 575–578, 582, 587, 593, 594, 598, 599, 601, 602, 604, 611, 615, 618, 627, 630, 631
Indigenous institutions, 439, 441
Industrialization, 48, 49, 316, 348, 368, 375, 458, 463, 469, 526, 629, 631
Inequality, 50, 68, 77, 115, 116, 203, 207, 220, 306, 315, 368–372, 402, 403, 526, 532, 601
Informal credit, 265
Inheritance, 12, 58, 180, 398, 566–568
Integrated Cooperative Model (ICM), 9, 367, 379, 382, 383, 387
International development, 18, 20–22, 34–36, 61, 459
Investment, 2–4, 8–11, 45, 46, 50, 51, 70–73, 77, 81, 83, 93, 115, 116, 120, 139–141, 155, 164, 206, 247, 250, 251, 254, 269, 271, 293, 302, 321, 324, 325, 327–329, 331, 347, 348, 376, 398, 401, 404, 426, 443,

444, 449, 457–463, 465–470, 476, 527, 528, 555, 571, 578, 579, 584, 590, 601, 602, 614, 629, 631, 635, 636
Irrigation, 7, 50, 51, 112, 164, 168, 170, 248, 249, 270, 271, 351, 376, 400, 483, 518, 630, 631

J
Job, 8, 9, 41–43, 45, 50, 60, 61, 69, 92, 100, 134, 136, 145, 176, 182, 203, 205, 206, 210, 292, 321, 341–345, 347, 350, 351, 354, 355, 358, 401, 403, 411, 417, 426, 466, 496, 497, 500, 516, 526, 545, 555, 571, 572, 574, 577, 578, 581, 582, 590, 591, 596, 597, 599–602, 605–607, 629

L
Labor demand, 53, 584, 590, 597
Labor force, 12, 28, 30, 32, 34, 41, 42, 44, 45, 50, 51, 58, 69, 70, 73, 74, 76, 83, 92, 95, 154, 162, 175, 176, 203, 342, 350, 357, 358, 496, 517, 526, 544, 554, 557, 572, 573, 578, 583, 587, 588, 593, 599, 605, 635
Labor market, 41–44, 49, 51, 59, 60, 69, 70, 74, 76, 92, 176, 179, 347, 349, 351, 357, 358, 575, 578, 605, 607
Labor migration, 82, 342–344, 347, 348, 350, 351, 358, 359
Labor supply, 69, 72–74, 76, 79, 82, 176
Labor use, 5, 6, 157, 175, 177–182, 185, 187, 188, 517
Land access, 51, 58, 294, 295, 306, 629, 633
Land acquisition, 10, 68, 136, 138, 139, 300, 457–459, 461–465, 467–470, 515, 567, 628, 629, 634, 635
Land investments, 4, 11, 135, 136, 138, 146, 292, 428, 431, 439, 514, 515, 520–522, 628
Land ownership, 50, 293–295, 305, 347, 516, 556, 560, 567, 635, 636
Land policy, 293, 633, 635, 636
Land security, 138, 295

Land use, 49, 293, 295, 305, 428, 513, 579, 636
Large-scale, 11, 49, 50, 117, 136, 138, 139, 156, 292, 306, 373, 427, 457, 460, 498, 513–515, 520–522, 566, 578, 628
Large-scale agricultural land investments (LALIs), 1, 9, 133, 427, 432, 627, 629, 632
Literacy, 3, 12, 43, 54–56, 249, 251, 567, 568
Livelihood, 1, 4, 19, 43, 49, 62, 109, 116, 119, 120, 133–138, 140, 147, 148, 154, 155, 204, 247, 248, 296, 299, 304, 317, 341, 342, 351–353, 358, 367, 369, 383, 403, 460, 461, 463, 515–517, 519, 526, 557, 563, 594, 602, 604, 606, 627–629, 632
Living Standards Measurement Study-Integrated Surveys on Agriculture (LSMS-ISA), 5, 10, 157, 351, 355, 430–432
Local capacity, 434, 449
Logit regression, 224

M
Maize, 7, 31, 58, 155, 168, 207, 248, 271, 295–298, 300, 301, 306, 516, 517, 535, 539, 541, 543, 578, 595, 631, 634
Malawi, 50, 52, 83, 92, 106, 248–254, 259, 460, 515, 578, 591
Male-headed households, 5, 188, 189, 192, 258
Manufacturing, 11, 32, 42, 48, 75, 76, 79, 291, 305, 357, 401, 495–497, 500–502, 540, 632
Market constraints, 30, 119, 120
Melon, 7, 271, 296–298, 302, 306
Micro-finance, 251, 264, 324, 325
Migrant, 67, 70, 71, 73, 74, 82, 83, 136, 342, 345–353, 357, 358, 576, 628, 630
Migration theories, 344, 345, 348
Millennium Development Goals (MDGs), 17–20, 22, 25, 206
Mobile phone technology, 112, 259

Mobility, 169, 347, 554, 557–559, 561, 563, 566, 578
Mozambique, 11, 12, 47, 52, 58, 83, 106, 134, 147, 372, 536, 571, 572, 575, 578–580, 583, 597, 629, 631

N
Namibia, 7, 52, 106, 249, 263–266, 270–272, 277, 284
Neoclassical, 69, 345, 348, 349, 479
New economics, 345
Niassa, 572, 573, 575–583, 585, 587, 591, 597, 599, 600, 604–607
Nigeria, 5–12, 49, 52, 58, 67, 68, 83, 106, 112, 121, 122, 134, 136, 137, 139–141, 147, 175, 177, 179–184, 186–188, 193, 199, 200, 202–204, 206–208, 211, 219–222, 230, 241, 249, 252, 292–296, 299–304, 306, 308, 323, 342–344, 350–352, 355, 358, 359, 367, 376, 398, 427, 428, 431, 476, 477, 480, 483, 487–489, 496, 497, 500–502, 504, 507, 508, 525, 527, 528, 531, 534, 536, 538–545, 553–558, 565, 567, 612, 613, 615–619, 622–624, 628, 629, 632, 634
Nigeria Health Care System, 221
Non-farm activities, 48, 341, 399–403, 407

O
Ogun State, 7, 137, 182, 294–297, 299–303, 305–308, 342, 351, 359, 557, 634
Ordinary least squares regression, 224
Organisation, 12, 121, 122, 206, 572, 573, 577, 580
Out-of-pocket expenses, 219

P
Panel analysis, 44, 51, 82, 92
Panel cointegration, 95, 96, 99, 101
Partial labor productivity, 178, 184

Participation, 12, 23, 42, 61, 69, 73, 74, 79, 95, 110, 119, 161, 164, 176, 181, 182, 201, 295, 296, 330, 332, 333, 359, 369, 399, 400, 402–404, 416, 418, 426, 430, 462, 463, 554–558, 560, 562–568, 631, 634
Pastoralists, 34, 304, 307, 428, 464
Performance, 7, 11, 18, 27, 34, 61, 101, 111, 114, 115, 164, 168, 169, 201, 280, 284, 298, 313, 323, 480, 484, 485, 497, 498, 500–502, 504–508, 613, 615, 623, 630, 632
Plantations, 11, 12, 137, 180, 181, 460, 462, 470, 488, 513, 514, 571–573, 578–584, 587, 588, 590–601, 603–605
Planting and harvesting activities, 5, 177, 187–189
Policies, 2, 10, 20, 23, 28, 31, 33, 45, 50, 52, 58–61, 101, 122, 163, 182, 203, 211, 219, 260, 263, 292, 293, 298, 315, 316, 318, 343, 346, 350, 375, 381, 384, 426, 430, 458, 461, 469, 470, 475–478, 480, 483, 486–488, 521, 534, 553, 568, 614, 624, 629, 630, 635, 636
Political economy, 10–12, 447, 458, 476, 514, 519, 521, 572
Population, 30, 31, 33, 41–45, 49, 51, 55–57, 59, 62, 75, 76, 92, 116, 118, 119, 122, 141, 153, 154, 156, 170, 180, 183, 199, 201–203, 207, 210–212, 222, 230, 247–252, 266, 267, 271, 272, 277, 291, 293, 297, 313, 314, 317, 320, 325, 341–343, 345–347, 349, 350, 352, 358, 367, 368, 377, 379, 380, 396, 404, 426, 430, 475, 476, 482, 485, 486, 488, 501, 517, 525, 526, 529, 531, 532, 558, 573, 576, 579–581, 590, 600, 604–606, 612, 627, 632, 633
Potato, 7, 8, 121, 253, 271, 297, 298, 303, 306, 537, 539, 578
Poverty, 6, 9, 11, 19, 25, 28–30, 33, 43, 44, 47, 67, 68, 76, 90, 92, 112, 114–116, 118–120, 148, 154, 156, 165, 170, 176, 199–203, 205–211, 219, 220, 314, 332, 367, 371, 387,

395, 401, 402, 404, 476, 496–498, 525, 529–533, 544, 627–629, 631, 633
Poverty reduction, 1, 4, 29, 68, 89, 101, 110, 114, 116, 119, 155, 201, 205, 206, 219, 248, 323, 325, 372, 382, 461, 497, 525, 526, 530, 543, 632
Poverty reduction strategies, 119, 525
Primary sector, 68, 69, 395, 630
Priority crop, 294, 295, 297, 298, 300, 302, 308, 634
Probit model, 181
Productive structure, 12, 572, 573, 575, 582, 583, 599, 605–607, 629
Productivity, 3, 5–7, 27–29, 31–34, 42, 43, 45, 48, 50, 51, 57–59, 68, 70–73, 76, 81, 82, 91, 93, 110–113, 118, 123, 153, 155, 160, 162, 166, 175–180, 182, 183, 248, 293, 305, 323, 331, 332, 355, 401, 402, 420, 432, 461, 496, 502, 534, 596, 597, 599, 607, 630, 632
Psychology, 478
Public sector health care services, 6, 228, 235, 241, 242
Push and pull factors, 348, 399

Q
Quality of care, 6, 220, 227, 240–242

R
Rational choice, 10, 476, 478–480, 486, 489
Remittances, 67–74, 79, 81–83, 348, 352, 358, 397, 398, 630, 631
Responsibilities, 9, 12, 26, 30, 357, 375, 386, 387, 444, 449, 480, 487, 488, 554, 556, 563, 565–568
Rice, 7, 8, 58, 112, 155, 182, 207, 209, 295, 297, 298, 301, 302, 306, 496, 534, 535, 542, 543, 557, 631, 632
Rural community, 137, 318, 327, 369, 481, 565
Rural development, 2, 3, 9, 11, 18, 28, 44, 46, 48, 52, 91, 101, 119, 136, 138, 313, 317, 343, 358, 368–370, 374, 378, 380, 382, 384–387, 636
Rural electrification, 4, 91–93, 95, 96, 98, 100, 101, 314
Rural employment, 52, 154, 401
Rural enterprise, 315, 331, 341, 370, 382
Rural financing, 316
Rural households, 74, 92, 155, 170, 224, 236, 259, 314, 341, 357, 402, 403, 407, 630, 632, 636
Rural livelihoods, 324, 331, 332, 460
Rural out-migration, 314

S
Savings and Credit Cooperative Societies (SACCOS), 8, 314–317, 320, 324–333, 375–377, 379, 382–384
Security, 1, 10, 18, 21, 137, 263, 267, 304, 330, 343, 371, 441, 449, 520, 598, 606, 635
Smallholder, 4, 7, 30, 109, 110, 112, 113, 115–123, 133, 136–138, 140, 157, 164, 175, 181, 247–251, 253, 259, 265, 268, 278, 285, 295, 296, 299, 306, 314, 323, 368, 373, 379, 516, 521, 526, 528, 541, 542, 581, 627, 629–633, 636
Smallholder farming, 153, 314, 632
Small-scale, 6, 7, 11, 28, 31, 33, 34, 45, 50, 59, 95, 118, 248, 263, 278, 292, 316, 368, 369, 372, 401, 460, 461, 496, 497, 500, 502, 507, 513, 516, 520, 573, 578, 632, 636
SME finance gap, 267, 268
Social arrangements, 43, 522
Social capital, 4, 110, 120–123, 137, 169, 318, 328, 345, 349, 499, 501
Social inclusion, 9, 47, 367, 369, 370, 374, 387
Social reproduction, 12, 572, 583, 593, 595, 598, 605, 607
Socio-cultural, 11, 211, 496–500, 502, 504, 505, 507, 508, 632
Socioeconomic changes, 343
South Eastern, 513

Sub-Sahara Africa, 61, 91, 93, 95, 97, 98, 100, 101
Sub-Saharan Africa, 396
Sugarcane, 514, 515, 518–522, 615
Sustainable development, 19, 22, 44, 461, 480, 495, 526, 529, 542, 545
Sustainable Development Goals (SDGs), 2, 17–19, 90, 483
System, 18, 24–27, 29, 30, 42, 46–48, 50, 51, 61, 72, 76, 82, 117, 119, 138–140, 169, 221, 226, 252, 293, 294, 304, 316, 317, 320, 325, 330, 333, 342, 345, 348, 349, 373, 382, 385, 386, 441, 480, 499, 504, 508, 513, 519, 521, 526, 528, 542, 555, 560, 567, 572, 582–584, 587, 588, 591, 594, 595, 597–599, 604, 606, 636

T

Tackling poverty, 210
Tanzania, 8–10, 52, 58, 83, 106, 112, 134, 137, 146, 147, 188, 252, 253, 313–315, 320, 323–325, 330, 332, 333, 367, 371–377, 379, 380, 382–385, 399, 427, 428, 430–432, 434, 436, 449, 450, 457–463, 465, 578, 580, 630, 631, 635
Technological adoption, 30, 111
Technological innovations, 109, 110, 114, 534
Technology adoption, 109, 114, 155, 156, 167–170, 249, 253, 636
Transformation, 1–4, 6, 8, 26, 28, 29, 44–46, 48, 50, 51, 53–55, 57, 58, 61, 77, 82, 89, 154, 156, 204, 315–318, 325, 326, 328–333, 355, 368, 385, 404, 496, 499, 571, 573, 582, 636

U

Uganda, 5, 8, 9, 26, 47, 49, 52, 58, 83, 106, 121, 137, 154–157, 163, 168, 169, 252, 269, 367, 371, 372, 374, 377–379, 383, 384, 580, 631, 632

Unemployment, 34, 41–44, 115, 179, 199, 200, 202–205, 207–211, 346, 401, 426, 444, 476, 495, 498, 582
Urban and rural areas, 6, 141, 220, 223, 234, 235, 241, 342, 351
Urban electrification, 91, 95, 96
Urbanization, 42, 44, 48, 74, 346, 348, 357

V

Value chain, 2, 4, 11, 45, 47, 50, 59, 101, 110, 113, 206, 207, 296, 521, 522, 527–529, 537, 540–545, 554–556, 564, 633, 636
Village Community Banks (VICoBA), 379

W

Wage, 6, 8, 42, 43, 45, 57, 69, 70, 73, 74, 138, 140, 154, 180–182, 187, 189, 232, 323, 347, 348, 353, 355, 357, 372, 497, 521, 572–578, 581, 590–594, 599, 601, 604, 607, 633
Well-being, 155, 176, 200, 202, 207, 255–257, 323, 325, 332, 359, 572, 600, 605, 606, 636
Willingness to pay, 6, 220, 223–225, 228, 229, 234–237, 240–242, 284
Women, 11, 12, 19, 33, 92, 176, 187, 205, 208, 224, 248, 270, 296, 324, 407, 412, 481, 482, 486, 515, 517–520, 522, 526, 553–561, 563–568, 588, 628, 634
Working conditions, 69, 247, 572, 575, 576, 579, 581, 582, 587, 591, 593, 599–601, 604, 605, 607

Y

Yam, 7, 8, 180, 181, 203, 296–298, 302, 303, 306, 537, 539, 634
Yield, 7, 11, 109, 110, 144, 154, 163, 168, 177, 247, 248, 297, 298, 300–303, 316, 330, 478, 481, 527, 528, 541–543, 613, 628, 630, 634

Youth employment, 3, 6, 10, 42, 44, 45, 47, 51, 53, 57, 59–61, 137, 343, 344, 350, 352, 359, 427, 430, 432, 436, 439, 441, 443, 444, 447

Youth unemployment, 3, 10, 42–45, 56, 57, 60, 203, 204, 342, 351, 352, 359, 425–428, 430, 434, 436, 441, 443, 449

Z

Zimbabwe, 11, 47, 52, 83, 106, 265, 367, 513, 514, 516, 517, 522, 578

Printed in the United States
by Baker & Taylor Publisher Services